DRINK DRIVING
LAW
AND
PRACTICE

AUSTRALIA
LBC Information Services Ltd
Sydney

CANADA and USA
Carswell
Toronto

NEW ZEALAND
Brooker's
Auckland

SINGAPORE and MALAYSIA
Thomson Information (S.E. Asia)
Singapore

DRINK DRIVING
LAW
AND
PRACTICE

NIGEL JOSEPH LEY, LL.M.
of Gray's Inn and the Northern Circuit;
Barrister-at-Law;
A member of the RAC Legal Committee

Author of medical sections
PETER MARKS, M.B. ch.B., M.R.C.P., M.SC., LL.B., M.A.
Barrister-at-Law

London
Sweet & Maxwell
1997

Published in 1997 by
Sweet & Maxwell Limited of
100 Avenue Road,
London NW3 3PF
Laserset by LBJ Enterprises Ltd,
Aldermaston and Chilcompton
Printed and bound in Great Britain by
Butler and Tanner Ltd, Frome and London

**A catalogue reference for this book is available
from the British Library**

ISBN 0–421–580–607

Addendum

The House of Lords

Please note after this edition had been printed the House of Lords, *The Times*, February, 21, 1997, reversed the decision of the High Court in *DPP v. McKeown* and *DPP v. Jones*, (see Chapter 15, above). Their Lordships held that the requirement of accuracy in P.A.C.E. section 69 only applied to the actual processing of information by a computer and therefore that legislation had no application if a computer printout reproduced what information had been fed into it, even though those imputed facts were wrong. If evidence was given about the breathalyser that the computer was working correctly (*i.e.* because of correct calibration) and its clock had no bearing on the processing of information from the analyser, then the printout was admissible in evidence. Also, because clocks have to be set to the correct time, the most likely explanation for the latter being slow was that the time had been incorrectly set and that, in any case, the clock mechanism was probably not part of the computer. In McKeown's case evidence was given by a director of the Lion laboratories. It is submitted that it would be a different matter if the only evidence was that of a police officer who said that he did not know whether the wrong time was or was not due to a processing error and the defence witnesses testified (1) that Lion sent a technician every six months to set the time correctly and over which activity was taken great care, (2) that the cause of the wrong time may have been due to an error in the processing of the signal from the clock and (3) that the same error could have effected the processing of the signal from the analyser. If such evidence was given, then it is submitted that the justices would be entitled (but not compelled) to conclude that the printout did not comply with section 69. In such cases, the DPP would probably seek to call an expert from the manufacturers to rebut such testimony. If the defence expert was qualified in electronics and could satisfy the magistrates that the circuit diagrams would be easily understood by him and would show whether or not a common error could have caused inaccurate processing of both the signal from the clock and the signal from the analyser, then their Lordships were of the view that the defence would be entitled to see the relevant circuit diagrams.

Their Lordships did not say whether the accuracy of the computer was to be judged objectively or subjectively, *i.e.* in accordance with design standards. The High Court in *Aston v. DPP*, *The Times*, July 14, 1995 had held the latter but had also said that if this were to cause prejudice to the defendant, then the court had power under P.A.C.E. section 78 to exclude any evidence of the result of the breath analysis.

Further their Lordships were also of the opinion that "a reasonable excuse" for not providing a specimen was not confined to a medical one and could include being asked to exhale into a breathalyser which was obviously faulty and incapable of carrying out an analysis. Such a machine nevertheless remained "an approved device".

FOREWORD

By the Rt Hon. Sir Frederick Lawton (a former Lord Justice of Appeal)

Reading the manuscript of Mr Nigel Ley's book brought back memories of
the times when as a barrister I prosecuted and defended in drink driving
cases. The relevant statute then was the Road Traffic Act 1930. Once it had
been adjudged that a charge of being under the influence of drink or drugs
was not bad for duplicity, the advocate had only the facts with which to
contend. I can still remember the usual police evidence: "I asked the
accused to get out of his car. When he did so there was a strong smell of
drink. He was unsteady on his feet and supported himself by leaning on
the bonnet of his car. His eyes were glazed and his speech slurred."
Evidence to the same effect would be given by a police surgeon, often
coupled with a statement that the accused's reaction to a knee-tapping test
had been sluggish. This was the nearest the evidence ever got to being
scientific. Occasionally the prosecution would rely on what the police
considered to be drunken behaviour. In one case in which I defended, the
police described how my client had climbed on to a table in the charge
room and had given them a demonstration of how he had bombed the
German warship Tirpitz. He had. He was acquitted.

In those days no cause was hopeless. The accused could, and usually did,
elect trial by jury. At London Sessions about 90 per cent of those tried on
indictment were acquitted. In one case in which I was instructed to defend
a docker at West Ham Quarter Sessions, I commented to my experienced
instructing solicitor that the case was hopeless because the accused had
admitted to the police on arrest, and was not denying, that he had drunk 10
pints of beer. "No it isn't hopeless," said the solicitor, "in West Ham only
boss's drinks like gin make anyone unfit to drive a car." My client was
acquitted.

The acquittal rate worried the Home Office and those concerned with
road safety. In the late 1950s, it was thought that science would be able to
bring certainty into trials. A series of tests were introduced, starting with
requests for urine samples and ending with the machine which records the
amount of alcohol in the breath. When I was in the Court of Appeal, I went
with one of my brethren to witness a demonstration of this machine. As we
came away he said: "Even with the knowledge I acquired nearly 40 years
ago reading the Natural Science Tripos at Cambridge, I can think of about
three reasons why that machine may not be all that reliable." How right he
was.

The introduction of scientific tests for establishing guilt, coupled with
the detailed statutory provisions there had to be for regulating the
circumstances in which they could be used, has brought both law and

science into the trial of drink driving cases. No longer can the advocate rely, as many of my generation did when defending, upon an ability to make the prosecution look ridiculous or to arouse sympathy for the accused. Every case now requires study of both the law and the science relied on by the prosecution. Mr Ley's book is where the relevant information can be found. I recommend it.

PREFACE TO THE SECOND EDITION

As Lord Diplock recognised in *Walker v. Lovell* [1975] 3 All E.R., page 111, motorists still take the view that it is more convenient to rely upon being defended by a sufficiently ingenious lawyer than to take care never to drive with more than the permitted level of alcohol. The result is that the case law has increased considerably since the last edition of this treatise and has led to the publication of this second edition containing an extra 100 pages. The two most litigated topics over the last three years are about the application of the Warren formula to the various, and in some cases widely different, procedures used by the various police forces throughout England and Wales for obtaining blood and urine specimens; and the associated issue of what redress is open to those who were convicted prior to the decision in the Warren Case and where the procedure followed did not comply with that laid down by Lord Bridge in the Warren Case. The other major development has been the application of section 69 of the Police and Criminal Evidence Act 1984 to the admissibility in evidence of breathalyser printouts, a matter which had given ingenious lawyers a field day.

The law stated in this treatise is that in force on January 1, 1997.

Gray's Inn Chambers, London WC1.   Nigel J. Ley
January 1, 1997

ACKNOWLEDGEMENTS

The Publishers and Author wish to thank the following for permission to reprint material from publications in which they have copyright:

Article by Wong, Keys, Scott and Peterson in (1991) 9 Alcohol 189; operating instructions from The Car and Medical Instruments Co.; table "Conversion factors for the distribution of ethanol between blood and other body tissues"; *The Daily Telegraph* for the article "The Legal Limit" January 3, 1996 © Telegraph Group Limited, London, 1996; The Incorporated Council of Law Reporting for England & Wales; table "Weight of Body Fluid as a Percentage of a Person's Total Weight" from the International Encyclopaedia of Pharmacology and Therapeutics, vol. 1, s.20 with kind permission from Elsevier Science—NL, Sara Burgerhartstraat 25, 1055 KV Amsterdam, The Netherlands; table of statutory limits of alcohol in blood and breath in various countries by A. W. Jones, and extract from the article "Absorption, Distribution, and Elimination of Alcohol: Highway Safety Aspects" by Dubowski reprinted with permission from *Journal of Studies on Alcohol*, Supplement No. 10 pp. 98–108, 1985. Copyright by Alcohol Research Documentation, Inc., Rutgers Center of Alcohol Studies, Piscataway, N.J. 08855; extract from a letter by M. J. Morris and A. C. Taylor "Drink Driving—Law and Practice" which appeared in *The Lancet*, January 3, 1987 © *The Lancet* 1987; table "The Impaired Driver Problem v. The Impaired Problem Driver" by H. M. Simpson.

Whilst every care has been taken to establish and acknowledge copyright and contact the copyright owners, the publishers tender their apologies for any accidental infringement. They would be pleased to come to a suitable arrangement with the rightful owner in each case.

CONTENTS

CONTENTS

CHAPTER 21. POLICE POWERS OF ARREST AND DAMAGES FOR THE AGGRIEVED MOTORIST

CHAPTER 22. APPEALS AND JUDICIAL REVIEW

A. Appeals to the Crown Court

CONTENTS

CONTENTS

TABLE OF CASES

TABLE OF STATUTES

TABLE OF STATUTORY INSTRUMENTS

Chapter 1

HISTORICAL PERSPECTIVE

A. The nineteenth century

Parliament has long been aware of the effects of alcohol and has passed **1-01** many statutes to try to prevent its abuse. The current legislation regulating drinking and driving dates back to 1831 when the London Hackney Carriage Act made it an offence for a London cab driver to allow drink to cause him to injure somebody or to damage property. However, the invention of the internal combustion engine put into the hands of previously unarmed citizens a potentially lethal weapon. Parliament responded to this danger by promptly enacting legislation to regulate the use of these new self-propelled vehicles. For example, a pedestrian carrying a red flag had to walk in front of such vehicles in order to warn people of their approach.

The first conviction for drunken driving of a horeseless carriage was in 1897 in the case of George Smith, a London taxi-driver, who on September 10, 1897 after having had two or three glasses of beer, allowed his electric cab to mount the pavement and "enter" 165 Bond Street (*The Daily Telegraph*, August 16, 1996). By 1904 it was noted in the United States that in 19 out of 25 fatal accidents involving "automobile wagons . . . drivers had used spirits within an hour or more of the disaster" (see *A Great and Graving Evil*, Royal College of Physicians, 1987). It was not only in America that precautions were taken to regulate drinking and driving. In Britain Parliament also regulated the circumstances in which a person was allowed to control a motor vehicle and as more traffic came on the road, more controls were brought into existence.

B. The introduction of specific drinking and driving laws

It was not until 1925 that an offence was introduced which was solely **1-02** concerned with the driving of motor vehicles by people who had been consuming alcoholic beverages. In that year the Criminal Justice Act 1925 was passed, which by section 40 made it an offence to be "drunk while in charge on the highway or other public place of any mechanically-propelled vehicle". The seriousness with which such conduct was regarded can be judged by the fact that a conviction carried a maximum of four months' imprisonment and an automatic disqualification from driving for one year (although an offender was allowed to apply to have his licence restored to him after three months).

That provision was extended by the Road Traffic Act 1930, s.15, which made it an offence:

" . . . when driving or attempting to drive, or when in charge of, a motor vehicle on a road or other public place [to be] under the influence of drink or a drug to such an extent as to be incapable of having proper control of the vehicle."

The penalty was increased to a maximum of six months' incarceration. The automatic disqualification remained, unless the court thought there were special reasons to order otherwise and there was no longer any power for the remainder of a driving ban to be remitted after three months.

C. A separate offence of "being in charge"

1-03 The Road Traffic Act 1956 made "being in charge" a separate offence from "driving", with a mandatory disqualification applying only to a second or subsequent conviction for this new crime. It also introduced a statutory defence for a person accused of "being in charge", namely that there was no likelihood of him driving while he remained unfit to do so and that he had not driven while unfit to do so. (This latter requirement was repealed by the Road Safety Act 1967 and the compulsory imposition of disqualification for a second offence was removed by the Road Traffic Act 1972.) The 1956 Act also altered the "in charge" offence to that of being in charge of motor vehicles when under the influence of drink or drugs which it defined as being: " . . . under the influence of drink or drugs to such an extent as to be incapable of having proper control of a vehicle."

D. Modern legislation

1-04 The Road Traffic Act 1960 substituted "unfitness to drive" in place of the 1930 Act's "driving under the influence". Two years later, Parliament in the Road Traffic Act 1962 reinterpreted the word "unfitness" to mean that the "ability to drive properly is for the time being impaired".

Exactly the same offence still remains part of today's drinking and driving laws, although it is now contained in the Road Traffic Act 1988, s.4.

E. Securing a conviction

The problem with these statutory provisions was that each individual had **1–05** his own tolerance level to alcohol and what made one person inebriated could have little apparent affect on somebody else. The consequence of this was that, in order to enforce the law, the police needed proof of a motorist's ability to drive and in order to obtain such evidence, they invented a series of ad hoc tests, such as walking along a straight line or pronouncing phrases such as "the Leith police dismisseth us". However, the idea of a person providing self-incriminatory evidence breached the whole tradition of the common law and found disfavour with the judiciary. This is well illustrated by the remarks of the Privy Council in *Lam Chi-Ming v. R.* [1991] 2 A.C. 212, 222: "The privilege against self-incrimination is deep rooted in English law . . . It is better by far to allow a few guilty men to escape conviction than to compromise the standards of a free society."

Accordingly, judges spoke out against arrested motorists having to **1–06** undergo tests to determine their sobriety. In *R. v. Tunnicliffe* (unreported) Swift J., at Liverpool Assizes between the Wars, held that if the defendant had been drunk, then he could not have consented to being tested by a doctor and the latter's evidence was inadmissible. If, however, the Crown was implying that the driver was not drunk when he consented, then he must also have been sober when he was driving. In the words of his Lordship:

> "It is the liberty of the subject I am concerned about. I object very much to these inroads on our British freedom.
> "If they say a man is willing to give consent, then they have no right to say he is drunk, because drunkenness destroys consent."

In the past, the judges took drinking and driving cases far less seriously than they do today. In a case at Nottingham Assizes in the 1950s, the prosecution evidence was that two constables had chased a suspected drunken driver but he had arrived at his home before they did, thereby avoiding being arrested. The policemen shouted to him to come out. He then appeared at a window. They asked him to give them a sample of urine, to which he replied, "P— off". Stable J., who was trying the case, then said to prosecuting counsel, "Can you think of a more concise and accurate way in which a suspect, wishing to exercise his legal rights, should do so?" (*ex relatio* Sir Frederick Lawton).

F. Body fluid analysis

There was nevertheless rising concern about the increasing number of **1–07** accidents on the road and various surveys were carried out to ascertain exactly what part alcohol played. One of the first reports to be published was by Holcomb in 1938. This showed that the alcohol level of Illinois

3

drivers involved in accidents was on average higher than that of a control sample of motorists selected at random. Similar studies were carried out in other countries confirming that the more liquor a driver consumed, the more likely he was to be involved in an accident. Nevertheless, the problems for a prosecutor in trying to prove that the accused's driving had been impaired still remained. The first statutory maximum alcohol level for drivers was introduced in 1936 in Norway (0.5mg/-g equals 53mg of alcohol/100ml of blood). It was followed in Europe by Sweden in 1941, with a limit of 0.8ml/-g but this reduced to 0.5mg/-g in 1957 and 0.2mg/-g in 1990 (equal to 21mg/100ml). Two states in America (Maine and Indiana) in 1939 defined the offence of driving under the influence as having a blood alcohol concentration in excess of 150mg per 100ml of blood. The Road Traffic Act 1962, s.2 introduced into Great Britain the concept of blood and urine analyses. The police could request a sample of body fluid for analysis and a refusal to provide one could be used in court as corroboration of the prosecution's case. However, the evidential burden was still on the prosecutor to show what effect the amount of alcohol found in the motorist's sample would have had on the latter's driving ability. (Urine specimens were preferred by police officers as these were easier to collect.) Such evidence would invariably be adduced by a medical practitioner whose opinion would normally be based upon publications by the British Medical Association. The amount of alcohol in a sample could never by itself found a conviction and juries were free to reject the testimony of a police surgeon about the impairment that would flow from the quantity of intoxicants in a motorist's body fluid.

1–08   At the same time the Government was becoming more and more concerned by the ever-increasing casualties on the road. The major problem was trying to convince juries to accept medical evidence showing that the defendant's driving had been impaired. The only solution was to make it illegal to drive with a blood alcohol level above a certain arbitrary limit. Around the same time, a major study was carried out by Borkenstein (at Grand Rapids in Michigan, United States). The results were published in 1964 and concluded that an alcohol level in excess of 80 milligrammes per 100 millilitres of blood produced a substantial risk of the driver being involved in an accident. In an article in *Alcohol, Drugs and Driving* (Vol. 4, No. 2, p. 106), A. W. Jones drew a schematic diagram based on the data from the Grand Rapids study.

G. The Road Safety Act 1967

1–09 In view of the Grand Rapids Study, H.M. Government decided to make it illegal in the United Kingdom for anybody to drive whose blood alcohol concentration exceeded a certain limit. This was achieved by the Road Safety Act 1967. Some means of ascertaining a motorist's alcohol consumption had to be introduced, and this was done by a method which necessitated the total abrogation of the rule against self-incrimination.

The original Bill to implement this innovation was introduced at the beginning of 1966 but fell with the General Election. The same legislation was again presented to Parliament in that winter. The reasons for such a law and what it was hoped it would achieve were distinctly set out by the Minister of Transport (Barbara Castle) when she opened the debate on the second reading (H.C. Deb., col. 981/2 November 7, 1966):

"The Bill is substantially the same measure as that which I brought before the House earlier this year. I am happy to say that most of the provisions of the Bill were welcomed by Hon. Members on both sides of the House. I think that we all saw the new principles introduced by the Bill as an important step forward in the continuing battle to reduce the intolerable number of casualties on our roads. This is a cause to which Members of all parties are dedicated. A cynic once said that road accidents are a measure of a nation's prosperity—the more accidents, the more affluence. If that is so, then Britain is rich indeed.

It is only nine months since I introduced the original version of the Bill and in that short time at least 5,500 people have been killed on our roads and another 73,000 seriously injured. These deaths and injuries are self-inflicted. In the sense that society inflicts this appalling damage on itself. We believe that it is primarily through a greater social awareness to accept discipline, restraint—and penalties—that society will cure itself of the disease.

The Bill makes a number of specific and, I believe, absolutely essential proposals for improving the situation, but its underlying purpose is to help in creating this greater consciousness of the problem and determination to deal with it.

The aim of Part 1 of the Bill is to make the sanctions against drinking and driving far more effective than they are under present legislation. To do this we propose a far-reaching change in the law, as the House knows. We are creating a new offence, namely, the offence of driving with more than a certain proportion of alcohol in the blood. By this means we shall be taking the guesswork out of the law on drink and driving.

Once the Bill has been brought into force, it will be an offence to drive with a blood alcohol level of more than 80 milligrammes of alcohol per 100 millilitres of blood. All the old arguments about what constitutes impairment and all the old devices for trying to decide whether or not a driver is impaired will go. Instead there will be a clear-cut level, and this 80 milligramme level which we have fixed has been arrived at on the recommendation of the B.M.A. and bearing in mind the views put forward by the Medical Research Council.

I would not like to suggest that this level is fixed for all time. I said it was a scientific standard, and, as such, the House might think it was subject to the eternal verity which the laws of science are supposed to possess. Certainly the medical authorities agree that, with a concentration of alcohol in the blood beyond this level, the ability to drive of the great majority of people is impaired.

Just how important it is to have this new standard Hon. Members will realise from the fact that at present prosecutions in this country are rarely brought against drivers having a concentration of less than 150 milligrammes, and even then a very high proportion are acquitted. With this new standard in force, we estimate that the saving in casualties each year will be between 18,000 and 32,000. None the less, there is a dispute about what the level should be, some people holding that it is too low."

1–10   A good historical perspective was given by Lord Bridge in *Fox v. Chief Constable of Gwent* [1985] A.C. 281, 296:

"For as long as most of us can remember the number of deaths and injuries caused by road accidents, year in and year out, has been one of the ugliest features of modern society. No one has ever doubted that a substantial fraction of that number was caused by persons driving when, to a greater or lesser extent, they were under the influence of alcohol. So long as the offence of drunken driving, however defined from time to time, could only be established by a jury's assessment of the outward manifestation of the driver's intoxication, convictions were hard to come by and the scourge remained. 'There but for the grace of God, go I,' said many a juror to himself as he voted for an acquittal.

The Road Safety Act 1967 . . . introduced for the first time an objective scientific criterion to determine the amount of alcohol in a driver's body and a new criminal offence defined by reference to a prescribed limit of the amount of alcohol in the body with which a person could lawfully drive."

H. The Breathalyser

1–11   Under the Road Safety Act 1967, drivers were obliged to blow into breath-testing devices at the roadside. These instruments were very soon christened "breathalysers" by the public. In addition, any motorist who failed or refused to take a breathalyser test was liable to be arrested and to find himself under a legal obligation to provide a blood or urine specimen for the purpose of an analysis.

As this was a novel departure from the ground rules in criminal law, and also to overcome likely opposition in Parliament, strict safeguards were laid down, breach of which would automatically result in an acquittal. Unless a motorist was involved in an accident, he could only be required to give a breath sample if he was still driving at the time of the request. Only if he had been afforded the opportunity to take a breath test could a motorist be required to provide a specimen of blood or urine, at his option, for a laboratory test. The Act made it clear that the sample had to be obtained strictly in accordance with the terms of the statute. Motorists, exercising their right to trial on indictment, argued that the statute had not been complied with, leaving it to a jury (of fellow drivers!) to acquit them for that sole reason, even though at the time of their driving they had consumed well over the prescribed limit of alcohol. Some idea of the approach taken by juries to such cases can be gained from the fact that in

Manchester a defendant could normally forecast the likely outcome of his trial on its first adjournment by noting whether the jury went to the coffee shop or the court bar.

The effect of the legislation was only temporary. In 1967, before the Act became law, 28 per cent of the drivers killed on the road had a blood alcohol concentration above what became the statutory limit. By the next year, when the Act was in force, that percentage had fallen to 17. However by 1981, the percentage of drivers killed with an alcohol level above 80 milligrammes was back to the level of the pre-Act days of the mid-1960s. Since the mid-1980s, there has been a "steady drop in drink-drive deaths. In 1985 the number of people killed in accidents involving illegal alcohol levels was 1,040, with a drink-drive casualty total of 27,220. In 1995 the number of deaths was 580, with a casualty total of 16,050." *The Guardian*, October 25, 1996. These figures are not meant to detract from the achievements of the statute. In a recorded programme on Radio 4 on February 11, 1991, Baroness Castle said that her officials had estimated that in its first year the Act would reduce the number of fatalities on the road by 200. In fact, during that period, it saved 1,200 lives. In 1968 the number of road fatalities fell by 15 per cent and total casualties fell by 11 per cent compared with the preceding year. Nevertheless, nearly 25 years after the introduction of compulsory breath tests, the debate about whether motorists should be subjected to them continues. **1–12**

I. The legislation of the 1970s

The provisions of the Road Safety Act 1967 were repealed and re-enacted *in toto* by the Road Traffic Act 1972. The Government decided to review the workings of the breathalyser legislation and in 1974 appointed a committee under the chairmanship of Frank Blennerhassett, Q.C. to report on, and to make recommendations about, the then current drinking and driving laws. The committee looked at other jurisdictions and was impressed by those that used breath alcohol measuring instruments able to give an instant analysis of a motorist's breath and to print out, within a couple of minutes, the results of the analysis, showing exactly what amount of alcohol was in the driver's breath. The committee was in favour of such machines becoming standard equipment for British police forces. It was also in favour of high risk offenders not having their licences returned until they had proved that their drinking habits would not constitute a danger on the road. A high risk driver was defined as somebody who was convicted either twice in a year or with a blood alcohol level of, or above, 200 milligrammes. As a result of their recommendations (the Blennerhassett Report), published in 1976, a study of this subject was undertaken by Home Office forensic scientists at Aldermaston during 1977 and 1978 which included field trials of three "breathalysers". These tests demonstrated the feasibility of using such devices in the United Kingdom. **1–13**

J. The abolition of jury trials

1-14 Other developments in the criminal field were occurring which would affect the drinking and driving laws, notably the abolition of trials by one's peers for such offences. The 1970s had led to a dramatic growth in the number of, and the consequent delay in, indictable offences coming before the Crown Court. The Government appointed a committee, under the chairmanship of James L.J., to make recommendations on the trial of offenders. That committee recommended that a defendant should no longer have the right to be tried by a jury for any crime for which the maximum period of imprisonment did not exceed six months. In those days a person had the right to be tried on indictment for any offence (except assault) for which a maximum sentence of four months or more in gaol was prescribed. The James Committee also recommended that the penalties for a number of misdemeanours be reduced so as to prevent the election of jury trial by those charged with such an offence. Much more preferable are the views expressed by Murphy J. in the High Court of Australia in *Barton v. R.* (1980) 47 C.L.R 109: "The trend to replace indictable offences by summary ones seriously erodes the institution of trial by jury, which is the most important safeguard for the liberties of the people."

1-15 Nevertheless, despite strong opposition from the Society of Labour Lawyers (and many others) the Callaghan administration passed the Criminal Law Act 1977 which removed all offences carrying no more than six months' imprisonment from the province of the jury. This spurning of jurors can best be described as "an unforgivable offence in the eyes of any true blooded Englishman" to quote the dicta of Donaldson M.R. (when describing the removal of the right to trial by jury in the Admiralty Court, in *The Goring* [1987] Q.B. 687 at 701). The Criminal Law Act accordingly reduced the maximum penalty for breathalyser offences from two years' incarceration to six months. Henceforth, and contrary to the principles enshrined in the Magna Carta (*i.e. nullus liber homo . . . nec sup eum ibimus, nec sup eum mittem nisi p judiciu legale piu suo*), drivers were denied the opportunity to be tried by jury and were forced to argue their case solely before magistrates. The new Government in 1979 decided to implement the recommendations of the Blennerhassett Committee, since this would save the rising cost of analysing samples of body fluid and also speed up the process of discovering how much liquor a driver had consumed. Accordingly, profound changes were introduced into the drinking and driving laws by the Transport Act 1981 and can best be summarised in the words of Lord Bridge [1986] A.C. 296:

> "What is undeniable is that the ingenuity of defence lawyers, deployed in searching the old provisions [*i.e.* the 1967 and 1972 Acts] for technical defences, provided many a drunken driver with an avenue of escape from conviction in circumstances in which even the characteristically sympathetic juror must have thought the conviction was richly deserved. As these loopholes in the law became widely known, the effectiveness of the new deterrent waned.

It was against this background that Parliament by section 25 of and Schedule 8 to the Transport Act 1981 replaced the old provisions by the new and radically redrafted sections 6 to 12 . . . "

K. The use of breath analyses to obtain convictions

Under these "new and radical" provisions, the circumstances in which a **1–16** motorist had to provide a specimen for analysis were greatly increased. The powers of the constabulary to require roadside breath tests were multiplied. Of far more significance, and in order to prevent acquittals based on matters other than the accuracy of the analysis, the police could simply demand the provision of a specimen (at a police station) for analysis if they suspected a motorist of having driven or been in charge of a motor vehicle while unfit or with excess alcohol in his body. No other pre-conditions were laid down. The choice of sample was given to the officer but he was normally required to demand (except in a few special circumstances) that the motorist blew into a breath alcohol measuring instrument which would carry out an "on the spot" analysis. Prior to the introduction of this new type of breathalyser, further field trials had been carried out on three models, two of which were subsequently approved by the Home Secretary for use by the police, namely the Intoximeter and the Camic. The prescribed limit for breath alcohol was 35 microgrammes, *i.e.* the approximate equivalent of the blood alcohol level.

L. Police perspective on the current legislation

The police were enthusiastic about these new instruments. In his annual **1–17** report for 1983, Sir Philip Knights, Chief Constable of the West Midlands Constabulary, wrote:

"The introduction in May of the Intoximeter evidential breath-testing machine for use in police stations, following the introduction of more positive roadside screening devices, has made the enforcement of drink-driving legislation simpler and less time-consuming."

M. The judicial reaction

The judiciary, however, still had no doubt as to the great infringement of **1–18** liberty involved in a person having to incriminate himself. Their view can be summarised in (once again) the words of Lord Bridge (*ibid.*): "Inevitably the means adopted to enable the amount of alcohol in the suspect's body to be determined in accordance with the appropriate scientific criterion involved a substantial encroachment on his civil liberties."

Accordingly, the courts have insisted that the police must follow, in the correct manner, the procedure laid down in the legislation (now the Road Traffic Act 1988) for requiring and obtaining a specimen for analysis. This was well expressed by Pill J. when he said in *Wareing v. DPP* [1990] R.T.R. 199 that the Road Traffic Act "provided a procedure which the police were required to follow". Thus the High Court made it mandatory for a constable to inform a motorist of the options open to him under the legislation, *e.g.* when he has the choice of providing blood or urine, to replace his breath specimen. This approach of the judges to the present legislation has not been universally welcomed in legal circles. An example of this is the commentary on the case of *Paterson v. DPP* [1990] R.T.R. 329 in the [1990] *Criminal Law Review*, p. 652. There the High Court held that a motorist must be told of his unfettered right to make representation as to which type of sample he would prefer to provide and whenever that was not done, there had to be an acquittal. The commentator on that decision stated that he "would be the last to suggest that this was a good rule" [1990] Crim L.R. 652. Logically, the judiciary must be correct in insisting that a driver must have explained to him what his rights are. Why should only lawyers, because of their legal knowledge, be in a position to exercise them, while the average member of the public would otherwise be prevented from taking advantage of them solely because of their unfamiliarity with the relevant statutory provisions? However, some of these privileges afforded to the motorist were severely curtailed by the House of Lords in *DPP v. Warren* [1993] A.C. 319 where their entitlement to state their preference for blood or urine was replaced by a more limited one, namely only to giving such reasons as prevented blood being taken by a doctor. Their Lordships also held that, but for the decisions of the High Court, they would not even have required the police to tell the motorist that the sample could be either of blood or of urine, the choice of which lay with the police.

N. The creation of the Crown Prosecution Service

1–19 The latest significant event to affect the motoring offender was the establishment in 1985 of the Crown Prosecution Service, a nationalised body set up by the Thatcher government to conduct all police prosecutions. It has been a mixed blessing for drivers. All cases now have to be reviewed by qualified lawyers which should prevent motorists having to come to court to face unjust prosecutions or those doomed to failure. Previously in some areas prosecutions were conducted by police officers without the case papers ever having been seen by a lawyer. This field of jurisprudence is very complex and can often only be found in specialist reports. Therefore it is possible to overlook the latest developments in this area, or indeed other technical rules, as happened in *Smith v. DPP* [1989] R.T.R. 148, which caused Farquharson J. to remark (at 152):

> "In a situation like this it is always distressing that an entirely unmeritorious appeal should succeed in this way, but the fact is that this perfectly simple procedure could have been followed by the prosecutor in adducing [his evidence] at the proper time."

Unfortunately, this lack of up-to-date knowledge has led to the finding of guilty of a number of people who as a matter of law could never have been convicted, *e.g. R. v. Penrith Justices, ex p. Marks* [1996] R.T.R. 207. To overcome such miscarriages of justice, the Criminal Appeal Act 1995 amended section 142 of the Magistrates' Courts Act 1980 to empower petty session to set aside a conviction wherever it is in the interest of justice to do so.

O. The end of the 1980s, and the 1990s

The history of this topic draws towards its close with the passing of the **1–20** Road Traffic Act 1988 supplemented by the Road Traffic Offenders Act 1988, both of which received the Royal Assent in November 1988, although neither came into force until May of the following year. No radical innovations were introduced into the law of drinking and driving by either of these Acts, which basically re-enacted the changes brought about by the Transport Act 1981. Certain modifications were made to those statutes by the latest piece of legislation in this field, namely the Road Traffic Act 1991, the major innovation being the introduction of a new offence of causing death by careless driving when either under the influence of drink or drugs, or having refused, within 18 hours of the fatal accident, to give a specimen for analysis.

Just how "popular" the breathalyser has become can be seen from an **1–21** examination of the criminal statistics released by the Home Office and reprinted in figure 1 (*Home Office Statistical Bulletin*, Issue 7/95: Breath Test Statistics England and Wales 1995).

These figures demonstrate that the police were carrying out an increasing number of tests, with an increasing number proving negative. The success of police campaigns can be seen, for example in the 1995 figures, where although more breath screening tests were carried out, the percentage of tests proving to be negative has increased by 1 per cent on the previous year.

Fig. 1

England and Wales

Outcome (In Thousands)	1985	1986	1987	1988	1989	1990	1991	1992[1]	1993	1994	1995
Total number of tests	250.3	303.0	399.8	443.3	540.9	596.6	562.5	531.3	599.6	678.5	702.7
Number positive or refused	95.7	97.8	111.4	111.7	108.0	102.4	90.3	87.8	89.4	93.3	94.4
% Positive or refused	38	32	28	25	20	17	16	17	15	14	13

[1] Reporting of breath tests is not comprehensive, negative tests are less well reported than positive tests. Up until 1992, breath test statistics were derived from a return to the Home Office by police forces in respect of each alcohol test required. Most forces returned information on negative tests on an aggregated basis. During 1992 a new return was introduced, which required police forces only to give the total number of screening tests, and the sum of positive and refused tests. The introduction of this new return may have altered the level of recording compared with earlier years.

The Home Secretary, Kenneth Baker M.P., asserted (*The Guardian*, July 25, 1991):

"Drink driving kills, and drivers should understand that the police are increasing their efforts to catch those who break the law."

P. Changing attitudes and the modern perspective

One thing is clear, attitudes to drinking and driving are hardening. In 1980 **1–22** a solicitor was sentenced by McNeil J. at St George's Hall (Liverpool) to four months' imprisonment for causing death by dangerous driving when totally intoxicated by alcohol and cannabis. Today he would have been considered to have been treated leniently if the sentence had been one of four years. A junior government minister resigned when arrested for drinking and driving as he drove home one night from the Conservative Party Conference. Even judges have been threatened with dismissal if convicted of such offences. The Lord Chancellor wrote to all full-time members of the judiciary with this warning (see *The Guardian*, April 21, 1995). This policy of Lord Mackay L.C. is reintroducing the standards of conduct which the judges had in the past previously voluntarily imposed upon themselves. In the 1960s the Recorder of Barrow was arrested for drunken driving and the very next day his letter of resignation was in the post. Things had altered towards the end of that decade when a member of the Court of Appeal who had pleaded guilty to contravening section 1 of the Road Safety Act not only continued to sit (see *The Times*, July 1, 1969) but later on became a Law Lord. Lord Elwyn-Jones L.C. announced the promotion of a puisne judge to the Court of Appeal just three days after the latter had been convicted under section 6 of the Road Traffic Act 1972 (see *The Sunday Times*, March 6, 1977). Lord Mackay has only very recently been converted to the idea of traffic regulations applying to his brethren. He had previously found it perfectly acceptable and had taken no action against one when he was convicted of drinking and driving for the second time (see *The Daily Mail*, June 2, 1993). To be fair to that judge, he had clearly been moderating his drinking habits as he was merely two-and-a-half times over the legal limit, while on the previous occasion he had consumed more than three times the permitted amount of alcohol for drivers. Such an attitude toward those who sit on the Bench is shared by few others, the general public much preferring the view expressed by Denning L.J. in *A Road to Justice*, published in 1955, when he wrote (at pp. 30–31):

"A judge should be beyond reproach.
The sixth principle I would suggest is that a judge should in his own character be beyond reproach, or at any rate should have so disciplined himself that he is not himself a breaker of the law. Time and time again he has to pronounce judgment on those who have offended against the law. He has to rebuke the evil and support the good. He cannot well do

this—he cannot without hypocrisy do it—if he himself has been found guilty of an offence against the law. I refer not to administrative offences like exceeding the speed limit but to grave offences which carry reproach in the eyes of the people, like being drunk in charge of a car. If a judge should be found guilty of such an offence, whilst holding office, most people would say he should resign: but a very difficult question may arise if a man should have been found guilty some years ago and then afterwards be considered for appointment as a judge.

The answer would seem to be therefore that a man should not be appointed a judge if he has been found guilty of a grave offence against the law: even though it is not generally known. And when it is publicly known it is worse because the people will then point a finger of scorn as they did long ago saying: 'Who made thee a ruler and a judge over us.' Such scornful remarks destroy the confidence which people should have in the judges."

1-23   On August 28, 1996 a semi-retired lord justice of appeal told a magistrates' court that he was deeply humiliated and depressed, when he was convicted of driving with twice the permitted amount of alcohol after having earlier that day sat in the Court of Appeal (*The Times*, August 29, 1996).

The Transport Minister has said that H.M. Government had no plans for reducing the permitted breath alcohol level for driving to 50μg as the British Medical Association and some police forces wanted, because then: "Support for the drink-driving campaign might disappear."

The Minister (Steven Norris) also pointed out that road fatalities due to drinking and driving had been reduced from 1,500 to a little over 500 (*The Guardian*, January 6, 1995). Despite the public revulsion against drinking and driving, its enforcement has not been immune from Government economies. In 1994 a rate-capped police authority in South Wales merely issued cautions to motorists whose breath alcohol level did not exceed 50μg and who exercised their option under section 8(2) of the Road Traffic Act by choosing to provide a blood specimen. There were no funds available to pay a doctor to take the sample or a scientist to analyse it.

1-24   The Transport and Works Act 1992 extended the breathalyser laws to those who work for a train or tramway company and either control or supervise the movements of those guided vehicles or who supervise or carry out maintenance. The Secretary of State can apply, and has applied, the provisions of the Transport and Works Act to those who also work for other transport systems which use guided vehicles, *inter alia*, for the carriage of members of the public.

1-25   The history of the drinking and driving laws can be summarised as the judiciary seeking to uphold the balance between the ancient tradition of the common law, that no man should be made to incriminate himself, and the need to enable the police to obtain sufficient evidence to secure the conviction of those who risk the lives of themselves and other road users. This conflict has made the law complex and, at times, has led to conflicting decisions (see Chapter 2).

Chapter 2

THE MODERN JUDICIAL ATTITUDE TO DRINKING AND DRIVING OFFENCES

A. Introduction

Many a judge today when hearing a breathalyser appeal will reiterate to **2–01** himself with reference to the present legislation the thoughts that Lord Morris of Borth-y-Gest expressed in *Bourlet v. Porter* [1973] R.T.R. 293, 295J:

> "My Lords, this case furnishes yet another example of the infinite and, perhaps, surprising variety of the sets of circumstances which give rise to prosecutions for an offence under section 1 of the Road Safety Act 1967."

In *Walker v. Lovell* [1975] 3 All E.R. 107, 111, Lord Diplock described what he believed to be the attitude adopted by many motorists towards the drinking and driving legislation:

> " . . . Drivers may take the view that it is more convenient to rely on being defended by a sufficiently ingenious lawyer than to take care never to drive with more than the permitted proportion of alcohol . . . "

Lord Diplock was not alone in his views. Four months later Viscount Dilhorne expressed similar sentiments in his speech in the House of Lords in the case of *Baker v. Foulkes* [1975] 3 All E.R. 651, 656:

> "I hope that the time will soon come when Parliament will amend these provisions so as to make their meaning and effect more intelligible and so as to reduce the chances of those proved to have an excess of alcohol in their blood avoiding conviction and punishment on pure technicalities. Just to increase the penalties for these offences will not improve the present highly unsatisfactory state of the law."

Ten years later those opinions were endorsed by Griffiths L.J. in *Lion* **2–02** *Laboratories v. Evans* [1985] Q.B. 526, 550:

> "The whole history of the drink and driving laws shows the lengths to which drivers will go to escape conviction on any technicality or bogus argument."

15

Lord Bridge in *Fox v. Chief Constable of Gwent* [1985] A.C. 281, 296 was at least prepared to put some of the blame on parliamentary counsel as well as lawyers in private practice:

> "How far the old provisions were drafted with a view to restricting this encroachment [of civil liberties] and how far the many difficulties revealed when the courts came to apply the old [*i.e.* pre-Transport Act] provisions were simply unanticipated in drafting the legislation is a matter of speculation. What is undeniable is that the ingenuity of lawyers, deployed in searching the old provisions for technical defences, provided many a drunken driver with an avenue of escape from conviction, in circumstances in which even the characteristically sympathetic juror must have thought that conviction was richly deserved."

2–03 Indeed, the law has become so technical that the *Criminal Law Review* expressed doubts as to the ability of circuit judges "to grasp the purport of [much of the technical and other] evidence" presented in such cases ([1988] Crim.L.R. 534). Hence the legion of appeals to the High Court. Nearly a quarter of a century later, things have not changed despite legislative efforts to improve them. The House of Commons on the second reading of the 1981 Transport Bill (H.C. Deb., vol. 966, col. 939) was told that the object of the proposed amendments and substitutions to the drinking and driving provisions of the Road Traffic Act 1972 was "to simplify, clarify, remove needless technicalities and thereby to make it more difficult for the guilty to get off by means of silly technical defences". In retrospect, much more accurate were the views of Lord Salmon in *Baker v. Foulkes* [1975] 3 All E.R. 651, 658 about the proposed reforms of the 1972 Act in addition to his views about the then current legislation:

> "My Lords, I am no more enchanted than are your Lordships by the draftsmanship of the Act with which this appeal is concerned. Many of its apparent obscurities and absurdities have, however, already been cured by recent decisions (including the present) of your Lordships' House. No doubt some grey areas remain, *e.g.* those exemplified by *Scott v. Baker* [1969] 1 Q.B. 659. Although I sympathise with the *cris de coeur* for amending legislation, I am by no means sanguine that it would improve the present situation. Indeed, I fear that it might have the contrary effect by blurring what has now been clarified by your Lordships' recent decisions."

B. Multiplicity and duplication of appeal

2–04 Since the amendments to the 1972 Act came into force on May 6, 1983, they have been under constant review in the courts. Indeed, lawyers in different parts of the country without any knowledge of what was happening in other magistrates' courts took the same legal points. The resulting volume of appeals to the Queen's Bench Divisional Court moved May L.J.

(in delivering the judgment in *Stepniewski v. Commissioner of Police of the Metropolis* [1985] R.T.R 330, 333) to assert that:

> "The number of appeals which come before the Court on the drink and driving legislation now contained in the Road Traffic Act 1972, as substituted, is legion."

In *Stokes v. Sayers* [1988] R.T.R 89, 94, Glidewell L.J. urged parties to abandon appeals where the point at issue had already been decided before their case came to be heard. As recently as 1988, new forensic submissions, this time by the prosecution in the case of *Gumbley v. Cunningham* [1989] A.C. 281, led to the introduction of another highly technical matter into the law, namely the metabolism of alcohol in human beings. In that case, the House of Lords held that proof of a motorist's alcohol content at the time of his driving could be obtained by retrospective calculations from a level which was below the statutory amount, and measured several hours after the driving had ceased.

C. Information to be given about the statutory option

The judges may blame counsel for the complexities which have crept into 2–05 the law, but their Lordships have not always applied a consistent interpretation to the same section of the Road Traffic Act. An example of the court "revising its previous opinion" can be seen in relation to the vexed question of what information must be given to motorists who either are under a mandatory duty, or have the option, to provide a sample of their body fluid for analysis. In *Lion Laboratories Ltd v. Evans* [1985] Q.B. 526, 540, *per* Stephenson L.J.:

> "The Statute also provides that if the breath test records a concentration of no more than 50 microgrammes, the suspect may claim an old-fashioned blood or urine test in replacement of the breath test. We are told that the suspect is in fact informed of that right on instruction to police forces, but there is no statutory requirement that he must be so informed."

Griffiths L.J. was of the same view (at 551): 2–06

> "In certain circumstances, namely a reading of over 50, an accused person is given no right to challenge the machine by a blood or urine test; even when there is a right to a blood or urine test between readings of 35 and 50, surprisingly there is no statutory obligation to tell the accused of his right."

These dicta were not followed in a case directly on this point, namely *Anderton v. Lythgoe* [1985] 1 W.L.R. 222, where Nolan J. said that a motorist must be informed that he had the option of giving a specimen of body fluid in substitution for the breath sample already provided. He dismissed the Court of Appeal's previous pronouncement (at 227):

> "[Defence counsel] asks us, and I for my part would accept his invitation, to view that remark [of Stephenson L.J.] as a dictum uttered without argument and not forming part of the decision reached in that case."

Nolan J. (at 228) continued:

> " . . . section[8(2)] contemplates two possible ways in which guilt or innocence may be established. One is by the breath sample. The other— if the subject so chooses—is by the sample of blood or urine. The alternatives must both be made available to the subject if the plain purpose of the subsection is to be achieved."

Relying on that dicta, the High Court in a series of cases (*e.g. DPP v. Byrne* [1991] R.T.R. 119, 125) went on to hold that before deciding which body fluid was required, the constable had to seek the motorist's views and take them into account. These cases were overruled by the House of Lords in *DPP v. Warren* [1993] A.C. 319, 331C (*per* Lord Bridge):

> "All [those cases were] based, as it seems to me, on a misreading of a few simple words in an earlier judgement as enunciating a proposition which simply cannot stand with the statutory language."

Lord Bridge said (at 893) that he understood Nolan J. to be saying that the motorist should be told that the choice was between breath and body fluid and not as meaning that the motorist had any say in which type of body fluid it should be.

2-07 Even today there is still a divergence of opinion among the judiciary as to how literally the pronouncements of Lord Bridge have to be followed. Some cases have treated them as if they were a statute and had to be followed literally (*e.g. R. v. Cheshire JJ., ex p. Cunningham* [1995] R.T.R. 287, 291G/H and *Breenan v. DPP*, unreported, October 13, 1994) while others have held that his Lordship's speech was not an Act of Parliament and it was sufficient if a motorist had been given enough facts to enable him to be in a position to decide whether or not to exercise his option, even though that did not literally comply with what Lord Bridge had laid down as the requisite information to be imparted to a driver: see *Baldwin v. DPP* [1996] R.T.R. 238. Indeed, the judges cannot even agree on whether or not a person must be told exactly why his option has arisen (*i.e.* because his lower breath reading did not exceed 50µg but was over the limit), or merely that it was between 40 and 50µg: see the conflicting decisions of *DPP v. Charles* [1996] R.T.R. 247 and *Noscoe v. DPP*, unreported, October 13, 1994, on the one hand and *DPP v. Hall-Brookes* [1996] R.T.R. 279 and *DPP v. Ormsby*, unreported, March 12, 1996, to the contrary.

D. Contradicting the breathalyser

A good example of the confusion in the law must be the overruling in 2–08
November 1987 of the view often expressed in the High Court as to the
nature of the evidence which may be adduced to undermine the accuracy of
the results of a breath analysis. In the case of *Hughes v. McConnell* [1985]
R.T.R. 244, the High Court ruled that only direct evidence of the
malfunctioning of the actual breathalyser used by the police was admissible
to impugn the result of its analysis. Evidence as to what the defendant had
drunk, prior to being breathalysed, was not admissible to challenge the
results of the test. It was further observed by Watkins L.J. in the case of
Price v. Nicholls [1986] R.T.R. 155, 161:

> "It is abundantly clear that the attempt being made in this case, as was
> made in *Hughes v. McConnell,* is to take this court and the courts below
> back to former days when there were long drawn out battles between on
> the one hand the prosecutor and on the other the defence as to the
> amount of drink taken by a defendant as compared with an analysis,
> usually produced as a result of the taking of a sample of urine.
> Parliament has by the legislation of more recent times set its face against
> contests of that kind . . . "

A further obvious class of relevant evidence which would appear to have 2–09
been excluded by *Hughes v. McConnell* [1985] R.T.R. 244 was the result of a
blood or urine analysis. Such evidence does not refer directly to the
functioning of a breath alcohol measuring instrument but clearly gives rise
to an inference about the accuracy or inaccuracy (as the case may be) of
such a device. However, in *Lucking v. Forbes* [1986] R.T.R. 97 such
circumstantial evidence was permitted to be given for the purpose of
challenging the results obtained by the use of a Lion Intoximeter 3000.
The justices were faced with a conflict between the breath analysis and two
blood analyses, one carried out on behalf of the police and the other by a
scientist employed by the accused. The High Court held that the result of
the defendant's analysis of his blood (which differed from that of the
prosecution) could be used to impugn the reliability of a breath alcohol
measuring instrument, even though the blood sample had been taken an
hour after the breath test. The court held that evidence as to standard
alcohol destruction rates was admissible and that the adjusted result of a
blood analysis could be used to undermine the accuracy of the breathalyser.
It should, however, be noted that a Home Office survey (*Report on Breath
Alcohol Measuring Instruments*, HMSO, 1985, ISBN 0 11340806 4) demonstrated quite clearly that the idea of a standard alcohol destruction rate was
not particularly helpful because of the wide variation between the liver
functioning of different individuals (see section 9–24 below).

This whole topic finally came to be reviewed by the House of Lords in 2–10
the case of *Cracknell v. Willis* [1988] A.C. 450. Their Lordships unan-
imously endorsed the rationale of the law expounded by Lord Griffiths who
stated (at 466–467) that he had the greatest difficulty in seeing any

indication in the statutory provisions that pointed to only one type of evidence being admissible to challenge the reliability of the breathalyser used in a particular case. However, the High Court has done its best to undermine that decision of the House of Lords (see *DPP v. Hill* [1991] R.T.R 351).

2–11   Despite the regret at that decision expressed by the High Court, this view of the law must still continue to have the approval of the House of Lords as their Lordships were in agreement with the sentiments expressed in the speech of Lord Ackner in *Gumbley v. Cunningham* [1989] A.C. 281, 287, when he said:

> "It would in my judgement be quite wrong to interpret the new statutory provisions as continuing to exclude evidence that was relevant to establishing the blood-alcohol concentration at a time when the defendant had been driving."

Under the unamended 1972 Act, there were conflicting decisions of the Court of Appeal as to whether the prosecution merely had to prove that the defendant's blood or urine analysis showed him to be over the prescribed limit, even though the analysis might not have been 100 per cent accurate (see *R. v. Coomaaswamy* [1976] R.T.R 21) or whether the prosecutor had to establish the analysis to be totally accurate (see *R. v. Porter* [1974] R.T.R. 273).

E. Which analytical result (if any) to found the prosecution

2–12 Some of the complexities of the legislation can be illustrated by the judgment of Robert Goff L.J. in the case of *Howard v. Hallett* [1984] R.T.R. 353. This was a case in which the driver did not initially provide two breath samples for the Intoximeter in one cycle because the police operator was inexperienced. It is not entirely clear from the judgment what actually occurred, but it can be inferred that the officer did not tell the defendant when he had to blow into the mouthpiece to provide a second specimen. In any event, the constable decided to start afresh and the result was that at the end of the procedure three breath samples had been provided. The Road Traffic Act 1972 (as substituted) only required two samples to be provided for analysis and only the lower of the two results could be used in court. The prosecutor chose the lower of the final two analyses as the basis of his prosecution. No evidence was given of the amount of alcohol in the very first sample. The High Court held that he had chosen the wrong two since the one excluded was prior to the other two and the Act only allowed two specimens to be required. Robert Goff L.J. expressed his view of the matter in the most forthright way by saying (at 360 H–J):

> "It would, it seems to me, be a most extraordinary consequence if, where the Act of 1972 lays down a careful and statutory procedure for

requiring a suspected motorist to provide specimens of breath and for analysing them and presenting them before a court, it is possible to disregard that procedure altogether. I cannot believe that was the intention of the legislature."

Robert Goff L.J. also held (at 360B/C and H) that the absence of a warning to a motorist that he might be prosecuted for failure to provide a specimen was fatal for any prosecution, even if the defendant had willingly provided the sample requested of him.

A further example of the same approach is the case of *Wakeley v. Hyams* **2–13** [1987] R.T.R. 49. In this case both parties were policemen. After his breath was shown to contain 50 microgrammes of alcohol, the defendant was required to provide a specimen of blood, instead of being informed that he could elect to give one, if he so wished, and have the analysis of that sample substituted for his breath analysis. The court held that the Intoximeter reading was inadmissible evidence since the driver had not been told that he had the choice of whether or not to give a blood sample. Similarly, the result of his blood analysis was inadmissible because the police had no power to demand a sample of body fluid (see s.7(3) of the Road Traffic Act 1988, which was substituted for s.8 of the Road Traffic Act 1972). In the words of Ralph Gibson L.J. (at 55E–F):

"The consequences of applying the principle in *Howard v. Hallett* [1984] R.T.R. 353 may include the sustaining of a defence to a charge under the Act which, on particular facts, may appear to be devoid of merits."

F. Large differences between the two analyses

The case of *Lodge v. Chief Constable of Greater Manchester* [1988] Crim.L.R. **2–14** 533 is a good example of the legal inconsistencies which the motorist faces and the element of luck in being acquitted or convicted. An analysis revealed a 23 per cent difference between the levels of alcohol in the two breath samples provided by Mr Lodge.

Sir William Paton, in his introduction to a report produced by the Home Office, had recommended that the machine should automatically abort if the difference between the two breath analyses was greater than 20 per cent. However, in *Lodge* above, the High Court said that it was solely for the tribunal of fact to decide if the difference was so large as to indicate that the machine used was unreliable. Accordingly, they dismissed Lodge's appeal.

Although they upheld the conviction, their Lordships made it clear that it was open for another court composed of different magistrates to come to the opposite conclusion on exactly the same evidence and on identical facts. Under the statutory powers to hear appeals, the High Court may only consider questions of law and the appeal court was accordingly absolutely right in its dismissal of the appeal. This is because the question of whether the machine was working correctly is a matter of fact with which the High Court cannot interfere. However, nothing is more likely to cause confusion than different courts reaching contradictory decisions on exactly the same evidence and facts.

G. Corroboration by the screening breath test

2–15 A further example of irreconcilable authorities are the decisions about whether the result of a roadside breath test is admissible in evidence to confirm the correctness of the analysis either of breath (by the Intoximeter) or of body fluid. It has been held to be admissible as corroborative evidence of a motorist's urine sample (see *Lomas v. Bowler* [1984] Crim.L.R. 178). However, in *Maharaj v. Solomon* [1987] R.T.R. 295, which was in turn approved in *Lodge* (reported on other matters [1988] Crim.L.R. 533) the High Court held that such evidence was not admissible to prove the accuracy of the Intoximeter. Whilst in *DPP v. Hill* [1991] R.T.R. 351, and *Lafferty v. DPP*, unreported, January 11, 1994, the court took the opposite view to that expressed in the last two mentioned cases.

H. Failure to produce a printout

2–16 The High Court has expressed diametrically opposed views over whether it is reasonable for a policeman to regard an Intoximeter as unreliable (and thus be entitled to require a specimen of body fluid) when its screen has displayed all the required information after the motorist has supplied two samples of breath, but it has failed to print out the results displayed on the screen. In *Morgan v. Lee* [1985] R.T.R. 409, it was held that it was not reasonable to regard such a machine as unreliable, while the opposite view was taken in *Badkin v. Chief Constable of South Yorkshire* [1988] R.T.R. 401.

I. Duplicity

2–17 Great confusion was caused by two conflicting decisions of the High Court (*DPP v. Corcoran* [1992] R.T.R 289 and *Shaw v. DPP* [1993] R.T.R 45) as to whether section 7(6) of the Road Traffic Act 1988 (failure to provide a specimen for analysis) created a single offence or two separate offences, each corresponding to the two different maximum sentences laid down in Schedule 2 to the Road Traffic Offenders Act 1988 (the penalty varied according to whether or not the defendant had or had not been driving a vehicle). The matter was finally settled by the House of Lords in *Butterworth v. DPP* [1994] R.T.R. 181, where it was held that Parliament had intended to create a single offence. At the same time their Lordships also settled the conflict between the cases which had held that the mandatory penalty of disqualification (subject to special reasons) was only to be imposed on those who had actually driven, *e.g. Crampsie v. DPP* [1993] R.T.R. 383 and those which had decided that such a sentence was to be inflicted when the police had merely suspected the defendant of having been driving, *e.g. Bunyard v. Hayes* [1985] R.T.R. 348. The House of Lords held the former statutory construction to be correct, which it is submitted is what justice required, although the wording of the Act strongly supported the other interpretation.

J. Hospital patients

Hospital patients are the latest category to cause disagreement between the judiciary in a number of instances over what is the correct procedure for dealing with them. *Duffy v. DPP* [1994] R.T.R. 241 held that they had to be told why they were not being required to provide breath specimens, while the opposite conclusion was reached in *R. v. Burton-upon-Trent JJ., ex p. Woolley* [1995] at 139. That latter case also disagreed with *White v. DPP ibid.* over whether a patient had to be asked if there were any reasons why a specimen of blood could not or should not be taken by a doctor. The latest judicial disagreement (so far!) is between Holland J. in *Webber v. DPP* [1995] T.L.R. 693 and Buxton J. in *Wheeler v. DPP*, unreported, June 28, 1994 over whether the procedure has to start all over again for a motorist who is required to provide a specimen at a hospital but is taken to a police station prior to its provision. **2–18**

K. Different philosophies

Most of the disagreements have been over statutory interpretation based on academic considerations. However, there is a clear difference of approach between two schools of thought on how the drinking and driving laws should be enforced. The majority who think that where Parliament has laid down safeguards for the motorist the courts should give effect to them even though it may on occasion mean the acquittal of a guilty driver. The minority take the opposite view, that "the means justify the end". This divergence is mirrored throughout the country in the debate on random breath tests. As this treatise is on what the law is, and is not designed to consider the morality or the theory of it, nothing further will be said, save that it helps to explain some totally inconsistent decisions. This view of the protagonists can be no better illustrated than by quoting the views openly expressed by two members of the higher judiciary over what both accepted to be the clearly established rule that a specimen for analysis which is not taken in accordance with the correct procedure cannot under any circumstance be admitted in evidence. Lord Bridge thought that anything else **2–19** would be "most extraordinary" ([1986] A.C. at 298), while Buxton J. thought that for the law to have been interpreted in this way was "a most striking conclusion" ([1995] R.T.R. at 152). The only comment the author proposes to make is to repeat with agreement what Lord Sailsbury said (though in a different context) during the rule of the Liberal government at the beginning of this century:

"Thank God for the House of Lords!"

The best example of this divergence of opinion is between those who think that the sacrifice of the licences of innocent motorists is justified *pour encouragez les autres*. So Paul Kennedy J. in *Dawes v. Taylor* [1986] R.T.R. 86 justified the condemnation of a driver for failing to provide a breath specimen even though the latter had done his best to provide such a specimen. Fortunately other judges have taken a view more in accordance with the principles of the common law such as Pain J. in *Cotgrove v. Cooney* [1987] R.T.R. 124, 127F that a person should not be punished for failing to do what he is incapable of achieving.

L. Conflicting decisions by the same judge

2-20 It is not only different judges who hold conflicting views; a judge may take another perspective of the law from that which he has taken in an earlier case. In *Cracknell v. Willis* [1988] A.C. 450, the House of Lords reversed a number of decisions of the High Court and held that a conviction for driving with excess alcohol could not be sustained on a single breath analysis, even where the lack of a second breath sample was due solely to the wrongful refusal of the motorist to provide one. It also stated specifically that *Duddy v. Gallagher* [1985] R.T.R. 401 should be overruled (*per* Lord Goff at 469, who also gave the leading judgment in *Duddy v. Gallagher*) where a conviction based on a single breath sample had been upheld.

In *Horrocks v. Binns* [1986] R.T.R. 202 McCullough J. held that before the prosecution could rely upon section 7(3)(a) to require a body fluid the constable had to believe what the motorist had told him, while four months later he expressed the opposite view in *White v. Proudlook* [1988] R.T.R 163.

A similar metamorphosis can be found in the dicta of Buxton J., when in construing Lord Bridge's speech in *DPP v. Warren, supra*, about the circumstances in which it is necessary to ask a hospital patient, before requiring a blood specimen, if there were any reasons why such could not or should not be taken by a doctor. In *White v. DPP* [1995] R.T.R. 287, he allowed an appeal because a hospital patient had not been asked that question (*ibid.*, 291L–292A). However, six-and-a-half months later, his Lordship took the opposite view and held that such a question was unnecessary because no specimen could be taken without the approval of the medical practitioner in charge of the motorist: see *R. v. Burton-upon-Trent JJ., ex p. Woolley, ibid.*, 149H–150B.

At the time of writing, the latest and most wide ranging judicial *volte face* **2–21** was by Leggatt L.J. in *DPP v. Ormsby*, unreported, May 12, 1996, where he said that the only parts of Lord Bridge's formula in *DPP v. Warren, supra*, which had to be told to a driver were those that represented a reproduction of the statutory requirements. Less than a year previously, in *ex p. Cunningham* [1995] R.T.R. 287, 291H, he had said that all of that speech by Lord Bridge had to be followed "literally". So much for *stare decisis*!

M. Confusion continues today

The government's hopes that the amendments to the 1972 legislation **2–22** would reduce acquittals on grounds unrelated to alcohol consumption remain unfulfilled, principally because the courts continue to protect the civil rights of motorists by insisting that the police follow, in its entirety, the statutory procedure laid down for the taking of samples. The removal of the need for a lawful arrest as a prerequisite for the statutory procedure certainly overcame one of the main bulwarks previously relied upon by drunken drivers. However, other defences came into existence and a fresh crop of problems arose through the more complex procedures necessary to deal with the introduction of another substance, namely breath, for the police to collect and to analyse, in addition to their existing powers in relation to body fluids.

Despite the conflicting views of the judiciary, in *DPP v. Magill* [1988] **2–23** R.T.R. 337, Watkins D.C.J. was hopeful that this state of affairs would not continue (at 341):

"It is, I think, most desirable that the police should know where this court once and for all stands upon this matter and are not called upon by contrary decisions coming from here to change their procedures time and again. That can only lead to confusion for both the police and public alike."

Unfortunately, one suspects that Parker L.J. was nearer to the mark in *Walton v. Rimmer* (reported on other matters [1986] R.T.R. 31) when counsel ventured to suggest that his Lordship's judgment would help to clarify the law:

"My Lord, may I ask that the Appellant's costs be paid out of central funds. The reason I make this application is that this case was really brought to clarify the wording which, although simple, is not clear. Your Lordship's decision will now make it clear to the police precisely what they must do, but those instructing me felt that clarification was required."

The response of Parker L.J. was much more sanguine:

"You may be unduly optimistic. My experience of the Road Traffic Act is that nothing ever makes anything clear."

Watkins D.C.J. now appears to share the opinion of Parker L.J. in view of this opening remark to defence counsel in *Renshaw v. DPP* [1992] R.T.R. 186 when he said: "Not another new defence!"

Chapter 3

THE ACTUS REUS AND MENS REA OF THE RELEVANT OFFENCES AND THEIR PUNISHMENTS; THE RELATIONSHIP BETWEEN THE OFFENCES AND THE DISCRETION OF THE POLICE TO INVESTIGATE AND PROSECUTE THEM

A. Introduction

The Road Traffic Act 1988, as amended by the Road Traffic Act 1991, **3–01** contains the statutory provisions relating to the offences of (a) driving, (b) attempting to drive, and (c) being in charge of a vehicle on a road or other public place, either while unfit or with an alcohol level above the prescribed limit. It also contains the related offences of failing to provide a specimen of breath, blood or urine, when required to do so. Some supplementary provisions regarding proof by written statements and the taking and analysing of specimens are to be found in sections 15 and 16 of the Road Traffic Offenders Act 1988. Sections 34 *et seq.* and Schedule 2 to the latter Act set out the penalties for those who commit drinking and driving offences. Both 1988 Acts came into force on May 15, 1989. Similar provisions were enacted by the Transport and Works Act 1992 for employees of railway and tram companies. In addition, there is still on the Statute Book one offence under the Licensing Act 1872 which punishes those who are drunk in the street, whether they are pedestrians or whether they are in charge of a vehicle and also even earlier legislation regulating the drinking habits of taxi-drivers.

Set out below are the *actus rei* of all 36 drinking and driving offences and their penalties. Subsequent chapters discuss how the courts have interpreted the statutory language creating those crimes. Parliament when empowering the judiciary to impose a driving disqualification has for some offences laid down a minimum period, unless there be special reasons to mitigate that, but has not proscribed any maximum duration. In March 1996 the DPP published a document entitled "Driving Offences Charging Standard". This gives guidance to Crown Prosecutors on what criteria should be applied when deciding which is the most appropriate charge to bring against a driver. A copy of these guidelines is reprinted in Appendix 11.

B. The offences

I. ROAD TRAFFIC ACT 1988

(a) Causing Death By Carelessly Driving A Mechanically Propelled Vehicle On A Road Or Other Public Place When Unfit To Drive Through Drink Or Drugs

3–02 This is a new offence created by the Road Traffic Act 1991, s.3, which inserted a new section 3A into the 1988 Act and is committed by causing a fatal accident by carelessly driving a mechanically propelled vehicle on a road or other public place while unfit to drive through drink or drugs.

Penalty for all offences contrary to section 3A

Fine	Unlimited
Penalty points	3–11
Imprisonment	10 years (maximum): Criminal Justice Act 1993, s.67(1)
Disqualification	Mandatory (two years minimum)

(b) Causing Death By Carelessly Driving A Motor Vehicle On A Road Or Other Public Place When The Proportion Of Alcohol In The Breath Exceeds The Prescribed Limit

3–03 This is contrary to section 3A of the 1988 Act as amended by the Road Traffic Act 1991, s.3. It is committed by causing a fatal accident through having driven a motor vehicle carelessly on a road or other public place with excess alcohol in the breath.

(c) Causing Death By Carelessly Driving A Motor Vehicle On A Road Or Other Public Place When The Proportion Of Alcohol In The Blood Exceeds The Prescribed Limit

3–04 This offence is created by the new section 3A and is identical in all respects to the preceding offence, save that the prosecution are relying upon an analysis of blood rather than of breath.

(d) Causing Death By Carelessly Driving A Motor Vehicle On A Road Or Other Public Place When The Proportion Of Alcohol In The Urine Exceeds The Prescribed Limit

3–05 This is contrary to section 3A, the only difference between this and the last two offences is that the prosecution must prove excess alcohol in urine rather than in breath or blood.

(e) Causing Death By Carelessly Driving A Motor Vehicle On A Road Or Other Public Place And Failing To Provide Without Reasonable Excuse A Specimen Of Breath, Blood Or Urine Within 18 Hours Of The Driving

This is like the previous four offences contrary to section 3A of the amended Road Traffic Act 1988 and is committed by causing a fatal accident by carelessly driving a motor vehicle on a road or other public place and then, within 18 hours of the driving, refusing to provide a specimen of breath, blood or urine, without a reasonable excuse. It carries the same penalty as all the other crimes created by section 3A. **3–06**

(f) Causing Death By Driving A Mechanically Propelled Vehicle On A Road Or Other Public Place Without Reasonable Consideration For Other Persons Using The Road Or Place When Unfit To Drive Through Drink Or Drugs

This offence, which is contrary to section 3A, is the same as (a), above, except that the motorist was driving without reasonable consideration for other road users rather than without due care and attention. **3–07**

(g) Causing Death By Driving A Motor Vehicle On A Road Or Other Public Place Without Reasonable Consideration For Other Persons Using The Road Or Place When The Proportion Of Alcohol In The Breath Exceeds The Pre-scribed Limit

This offence, also contrary to section 3A, is the same as (b), above, except that the motorist was driving without reasonable consideration for other road users rather than without due care and attention. **3–08**

(h) Causing Death By Driving A Motor Vehicle On A Road Or Other Public Place Without Reasonable Consideration For Other Persons Using The Road Or Place When The Proportion Of Alcohol In The Blood Exceeds The Pre-scribed Limit

This offence, contrary to section 3A, is the same as (c), above, except that the motorist was driving without reasonable consideration for other road users rather than carelessly. **3–09**

(i) Causing Death By Driving A Motor Vehicle On A Road Or Other Public Place Without Reasonable Consideration For Other Persons Using The Road Or Place After Driving When The Proportion Of Alcohol In The Urine Exceeds The Prescribed Limit

3–10 This offence, contrary to section 3A, is the same as (h), above, except that here the excess alcohol is in the urine and not in the blood.

(j) Causing Death By Driving A Motor Vehicle On A Road Or Other Public Place Without Reasonable Consideration For Other Persons Using The Road Or Place And Failing To Provide Without Reasonable Excuse A Specimen Of Breath, Blood Or Urine For Analysis Within 18 Hours Of Driving

3–11 This is the same offence as (f), (g) and (h), above, save that instead of having provided a specimen for analysis, one has been refused without a reasonable excuse within 18 hours of the driving. It is also contrary to section 3A.

(k) Driving A Mechanically Propelled Vehicle On A Road Or Other Public Place While Unfit Through Drink Or Drugs

3–12 This is contrary to section 4(1) of the Road Traffic Act 1988, as amended by the Road Traffic Act 1991, s. 4.

A person commits an offence if he drives a mechanically propelled vehicle on a road or other public place when he is unable to drive properly on account of this consumption of alcohol and/or, through taking drugs.

Penalty

Fine	Level 5
Penalty points	3–11
Imprisonment	Six months (maximum)
Disqualification	Mandatory (minimum 12 months)

(l) Attempting To Drive A Mechanically Propelled Vehicle On A Road Or Other Public Place While Unfit Through Drink Or Drugs

3–12A This offence is identical to, carries the same penalty as, and was created by the same subsection of the Road Traffic Act 1988 as offence (k), save that the prosecution merely have to prove an attempt to drive and not the full offence.

(m) In Charge Of A Mechanically Propelled Vehicle On A Road Or Other Place When Unfit Through Drink Or Drugs

This is contrary to section 4(2) of the Road Traffic Act 1988, as amended **3–13** by the Road Traffic Act 1991, s. 4.

A person commits an offence if he is in charge of a mechanically propelled vehicle on a road or other public place when he is unable to drive properly on account of his consumption of alcohol and/or through taking drugs. It is a statutory defence for the accused to prove that he would not have driven nor attempted to drive whilst his ability to do so was impaired.

Penalty

Fine	Level 4
Penalty points	10
Imprisonment	Three months (maximum)
Disqualification	Discretionary (even though the evidence showed that the defendant was not merely in charge but was also actually driving the vehicle, a conviction for this offence still only carries a discretionary disqualification; see *George v. DPP* [1989] R.T.R 217)

(n) Driving A Motor Vehicle On A Road Or Other Public Place When The Proportion Of Alcohol In The Breath Exceeded The Prescribed Limit

This is contrary to section 5(1)(a) of the Road Traffic Act 1988. **3–14**

A person commits an offence if he drives or attempts to drive a motor vehicle on a road or other public place when his breath alcohol concentration exceeds the prescribed level.

Penalty

Fine	Level 5
Penalty points	3–11
Imprisonment	Six months (maximum)
Disqualification	Mandatory (minimum 12 months)

(o) Driving A Motor Vehicle On A Road Or Other Public Place When The Proportion Of Alcohol In The Blood Exceeded The Prescribed Limit

This is an identical offence to, carries the same penalty as, and was created **3–15** by the same subsection of the Road Traffic Act as (n) above, save that the prosecution are relying on a blood analysis rather than a breath analysis to prove the excess alcohol.

(p) Driving A Motor Vehicle On A Road Or Other Public Place When The Proportion Of Alcohol In The Urine Exceeded The Prescribed Limit

3–16 This is also contrary to section 5(1)(a) and is identical to the previous two offences save that the prosecution are relying on an analysis of urine rather than one of blood or breath. It carries the same penalty as offences (n) and (o) and was created under the same subsection.

(q) Attempting To Drive a Motor Vehicle On A Road Or Other Public Place When The Proportion Of Alcohol In The Breath Exceeded The Prescribed Limit

3–16A This offence is identical to, carries the same penalty as, and was created by the same subsection of the Road Traffic Act 1988 as offence (n), save that the prosecution merely have to prove an attempt to drive and not the full offence.

(r) Attempting To Drive a Motor Vehicle On A Road Or Other Public Place When The Proportion Of Alcohol In The Blood Exceeded The Prescribed Limit

3–16B This offence is identical to, carries the same penalty as, and was created by the same subsection of the Road Traffic Act 1988 as offence (o), save that the prosecution merely have to prove an attempt to drive and not the full offence.

(s) Attempting To Drive a Motor Vehicle On A Road Or Other Public Place When The Proportion Of Alcohol In The Urine Exceeded The Prescribed Limit

3–16C This offence is identical to, carries the same penalty as, and was created by the same subsection of the Road Traffic Act 1988 as offence (p), save that the prosecution merely have to prove an attempt to drive and not the full offence.

(t) In Charge Of A Motor Vehicle On A Public Road Or Other Public Place With Excess Alcohol In The Breath

3–17 This is contrary to section 5(1)(b) of the Road Traffic Act 1988.

A person commits an offence if he is in charge of a motor vehicle on a road or other public place when his breath alcohol concentration exceeds the prescribed limit. It is a statutory defence to prove that the motorist would not have driven while his alcohol level was above the prescribed limit.

Penalty

Fine	Level 4
Penalty points	10
Imprisonment	Three months (maximum)
Disqualification	Discretionary (*q.v.* under the heading "Disqualification" in offence (m)—in charge of a vehicle while unfit)

(u) In Charge Of A Motor Vehicle On A Road Or Other Public Place With Excess Alcohol In The Blood

This is an identical offence, with the same statutory defence, with the same **3–18** penalty and under the same subsection of the Road Traffic Act as offence (t), save that the excess alcohol is in the blood and not the breath.

(v) In Charge Of A Motor Vehicle On A Road Or Other Public Place With Excess Alcohol In The Urine

Apart from the fact that the prosecution are relying on a urine analysis, this **3–19** offence is identical to, created under the same subsection of the Road Traffic Act, and carries the same penalty, as the previous two offences. It is also subject to the same statutory defence.

(w) Failing To Provide Without A Reasonable Excuse A Specimen Of Breath For A Breath Test

This is contrary to section 6(4) of the Road Traffic Act 1988. **3–20**
   A person who is or was driving or attempting to drive or is or was in charge of a motor vehicle on a road or other public place commits an offence when he fails or refuses without a reasonable excuse to provide a specimen of breath for a screening test when required to do so. This offence must not be confused with the much more serious offence under section 7(6) of failing at a hospital or a police station to supply a specimen of breath for analysis by a Lion Intoximeter or Camic breath alcohol measuring device or failing to supply a specimen of blood or urine.

Penalty

Fine	Level 3
Penalty points	4
Disqualification	Discretionary

(x) Failing To Provide Without A Reasonable Excuse A Specimen For Analysis, After Having Been Required To Do So During The Course Of An Investigation Into Whether An Offence Under Sections 3A, 4 Or 5 Had Been Committed

This is contrary to section 7(6) of the Road Traffic Act 1988. **3–21**

A person commits an offence if he refuses without a reasonable excuse to provide a specimen for analysis when requested to do so during an investigation into a possible offence under sections 3A, 4 or 5. Unlike an offence under that latter section, separate offences are not created according to which type of substance the defendant has failed to supply.

Penalty
If having driven or attempted to drive
Fine	Level 5
Penalty points	3 to 11
Imprisonment	Six months (maximum)
Disqualification	Mandatory (minimum of one year)

If having not driven or attempted to drive
Fine	Level 4
Penalty points	10
Imprisonment	Three months (maximum)
Disqualification	Discretionary

In *Butterworth v. DPP* [1994] R.T.R. 330, the House of Lords laid down that if the prosecution and defence disagree on whether or not the accused had been driving, that question must be determined by the tribunal of fact in accordance with the normal rules of evidence (*i.e.* a *Newton* hearing (1982) 77 Cr. App. R. 13).

(y) CYCLING WHEN UNDER THE INFLUENCE OF DRINK AND DRUGS

3-22   This is contrary to section 30(1) of the Road Traffic Act 1988.

A person commits an offence if he rides a cycle on a road or other public place while unfit through drink or drugs so that he is unable to have proper control of his cycle.

Penalty
Fine	Level 3

II. LONDON HACKNEY CARRIAGE ACT 1831

(a) DRIVER OF HACKNEY CARRIAGE, THROUGH BEING INTOXICATED, INJURES ANY PERSON IN HIS LIFE, LIMBS, OR PROPERTY

3-22A   It is an offence under section 56 of the London Hackney Carriage Act 1831 for a taxi driver, through drink, to cause injury to somebody or to damage property within both the City of London and the Metropolitan Police Area.

Penalty
Fine
Level 1 (Criminal Justice Act 1982, s.46) and on conviction, an Assistant Commissioner of Police can revoke the holder's hackney carriage licence (*vide* the Metropolitan Police Carriage Act 1869, s.15 and the London Cab Order, [SR and O 1346 of 1934] paragraph 7, as amended by S.I. 1955 No. 1853 and paragraph 19, as amended by S.I. 1955 No. 1853 and S.I. 1962 No. 289).

III. LONDON HACKNEY CARRIAGES ACT 1843

(a) A HACKNEY CARRIAGE DRIVER WHO IS DRUNK WHILE WORKING

It is an offence under section 29 of the London Hackney Carriage Act 1843 **3–22B** for a taxi driver in the City of London or the Metropolitan Police District to be drunk during working hours.

Penalty
Fine
Level 1 (*vide* Criminal Justice Act 1982, s.46) OR Imprisonment, 2 months (maximum)

IV. TOWN POLICE CLAUSES ACT 1847

(a) DRIVING A HACKNEY CARRIAGE WHILE INTOXICATED

It is an offence under section 61 of Town Police Clauses Act 1847 to drive a **3–22C** taxi while drunk, anywhere in England and Wales (*vide* section 15 of the Transport Act 1985), except the Metropolitan Police District and the City of London.

Penalty
Fine
Level 1 (*vide* Criminal Justice Act 1982, s.46)

V. THE LICENSING ACT 1872

(a) DRUNK ON THE HIGHWAY OR OTHER PUBLIC PLACE WHILE IN CHARGE OF A CARRIAGE

This is contrary to section 12 of the Licensing Act 1872. **3–23**

A person commits an offence, under this section, if he is drunk while in charge of a carriage or steam engine on a road or other public place. By section 191 of the Road Traffic Act 1988, all motor vehicles are deemed to be carriages (even for the purpose of the Licensing Act). The word "carriage" also includes a pedal cycle and a person is still in charge of it, even if he is merely pushing it (see *Corkery v. Carpenter* [1951] 1 K.B. 102).

Under section 5 of the Road Traffic Offenders Act 1988 a person who is liable to be charged with any of the preceding offences under the R.T.A. 1988 cannot be charged with this offence.

Penalty
Fine   Level 1
Imprisonment   One month (maximum)

VI. UNDER THE TRANSPORT AND WORKS ACT 1992

(a) CARRYING OUT WORK WHILE UNFIT THROUGH DRINK OR DRUGS

3–24 It is an offence under section 27(1) of the Transport and Works Act 1992 for any of the following persons to carry out their work while unfit through drink or drugs; namely a train or tram driver, guard, conductor or signalman or anybody who works on a transport system in which he can control or affect the movement of a vehicle or works in a maintenance capacity or as a supervisor or lookout for persons working in a maintenance capacity.

Penalty
Fine   Level 5
Imprisonment   Six months (maximum)

(b) CARRYING OUT WORK WITH EXCESS ALCOHOL IN THE BREATH

3–25 It is an offence under section 27(2) for any of the following persons to carry out their work after having consumed more alcohol than the prescribed limit, namely a train or tram driver, guard, conductor or signalman or anybody who works on a transport system in which he can control or affect the movement of a vehicle or in a maintenance capacity or as supervisor or lookout for persons working in a maintenance capacity.

Penalty
Fine   Level 5
Imprisonment   Six months (maximum)

(c) CARRYING OUT WORK WITH EXCESS ALCOHOL IN THE BLOOD

3–26 Save that the substance is blood not breath, everything about this offence is the same as the preceding one.

(d) CARRYING OUT WORK WITH EXCESS ALCOHOL IN THE URINE

Except that the substance is urine, this offence is identical in all respects to **3–27** the two previous ones.

(e) OFFENCES BY OPERATORS OF TRANSPORT SYSTEMS

Under section 28(1) of the Transport and Works Act 1992, the responsible **3–28** operator (and, if different, his employer also) shall be guilty if anybody for whom he is responsible commits an offence under section 27. He shall not be guilty if he used all due diligence to try to prevent the commission of an offence under section 27.

Penalty

Fine	Level 5
Imprisonment	Six months (maximum)

(f) FAILING TO TAKE A BREATH TEST

It is an offence under section 29(5) for any of the following people, namely **3–29** a train or tram driver, guard, conductor or signalman or anybody who works on a transport system in which he can control or affect the movement of a vehicle or in a maintenance capacity or as a supervisor or lookout for persons working in a maintenance capacity, to refuse to take a breath test without reasonable excuse (a) if a constable reasonably suspects him of working or, of having worked, with alcohol in his body, or (b) if a constable reasonably suspects him of having been working at the time of an accident or serious incident and that an act or omission by him may have been a cause of the accident or incident.

Penalty

Fine	Level 3

(g) FAILING TO PROVIDE WITHOUT REASONABLE EXCUSE A SPECIMEN OF BREATH, BLOOD OR URINE FOR ANALYSIS

It is an offence under section 31(8) for a person, without reasonable excuse, **3–30** to fail to give a sample for analysis when lawfully required to do so during an investigation into an offence under section 27.

Penalty

Fine	Level 5
Imprisonment	Six months (maximum)

VII. MENS REA

On the authority of *Blayney v. Knight* [1975] R.T.R. 279, *mens rea* is **3–31** required for the actual act of driving or being in charge but, by analogy with *R. v. Miller* [1975] Crim. L.R. 723 (a case of driving without insurance), strict liability will be imposed concerning the motorist's knowledge of the rights exercised by the public over the *locus in quo* of the driving. The rationale of the latter case was *salus populi suprama lex*, which principle is equally applicable, if not more so, to drinking and driving offences. For the same reason, no *mens rea* is required of the motorist about the state he is in or of the amount of alcohol consumed (see *Tucker v. DPP* [1995] R.T.R. 9).

No *mens rea* would appear to be required for any of the relevant offences under the Transport and Works Act.

C. Penalties for aiding, abetting, counselling and procuring

3–32 Chapter 4, below, considers the question of what conduct makes a person an aider, an abettor, a counsellor or a procurer. Such a person is subject to the same penalty as the principal offender except that any power to impose a driving disqualification shall be at the discretion of the court (see Magistrates' Court Act 1980, s. 44; Accessories and Abettors Act 1861, s. 8; and Road Traffic Offenders Act 1988, s. 34(5)).

I. TIME LIMITS AND MODE OF TRIAL

3–33 Information must be laid in respect of any of the crimes mentioned in this chapter (other than one contrary to s. 3A) within six months of its commission. Save for proceedings under section 3A which can only be tried on indictment, all the other drinking and driving offences are summary and must be tried in the magistrates' court. In addition, when an either way offence is committed to the Crown Court for trial by jury, magistrates may commit to the Crown Court at the same time (by virtue of Criminal Justice Act 1988, s. 41(1)) any drinking and driving offence, provided it arose out of the circumstances giving rise to the either way offence (Section 41[1] does not apply where the connected offence is triable only on indictment: see *R. v. Miall* (1991) 155 J.P. 875.) If the motorist is convicted of the either way offence and pleads guilty to the summary offence, the latter can be dealt with by the Crown Court. If either of those pre-conditions does not apply, or the conviction on indictment is quashed on appeal, the summary matter must be returned to petty sessions for disposal by the justices.

D. The Relationship between the offences

I. ALTERNATIVE VERDICTS

3–34 Until the Road Traffic Act 1991, there was no provision whereby magistrates could convict of an alternative offence instead of the one to which the defendant had originally pleaded, without an amendment of the charge. Such an amendment was not possible on the hearing of an appeal; see

Garfield v. Maddocks [1974] Q.B. 7. Under section 24 of the Road Traffic Act 1991, the following alternative verdicts are available to justices at first instance, a jury, and the Crown Court on appeal. Therefore, a defendant will no longer be able to escape punishment by being convicted on an information which is inappropriate for the circumstances giving rise to the offence and then being acquitted by successfully appealing; by which time it would usually be too late to lay a new and more appropriate information.

Offence charged	*Alternative verdict*
Section 3A (causing death by careless driving when under the influence of drink or drugs).	Section 3 (careless and inconsiderate driving). Section 4(1) (driving when unfit to drive through drink or drugs). Section 5(1)(a) (driving with excess alcohol in breath, blood or urine). Section 7(6) (failing to provide specimen).
Section 4(1) (driving when unfit to drive through drink or drugs).	Section 4(2) (being in charge of a vehicle when unfit to drive through drink or drugs).
Section 5(1)(a) (driving or attempting to drive with excess alcohol in breath, blood or urine).	Section 5(1)(b) being in charge of a vehicle with excess alcohol in breath, blood or urine).

Where a person is charged under section 4(1) or 5(1)(a)—but not under section 3(A)—with driving in contravention of the relevant section, he can be convicted of an attempt to commit the offence.

As the alternatives for a section 3A offence are only summary matters, no separate count for any of them can be included in an indictment, see *R. v. Davis*, unreported, April 19, 1996.

II. AUTREFOIS ACQUIT OR CONVICT—SEPARATE OFFENCES

Excess alcohol in one substance is a separate and distinct offence from 3–35 excess alcohol in another substance. That is in effect the *ratio* of *Evans v. DPP*, *The Times*, May 30, 1995, where the High Court held that a motorist who had been charged with driving with excess alcohol in urine could only be convicted on the admissible evidence of the result of an analysis of that fluid and not on his Intoximeter reading. The High Court overruled Judge Robin David, Q.C. who had held that the offence was merely driving with excess alcohol and the description of which type of substance had been analysed was mere surplusage. In *Williams v. DPP* [1991] 1 W.L.R. 1160 the High Court also held that a motorist who had been acquitted of having excess alcohol in his breath could still be tried for excess alcohol in the blood because these were separate offences. (The defendant in that case had exercised his option under section 8(2) and had supplied a specimen of his body fluid.) Since the accused could not have been convicted at this first trial of driving with excess alcohol in his blood, there was nothing to prevent him being tried later for such an offence. The rationale of this decision was described by Rougier J. in these words:

" . . . Since the prosecution had framed the [first] charge incorrectly, the defendant could never have been convicted and he was therefore never in jeopardy within the meaning of *autrefois acquit* [on the present charge]."

To the same effect is *Lucking v. Forbes* [1986] R.T.R. 97, 104J/K, *per* Lloyd L.J:

"This was not a case in which the information laid against the defendant charged him with an excess of alcohol in his blood. The only question is whether the prosecution proved the offence as charged [*i.e.* excess alcohol in breath]."

Indeed, the prescribed blood and breath alcohol levels are only equivalent if the *ratio* adopted for the Road Traffic Act and the Transport and Works Act of 2300:1 is used. The actual difference varies from one individual to another (see Chapter 9, below). Thus a person could have a breath alcohol concentration above the prescribed limit and at the same time a blood alcohol level below it and vice versa.

3–36   In *R. v. Truro and South Powder Justices, ex p. McCullagh* [1991] R.T.R. 374, the defendant was found sitting in the driver's seat of a car on the forecourt of a garage. He did not possess the ignition key. He was arrested and taken to the police station, where he provided a sample of breath for analysis. He was acquitted of an offence under section 5(1)(b) of being in charge of a vehicle with an alcohol level above the prescribed limit, on the grounds that he had proved that he did not intend to drive the car. The police subsequently learnt from the garage proprietor that the accused had driven on to the forecourt a very short time before his arrest. He was therefore charged with an offence under section 5(1)(a), *i.e.* of actually driving. He moved for an order of prohibition in the High Court to prevent this new prosecution because he had already been acquitted of the charge under section 5(1)(b). His application was refused. The High Court held that the driving charge related to a time prior to his arrival at the garage, while the acquittal related to when he was in the garage. As they related to separate incidents, there was no reason why he should not face the second charge under subsection 5(1)(a). The magistrates in the first case had not disbelieved the police, but had merely found that the accused had proved the statutory defence of not intending to drive.

In *Sharpe v. Perry* [1979] R.T.R. 235, it was held that a defendant could, in relation to the same piece of driving, be convicted of both driving while unfit and driving with excess alcohol.

In *DPP v. Gane* (1991) 155 J.P. 846 it was held that if justices convict of the driving offence, they cannot just dismiss an in charge offence, based on the same facts. They can, however, impose a nominal penalty or adjourn it pending the outcome of any appeal against the conviction for the driving offence.

In *Dixon v. DPP*, unreported, December 14, 1995 it was held that driving was a separate offence from attempting to drive.

III. SEPARATE TRIALS

In *R. v. Chichester JJ., ex p. DPP* [1994] R.T.R. 175 the High Court held **3–37** that the justices were wrong to order separate trials for offences of failing to provide a breath specimen for analysis and an alternative charge of failing to provide blood for analysis. The court held that the charges arose out of the same incident and therefore they should be heard together. The dicta of Evans L.J. (at 180) that section 7(6) might well create one offence of just failing to supply a specimen for analysis became the *ratio* of *Worsley v. DPP* (see below).

E. Duplicity

I. A SECTION 3A OFFENCE

It is duplicitous to allege both driving without due care and attention and **3–38** driving without reasonable consideration in the same information (or count in an indictment): see *R. v. Surrey JJ., ex p. Witherick* [1932] 1 K.B. 450. Just as it is duplicitous to allege alcohol in more than one substance for an offence under section 5, so must the same apply to section 3A. By analogy it must also be duplicitous to allege in the same count facts from more than any one of the three subsections in section 3A.

II. A SECTION 4 OFFENCE

In *Thomson v. Knights* [1974] K.B. 336 it was held that an information **3–39** alleging unfitness to drive through drink or drugs was not bad for duplicity, because the statute had created only a single offence of self-induced incapacity to drive due to drink or drugs.

III. A SECTION 5 OFFENCE

The effect of the decision in *Williams v. DPP* [1991] 1 W.L.R. 1160 and **3–40** *Evans v. DPP, The Times,* May 30, 1996 (see above) is that an information charging driving, or in charge, with excess alcohol in more than one substance (*e.g.* blood and urine) is duplicitous.

IV. A SECTION 7 OFFENCE

3–41 The House of Lords in *Butterworth v. DPP*, above, held that section 7(6) created one offence even though the maximum penalty varied according to the presence or absence of certain facts, *i.e.* whether or not the accused had been driving. That is the law. It is submitted that the views expressed by Lord Diplock in *R. v. Courtie* [1984] A.C. 463, 471 are preferable:

> "My Lords, where it is provided by a statute that an accused person's liability to have inflicted upon him a maximum punishment which, if the prosecution are successful in establishing the existence in his case of a particular factual ingredient, is greater than the maximum punishment that could be inflicted on him if the existence of that factual ingredient was not established, *it seems to me to be plain beyond argument that Parliament has thereby created two distinct offences*, whether the statute by which they are created does so by using language which treats them as being different species of a single genus of offence, or by using language which treats them as separate offences unrelated to one another." (Emphasis added.)

Thus *Butterworth v. DPP* overruled *DPP v. Corcoran* [1992] R.T.R. 289, where Pill J. held that section 7(6) created two separate offences because the maximum sentence for contravening that section depended on the presence or absence of certain conduct. The author entirely agrees with the rationale of his judgment:

> "There are two offences. Lord Diplock's statement in *R. v. Courtie* [1984] A.C. 463, 471 D–F covers the present situation. Further the good sense of the approach he lays down, if I may say so with respect, is illustrated by the difficulties which have arisen in other cases where informations have been laid upon a different basis, namely, the basis of the information in the present case. There must be a single rule covering this point." (At 298h.)

Worsley v. DPP, unreported, November 11, 1994, held that there was a single offence of failing to provide a specimen for analysis and it was irrelevant which type of specimen had been required. An information was not duplicitous if it alleged the failure to supply "a specimen of breath/ blood/urine".

F. The discretion to prosecute

3–42 The police must investigate all suspected cases of drinking and driving. In *R. v. Coxhead* [1986] R.T.R. 411 a jury found a police sergeant guilty of attempting to pervert the course of justice when he refrained from requiring a specimen for analysis from the son of a local inspector, since the latter had suffered a heart attack and the sergeant thought that knowledge of his son having been breathalysed would make that condition worse. In so convicting the jury were answering, in the affirmative, the judge's question of whether, in not pursuing his investigation into an offence under section 5, Sergeant Coxhead had acted outside the discretion given to him. Once an investigation is completed, it is another matter and then, when all the facts are known, the police have a discretion not to prosecute somebody whose alcohol level is just over the prescribed limit on the basis of *de minimis*. In *R. v. Anderson* [1972] R.T.R. 113, 117C (where the blood alcohol concentration was 81ml) the Court of Appeal approved the words of Lord Parker C.J. in *Watson v. Last* [1969] 2 Q.B. 208 at 215H–216A (where the blood alcohol level was certified to be not less than 82ml):

> "If in any case the amount is truly minimal, this would, we hope, provide a good reason for not prosecuting the offender . . . "

As far as the author can gather, the above quoted words of the Lord Chief Justice fall on deaf ears so far as the present Director of Public Prosecutions is concerned. In accordance with Home Office Circular 46/83, prosecutions are only brought where the breath alcohol concentration is $40\mu g$ or more. This is because the approved breathalysers are only accurate to $+/- 3\mu g$.

Chapter 4

INCHOATE OFFENCES, ACCESSORIES, THE STANDARD OF PROOF AND SPECIAL DEFENCES

A. Attempts

Sections 4 and 5 of the Road Traffic Act 1988 create separate offences of driving and attempting to drive, see *Dixon v. DPP*, unreported, December 12, 1995.

I. THE COMMON LAW DEFINITION

A person who attempts to drive is equally as guilty as a person who actually **4–01** drives. The common law definition of an attempt was given by the House of Lords in *Haughton v. Smith* [1975] A.C. 476, 492 (*per* Lord Hailsham):

> "(3) The act relied on as constituting the attempt must not be an act merely preparatory to commit the completed offence, but must bear a relationship to the completion of the offence referred to in *R. v. Eagleton* (1854) Dears C.L. 376 as being 'proximate' to the completion of the offence and in *Davey v. Lee* [1968] 1 Q.B. 366, 370 as being immediately and not merely remotely connected with the completed offence . . . Obviously whenever the test of proximity becomes crucial in a particular case, difficult questions of fact and degree will arise . . . "

The accused must also have intended to commit the full offence. **4–02** Foresight is not sufficient, although such can be used to infer the necessary *mens rea*: see *R. v. Pearlman* [1985] R.T.R. 38, where the prisoner was charged under the Offences against the Person Act 1861, s. 18. He had driven his car at a policeman. The Court of Appeal held that it was a misdirection for the judge to have summed up to the jury that they should return a verdict of guilty if Pearlman had foreseen that the probable consequences of his actions would be to cause grievous bodily harm, even though he did not desire to do so.

II. REMOTENESS

Bearing in mind those words of caution from the Lord Chancellor in **4–03** *Haughton v. Smith*, it is submitted that generally speaking an attempt to drive will only occur either when a person starts to board a vehicle or starts to push it; merely approaching a vehicle, key in hand, would be too remote. In *Shaw v. Knill* [1974] R.T.R. 142, it was held that a motorist who pushed his motorcycle six yards toward the entrance of the road where he intended to drive it was guilty of attempting to drive while disqualified. In *Harman v. Wardrop* [1971] R.T.R. 127 it was held that merely asking for the car keys could not amount to an attempt to drive.

III. IMPOSSIBILITY

4-04 As well as being "proximate", the action of the accused must, if uninterrupted, have led to the commission of the full offence, but merely using tools which are inadequate for that purpose does not amount to a defence (*per* Lord Hailsham L.C. in *Haughton v. Smith* [1975] A.C. 476, 492). In *R. v. Farrance* (1977) 67 Cr.App.R. 136, it was held that sitting in the driver's seat and endeavouring to start a vehicle or to put it into gear or to accelerate the engine in order to try to make it go forward all amounted in law to "attempts to drive". It was also held that there could still be an attempt even though a mechanical defect made it impossible to set the vehicle in motion. In this case the accused was sitting in his van "revving up" the engine but remained stationary because the clutch was burnt out.

4-05 Another view of the law was taken the following month by a differently constituted Court of Appeal in *R. v. Neilson* [1978] R.T.R. 232, where it was held that if a car could not be driven by anybody, then its "driver" could not be guilty of driving or attempting to drive, as a person cannot be convicted of attempting to do the impossible. In this case the vehicle's tyres were hot and its rear off-side axle had seized up, so that any motion of the wheels was impossible. In *Farrance*, above, Watkins J. had compared the burned-out clutch with a burglar who used an inadequate tool and was therefore unable to force an entry.

4-06 It is submitted that the reasoning in *R. v. Neilson*, above, is preferable to that of Watkins J. in *Farrance*. In his Lordship's example it was possible to commit the burglary as the premises contained property which could be stolen. Somebody else with the correct tool could have entered and run off with the chattels in the house. Therefore burglary was not *ipso facto* impossible. However, a car with a burnt-out clutch cannot be driven any more than a pickpocket can steal from an empty pocket. The other ground on which Watkins J. founded his judgment was that the van was going downhill and had stopped only because it had hit the curve. Its driver had a heart condition which prevented him from pushing the van but a healthy man could have manoeuvred the van away from the pavement and it could then have continued its journey by coasting down hill. On the special facts of that case (namely, that somebody else was capable of "driving" the van), Watkins J. reached the correct decision. Nevertheless, it is submitted that in the context of driving, the normal test at common law applies to determining what amounts to an attempt and that total impossibility is a defence to a charge of attempting to drive.

4-07 In *Kelly v. Hogan* [1982] R.T.R. 352, the defendant was held to be "attempting to drive" when he sat in the driver's seat trying to insert a key in the ignition, but was unable to do so as he had the wrong key. It is submitted that this is correct, since somebody with the right key could have driven the car. It was not impossible to have driven the vehicle but the accused's endeavours to do so were frustrated solely because he had the wrong tools with him. Donaldson L.J. stressed the fact that another key could have started the car. By the way his Lordship stressed this fact, if no key in the world would have started the car, then Donaldson L.J. would have ordered an acquittal.

IV. CRIMINAL ATTEMPTS ACT 1981

In 1981 Parliament passed the Criminal Attempts Act in order to codify the **4–08** law of attempt. This Act does not affect the interpretation of "attempting to drive" in sections 4 and 5 of the Road Traffic Act 1988, which still have to be construed in the same way as they were prior to 1981. The reason for this is that section 1 of the 1981 Act limits the statutory definition of "an attempt" to attempts to commit indictable offences. Section 3 of this Act does apply the new codified definition to an attempt to commit a statutory offence, which is defined in section 3(2)(b) as:

" . . . an offence of attempting to commit another offence (. . . referred to as the 'relevant full offence')."

The commentary in *Current Law Statutes* says that:

"This formula appears to exclude from the scope of the section a specific attempt offence created, as it were, in the same breath as the corresponding full offence . . . "

In other words, section 3 applies the Act's definition of an "attempt" to an endeavour to commit an offence created by statute, but has no application where the actual attempt is itself made a crime by another Act. The 1981 Act did not alter the *mens rea* required to commit an attempt: see *R. v. Pearlman* (above).

B. The burden of proof

In *Patterson v. Charlton* [1986] R.T.R. 18, the police spoke to the defendant **4–09** about a car parked in a street. He was arrested and subsequently gave a breath sample which showed his alcohol level to have been over the legal limit. He also admitted that earlier in the day he had driven the car. It was held to be sufficient prima facie evidence that he had committed an offence under section 5 (driving with excess alcohol), and it was incumbent on him to rebut the presumption of guilt in accordance with section 15(3) of the Road Traffic Offenders Act 1988, *i.e.* the accused must prove that his alcohol level was above the prescribed limit *solely* because of his post-driving consumption of liquor (see Chapter 9). That decision was followed in *DPP v. Williams*, unreported, July 15, 1990, where the defendant admitted to the police that he had driven five hours previously. It was held that it was up to the accused to show that his excess alcohol level was caused solely by consumption of intoxicants after he had ceased to drive.

4–10   In *DPP v. Plumb*, unreported, April 7, 1995, the defendant was in his van in a wood 300 yards from the road. The justices found that he had driven it there. The High Court held that accordingly section 15(3) applied and it was for the defendant to prove that his post-driving imbibing was the *sine qua non* of his alcohol level having exceeded the prescribed limit. In theory, once it has been proved that at sometime in the past the defendant has driven, the presumption in section 15(3) will arise. However, the longer the time interval, the easier it will be for a person to rebut it, *e.g.* by demonstrating that all the alcohol in his breath would have been metabolised in the interval between when he supplied his specimen and when he had proved that he last drove.

C. Evidence

4–11 In *Baker v. Oxford* [1980] L.S.Gaz. 94 the High Court held the presumption to be applicable in criminal cases that the registered keeper was the driver of the vehicle. Even though there is no witness who actually saw the defendant driving, a court is entitled to draw that inference when the facts lead to that conclusion. Of course, as Judge Holman said in *Hall v. DPP*, unreported, June 26, 1995, in criminal cases an inference can only be drawn if the facts can lead to no other conclusion. Such an inference (that the defendant had been driving) was, in view of the High Court, rightly drawn by the justices in *Whelehan v. DPP* [1995] R.T.R. 177, 181D/E, *per* Curtis J.:

> "The time of 1.20 a.m., the place and the circumstances, in particular the defendant being found alone in a motor car with the keys in the ignition, afforded sufficient evidence . . . on which it could be inferred by necessary and proper deduction by the court that [the defendant] had driven the motor car in which he was sitting on a road."

D. An accessory before the fact

I. ACTUS REUS

4–12 To aid, abet, counsel or procure a person to commit a summary offence is also a crime, and a person guilty of so doing can, by virtue of section 44 of the Magistrates' Courts Act 1980, be charged as if he was an actual perpetrator of the crime. (The same applies to indictable offences by section 8 of the Accessories and Abettors Act 1861.) Consequently, a person can be convicted under sections 4 or 5 of the Road Traffic Act 1988 solely on the basis of somebody else's driving. In *Attorney-General's Reference (No. 1 of 1975)* [1975] Q.B. 773, 779, it was held that for the aiding, abetting or counselling of an offence, there must be an agreement between the principal and the accessory about the commission of the actus reus. It was also held that there need be no consensus between a person who procures an offence and the actual offender.

II. MENS REA

In *Attorney-General's Reference (No. 1 of 1975)*, above, it was held that in **4–13** order to be guilty of procuring the offence of driving with excess alcohol, the alleged accessory had to know both that the principal offender was going to drive and that the ordinary and natural result of the lacing of his drink would be to raise the driver's alcohol level over the prescribed limit. The Court of Appeal specifically used the word "knowledge" when considering the necessary *mens rea*. However, it will often be difficult to prove that the "lacer" actually knew that the driver had not already drunk more than the prescribed limit and that the laced drink would be solely responsible for him driving with excess alcohol. The "lacer" is more likely to be reckless as to such matters, so the question arises of whether "recklessness" is sufficient *mens rea* to secure a conviction for this offence. This question was considered in *Blakely v. DPP* [1991] R.T.R. 405 where it was held that while the *mens rea* of an alleged accessory before the fact might be advertent recklessness as to the consequences of his deliberate act, it was clear that inadvertent recklessness was not sufficient to found a conviction. In that case the defendants were held not to be guilty of procuring a man to drive in contravention of section 5(1) of the Road Traffic Act 1988 when they had laced his drinks in the hope that he would be unable to drive home and would therefore stay the night. The man had, however, driven off before they had had a chance to tell him about the extra alcohol added to his beverages. In *DPP v. Anderson* (1991) 155 J.P. 157, it was held that ordinary recklessness was sufficient *mens rea*. The accused had been a pillion passenger on a motorcycle knowing that the driver had drunk half a bottle of wine, half a bottle of cider and a mixed spirit drink. He held a full driving licence and had been giving some form of supervision to the driver who only held a provisional one. It was this latter fact plus knowledge of the drinking that made the accused guilty of aiding and abetting the driving with excess alcohol.

Recklessness was defined by the House of Lords in *R. v. Lawrence* [1982] A.C. 510 as either never considering the consequences of one's actions or, having done so, continuing to go ahead in the knowledge that the *actus reus* might be perpetrated.

III. PRINCIPAL OFFENDER

There can be no aiding and abetting unless the *actus reus* of the crime is **4–14** committed, although that need not be perpetrated with *mens rea*: see *R. v. Loukes* [1996] R.T.R. 164.

IV. THE GENEROUS HOST AND LACED DRINKS

4-15 In theory there should be no distinction between the lacer and, say, a barman who openly serves customers with alcohol specifically requested by them. However, that is not the law. In *Attorney-General's Reference (No. 1 of 1975)* [1975] Q.B. 773 the Court of Appeal drew a distinction between the surreptitious adding of alcohol to the glass of a driver and a "generous host". Lord Widgery said (at 780/1):

> "The first point to notice in regard to the generous host is that that is not a case in which the alcohol is being put surreptitiously into the glass of the driver. That is a case in which the driver knows perfectly well how much he has to drink and where to a large extent it is perfectly right and proper to leave him to make his own decision.
>
> In those circumstances the matter must be approached in accordance with well-known authority governing the provision of the tools for the commission of an offence, and never forgetting that the introduction of the alcohol is not there surreptitious, and that consequently the case for saying that the offence was procured by the supplier of the alcohol is very much more difficult."

V. JOINT ENTERPRISE

4-16 In *Smith v. Mellows* [1987] R.T.R. 210, it was held that even if the prosecution could not establish who was actually driving, the two occupants of a car would both be guilty of an offence under section 5 if it could be proved that they were involved in a joint enterprise, and each knew that the other had drunk too much. Both could be convicted on the basis that he must have at least aided and abetted the contravention of section 5. Thus a driving instructor can be found guilty of that offence through giving tuition to a pupil whom he knows has an alcohol concentration above the prescribed limit, on the basis that he is aiding and abetting his student (see *Carter v. Richardson* [1974] R.T.R. 314). The High Court (at 320) held that the justices were entitled to infer that the instructor knew of his pupil's consumption of intoxicating liquor because he had pretended to the police that he had been driving. However, merely being a passenger is not normally sufficient to found criminal liability, as Peter Pain J. pointed out in *Smith's case* (at 220B):

> " . . . this was not a case of one driver simply giving a passenger a lift home, in which case the passenger would not be ordinarily aiding and abetting the offence which was committed by the driver quite independently."

E. The defence of duress and necessity

4-17 If a person drives when his alcohol level exceeds the legal limit or whilst unfit, the reason why he did so is usually irrelevant to the question of guilt although it may mitigate the penalty that would otherwise be imposed (see Chapter 20, below).

If a person is forced to drive through threats or fear of violence, he will escape conviction. In *R. v. Martin* [1989] 1 All E.R. 652, duress was held to be a defence where the accused only drove whilst disqualified because of the threat by his wife to commit suicide if he did not drive their son to work.

In *DPP v. Jones* [1990] R.T.R. 33, the accused had been attacked and in order to avoid being hurt drove away. On route he was stopped and subsequently found to be over the legal alcohol limit. His initial reason for driving was held to amount to the defence of duress of circumstances. However, he was still disqualified from driving as he had driven for one-and-a-half to two miles without seeing if he was being followed. Once any pursuit ceased, the threat no longer existed, so the defence of duress was no longer be open to him.

In *Williams v. Tierney* [1988] R.T.R. 118, the defendant drove off with his wife as she was likely to be attacked by her ex-husband. The latter then pursued them for about four-and-a-half miles into the driveway of the residence of the wife's parents. The ex-husband then drove away, thus ending the emergency. The defendant entered the house, telephoned the police and then drove home (a journey of two minutes) with his spouse. Both of them were suffering from shock. The justices held that special reasons existed for not disqualifying the defendant and that was upheld by the High Court. After the emergency was over, he had driven home, a distance of about three-quarters of a mile. That was held not to preclude special reasons, *per* May J. (at 123C/E):

> "The justices in their findings then stated:
> '(v) a reasonable man would not have considered other means of transport at that particular time of night and in those circumstances, to travel such a short distance; (vi) the special reasons extended after the initial emergency had ceased to exist.'
>
> That is a specific reference to the last few words of the passage from the judgement of Lord Widgery C.J. in *Jacobs v. Reed* [1974] R.T.R. 81, 87K, which I have read,
>
> 'Although it may be that it can be extended within reasonable limits thereafter.' "

Although that was a case on special reasons, nowadays it would be treated as one about duress of circumstances: see *DPP v. Whittle* (below). In *DPP v. Bell* [1992] R.T.R. 329, the accused was acquitted on the grounds that he had committed the *actus reus* of an offence under section 5 of the Road Traffic Act 1988 under duress. He had been forced to beat a hasty retreat from a night-club car park in order to avoid being attacked after he had got into an argument with some of the other customers. The High Court held that the fact that he always intended to drive home was irrelevant as the actual driving which led to his arrest was due solely to the threatened assault on him.

In two appeals heard at the same time, *DPP v. Davis* [1994] Crim L.R. 600 and *DPP v. Pittaway*, *ibid.*, the High Court held that the defence of duress was subjective but it had objective elements to it: whether there was good reason for the defendant to fear that he would suffer death or serious bodily injury unless he acted in the way which he did; and whether a sober and reasonable person with the same characteristics as him would have acted as he had done. In *Davis' case* the respondent went to the home of a male acquaintance where he was subject to a homosexual advance, the other man undoing his shirt buttons. The High Court held that duress did not exist. There had been no finding by the justices that the respondent was in fear of his life or serious injury when he got into his car. The other man had attempted to pull him out of the vehicle but this was only accompanied by verbal abuse. No blows were struck. It is submitted that somebody pulling a driver out of car after making a homosexual advance could well cause a person to fear a more violent reaction. The case is best explained by the fact that there was no need for him to have driven two miles. If he was not being followed after a short distance, say half a mile or so, the respondent should have stopped. Also, there was no finding that he continued to be frightened after he had left the *locus in quo*. In *Pittaway's case*, the accused was a female motorist. After threats of violence by her boyfriend at a party, she ran 200 yards home. She did not go inside but hid in her car for five minutes and then drove 200 yards before being stopped by the police. The High Court ordered the justices to convict for two reasons. First, there was no finding of fact that the threats were of serious injury or death. Secondly, her boyfriend was not around when she drove off, *i.e.* the threat was no longer operative.

4–19   In the recent case of *DPP v. Whittle*, [1996] R.T.R. 154, Simon Brown L.J. was of the opinion that a sudden emergency which caused somebody to drive "may be a complete defence" to a drinking and driving charge. Such would amount to what is now called "duress of circumstances", as had occurred in *R. v. Martin*, above. Previous decisions had usually treated an emergency as being merely a special reason for not imposing any disqualification (see Chapter 20, below). In none of those cases did counsel argue that their client was innocent because of the reason why he drove. It is submitted that the view put forward by Simon Brown L.J. is a just concept, because although a person escapes losing his licence because special reasons caused him to drive, should he be convicted again of a similar offence within 10 years, he must suffer a minimum disqualification of three years, while if on the previous occasion he had been acquitted, he need only lose his licence for one year. Also, the test of duress of circumstances is wider than necessity. It is based on what the Europeans call proportionality. Does the risk of the harm caused by not driving justify the risk caused by the driving?

Chapter 5

DRIVING OR ATTEMPTING TO DRIVE

A. Generally

A *sine qua non* of any conviction for being unfit to drive or for having 5–01
consumed alcohol above the prescribed limit is that the defendant was
either driving, attempting to drive or was in charge of a motor vehicle.
This chapter considers what is meant by the words "driving" or "attempting to drive" in the context in which they are used in the Road Traffic Act
1988, ss.3A *et seq.*

B. Driving

I. ROAD TRAFFIC ACT 1988

Very little guidance, if any, is to be found in the statute as to the meaning 5–02
of "driving". The only reference to any definition of that word is to be
found in section 192:

> "(2) In this Act —
> . . . 'driver,' where a separate person acts as a steersman of a motor
> vehicle, includes (except for the purpose of section 1 of this Act) that
> person as well as any other person engaged in the driving of the vehicle,
> and 'drive' is to be interpreted accordingly."

Consequently, it is necessary to see what interpretation has been given to 5–03
it by the judiciary. The leading decision is *R. v. McDonagh* [1974] Q.B. 448
(a case on driving while disqualified) where Lord Widgery C.J. stated (at
451):

> "The Act does not define the word 'drive' and in its simplest meaning
> we think that it refers to a person using the driver's controls for the
> purpose of directing the movement of the vehicle. It matters not that the
> vehicle is not moving under its own power, or is being driven by the
> force of gravity, or even that it is being pushed by other well-wishers.
> The essence of driving is the use of the driver's controls in order to

direct the movement, however movement is produced. There are an infinite number of ways in which a person may control the movement of a motor vehicle, apart from the orthodox one of sitting in the driving seat and using the engine for propulsion. He may be coasting down a hill with the gears in neutral and the engine switched off; he may be steering a vehicle which is being towed by another. As has already been pointed out, he may be sitting in the driving seat whilst others push, or half sitting in the driving seat but keeping one foot on the road in order to induce the car to move. Finally, as in the present case, he may be standing in the road and himself pushing the car with or without using the steering wheel to direct it. Although the word 'drive' must be given a wide meaning, the courts must be alert to see that the net is not thrown so widely that it includes activities which cannot be said to be driving a motor vehicle in any ordinary use of that word in the English language. Unless this is done, absurdity may result by requiring the obtaining of a driving licence and third party insurance in circumstances which cannot have been contemplated by Parliament."

5-04 In other words, a driver is a person controlling the movement of the vehicle, provided a layman would also call him "a driver". Accordingly, in this case, the court held that the ordinary meaning of the word "drive" did not extend to include the activity of the defendant who was not in the motor car but was merely pushing it with his two feet on the ground and was making no use of the controls apart from an occasional adjustment of the steering wheel. The Lord Chief Justice went on to give examples (at 452) of people driving or not driving by reference to previous decisions. In *Saycell v. Bool* [1948] 2 All E.R. 83, the owner of a lorry which had run out of petrol released the hand-brake and, while sitting in the driving seat, had steered the vehicle down an incline for a distance of 100 yards. In the view of Lord Goddard C.J. (at 84):

" . . . but it seems impossible to say that in those circumstances he was not 'driving' the vehicle."

II. CONTROL

5-05 In *R. v. Roberts* [1965] 1 Q.B. 85, the Court of Criminal Appeal declined to say that the appellant was "driving" when he had maliciously released the hand-brake of a motor vehicle and thus allowed it to run down a hill unattended. Lord Parker C.J. said (at 88):

"On the authorities, a man cannot be said to be a driver unless he is in the driving seat or in control of the steering wheel and also has something to do with the propulsion . . . There are no cases, so far as this court knows, where a man has been held to be guilty of taking and driving away if, although he has something to do with the movement and the propulsion, he is not driving in any ordinary sense of the word."

In *Wallace v. Major* [1946] K.B. 473, the person at the steering wheel of a towed vehicle was held not to be the driver. The correctness of that decision was doubted in *R. v. McDonagh* [1974] Q.B. 448 and in *R. v. Challinor* (1985) 80 Cr.App.R. 253 it was held that the accused was driving when he sat behind the wheel of a vehicle being towed by means of a rope. Nowadays, by the Road Traffic Act 1988, s.192, the word "driver" includes a steersman.

In other words, the courts have laid down a twofold requirement before a person can be said to be driving. First, he must be in the driving seat or in control of the steering wheel and, secondly, what he was doing must come within the usual meaning of the word "driving". Therefore, in *Jones v. Pratt* [1983] R.T.R. 54, it was held that a passenger who suddenly grabbed the steering wheel and put the car in a field had not been "driving" it.

That decision was followed by the acquittal of the front-seat passenger in the similar case of *DPP v. Hastings* [1993] R.T.R. 205, where the latter had momentarily seized the wheel of the car to steer it towards a pedestrian in order to scare him. The High Court held that this amounted to an interference with the driving rather an act of driving.

In *Burgoyne v. Phillips* [1983] R.T.R. 49 a man sat in the driver's seat after 5–06 letting the car roll forward but was unable to steer it as he did not have the keys to the ignition/steering lock. He was held to have been "driving". He was in control of the car while it was moving. On the other hand, in *Leach v. DPP* [1993] R.T.R. 161 it was held that a person was not "driving" just because, while sitting in the driving seat of a stationary car, he switched the ignition on and placed his hands on the steering wheel. The cases state that a *sine qua non* of "driving" is that movement is brought to the vehicle. So in *Rowan v. The Chief Constable of Merseyside, The Times*, December 10, 1985, the High Court upheld a conviction for driving with excess alcohol of a defendant who had knelt on the driving seat, released the hand-brake and thereafter attempted to stop the movement of the vehicle. Watkins L.J. said it had to be shown that the defendant had brought movement to the vehicle and had endeavoured to control it once it was in motion. Nolan J. said that if he had been in the vehicle trying to control it, then there was material on which a court could find that the defendant was driving it. In *McKoen v. Ellis, The Times*, July 11, 1986, the High Court held that it was a matter of fact and degree as to whether or not a person was driving. In that case it upheld the conviction for driving with excess alcohol by the accused. He had been wearing a motorcyclist's clothing and a crash helmet and, while standing with his legs astride a motorcycle, he had, for an unspecified distance, been controlling the movement and direction of the vehicle by pushing and steering it while the ignition was on and its lights were illuminated. That decision was followed in two similar cases where moped riders were held to be "driving" when they sat astride their vehicles and propelled them with their feet: see *Gunnel v. DPP* [1994] R.T.R. 151 (where the engine would not start because of a faulty spark plug) and *Selby v. DPP, ibid.*, at 157. In the latter case Henry J. said that just as a person sitting astride a pedal cycle and propelling it with his feet would be considered to be driving it, so it would be strange if the same did not apply to a bicycle merely because it was motor assisted.

5-07 It should be noted that in all of the last three mentioned cases the defendant was controlling the movement of a vehicle. This requirement for control and motion can be seen in the case of *Blayney v. Knight* (1975) 60 Cr.App.R. 269. In that case the High Court upheld Mr Knight's acquittal of driving with excess alcohol. The facts were that a taxi driver alighted from his cab to go to where he believed his fare was waiting. He left his engine running and his door open. Two men sat in the back seat of the taxi. The defendant, seeing his friends in the back of the vehicle and wishing to talk to them, went and sat in the driver's seat. The cabby returned and tried to eject him. In the course of this struggle the accused's foot accidentally operated the accelerator pedal, thus moving the cab forward and injuring the driver. The High Court held that Mr Knight had not been driving or attempting to drive. Although he had put the cab into motion, he had not intended to do so and had made no attempt to control that moment, *e.g.* by steering. (He was also found not to have been in charge of the hackney carriage either. See section 6–03 below.)

III. THE INTRODUCTION AND REJECTION OF AN EXTENDED DEFINITION

5-08 The Road Safety Act 1967 made the requirement for a breath test a prerequisite for a conviction for driving with excess alcohol (see *Scott v. Baker* [1969] 1 Q.B. 659) and, unless there had been an accident, the police could only require a person to undergo such a test who was, at the actual time of the request, either (a) "driving" or (b) "attempting to drive". However, if those words were to be given their normal meaning, then it would have been almost impossible ever to make a lawful request for a breath test. This is because the person to whom the request was made must, at the very time of being asked, have actually been controlling a vehicle in motion (or attempting to do so). To overcome "this problem", the House of Lords in *Pinner v. Everett* [1969] 1 W.L.R. 1266 gave a very broad interpretation to the words "driving or attempting to drive", which would include a person who had stopped his vehicle during his journey but was still doing something connected with it, *e.g.* checking the pressure of its tyres. In other words, a person who would not normally have been described as driving was to be regarded as such under that legislation.

In *Edkins v. Knowles* [1973] Q.B. 748, it was decided that the test to be applied in determining whether a motorist was "driving" within the meaning of that word in the Road Safety Act 1967 was as follows (at 756F–757B):

> "(1) The vehicle does not have to be in motion; there will always be a brief interval of time after the vehicle has been brought to rest and before the motorist has completed those operations necessarily connected with driving, such as applying the handbrake, switching off the ignition and securing the vehicle, during which he must still be considered to be driving.

56

(2) When a motorist stops before he has completed his journey he may still be driving; an obvious example is when he is halted at traffic lights. Each case will depend on its own facts, but generally the following questions will be relevant: (a) What was the purpose of the stop? If it is connected with the driving, and not for some purpose unconnected with the driving, the facts may justify a finding that the driving is continuing although the vehicle is stationary (b) How long was he stopped? The longer he is stopped the more difficult it becomes to regard him as still driving (c) Did he get out of the vehicle? If he remains in the vehicle it is some, though not a conclusive, indication that he is still driving.

(3) If a motorist is stopped by a constable in uniform who immediately forms the suspicion that the motorist has alcohol in his body, the motorist should be regarded as still driving at the moment when the suspicion is formed; but if an appreciable time elapses before the constable's suspicion is aroused it will be a question of fact and degree whether the motorist is still to be considered as driving at that time.

(4) When a motorist has arrived at the end of his journey then subject to the brief interval referred to in (1) above he can no longer be regarded as driving.

(5) When a motorist has been effectively prevented or persuaded from driving he can no longer be considered to be driving."

Under the present legislation, a policeman can demand a breath test from a person who has been, but is no longer, driving. In view of the extended powers of the constabulary, there is clearly nowadays no need for Parliament to have intended a specially wide meaning of the words "driving or attempting to drive". As Lord Bridge said in *Fox v. Chief Constable of Kent* [1986] A.C. 281, 297A/B:

"[The new section 7(1) (c) of the amended Road Traffic Act 1972] has rendered obsolete the nice distinctions drawn by the courts to determine whether a person who was no longer at the wheel of a vehicle could or could not still be regarded as driving it."

In *Blake v. Pope* [1986] R.T.R. 77, 85E/F Hirst J. agreed with Stocker L.J. when the latter stated:

"In my view, *Edkins v. Knowles*, above and *R. v. Bates* [1973] R.T.R. 264 are not authorities for the proper construction of the Road Traffic Act 1972 as amended by the provisions of the Transport Act 1981."

The actual point in that case was whether the motorist still had to be driving when a breath test was required; but that issue was, of course, linked by pre-Transport Act cases to the definition of "driving". It is submitted that the above quoted dicta of Stocker L.J. also applies to the definition of "driving". Although not expressly stated, that view has been followed in other decisions. Hence the dicta in *Rowan v. Chief Constable*, see above, and the absence of dissent by the High Court in *Leach v. DPP*, above, to the justices having held that the answer to the question of whether or not a person had been "driving" was to be determined by the test laid down in *R. v. McDonagh* (see para. 4–03 above). Accordingly, it is submitted that no longer would the man filling up the petrol tank of his car on a garage forecourt be considered, in the eyes of the law, to be also driving it at the same time as he was refuelling it.

IV. MORE THAN ONE DRIVER

5–09 In *Longman v. Valentine* [1952] 2 All E.R. 803, it was held that two people could in law be driving the same vehicle simultaneously. There, one person sat in the passenger seat, with one hand on the brake and the other on the steering wheel and could switch the ignition on and off while somebody else sat in the driving seat, controlled the foot-brakes and accelerator pedals and steered the car. Thus, as the first-mentioned gentleman was able to start, stop and steer the car, the High Court held that both he and the person in the driver's seat were, in law, driving the car at the same time. That case was distinguished in *Evans v. Walkden* [1956] 1 W.L.R. 1019. There the driver did not possess a licence but the defendant merely sat next to him in the front passenger seat, ready to take control of the car if need be. Unlike the previous case, he did not have sufficient control over the vehicle to be driving it but would be in charge of it (see Chapter 6, below). The distinction between these two appeals appears to be that for a passenger to be considered to be jointly driving, he must have his hands on the instruments of control and it is not sufficient merely to sit there, ready to take command, if an emergency should arise. Although these two cases were concerned with the offence of driving without insurance, it is submitted that their *ratios* would apply to all charges under the Road Traffic Act 1988. In *Tyler v. Whatmore* [1976] R.T.R. 83, the defendant, who was a young woman, was in the front passenger seat of a car steering it, with both hands on the wheel, while the car was propelled by its own power. She was sitting beside a man in the driving seat, whose view of the road ahead was obstructed as she leant across him, and he was not holding the steering wheel or controlling the steering; the hand-brake was below her and within her reach and she was in a position to operate the ignition. The justices were of opinion that, although she did not control the car's propulsion, nevertheless she (as steersman) and the man operating the gears and foot controls were together engaged in driving the car in pursuance of a common agreed arrangement. The defendant was convicted and appealed. The High Court upheld the conviction stating that no authority required that, for a person to be driving, she had to be not merely steering but also controlling the propulsion of the vehicle in some way; that it was not impossible for two people to be controlling a vehicle so that each was a driver, and every case had to be decided on its own facts; and that the justices had reasonably concluded on the facts that the defendant was driving. However, a passenger who momentarily seizes and turn the steering wheel is not driving it (see section 5–05, above).

C. Burden of Proof and Sufficient Evidence

This is on the prosecution. In *Selby v. DPP* [1994] R.T.R. 157, the **5–10** appellant was driving his motorcycle on private land. His conviction was quashed. There was no evidence as to how he got there. Although he would have had to use public roads, he could have pushed his motorcycle there. The prosecution could not show that he must have driven on a public highway.

In *McShane v. DPP*, unreported, December 12, 1995, the appellant and his girlfriend were found arguing outside his car which was parked in the middle of the road, without lights, in a damaged condition and with one of its wheels buckled. Its bonnet was warm. He was holding the car keys in his hand and his girlfriend's shoulder bag was between the front two seats. He said that his friend had crashed it as he and his girlfriend were walking past. The High Court held that there was sufficient evidence of the appellant having driven it.

D. Discretion to Exclude Evidence

Section 78 of the Police and Criminal Evidence Act 1984 gives a court a discretion to exclude any evidence which they think will be unfair to admit. (See section 14–05 *et seq.*) In *McShane v. DPP*, above, on arrival at the police station the appellant provided a breath specimen which, on analysis, had shown an amount of alcohol four times the prescribed limit. He was then locked in a cell. Later he asked to see the custody officer without being asked anything, he stated of his own volition: "Look, I can talk to you. I don't want to talk to him (indicating the arresting officer), it was [his passenger's] fault; I was driving along and she pulled the wheel and we hit the kerb."

Defending counsel argued that his client had been highly intoxicated and therefore anything he said was likely to be unreliable; also he had been in a vulnerable position which could be equated to that of a person with the mental ability of a child. The High Court held that the refusal of the justices to exercise their discretion under section 78 to exclude the oral admission of driving could not be said to be such a decision which no reasonable bench of magistrates could have reached.

E. Attempting to Drive

This is considered in section A of Chapter 4.

Chapter 6

BEING IN CHARGE
(AND THE DEFENCE THERETO)

A. The offence

A person who is not driving can still contravene the drinking and driving **6–01** laws if he is "in charge" of a vehicle. Under section 4(2) of the Road Traffic Act 1988, it is an offence to be in charge of a mechanically propelled vehicle while unfit through drink or drugs, whereas under section 5(1)(b) it is an offence to be in charge of a motor vehicle while one's alcohol level is over the statutory limit. In both cases the conveyance must have been on a road or other public place.

B. In charge

Until recently there was some confusion over exactly what the words "in **6–02** charge" meant. This has now been made clear by the judgment in *DPP v. Watkins* [1989] 1 All E.R. 1126. Taylor L.J. (at 1132–1133) set out the law on this point and listed the different criteria which will apply, depending on whether or not the accused had been lawfully in possession of the vehicle or whether he has merely been a trespasser who has taken charge of somebody else's property:

> "Broadly there are two distinct classes of case. (1) If the defendant is the owner or lawful possessor of the vehicle or has recently driven it, he will have been in charge of it, and the question for the court will be whether he is still in charge or whether he has relinquished his charge. That is the class of case to which the *Haines v. Roberts* rule [(1953) 1 W.L.R. 309] was directed. Usually such a defendant will be prima facie in charge unless he has put the vehicle in somebody else's charge. However, he would not be so if in all the circumstances he has ceased to be in actual control and there is no realistic possibility of his resuming actual control while unfit, *e.g.* if he is at home in bed for the night, if he is a great distance from the car or if it is taken by another. (2) If the defendant is not the owner, the lawful possessor or the recent driver but is sitting in the vehicle or is otherwise involved with it, the question for

61

the court is, as here, whether he has assumed being in charge of it. In this class of case the defendant will be in charge if, whilst unfit, he is voluntarily in *de facto* control of the vehicle or if, in the circumstances, including his position, his intentions and his actions, he may be expected imminently to assume control. Usually this will involve his having gained entry to the car and evinced an intention to take control of it. But gaining entry may not be necessary if he has manifested the intention in some other way, *e.g.* by stealing the keys of a car in circumstances which show he means presently to drive it.

The circumstances to be taken into account will vary infinitely, but the following will be relevant: (i) whether he is in the vehicle, or how far he is from it; (ii) what he is doing at the relevant time; (iii) whether he is in possession of a key that fits the ignition; (iv) whether there is evidence of an intention to take or assert control of the car by driving or other wise; (v) whether any other person is in, at or near the vehicle and, if so, the like particulars in respect of that person."

6–03   Taylor L.J. cited with approval the case of *Blayney v. Knight* (1976) 60 Cr.App.R. 269, that merely sitting in the driver's seat without the owner's consent does not automatically make that person "in charge" of the vehicle. In that case (see section 5–07), the other four criteria mentioned in *DPP v. Watkins* were absent. In *Sheldon v. Jones* [1970] Crim.L.R. 38, it was held that the possessor of a full driving licence was in charge of the vehicle while it was being driven by a learner driver under his supervision.

6–04   Since *DPP v. Watkins*, above, some of the old cases can no longer be regarded as correctly decided, such as, it is submitted, *Ellis v. Ellis* [1962] 1 W.L.R. 1486. There it was held that a bus driver, who went off duty leaving his vehicle on the highway, remained in charge of it until his relief had arrived and taken control of it. Nowadays, once he had left the omnibus, he would cease to be in charge of it even if nobody else took control of the vehicle.

6–05   In *Norman v. Gill* [1972] R.T.R. 81 the defendant had been driving . His passenger had alighted and gone shopping, taking with her the ignition key. The accused was held to be still in charge of the car during the absence of his passenger. He was in the driver's seat, even though he could not start the vehicle. In *Drake v. DPP* [1994] R.T.R. 411, it was held that the owner of a motor car which had been wheel-clamped was still in charge of it. The Scottish High Court of Justiciary in *Dean v. Wishart* 1952 S.L.T. 86 found that the appellant was not in charge of a car in which he had been placed by his friends while in a drunken sleep and of which fact he was unaware until awakened by the police.

C. The statutory defence

I. NO LIKELIHOOD OF DRIVING

6–06 The Road Traffic Act, ss. 4(3) and 5(2) respectively provide a defence for motorists who are alleged to have been in charge of a vehicle while unfit or when over the prescribed alcohol limit. This is that a person shall not be deemed to have been "in charge" of a motor vehicle if he proves that "at the material time the circumstances were such that there was no likelihood of his driving it so long as he remained unfit" (for the section 4 offence), or "there was no likelihood of his driving the vehicle whilst the proportion of alcohol in his breath, blood or urine remained likely to exceed the prescribed limit" (for the section 5 offence). In *Morton v. Confer* [1963] 1 W.L.R. 763 those words were held to mean that the defendant must prove, on a balance of probabilities, that there was no likelihood of him driving and not merely that he had no intention to drive, although the latter fact was something which the magistrates could take into account in reaching their decision. In *Northfield v. Pinder* [1969] 2 Q.B. 7, the justices had, in effect, found that "material time" meant "the time of arrest" so that if a person was not about to drive at the time of his apprehension, then he could rely on the statutory defence. The High Court did not accept that proposition and said that the relevant words had a wider meaning but held that it was not necessary for their decision to have to define them. It specifically refused to consider whether the prosecution was correct in arguing that "material time" meant "so long as the driver was unfit or over the limit". However, that latter definition was assumed, without argument, by the High Court in *DPP v. Frost* [1989] R.T.R. 11, where the court was more concerned with what proof was necessary to establish that the man in the dock had actually been in charge of the vehicle. If taken literally, the statutory defence would apply to everyone, since once detained the police would prevent a person from driving in contravention of sections 4 and 5. Thus the correct test is probably whether or not the motorist would have driven in breach of those sections if he had not been arrested.

II. THE NECESSITY FOR EXPERT EVIDENCE

In *DPP v. Frost* [1989] R.T.R. 11, it was held that magistrates could use **6–07** their own judgment as to whether or not a defendant would have been fit to drive at the time which he had proved would have been the earliest occasion when he would next have driven. However, their Lordships also said that in the case of a person who had been in charge of a vehicle when over the legal alcohol limit, then, unless it was obvious, he must call expert evidence to establish that he would have been below the prescribed limit when he would next have driven. If, for example, a motorist had been just over the limit when arrested but proved that he would not have driven for a long time, so that, by then, the excess alcohol must have dissipated, then, in those circumstances it would not be strictly necessary to call an expert to testify about alcohol metabolism. However, as justices are bound to take note of the comments of the High Court in *DPP v. Frost*, above, it will *always* be advisable to call an appropriately qualified witness to establish at what time the quantity of alcohol inside the accused would have been below the prescribed limit or would no longer have rendered him unfit to drive.

In *R. v. Sunderland JJ., ex p. Dryden, The Times*, May 19, 1994, it was held that if an expert was called by one party without giving prior warning to the other side, the latter were entitled to an adjournment to consider the evidence of that witness.

III. INJURY TO THE DRIVER OR DAMAGE TO HIS VEHICLE

6–08 Sections 4(4) and 5(3) of the Road Traffic Act 1988 both afford the court a discretion "to disregard any injury to the accused and any damage to his vehicle" when determining the likelihood of the defendant driving at the material time. In *R. v. Lawrence* [1973] 1 W.L.R. 329, Lord Widgery C.J. said about these statutory provisions:

> "For myself I find this a difficult subsection to understand in this sense: that its purpose escapes me. One would have thought that the concern of the draftsman was to ensure that a drunken man should not drive again until he ceases to be in that condition, and in deciding whether it was likely that he would drive again within the danger period, if one may so describe it, the condition of the car and the condition of himself in the sense of injury one would have thought at first sight would have been matters of considerable relevance."

It is submitted that the purpose of sections 4(4) and 5(3) is to enable magistrates to convict if they think that the intention of a person in charge of a vehicle was to have driven it, even though that intention may have been frustrated either because of an injury he had received or because of damage to his vehicle which would have prevented it from being driven.

6–09 Damage was given an extended definition in *Morphitis v. Salmon* [1990] Crim. L.R. 48, where it was held to include the removal of any part that temporarily or permanently impaired the value or usefulness of the vehicle. That was a case under the Criminal Damage Act. It was distinguished in *Drake v. DPP* [1994] T.L.R 411 where it was held that adding to a vehicle (a wheel-clamp) was not damage. The High Court held that for there to be damage there must be "some intrusion into the integrity of the object in question" (*ibid.*, at 418C). The wheel-clamp was not such an intrusion and did not amount to "damage". Therefore the court had to take it into account in determining the likelihood of the vehicle being driven. Since the clamp prevented the car being driven and the defendant had refused to pay the £35 unclamping fee, he must be acquitted as there was no possibility of him driving. (His attempts to remove the clamp had proved fruitless and it was pure speculation that he might be able to remove the clamp himself.)

D. Summary

6–10 A motorist can still be convicted of a drinking and driving offence, even though he has not been driving a vehicle. It is sufficient that he is in charge of one. Unless somebody else has taken control of his vehicle, an owner remains in charge of his vehicle until he has locked it away in a garage or he had gone to bed for the night. Even though an accused may have been in charge either whilst unfit through drink or drugs or when his alcohol level was above the prescribed limit, he can still avoid a conviction if he can show, on a balance of probabilities, that when he would next have driven, he could have done so without committing the offence of which he now stood charged.

Chapter 7

MOTOR VEHICLES, MECHANICALLY PROPELLED VEHICLES AND GUIDED TRANSPORT

A. Introduction

Under the Road Traffic Act 1988, as originally enacted, those people who **7–01** drove, attempted to drive or were in charge of a "motor vehicle" were subject to its drinking and driving provisions. This has been extended by section 4 of the Road Traffic Act 1991, so that sections 3A and 4 of the 1988 Act also apply to drivers of all "mechanically propelled vehicles". In practice this alteration in the law will have very little effect. This is because virtually all vehicles will fall within the statutory definitions of both "mechanically propelled" and "motor" vehicles, although there will be the occasional exception where one in the former category is not covered by the definition of the other type.

B. A motor vehicle

I. GENERALLY

In the Road Traffic Act 1988, s. 185(1), a motor vehicle is defined as: "A **7–02** mechanically propelled vehicle *intended or adapted for use on roads*." (Author's emphasis). It is submitted that the words "mechanically propelled" are intended to have a very wide meaning and will cover any transmission of power from the engine to the wheels by mechanical means. The source of the energy that drives it will be irrelevant, and the definition will include electrically propelled vehicles. The rationale of this is that Parliament could never have intended drunken drivers whose cars happened to be battery-driven to be able to endanger the safety of pedestrians and other road users with impunity from the drinking and driving provisions of the Road Traffic Act. Also, if mechanically propelled vehicles did not include electric ones, there would have been no need for Parliament to have included a special provision in (the now repealed) paragraph

2 of Schedule 4 to the Road Traffic Act 1988 to exempt tram drivers from being subject to section 4(1)(a), or to have enacted section 189(1)(c) to exclude "electrically assisted pedal cycles" from being within the definition of "motor vehicle".

In *Floyd v. Bush* [1953] 1 W.L.R. 242, a cycle fitted with an auxiliary motor was held to remain a motor vehicle even when it was only being propelled by its pedals (see also section 7–04).

II. INTENDED OR ADAPTED FOR USE ON A ROAD

7–03 The classic definition of the above phrase is that of Lord Parker C.J. in *Burns v. Currell* [1963] 2 Q.B. 433, 440:

> "I think that the expression 'intended', to take that word first, does not mean 'intended by the user of the vehicle either at the moment of the alleged offence or for the future'. I do not think it means the intention of the manufacturer or the wholesaler or the retailer . . . but I prefer to make the test whether a reasonable person looking at the vehicle would say that one of its users would be a road user.
>
> In deciding that question the reasonable man would not, as I conceive, have to envisage what some man losing his senses might do with a vehicle; nor an isolated user or a user in an emergency. The real question is: is some general use on the roads contemplated as one of the users?"

In that case a go-kart being driven on the highway was held not to be a motor vehicle. In *Percy v. Smith* [1986] R.T.R. 252, the High Court upheld the justices' decision that a fork-lift truck was intended for use on roads. In *Chief Constable of Avon & Somerset Constabulary v. Fleming* [1987] 1 All E.R. 318, 322, Glidewell L.J. stated:

> "In my view once a vehicle has been manufactured as one which is intended or adapted for use on a road, it would require very substantial, indeed dramatic, alteration if it could be said no longer to be a 'motor vehicle'."

His Lordship was of the opinion that a motorcycle remained a motor vehicle even though its registration plate, reflectors, lights and speedometer had been removed so as to adapt it for scrambling. Glidewell L.J. made it clear that at the end of the day it was solely a question for the tribunal of fact.

In *Nichol v. Leach* [1972] R.T.R. 476 the accused bought himself a Mini motor car as scrap. He rebuilt it for autocross racing, never intending it to run on a road under its own power. (It would always be towed.) The High Court held that a Mini was intended to be driven on a road and remained a motor vehicle irrespective of the intention of its present owner.

By section 188 of the Road Traffic Act 1988, a hover vehicle is a "motor vehicle", irrespective of whether or not it was intended or adapted for use on the road.

III. REMOVAL OF THE ENGINE OR LACK OF REPAIR

In *R. v. Tashin* [1970] R.T.R. 88, it was held that a moped was designed to **7–04** be used on roads and did not cease to be a motor vehicle because some temporary mechanical fault prevented the vehicle being driven. In this case the defendant was convicted of driving with excess alcohol. He had been pedalling his moped because he had been unable to start it through some fault on the engine. That case must be distinguished from *Lawrence v. Howlett* [1952] 2 All E.R. 74, where the defendant was held not to be driving a motor vehicle when he was riding his pedal cycle. It had previously had an engine connected to it so that it was power-assisted, but, at the relevant time, the engine had been disconnected from the wheels. It was held that the conveyance was a pedal cycle. It could be altered but, so long as it was not capable of being powered by its motor, it remained a pedal cycle and not a motor vehicle. The court emphasised the dual propulsion system of the vehicle, and that only one of those systems was available for use at the relevant time. To the same effect as *R. v. Tashin* is *Floyd v. Bush* [1953] 1 W.L.R. 242.

In *Smart v. Allan* [1963] 1 Q.B. 291, the defendant had bought a car for **7–05** £2 from a scrap yard. The engine did not work and was very rusty. It had no gearbox or battery and had one tyre missing. It had been towed from the scrap yard on two wheels. The cost of making the conveyance road worthy was far in excess of what its value would be worth if it were ever repaired. On that basis, the High Court held that since the car had no reasonable prospects of ever being driven again, it was not a mechanically propelled vehicle. Accordingly, the court ordered an acquittal. As it was left on the road, the defendant had been charged with using it without insurance and without paying any road fund duty. The *ratio decidendi* of that case is that a conveyance ceases to be a "mechanically propelled" and therefore a "motor" vehicle only if there was no practical likelihood of it being made road-worthy, either because it is impossible to do so, or because the cost of so doing would be out of all proportion to its value once the repairs had been satisfactorily completed. In *Newbury v. Simms* [1961] Q.B. 345, Widgery J. said (at 350) that a car did not cease to be a mechanically propelled vehicle upon the mere removal of its engine, if the evidence admitted the possibility that the engine might be replaced and the motive power restored.

IV. STATUTORY EXCEPTIONS

The definition in the Road Traffic Act 1988 was specifically made subject **7–06** to section 20 of the Chronically Sick and Disabled Act 1970, which provides that an invalid carriage is not to be regarded as a motor vehicle.

Under section 189 of the Road Traffic Act 1988, a lawnmower and an electrically assisted pedal cycle are not motor vehicles for the purposes of that Act. In addition, by section 192A of the same statute, a tramcar is not within the provisions of sections 4 to 11 of the 1988 Act (section 192A was inserted by section 39 of the Transport and Works Act 1992).

V. EVIDENCE

7–07   In *R. v. Challinor* [1985] R.T.R. 373 it was held that if a contraption had the appearance of being a motor vehicle, that raised a presumption that it was one. In that case the defendant had been steering a towed Austin 1300 motor car. There was no explanation as to why it was being towed or whether it was capable of being driven under its own propulsion. The Court of Appeal held that as the vehicle looked liked a motor car it raised a presumption that it was one, the burden of rebutting which lay on the defendant. As no evidence was given on this matter, the conviction was upheld.

In *Newbury v. Simmons* [1961] 2 Q.B. 345, 350/1, Lord Widgery J. said that once a conveyance had been shown prima facie to be a motor vehicle, the burden of proof shifted to the defendant to show that it was not one. However, in *Chief Constable of Avon and Somerset v. Fleming*, above, the High Court upheld an acquittal because the condition of the motorcycle was so "vague and unsatisfactory" that the justices could not be satisfied that the reasonable man would still have regarded the bicycle as being intended for use on a road. In *Reader v. Bunyard, ibid.*, at 406, the High Court held that where the magistrates had made findings about exactly what state a vehicle was in, then it was for the prosecution to prove that it was "a motor vehicle". In the latter case, the vehicle was being towed. It had no engine nor gear box but its lights and brakes worked. It was held that in those circumstances it was for the prosecution to negative the proposition that there was no reasonable prospect of it ever being made mobile again as a mechanically propelled vehicle.

To sum up, if the only evidence is that a vehicle looked like a motorised one, this raises a presumption to that effect. Once more evidence is given about its condition, the presumption ceases, although the cases are silent on to how detailed that evidence must be to shift the burden on to the prosecution of proving that the vehicle comes within the statutory definition.

C. A mechanically propelled vehicle

7–08   A new section 3A was inserted into the Road Traffic Act 1988 (by section 3 of the Road Traffic Act 1991), which made it an offence to cause death by carelessly driving a mechanically propelled vehicle while unfit and section 4 of the 1991 Act also extended the offence of driving while unfit to those who were driving or in charge of such a vehicle, instead of, as previously, a motor vehicle. No definition of "a mechanically propelled vehicle" is included in the 1991 Act. Under sections 185(2) and 189 of the 1988 Act, a motor vehicle had to be mechanically propelled but subject to two conditions, *i.e.* that it was intended for use on a road and was not an invalid carriage, a lawnmower or an electrically assisted pedal cycle. By introducing the reference to mechanically propelled vehicles in sections 3A and 4 of the 1988 Act, Parliament intended to widen the types of vehicles subject to those sections by excluding the limitations placed upon the definition in sections 185 and 189. The law relating to the circumstances of when a mechanically propelled vehicle would cease to be such through lack of repair will be the same as laid down by the High Court in *Smart v. Allan* [1963] 1 Q.B. 291.

D. Guided Transport

Offences under the Transport and Works Act 1992, Chap. 1, P. II (*i.e.* those 7–09 involving drink and drugs) can only be committed by employees of a railway or tramway company or by those who work for "a system which uses another mode of guided transport" specified by the Secretary of State [see section 26(1)(c)], provided that it transports, *inter alia*, the public. The definition of such transport is contained in section 40(4):

> " 'guided transport' means transport by vehicles guided by means external to the vehicles (whether or not the vehicles are also capable of being operated in some other way), and 'vehicle' includes 'mobile traction unit'."

The same definition is contained in section 192A(iv) of the Road Traffic Act 1988.

The Secretary of State by the Transport (Guidance Systems) Order (S.I. 1992 No. 2044) has extended the provisions of the Transport and Works Act 1992 to the following transport systems:

Mode	Location	Terminal points	Operator
Magnetic levitation	Birmingham International Airport, Solihull, West Midlands	Birmingham International Airport and Birmingham International railway station	Birmingham International Airport Plc
Monorail	Merry Hill Centre, Brierley Hill, Dudley, West Midlands	Boulevard station and Waterfront East Station	Von Roll Transport Systems U.K. Ltd
Track-based with side guidance	Gatwick Airport, Crawley, West Sussex	South Terminal and North Terminal	Gatwick Airport Limited
Track-based with side guidance	Gatwick Airport, Crawley, West Sussex	South Terminal and South Terminal satellite/pier 3	Gatwick Airport Limited
Track-based with side guidance	Stansted Airport, Uttlesford, Essex	Airport terminal and satellite 1	Stansted Airport Limited

Chapter 8

ROADS, PUBLIC PLACES AND OTHER LOCATIONS SUBJECT TO THE ROAD TRAFFIC ACT

A. Road or other public place

I. ROAD TRAFFIC ACT 1988

The word "road" is defined in section 192(1) of the Road Traffic Act 1988 **8–01** as:

> " . . . any highway and any other road to which the public has access, and includes bridges over which a road passes, . . . "

II. COMMON LAW

At common law a highway is a path dedicated to the public over which all **8–02** its members have the right to pass and repass at any time of the day and night. The classic definition is probably that given in *ex p. Lewis* (1888) 21 Q.B.D. 191, 197, *per* Willis J:

> "The only 'dedication' in the legal sense that we are aware of is that of a public right of passage of which the legal description is a right for all Her Majesty's subjects at all seasons of the year freely and at their will to pass and repass without let or hindrance."

III. PRIVATE ROAD

(a) DEFINITION

What would constitute a road but not a highway was considered in *Cox v.* **8–03** *White* [1976] R.T.R. 248, 251 by Lord Widgery C.J., who approved the definition given by Lord Sands in *Harrison v. Hill* 132 S.C.(J.) 13, 17:

"Any road may be regarded as a road to which the public have access upon which members of the public are to be found who have not obtained access either by overcoming a physical obstruction or in defiance of a prohibition express or implied."

A road must be a right of way open to all the public and not just a limited section, *e.g.* the inhabitants of a parish (see *Poole v. Huskinson* (1843) 11 M. & W. 827). In *Oxford v. Austin* [1981] R.T.R. 416, the court stated that one must first find a road and then ask if it is open to the public. In *Deacon v. A.T. (A Minor)* [1976] R.T.R. 244, it was held that an access road to a council estate was not a road within the meaning of the Act without evidence that it was used by the public at large. It was not sufficient that it was used by estate residents and their guests. The High Court also held that there must be some evidence of tolerance by the owner to the public at large using the access road. The only case contrary to the above line of authority is *Adams v. Commissioner of Police of the Metropolis; Aberdeen Park Maintenance Co. (Third Party)* [1980] R.T.R. 289. There the plaintiffs were residents living on a private road with signs indicating that it was not open to the public. They were fed up with motorists who used it as a short-cut, driving at great speed. The signs indicating that it was a private road were removed and a declaration was sought that it was a road subject to the Road Traffic Act 1972. Jupp J. granted the declaration. As, at the time of the hearing, there was nothing to indicate any prohibition on public use, it is submitted that the judge was right. He also held (*obiter*) that as the public took no notice of the express prohibition on using the road, it was always a road within the meaning of section 192. It is submitted that this dicta was wrong. Unlawful acts should not be recognised by the law. If Jupp J. was right, it would mean that if the public wanted to use a short-cut, and the owner was unable to prevent this due to the large number of people taking advantage of it, he would not be able to seek an injunction, as the usage had made it a public right of way. This cannot be correct.

In *Heath v. Pearson* [1957] Crim.L.R. 195, it was held that, on the facts of that particular case, a yard serving several houses was not a road; and in *Griffin v. Squires* [1958] 1 W.L.R. 1106, Streatfeild J. said that nobody would consider a car park to be a road in the ordinary sense of the word. In *Randall v. Motor Insurers' Bureau* [1968] 1 W.L.R. 1900 a vehicle was held to be on a road when it was partly on a road and partly on private land.

B. Crown land

8–04   Under section 131 of the Road Traffic Regulation Act 1984 the Secretary of State may by order extend the provisions of the Road Traffic Act to Crown lands.

8–05   In *Kellett v. Daisy, The Times,* June 28, 1977, the court rejected the contention that the prosecution had to prove that "a road" came within the definition of what is now section 196 of the Road Traffic Act 1988, that this section did not apply to the Crown (*ibid.*, s.183), and therefore no offence under the Road Traffic Act could be committed on land owned by the Crown. The court held that the question was not whether the Crown was bound by the statute but whether the defendant was, and in that case he was.

C. Public places

A motorist is still at risk of a conviction under the drinking and driving **8–06** legislation if he is in a public place. This means a place to which all members of the public are allowed to go if they so wish. In *Elkins v. Cartlidge* [1947] 1 All E.R. 829 a car park attached to a public house was held, during opening hours, to be a public place as it was attached to a tavern which offered its services of food and drink to all members of the public. However, the same car park would not be regarded as a public place if it were attached to a private club: see *Pugh v. Knipe* [1972] R.T.R. 286. In that case the defendant's car had been parked adjacent to an unfenced public footpath by the front entrance to a club and members' car park. Lord Widgery C.J. (at 289) said that the defendant had to be acquitted because there was no evidence that the public used the private car park, even though his Lordship felt that "it was very unlikely that the public [did] not use the car park". In *Capell v. DPP* (1991) 155 J.P. 361, the defendant was parked in what was described as an "off the road parking bay" adjacent to a public road on a private housing estate. The High Court held that the bay was a public place as there was no physical barrier, impediment or notice to indicate that it was private, nor anything to distinguish the highway from the parking bay in a material respect. Accordingly, there was nothing to displace the inference that the bay formed part of the land in public use in the relevant area. In *Thomas v. Dando* [1951] 1 All E.R. 1010 it was held that a forecourt which was not separated from the road was not a public place because it was private property which the public did not habitually use. The material finding was this latter fact.

In essence, a public place is a location frequented by the public where **8–07** their presence is not objected to by the owner of the land. This was stated by McNair J. in *Buchanan v. Motor Insurers' Bureau* [1995] 1 W.L.R. 488 when he approved the words of the Lord Justice General in *Harrison v. Hill* 1932 S.C. (J.) 13, 16:

"There must be, as a matter of fact, walking or driving by the public on the road, and such walking or driving must be lawfully performed— that is to say, must be permitted or allowed, either expressly or implicitly, by the person or persons to whom the road belongs. I include in permission or allowance the state of matters known in right of way cases as the tolerance of the proprietor."

In that case, the court was concerned with whether a road was public or private. It is submitted, however, that the same principles would apply in deciding whether a place was a "public" one. Therefore, where land is utilised as a car park for the users of adjoining premises, the type of place that it is will depend on who is entitled to use those neighbouring premises. If the latter is open to the public then the car park will be a public place. Thus a cinema car park, for example, would be a public place if the cinema itself were open to any member of the public. On the other hand, if only members of a film club were allowed in, the car park would be a private place. Indeed, the same piece of land can at one time be a public place and at another time a private one. In *Sandy v. Martin* [1974] R.T.R. 263, the High Court upheld an acquittal when the prosecution was unable to prove that a "pub" car park was open to the public one hour after closing time. In *R. v. Collinson* (1931) 23 Cr.App.R. 49, a private field to which the public were temporarily invited to watch point-to-point races was held to be a public place during the meet.

8–08   That decision was explained in *Elkins v. Cartlidge* [1947] 1 All E.R. 829, where Lord Goddard C.J. succinctly set out the law (at 829):

> "It was a private field, and no doubt it could have been closed at any time, and I have no doubt that the proprietor of the field could have objected to any particular person going into it. The public had not a legal right which they could enforce of access to the field, but it was a public place for the purposes of this section [now section 4] because at the relevant time the public were being invited to use it. That is the *ratio decidendi* of the case . . . "

In *Bowman v. DPP* [1991] R.T.R. 263, the accused parked his car in a Tesco's car park in the very early hours of the morning. The High Court upheld the justices' view that this was a public place. The rationale of the magistrates' decision was that the barrier had been left open and a few cars were parked there at the relevant time, so this indicated that Tesco were allowing the public to use it.

8–09   In *DPP v. Vivier* [1991] 4 All E.R. 18 a caravan and camping holiday site was held to be a public place, as it was open to all members of the public who were prepared to pay the admission fees. The court held that the test was whether (a) members of the public actually used the place and (b) whether or not the owner of the land allowed anybody on to it or merely restricted access to a special class of person. Here the proprietor would allow all and sundry onto the site if they were prepared to pay the admission fee and to abide by the rules. As the commentary at [1991] Crim. L. R. 639 points out, "everyone is 'a member of the public'". It is submitted that the court was saying that in the case of a commercial organisation, if anyone is allowed in on payment of the appropriate sum, then it is a public place.

8–10   In *Havell v. DPP* [1993] Crim L.R. 621, a car park of a club (a community centre) was held not to be a public place. A member had to be proposed and seconded. As membership was not a formality open to anybody on payment of the prescribed fee (as it was in *Vivier v. DPP* above), then its car park was held not to be open to the public, *i.e.* it was not a public place.

In *DPP v. Coulman* [1994] R.T.R. 230 the defendant had disembarked **8–11** from a ship on to the Freight Immigration Lanes (*i.e.* a dock road). The court said that the test to be applied was whether the people who used the dock road did so for the purposes of the occupiers (*e.g.* to visit them or to deliver something to them) or did they enter solely for their own purpose, even though they were screened, *i.e.* had to satisfy certain conditions for entry. If the latter, it was a public place. Here people were allowed on to the dock road for their own purpose, *i.e.* to land in England and, accordingly, it was a public place. The court held *obiter* that it was otherwise for embarking passengers as entry to the road was restricted to those holding passports and a ticket or who had been given a special pass, *e.g.* an employee. Such people were not members of the public but those who had special characteristics. That dicta was not followed in *DPP v. Neville*, unreported, December 4, 1995, where it was held that once a place was a public place, it was such for all who frequented it and that *DPP v. Coulman*, above, was wrong to draw a distinction between different categories of users. That does seem logical and, accordingly, *DPP v. Neville*, above, held embarking passengers on an airport road (pier 7 at Heathrow) to be in a public place, thus reversing the decision of the justices who had acquitted on the authority of *DPP v. Coulman*, above.

In that latter case (a case of driving with excess alcohol) Mann L.J. (at 234G) stated that he reached his conclusion with satisfaction because it was the presumed policy of Parliament that the Dover Immigrations Lanes should be subject to the regime of the Road Traffic Acts. In saying that he was right but, it is submitted, had not correctly applied that policy. In 1963 Parliament made dock roads in Dover Harbour subject to certain sections of the Road Traffic Act, including the offence of driving while unfit. If dock roads were public places there would have been no need for the Legislature to have done so and Parliament is presumed not to have done anything in vain. The Dover Harbour Act does not seem to have been cited to the court. Thus it could be argued that the decision was reached *per incuriam*. Nevertheless, the modern judicial approach is to afford protection against the dangers caused by those who drink and drive and later cases will almost certainly adopt the test laid down in that decision.

In *DPP v. Cargo Handling Ltd* [1992] R.T.R. 318, the roads at London Airport were held to be public places. Although they had signs saying "not open to the public", there were no barriers. The airport roads were used by anybody who had business at the airport, and visitors. These people amounted to several million a year. The High Court held that user by several million people clearly meant that the roads were places to which the public had access. Contrasted with that decision is *Deacon v. A.T. (A Minor)* [1974] R.T.R. 244, where the residents and visitors to a council estate were considered a restricted class of persons, so that the private estate roads were not public places. If the estate roads had been used as a short cut by non-residents, it would have been another matter. In *Edwards v. DPP*, unreported, March 10, 1994, the High Court said the test is not whether the public had a right to use the land but whether they did in fact do so.

The authorities seem to establish the following proposition: a public place need not be somewhere to which the public have a legal right of access. It also includes any privately owned location frequented by members of the public for their own purposes, where that is allowed or tolerated by the owner. This applies even where conditions are imposed (*e.g.* payment) but where entrance is allowed to all people complying with those conditions. Thus a car park attached to, say, a bingo club which is open to anybody who is prepared to pay to join is a public place but a club car park is a private place when membership of the club is subject to election and applicants have been known to be refused membership.

I. BURDEN OF PROOF

8–12 It is, of course, for the prosecution to prove the *locus in quo* to be a public place. In *Robinson v. DPP*, unreported, March 10, 1995, the accused had driven along an unmade-up and unlit lane, 70 yards long and at the top of which he lived. There was evidence of a man walking his dog there. The defence submitted that there was no evidence that the man had not also been a resident. The High Court held that one could assume that the man with the dog was a member of the public in the absence of testimony to the contrary. Presumably the presumption would not apply if witnesses were called to show that it was only used by a special class of people. In that case there was some evidence of a public footpath leading from the top of the lane, while at the other end it ran directly off the High Street.

D. Private property subject by legislation to the Road Traffic Act 1988

8–13 Various statutes have extended the ambit of the Road Traffic Act 1988 so that a motorist remains subject to some of its provisions, even though he is driving on property which is not open to the public at large.

Under the Dover Harbour Act 1963, an offence under section 4 of the Road Traffic Act 1988 can be committed on a harbour road, even though there is no right of way for the general public. Somewhat similar provisions apply to nationalised docks under the British Transport Commission Act 1961, and the Port of London Act 1968 as amended. Under section 65 of the Airports Act 1986, the Secretary of State can, by order, designate certain roads in specified airports, and anybody who drives on such a designated road will be subject to the provisions of the Road Traffic Act 1988. Other local Acts (*e.g.* the London Hackney Carriage Act 1831) also have the effect of extending the jurisdiction of the Road Traffic Act 1988 to certain types of private property situated in a particular locality. Under the Channel Tunnel Act 1987, s.23, all Channel Tunnel roads whether or not open to the public are made subject to the Road Traffic Act but the Secretary of State can make an exception in regard to any such roads. Section 23 was brought into force on April 5, 1994 (see S.I. 1994 No. 970).

E. Abroad

With two exceptions, the drinking and driving provisions of the Road **8–14** Traffic Act 1988 only apply to England, Wales and Scotland. First, those persons subject to service discipline may be convicted of the relevant service disciplinary offence if, anywhere in the world, they drive or are in charge of a motor vehicle on a road or other public place whilst unfit or with an alcohol level above the prescribed limit or they fail to take a breath test or fail to provide a sample for analysis, when lawfully required to do so: see sections 184 and 197(3) of the Road Traffic Act 1988.

Secondly, under section 31(1) of the Criminal Justice Act 1948, a Crown servant who kills somebody when driving on official business on any road or other public place anywhere in the world can be tried in England and convicted of an offence under section 3A of the Road Traffic Act 1988.

F. Transport and Works Act 1992

The offences created by the drinking and driving provisions of the above **8–15** Act may be committed anywhere in England, Wales or Scotland.

G. Justices' own knowledge

In *Cliffe v. Long* [1961] Crim.L.R. 121 the High Court affirmed the age old **8–16** principle that justices can use their own knowledge, in that case whether the *locus in quo* (a car park) was a public place. It is a question of fact for the justices: see *Griffin v. Squires* [1958] 3 All E.R. 468.

Chapter 9

ALCOHOL AND THE MOTORIST

A. Introduction

"Scientific investigations have produced fifty years of accumulated **9–01** evidence showing a direct relationship between increasing alcohol concentrations in drivers and increasing risk of a motor vehicle crash. There is scientific consensus that alcohol causes deterioration of driving skills at 0.05% or even lower and progressively serious impairment at higher blood alcohol concentrations . . . Alcohol impairs driving skills by its effects on the central nervous system, acting like a general anaesthetic. It renders slower and less efficient both information acquisition and information processing, making divided attention tasks such as steering and braking more difficult to carry out without error. The influence of alcohol on emotions and attitudes may be a crash risk factor relating to driving style in addition to driving skill.

A driver's relative risk of having a road crash shows a dramatic rise as the driver's blood alcohol concentration increases. Alcohol impaired drivers are believed to be responsible for 25 to 35% of all serious crashes causing injury and 6% of all crashes. In single vehicle crashes, 55–65% of fatally injured drivers have blood alcohol concentrations of 0.10% or greater." (P. E. Walker *et al* (1986) 256 J.A.M.A. 1461.)

However, its effect on individuals varies so greatly that one can merely **9–02** generalise. One of the leading researchers in this field commented as follows:

"Alcohol is unusual, if not unique, among drugs in several aspects of its pharmacokinetics. Particularly striking are the great biological inter-subject variabilities in alcohol consumption tolerance and in alcohol elimination, in the pattern of short term fluctuations from the trend line of the time course of the blood and breath alcohol concentrations and in alcohol participation between blood and other body fluids and tissues even at equilibrium. Also significant is that alcohol is absorbed and distributed in an unaltered state and bound to proteins or complexed with other transport systems." (R. K. Dubowski [1985] J. Studies on Alcohol 98.)

B. The absorption of alcohol in the human body

9–03   The unique feature of alcohol is that its molecule contains an oxygen and hydrogen atom linked together, called a hydroxyl. Its molecule also contains hydrogen and carbon atoms. There are various types of alcohol, each of which contains different combinations of those substances in its atomic structure. The specific type found in alcoholic beverages is ethyl alcohol or ethanol. On being consumed, a very small quantity of the alcohol is absorbed by the mucous membranes of the mouth and the oesophagus, the remainder passing to the stomach and through the duodenum to the intestines, from where it is absorbed into the bloodstream, circulating to all the organs including the brain and liver. The alcohol is continuously being broken down by the enzyme alcohol dehydrogenase. That enzyme is found in the stomach and in the liver. Well over 90 per cent of the alcohol is metabolised in the liver first into acetaldehyde, then acetate and finally carbon dioxide, in which form it is exhaled from the body. The rest of the alcohol will be eliminated either by urination or perspiration upon entering the pulmonary circulation, will cross the alveolar walls and enter the airspace of the small alveolar sacs from which it is breathed out into the air. (Those sacs contain air which is in the deepest part of the lungs and which is inhaled and exhaled.) Usually less than 6 per cent of the alcohol will pass out of the body this way, *i.e.* via the lungs or in urine or by perspiration (Harger and Forney, 1963).

9–04   Alcohol need not just be drunk. Ethanol can be inhaled since there are a number of chemicals which contain that fluid and in which it evaporates. According to a report in 1990, sugar in the stomach can ferment and produce alcohol. 510 volunteers with a nil blood alcohol concentration ate five grammes of glucose. An hour later, 310 of them had ethyl alcohol present in their blood. Tests in Sweden found volunteers capable of producing levels of 19.7mg of alcohol solely by eating glucose. Indeed, the study showed that quite a number of people suffered from fermentation of yeast in their gut or small intestine which caused them to produce alcohol (see S. Davies *et al.* [1990] *Journal of Nutritional Medicine* 33). There are also widely-used drugs on the market which can prevent the breakdown of the alcohol in the body, thereby causing more alcohol to enter and to remain in the blood than otherwise would have done. A survey found that Zantac (ranitidine) and Tagamet (cimetidine) had this effect, thereby increasing the expected blood alcohol concentrations by 34 per cent and 92 per cent respectively in a group of 20 healthy males aged 24 to 26 years (see M. Walker, "Glaxo Drug Names as Alcohol Risk", *The Times*, January 2, 1992). These are medicines designed to treat ulcers by preventing acid entering the stomach. One of their side effects is to inhibit the enzyme alcohol dehydrogenase from metabolising alcohol.

C. The consumption of alcohol

In *DPP v. Tucker* [1995] R.T.R. 9 it was held that the word "consumed" in **9–05** section 5 of the 1988 Road Traffic Act was not confined to oral consumption but included any intake of alcohol, in that case by intravenous injection. Indeed, although that fluid is usually imbibed through the mouth, it can also enter the body through breathing, but not apparently by absorption through the skin. According to Kalant:

> "The factor which limits the uptake of alcohols by the respiratory system is the maximum tolerable concentration in the inspired air, which Lester *et al.* found to be in the order of 20mg/1. Higher concentrations are quite irritating. If the tolerable level is not exceeded, the rate of absorption is not much above the rate of metabolism and excretion by other routes, so that blood alcohol levels do not exceed 50mg/100ml (Bagchi and Ganguly, 1943; Lester *et al.*, 1951). However, if by accident or design the alcohol concentration in the inspired air is raised, regardless of discomfort to the subject, it is possible to produce blood alcohol levels giving rise to severe intoxication or even death (Loewy and von der Heide, 1918; Carpenter, 1929; Bowers *et al.*, 1942). The best study was that reported by Bowers *et al.* (1942), who applied dressings soaked with 95% ethanol to the legs of the five subjects and then wrapped them with impermeable rubber sheet, in effect antedating the occlusive dressing technique now used in dermatology. Blood alcohol measurements, made at 3-hr intervals for a period of 12 hr, showed no evidence of alcohol absorption through the intact skin, even under these most favourable conditions."

D. The prescribed limit

The legal limit for driving is prescribed by section 11(2) of the Road Traffic **9–06** Act 1988, namely 80 milligrammes (mg) of alcohol in 100 millilitres (ml) of blood or 35 microgrammes (μg) of alcohol per 100ml of breath. Urine will contain less ethanol than blood, as long as the alcohol is still being absorbed. Once absorption finishes and elimination begins, the alcohol level in the urine will become greater than that in the blood in the ratio of around 4:3. This is because, unlike that in the blood, the ethanol in the urine in not in a state of continual (or indeed any) metabolism. Accordingly, the prescribed limit was fixed at 107mg of alcohol per 100ml of urine. In *McCarry v. Chief Constable of Bedfordshire*, unreported, May 18, 1982, it was held that where urine had been analysed, there was no requirement that the forensic scientist had to make a further calculation to ascertain what the equivalent blood alcohol concentration was.

In *Oswald v DPP* [1989] R.T.R. 360 the High Court held that the defendant was guilty even on the basis of his own analysis, which had revealed a blood alcohol concentration of 80.2mg. The court said that any amount over 80mg, no matter how small, made the motorist guilty of an offence under section 5 of the Road Traffic Act 1988 (of driving, etc., with excess alcohol).

E. Ascertaining the amount in the body

9–07 In a drinking and driving case, the court may be presented with evidence of one of three methods used to discover the amount of alcohol in the defendant's body. The first and most common one is a breath analysis using the principle of infra-red absorption. The second is the analysis of a body fluid, which is invariably carried out by gas chromatography. The third modus, which cannot found a conviction, is by mathematical calculation involving a number of variables, such as what has been imbibed, the amount of food eaten, etc. Unfortunately this suffers from a major disadvantage, namely, that motorists tend to underestimate what they have been drinking! Each of these methods will be discussed separately. As to the accuracy of the results of an analysis, this is a topic to which Chapter 14 is devoted.

I. THE ANALYSIS OF BREATH

9–08 Prosecutions for drinking and driving offences must normally be based on the amount of alcohol in the defendant's breath as ascertained by a breath alcohol measuring instrument which has been approved by the Secretary of State. At the date of publication only two such devices have received approval, namely the Camic and the Intoximeter. Both work on a similar principle, namely that of infra-red absorption. They are designed to analyse the gaseous ethanol which has been mixed with air in the deepest part of the lungs. In order to obtain such air, the Intoximeter requires a minimum of 1.5 litres of breath before it will carry out an analysis. A person with a large lung capacity might satisfy that requirement with a specimen which need not be representative of his alveolar air and thereby obtain a reading which indicates a smaller amount of ethanol than is actually present in his lungs. In addition, there is always the possibility that the machine might analyse something else besides gaseous alcohol and produce a result, without indicating that the wrong substance has been analysed. The most common error is the analysing of liquid alcohol. This will produce a very high reading. The effect of such an error is easily demonstrated by the fact that 100ml of beer contains over 1,500mg of alcohol, while the legal limit for driving is merely $35\mu g$ of alcohol in 100ml of breath. Such an occurrence can normally be prevented by following the manufacturer's instructions, namely that breathalysers should not be used until 20 minutes after the driver's last drink, by which time any residual alcohol in the mouth will have evaporated.

For a fuller description of the Camic and Lion Intoximeter and how they function, the reader is referred to Chapter 13. For a discussion about their reliability, the reader is referred to Chapters 13 and 16.

II. THE MEASUREMENT OF ALCOHOL IN BODY FLUIDS

Defining an offence in terms of a stated level of blood alcohol means that **9–09** the method of measurement of ethanol must be accurate and specific. Early methods of blood alcohol measurement were solely chemical in nature, but in the last 20 years enzymatic and physico-chemical methods have been developed and have been found to be both accurate and reproducible.

It has previously been stressed that the absorption and distribution of alcohol vary greatly with the individual person concerned, yet, with this reservation, it is theoretically possible to determine the alcohol content of any tissue of the body from a sample taken elsewhere when equilibrium has been reached. Muehlberger in 1959 published a table indicating that the alcohol content for the whole blood could be obtained by dividing the alcohol content of other parts of the body by an appropriate conversion factor (see C. W. Muehlberger, *The Physiological Action of Alcohol: Chemical Tests for Intoxication* (1959, Chicago), p. 6).

Table 1

Conversion factors for the distribution of ethanol between whole blood and other body tissues and fluids

Tissue	Factor
Whole blood	1.00
C.S.F.	1.10
Urine	1.33
Saliva	1.18
Plasma or serum	1.15
Brain	0.85
Liver	0.90
Kidney	0.83
Alveolar breath	0.000476

Source: Muehlberger, *The Physiological Action of Alcohol: Chemical Tests for Intoxication* (1959).

These conversion ratios are shown in Table 1 (see para. 9–11). Many of **9–10** these ratios are highly controversial. For breath, there is great argument as to whether the ratio for a volume of breath containing the same amount of alcohol as blood should be 2 or 2.3. For urine, likewise, the ratio of 1.33 is arguable since this is an eliminated fluid and therefore not truly in equilibrium with the rest of the body. The table of conversion factors is interesting and important, even if not universally agreed.

The chemical method of alcohol measurements has been superseded by enzymatic and physico-chemical ones, but it is still historically important and is described for interest. In this method, the ethanol is mixed with potassium dichromate in sulphuric acid. Most procedures are based upon determining the amount of unreacted potassium dichromate by titration and calculating the quantity used for the oxidation by difference. The alcohol is distilled and thus separated from non-volatile components of the sample and consequently any interference by proteins or preservatives is avoided. However, the four-stage process of precipitation, distillation, oxidation and titration is arduous and lengthy.

The two methods recommended by the Royal Institute of Chemistry were those of Kozelka and Hine, and Cavett (a micro-method) (see Kozelka and Hine [1941] *The Analyst* 174 and Cavett [1937/1938] *Journal of Laboratory and Clinical Medicine* 543).

(a) Biochemical Methods

9–11 The basis of a biochemical method is the enzymatic oxidation of ethanol to acetaldehyde. The co-enzyme nicotinamide adenine dinucleotide (NADH) is used in conjunction with this reaction as shown in Table 2. The amount of reduced coenzyme NADH is proportional to the concentration of alcohol present in the sample. This can be conveniently measured using a spectrophotometer at wavelength 340nm.

Table 2

alcohol dehydrogenase

$$CH_3CH_2OH + NAD^+ = CH_3CHO + H^+$$

inhibited by Hg^{2+}

This is a simple method which forms the basis of the automatic analyser and is used frequently in research. It is also the basis of several kits. It was claimed by J. E. L. Corry in 1978 (in 44 *The Journal of Applied Microbiology* 1) that this enzymatic method was not appropriate for samples which had been preserved with mercurial-type preservatives since the Hg2 + was used to inhibit activity (see G.C. Davis *et al.*, (1979) 2 *The Journal of Lipid Chromatography* 663). It is usual to deproteinise blood samples with trichloroacetic or perchloric acid before analysis. However, if samples are diluted by a factor of 10, it is not necessary to deproteinise before using the ADH procedure. The enzymatic method lacks the specificity of gas chromatography. There is also cross reactivity with 2-propanol and butanol and other longer chain alcohols. However, the ADH method does not oxidise any methanol or acetone present. Although the enzymatic method is quite reliable it can be difficult to persuade a court of its absolute value and thus it is mandatory to base any challenge on the gas chromatography method.

(b) PHYSICO-CHEMICAL METHODS

The major advantage that gas chromatography has over other analytical **9–12** procedures is that there is complete separation of ethanol from the other volatile components that may be present. Thus gas chromatography will measure separately 2-propanol, which is commonly consumed and which gives a cross-reaction with the enzymatic method.

The basic principle of this method is that the vaporised sample is transported in a continuous flow of an inert carrier gas over an adsorbent which causes a complete separation of components. Each individual substance is detected as it leaves the adsorbent and is measured by a signal from the detector which causes a recorder to produce a peak on a chart proportional to the amount of substance separated (see S. B. Rosalki (1984) *Clinical Biochemistry of Alcohol*).

The standard version of gas chromatography for mass sampling of alcohol in blood, urine serum and tissue extracts is that of Hachenberg and Schmidt (see H. Hachenberg, and A.P. Schmidt, *Gas Chromatograph Headspace Analysis*, (1977, London)). This is the head-space technique. In this method a measured quantity of the sample is placed in a small container fitted with a rubber septum cap. The rationale is that the vapour in equilibrium with a liquid has a representative composition with the fluid itself. The unknown is measured in tandem with a series of known standards. Thus the composition of the original can be calculated. In practice, to improve the accuracy of this method, an internal standard such as either propanol or isopropanol is used. The vapour above the liquid is then sampled with a syringe and injected upon the gas chromatography column. Usually the column temperature is about 100°C and the inert carrier is helium with a flow rate of 40ml/min. A flow ionisation detector completes the preferred method for measuring alcohol in biological fluids.

Owing to its accuracy and specificity, gas chromatography is the method **9–13** of choice for any legal challenge. Although the enzymatic method is normally very accurate, it is difficult to persuade a court of this because of the danger of cross-reactivity. Table 3 is a summarised critique of this method. The head-space procedure can be applied equally to blood and urine samples, as can the enzymatic method. Medico-legal samples are stored in sealed containers with the necessary preservative.

Preservatives for blood samples are sodium fluoride as a bacteriostat and potassium oxalate as an anticoagulant. The latter is not needed for urine samples and these require only sodium fluoride as a preservative.

In post-mortem samples, alcohol may be generated by fermentation of glucose or amino-acids. The presence of glycosusia is especially important since fermentation can give falsely raised alcohol levels. In addition, ethanol may be reduced by evaporation or oxidation.

Before analysis, the integrity of the seals of medico-legal samples must be checked. Confidence in the integrity of samples and essential modes of presentation is mandatory and any failure of the seal opens the prospect of speculation.

Table 3

Method	Advantage	Disadvantage
Gas chromatography	Very specific. Can distinguish between methanol and 2-propanol and butanol.	None.
Enzymatic method	Several kits available. A rapid method suitable for screening or research.	Potential cross-reactivity, *e.g.*, propanol, butanol.

(c) GAS CHROMATOGRAPHY IN PRACTICE

9–14 A control sample containing a known quantity of alcohol is taken as the reference sample. Then a known amount of another chemical is added, *e.g.* N-propanol. They are then heated together in a sealed container and some of the alcohol and propanol evaporates and mixes with the air in the head-space (*i.e.* above the blood) in the sealed container. The body fluid is heated until equalisation has taken place, *i.e.* until the evaporated alcohol and N-propanol are in the same proportion in the head-space as they are in the body fluid below. The air in the head-space is then placed in a gas chromatograph and forced along a cylinder under pressure from a gas jet. The cylinder contains a wadding with chemical on it which absorbs the ethanol and the alcohol. The jet forces these latter substances out of the wadding. Owing to the differences in their respective atomic weights, the alcohol and the N-propanol emerge separately and continue their respective journeys along the tube at different speeds and remain separated. The alcohol is then mixed with hydrogen and is burnt in a small jet in a process known as flame ionisation. The same happens to the N-propanol. The burning takes place below a collecting electrode, which may be a wire or a ring which has a polarising potential between the jet and the electrode. When burnt, both the alcohol and the N-propanol give off ions, which are attracted to the electrode and cause a resistance to be set up in the current flowing through it. This resistance is plotted on a chart recorder which traces in graph form the ethanol ions detected by the electrodes. The same thing happens to the N-propanol and the recorder prints out a graph showing the peaks of the alcohol and the N-propanol (*i.e.* the maximum amounts of ions). As the amount of these two substances are known, it is then possible to calculate the ratio between them.

9–15 The Home Office Forensic Science Service uses a micro-processor to carry out this calculation. After the ratio has been determined, the gas chromatograph is ready for ascertaining the (unknown) amount of alcohol in the body fluid provided by the motorist. The analyst carries out the same test procedure on that sample and uses the same controlled amount of N-propanol as was used in the test run. The chart recorder will indicate the peaks showing the amount of N-propanol and ethanol ions that have been detected. By applying the same ratio as was obtained from the test, it is possible to calculate the (previously unknown) amount of alcohol in the sample of body fluid.

(d) THE RAW DATA

The blood sample is analysed at least twice. In the case of the Home Office **9–16** Laboratories, these are carried out by two different gas chromatographs, each using a different chemical as the control substance and a different type of wadding. In the case of *DPP v. Swift*, St Helen's Magistrates' Court, January 7, 1993 (reported only on appeal [1995] R.T.R. 287) the wadding used in one of the gas chromatographs was polyethelene glycol, and in the other it was carbowax glycol. The average result of the analyses is then calculated, from which government scientists make a standard reduction to allow for any error. The greater of 6μg or 6 per cent is always subtracted from the result, *i.e.* three standard deviations.

In *Walker v. Hodgkins* [1984] R.T.R. 34, the High Court upheld the decision of the magistrates who had, of their own volition, made the standard 6mg deduction from the uncorrected result of the defendant's own analysis and then, on that basis, acquitted him.

That decision was not cited in *DPP v. Welsh*, unreported, November 11, 1996, where in a similar factual context the High Court held that justices were not entitled to make their own deduction of 6μg where the defence analyst had not done so. It is submitted that Welsh's case was decided *per incuria*. Also because the standard of proof is beyond all reasonable doubt, then if the Home Office considered that in order to avoid obtaining too high a result, three standard deviations must always be deducted from the results obtained from the gas chromatograph, then how can a court be satisfied so as to be sure of the alcohol content of a motorist's blood specimen without likewise making a similar reduction from the actual results of the analysis?

(e) CONTAMINATION OF THE SAMPLE

In *Collins v. Lucking* [1993] R.T.R. 312 the prosecution scientist said that **9–17** micro-organisms were found in the urine. These would not have affected the result of the analysis unless the accused was a diabetic. In the absence of any evidence as to the defendant's medical health, the High Court held that this created sufficient doubt for the justices not to be sure of the defendant's guilt. This topic is further discussed in Chapter 16.

However, the mere theoretical possibility of such contamination will not prevent a conviction. Thus the High Court upheld the verdict of guilty in *Sophocleous v. Ringer* [1988] R.T.R. 52. A forensic scientist had testified that there was always a possibility of blood producing micro-organisms which manufactured alcohol, but that she had never personally come across this. The High Court held that this testimony did not raise a sufficient reasonable doubt that no contamination of the blood sample had occurred. In other words, where there is an allegation of contamination, there must be some evidence of this having been a real, as opposed to a mere theoretical, possibility, if there is to be an acquittal.

III. DIFFERENCES BETWEEN THE PROSECUTION AND DEFENCE ANALYSES

9–18 It has been held that whenever the prosecution and defence analyses differ, it is entirely a question for the tribunal of fact to decide which they prefer and an appeal court will not overrule their preference (see, *e.g. R. v. Sodo* [1975] R.T.R. 357 and *R. v. Marr* [1977] R.T.R. 168). In *Walker v. Hodkins* [1984] R.T.R. 34, the prosecution analysis of the defendant's blood revealed 96mg of alcohol, while the latter's own analysis showed an uncorrected result of 83mg, *i.e.* the normal reduction had not been made. The magistrates themselves applied the standard deduction of 6mg and dismissed the charge under section 5. The High Court upheld that decision as it was a question of fact for the lower court to determine which one of the two conflicting results was to be accepted as accurate.

IV. THE MATHEMATICAL METHOD

(a) CALCULATING THE AMOUNT IN THE BLOOD

9–19 On average, half a pint of beer or a single "pub" measure of a spirit will contain the equivalent of 13mg of alcohol per 100ml of blood.

A more accurate method to determine the amount of alcohol in the body at a given time is to divide the weight of the liquor consumed by that of the body fluid and then subtract the amount of alcohol metabolised since the drinking began down to the time for which the calculation is made. Although that sounds simple, it is made complicated by two factors. First, it is necessary to convert the relevant data from imperial to metric measurements. Secondly, it is necessary to ascertain the certainty of five variables, namely, (i) the weight of the motorist's body fluid, (ii) the weight of the alcohol which has been consumed, (iii) the length of time that the alcohol took to enter the bloodstream, (iv) other substances consumed and (v) his metabolic rate.

(i) The weight of the body fluid

9–20 The weight of a person's body fluid is a percentage of his total weight, and this, in turn, depends on his build: the more fat, the less fluid. Therefore, it varies from one individual to another. Various tests have been carried out with different results (see Table 4).

Table 4

Weight of body fluid as a percentage of a person's total weight

Species	Number of observations	Mean	Range	Reference
Humans, male		0.68		Widmark (1932)
female	30	0.55	0.46–0.86	
Humans, male		0.76		Jungmichel (1933,
female	17	0.66	0.64–0.85	according to Elbel and Schleyer 1956)
Humans	57	0.82	0.50–1.15	Schmidt (1937, according to Elbel and Schleyer, 1956)
Humans	39	0.71		Goldberg (1943)
Humans, male	19	0.72	0.59–0.90	Jopikii (1951)
female	23	0.66	0.52–0.86	
Man	51	0.72	0.52–0.89	Alha (1951)
Man	16	0.71	0.51–0.94	Elbel (1956, in Elbel and Schleyer (1956))

(Table reproduced from the *International Encyclopedia of Pharmacology and Therapeutics*, Vol. 1, s. 20.)

The mean of Widmark's results is known as the Widmark Factor. Simpson found this factor to be accurate for 7 per cent of the male population.

(ii) The weight of the alcohol

This is calculated as follows: **9–21**

(1) Convert the proof strength (which is on the label and can always be obtained from the manufacturer) into percentage terms of alcohol. To convert proof into volume one multiplies the former by 1.75, *e.g.* 7.2 per cent proof of low calorie beer means that it comprises 4.2 per cent alcohol by volume.

(2) Convert the quantity of the beverage into metric, *e.g.* 10 pints of beer is the same as 5.683 litres. Accordingly, 10 pints of low calorie beer contain 0.238986 litres of alcohol.

(3) Multiply the volume of the alcohol by its specific gravity (0.776) and this will give the weight in grammes of the alcohol which has been consumed.

(iii) The length of time for alcohol to enter the bloodstream

For the calculation to be accurate, all the alcohol must have entered the **9–22** bloodstream. The time taken for this to occur depends on the contents of the stomach (*i.e.* the amount of both food and drink) as well as a multitude of physical factors, such as the opening and closing of the pyloric sphincter which controls the opening between the stomach and the duodenum, through which the alcohol passes on route to the bloodstream. In experiments carried out in the mid-1970s, Dubowski found that the time taken from the cessation of drinking until the blood alcohol level in the drinker had reached its peak varied from 14 minutes to two hours and 18 minutes, a near tenfold variation, with mean times for men and women being 57 and 42 minutes respectively.

Batt and Couchman, and Abele and Kropp found that a full meal taken before imbibing could reduce the maximum blood alcohol concentration by half in the case of the consumption of spirits and wine. Likewise, the more carbohydrates in the liquor (*e.g.* beer) the longer the ethanol takes to enter the bloodstream, during which period some of it is being continually metabolised. Dussault and Chappel found consistently that the peak alcohol concentration from beer occurred about an hour after the last drink and was 25 per cent lower than in the case of whisky containing a similar amount of alcohol. The greater the volume of alcohol, the greater the difference. Studies by Grecant (cited by Elbel and Schleyer, 1958) showed that:

> "In fed subjects the blood alcohol after oral ingestion was only about one-half to two-thirds of the value achieved with the same amount of alcohol consumed on an empty stomach."

(iv) Consumption of other substances

9–23 There are other substances which will produce a much higher alcohol level than normally expected. A recent study has discovered that aspirin is one of these (see R. Roine, R. Thomas Gentry, R. Hernandez-Munoz, E. Baraona, and C.S. Liber, "Aspirin Increases Alcohol Concentrations in Humans After Ingestion of Ethanol" (1990) 264 J.A.M.A. 2406). The survey showed that two aspirin tablets taken with a full breakfast an hour before drinking produced a blood alcohol level which was, on average, 20 per cent higher than expected and it was not until about an hour-and-three-quarters after the last drink that the alcohol level was down to normal for the amount of liquor consumed. This was probably due to the tablets inhibiting metabolism by the enzyme ADM. Women taking oral contraceptives had lower levels of alcohol for the same amount of intoxicants than those who were not. There are other substances which will effect the blood alcohol concentration, *e.g.* sugar might ferment in the stomach.

(v) Metabolism of alcohol

9–24 A person's metabolism of alcohol is the rate at which he dissipates ethanol from his body. Dubowski found a mean rate of 14.94mg per 100ml of blood per hour. In England, the Home Office Forensic Science Service work on an average rate of 15mg per hour. Dubowski also reported other surveys which showed a mean rate of 18.6mg. The alcohol decrease rate can vary enormously from one individual to another. In *Alcohol and Road Traffic* (J. D. J. Howard (ed.), B.M.A., 1963) Dubowski commented (at 209):

"Numerous recent studies confirm the extreme variability of the blood clearance rate . . . with most investigations disclosing significant numbers of individual clearance rates which exceeded or trailed the average by factors of 2–4 and some extremes differing by factors of 8."

He also published an article entitled "Absorption, Distribution and Elimination of Alcohol: Highway Safety Aspects" in (1985) 10 *Journal of Studies in Alcohol 98*:

"Quantitative data on alcohol elimination have been obtained in profusion, mostly from repeated measurement of blood or breath alcohol concentrations. In addition to these controlled pharmacokinetic studies, considerable information has been published on blood alcohol concentration changes with time in drivers who drink, usually by calculation from testing at two points along the elimination curve. The number of subjects tested and the variability of the results encountered have been much greater than in the laboratory studies. Moreover, the blood alcohol concentrations involved were usually much higher in the studies of drivers who drink. For example, in 922 men traffic offenders, Abele (1955) found a blood alcohol decrease rate range of 6 to 40 mg/dl/hr, with a mean of 18.4 and a mode of 18.0. In other studies in which two samples were tested, ranges of 1 to 80 mg/dl/hr (mean approx. $+/-$ SD, 20.4 $+/-$ 10.5) among 1512 subjects (Schweitzer, 1968), 0 to 26 mg/dl/hr (mean, 17.2 $+/-$ 9.1) among 1655 subjects (Ponsold and Heite, 1960) and 9 to 30 mg/dl/hr (mean, 18.6 $+/-$ 6) for 1142 subjects (Hilgermann and Schleyer, 1971) were reported. In 16 traffic offenders, the breath alcohol decrease range measured by two tests was 7 to 17 mg/210 L/hr (mean, 11.1 $+/-$ 2.8) (Loomis, 1974). Several of these other authors found alcohol elimination rates to be normally distributed (Lund, 1979), as has the present author.

Results of observations limited to two points on the elimination curve have many obvious shortcomings and limitations for determining functional blood or breath alcohol decrease rates, but they do illustrate the wide range encountered."

Dubowski also found the blood alcohol decrease rate in females to be 23.6 per cent greater than in males. Women taking oral contraceptives were found to have significantly lower metabolisms than those who were not. However, a person will normally dissipate alcohol at a constant rate and this can easily be discovered by tests, usually carried out by a doctor: a motorist is fed alcohol in the presence of the doctor who waits two hours to be certain that all the ethanol has entered the bloodstream. He then takes four blood samples from the motorist at half-hourly intervals and analyses them for their alcoholic content. The difference between the blood alcohol concentrations in the samples enables the dissipation rate to be accurately ascertained.

9-25 The Paton Report's findings are as follows (at 45):

"Approximately 5% of subjects showed a higher result for the 2nd breath test than the first which is evidence that they were still in the absorption phase at the time of the tests. The modal value of 8–9µg/(100ml/h) (18.4–20.7mg/(100ml/h) in blood at an apparent blood to breath ratio of 2300:1) agrees well with the modal value of 19mg/(100ml/h) obtained by Isaacs during laboratory trials. The distribution is skewed towards the lower values also suggesting that many subjects, when in the elimination phase, eliminate alcohol from their breath at a rate of at least 5µg/(100ml/h) (11.5mg/(100ml/h) in blood) then 20% of subjects had not fully entered the elimination phase at the time of their first breath test.

Table A15 shows that there were 139 cases where the elimination rate was over 13µg/(100ml/h) (~30mg/(100ml/h) in blood) and 18 cases where the elimination rate exceeded 20µg/(100ml/h).

In order to increase confidence in the calculated elimination rates the breath test data were examined critically and only those cases which met the following selection criteria were included for further consideration.

a) Difference between the two breath samples in both breath tests was less than 7.

b) No acetone indication on first or second test.

c) The time difference between the two breath tests was greater than 20 minutes.

Table A16 gives the resultant table of elimination rates. Although the number of very high elimination rates has been reduced, approximately 5% of subjects appear to have an elimination rate of at least 13µg/(100ml/h) (30mg/(100ml/h) in blood). There were 5 cases (Table A17) where extremely high elimination rates were observed but other parameters were within expected ranges."

Tests by Isbell *et al.* (1955) and Mendelson and La Doy show that alcoholics have much higher elimination rates than non-alcoholics.

"Disappearance rate of alcohol from the blood of drunk drivers calculated from two consecutive samples; What do the results really mean?" by W. Neuteboom and A.W. Jones in (1990) 45 *Forensic Science International* 107, reached the following conclusions:

'Based on a large material (N = 2354) of double blood specimens from drunk drivers apprehended in The Netherlands, we selected 1814 cases for further evaluation. The difference BAC2—BAC1 was used as index of alcohol elimination rate from the blood. The results ranged from below 0.10 to 0.64mg/ml/h with a mean of 0.22mg/ml/h. At least about 2% of drivers were still absorbing alcohol as indicated by a rising BAC.' "

Table 5
(Table A15 in the Paton Report)

LION INTOXIMETER 3000: Rate of elimination of alcohol from breath **9–26**
calculated from the mean result in each of two breath tests.

Elimination rate ($\mu g/(100ml/h)$)	Frequency	Relative frequency (%)	Cumulative frequency (%)
Absorbing	70	5.0	5.0
<1	5	0.4	5.4
1–2	44	3.2	8.6
2–3	42	3.0	11.6
3–4	53	3.8	15.4
4–5	63	4.5	19.9
5–6	98	7.1	27.0
6–7	135	9.7	36.7
7–8	128	9.2	45.9
8–9	171	12.3	58.3
9–10	158	11.4	69.6
10–11	115	8.3	77.9
11–12	95	6.8	84.2
12–13	72	5.2	89.9
13–14	48	3.5	93.2
14–15	23	1.7	95.1
15–16	22	1.6	96.7
16–17	7	0.5	97.2
17–18	9	0.6	97.8
18–19	7	0.5	98.3
19–20	5	0.4	98.7
20–21	1	0.1	98.8
21–22	2	0.1	98.9
22–23	3	0.2	99.1
23–24	4	0.3	99.4
24–25	1	0.1	99.5
25 and over	7	0.5	100.0
TOTAL	1,388		

Table 6
(Table A16 in the Paton Report)

9-27 LION INTOXIMETER 3000: Rate of elimination of alcohol from breath calculated from the mean result in each of two breath tests—refined data.

Elimination rate ($\mu g/(100ml/h)$)	Frequency	Relative frequency (%)	Cumulative frequency (%)
Absorbing	41	3.8	3.8
<1	5	0.5	4.2
1–2	39	3.6	7.8
2–3	34	3.1	10.9
3–4	42	3.9	14.8
4–5	51	4.7	19.5
5–6	81	7.5	27.0
6–7	107	9.8	36.8
7–8	106	9.8	46.6
8–9	131	12.1	58.6
9–10	140	12.9	71.5
10–11	81	7.5	78.9
11–12	82	7.5	86.5
12–13	61	5.6	92.1
13–14	31	2.9	94.9
14–15	18	1.7	96.6
15–16	12	1.1	97.7
16–17	5	0.5	98.2
17–18	7	0.6	98.8
18–19	4	0.4	99.2
19–20	4	0.4	99.5
20–21	0	0.0	99.5
21–22	1	0.1	99.6
22–23	2	0.2	99.8
23–24	1	0.1	99.9
24–25	0	0.0	99.9
25 and over	1	0.1	100.0
TOTAL	1,087		

(b) THE WIDMARK FORMULA

9-28 A quick way of calculating the *theoretical* maximum alcohol level is by applying a formula devised by Widmark, namely:

$$C = \frac{A \times 100}{D \times W}$$

C is the peak alcohol concentration in blood in milligrammes per 100ml of blood, where A = the amount of alcohol consumed in grammes, D = the weight of the drinker in kilogrammes, and W = the *Widmark Factor, i.e.* 0.68 for men and 0.55 for women (see above). In practice, the maximum concentration will never be reached in view of the time taken for all the alcohol to enter the bloodstream because it is being metabolised continuously from the moment it is first imbided through the mouth.

(c) CALCULATING THE AMOUNT IN BREATH OR URINE

The 1988 Road Traffic Act and 1992 Transport and Works Act have used a **9–29** blood: breath ratio of 2,300:1 to make 80ml of blood the equivalent of 35µg of breath. However, this varies considerably for individuals, from less than 1,800:1 to more than 2,800:1 Other countries use different ratios from that adopted by our legislation (see Table 9, p.102). To quote the summary of an article entitled "Variability of the Blood: Breath Alcohol Ratio *in Vivo*" by A.W. Jones and published in (1978) 39 *The Journal of Studies of Alcohol* 1931:

> "The blood:breath alcohol ratio, commonly used to translate the result **9–30** of breath alcohol analysis into the co-existing blood alcohol concentration, varies from person to person and within one person over time."

That summary is demonstrated by table 7 (drawn by A. W. Jones).

Table 7

Mean blood:breath alcohol ratios at different sampling times after drinking and significance of the differences from the customary 2,100:1 ratio, by student's test.

Sampling time (min)	Mean ± SD (N = 21)	Range	Coefficient of variation (%)	Mean difference from 2,100 (%)
30	1870 ± 210	990–2280	13.97	− 10.95
60	2055 ± 120	1794–2256	5.81	− 2.4
90	2070 ± 137	1797–2404	6.42	− 1.43
120	2104 ± 120	1896–2449	6.33	0.19
180	2111 ± 199	1870–2513	9.34	0.52
240	2201 ± 142	2025–2493	6.46	4.81
300	2181 ± 158	1837–2482	7.15	3.86
360	2284 ± 262	1875–2863	11.46	8.76
(1)p<.05	(2)p<.01	(3)p<.001		

The Paton Report found that in the Lion Intoximeter group of 815 **9–31** subjects for whom the blood:breath ratio was calculated from samples of those substances taken simultaneously, 37 per cent were in the range 2,200–2,400, 52 per cent over 2,400 (maximum 3,100), and only 11 per cent below 2,200 (minimum 1,900).

When calculating the amount of alcohol imbibed by the man in the dock, based on his admitted consumption, the Home Office Forensic Science Service first work out the quantity of alcohol in the blood. Where relevant, they convert that into breath alcohol, by dividing by 2.3 and that will give, in microgrammes, the level of alcohol per 100ml of breath. To ascertain the amount in urine, the breath alcohol level is multiplied by 3.06 and the figure obtained would give, in milligrammes, the level of alcohol in 100ml of urine.

Sometimes the amount of admitted drinking by a motorist using the above factors may be incompatible with the actual breath analysis. In such cases, if a different conversion figure is used which is within the recognised bracket, it may turn out that the driver's consumption is after all *ad idem* with the breathalyser.

F. The statutory presumption and drinking after driving

9–32 Since it takes on average approximately 45 minutes to an hour after finishing drinking for the alcohol content of the body to reach its peak (see above), it is quite possible for a motorist to have been under the prescribed limit at the time of driving, but over it by the time he came to provide his specimen. However, as a matter of law, it is not open to a person to make that submission to a court hearing a charge under the Road Traffic Act, ss. 3A, 4 or 5 or the Transport and Works Act, s. 27(2), unless he can prove post-driving consumption of liquor. The rationale of this was explained in *Millard v. DPP* [1990] R.T.R. 201, where the court stated that section 15(2) of the Road Traffic Offenders Act 1988 (see section 9–34) provided an irrebuttable presumption that the alcohol level at the time of driving was not less than that ascertained by the analysis. The only exception to this was that permitted by section 15(3), *i.e.* where an accused was able to prove he had imbibed alcohol after ceasing to drive and that the amount of such consumption was the sole reason for him being over the legal limit or unfit to drive (according to the allegation against him), at the time he gave his sample for analysis.

Wherever section 15(3) is invoked, an expert should be called to show that it was only the post-driving consumption which had caused the analysis to reveal an alcohol level above the prescribed limit (see *Dawson v. Lunn* [1986] R.T.R. 234). In *DPP v. Lowden, The Times*, April 10, 1992, the High Court held that justices could accept the account given in the witness box by the accused of what he had drunk after ceasing to drive, even though this contradicted what he had told the police at the time.

It should be noted that section 15 is not a presumption of the accuracy of the analysis (see *Cracknell v. Willis*) [1988] A.C. 450 at 467C). The presumption only arises after the accuracy of the analysis relied upon by the prosecution has been proved beyond all reasonable doubt.

G. Back calculations

In *Gumbley v. Cunningham* [1989] A.C. 281, it was held that the presump- **9–33** tion in section 15(2) only related to the *minimum* quantity of alcohol in the defendant at the time of driving, and there was nothing to stop the prosecution showing that when he had actually been driving, his alcohol level had in fact been higher than that disclosed by the analysis. The House of Lords emphasised that this should only be done in the clearest cases and not when there were differing scientific views about how much ethanol had been dissipated in the interval between the driving and provision of the sample. In effect, this means that the prosecution must work on the lowest known rate of metabolism. In making such a calculation, allowance must be made for the alcohol to have reached its peak at least two-and-a-quarter hours after the accused had ceased drinking, as this is approximately the longest duration it could take for all the alcohol to have been absorbed into the blood stream (see section 9–22). Until that point in time has been reached, it is not possible to carry out an accurate back-calculation.

In *R. v. Forest of Dean Justices, ex p. Farley* [1990] R.T.R. 228, the **9–34** applicant had been charged with two offences, both arising out of the same incident, one under section 3A and the other under section 5. He had been breathalysed just over 10-and-a-quarter hours after the occurrence of the fatal accident and the reading was 31µg. The DPP submitted that this meant that his alcohol level at the time of the accident was at least 98µg. Without argument, the High Court accepted that if the prosecutor used back-tracking to calculate the quantity of alcohol, the result was automatically presumed to be the amount at the time of driving, unless section 15(3) could be invoked. In other words, the defendant had to prove that he had consumed 67µg of alcohol after the accident. It is submitted that such reasoning is totally fallacious. The presumption in section 15 is as follows:

> "15(2) Evidence of the proportion of alcohol or any drug in a specimen of breath, blood or urine provided by the accused shall, in all cases (including cases where the specimen was not provided in connection with the alleged offence), be taken into account, and subject to subsection (3) below, it shall be assumed that the proportion of alcohol in the accused's breath, blood or urine at the time of the alleged offence was not less than in the specimen.
>
> (3) The assumption shall not be made if the accused proves —
> (a) that he consumed alcohol before he provided the specimen and —
> > (i) in relation to an offence under section 3A, after the time of the alleged offence, and

(ii) otherwise, after he had ceased to drive, attempt to drive or be in charge of a vehicle on a road or other public place, and

(b) that had he not done so the proportion of alcohol in his breath, blood or urine would not have exceeded the prescribed limit and, if the proceedings are for an offence under section 4 of that Act, would not have been such as to impair his ability to drive properly."

Sections 34(1) and (2) of the Transport and Works Act 1992 are framed in similar terms, save that the relevant permitted drinking period is from ceasing work until the provision of the specimen.

9–35 The above quoted statutory wording means literally that a motorist's alcohol level when he was driving is presumed to be no less than in the specimen which he provided and which was subsequently analysed. It is submitted that it does not mean that the alcohol at that time must be presumed to be such as is ascertained by the analysis plus the theoretical amount which would have been metabolised in a time-span equal to that which occurred between the ceasing to drive and the taking of the sample. Even if the statute was ambiguous, which it is not, it would still have to be construed in favour of the accused. Accordingly, in ex p. Farley, it should have been for the DPP to prove that between the time of the accident and the provision of the breath specimen, the defendant had not consumed any alcohol. It may be said that to put this burden of proof on to the prosecution would give them an impossible task. That is no reason in law for altering the normal principles of the criminal law, as is illustrated by the decision in Collins v. Lucking [1983] R.T.R. 312. There the urine sample was found to contain micro-organisms which were capable of producing alcohol but which would only have significantly affected the result of the analysis, if the accused was a diabetic. The High Court ordered an acquittal as there was no evidence that the latter gentleman did not suffer from diabetes. It is submitted that it was just as hard for the Crown to have to prove the negative in that case as it would have been for them to have done so in R. v. Forest of Dean Justices, ex. p. Farley [1990] R.T.R. 228.

H. Effects of alcohol

9–36 The reaction to ethanol varies enormously from one person to another. The only way to discover what effect a particular amount of liquor would have on any one individual is for a doctor to observe him drinking a specific quantity and watch how he reacts to it. Set out below in Table 8 is a rough guide to the general effects that alcohol has on a human being, although it must always be remembered that the same quantity can produce widely varying reactions amongst different people. The guide is based to a large extent on evidence given in a number of cases, and on the pamphlet, "Drink or Drive" produced by the Commission of the European Community.

Table 8

Blood/alcohol concentration	Effect on motorist
30mg	Driving skills start to become impaired. Tendency to take risks.
50mg	Carefree and loss of inhibitions. Problems in making judgments and severe impairment of the ability to react.
80mg	Driving skills seriously affected.
100mg	Obvious clumsiness and impaired emotional judgment. Euphoria starting to set in. Increased impairment of the eyes' reaction to light and dark
120mg	Beginning of complete unfitness to drive. Serious impairment of concentration. Extreme euphoria.
200mg	Those parts of the brain which control movement and emotional behaviour are clearly impaired.
300mg	Very intoxicated, confusion, passing-out and progressive stupor.
500–800mg	Fatal.

In the Intoximeter handbook, Lion Laboratories give the following **9–37** description of the effects of alcohol (see Table 9). (The author has converted the breath alcohol figures into approximately those for alcohol in 100ml of blood):

Table 9

Amount	Symptoms
0–45mg	Sobriety
35–115mg	Euphoria
90–230mg	Excitement
161–276mg	Confusion
255–370mg	Stupor
345–460mg	Coma
437 + mg	Death

The Mellanly Factor states that, in an individual, the same amount of **9–38** alcohol will have a greater effect in the absorption phase.

I. Other European countries

It may well be thought, from the above table showing its effects, that the **9–39** British Isles are too tolerant of those who drink and drive. In Europe, no other country allows its motorists to drive legally with more alcohol in their system than in the United Kingdom. As a matter of comparison, the prescribed limits for the blood alcohol content allowed by various European countries for their motorists are set out in Table 10. All figures are the maximum permissible amount in milligrammes per 100ml of blood.

Table 10

Other European Countries

Austria	.80	Luxembourg	.80
Belgium	.80	Netherlands	.50
Bulgaria	0	Norway	.53
Czechoslovakia	0	Poland	.20
Denmark	.80	Portugal	.50
Eire	.80	Romania	0
Finland	.50	Russia	0
France	.50	Sweden	.21
Germany	.80	Spain	.80
Greece	.50	Turkey	0
Hungary	0	Yugoslavia	.50
Italy	.80		

The legal limit in Eire was lowered from 100mg in December 1994 and this led to "hate mail" being sent to the Minister of Transport. The French altered their limit from 80 to 50mg on September 17, 1995.

9–40   Other countries also use a different breath:blood ratio and set out below in Table 11 (by A.W. Jones) is the statutory limit of alcohol in blood and breath in various countries compared to that of the United Kingdom.

Table 11

Statutory limits of alcohol in blood and breath in various countries.

Country	Statutory blood alcohol	Statutory breath alcohol	Conversion (blood:breath)
Britain	80mg/100ml(i)	35μg/100ml	2,300:1
Sweden	0.20mg/g(ii)	0.10mg/l	2,100:1
Norway	0.50mg/g(ii)	0.25mg/l	2,100:1
Austria	0.80g/l	0.40mg/l	2,000:1
Holland	0.50mg/ml	0.22mg/l	2,300:1
Germany	0.80g/kg(ii & iii)	(iv)	2,100:1
France(v)	0.80mg/ml	0.40mg/l	2,000:1
United States	0.10g/100ml(vi)	0.10g/2101	2,100:1

Notes

(i) Because 1ml of whole blood weighs, on average, 1.55g, 80mg/100ml corresponds to 76mg/100g.

(ii) 1ml of whole blood weighs 1.055g.

(iii) Concentrations of alcohol are determined in serum, and the result is converted into the presumed concentration in whole blood by dividing by 1.2.

(iv) Breath tests are used for roadside screening and not for evidential purposes.

(v) The level was lowered to 50mg on 17/9/95.

(vi) Applies in most American states.

Chapter 10

THE SCREENING BREATH TEST

A. Introduction

The Road Traffic Act 1988 draws a distinction between a breath test and a **10–01**
breath analysis. Both involve the motorist blowing into a scientific
instrument approved by the Secretary of State. Section 11(2) defines the
former as:

"A preliminary test for the purpose of obtaining, by means of a device
of a type approved by the Secretary of State, an indication whether the
proportion of alcohol in a person's breath or blood is likely to exceed the
prescribed limit."

A breath analysis, on the other hand, is designed to ascertain the exact
amount of alcohol which is contained in a person's breath. The circumstances in which a breath test may be required are limited. A proposed
amendment of the Road Traffic Bill 1991 to allow random breath testing of
motorists was defeated in the House of Commons. This chapter first
considers what devices have been approved and secondly discusses the
powers of the police to invoke their use. It should be noted that a motorist
has no right to be shown the results of his test displayed on the
breathalyser (see *Mallows v. Harris* [1979] R.T.R. 404).

B. Approved devices

I. IN BRIEF

The following devices are approved under the Road Traffic Act: **10–02**

(a) the DRAEGER ALCOTEST 80 (by Breath Test Device (Approval)
(No. 1) Order 1968);
(b) the DRAEGER ALCOTEST 80A (by Breath Test Device
(Approval) (No. 1) Order 1975);
(c) the LION ALCOLYSER (by Breath Test Device (Approval) (No.
1) Order 1979);

(d) the LION ALCOLMETER (by Breath Test Device (Approval) (No. 2) Order 1979);

(e) the DRAEGER ALERT (by Breath Test Device (Approval) (No. 1) Order 1980);

(f) the LION ALCOLMETER S-L2A (by Breath Test Device (Approval) Order 1987);

(g) the DRAEGER ALCOTEST 7410 (by Breath Test Device (Approval) Order 1993);

(h) the LION ALCOLMETER SL-400 (U.K.) (INDICATING DISPLAY FORM) (by Breath Test Device (Approval) (No. 2) Order 1993).

Breathalysers (a) to (f) were approved in 1992 under the Transport and Works Act and breathalysers (g) and (h) were similarly approved in 1993.

(a) EVIDENCE OF THE APPROVAL

10–03   In *R. v. Skinner* [1968] 2 Q.B. 700, it was held that an official authorised by the Secretary of State could give the necessary approval and in law that was regarded as the Secretary of State's approval. In *R. v. Jones (R.W.)* [1970] 1 W.L.R. 16, it was held that a court could take judicial notice of the approval without an HMSO copy of the relevant order having to be produced in evidence. In *Cooper v. Rowlands* [1971] R.T.R. 291 the High Court was of the opinion that any reference by the police to a breath testing device was to be construed as a reference to "an approved device" unless the defence were to raise the matter and take issue with the prosecution over it.

In *Bentley v. Chief Constable of Northumbria* [1984] R.T.R. 277 the High Court followed *R. v. Jones*, above. *Cooper v. Rowlands, supra,* was not cited in *Roberts v. DPP* [1994] R.T.R. 31 which latter case held that the Crown had to prove the Home Secretary's approval of the Kustom Falcom, which is a device used to measure, by radar, the speed of vehicles. It was not sufficient for the police officers in the case to say that they had used this equipment on numerous occasions. The justices had no judicial experience of this radar gun. If they had, then it would appear that such experience could enable them to take notice of its approval. The court said, *obiter*, that this could be established by oral evidence from a police officer or by a copy of the written approval by the Home Secretary. A new generation of breathalysers are waiting to be approved. It is submitted that *Roberts v. DPP*, above, was correctly decided and its *ratio* should apply to the new generation of breathalysers. However, it is almost certain that the judiciary would not take kindly to counsel raising such a defence and will confine *Roberts' case*, above, to radar guns on the grounds that they are not well known to the public, unlike breathalysers, which are, and this will include the next generation of them. The good old days of *Scott v. Baker* [1969] 1 Q.B. 659 will not be allowed to return, where the prosecution had to establish by admissible evidence the Home Secretary's approval if the matter was raised by the defence.

(b) Loss of Approval

In *Rayner v. Chief Constable of Hampshire* [1971] R.T.R. 15 it was held that **10–04** an Alcotest with a hole in its bag was not an approved device, even though this defect had not prevented the test being carried out accurately. *R. v. Kaplan* [1977] R.T.R. 119 held that there was a valid breath test when the bag only exploded while it was being blown into and after the crystals have changed colour (*i.e.* after giving a positive result). The House of Lords in *Webber v. Carey* [1970] A.C. 1072 held that a breathalyser which was not assembled in accordance with its manufacturer's instructions was not an approved device.

II. THE ALCOTEST® 80 AND THE ALCOLYSER

The Alcotest® 80 was the original "breathalyser" of Swedish manufacture **10–05** and was approved by the Breath Test Device (Approval) (No. 1) Order 1968. It is a tube into which a person has to exhale for between 10 and 20 seconds. It contains crystals of acid bichromate and if these turn green beyond a line marked on the tube (and not merely up to it; see *R. v. Sittingbourn JJ., ex p. Parsley* [1978] R.T.R. 153), this indicates that the motorist had probably consumed more alcohol than the prescribed limit. Later versions have also been approved: the 80A in 1975 and the 7410 in 1993.

The Alcolyser, made by Lion Laboratories, works on the same principle. Both are rarely used these days, as the police prefer electronic breath screening devices (see below).

III. THE ALCOLMETER

The Lion Alcolmeter S-L2 was approved by the Breath Test Device **10–06** (Approval) (No. 2) Order 1979 and eight years later, a more up-to-date version (the S-L2A) came into service and was approved by the Breath Test Device (Approval) Order 1987. The Alcometer is designed round a fuel cell. Whenever alcohol is blown into the device, the ethanol will cause the fuel cell to produce electricity which in turn passes through an amplifier and which, according to its strength, causes various lights to become illuminated.

Its mode of operation is fairly simple. First, the operator must hold the "read" button down for 10 seconds and two green lights should come on. The mouthpiece is then attached and the motorist starts blowing into it through an open-ended tube, about four inches long, attached to the mouth-piece. The exhalation must be of sufficient strength for light A to come on (*i.e.* a minimum flow of 28 litres per minute) and provide sufficient breath for light B to illuminate (*i.e.* the flow rate must be maintained for at least 2.7 seconds, giving a minimum expired volume of 1.25 litres). If this is done then light B illuminates which is the signal to stop blowing. The operator then depresses the "read" button for 40 seconds after which time the result will be displayed as follows:

Colour of light	Amount of alcohol per 100ml of blood
Red	Over 80mg
Red and amber	70–80mg
Amber	6–70mg
Green	0–6mg

The latest version is the SL-400. It is totally automatic once the switch has been pressed. It works on a traffic light basis, the same as the S-L2A, but the operator does not have to press any buttons to obtain a reading.

IV. THE ALERT

10–07 The Alert is manufactured by the Swedish company Draeger and was approved by the Breath Test Device (Approval) (No. 1) Order 1980. It works on the following principle. As the alcohol in the breath sample passes over a semi-conductor, it increases the ability of the latter to conduct electricity and this change in voltage causes the device's lights to illuminate. Once it is switched on, the operator waits for around two minutes until the "ready" light comes on, when the motorist must commence blowing within 15 seconds. The "test" light will then also become illuminated. When sufficient breath has been blown in, both the ready and test lights will go off. The motorist can then stop blowing and the result is displayed immediately in the following manner:

Illuminated light	Blood alcohol concentration (per 100ml of blood)
Fail	Over 80mg
Warn	Between 2–80mg
Pass	Not more than 2mg

V. THE MANUFACTURER'S INSTRUCTIONS AND THE EFFECT OF NON-COMPLIANCE

10–08 In *DPP v. Carey* [1970] A.C. 1072, the House of Lords held that the mere fact that a constable had not followed the manufacturer's instructions when using a breathalyser did not of itself invalidate a breath test, provided there was no mala fides on the part of the police officer. It would be another matter if the defendant could show that he had been prejudiced by this. The only exception to this was stated by Lord Diplock (at 1096):

"The instructions for dealing with the method of assembly . . . must be strictly complied with for unless this is done the product of the assembly is not of a type approved by the Secretary of State."

In *Rendel v. Hooper* [1970] 1 W.L.R. 747, it was held that there was a **10–09** rebuttable presumption of bona fides on the part of the police. In *DPP v. Carey*, above, it was held that a police officer was under no duty to inquire when the motorist last drank or smoked, even though the instructions provided by the manufacturers of the various breath testing devices lay down a minimum length of time which should elapse after drinking or smoking before the test should be administered. If the constable does not know that the motorist has been smoking, then he need not wait before administering the test: see *Darnell v. Portal* [1972] R.T.R. 483. If the police have reason to suspect that smoking or drinking has occurred within the prescribed time, there will not be a valid breath test if the time limits are not adhered to by the constable. In *Attorney-General's Reference (No. 1 of 1978)* [1978] R.T.R. 377 it was held that even if the accused told the officer that his last drink was a quarter of an hour ago but the policeman bona fide disbelieved him, then the constable could demand a test straight away and would not have had to wait another five minutes in accordance with the manufacturer's instructions. In *Attorney-General's Reference (No. 2 of 1974)* [1975] 1 W.L.R. 328, it was held that a policeman could not be considered to have been acting bona fides if he did not know what the manufacturer's instructions were. The force of that decision was weakened by *Blake v. Bickmore* [1982] R.T.R. 167, where it was held that there was no need for the prosecution to give evidence of what the instructions were for the device in question. It was for the defendant to show that non-compliance with the instructions had produced a result favourable to the prosecution. Nowadays the importance of how the test is administered is of much less consequence since such is no longer a prerequisite of a requirement by the police for a sample for analysis.

The position of a motorist who provides a breath sample in a manner **10–10** which is contrary to the manufacturer's instructions is considered in Chapter 20. Essentially, the law states that if the test produces a positive reading (*i.e.* shows him to be over the limit), then he is deemed to have taken the test satisfactorily (see *Woon v. Maskell* [1985] R.T.R. 289). If a negative reading is obtained after not complying with the manufacturer's instructions, then it is a question of fact as to whether this non-compliance would have prevented a positive reading being obtained. Only if the answer is that it would have made no difference will a satisfactory test have been taken (see *Corp v. Dalton* [1983] R.T.R. 160, 165K, where it was held that these instructions were not incorporated into the approval order).

C. The prerequisites of a requirement

The Road Traffic Act allows the police in certain circumstances to require a **10–11** motorist to blow into a breath testing instrument, namely:

(1) Under section 6 (1), where a constable in uniform can demand a breath test to be taken if he has reasonable cause to suspect:

(i) that a person driving, attempting to drive or in charge of a motor vehicle on a road or other public place has alcohol in his body or has committed a traffic offence while the vehicle was in motion (see (iii), below); or

(ii) that a person has been driving, attempting to drive or had been in charge of a motor vehicle on a road or other public place with alcohol in his body and that the suspect still has alcohol in his body; or

(iii) that a person has been driving, attempting to drive or has been in charge of a motor vehicle on a road or other public place and has committed, while the vehicle was in motion, one of the following crimes:

(a) any offence under the Road Traffic Act, except under those contrary to sections 123–142, inclusive; or

(b) any offence under the Road Traffic Regulation Act 1984; or

(c) any offence under the Road Traffic Offenders Act 1988 (other than one in P. 3); or

(d) an offence under Part 2 of the Public Passenger Vehicles Act 1981;

(e) also included would probably be an offence created by any regulation made under one of those statutes (see *Bingham v. Bruce* [1962] 1 W.L.R. 70 and *Rathbone v. Bundock* [1962] 2 Q.B. 260).

In *Morriss v. Lawrence* [1977] R.T.R. 205, it was held that if the prosecution based its case on the grounds for the breath test as being "suspicion of the consumption of alcohol", then it was not open to the justices to convict on the basis of a moving traffic offence, at least not without informing the accused of what was in their minds and allowing him an opportunity to meet that allegation.

10–12 Under section 6(2) a constable (whether or not he is in uniform) may require a breath test from a person whom he believes to have been driving, attempting to drive or in charge of a vehicle, the presence of which had caused an accident on a road or other public place. Two things should be noted about this section. Unlike section 6(1), which merely requires suspicion, section 6(2) requires belief in the existence of certain facts. Secondly, for this power to be exercised, there must actually have been an accident (see *R. v. Vardy* [1978] R.T.R. 202) but the accident (see above) need only involve one vehicle, *i.e.* that driven by the accused (see *R. v. Pico* [1971] R.T.R. 500, where the defendant's car hit the curb and a gatepost, damaging the latter).

Under section 29(1) of the Transport and Works Act 1992, a constable in uniform may require a breath test from a train or tram driver, (or indeed anybody who controls or affects the movement of such a vehicle or who supervises or carries out maintenance on a transport system (see Chapter 7), if the officer has reasonable cause to suspect that person of:

(a) working on a transport system with alcohol in his body [s.29(1)(a)]; or

(b) having been working on a transport system with alcohol in his body and of still having alcohol in his body [s.29(1)(b)]; or

(c) working on a transport system at the time of an accident or a dangerous incident where his act or omission may have been a cause of that accident or dangerous incident.

Although the statute uses the word "may require a breath test", a police officer who refrains from demanding a test without good cause is himself guilty of attempting to pervert the course of justice: see *R. v. Coxhead* [1986] R.T.R. 411, which was approved and followed in *R. v. Ward and Hollister* [1995] Crim.L.R. 398.

D. Restrictions on making a requirement for a breath test

The remainder of this chapter is concerned with the restrictions placed on the local constabulary with regard to their powers to require a breath test. **10–13**

I. A CONSTABLE IN UNIFORM

(a) CONSTABLE

Section 6(1) of the Road Traffic Act 1988 has only conferred the power to require a breath test upon "a constable in uniform". About the only thing that counsel has not thought worthwhile to argue on appeal is that "constable" means only the lowest rank in the police force. It is submitted that as a matter of common sense it embraces anybody who has been sworn in as a policeman, irrespective of his actual position in the constabulary hierarchy. This accords with the Police Act 1964 which enacts that a member of a police force shall, on appointment, be attested as a constable (*ibid.*, s. 18) and shall have all the powers and privileges of a constable throughout England and Wales (*ibid.*, s. 19[1]). **10–14**

(b) UNIFORM

The officer need not be in full uniform, according to *Wallwork v. Giles* (1969) 114 S.J. 36. There it was held that the requirement of the Act had been complied with, even though the officer was not wearing his helmet. The court said that the object of the provision was to ensure that the constable might be easily recognisable as such. So in *Taylor v. Baldwin* [1976] R.T.R. 265 it was held that the uniform need only be worn when the motorist is asked to take a breath test and not necessarily when the suspicion arose. In that case it was held to be sufficient for the sergeant to be wearing a civilian raincoat over his uniform. It has also been held that in the absence of direct evidence that the constable was in uniform, the **10–15** court may infer that fact from the circumstances, *e.g.* in *Cooper v. Rowlands* [1971] R.T.R. 291, where the policeman was a motor patrol officer and in *Richards v. West* [1980] R.T.R. 215, where the arresting officer was a special constable because the justices knew that when on duty "specials" always wore uniform. Indeed, in *Gage v. Jones* [1983] R.T.R. 508, the High Court went so far as to hold that there was a presumption that a policeman who required a motorist to give a breath test was in uniform. Griffiths L.J. also held that the justices could have drawn such an inference from any of the following facts:

(1) Only an officer in uniform would make the requirement for the test as otherwise it would be pointless. [The author would merely point out that in *DPP v. Harrington, Great Marlborough St Magistrates' Court*, November 25, 1994, a plain clothes member of the Vice Squad made such a request and arrested the defendant when he refused to await the arrival of the breathalyser.]

(2) The officer was a sergeant on duty on the highway.

(3) A pedestrian who witnessed the accident approached the sergeant and gave him the registration number of the defendant's car, presumably because he was identified as a police officer by the passer-by.

II. THE WORDS OF THE REQUIREMENT

10–16 In *R. v. O'Boyle* [1973] R.T.R. 445, it was held that any form of words may be used by the police to signify their wish that the motorist undergo a breath test, provided that the actual words spoken would be reasonably understood to mean just that. There it held that the words, "I intend to give you a breath test" were sufficient. Likewise, in *Johnson v. Whitehouse* [1984] R.T.R. 38 it was held that the requirement for the test was not invalidated where the officer used the word "suspect" instead of "believe" when requiring a breath test under section 6(2) of the Road Traffic Act 1988. (The facts known to the policeman justified him in believing, rather than merely suspecting, the defendant to have been involved in a road accident.) In *R. v. Nicholls* [1972] 1 W.L.R. 502 it was held that a valid request had been made if the constable reasonably believed that the request had been heard by the defendant, even if in fact he had neither heard nor understood it. That appeal was not cited in *Chief Constable of Avon and Somerset v. Singh* [1988] R.T.R. 107, where the contrary decision was reached.

In *R. v. Burdekin* [1976] R.T.R. 27, the Court of Appeal held that the police could justify a breath test on any suspicion which they could have reasonably possessed from the facts actually known to them at the time of the requirement, and were not restricted to relying just on the grounds which they had told the motorist when asking him to take the test. In *McKenna v. Smith* [1976] Crim.L.R.256, it was held that when requesting a breath test, no reason need be given by the constable to the motorist as to why he was making the requirement. In *Atkinson v. Walker* [1976] R.T.R. 117, it was held that even if the constable gave a wrong reason for requiring a test, that did not invalidate the requirement, provided facts actually existed which entitled the officer to ask for a test. In *Williams v. Jones* [1972] R.T.R. 5 the prosecutor argued for the first time on appeal that if the police could not reasonably have suspected alcohol in the accused, he would rely upon a speeding offence as entitling them to require a breath test, although this had not been told to the driver as the reason why the test was being requested. The High Court held that it was too late to take this point for the first time on appeal because, had it been raised in the lower court, the defence might have been conducted differently, *e.g.* by cross-examining the police about the speeding allegation.

In view of the decision in *DPP v. Warren* [1992] A.C. 319 the correctness **10–17** of the decisions in *McKenna v. Smith* and *Atkinson v. Walker* is now highly circumspect. In *DPP v. Warren*, Lord Bridge said (at 328B) that the police had to tell a motorist the reason why under section 7(3) a specimen of body fluid was being required instead of one of breath. The reason for this was that the driver might wish to contradict the constable on a factual point or at least be informed for the purposes of future legal proceedings, *per* Buxton J. in *R. v. Burton-upon-Trent JJ., ex p. Woolley* [1995] R.T.R. 139, 150. Since the law demands that a person must be told the reason why the police are requiring blood or urine, so surely the law must also require the police to inform a motorist as to why he is being required to undergo a breath test. It is true that Lord Bridge did not state that a person should be told the reason why a specimen was required in the first place, but in that case the driver will (unless at a hospital) almost invariably be under arrest either for having taken a breath test which gave a positive result or for having failed to take the test correctly. In either case he will have been told what was the reason for his apprehension. It will also be obvious that he is being required to provide a specimen for analysis at the police station for the same reason as that for which he had been arrested. However, just as he will not know at the station why he was being required to provide a specimen of blood or urine rather than one of breath, so at the road side he may well not know why he is being asked to take a breath test. Justice requires that he should be informed of not just the reason for the former but also for rationale of the latter as well.

III. ACCIDENT

(a) Definition

The definition of "accident" given by Lord Robertson in *Fenton v. Thorley* **10–18** *& Co.* [1903] A.C. 443 was followed by the Court of Appeal when interpreting that word in the Road Traffic Act in *R. v. Morris* [1972] 1 W.L.R. 228, namely "an unintended occurrence with adverse physical result", subject to the *de minimis* rule, *i.e.* where "the adverse physical effect is so trivial that no normal person would regard the occurrence as an accident at all". However, in later cases, the word "accident" was, as a policy decision, extended to include a deliberate act which had the same effect. Such an incident occurred in *Chief Constable of West Midlands Police v. Billingham* [1979] 1 W.L.R. 747, where the High Court held that the magistrates were wrong to acquit somebody who had deliberately released the hand-brake of a stationary car with the intention that it should be damaged. It held the test to be applied was: "Would an ordinary man conclude on the facts of the particular case that there had been an accident?"

In other words, would the archetypal person in the street who saw the event or its aftermath return home and report to his family that "there had been an accident"? That case was followed in *Chief Constable of Staffordshire v. Lees* [1981] R.T.R. 506, where the defendant had deliberately driven through a locked gate. The test was described as whether an ordinary man would conclude that there had been an accident. It is submitted that this conclusion must be on the basis of what damage was caused and how it occurred, without considering the *mens rea* or intention of the driver. The rationale of this latter decision is set out in the judgment of Bingham J. (at 510):

> "It would be an insult to common sense if a collision involving a motor car arising from some careless and inadvertent act entitled a constable to exercise his powers under the Act but a similar result caused by a deliberate anti-social act did not."

10–19   It may well be sensible not to allow a deliberate piece of drunken driving to go unpunished while the same piece of driving through mere recklessness on the part of an inebriated motorist would have caused the latter to lose his licence. However, in a democratic society it is questionable as to how far the judiciary should be entitled to improve the law if that involves giving a strained meaning to the words used in a statute. One view on this topic is that expressed (on different facts) by Fisher J. in *Waite v. Redpath Dorman Long Ltd* [1971] 2 Q.B. 294, 298:

> "There is a *lacuna* in the Act but it is well established that the Courts are not entitled to fill gaps in Acts of Parliament. This was laid down by the House of Lords, of course, in *Magor and St Mellons Rural District Council v. Newport Borough Council* [1952] A.C. 189, and has been reiterated in later cases in the House of Lords."

10–20   In construing the word "accident", Bingham J. referred to the *Oxford English Dictionary* definition of that word, namely "an unfortunate event, a mishap", and said that this was wide enough to include "an event not occurring in the ordinary course [of things]". He also referred to Shakespeare's use of the word in *Othello*. It is submitted that if Parliament has intended "accident" to mean anything other than its natural meaning, it would have said so. The use of Shakespearean English by a judge was not approved of by the Court of Appeal and caused them to order a new trial in *Holden v. Chief Constable of Lancashire* [1987] Q.B. 380, where the judge's use of the word "ample" would only have been correct if that word had been given its Shakespearean use as spoken by Falstaff, which was in fact the interpretation intended by the trial judge, though that information was not imparted to the jury.

(b) INVOLVEMENT OF VEHICLE

In *Quelch v. Phipps* [1955] 2 Q.B. 107 it was held that the defendant's **10–21** vehicle must not just have been the *causa sine qua non* of the accident but must also have been the *causa causans* of it. In that case a passenger injured himself when he jumped on a moving bus in Oxford. It was held that the accident did occur owing to its presence on the road; but the court said that it would have been different if somebody had started to cross the road, seen the bus coming and had stepped back into the person behind him, thereby injuring himself or the pedestrian to his rear.

(c) THE LOCATION

Section 6(2) of the Road Traffic Act 1988 states that the accident must **10–22** occur "owing to the presence of a motor vehicle on a road or other public place". This means that the actual collision need not have occurred in either of those locations. In *M (A Minor) v. Oxford* [1981] R.T.R. 246, a lorry ran off the street into a house. The High Court held that this accident occurred "owing to the presence of a motor vehicle on a road". Lord Lane C.J. quoted with approval a passage from *Redman v. Taylor* [1975] Crim L.R. 348:

> "Held, dismissing the appeal, that since the justices had found that the land was a public place the conviction was justified. The prosecution would have been simpler if it had been based on the accident having occurred as a result of driving 'on a road' because the mishap which led to the prosecution started on the roadway [*per* Bridge J.] Any accident resulting from such driving on a road as resulted in the vehicle running off the road and then colliding with some stationary object was clearly an accident which occurred 'owing to the presence of a motor vehicle on a road' within section 6(2) notwithstanding that the vehicle was off the road before the impact occurred."

(d) DANGEROUS INCIDENT

The Transport and Works Act s.29(3) defines a "dangerous incident" as an **10–23** "incident which in the Constable's opinion involved a danger of death or personal injury".

IV. THE REASON WHY

(a) RANDOM TESTS

(i) *The views of the public*

The original Road Safety Bill proposed to allow random testing. The Bill **10–24** fell with the 1966 election. When reintroduced into Parliament, it only allowed motorists to be breath tested if involved in an accident, suspected of committing a moving traffic offence or suspected of having consumed alcohol. This change was made after representations by the RAC and the AA. Indeed, during its passage through Parliament in 1967, the incumbent Secretary of State for Transport gave an undertaking that the resulting legislation would not provide for random breath testing. (This led her then junior minister, (now) the Rt Hon. Jon Morris, Q.C., M.P., many years later, to give to a meeting of Justice that statement as an example of how promises given by one minister can never be relied upon to be honoured by others, in that case the police.) Needless to say, random tests are not looked upon with favour by those who are subjected to them. In a letter to *The Times* dated July 7, 1991, Sir Hugh Cubitt wrote:

> "Chief Superintendent Sanderson, who . . . is to conduct an enquiry . . . into what makes motorists angry could well start by interviewing some of the 251 law-abiding ones (including myself) who . . . were inconvenienced by being randomly breath tested under the specious guise of 'road safety checks' by the Thames Valley police as they were driving away from Ascot races last month. He should, of course, avoid speaking to the ten who, when thus tested, were found to be positive."

The Association of Chief Police Officers takes a different view. Referring to the increase in the number of positive tests in the run-up to Christmas 1991, their spokesman said:

> "This highlights the police service's need for the unfettered discretion to demand a breath test in order to target these selfish hard-core drink drivers." (*The Daily Express*, December 23, 1991.)

10–25 The controversy over random testing still continues, nearly 30 years after the introduction of the breathalyser, as witnessed by two articles published on January 3, 1996 in *The Daily Telegraph*. It was reported that a spokesman for the Campaign Against Drink-Driving was advocating extra powers for the constabulary:

> "We think the introduction of random breath testing would make such a difference because a large number of drivers think that they will not get caught unless involved in an accident."

A leader writer took a different view in a column headed "The Legal Limit":

> "As figures for the Christmas holiday proclaim, the police were busy discouraging drink-driving. And, as these figures imply and a number of motorists will have discovered for themselves, the notion that random breath tests are outside the law is more honoured in the breach than the observance.
>
> The police officer who stops a vehicle and then finds reason to suspect that the driver has been drinking is entitled to apply the breathalyser test. Confusion in the public mind on this point is excusable, because Parliament has not in fact declared any change in its intention since the

Road Safety Act came before it almost 30 years ago. After considerable controversy, the random test was then ruled out.

What the Act of 1967 laid down was that police were entitled to stop motorists for suspected drink-driving only when they had been involved in an accident or had committed a 'moving traffic offence'. Parliament confirmed that attitude when, five years ago, an attempt to give the police powers to carry out random roadside tests was defeated by 265 votes to 157.

What has happened is that after a series of test cases in the courts, the law has been altered in a way that enables the police to act contrary to Parliament's original intention. The Road Safety Act was replaced by the Road Traffic Act of 1972, which was again updated in 1988. Under section 6 of that Act, a police officer is entitled to carry out a test if he has reasonable cause to suspect the ingestion of alcohol. Under section 163 of the same Act, a person driving a mechanised vehicle must stop if required to do so by a constable in uniform.

By operating the law under these two heads, the police can in effect force the breathalyser on whoever they choose. They can and do claim that in doing so they are acting wholly in the public interest. Drink-driving has entered the most heinous category of human offences. Policemen see more road smashes, some of them alcohol-related, than most people. Their zeal in catching principal offenders is understandable.

However, the present position is unsatisfactory on at least two counts. Parliament appears to have contrived with its left hand a situation that its right hand rejected.

Worse, the motorist who is halted and tested in this fashion is left believing that he is the victim of trickery. Yet he is a citizen whom the police need to have on their side. The police have no authority to carry out random testing, and Parliament should remind them of this. Liberties are always most easily eroded when people approve of the purpose behind that erosion: this does not make the erosion right."

(ii) *The law*

As mentioned by the leader in *The Daily Telegraph*, under the present state **10–26** of the law, a random breath test is in theory illegal. This is because the police would have no reasonable suspicion of the existence of any of the facts which would entitle them to administer a breath test. In practice this requirement does not produce any significant obstacle for an officer on traffic duties. Under sections 164 and 165 of the Road Traffic Act 1988, a constable is empowered to stop any motorist in order to inspect his licence, insurance and test certificate (See *Lodwick v. Saunders* [1985] 1 W.L.R. 382). If his suspicions are then aroused, usually because of the smell of alcohol, he is entitled to require a breath test. In *Such v. Ball* [1982] R.T.R. 140, it was held that whether or not a police officer was entitled to stop the vehicle was irrelevant. The issue was whether or not he had suspected the defendant of having alcohol in his body. If he did, he was entitled to require a breath test and the fact that he was only able to gain his suspicion because he had wrongly stopped the vehicle was of no relevance, provided that the police were not halting drivers at random for the sole purpose of ascertaining whether or not they had been drinking. (No such allegation had been made in that case.) If such was to occur, it would amount to malpractice in the view of Donaldson L.J., with which sentiments Forbes J. expressed his agreement. However, that latter judge also concurred with the opinion of Griffiths L.J. in *Steel v. Goacher* [1992] Crim L.R. 689, that it was perfectly acceptable to stop a vehicle late at night because it was not registered in the area and there had been a number of crimes in the locality. In the words of the Lord Justice:

> "If the public wish the police to contain and detect the ever increasing amounts of crime . . . they must be prepared to put up with the occasional inconvenience of being stopped and questioned."

10–27   Thus Forbes J. clearly drew a distinction, with which all motorists would agree, between proper crimes and mere infringements of the road traffic legislation. However, the *obiter dicta* of Donaldson L.J. in *Such's case*, above, was not followed in an appeal where the local constabulary had done exactly that about which he had expressed his disapproval. In *Chief Constable of Gwent v. Dash* [1985] Crim. L.R. 674 it was held that there was nothing unlawful in the police stopping cars to ascertain if they could smell alcohol on the driver's breath and, if there was such an odour, then requiring a breath test. The court (Lloyd L.J. and MacPherson J.) could see nothing wrong with that at all and it is definitely a view now in vogue with the judiciary, as was aptly illustrated by two cases heard at the same time before the Divisional Court. In *DPP v. Godwin* [1991] R.T.R. 303 a police officer stopped the defendant's vehicle and required a breath test. The prosecution argued that the manner of his driving would have given rise to a suspicion that he had been drinking. That submission was rejected and the justices held there to be no reasonable grounds for such a suspicion. (Although the officer had asked the defendant if he had been drinking, he had received a reply in the negative.) In these circumstances the High Court held that the policeman was acting unlawfully, whereas, in *DPP v. McGladrigan, ibid.*, at 297, the accused was stopped by a constable on grounds unrelated to any suspicion of alcohol, but the latter subsequently formed such a suspicion on reasonable grounds. Only after his suspicions were aroused did he request a breath test. It was held that he was entitled to require the motorist to blow into the roadside breathalyser. In *R. v. Downey* [1970] R.T.R. 257 it was held to be irrelevant that the suspicion turned out to be ill founded.

(b) WHOSE SUSPICION?

10–28   The suspicion or belief must be that of the constable making the requirement for the test, but need not be based on facts within his own personal knowledge. It can arise from what has been told to him, provided it was reasonable for him to rely upon that information, which can be from another officer (see *Erskine v. Hollin* [1971] R.T.R. 199 and *R. v. Evans* [1974] R.T.R. 232) or can even be an anonymous tip-off that the defendant was drunk, as happened in *DPP v. Wilson* [1991] R.T.R. 284. There the police lay in waiting for the accused's car after being informed by an unknown person that the former was drunk and was going to drive. At first instance the magistrates dismissed the charge because in their view the police has acted unfairly. Their decision was reversed on appeal by the High Court. The latter held that the conduct of the police was at all times perfectly proper and within the law.

(c) Difference Between Suspicion and Belief

Under section 6(1) suspicion is all that the officer requires to administer a **10–29** breath test while under section 6(2), he must have a belief in the existence of certain facts. This section considers what is meant by those words and what is the difference between them. Further sections will consider examples of what has been held to amount to such perceptions. In *Holtham v. Metropolitan Police Commissioner, The Times*, November 28, 1987, the Court of Appeal said that:

"Suspicion was a state of conjecture or surmise where proof was lacking. It was nothing more and was not to be confused with the provision of evidence."

In *Hussein v. Kam* [1970] A.C. 492 the Privy Council stated:

"Their Lordships have not found any English authority in which reasonable suspicion has been equated with prima facie proof."

In *Dumbell v. Roberts* [1944] 1 All E.R. 326, 239, Scott L.J. said:

"The protection of the public is safeguarded by the requirement, alike of the common law and, so far as I know, of all statutes, that the constable shall before arresting satisfy himself that there do in fact exist reasonable grounds for suspicion of guilt. That requirement is very limited. The police are not called upon before acting to have anything like a prima facie case for conviction . . .

There is another distinction between reasonable suspicion and prima facie proof. Prima facie proof consists of admissible evidence. Suspicion can take into account matters that could not be put in evidence at all. There is a discussion about the relevance of previous convictions in the judgement of Lord Wright in *McArdle v. Egan* (1934) 150 L.J. 412. Suspicion can take into account also matters which, though admissible, could not form part of a prima facie case."

In *Johnson v. Whitehouse* [1984] R.T.R. 38, 47 Nolan J. stated:

" . . . the submission which she makes to the court now as to the importance of the distinction between the word 'suspect' and the word 'believe'. I should make it clear for my part that the greater force of the word 'believe' is an essential part of the law and that the requirement for a breath test under section [6(2)] can only be justified if there are reasonable grounds for believing—in the full sense of that word—that the person concerned was the driver of the vehicle."

10–30   The difference between suspicion and belief is well illustrated in the case of *Bunyard v. Haynes* [1985] R.T.R. 348. There a car owner heard a crash while in his living-room and went outside. He saw that his vehicle had been damaged by another motor. His neighbour was also present and said that the other car was his and it must have been stolen. The magistrates were of the opinion that those facts gave rise to a reasonable suspicion that the neighbour had in fact been driving his own car at the time of the accident but did not justify a belief in that fact. It is submitted that all "suspicion" means is that the constable thought that the person may have committed the offence or may have done whatever is suspected, whilst "belief" means that the constable is sure of those facts. In considering a previous authority on this point, it must always be borne in mind whether or not the incident giving rise to the case had occurred before or after the coming into force of the relevant provisions of the Transport Act 1981 in May 1983. The reason for this is that prior to that legislation, unless there had been an accident, the police could only justify their suspicions by facts known to them before the motorist had ceased "driving". Since May 1983, the police can rely on all facts known to them when they make a requirement for a breath test, even though they only learned of them long after the driving had ceased. From *Mulcaster v. Wheatstone* [1980] R.T.R. 190 and *Godwin v. DPP* [1991] R.T.R. 297 it is clear that a policeman can justify his administration of a breath test only by relying on facts known or suspected by him at the time when he made the requirement.

The words "to believe" have been interpreted to mean both "belief based on facts which are reasonably believed to exist" (see *Liversidge v. Anderson* [1942] A.C. 206) and as meaning that the facts on which the belief is based must actually exist (see *Nakkuda Ali v. M. F. de S. Jayaratne* [1951] A.C. 66). As the police on some occasions rely on "tip-offs" for breathalysing a driver, especially one who fails to stop after an accident, the former depiction is most likely what Parliament intended.

(d) EXAMPLES OF REASONABLENESS

10–31   Often the police will stop a vehicle at random and ask the driver whether or not he has been drinking. In *R. v. Needham* [1974] R.T.R. 201 and *DPP v. McCladrigan* [1991] R.T.R. 297, it was held that an affirmative answer to such a question would arouse sufficient suspicion to enable a policeman to require a breath test. In *Clements v Dams* [1978] R.T.R. 206 the police based their grounds for a breath test on suspicion of the accused having been involved in an accident, but they also said in evidence that they thought that there had been signs of alcohol on the driver's breath but had not really considered the matter. The High Court held that the latter did not amount to reasonable suspicion of the driver having taken alcohol. If the officers had been questioned further about the matter, they may well in fact have had the necessary suspicion but that was not disclosed on the evidence before the justices.

In *Baker v. Oxford* [1980] R.T.R. 315 a car was involved in an accident and two men alighted from it and ran away. A constable carried out a computer check and ascertained that the defendant was the registered keeper of the car and arrested him (and the other man). The High Court held that as there was a presumption that the registered keeper was the driver, that was sufficient evidence to show that it was reasonable for the officer to have believed that the defendant had been the driving.

(e) MANNER OF DRIVING

In *Williams v. Jones* [1972] R.T.R. 5, it was held that it was not reasonable **10–32** to have suspected a motorist of having consumed alcohol merely because the latter, at 3.30 a.m., had done a U-turn when starting off, switched on his right-hand indicator to show that he intended to take the second of two left-hand exits off a roundabout, and had exceeded the speed limit by eight miles per hour. If a driver had done that on a busy road in the rush hour, it might have been another matter. In *Everitt v. Trevorrow* [1972] Crim.L.R. 566, the court held that it was reasonable to suspect a driver of having alcohol in his body where the latter had exceeded the 30 miles per hour speed limit and, after rounding a bend, had driven for 100 yards on the wrong side of the road without causing inconvenience to other traffic. The difference between these two cases is clear. In the former, the defendant did what any driver might well do even when perfectly sober, whilst, in the latter case, driving for 100 yards on the wrong side of the highway was something that a sober driver just would not do. Essentially it is a question of fact as to whether the way in which the accused had controlled his vehicle was such as to lead to the conclusion that a sober person would not have driven in such a manner.

In *R. v. Fardy* [1973] R.T.R. 268 the Court of Appeal held that it was not **10–33** easy to give an answer to the question of how far bad driving, which was possible from all drivers, drunk or sober, could support a reasonable suspicion that a driver had consumed alcohol. In that case, the defendant, at 3.30 a.m., had driven out of a minor road and stopped two feet into the major road, causing an approaching police car to brake hard in order to avoid a collision. The Court of Appeal upheld the jury's conviction on the grounds that the manner of his driving could give rise to a reasonable suspicion of the accused having consumed alcohol, the basis for this being that the driving would have caused an accident but for an emergency stop by another car. The jury, and the police, were entitled to conclude that a sober driver would have seen the approaching police car and stopped inside the minor road. Therefore the error made by the accused, coupled with the time when it occurred, gave rise to the suspicion that he had been drinking. The contrary decision was reached in *Mulcaster v. Wheatstone* [1980] R.T.R. 190, where it was held not to be a reasonable suspicion of drinking that a driver had pulled away from a stop sign and then suddenly braked to avoid a collision with two cars on the major road. It is submitted that this is a correct decision as the failure to see the cars could easily have been momentary inadvertence, totally unconnected with the consumption of alcohol. In *R. v. McGall* [1974] R.T.R. 216, the court refused to disturb a jury's verdict of guilty when the police suspected the accused of having consumed alcohol as they followed his car late at night. He was driving slowly in the outside lane with his offside indicator flashing. He came to a road junction but continued straight across it. The police signalled to him to show that his indicator was on, so he turned it off but a little later he switched it on again although there was no junction in the immediate vicinity.

10–34 In *Pamplin v. Fraser (No. 1)* [1981] R.T.R. 499 it was held to be reasonable to suspect of having alcohol in his body, a driver who had driven at an excessive speed and when, on approaching a "Give Way" line at a roundabout, the front end of his vehicle dipped drastically but he did not stop. Instead, he went across the "Give Way" line and turned left.

10–35 In *Clark v. Price* (1984) 148 J.P. 55 it was held that the police were entitled to suspect the defendant of having consumed alcohol when, on being followed by the police, he stopped his car on a bend, blocking half the road. He alighted and ran off, leaving his jacket and ignition keys in the car. On returning he told a policeman that the car was his. The High Court held that, in those circumstances, a constable could reasonably have suspected the defendant of having consumed alcohol. In *Griffiths v. Willett* [1979] R.T.R. 195 the police found a blood-splattered van in a ditch. It was held that this did not give rise to a reasonable suspicion that its driver had been drinking. There could have been many reasons why the vehicle ended up where it did. In *Fox v. Chief Constable of Gwent* [1984] R.T.R. 402 it was held that merely because a car had been involved in an accident, that did not give rise to a reasonable suspicion that somebody had been injured. That proposition was not disturbed on appeal to the House of Lords [1986] A. C. 281.

10–36 In the case of *Monaghan v. Corbett* (1983) 147 J.P. 545, a policeman went round to the defendant's home and breathalysed him at 2.30 p.m. on a Sunday. It was held that it was not reasonable to have suspected the motorist, at the time of the test, of having alcohol in his body merely because the officer, on the previous day, had smelled alcohol on his breath and had been told by neighbours that he invariably frequented a public house at Sunday lunch-time and that he had seen the defendant drive off at lunch-time that day. In the words of the High Court:

"It would be a very dangerous extension of the law to permit reasonable suspicion to be founded on facts wholly unconnected with the driving of a motor vehicle at the time to which the suspicion related."

In *R. v. Furness* [1974] Crim. L.R. 750 the defendant was seen by a constable outside licensed premises, staggering and smelling of drink. Half an hour later the same officer saw him drive out of the car park of that inn. Those facts were held to amount to reasonable suspicion that the defendant had alcohol in his body. However, the court deprecated the idea of police officers lying in wait outside public houses at closing time to stop at random departing motorists. No case has decided if it is reasonable to suspect a person of having alcohol in his body merely because he is seen coming out of a public house. It is submitted that the answer is "no", for two reasons: first, the decision in *Monaghan v. Corbett*, above, decided by a strong court consisting of the future Chief Justice and Deputy Chief Justice. Secondly, as was said by Viscount Dilhorne in *Spicer v. Holt* [1977] A.C. 987, 996F/G:

> "It is a matter of common knowledge of which one can in my view properly take judicial notice, that at the time when the creation of the new offence was under consideration, there was great concern about the possibility of random tests and the possible harassment of motorists with the result that Parliament required certain conditions to be complied with for an analysis to be admissible."

(f) THE RELEVANCE OF INFORMATION SUPPLIED TO THE MOTORIST

The High Court in *Vernon v. Lawrence* 137 J.P. 867 held that a reference to **10–37** "drinking" by a police officer can be construed as meaning "drinking alcohol".

(g) PRESUMPTIONS

The prosecution must always prove beyond reasonable doubt that the **10–38** officer who required the breath test had indeed reasonable suspicion. It was held in *Siddiqui v. Swain* [1979] R.T.R 454 and *DPP v. Godwin* [1991] R.T.R. 303 that there was no presumption of this and the mere fact that an officer had required a breath test was no evidence that he had possessed the necessary suspicion enabling him to make the request.

V. SPECIAL PROTECTION FOR HOSPITAL PATIENTS

(a) A PATIENT AT A HOSPITAL

(i) *Hospital*

Section 11(2) of the Road Traffic Act 1988 and section 38(1) of the **10–39** Transport and Works Act 1992 define "a hospital" as:

> "An institution which provides medical or surgical treatment for in-patients or out-patients."

(ii) *Patient*

The statute does not attempt to offer any definition of the word "patient". **10–40** In *R. v. Crowley* [1977] R.T.R. 153, it was held that once a person had arrived at a hospital he became a patient, even though his treatment had not commenced. In *Attorney-General's Reference (No. 1 of 1976)* [1977] 1 W.L.R. 646, the Court of Appeal held that "a patient at a hospital" was a person who was physically present in a such an institution for the purpose of obtaining treatment and that encompassed anywhere within its curtilage. The Court went on to state that a person would only cease to be one when he had received all the treatment for which he had visited the hospital and had started to leave for home. Accordingly, in the view of their Lordships, if a doctor were to tell him to sit down for 30 minutes before he left, he would still remain a patient for those 30 minutes. In that case, the Court upheld the validity of a breath test on somebody who was in the car park on his departure from the hospital. Also, a person who is travelling to such an institution in an ambulance does not fall within the definition of "a patient at a hospital" (see *Hollingsworth v. Howard* [1974] R.T.R. 58).

10–41   In *Askew v. DPP* [1988] R.T.R. 303, the defendant was found not to be a patient when he was arrested in the hospital car park immediately after having been discharged, even though he was readmitted the next day. In giving his judgment, Watkins L.J. said (at 308) that the expression "patient at a hospital" should be given "a wide interpretation". His Lordship went on to give guidance (at 309) on how a court should answer the question of whether or not a person had ceased to be a patient:

> "In any event, I think it is in essence a question of fact for the jury in the particular circumstances to conclude whether or not a person is a patient at a hospital when spoken to for the purpose of requesting that he take a breath test. The commonsense approach to that problem obviously will involve ascertaining among other things whether or not a person has had treatment at the hospital, whether the treatment has come to an end, whether the doctor in charge of the treatment has informed the police that the treatment has come to an end, or a nurse has said so, as the case may be, and whether that fact having been ascertained the patient has begun at least to prepare himself for making his way out of hospital. It does not seem to me that justices need be influenced in their conclusion by the fact that a person has not actually left the precincts of a hospital when a request by a police officer is made to him to provide a specimen of breath."

10–42   The last part of the penultimate sentence must be interpreted in the light of the fact that Watkins L.J. approved the decision of the Scottish Court of Justiciary in *Watt v. MacNeil* [1988] R.T.R. 310, where it held that a person whose treatment had concluded but who was sitting on a trolley naked from the waist upwards was still a patient. It is accordingly submitted that a person remains a patient until he has dressed himself and is ready to leave the hospital; or, to use the picturesque words of the Sheriff of Aberdeen, (at 312):

> "He was not miraculously transformed into a creature of some other nature at the moment when the last bandage was secured or the last X-ray photograph taken."

(b) Information to, and Objection by, the Doctor

(i) The requisite information

Under section 9 of the Road Traffic Act 1988 and section 33 of the **10–43** Transport and Works Act 1992, a breath test cannot be administered to a patient at a hospital unless the doctor in immediate charge has been informed and he has not raised any objection on the grounds that the requirement for, or the provision of, a breath sample would be prejudicial to the proper care and treatment of the patient. In *Baker v. Foulkes* [1975] R.T.R. 509 the House of Lords stated that the doctor need only be told of what the police intended to do. There was no requirement that he be told of his right of objection to the proposals of the local constabulary.

(ii) In immediate charge

In *Jones v. Brazil* [1970] R.T.R. 449, the police saw the patient being **10–44** attended to by a doctor who was accompanied by some nurses. The police assumed that this medical practitioner was the one in immediate charge of the patient. The High Court held that if a certain doctor appeared to the police to be "in immediate charge", this was sufficient prima facie evidence of that fact. It is submitted that it would always be open to the defence to rebut such a prima facie case. In *R. v. Crowley* [1977] R.T.R. 153 it was held that "in immediate charge" meant the doctor who was directly responsible for the patient and in the ordinary case it would be the casualty officer.

(iii) Overheard by patient

In *R. v. Walters* [1972] Crim. L.R. 381, Bridge J. held that notification to **10–45** the doctor pursuant to section 9 must be made out of the hearing of the patient, as there was always a possibility that, depending on his medical condition, knowledge of what the police wanted might cause a heart attack. As that had not been done, the judge directed an acquittal. Unfortunately the authority of that decision has been somewhat weakened by the judgments of Lord Widgery C.J. and Wien J. in *Oxford v. Lowton* [1978] R.T.R. 237. There it was held that, in the absence of express words in the statute, there was no requirement for the patient to be out of earshot when the police spoke to the doctor about, and prior to, their making their request for the provision of a specimen. It is submitted that the better view is that propounded by Bridge J., which is supported by the observations of Viscount Dilhorne in *Foulkes v. Baker* [1975] 1 W.L.R. 1551:

> "Let me assume that a patient with a weak heart is in hospital after suffering injuries in a road accident. A visit by a police officer or officers to his bedside might be a considerable shock to him . . . In such a case the doctor might well object to the police officer or officers seeing the patient and requiring a specimen."

10–46   Hearing a police officer speaking about administering a breath test or of an intention to require blood could easily have the same effect on a patient as actually seeing a constable. Accordingly, it is submitted that it would have been illogical for Parliament to have made it illegal for a policeman to request a sample without having notified the doctor beforehand, while at the same time allowing the patient to overhear that conversation informing the medical practitioner of the future plans of the police in that regard. Therefore, it is submitted that *Walters* was correctly decided. This is especially so since the medical practitioner can object not only if the motorist is unfit to give a specimen, but also if he is not well enough to be told of such a request, irrespective of his ability to provide the sample.

(iv) Revocation of consent

10–47   In *Bosley v. Long* [1970] 1 W.L.R. 1410 the High Court was of the opinion that although a doctor had initially raised no dissent when spoken to by the police, he could at any time prior to the actual taking of the sample object to that course of action for the reasons laid down in the statute. In *Bourlet v. Porter* [1973] R.T.R. 293, Lord Morris of Borth-y-Gest agreed with the views expressed in *Bosley v. Long*, above, but two of his noble and learned friends (Viscount Dilhorne and Lord Diplock) took the opposite view. Their Lordships' pronouncements on this matter were *orbiter*. It is submitted that the opinion of Lord Morris is preferable. The mandatory requirement of having to inform the doctor was enacted by Parliament as a safeguard for the injured motorist. If he were to have a relapse after the medical practitioner had originally considered him well enough to supply a specimen, he should still be entitled to the protection of the doctor being able to veto any sample being taken. This is probably of academic interest only, because (as Viscount Dilhorne pointed out) no policeman would insist on a specimen if a doctor told him that a patient should not provide one.

(v) A requirement made before arrival at a hospital but sample provided afterwards

10–48   In *R. v. Crowley* [1977] R.T.R. 153 it was held that if the request for breath was made prior to the arrival at the hospital, but the specimen was not taken until the motorist had become a patient, then the procedure laid down in section 9 had to be followed before a breath test could be administered.

(vi) Hearsay

10–49   In *R. v. Chapman* [1969] 2 Q.B. 436 and *Burn v. Kernohan* [1973] R.T.R. 82 it was held that it was not hearsay evidence for a policeman to say that the doctor did not object.

VI. VENUE

10–50   Under section 6(3) of the Road Traffic Act 1988 and section 27(4) of the Transport and Works Act 1992 a person must be asked to undertake the breath test "at or near" the place where the requirement is made, unless there has been an accident (in a case under the Transport and Works Act, a serious incident) when he can be made to go to a police station and to take the test there. In *Donegani v. Ward* [1969] 1 W.L.R. 1502, the High Court upheld the decision of the Carlisle justices that a distance of 160 yards was not "there or nearby". In that case the officer sent for the breathalyser and asked the defendant if he would walk with him in the direction of the police station. After walking 160 yards they came across the officer who was bringing the equipment. In *Hill v. Wilson* (1984) 149 J.P.(R.) 252 the prosecutor argued at petty sessions that 160 yards might not be "near or thereby" in Carlisle but one-and-a-half miles was "there or nearby" in Lancaster! The High Court did not make any comment on this point, as it allowed the appeal on another ground and did not consider it necessary to give judgment on any other matter. It should be noted that the statutory wording under the legislation now in force is "at or near" instead of "there or nearby", as it was under the Road Safety Act 1967 and the unamended Road Traffic Act 1972. It is submitted that the words "at" and "there" have an identical meaning, *i.e.* "in the same place as", since it is hard to see what difference there is in these two words or what other meaning either of them could have. This is supported by *Donegani v. Ward* (at 1505) where Lord Parker C.J. explained what the word "nearby" meant:

> "It seems to me, however, that one must judge 'nearby' in the purely geographical sense, and I can only think that the words 'or nearby' were inserted in order to cover the case where it was necessary to take the test, not on the main road, but in a lay-by or in some such circumstances as that."

VII. POWERS OF ENTRY

(a) Express Statutory Powers

The main curb on the police attempting to breathalyse drivers is that they **10–51** only have a very limited power of entry, without the consent of the occupier, on to private premises where a suspect is lawfully present. If the motorist is a trespasser then he cannot rely upon the police being in the same position. Therefore a drunken driver cannot escape arrest by jumping over the nearest hedge, as was attempted in *R. v. Burdekin*, above. If only the police are trespassers, then they have no legal right to request a breath test and if a driver in those circumstances should refuse to blow into a breathalyser, he commits no offence (see *Anderton v. Lythgoe* [1985] 1 W.L.R. 222).

Under the Road Traffic Act the police are only allowed to enter private property uninvited to administer a breath test where (a) there has been an accident owing to the presence of a motor vehicle on a road or other public place which they reasonably suspect has caused personal injury to a person other than the one to be breathalysed, and (b) they have reasonable cause to suspect that there was on the premises a person whom they reasonably believe to have been driving a motor vehicle which had been involved in that accident: see *Clowser v. Chaplin* [1981] 1 W.L.R. 837, *Anderton v. Lythgoe* [1985] 1 W.L.R. 222 and section 6(6) of the Road Traffic Act 1988. Under section 30(4) of the Transport and Works Act 1992 a constable may also enter any property uninvited to administer a breath test to a person who works on a transport system as a driver, guard, conductor or signalman or in any other capacity where he can control or effect the movement of a vehicle or is involved in its maintenance (including in a supervisory capacity), on look-out where there has been an incident which the officer reasonably suspected involved the death of, or injury to, a person other than the one to be breathalysed and that the act or omission of the person to be breathalysed may have been a cause of that incident.

In *Clowser v. Chaplin* the court left open the question of whether the law still recognises the doctrine of trespass *ab initio* (see *The Six Carpenters' case* (1610) 8 Co. Rep. 146a), which makes a lawful entry become *ex post facto* a trespass, where, once he is on the premises, the entrant abuses his position. This principle only applies where the right to enter is given by law and not by the agreement of the occupier or owner. Also, the legislation allows a constable to enter by force "if need be".

Swales v. Cox [1981] Q.B. 849 held that the words "if need be" meant that force could only be used as a last resort. The police must first take all reasonable steps to obtain the occupier's permission.

(b) IMPLIED PERMISSION

(i) *The grounds of a house*

10–52 Common law considered that everybody (including the police) had an implied permission from the occupier to enter the curtilage of his private premises and to knock at the door of (see *R. v. Allen* [1981] R.T.R. 410), but not to enter inside, his house (see *Fox v. Chief Constable of Gwent* [1986] A.C. 281). The law even thought that an occupier was willing to allow members of his local constabulary to go upon his land solely for the purposes of breathalysing him! Thus the police can lawfully make a requirement for a breath test while legally present upon any premises, so long as they do this before they are ordered to leave (see *Faulkner v. Willets* [1982] R.T.R. 159). On being told to depart, they must do so forthwith (see *R. v. Allen*, above). Merely telling the police to "f—off" may not amount to a withdrawal of their implied licence to enter the property. In *Gilham v. Breidenbach* [1982] R.T.R. 328 the High Court upheld the decision of the magistrates that those words were mere vulgar abuse. It is submitted that much more preferable, and in accordance with common sense, is the view of Judge A.A. Edmondson at Carlisle Crown Court in the case of *R. v. McMillan*, unreported, July 9, 1986. His Honour was clearly of the opinion that words like "f— off" by a tenant to a policeman on his demise who wished to breathalyse him manifestly meant that the local constabulary should forthwith depart from his property and leave him alone. Similarly, the High Court has held that when pursued by police cars, the mere act of driving into his backyard, winding up his car windows and locking himself in the vehicle while the police attempt to unlock its door, did not mean that the driver wanted the police to leave his backyard! The above factual situation occurred in the case of *Pamplin v. Fraser (No.1)* [1981] R.T.R. 494, where the accused was duly convicted of failing to provide a breath test. As the motorist's actions in that case did not amount to the revocation of a person's implied licence to enter the grounds of a house, it would appear that only words expressly stating this can end the permission to enter which the owner had (impliedly) granted to the policeman. Accordingly, in *Lambert v. Roberts* [1981] 2 All E.R. 15, 19, Donaldson L.J. helpfully suggested that a householder could always prevent a constable from going on to his property by the simple expediency of displaying a notice on his land stating "Police Keep Out"! In *Robson v. Hallett* [1967] 2 Q.B. 939, 954B, Diplock L.J. suggested a notice on the front gate saying "No Admittance to Police Officers". His Lordship also held that once such people were told to leave they must do so forthwith.

(ii) The dwelling-house

Although there is no implied permission to enter inside a dwelling-house, a **10–53** licence to do so can be inferred from conduct. In *Faulkner v. Willets* [1982] R.T.R. 159 a policeman knocked at the defendant's front door which was opened by his wife who then walked back inside her home. She was followed by the officer, who was at no time requested to leave. The High Court held that this amounted to an implied invitation to enter.

(iii) Joint owners and landlords

The rights of co-owners over their property are concurrent. When one joint **10–54** tenant invites the police inside the property, another joint tenant cannot revoke that licence (see *R. v. Thornley* (1981) 72 Cr.App.R. 302). In *Faulkner v. Willets*, above, it was held that a licence to enter the matrimonial home by a wife enabled a constable to require her husband to take a breath test and to arrest him when he refused to comply with that demand. A freeholder has no power to grant or to revoke a licence to enter premises which he has demised to a tenant (see *Preston Borough Council v. Fairclough, The Times*, December 15, 1982, C.A.).

(iv) Police and Criminal Evidence Act 1984

Section 17(5) of the Police and Criminal Evidence Act 1984 abolished all **10–55** common law rights of a constable to enter premises without a warrant, except to prevent a breach of the peace. Strictly speaking, the doctrine of an implied licence is not a right of entry at common law which could be exercised irrespective of the will of the lawful occupier, but is based on a presumed grant which is deemed to have been given by the occupier and which remains in force until revoked. Therefore section 17(5) will not have altered the position of policemen who wish to administer breath tests while on private property.

VIII. WARNING OF PROSECUTION

10–56   In the case of a requirement for a specimen for analysis, the police are under a statutory duty to warn a driver of the possibility of prosecution should he refuse to supply such a specimen; and a failure to give such a warning automatically renders the results of the analysis inadmissible in evidence (see Road Traffic Act, s. 7 and *Murray v. DPP* [1993] R.T.R. 209). No such procedure is laid down with regard to the roadside screening breath test. It is difficult to see why Parliament has differentiated between a requirement for a breath test at the roadside and one at a police station. It may possibly be because the failure to supply the latter carries a mandatory disqualification. Under section 78 of the Police and Criminal Evidence Act 1984, any court can exclude evidence on the grounds of unfairness (see section 14–05 *et seq.*). No doubt if a court was satisfied that the defendant did not know that his refusal would lead to a prosecution, it could use its powers under section 78 on the grounds that it was unfair of the police not to have warned the defendant of the risk of prosecution.

In *Bryant v. Morris* [1972] R.T.R. 214, it was held that a breath test was not obtained by duress where the police had erroneously exaggerated the penalty which could be imposed on a person who had failed to take such a test. The constable had told the accused that he could be imprisoned, which was not, in fact, the case.

E. The consequences of failing to take a breath test or taking and failing the test

10–57   Except in the case of a patient in a hospital, the police can arrest a person whose test indicates that his alcohol level is above the prescribed limit. Likewise, the police may arrest anyone, except a patient at a hospital, who fails satisfactorily to take a breath test or who refuses to take one, irrespective of the reason for the failure to do so. The question of an arrest is discussed in detail in Chapter 21. If the refusal is made without any reasonable excuse, then an offence will have been committed, contrary to section 6(4) of the Road Traffic Act 1988 (or section 29(5) of the Transport and Works Act 1992). What can amount to a "reasonable excuse" is discussed in section 17–37 *et seq.* Unlike under the old Road Safety Act 1967, a breath test is no longer a *sine qua non* of a conviction for driving with an alcohol level above the prescribed limit.

F. Summary

10–58   To save the expense and trouble of all motorists who were suspected of driving with excess alcohol having to be taken to a police station, Parliament introduced a roadside screening procedure which would give a rough and ready idea of whether or not the motorist had been imbibing more alcohol than the law allowed. Although the law regarding the screening roadside breath test became very complex over the years, it ceased to be of great importance after *Fox v. Chief Constable of Gwent* [1986] A.C. 281 which decided that, in the absence of mala fides, the events prior to the motorist's arrival at the police station were irrelevant to a charge of driving with excess alcohol. Accordingly, lawyers in such cases no longer bothered to raise the issue of what happened at the roadside. However, that has all been altered by the Police and Criminal Evidence Act, which gave the judiciary a discretion to exclude the results of a breath or body fluid analysis if any procedural impropriety had occurred at the roadside, even in the absence of any bad faith on the part of the police (see *Godwin v. DPP*, above). Nevertheless, the powers to demand a screening breath test are very much wider today than they were under the original legislation and any authority on this matter decided before the coming into force of the Transport Act 1981 must be viewed with caution.

The real debate has been over whether or not the police should be **10–59** allowed the right to breath test any motorist at any time, or whether, as now, only when they suspect a person has been drinking or has been involved in an accident or has committed a moving traffic offence. Due to the opposition to the former proposition when the breathalyser legislation was first introduced into Parliament, the power to conduct such tests was strictly prescribed and the then Secretary of State for Transport gave an undertaking to the House of Commons that random tests would not be authorised under the Road Safety Act. The Transport Act 1981 did not abolish that principle altogether but greatly weakened it by repealing the provisions which the courts had interpreted to mean that an acquittal must follow whenever the police had exceeded their powers to demand a roadside breath test. Today, there is great support for the introduction of random breath tests because of their deterrent effect on drivers who might otherwise commit drinking and driving offences. Indeed, attempts have been made in Parliament to introduce such tests, the latest one being during the report stage of the 1991 Road Traffic Bill. That was opposed by the government and defeated. Apart from the possible psychological effect which will almost certainly only last for a year or two, it is difficult to see how the introduction of true random breath testing would make any difference in practice. The odour of intoxicants is all that is required to enable such a test to be carried out and the police may stop anybody to smell their breath. Whether this has public approval is a moot point.

Chapter 11

WHEN A SAMPLE FOR ANALYSIS CAN BE REQUIRED

A. Introduction

The previous chapter has considered when a roadside breath test may be **11–01** requested. This chapter considers when a specimen for analysis can be demanded.

B. Investigation

As previously mentioned, a novel and great infringement of the liberty of **11–02** the subject was caused by the Road Safety Act 1967, in that it compelled motorists to provide samples of their own body fluids so these could be used in evidence against them. In order to calm the resentment caused by this proposal and to ease its passage through Parliament, the Road Safety Act laid down strict rules as to when a specimen for a laboratory test could be obtained from a motorist. The present road traffic legislation has greatly extended the powers of the police in relation to the circumstances when they can require motorists to supply samples of their breath, blood or urine for analysis. There is now only one pre-condition imposed upon the police by the Road Traffic Act, namely that they must genuinely have been holding an investigation into an offence involving drinking and driving under sections 3A, 4 or 5 of the Road Traffic Act 1988 (see s.7(1)). Also, under section 31(1) of the Transport and Works Act 1992, a constable may also require a specimen for analysis during an investigation into an offence under section 27 of that Act. In *Graham v. Albert* [1985] R.T.R. 352, 358, May L.J. held that "an investigation" meant nothing more than merely "inquiring into" whether a person had committed an offence under the relevant sections of the Road Traffic Act 1988. That decision was followed in *Timothy v. DPP* [1989] Crim. L.R. 893. In *Hawes v. DPP* [1993] R.T.R. 116, the defendant had been driving in a car park which the police believed to be a public place. (In fact this was not the case.) As the police also suspected the accused of having been drinking, they required him to give a specimen of breath for analysis, which he declined to do. The High Court held that such a requirement was perfectly valid, provided that the police were inquiring into a possible offence under section 4 or 5, which was what they were doing in that case. The fact that it later turned out that no such crime had been committed was irrelevant.

C. Authenticity of the investigation

11–03 In *Anderton v. Lythgoe* [1985] 1 W.L.R. 222, a motorist drove home but his car's spotlights did not comply with the Construction and Use Regulations. He was followed by two constables who went to his front door. Despite his request to leave, they insisted that he take a breath test and when this was refused, they arrested him. He was taken down to the station where he was required to provide two specimens for analysis by the Intoximeter, which he did. The High Court held that the results of the analysis were inadmissible in evidence because there was nothing to warrant the police holding an investigation into whether he had been drinking and driving. There was nothing to arouse their suspicions that he had been drinking. It is submitted that this decision is correct, otherwise the police could require anybody who happened to be in a police station to provide a specimen for analysis. Although not cited, the rationale of that decision was applied in *Haghigat-Khou v. Chambers* [1988] R.T.R. 95, where Ralph Gibson L.J. stated that once a constable had seen the results of the two breath analyses on the screen of the Intoximeter, he could not demand a specimen of blood, even if no printout was produced. This was because there was nothing left to be investigated. Neither of those two appeals were cited in *R v. South Norfolk JJ., ex p. Keymer*, unreported, October 12, 1994, when it was held to be sufficient if the investigation was conducted without mala fides even though the officer had no reasonable grounds for undertaking the investigation in the first place. It is submitted that this latter case is inconsistent with the intention of Parliament. When enacting the Road Safety Act and subsequent legislation, the constabulary were only empowered to ask for roadside breath tests on limited grounds and only when they had reasonable suspicion that certain facts had occurred. Thus, it is inconceivable that Parliament wanted the same people to be able to exercise capriciously the far greater and draconian power of forcing men and women to provide specimens for analysis, which could involve compulsory veinapuncture.

D. More than one suspect

11–04 A policeman can require specimens from two or more people if he suspects that one of them must have been driving but does not know which one it was. In *Pearson v. Commissioner of Police of the Metropolis* [1988] R.T.R. 276 a constable saw three youths by the side of a car. The driver's door was open, the key was in the ignition switch and the engine was still warm. They were arrested on suspicion of theft and interfering with a motor vehicle. It was also apparent that all three had been drinking. On being questioned, each denied having been the driver. So at the police station a sergeant, suspecting that one of these must have been driving, requested all of them to provide two breath specimens for the Intoximeter. They all refused. Their convictions for refusing to provide a sample were upheld by the High Court. In the words of Kennedy J. (at 280):

" . . . it seems to me in the context of section [7(1)] of the Road Traffic Act [1988] when, as occurred in this case, a police officer has good reason to believe that one of three persons and no one else, was the driver of the vehicle, and each of those three persons had consumed alcohol to such an extent that it was appropriate for the officer to require that person to provide a sample, then, what he was doing in making his request, if I may use the words of the section, was 'in the course of an investigation whether (the person to whom the request was addressed) has committed an offence'."

E. Knowledge of the constable making the request

It must, of course, be proved that the officer who made the request for the **11–05** specimen had the requisite knowledge to enable him to do so. In *Moss v. Jenkins* [1975] R.T.R 25 a motorist had been involved in an accident and had been escorted to the police station. On arrival the station sergeant asked him for a specimen for a laboratory test. He provided it and was charged with, and acquitted by the magistrates of, driving with excess alcohol. The High Court upheld that verdict. It held that there was no evidence to show that the sergeant had suspected the accused of being in an accident. The inference was that the arresting officer had transmitted that information by wireless to the station, but that was not sufficient to found a conviction. Therefore the prosecution must always prove that the actual officer who required the sample had sufficient knowledge for him to think that a drinking and driving offence may have been committed and therefore needed to be investigated.

F. Arrest

In *Anderton v. Royle* [1985] R.T.R. 91 it was held that there was no necessity **11–06** for a motorist to be under arrest when he was required to provide a specimen for analysis.

G. Specimen requested after illegal arrest

Although the requisite grounds may have existed to justify the police **11–07** making a requirement for the accused to provide a sample for analysis, the courts have a discretion to refuse to admit the result of the analysis if the motorist had been illegally arrested and was being unlawfully detained when the requirement for the specimen had been made (see Chapter 14, below).

H. Discretion

11–08 Although the relevant legislation says that a constable "may" require a specimen, that does not give him an unfettered discretion. If the circumstances permit him to require a specimen, he can only decline to do so if there are special circumstances justifying him not exercising his powers under the Road Traffic Act, s.7(1), or the Transport and Works Act, s.31(1) (see Chapter 3, above).

Chapter 12

WHICH TYPE OF SPECIMEN: BREATH, BLOOD OR URINE

A. Introduction

Under the Road Traffic Safety Act, the arrested motorist had the option of **12–01** choosing which body fluid would be analysed for its alcoholic content. That was altered by the Transport Act 1981 and currently a motorist will normally have to supply a breath sample. The change and the new legal regime were summarised by Lord Griffiths in *Cracknell v. Willis* [1988] A.C. 450, 457:

> "For some years the offence was proved by producing an analysis of a blood or urine sample provided by the motorist but then a new device was invented that enabled the proportion of alcohol in the breath to be determined by immediate analysis. Provided that such a machine is reliable it has obvious advantages over the use of urine or blood samples. It can be operated by a trained police officer and prints out an immediate analysis of the breath, cutting out the delay involved in the laboratory analysis of urine and blood samples and the attendance of a doctor in the case of a blood sample."

This chapter considers when, during an investigation into a possible offence under sections 3A, 4 or 5, an officer can request, or a motorist can opt to supply, a specimen of blood or urine.

B. Whether the substance required for analysis is to be breath or a body fluid

I. THE STATUTORY REQUIREMENTS

(a) ROAD TRAFFIC ACT 1988

The present position is that a sample of blood or urine may be required **12–02** from a motorist who is either at a police station or is physically present in a hospital. He need not be a patient there. (For the definition of a "hospital", see section 10–39.)

Section 7(2) of the Road Traffic Act 1988 allows the police to require a breath sample from a driver who is at a police station and section 7(3) limits the freedom of the police to demand anything besides that substance from such a driver. Only in the limited circumstances set out in the subsections of section 7(3) can they make a mandatory request to a motorist at a police station to supply a specimen of his body fluid. Such a requirement can be made if:

"(a) the constable making the requirement has reasonable cause to believe that for medical reasons a specimen of breath cannot be provided or should not be required, or

(b) at the time the requirement is made a device or a reliable device of the type mentioned in subsection (1)(a) above [*i.e.* approved by the Secretary of State] is not available at the police station or it is then for any other reason not practicable to use such a device there, or

(bb) a device of the type mentioned in subsection (1)(a) above has been used at the police station but the constable who required the specimens of breath has reasonable cause to believe that the device has not produced a reliable indication of the proportion of alcohol in the breath of the person concerned, or [inserted by section 63 of the Criminal Procedure and Investigations Act 1996].

(c) the suspected offence is one under section 4 of this Act [driving while unfit] and the constable making the requirement has been advised by a medical practitioner that the condition of the person required to provide the specimen might be due to some drug, or

and may be made notwithstanding that the person required to provide the specimen has already provided or been required to provide two specimens of breath."

To use the words of Mustill L.J. in *Johnson v. West Yorkshire Police* [1986] R.T.R. 167, subsections (a) (b) and (c) are the "gateways" to the right to require blood or urine: see *Dempsey v. Catton* [1986] R.T.R. 194, 198J. At the time of writing subsection (bb) was not yet in force. It is anticipated that section (bb) will be brought into force in 1997 when the new generation of breathalysers is approved.

(b) TRANSPORT AND WORKS ACT 1992

12–03 Section 31 enacts similar provisions to section 7 of the Road Traffic Act 1988. Subsections (3) and (4) allow the police to demand a body fluid rather than breath only for the same reasons as the Road Traffic Act 1988, s.7(3) empowers them so to do.

II. MEDICAL REASONS

12–04 Under section 7(3) (a) of the Road Traffic Act 1988 and section 31(4) (a) of the Transport and Works Act 1992, a constable can require a specimen of body fluid if he believes that for medical reasons a breath sample cannot or should not be provided. The authorities are divided over whether the policeman has actually to believe what the motorist has said to him, or whether it is sufficient if the information given to the constable, judged objectively, amounted to a medical reason, even though the officer did not himself believe what he had been told. The present Chief Justice (Lord Bingham) is of the latter view and expressed a very strong dissent from the first relevant reported decision, namely *Horrocks v. Binns* [1986] R.T.R. 202, where the motorist said that he could not blow into the breathalyser because of the cut he had on his head. The officer did not believe that the cut had that effect but gave the motorist the benefit of the doubt. The High Court upheld the acquittal for failing to supply a specimen of blood because, since the constable did not believe the defendant, he had no legal right to demand blood. In the words of McCullough J.:

> "Whether a driver can or cannot blow into a machine is a question of an objective fact and is not to be determined by what the driver says about his own ability or the officer's belief about the ability. The magistrate found as a fact that the defendant could blow into the machine. That being so it was practical for the device to be used." (At 206G/H.)

Four months later, in *White v. Proudlock* [1988] R.T.R. 163, McCullough J. agreed with Robert Goff L.J. when he held that the question to be determined was whether the constable, judged objectively, had reasonable grounds for believing that for medical reasons a breath specimen could not be given, and not whether he personally believed the motorist had medical reasons (at 170 F/G). There the motorist blew into the machine on four occasions, causing it to abort. He was asked by a constable if he had a medical reason for not supplying sufficient breath, to which he replied "no". He then went to the charge office where he told the custody sergeant that he could not blow any harder and would bring his doctor to court. This caused the constable to ask him again about medical reasons, to which he replied, "I just couldn't blow it". On being asked what the medical condition was, he said, "You'll see. It will get me off in court". That was held to give rise to a reasonable belief that, for medical reasons, a breath specimen could not be provided. However, in *DPP v. Boden* [1988] R.T.R. 188, 191C, Mann J. doubted if a constable could reasonably believe that there was a medical reason if the motorist told him that he had one but refused to divulge what it was. One can see the logic in the reasoning of Mann J. If a driver is not prepared to state what the medical condition is which makes him unable to supply a breath specimen, then that must raise serious doubts about his bona fides, in which case can it be said that it was reasonable for the constable to believe that grounds existed which enabled him to require a specimen of body fluid?

Dempsey v. Catton [1986] R.T.R. 194, 201 held that gateway 7(3) (a) was not open to the prosecution in *Horrocks' case*, above, because the constable had said that he did not think that the defendant had any reason for not supplying breath. In *Dempsey's case*, above, the officer had believed the defendant when he told him that he had a phobia of machines. However, the policeman was not certain whether that was a medical reason, but in case it was, he required a specimen of blood. The High Court upheld the conviction for failing to supply blood, stating that if a motorist gave a reason which caused a layman to conclude that it could be a medical one, then gateway (a) was opened in that case. In *Davis v. DPP* [1988] R.T.R. 156, 162F Bingham L.J. said "without any hesitation" that if *White v. Proulock, above*, was inconsistent with *Horrocks v. Binns, above*, the former decision correctly stated the law. His Lordship held unequivocally that subsection 7(3) (a) meant that a constable could require blood or urine if what the motorist had told him could lead a reasonable policeman to decide that breath should not be required on medical grounds. The fact that the sergeant who was administering the test did not believe that a medical reason had been disclosed by the defendant was irrelevant. In this case, the driver had informed the sergeant that he had asthma and a heavy cold and could not blow properly. The officer thought that the defendant was capable of blowing into the Intoximeter but requested a blood sample. The High Court upheld the conviction for driving with excess alcohol in the blood on the grounds that the sergeant had reasonable cause to believe that medically a breath specimen could not be provided. In *Webb v. DPP, The Independent*, March 23, 1992, the High Court held that a police officer was entitled to demand body fluid when he had formed the opinion from the defendant's condition that she was unable to supply a breath sample, even though she had assured the constable that she was perfectly capable of supplying sufficient breath for an analysis.

12-05   It is submitted that the approach of Bingham L.J. in *Davis' case, above*, is the more preferable, even though it strains the statutory language. Literally, when an Act says if a constable "has reasonable cause to believe", it means just that and the constable must hold such a belief. However, it is much fairer on a motorist that a sceptical constable gives him the benefit of the doubt, which is the very point made by Bingham L.J. It is to be hoped that his approach to the statutory construction of section 7(3) (a) will in future be followed by other members of the judiciary. In *DPP v. Boden* [1988] R.T.R. 188, 191L, Mann J. held that the test of reasonable belief was an objective one. Bingham L.J. delivered a concurring judgment. In *R. v. Chichester JJ., ex p. DPP* [1994] R.T.R. 175, 178D/E, Moreland J. held:

> "It is clear from the decisions of the Divisional Court in *White v. Proudlock* (Note) and in the more recent case of *Davis v. DPP* [1988] R.T.R. 156 that the test is not a subjective test, that is a test of whether the constable concerned actually believes that there are medical reasons, but is an objective test, that is, whether there were reasonable grounds or cause for believing that there was a medical reason why a specimen of breath could not be provided."

In *Davies v. DPP* [1989] R.T.R. 391, the defendant informed the policeman that he was taking a specific medicine which he had been told would effect his blood alcohol concentration. Accordingly, the officer demanded a specimen of urine, instead of one of breath. He was held by the High Court to have acted lawfully, as it was reasonable for him to assume that, for medical reasons, a specimen of breath should not be supplied. The court did not elaborate on this. Of course, the alcohol which is exhaled only reaches the breath via the blood, so any false increase in the latter would automatically be passed on to the alcohol in the breath. However, the alcohol in the urine also only arrives there via the blood, so that a urine analysis would be no more accurate than a breath analysis. Thus it is arguable that in these circumstances the officer was unreasonable to think that there were medical reasons why a breath sample should not be given, since the same rationale would also apply to the taking of any other type of sample.

In *Young v. DPP, The Times*, March 27, 1992, it was held that a motorist's intoxication was a medical reason which enabled the police to demand blood or urine rather than a breath specimen.

The decision of the constable about whether or not there are medical reasons can only be challenged on the *Wednesbury* principles: (see *Associated Provincial Picture Houses Ltd v. Wednesbury Corp* [1948] 1 K.B. 223) or, in the words of McNiel J. in *Dempsey v. Catton* [1986] R.T.R. 194 at 201B:

> " . . . provided there is sufficient material to justify his decision [not to require a breath specimen], the decision is the constable's alone. There is no provision or requirement at that stage for a doctor to be summoned or to give an opinion."

III. THE UNAVAILABILITY OF, OR IMPRACTICALITY OF USING, THE BREATHALYSER

(a) THE RELEVANT TIME

Section 7(3)(b) of the Road Traffic Act 1988 and section 31(4)(b) of the **12–06** Transport and Works Act 1992 allow a specimen of body fluid to be required if the police do not have a reliable breath alcohol measuring instrument available or if it is not practical to use one. In number of cases (*e.g. Cotter v. Kamil* [1984] R.T.R. 371), it has been held that the relevant time at which the factual situation laid down in subsection (b) must have existed is when the police first made their requirement for the provision of a body fluid from the motorist. In *Chief Constable of Kent v. Berry* [1986] R.T.R. 321 the Intoximeter was not working correctly so the defendant was asked to supply blood, to which he agreed. The High Court held that once the police had lawfully requested blood, then that was the end of the matter, and that it was irrelevant that, prior to the actual supply of the sample, a reliable Intoximeter had become available which could have been used. In *Oxford v. Baxendale* [1987] R.T.R. 247, at just after 3 p.m., the defendant took a breath test on an Intoximeter. At 4.35 p.m., the police realised that the machine's calibration was wrong. Seven minutes later they required a blood sample but this was refused. The defendant was acquitted by the magistrates because there was no evidence that the machine was still defective when the request for blood was made. The High Court upheld an appeal by the Chief Constable of Merseyside. In the words of Schiemann J.:

"... it is not incumbent upon the police to adduce further evidence to show that a device or a reliable device is not available at the time the request for blood or urine is made, but the evidence that the prosecution adduced was evidence from which the magistrates could come to the conclusion that such a device was not available."

12-07 The High Court in effect held that the magistrates did not have to hear any testimony that immediately before the requirement for a body fluid was made the police had checked the breathalyser, but a court could draw inferences about the state of that device from what had occurred sometime beforehand. Consequently, the case was sent back to the magistrates for them to decide what inferences, if any, they would draw about the relevant Intoximeter. There the second calibration ("STD" on the Intoximeter printout) showed "0 LOW". However, the usual fault is an STD reading which is only a few microgrammes out from the correct standard of 32–37μg and which is caused by the vapour in the simulator having either risen above, or dropped below, the correct temperature. (Each 1° change of temperature in the simulator will produce a 6μg difference in the calibration.) In such circumstances it is quite likely that the temperature in the simulator would have reverted to normal after a brief interval. Consequently, if the police do not require a blood sample within a very short time of an unacceptable STD reading, it is submitted that the justices could not then be satisfied, beyond all reasonable doubt, that this had not occurred and that the Intoximeter was still malfunctioning when the police made their request for a specimen of body fluid. The High Court did not consider the question of whether it was reasonable for the police to believe that the Intoximeter was still unreliable. It is submitted that the only answer to that question could be "no", as the operator's handbook makes it plain that such an error was probably due to the simulator over- or under-heating, a malfunction which soon corrects itself and the Merseyside police had waited an hour-and-a-half before making their request for blood.

(b) No Trained Operator at the Station

12-08 In *Chief Constable of Avon and Somerset Constabulary v. Kelliher* [1987] R.T.R. 305, it was held not to be practicable to use the breathalyser when there was no trained officer then available in the police station to operate the machine. The police did not have to try to find one and to ask him to come to the station. In *Denny v. DPP* [1990] R.T.R. 417 it was held that if there was not a reliable device available at the police station where the defendant was, he could be taken to another police station where there was a fully operative Intoximeter and could there be lawfully required to supply a breath sample.

(c) WRONG TIME, DATE OR SPELLING ERRORS ON THE PRINTOUT

The majority of cases on section 7(3) have been about what is meant by **12–09** "reliable". As originally designed the Intoximeter displayed the date but could not deal with leap years. So in *Slender v. Boothby* [1986] R.T.R. 385 the printout showed the date as March 1 instead of February 29. The High Court upheld the validity of the request to supply blood because (*per* McCullough J. at 387):

> " . . . the phrase 'reliable device' in section [7(3)(b)] means a device which is capable of producing a statement, reliable not only to the proportion of the alcohol in the breath, but reliable also as to date and time. This device was not reliable because it produced a printout bearing a false date."

As a result of this case the software of the Intoximeter was modified to deal with leap years. That decision was followed in *Badkin v. Chief Constable of South Yorkshire* [1988] R.T.R. 401, 408K/L, where the device showed the wrong time. (It was five minutes fast.)

In two Crown Court appeals the Intoximeter was held to be unreliable where its clock was two minutes slow (see *Hall v. DPP*, June 26, 1995, *per* Judge Holman, and *Stibbard v. DPP*, February 15, 1995, *per* Judge Bathurst-Norman).

In *Burditt v. Roberts* [1986] R.T.R. 391 the printout contained mis-spellings. The High Court held that, since these were due to the mis-typing of the police officer, the Intoximeter in question was a reliable device. It had in fact printed out exactly what the officer had typed into it. To the same effect is *Toovey v. Chief Constable of Northumberland* [1986] Crim L. R. 475, where the wrong Christian name was typed into the breathalyser.

(d) BELIEF OR ACTUAL FACT

The literal wording of the subsection allows a request for blood or urine **12–10** only if the actual conditions prescribed in the subsection existed. This is how some of the early cases, without argument, interpreted the legislation, *e.g. Oxford v. Baxendale, above, Dye v. Manns* [1986] Crim. L.R. 377 and *Slender v. Boothby*, above. Since then the judiciary have held the requirements of the subsection to have been complied with where a constable, on reasonable grounds, believed that the factual situation described therein existed. Hence in *Haghigat-Khou v. Chambers* [1988] R.T.R. 95 it was held that if an officer knew in advance that the printer was not working and believed that this made the device unreliable, then that was reasonable and he was entitled to require a blood or urine sample. In the words of Ralph Gibson L.J. (at 100L):

> "For all these reasons, in my opinion, the words, 'a reliable device' are to be given the meaning 'a device which he reasonably believes to be reliable'."

12–11   To the same effect is the judgment in *Thompson v. Thynne* [1986] R.T.R. 293, which upheld the conviction for excess alcohol in blood. There it was held that the officer was entitled to demand a blood sample in view of the large difference between the two breath analyses, even though the relevant Camic was thoroughly inspected by the manufacturers two days later and shown to be functioning correctly. However, in *Jones v. DPP* [1991] R.T.R. 41 it was held that before a constable can *reasonably* believe that a device is unreliable he must have followed its routine operating procedures. In that case, the Intoximeter did not print out the result of the analysis. The High Court held that the officer ought to have checked that the switch controlling the printer had been placed in the "on" position, and this applied even though he had thought that it would have been left in its usual "on" position. As he failed to do this, he had no legal right to ask for blood or urine. Schiemann J. also made it clear that if a policeman found nothing happened when he came to use an Intoximeter, he must first check that it was switched to "on". In other words, the court was ruling that before a constable can give up hope of using an evidential breath testing device, he must attempt to do any simple and obvious task necessary to get it working. In the words of Schiemann J. (at 48):

> " . . . I am not persuaded that the sergeant could *reasonably* believe that a reliable device was not available . . . As I read the case, not only was there nothing wrong with the device but, also, this would have been disclosed by following the routine procedures which could and should have been operated by a constable. The situation was analogous to never switching the device on in the first place."

12–12   In *Hague v. DPP* (reported on other issues [1995] T.L.R. 589) the High Court had very grave doubts as to whether a police officer's mistaken belief as to what the correct calibration readings were could ever be considered to be reasonable. In *DPP v. Dixon* [1993] R.T.R. 23, Watkins D.C.J. stated that justices must find as a fact that the constable actually held the reasonable belief that the machine was unreliable. In the words of the Deputy Chief Justice:

> "[Blood can be required] if it be found that the police officer is charge of the procedure holds the belief not that the device might be unreliable but the reasonable belief that it was at the material time unreliable."

The facts were that the defendant's two breath readings were 198 and 191μg. The operator told the custody officer that the Intoximeter might not be reliable because of the high reading compared to the motorist's failure to display any symptoms of intoxication.

The custody sergeant then required a blood sample, which, on subsequent analysis confirmed the Intoximeter reading. The sergeant said he did this because of what he had been told by the Intoximeter operator. Thus the sergeant had not required a blood sample because he had formed a belief that the Intoximeter was unreliable but merely because it might be unreliable. That is not a sufficient belief to open the gateway to subsection 7(3)(b). That decision was distinguished in *Rathbone v. DPP*, unreported,

January 20, 1995. There the defendant had to blow into the device on three occasions but no printout was produced showing "no sample". The constable thought that the defendant had not blown sufficiently hard to obtain an analysis but also believed that the failure to produce a printout meant that the Intoximeter was malfunctioning, but he was not absolutely certain of this, as he did not fully understand the workings of the machine. The High Court held that the subsequent request for blood was lawful. A constable merely had to hold a reasonable belief and certainty was not required. The effect of those two appeals is that if the facts merely lead a constable to the view that there might be something wrong with the breathalyser, that does not justify him requiring a body fluid. To be able to make such a requirement, the facts must have made him believe reasonably that the machine was in fact malfunctioning, even though he realised that his belief might be mistaken.

In *Stokes v. Sayers* [1988] R.T.R. 89, the High Court upheld the acquittal of the defendant for driving with excess alcohol in his blood. According to the case stated, the reason why that fluid was required was because the Intoximeter operator saw the words "34 low abort" displayed on his screen and therefore concluded that the breathalyser was unreliable. Glidewell L.J. held that the prosecution had to prove (1) that the officer believed the breathalyser to be unreliable and (2) that such a belief was reasonable. The acquittal was upheld since the justices had no idea what the display on the screen meant and therefore were not in a position to judge if the operator's belief was, or was not, reasonable.

In *Dixon v. DPP* [1993] R.T.R. 22 at 30F, Watkins D.C.J. stated that **12–13** there was nothing in his judgment in *Morgan v. Lee* [1985] R.T.R. 409 to suggest that the objective test was the one to be applied, *i.e.* whether, as a fact, the machine was or was not working correctly. In *Morgan's case* the Intoximeter at the police station had analysed the motorist's breath and the results had appeared on its screen, but no printout was expelled. The police then demanded a blood sample which was refused. The prosecutor argued that such a demand was lawful as the Intoximeter was inoperative, *i.e.* not available for use, or it was not practicable to use it. Lee's acquittal of failing to provide a blood sample was upheld on appeal because all the results had been displayed on the screen, so there were no grounds for the officer to have regarded the breathalyser as not working properly. Accordingly, he was not entitled to require a specimen of body fluid. *Haghigat-Khou v. Chambers*, above, distinguished that case because there the results of the analysis of the defendant's breath had been displayed on the Intoximeter screen, and "there was no further investigation into whether a person had committed an offence under sections [4] or [5] which the officer [could] properly carry out under section [7]" (*per* Ralph Gibson L.J. at 100B). Haghigat-Khou was never asked to blow into the Intoximeter because it was known that the printer was not working. Thus, when the latter was required to supply a specimen of his blood, it was not known whether an offence under section 5 had or had not been committed, so that the investigation was still in progress. However, Ralph Gibson L.J. clearly dissented from part of the *ratio* of Watkins L.J. as he went on to say (at 101D/E):

"The inability of the machine to produce this printout meant that it was not able to function, in one important way, in the way it was intended to function. There was not available to Srg. Rigler [the Intoximeter operator] a device which he reasonably believed to be reliable."

12–14   In *Badkin v. Constable of South Yorkshire* [1988] R.T.R. 401 exactly the same facts occurred at the police station as had happened in *Morgan's case*, above, save that the defendant complied with the request for a blood specimen, which was analysed. The High Court held that if an officer at any time reasonably concluded that the machine was not reliable, he could require a specimen of body fluid, and the failure to expel a printout was a malfunction which justified the officer asking for blood (at 408F/G). In that case the High Court quashed Badkin's conviction for driving with excess alcohol in his breath. Those cases can be reconciled because in *Badkin's case*, above, Glidewell L.J. went on to say that once a police officer had decided that an Intoximeter was not reliable and had required, and obtained, a blood sample, then any prosecution must be based on the results of the blood analysis (*i.e.* a charge of driving with excess alcohol in blood). It is to be noted that Glidewell L.J did not say "reasonably decided", but clearly must have meant "reasonably" in view of his judgment five months earlier in *Stokes v. Sayers*, above. This last proposition (that in such circumstances any prosecution had to be based on the blood analysis) was approved and followed in the case of *McLellan v. DPP* [1994] R.T.R. 401 where there was a difference of over 20 per cent between the two Intoximeter readings (see section 16–39 *et seq.* below), so the operator believed there was something wrong with the breathalyser. (On the evidence of the marketing director of Lion Laboratories, the Crown Court held this opinion to be reasonable.) The constable then required blood but did not give the requisite information to the appellant so the blood analysis was not admissible in evidence. Accordingly, the latter was charged with driving with excess alcohol in his breath. The High Court (at 405) rejected the Crown's argument that the proposition laid down by Glidewell L.J. in *Badkin's case* did not apply either where the Intoximeter was proved to be reliable by the results of the blood analysis or where the correct procedure for the taking of the blood specimen was not followed. (For the sake of completeness it should be noted that the prosecution, for reasons known only to themselves, did not adduce in evidence the results of the analysis of Badkin's blood.) Where it is not reasonable for the constable to have believed that the breathalyser had malfunctioned, then any prosecution must be for excess alcohol in breath, based on the results of the breathalyser and not on the subsequent body fluid analysis: see *Evans v. DPP* [1996] T.L.R. 339.

12–15   The appeals of Badkin and McLellan were not cited in *Hague v. DPP* [1985] T.L.R. 589 where the defendant provided two breath specimens which were analysed but the operator erroneously believed that the machine had malfunctioned. So he required a specimen of blood, which was refused. In fact the Intoximeter was working correctly but, solely for the purposes of the appeal, the High Court assumed that the officer's belief was reasonable. It upheld the conviction for driving with excess alcohol in breath. The court based its decision on section 15(2) of the Road Traffic Offenders Act, *i.e.* that the amount of alcohol in any specimen properly obtained (see *Fox's* case, [1986] A.C. at 298) must be given in evidence. However, Scott Baker J. also stated in *Hague's* case that an accurate breath analysis could be relied upon unless and until replaced by an "admissible" blood or urine sample. That dicta about the blood analysis having to be admissible in evidence was *obiter*, as no such specimen was in fact provided. It was contrary to *McLellan v. DPP* and should be regarded as having been uttered *per incuriam*. It is submitted that if no body fluid is provided, then the prosecutor can rely upon the breath specimen. However, where a specimen of the former type could be lawfully requested and was in fact provided, then any prosecution must be based on the analysis of the body fluid and, if the correct procedure had not been followed for taking the specimen of blood or urine (see section 14–02), then there must be an acquittal.

(e) THE PRESENT LEGAL POSITION

Despite earlier decisions supporting the contrary view, the law, as it now **12–16** stands south of the Border, is that a policeman need not use an Intoximeter or Camic if he reasonably believes it not to be reliable, provided that he has carried out the normal operating procedures within a reasonable period beforehand. These procedures will be those set out in the device's handbook. It is submitted that this is not what Parliament intended. Having to give blood is a far greater infringement of a person's civil liberties than merely exhaling into a machine. It is submitted that this is the rationale for Parliament omitting any reference to "reasonable belief" in subsection (b) when it had specifically incorporated such criteria into subsection (a) (reasonable belief in a medical reason preventing a motorist from blowing into a breath alcohol measuring device); and that subsection (b) was intended solely to empower the police to be able to require a specimen of body fluid if, but only if, the relevant Intoximeter or Camic was in fact unreliable (or if it was impractical to use such a device). The author agrees with the commentary on *Waite v. Smith* at [1986] Crim. L. R. 406:

"The Divisional court agreed to read the subsection as though it contained the words the 'operator has reasonable cause to believe' a reliable device is not available. This, though it may seem convenient in some cases, seems astonishing, particularly as Parliament has seen fit to include such words in section 7(3)(a), and an equivalent formula in 7(3)(c), the clear inference being that the power under (b) turns on a state of facts, not the operator's state of mind. Where the instructions for use of the Intoximeter are so clear, it seems ridiculous to read extra words into the subsection which are more likely to create confusion than solve it."

Similar reasoning was accepted by the Scottish High Court of Justiciary **12–17** in *Hodgins v. Smith* [1989] S.L.T. 514 when it held that the test under section 7(3)(b) was whether or not the Intoximeter was actually working correctly. However, that case was not cited in *Burnett v. Smith* [1990] S.L.T. 537 where the Scottish court followed *Haghigat-Khou v. Chambers*, above, on the grounds that any other interpretation would make that subsection unworkable. All the author can do is to ask rhetorically why did the Legislature use different wording for subsections (a) and (b), if it intended them to have the same meaning?

Save in one possible respect, subsection (bb) (when it comes into force) does not add anything new to the law as laid down in *Oxford v. Baxendale*, *supra*. The only difference is that subsection (bb) makes it clear that if what the constable is relying on to support his contention about the device being unreliable only occurred after two breath specimens had been provided, then it is sufficient for the officer to have reasonably believed the machine to have been unreliable, even though in fact it may have been working correctly. This was inserted because the next generation of breathalysers will give far more information than those now in service. *e.g.* they will show if the reading is based on mouth alcohol (see section 16–59). As Parliament does nothing in vain, the only rationale for the new (bb) is that the requisite facts set out in (b) must have actually existed to enable a specimen of body fluid to be demanded, while under (bb) the officer need only have a reasonable belief in their existence. Whether that will cause the English judiciary to interpret (b) any differently from that done at present (*e.g.* as in *Haghigat-Khou v. Chambers*) is another matter.

(f) THE BREATHALYSER FAILING TO ANALYSE THE BREATH SPECIMEN PROVIDED

12–18 In *Ward v. Elsbury*, May 14, 1986, the High Court held that if a defendant supplied sufficient breath for an analysis but the machine did not analyse it, he could not be asked for another breath sample but only for one of blood or urine. In that case the motorist was asked to blow for a second time into the same breathalyser. It would have been a different matter if he had been told to exhale into a different device, as such a requirement would be perfectly valid, as happened in *Denny v. DPP* [1990] R.T.R. 417 when the second calibration was outside its permitted parameters.

(g) EVIDENCE

12–19 If the prosecution is relying upon a requirement made under subsection (b), then in order to secure a conviction they must prove that the necessary facts existed to enable them to invoke that subsection. The normal rules of evidence will apply. In *Dye v. Manns* [1987] R.T.R. 90, it was held that the requirements of subsection (b) could not be proved merely by a policeman telling the court that he had heard the constable who made the requirement saying that the breathalyser was not working correctly. It is submitted that it would have been sufficient for the constable making the requirement merely to have testified that he had not used the Intoximeter because of what he had been told by another officer (provided, of course, that this had amounted to reasonable cause for not using the device). In other words, the *ratio* in *Dye v. Manns* is that the belief of the officer making the requirement can only be proved by actually calling that person to testify at court. It is submitted that it might be possible for justices (and a jury) to infer that officer's belief if evidence was given of what information had actually been relayed to him. What is not permissible is for somebody else to give evidence of what he had been told by the constable making the requirement were his reasons for not using the breathalyser. Furthermore, the court also held that it could not infer that what the operator said must have been true on the basis that he was not contradicted and he did not indeed use the Intoximeter.

In *Tobi v. Nicholas* [1988] R.T.R. 343, the sergeant gave evidence of the reason given by him to the defendant for requesting a blood sample. It was held that it was implicit in such testimony that this was also the reason why he had in fact asked for that fluid. In *Jarvis v. DPP* [1996] R.T.R. 192 the constable testified that the Intoximeter failed to work when he pressed the start button and "therefore it was not possible to take a breath specimen". The court held the words in inverted commas to mean that there was no other Intoximeter in the police station.

IV. SUSPICION OF DRUGS

Section 7(3)(c) of the Road Traffic Act 1988 and section 31(4)(c) of the **12–20** Transport and Works Act 1992 allow the police to require a sample of body fluid if they had suspected an offence under section 4 of the Road Traffic Act 1988 or section 27(1) of the Transport and Works Act, and a doctor had advised that the suspect's condition might be due to drugs. In *Cole v. DPP* [1988] R.T.R. 224, the surgeon failed to give a clear oral statement that in the absence of a positive Intoximeter reading, the defendant's condition might be due to drugs. Accordingly, the High Court held that the police were not entitled to demand a blood sample under subsection (c).

V. THE CONSEQUENCES OF SUBSECTIONS (A), (B) OR (C) BEING FULFILLED

If any of the conditions prescribed in subsections (a), (b), (bb) when in **12–21** force or (c) are fulfilled, then a person can be requested to supply blood or urine, notwithstanding that he has already been asked to supply two specimens of breath or, indeed, has already done so; see Road Traffic Act 1988, s. 7(3) and Transport and Works Act 1992, s. 31(5).

VI. CHANGE OF VENUE

The question has arisen of what is the legal position of a motorist who has **12–22** been required to supply a specimen of blood or urine at a hospital but, before providing it, is taken to a police station. The Road Traffic Act, s. 9(1)(a) and the Transport and Works Act, s. 33(1)(a) enact:

"While a person is at hospital as a patient . . .
    (a) if the requirement is then made, it shall be for the provision for a specimen at *the hospital*." (Author's emphasis.)

Those words led Buxton J. in *Whelan v. DPP*, unreported, July 28, 1995, to say:

"In my judgment it is very doubtful whether that could be extended to cover a specimen which is in fact taken outside the hospital. It seems that it may be the case, that if the patient leaves the hospital before the specimen can be taken, even though through no fault at all of the police officers, the process may have to start again. Again, however it is not necessary, in my judgment, to decide that."

That *obiter dicta* was not followed in a case on the very point, namely *Webber v. DPP*, unreported, December 4, 1995, where it was held that in those circumstances the police did not need to start all over again at the police station and to make another requirement for a specimen. (Such a requirement would normally have to be for breath: see section 7(3)). The court held that once the section 9 procedure had started it was in no way abrogated just because the patient then left hospital. The police could abandon the hospital procedure and start again at the station but would only be held to have done so if, by word or deed, it was clear that such abrogation had taken place. One is tempted to ask why section 9 says that the police shall require a person to provide his specimen at the hospital, if the law allows the specimen to be taken elsewhere. The judgment in *Webber's case* does not provide an answer. Of more significance, but not cited to the court, was a case decided 25 years previously on exactly the same facts, namely *Bosley v. Long* [1970] R.T.R. 432. There the High Court reached the opposite conclusion in a judgment subsequently approved on that point by the House of Lords in *Bourlet v. Porter* [1973] 2 All E.R. 800. In the words of Cooke J. in *Bosley's case*: "It is merely a case where, if one of two procedures are not carried to a conclusion, the other must be followed."

In *Chief Constable of Kent v. Berry* [1986] R.T.R. 321, the defendant was asked to provide blood at Faversham police station as there was no reliable Intoximeter there. He was taken to another one at Canterbury where the blood was taken. He was acquitted by the justices because there was no evidence to show that he could not have been breathalysed at that second station. The High Court reversed that decision, holding that once a valid requirement for blood had been made, then that procedure could be carried through; and there was no novation merely because at the second police station he was again required to provide blood. It is an open question as to whether the same decision would have been reached if the above quoted dicta of Cooke J. in *Bosley v. Long* had been cited to the court.

In *Denny v. DPP* [1990] R.T.R. 417, it was held that a constable can at one police station make the requirement for breath and then take the motorist to another station where the Intoximeter into which he has to provide his specimen is situated. There was no obligation to require a specimen of body fluid at the first location just because there was no working breathalyser there. (It had failed to carry out correctly its second standard check.)

C. A breath analysis not exceeding 50μg

By virtue of section 32(2) of the Transport and Works Act 1992 and section 8(2) of the Road Traffic Act 1988, a prosecution must be based upon the result of a urine or blood analysis, if the police have followed the correct procedure and have obtained two specimens of breath which have been analysed and one of which has been shown to contain no more than 50μg of alcohol and the motorist has then opted to give an alternative sample of body fluid and has actually done so. (In *Reeves v. Enstone, The Times,* February 15, 1985, the High Court rejected the argument that because the Intoximeter was only accurate to within a couple of microgrammes, a reading of 51 or 52μg entitled the motorist to exercise the section 8(2) option.) Once the alternative specimen has been provided, the police can no longer rely upon the breath analysis for any purpose whatsoever, save to justify the taking of the alternative specimen. In *Archbold v. Jones* [1986] R.T.R. 178 it was held that where the defendant had exercised his option and had supplied blood, the prosecutor could not rely upon the result of the breath analysis even though that fluid had been subsequently dis-covered to be incapable of accurate analysis. This does not prevent the magistrates learning of the Intoximeter reading. In *Yhnell v. DPP* [1984] R.T.R. 250 it was held that justices could be told the amount of the reading despite the fact that the accused had given an alternative specimen. Such evidence is admissible solely to establish that reasons existed which enabled the police to rely upon the blood analysis but cannot be used for any other purpose, *e.g.* to confirm the accuracy of the blood or urine analysis. One can only speculate how many motorists are really aware of the potential advantage of exercising this option. In 1989 the option was exercised by only 48 per cent of those eligible, 22 per cent of whom were found to be below the statutory limit (see the *New Law Journal*, September 21, 1990). The figures for 1991 (the last year for which such statistics were kept) show that 24 per cent of those who exercised their section 8(2) option were found to be below the prescribed limit.

12–23

D. Which type of body fluid?

I. WHOSE CHOICE?

In *DPP v. Warren* [1993] A.C. 319, the House of Lords held that the choice of which body fluid was to be provided by the motorist lay with the police.

12–24

II. MEDICAL OBJECTIONS TO GIVING BLOOD

12–25 In the words of Bingham L.J. in *Andrews v. DPP* [1992] R.T.R. 1, 12F/C:

> "The scheme was a simple one. The constable was to decide which of the two specimens should be given, subject to the over-riding opinion of the medical practitioner."

Thus, although the choice of which type of specimen may be required is given to a policeman, the latter cannot request blood if a doctor is of the opinion that the sample should be of urine (see section 7(4) of the Road Traffic Act 1988 and section 31(6) of the Transport and Works Act 1992). The courts, with the approval of the House of Lords in *DPP v. Warren*, above, have extended these subsections to mean that if a potential medical reason is put forward by a motorist, the police must either request urine or obtain a doctor's opinion. If, in such circumstances, they insist on blood without consulting a doctor, the accused must be acquitted whether or not he actually provides one, as the correct procedure will not have been followed. (The latter is a *sine qua non* of a conviction: see *Fox's* case [1986] A.C. at 298.) Such an acquittal occurred in *Johnson v. West Yorkshire Metropolitan Police* [1986] R.T.R. 167. There the defendant provided a breath sample containing 40µg. On being told of the option under section 8(2) of the Road Traffic Act 1988 he opted for a substitute sample. The constable decided to ask for a blood specimen. The motorist demurred and said that he did not like needles and had once fainted at hospital when giving a sample of blood during an investigation into the possibility of diabetes. The officer asked him if he had diabetes and he replied in the negative and declined to give blood. Nevertheless, the officer refused to accept a sample of urine. The defendant was acquitted because the question of whether or not he had a medical condition, within the meaning of section 7(4) of the Road Traffic Act 1988, was exclusively for a doctor. This usurpation of this decision-making role by the police had deprived the driver of his right under section 8(2) to provide an alternative sample to replace the one already given. The Intoximeter printout was, therefore, inadmissible because the provisions set out in section 8(2) had not been followed.

12–26 In *Grix v. The Chief Constable of Kent* [1987] R.T.R. 193, the court, in commenting on that decision, made it clear that the judgment should not be understood as placing upon the police a duty to seek the advice of a doctor on every occasion when the supply of a sample of blood was refused on grounds unrelated to any medical condition. However, the police must always give the motorist an opportunity of objecting on medical grounds to giving blood (see *DPP v. Warren*). In *R. v. Epping JJ., ex p. Quy* [1993] Crim. L.R. 970, the defendant said that he was afraid of needles. As this was a potential medical reason, the police had to consult a doctor if they wanted a blood specimen. As that was not done, the applicant was ordered to be acquitted. The High Court said that if further questions had been asked of him, it might have turned out that this was not a medical reason. In *Wade's Case* [1996] R.T.R. 177 the defendant accepted his option under section 8(2) and was asked to provide blood. He said that he took pills. He also said that he did not have a medical reason for not giving blood. A doctor came and took a blood specimen but was not consulted about the taking of the pills. The High Court acquitted the appellant because by saying that he took pills, he had raised a medical question and, since the doctor had not been consulted, the correct procedure had not been followed. The fact that he also said that he had no medical reason was irrelevant as he might not have known if medical reasons existed. The use of tablets could have affected the accuracy of any analysis of the blood or have made its provision medically unwise. In *DPP v. Wyeth*, unreported, July 19, 1995, no breathalyser was available, so the motorist was given the full *Warren* formula (see Chapter 14) ending with the question about whether there were any reasons why a blood specimen could or should not be taken by a doctor. He replied:

"Yes, I am a diabetic and need two injections a day. I haven't been to a diabetic clinic for five years because I don't want other people putting needles in my arms and skin."

The constable, in the light of the admission that the accused had pierced ears and tattoos, and without further questioning or consideration, required him to supply a specimen of blood. When asked if he would do so the accused replied: "If you take it out of my finger, yes; if it is going to come out of my arm, no." He was then seen by a police surgeon. No evidence of what happened thereafter was adduced, save that no specimen was provided. Thus it was not known if the doctor was, or was not, of the opinion that medical reasons prevented a blood sample being provided.

Butterfield J. (with the agreement of Stuart-Smith L.J.) upheld the acquittal:

"For my part, I do not accept the words used by the Respondent were, in fact and in law, a failure without reasonable excuse to provide a specimen of blood. The Respondent was advancing reasons connected with his medical condition why he should not give a specimen of blood in response to the constable's warning. They may have been unconvincing reasons, but it was not for the constable to substitute his opinion for that of a medical practitioner unless, of course, the reasons were so obviously frivolous that they could not, in any circumstances, amount to a medical condition providing significant reasons for refusing to provide a specimen."

Earlier in his judgment, he stated:

"However the decision in *Leonard* [1993] W.L.R. 483 related to the issue at trial of what was capable of amounting to a reasonable excuse for failing to provide a specimen of blood. It was not directed to the quite separate question of how police officers should deal with a driver who gives an explanation of why he does not wish to provide a specimen."

In *Sainsbury v. DPP*, unreported, March 29, 1995 (an option case), the **12–27** defendant, on being asked if he wished to supply blood or urine, replied, indicating the latter. He was then asked the reason, which he gave as "not liking needles". He was then asked if there were any reasons why a specimen of blood could not or should not be taken by a doctor, to which the reply was "none at all". He was then required to provide such a specimen but stated: "I don't want to give a sample then. I am scared of needles."

The officer then repeated his requirements for blood, but the defendant declined to supply it. The High Court upheld the conviction. Buxton J. stated that the defendant had replied in the negative when asked if there was any reason why a specimen of blood could not or should not be taken by a doctor. That judgment is contrary to the more logical decision the previous month in *Wade v. DPP*, above. Sainsbury may not have realised that a fear of needles could amount to medical grounds for not providing blood. As McCowan L.J. said in *Wade's case*, a motorist may not appreciate that he was giving a medical reason. Wade had actually said that he preferred to give blood, being unaware that the taking of pills could, in some circumstances, amount to a medical reason. Indeed, fear of needles is much more likely to be recognised by a lay person as a medical reason than the taking of pills. The two decisions cannot be reconciled, any more than other conflicting cases involving those two judges can be, *e.g. Breenan v. DPP*, unreported, October 13, 1994 and *DPP v. Hill-Brookes* [1996] R.T.R. 279.

12–28   *Andrews v. DPP* [1992] R.T.R. 1 was an option case. The accused told a sergeant that he had a phobia of needles. So the latter rang a police surgeon, who, over the telephone, ridiculed the idea. So the sergeant required a blood sample but that was refused. The High Court held that if a medical reason were proffered by the motorist as to why he could not supply blood, the constable should either require urine or consult a doctor. Failure to do this would automatically lead to an acquittal. However, if the police took a doctor's opinion, they were entitled to rely upon it, even if it was wrong. However, if the medical opinion was proved to be erroneous or irrational, a court could always use its powers under section 78 of the Police and Criminal Evidence Act 1984 to exclude all evidence of the breath test and of the requirement to give blood.

III. THE WEDNESBURY PRINCIPLES

12–29 It should not be forgotten that the constable's choice of specimen is an executive decision, expressly conferred by statute on a public officer. Therefore, in accordance with the views expressed by Lord Diplock in *Mohammed-Holgate v. Duke* [1984] A.C. 437, 443B, that decision-making power is subject to the *Wednesbury* principles (see *Associated Provincial Picture Houses Limited v. Wednesbury Corporation* [1948] 1 K.B. 223). A constable is under no duty to ask a motorist for the latter's preference. If, however, a person does give reasons as to why he would prefer to supply one type of body fluid rather than another, it is submitted that the constable must consider those reasons to see if there is anything exceptional in them that would cause him to depart from his normal policy as to which type of sample should be required (see *R. v. Torquay Licensing Justices, ex p. Brockman* [1951] 2 K.B. 784).

IV. LEGITIMATE EXPECTATIONS

Despite the fact that a motorist has no legal right to state a preference, **12–30** some police officers still do the "decent thing" and ask a motorist whether he would prefer to give blood or to give urine. It is submitted that if such a question is asked, then the driver has a legitimate expectation that his view will be taken into account by the constable before the latter decides on which type of specimen should be provided. This is because an undertaking once given creates an expectation that the constable will act in accordance with that assurance (see *New Zealand Maori Council v. Att.-Gen. for New Zealand* [1994] 1 A.C. at 485E); and also since (to quote the advice of the Privy Council in *ex p. Bennett, ibid.*, at 61F) there is a clear public interest in holding an officer of the Crown to his promises. Thus, if a motorist is asked to state a preference, the police must take due account of his wishes before deciding on which type of fluid the specimen should be. An example of this principle in another context is that a convicted prisoner was held to have had a legitimate expectation that he would not receive a custodial sentence if the social inquiry report ordered by the justices was favourable (see *R. v. Isleworth Crown Court* [1991] T.L.R. 557), where the expectation arose because, at the time of seeking reports, the magistrates did not state that all the sentencing options were still open for them.

V. A CHANGE OF MIND BY THE CONSTABLE

Once a constable has told a motorist what type of specimen he must **12–31** provide, the officer can always change his mind at any time until the sample has actually been provided, as happened in *Winstaley v. DPP* [1993] R.T.R. 222 and *Hayes v. DPP* [1994] R.T.R. 163. In *Garrett v. DPP* [1995] R.T.R. 302, the High Court held that a policeman was entitled to require a urine specimen after the surgeon had unsuccessfully tried to take blood from the defendant. He had inserted a needle into the defendant's arm but his vein had collapsed. However, in *Poole v. Lockwood, The Times*, August 1, 1980, it was held that once the first specimen of urine had been provided, it was then too late for the constable to ask for blood.

D. Summary

If the police wish to obtain evidence of the amount of alcohol which a **12–32** driver has consumed, they must normally use a breathalyser. Only in a few specified cases can they rely upon an analysis of blood or urine to show how much a motorist has drunk. It is a decision for the police as to which type of body fluid should be sent to the laboratory but, before reaching that decision, they must afford the accused an opportunity to object to supplying blood and, if any medical reason is proffered, they must consult a doctor. Until overruled by the House of Lords, the High Court had in numerous cases insisted that a motorist must be asked which type of body fluid he would prefer to give and, if he expressed a preference, his reasons for that choice had to be taken into account by the constable in deciding whether to require blood or urine from him. It is most unfortunate that this limited right has been taken from the motorist. It created no problems for the police and gave them a good image, as they were seen to be trying to cause the least inconvenience to the road user by seeking his views as to how he would prefer to supply what could be the most damning evidence against him.

Chapter 13

BREATH ALCOHOL MEASURING INSTRUMENTS

A. Introduction

This chapter considers the breath alcohol measuring instruments used by **13–01** the police to analyse breath samples, in order to ascertain their exact alcoholic content. These machines must not be confused with the screening devices used mainly at the roadside to gain a rough idea as to whether or not a driver's alcohol concentration is above the prescribed limit. These latter contraptions have already been considered in Chapter 10.

B. Approval by the Secretary of State

I. POWER TO APPROVE

By section 7(1)(a) of the Road Traffic Act 1988, and section 37(1) of the **13–02** Transport and Works Act 1992, the police can only use breath alcohol measuring machines which have been approved by the Secretary of State. To date, only two such devices have been approved. (The Breath Analysis Devices (Approval) Order 1983, published by HMSO, ISBN 340 787 4, is now out of print but is reproduced in Appendix 2.) The fact that these devices were approved prior to the commencement of the legislation authorising their use does not invalidate their approval (see *Hayward v. Eames* [1985] R.T.R. 12).

At the time of writing the Home Secretary is evaluating second generation breathalysers and it is anticipated that they will be approved and in service in the not too distant future. The author has been informed by the Home Office that it is expected that the Home Secretary will be in a position to give them his approval in the spring of 1997.

II. WHICH DEVICES ARE APPROVED

13–03   The following two machines were both approved on April 18, 1983:

> 1."The device comprised of two components which are respectively known as the Camic Simulator and the Camic Breath Analyser, each being manufactured by the Camic Car and Medical Instrument Company Limited."
>
> 2."The device comprised of two components which are respectively known as the Lion Breath Simulator and the Lion Intoximeter 3000, the first mentioned component being manufactured by the Camic Car and Medical Instrument Company Limited and the other component being manufactured by Lion Laboratories Limited."

In fact the word "Camic" is merely the acronym of the Car and Medical Instrument Co. Ltd and there is no such company as the "the Camic Car and Medical Instrument Company Limited". However, in *Chief Constable of Northumbria v. Browne* [1986] R.T.R. 113, it was held that the manufacturer's name was not an essential part of the approval, so the misnomer did not invalidate the approval of the breathalysers named in the order. The same machines were approved for use under the Transport and Works Act 1992 by the Breath Analysis Devices (Approval) Order 1992.

In *R. v. Skegness JJ., ex p. Cardy* [1985] R.T.R. 49 at 59H–K and 60C/D, the High Court held that provided the device could fairly be called an Intoximeter, it was an approved device. An issue raised in the case was whether minor modifications caused a breathalyser to lose its seal of approval. The High Court held that the answer was "no".

III. THEIR USERS

13–04   In England and Wales all police forces use the Lion Intoximeter 3000, except for four of the smaller constabularies in the North of England (Northumbria, Cleveland, North Yorkshire and County Durham) which, like all police authorities in Scotland, use the Camic Breath Analyser. Both devices work on a similar principle, namely the technique of infra-red absorption.

IV. INCORRECT ASSEMBLY AND MALFUNCTION

13–05   In *DPP v. Carey* [1970] A.C. 1072, 1096, the House of Lords held that an incorrectly assembled breathalyser was not an approved device. Consequently, if a policeman used an Intoximeter without inserting the mouthpiece, he would not be using an approved device.

In *Rayner v. Chief Constable of Hampshire* [1971] R.T.R. 15, the High Court held that an Alcotest 80 with a broken bag was not an approved breathalyser, even though it had accurately showed the defendant's breath to have exceeded the prescribed limit. In *Slender v. Boothby* [1986] R.T.R. 385 the High Court said that an Intoximeter which did not show the correct date or time was not an approved device as Parliament only intended that reliable Intoximeters were approved. This applied even though the Intoximeter was working in accordance with the manufacturer's specification. There it was not an approved device because it showed February 29 as March 1, even though that was what it was designed to do. So in *Jones v. DPP* [1995] Crim L.R. 69, the High Court held that an Intoximeter with a slow clock was not an approved device. In a number of Crown Court appeals (*e.g. Hall v. DPP*, July 26, 1995, *per* Judge Holman and *Stibbard v. DPP*, February 15, 1995, *per* Judge Bathurst-Norman) it has been held that two minutes' slowness in an Intoximeter's clock meant that it was not an approved device.

V. ESTABLISHING THE APPROVAL IN COURT

Courts can take judicial notice of those devices which have been approved **13–06** by the Secretary of State and there is no need for the prosecution to establish approval in every case (see *R. v. Jones (R.W.)* [1970] 1 W.L.R. 16 and *Chief Constable of Northumbria v. Browne* [1986] R.T.R. 113). Indeed, if the police refer to a breathalyser, the High Court is of the view that it can be assumed that this is a reference to an approved device, unless the defence raises the matter (see *Cooper v. Rowlands* [1971] R.T.R. 291). These appeals must now be considered in the light of *Roberts v. DPP* [1994] R.T.R. 31 (see section 10–03), where judicial notice was held to be based on knowledge gained from previous cases.

C. The Lion Intoximeter 3000

In *Mayon v. DPP* [1988] R.T.R. 281, 283E, Glidewell L.J. stated: **13–07**

"I do not suppose that the inventor of the Intoximeter device realised how much it was going to exercise the minds of those who sit in the Divisional Court, but that it has exercised our minds and no doubt will continue to do so is a fact. This is yet another appeal arising out of the operation of an Intoximeter at a police station."

I. OPERATION

(a) GENERALLY

The Intoximeter is an American-designed machine, originally manufac- **13–08** tured under licence from the United States by Lion Laboratories Limited in South Wales. The machine is not normally for sale in this country, but is mainly leased to the majority of police forces in England and Wales. It works on the principle of infra-red absorption in the following way. The Intoximeter has a mouthpiece 7cm long with an internal diameter of 7mm which is connected to a long piece of tubing with a diameter of 7mm. It also contains two chambers, one being the analytical chamber and the other being the reference chamber, running parallel and separated by a partition wall. When the device is switched on an infra-red beam is continually transmitted. Some of the beam shines through the reference chamber, the other part through the analytical chamber, both being about 3cm long. The infra-red is beamed through at a wavelength of between 3.39 and 3.42 microns and centred at 3.41 microns. This frequency was chosen as it is the same as that of the energy emitted from the carbon hydrogen bonding in ethanol. The energy emitted from those bondings will absorb some of the infra-red radiation.

When a motorist blows into the device, his breath is channelled into the analytical chamber where some of the infra-red radiation will be duly absorbed by the energy from the carbon hydrogen bondings in the alcohol in the breath. (The higher the amount of alcohol, the greater the absorption of the infra-red beam.) At the end of the analytical and reference chambers is a photoelectric cell. Between the chambers and the cell is a chopper. It is shaped and moves like the rotor blades of a helicopter, alternately allowing infra-red from the analytical and reference chambers to reach the cell. The latter is sensitive to infra-red radiation with a special filter which will only allow a beam of the correct frequency to reach it. The infra-red radiation reaching the photo-electric cell causes a current to flow from the cell, the strength of which depends on the amount of infra-red entering the cell. The resistance caused by the current is measured in the form of an analogue, *i.e.* a curve, since the resistance decreases as the infra-red radiation is absorbed by the energy emitted from the carbon hydrogen bonding of the alcohol in the motorist's breath. This is similar to the needle on the dial of a battery charger that descends in a curve as a battery becomes charged.

The difference between the resistances generated by the currents from the analytical and reference chambers will be due to one of the infra-red beams having been partly absorbed by the energy emitted from the carbon hydrogen bonding of ethanol and other substances in the breath.

(b) ACETONE AND THE TAGUCHI CELL

13–09 Alcohol is not the only substance which absorbs infra-red on a frequency centred at 3.41 microns (see section 16–56, below). The most common substance to cause such absorption is acetone, which occurs naturally in breath. Its atomic structure is very similar to that of ethanol and is set out in Figure 2. (The molecular structure of alcohol is set out in Figure 1.)

Figure 1

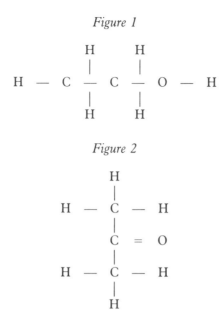

Figure 2

On being exhaled into the intoximeter, part of the breath specimen enters the analytical chamber while the other part is channelled onto a Taguchi cell, model TSG 822. This is essentially a semi-conductor made of tin oxide and which is especially sensitive to acetone. The change in the resistance in the semi-conductor due to the presence of acetone is duly measured. The TSG 822 is about three times more sensitive to acetone than the infra-red beam in the analytical chamber. By comparing the difference between the resistance in the two cells (*i.e.* photoelectric and Taguchi), the microprocessor is able to calculate the amount of acetone in the breath sample. If any acetone is detected, it should be indicated on the screen and also on the printout, if in the latter case it is detected in the second specimen.

(c) THE ANALOGUE/DIGITAL CONVERTER AND MICRO-PROCESSOR

All the analogue measurements are converted into a digital (*i.e.* binary) **13–10** system by an analogue digital converter, consisting of eight bits. The data, now in digital form, is fed into a micro-processor which calculates the amount of alcohol in the breath sample by comparing the difference in the amount of resistance caused by the two infra-red beams (and also making due allowance for any of the resistance that has been caused by acetone in the Taguchi cell). The result of the calculation is then displayed in Arabic numerals on a screen at the top of the Intoximeter.

(d) THE BREATH VOLUME REQUIREMENT AND ITS MEASUREMENT

In order to obtain an analysis, a minimum of 1.5 litres of breath should be **13–11** blown into the Intoximeter without interruption in no more than nine seconds. This is to ensure that the deep alveolar air is measured, as that contains the true amount of alcohol. However, the harder the motorist blows, the more breath is required to obtain an analysis. The strength of the blow is shown by bars on the screen.

The pressures required for the various numbers of bars to come up are as follows:

Bars	Flow rate litres/ minutes necessary to obtain an analysis	Pressure cm water	Amount of breath in litres
2	10–15	7–11	1.5
3	15–24	11–19	2.3
4	24–30	19–29	2.6
5	30–55	29–76	3.8

(The above figures supplied by M. J. Morris.)

It is possible to bring up three or four bars on the screen despite a small leak, but the bars will not be evident for as long a time as they would if there was no leak.

13–12   Thus it will be seen that the stronger a motorist exhales, the more breath he must supply in order to obtain an analysis. (The lung capacity of the average male is 4–5 litres and of the average female 3.5 litres.) There is a flow sensor which is designed to detect the commencement of a breath sample and its continuity. It contains a heated element called a Theristor which, when the instrument is not being used, maintains a steady temperature owing to the stillness of the air around it. When breath is blown past it, the element cools. It is rather slow to activate and may take 4–5 seconds, which is why a person must blow for a minimum length of time, irrespective of how much breath he happens to exhale into the machine. This cooling affects its electrical resistance and, accordingly, produces a triggering signal indicating that a sample has begun to pass. This cooling effect must continue for the requisite time, showing that an adequate sample of breath has been obtained. Once the flow of breath ceases, the element will immediately begin to warm up again and this is the signal which indicates that the sample has stopped or been otherwise interrupted. Unless sufficient breath has already been exhaled to obtain an analysis to be carried out, this will cause the machine to display the word "Aborted" i.e. the motorist will have to start all over again to provide sufficient breath for an analysis. The word "Aborted" on the screen must not be confused with the word "Abort" (see below).

According to a letter written to The Lancet, January 3, 1987, by M.J. Morris and A.C. Taylor, sustaining the exhilaration was crucial:

"The handbook for the Intoximeter specifies that at least 1.5 litres of breath be delivered at a flow rate of 10l/min or more. With the co-operation of the Thames Valley police we have done tests on two Intoximeters. On the first occasion we found that we had to breathe out close to our full vital capacities, 3.6 litres (A.G.T.) and 3.8 litres (M.J.M.), to get the machine to accept the sample. Using four subjects to re-test a second Intoximeter with a pocket spirometer in the line, we found considerable variation in the volumes accepted and rejected by the Intoximeter. Seven attempts were unsuccessful (volumes of 1.2, 1.2, 1.7, 2.4, 2.7, 3.1 and 2.9 litres) and five were successful (1.90–3.2 litres). It was our impression that sustaining the breath for many seconds was crucial to the Intoximeter accepting the sample for analysis—*i.e.*, a smaller volume was accepted if delivered over a longer time interval. The manufacturers have told us that if the flow rate is increased, the volume required rises to 2.6 litres or more. In addition there is a minimum breath time of 9 seconds which may decrease with increasing flow rate."

(e) INTERNAL CHECKING DEVICES

The Intoximeter has a built-in checking mechanism to try to ensure that, **13–13** prior to it receiving a breath specimen, it is functioning correctly. It checks itself and displays and prints out the result which is shown as "STD" on the printout. The check is as follows: before and after the two breath specimens are provided, it tests itself with a Lion breath simulator. This is a glass jar containing a solution of alcohol and water in the ratio of 0.893g of alcohol per litre of water, at a constant temperature of 34°C. (The simulator has its own heater.) Air is blown through the solution, creating a vapour containing 35µg of alcohol per 100ml, in accordance with Henry's Law. The vapour then enters the analytical chamber of the Intoximeter and is treated in exactly the same way as if it were a breath sample. (The air should produce a reading of 35µg on the screen and on the printout.) If cither of the two chccking analyscs is not within thc pcrmittcd rangc (*i.e.* between 32–37µg, inclusive—see Home Office Circular 32/84), then the result of any breath analysis will not be admissible in court (see *Mayon v. DPP* [1988] R.T.R. 281). The normal cause of a wrong check result is that the simulator has either not warmed up or has overheated. This is because a change of one degree in the temperature inside the simulator will alter the alcohol in the vapour by 6 per cent. If the first check is outside its permitted limit, the machine will display the word "Abort" and will close itself down. If the second check is wrong, it will print the results together with the final check result, followed by the words "high" or "low" as the case might be. This should warn the operator to ask for a blood or urine sample and, if he does not do so, the motorist must be acquitted. This is because the courts have insisted that the prosecution must prove both checks to have been within the range laid down by Home Office Circular 32/84. These checks are commonly, but erroneously, referred to as "calibration". They are not calibration because that is, strictly speaking, the alteration of an instrument's tolerance or accuracy, so that the latter corresponds with the results which should have been obtained. The police do not carry out such alterations. In addition, after the first check and after the analysis of each of the breath samples, the device will keep sucking in air and analysing it until the latter indicates that the device is completely free of alcohol. These checks are indicated by the words "BLK 0" on the screen and on the printout. If the "BLK" reading shows any other figure except zero, the result of the next analysis is unreliable as it could well have analysed both the defendant's breath and the alcohol left in the chamber from the previous analysis.

II. ACCURACY AND RELIABILITY

(a) In General

13–14 How reliable is the Intoximeter? The best answer is probably the evidence of Professor V. Marks to the Dewsbury Justices on December 11, 1990, in the case of *DPP v McAll*:

> "I have no doubt whatever. I would personally say that the machine is extremely reliable and that is why I haven't appeared in a case like this for a long time [*i.e.* as a defence witness], because I have always maintained that the machine is generally reliable . . . The machine is extremely reliable but like all machines *it is not infallible*." (Author's emphasis.)

Or as Lord Griffiths in *Cracknell v. Willis* [1988] A.C. 450, 467 put it: "We all know that no machine is infallible."

Owing to public concern about the accuracy of these devices when they were first introduced (see *Lion Laboratories v. Evans* [1985] Q.B. 526) the Home Secretary commissioned a survey by P.G.W. Cobb and M.D.G. Dabbs, which was subsequently published with a foreword by Sir William Paton ("The Paton Report", 1985, ISBN 0 11340806 4). It compared the results of breath analyses with those of blood samples obtained voluntarily from drivers at about the same time as they were compulsorily breathalysed at police stations. The report recognised that errors did on occasion occur. The Intoximeter would give a high and wrong reading for glue sniffers and could do so for others who had taken substances which the machine falsely treated as alcohol. There were in fact 21 cases out of a total sample of 12,066 analyses where the difference between the results of the analyses of 11 blood and 10 urine samples could not be reconciled with the Intoximeter's breath analyses and where the discrepancies could not be explained, *e.g.* by the difference in time between the provision of the breath and the blood or by other known reasons, such as glue sniffing. The Intoximeter can thus, on rare occasions, make an error even though it has correctly tested and purged itself. The concern is that when an error occurs, it can result in the conviction of an innocent motorist with potentially disastrous consequences, *e.g.* loss of job. Likely causes of such errors are discussed in some detail in Chapter 16.

(b) An Analogue/Digital Conversion Error

The most likely cause of an inaccurate analysis will be the malfunctioning **13–15**
of the analogue/digital converter. The Intoximeter has an eight bit converter to change the analogue into a digital signal using the binary system.
In *DPP v. McAll*, above, Professor Howes (who holds the chair in
Electronic Engineering at Leeds University) gave unchallenged evidence of
the problems that could arise with the conversion. He told the justices that
an eight bit converter has the capacity to change an analogue signal into
256 different digital combinations of noughts and ones. (Each of those
combinations is called a "word".) There is a constant signal to a transducer,
which at the appropriate moment indicates when the relevant analogue
signal begins and ends. The converter incorporates a "clock-like" mechanism to keep the signals in synchronisation. If the clock becomes a
microsecond out, it may or can misread the signal informing it when the
analogue is starting and finishing and thus misread noughts as ones or vice
versa, accordingly translating the analogue into an erroneous digital form,
with the result that the number which comes out of the converter may be
either higher or lower than the true figure. There is nothing to indicate to
the operator that this is occurring and just as it may become
unsynchronised, so it could also suddenly revert to normal. The signals
could go out of sequence for a number of reasons, but usually because of
pulse jitter. The latter would be caused by some interference, such as the
voltage being disturbed or by electrical noise. Such "noise" is usually
inaudible to a human being and in this context bears a different meaning
from the sound perceived by the ear and means "waves" emitted from an
unsuppressed or partly suppressed source. Hence, Home Office Circular
39/88 warned the police not to transmit on their personal radios in the
same room as an Intoximeter or Camic breath analysing device. The
Professor also told the court that these "interferences" could never be
entirely avoided but very expensive equipment can be installed to lessen
their occurrence, although the use of such equipment in the Intoximeter
would have priced it out of the market.

(c) Other Substances Wrongly Analysed

The other most likely cause of an inaccurate breath analysis would be if an **13–16**
Intoximeter were to analyse another substance beside gaseous ethanol.
Whether such an occurrence is a real possibility and the chances of it
happening are considered in section 16–56 *et seq.*, below.

III. OPERATING AN INTOXIMETER

So far as the police are concerned, operating an Intoximeter is fairly **13–17**
routine. Full details are set out in the operator's handbook. The following
account is based on the evidence relied upon by the prosecution in a
number of cases.

In order to obtain an analysis the following sequence of events must occur:

(1) The operator presses the start button and checks the memory. The machine shows how many further results can be stored in its memory. If the latter is full and the instrument is then used, the oldest result is erased, thus enabling the latest test result to be stored. When satisfied with the capacity of the memory, he presses the start button once again.

(2) The operator types in his name, rank, number and his code. (Each operator has his own secret code number.) He then types in the motorist's name and date of birth.

(3) The words "STAND BY" appear on the screen, unless the machine has been used in the last half hour.

(4) The device next purges itself of any residual alcohol by pumping through fresh air. This is indicated by a flashing "PRG" on the screen.

(5) To ensure that the purging is complete, the device analyses the air in the analytical chamber. This is indicated by a flashing "BLK" on the screen.

(6) When the device is satisfied that no alcohol remains in the analytical chamber, it will carry out its first standard test by analysing a solution containing 35µg of alcohol. While this is happening "XST" will flash on and off the screen and a click should be heard as the solution is passed over the acetone detector. (If there is a fault on the detector "*AD.FAULT*" will appear on the screen.) The screen will then show the results of the analysis by displaying "XST", followed by the amount of alcohol that has been detected. (This is shown on the printout as "STD" followed by the amount of alcohol.) If the alcohol detected is not within the range 32–37µg, the device will automatically close itself down, displaying "high" or "low" "abort", depending on the result of the analysis.

(7) If the test was satisfactory the device then purges itself again and this time the result should be displayed as "BLK 0". The appearance of any other figure indicates that the machine had not expelled all the alcohol used in its standard test, and the results of the subsequent analysis will not be accurate. (During this purging, the operator should attach the mouthpiece to the machine.)

(8) The machine next displays "BLOW UNTIL STAR"; also, the word "SUB" will flash on the screen. The motorist then has three minutes to provide a satisfactory breath sample. Once he has blown hard enough to activate the flow sensor, bars will appear on the screen. The stronger he blows the more bars appear. If he provides the requisite amount of breath within nine seconds, a star will appear and the motorist can stop blowing. If the motorist has blown sufficiently hard for a bar to appear but has not provided sufficient breath in the time allowed, then the word "ABORTED" will appear on the screen. The machine will then expel all the breath that has been blown in and start flashing "SUB" again. The motorist can then try again until the requisite time has expired. If after three minutes and four seconds no satisfactory sample has been provided then the words "NO SAMPLE" will be displayed and the machine will automatically close itself down.

(9) If a reading has been obtained, the machine will indicate the result of the analysis by flashing "SUBJ" followed by a figure indicating the amount of the alcohol. (On the printout the word "SUBJ" is replaced by "ONE" or "TWO," depending on whether it is the first or second analysis.)

(10) The machine then repeats stages (7) (8) and (9) in order to obtain a second analysis.

(11) If a second analysis has been obtained, the machine then tests itself as in (6), save that if the result is not within the range 32–37, it will also display the words "high" or "low" as the case may be, and this will also be shown on the printout.

(12) If it is switched on, the printer will now provide a written record of the result. (A sample printout is set out in Appendix 3.) Each police force can choose the number of copies (between one and 10) that will be printed out automatically if the printer is switched on. (Usually the chosen amount is either three or four.) Also, by pressing the "print" button, the operator can obtain further copies.

A copy of the operator's instruction card is reproduced in Appendix 3.

IV. STILL AN APPROVED DEVICE

The Intoximeter has been modified since its approval. This was indeed the **13–18** evidence provided by an employee of Lion Laboratories in *Young v. Flint* [1987] R.T.R. 300, but he also stated that the alterations did not affect its approval by the Home Secretary. The High Court subsequently quashed the conviction because of the magistrates' refusal to allow the defence to cross-examine that witness or to call evidence in rebuttal, in an attempt to show that the alterations to the Intoximeter had caused it to forfeit its approved status on the grounds that it was no longer the same instrument as had been approved by the Home Secretary. That decision is clearly an authority for the proposition that modifications to "an approved device" can *ipso facto* deprive it of its seal of approval, without any intervention on the part of the Home Secretary. What the case did not determine, however, is how fundamental the alterations have to be before approval is lost.

From the instructions supplied to Mr Young's counsel, it would appear that the modifications did not affect the basic operation of its infra-red absorption system. Changes were made to the micro-processor unit, to the interface unit and to the power supply unit, which in the latter case included the addition of filters and improved grounding to try to smooth the power output in order to minimise the fluctuations which had led to corruption in the micro-processor unit. Indeed, that computer had been to some extent redesigned with the aim of reducing its susceptibility to voltage fluctuations, including grounding revisions and various chips being replaced by ones less affected by voltage reductions. The infra-red detector resistor had been changed. The interface board had also undergone various modifications.

It is a reliable assumption that, more than a decade after its approval, the **13–19** courts will hold that the Intoximeter's modifications have not prevented it being an approved device. The basis of such a decision will be threefold. First, none of the alterations have affected its basic infra-red absorption technology. Secondly, the Home Secretary did not choose to approve a specific design but merely the instrument known as the Lion Intoximeter 3000. By so doing, he contemplated that those manufactured after April 18, 1983 might well contain minor design changes but, provided the instrument could still legitimately be described as an Intoximeter, it would retain his approval. Thirdly, because hundreds of thousands of motorists have been convicted solely on the basis of the analytical results obtained by an Intoximeter, it would produce administrative chaos to cast doubt upon the validity of those findings of guilt.

D. The Camic breath analyser

13–20 The Camic is a British-designed instrument and is manufactured in North Shields by the Car and Medical Instrument Co. Ltd. The Camic works on the principle of infra-red absorption. It uses an interference filter centred at 3.4μm to detect any alcohol present in the breath sample. It should eliminate the possibility of acetone interference by means of the very narrow pass-band (plus or minus 0.17μm) of the filter. It does not have a separate acetone detection system. Its standard is 32–38μg inclusive: see Home Office circular 32/84.

The Paton Report evaluated the performance of the Camic breath analyser. No acetone was detected in any of the blood or urine samples obtained from motorists who had also undergone a breath test on it, and "therefore no opportunity arose to evaluate the performance of this instrument with respect to acetone". The authors of the Paton Report compared 576 analyses of a body fluid with a similar number of analyses of breath performed by the Camic, where both substances had been supplied by the same person on the same occasion. Only one (0.17 per cent) was found to be anomalous. That is approximately the same percentage of the analyses which were found to be anomalous in a similar survey with regard to the Intoximeter.

13–21 The Camic's operating sequence is very similar to that of the Intoximeter. The operator enters the requisite details into the Camic and then presses the start button. The machine purges and tests itself and a green light illuminates. The motorist then has three minutes in which to provide the first sample. Sufficient breath must be blown in within six seconds, as opposed to the nine seconds allowed by the Intoximeter. The green light must go off and the red light become illuminated. This shows that sufficient breath has been exhaled into the machine to enable it to perform an analysis. The sequence is then repeated for the second specimen. The device then tests itself again and will only print out the result if it has analysed both samples and if the two self-checking exercises are within the prescribed tolerances.

E. Operational instructions for the Camic

The following are the instructions issued for its use by the manufacturers: **13–22**

"Check that the analyser and simulator units are both switched on. If the analyser has been switched off for any reason allow a 30 minute warm up period to elapse before taking any breath test.

TO START TEST, SIMPLY PRESS TEST BUTTON.

The instrument will now calibrate itself and after approximately one minute the green 'blow now' lamp will come on requesting the subject to blow.
A CONTINUOUS breath of at least six seconds is required to provide an accurate sample and bring on the 'stop blow' lamp.
The subject has a total of 3 minutes to provide a correct sample. The subject may make as many attempts as necessary to provide a six second continuous sample.
If, after providing a correct breath sample, the subject attempts to suck the gas back out of the breath pipe, the instrument will sense this and immediately reset and print out 'Breath Invalid'.
After the first breath test has been completed the instrument will request a second breath sample exactly as before.
After the second breath test the instrument will again check its calibration and if accurate then the results will be printed out, together with the date and time of test."

F. Summary

The Intoximeter and Camic breath alcohol measuring instruments are the **13–23** two devices which have currently been approved by the Home Secretary for use by the police to analyse breath. The motorist must accept that both of these are very reliable and accurate. In less than two tests per thousand will a mistake occur. It is clearly impossible to challenge their general reliability and, in any case, such evidence is inadmissible: see *Healy v. DPP* [1996] R.T.R. 247. However, the courts will, occasionally, accept that the result of an analysis is erroneous. If such an error is not apparent from the printout, then it will need very strong evidence to convince a court of that fact. The usual method is by the motorist adducing evidence that neither his consumption of alcohol, nor the prosecution's account of his state and condition at the time of arrest, were consistent with the amount of alcohol disclosed by the analysis (see section 16–31 *et seq.*, below).

Chapter 14

THE ADMISSIBILITY IN EVIDENCE OF
THE RESULT OF THE ANALYSIS

A. Introduction

"Every day throughout the world, lawyers are getting people off drink- **14–01** drive cases through errors found in drink-drive procedures, even though the accused person was above the legal driving limit at the time of the incident" (*The LIBIS Newsletter*, June 1996, published by Sound Techniques Limited.)

The same sentiments as those quoted above have also been expressed by the judiciary. In *Hobbs v. Clark* [1988] R.T.R. 36, 39K/L, May L.J. stated:

> "The code of procedure set out in the [the Road Traffic Act], as has been said in so many cases, is a simple one. It can and should be followed by police officers without any difficulty at all. Appropriate instructions can be given by police forces precisely about the procedure to be adopted. If that procedure is adopted without fail, then the appropriate result will be achieved, namely, that justice will be done without artificiality between prosecution and defendant, depending on the facts and circumstances of a given case. What happens so many times is that the procedure is not followed completely and defences are thereby enabled to be raised artificially or otherwise, in cases in which, having regard to the justice of the matter, in truth there should be no defence at all."

The statutory powers of the police to require a specimen for analysis have already been considered in Chapter 11. This chapter examines the circumstances in which the judiciary have held the results of the analyses of such specimens to be inadmissible in evidence, even though their accuracy was never in dispute and, moreover, may well have been in agreement with the result reached by a scientist employed by the motorist. The law on this point varies according to whether the court is dealing with events which occurred prior to, or after, the arrival at the police station.

B. Failure to follow the correct procedure

I. IMPROPRIETY BY THE POLICE PRIOR TO THE ARRIVAL AT THE POLICE STATION

(a) COMMON LAW

14–02 The status of evidence obtained unfairly or illegally has been considered by the courts on a number of occasions. The leading case is *R. v. Sang* [1980] A.C. 402, where the appellants alleged that they had only committed offences relating to the forgery of a document because a police sergeant had acted as an *agent provocateur*. Lord Diplock was of the view (*ibid.*, at 436) that the only type of evidence which could be excluded was incriminating evidence emanating from the accused and which did not exist at the time of the commission of the offence:

> "[Evidence could only be excluded if it was] tantamount to a self-incriminatory admission which was obtained from the defendant after the offence has been committed, by means which would justify a judge in excluding an actual confession which had the like self-incriminating effect."

A somewhat wider view was taken by Lord Scarman (*ibid.*, at 546):

> "The principle of fairness, though concerned exclusively with the use of evidence at trial, is not susceptible to categorisation or classification and is wide enough in some circumstances to embrace the way in which, after the crime, evidence has been obtained from the accused."

14–03 Nearly six years later, in the case of *Fox v. Chief Constable of Gwent* [1986] A.C. 281, this aspect of the law came to be considered by the House of Lords specifically in relation to drinking and driving cases. The facts were that the police had unlawfully entered the appellant's home and illegally arrested him. He was taken to a police station, where he provided the two requisite breath samples for analysis by the Intoximeter. The defence conceded that there was no mala fides on the part of the police and that they had merely been under a misapprehension as to the extent of their powers. That concession prompted Lord Edmund-Davies to say (at 295):

> "It has to be added that the appellant has throughout accepted that the police have not acted 'deliberately or maliciously', but simply because of a mistaken view of their powers. Some might think that a police cadet might very soon have learnt how limited are the rights of entry on private property without consent and without a warrant and that no policeman could be heard to assert the contrary."

14–04 Accordingly, their Lordships upheld the conviction on the basis that the accidental disregard of one of the most basic principles of the common law, namely that an "Englishman's home is his castle" (see *Semayne's case* (1604)

5 Co. Rep. 91a) was acceptable in the quest to stop the slaughter on the roads. Their Lordships held that, provided the police officers were acting without bad faith and were bona fide investigating an offence under the relevant sections of the Road Traffic Act, then the result of the analysis could never be ruled inadmissible, subject to one important caveat (*per* Lord Bridge at 298), namely that the procedures prescribed for the actual taking of the specimen for analysis at a police station or a hospital had been correctly followed. (What those procedures are is discussed later in this chapter.)

(b) POLICE AND CRIMINAL EVIDENCE ACT 1984

Since the decision in *Fox v. Chief Constable of Gwent* [1985] A.C. 281, **14–05** section 78 of the Police and Criminal Evidence Act (P.A.C.E.) 1984 has been enacted. This provides:

> "(1) In any proceedings the court may refuse to allow evidence on which the prosecution proposes to rely to be given if it appears to the court that, having regard to all the circumstances, including the circumstances in which the evidence was obtained, the admission of the evidence would have such an adverse effect on the fairness of the proceedings that the court ought not to admit it.
> (2) Nothing in this section shall prejudice any rule of law requiring a Court to exclude evidence."

Section 82 makes it clear that the above provisions are intended to strengthen the existing powers of exclusion as it expressly enacts:

> "(3) Nothing in this Part of this Act shall prejudice any power of a court to exclude evidence (whether by preventing questions from being put or otherwise) at its discretion."

(c) MALA FIDES

The first reported case of section 78 being invoked by a motorist appears to **14–06** be *Matto v. Wolverhampton Crown Court* [1987] R.T.R. 337. From the case stated, it is not altogether easy to discover exactly what facts were found by the Crown Court. (The author is informed by prosecuting counsel that one of the difficulties with the case was that the recorder had dissented from the views of the justices.) It would appear that two constables saw a motorist speeding. They signalled him to stop, but he took no notice. They pursued him as he drove into his driveway. The motorist then determined their implied licence to be on his property but the officers took no notice of this. Instead, they deliberately and knowingly committed trespass to arrest him. As they were well aware that they were acting unlawfully, the High Court held that the Crown Court was wrong to rule that it had no power to exclude the evidence of the results of the blood analysis. The High Court stated that when a lower court had failed to consider how it should exercise a discretion vested in it, the case would normally be remitted for it to make that decision. Here, instead of the case being sent back, the conviction was quashed because (*per* McCullough J.) there was only one way in which the justices could exercise their discretion. (This was obviously because of the unfairness caused to the accused by the deliberate disregard of the law by the police.) The High Court appeared to be stating that its decision was, and could only have been, based on the finding of fact that there had been mala fides on the part of the arresting officers. In *Sharpe v. DPP* [1993] R.T.R. 392, Staughton L.J. and Buckley J. held that even in such circumstances as *Matto*, magistrates still possessed a discretion as to whether or not to admit evidence of the results of the analysis.

(d) A Bona Fide Mistake

14–07   In *Thomas v. DPP* [1991] R.T.R. 292, the facts were similar to those in *Matto v. Wolverhampton Crown Court*, above, but there was no finding of bad faith so the High Court upheld the conviction, stating that section 78 only applied in cases of mala fides. However, in two cases heard together on April 22, 1991, namely *DPP v. Godwin* [1991] R.T.R. 303 and *DPP v. McGladrigan* [1991] R.T.R. 297, the High Court held that *Thomas v. DPP* had been decided *per incuriam*, since that court had been unaware of, and had therefore not taken into account, the decision of the Court of Appeal in the case of *R. v. Samuel* [1988] Q.B. 615, where it had been held that the exercise of the court's discretion to exclude evidence under section 78 did not depend of there being any bad fact or malice on the part of the police. In *Daniels v. DPP* [1992] R.T.R. 140, 150J/k, Woolf L.J. said that if people thought that his judgment in *Matto's case*, above, meant that section 78 only applied if the local constabulary had acted with mala fides, then they were mistaken. In *DPP v. Godwin* the High Court upheld the acquittal of the defendant for driving with excess alcohol as he had been illegally arrested. Bingham L.J. held that this trespass to the person gave the justices the discretion under section 78 to exclude evidence of the breath analysis and that, whichever way that power was exercised, it could not be challenged in the High Court. Indeed, his Lordship stated that some might consider the defendant fortunate. However, he also said that others may take the view that if their breach had no sanction, any safeguards for the motorist provided for by Parliament would be rendered nugatory. In the words of Bingham L.J. at 308H/J:

> "The justices were entitled to conclude that the substantial breach by the constable of the protection afforded to members of the public by section 6 was denied to the defendant, that as a result the prosecutor obtained evidence which he would not otherwise have obtained, and that as a result the defendant was prejudiced in a significant manner in resisting the charge against him."

"*Ignorantia facti excusat, ignorantia iuris non exusat*" is an old maxim of the common law (see *Mildmay's case* (1584) 1 Co. Rep. 175a, 177b). There can be no mitigation if a police officer does not know the law. The author can only hope that every member of the judiciary will be guided by the words of Lord Griffiths when delivering the advice of the Privy Council in the case of *Lam Chi-ming v. R.* [1991] 2 A.C. 212, 222: "It is better by far to allow a few guilty men to escape conviction than to compromise the standards of a free society."

In *Braham v. DPP* [1994] T.L.R. 684, it was held that section 78 cannot be raised for the first time on an appeal to the Queen's Bench Division. It must be taken in the lower court. Despite what Latham J. says, the point was indeed taken at first instance in that case but the junior counsel who had appeared at petty sessions was replaced by a Queen's Counsel for the hearing of the appeal, so the High Court was not informed that the issue had been raised before the justices.

II. IMPROPRIETY AND IRREGULARITIES ARISING FROM CONDUCT AT A POLICE STATION OR HOSPITAL

(a) The Procedure to be Followed

(i) An investigation

What is a bona fide investigation and when it can be held are considered in **14–08** Chapter 9. Unless there was such an investigation being properly undertaken, any specimen obtained can not be put in evidence.

(b) Warning of Prosecution

The Road Traffic Act, s.7(7) and the Transport and Works Act, s.31(9) both **14–09** enact that any person asked to provide a specimen for analysis must be told that if he fails to do as required of him, he may be prosecuted. *Murray v. D.P.P.*, above, held that this warning was a *sine qua non* of any conviction under the Road Traffic Act 1988, ss.3A, 5 and 7. That case distinguished *R. v. Brush* [1969] 1 W.L.R. 740 as being under different legislation. (Under the Road Safety Act a judge was given power to direct a jury to ignore the absence of such a warning if no prejudice was caused to the defendant but that provision has not been re-enacted in the Road Traffic Act 1988.) An erroneous and exaggerated account of the penalties which could be imposed upon conviction for failing to provide a specimen would not invalidate the requirement (see *Bryant v. Morris* [1972] R.T.R. 214).

In *R. v. Chippendale* [1973] R.T.R. 236, it was held that the warning of **14–10** prosecution need only be given when the requirement was initially made and there was no need to repeat it when the time came for the sample to be actually provided, *e.g.* when the doctor arrived. In *Foulkes v. Baker* [1975] R.T.R. 50, it was held that there was no presumption that a warning of prosecution had been given and it was for the prosecution to prove this if they asserted that such a warning had been given. In *Murray v. DPP*, above, the constable had merely said that she had followed the standard procedure form. Watkins D.C.J. held that since the officer had referred to using a form, the justices were entitled to look at it and to see if had printed in it a warning of prosecution. That dicta was followed in *Braham v. DPP* [1994] T.L.R. 684. However, in *Lyons v. DPP*, unreported, February 17, 1995 (an application for the case to be remitted), Rose L.J. said that just because a police sergeant had said he had used the local constabulary's drinking and driving *pro forma*, "that did not of itself mean that he followed all of it. He may have done so or he may not have done so". The evidential status of such a *pro forma* is considered in section 15–36.

(c) Breath Specimens

14–11 Unlike requirements for blood and urine, no cases have decided how breath specimens for analysis have to be requested. Some guidance can no doubt be gained from decisions under the Road Traffic Act 1972 regarding body fluids. In *R. v. Coward* [1976] R.T.R. 425, it was held that the words "for a laboratory test" had to be used so that the motorist knew why the sample was being required and what was going to happen to it. Lord Bridge in *DPP v. Warren* (see below) said that a defendant should be told "no more and no less" than was told to Warren. He was told that the specimen of blood or urine "would be submitted for laboratory analysis". By analogy, when a person is required to provide a breath specimen he must also be told that it is for "analysis". In *R. v. O'Boyle* (1973) 137 J.P. 280 the Court of Appeal held that the word "require" need not be used, provided that the motorist knew that he was under a mandatory duty to supply the specimen.

The breathalyser into which the suspect has to exhale must be "an approved device": see Road Traffic Act, s.7(1)(a) and Transport and Works Act, s.31(1)(a). What is an approved device is discussed in Chapters 11 and 13.

(d) Simultaneous or Consecutive Requirements for Two Specimens of Breath or Urine

14–12 Both section 6(3) of the Road Safety Act and section (9)(5) of the unamended Road Traffic Act 1972 enacted: "(b) He is then requested to provide two specimens of urine within one hour of the request."

R. v. Reynolds [1976] R.T.R. 229, 233, and *R. v. Trott, ibid.*, at 234J/K held that the wording of the Act meant that the motorist must be told all at once that he had to provide two specimens of urine. Not cited by counsel nor referred to in the judgments of either of those cases was the earlier and contrary decision in *R. v. Pursehouse* [1970] R.T.R. 494. However, the Road Traffic Act 1988, s.7(1) and Transport and Works Act, s.31(1) now provide:

" . . . A constable may . . . require him —
(a) to provide two specimens of breath for analysis . . . or
(b) to provide a specimen of blood or urine for a laboratory test."

Section 7 in subsection (5) and section 31 in subsection (7) go on to state:

"A specimen of urine shall be provided within one hour of the requirement for its provision being made and after the provision of a previous specimen of urine."

In view of the different wording of the statute regarding the requirement for specimens, on the one hand, of breath and, on the other hand, of urine and the last two mentioned decisions of the Court of Appeal, it is submitted that the present day position is that a motorist must be asked at the same time for two breath specimens but there is no requirement for contemporaneous requests in the case of urine. Also, in *DPP v. Warren* [1993] A.C. 319 at 328A/B, Lord Bridge, in stating what must be told to a motorist, merely said: "Tell him that . . . he is required to give a specimen of blood or urine."

That was all that was told to the respondent in that case, so clearly the *Warren* formula does not require that, when urine is initially requested, the driver must be told that two specimens must be provided. However, this particular point may well not have been in Lord Bridge's mind when he delivered his speech.

(e) THE PROCEDURE FOR OBTAINING BODY FLUID SAMPLES

The circumstances where a specimen of body fluid rather than one of **14–13** breath can be supplied by a motorist is discussed in Chapter 12. The following sections consider what information must be given to the motorist, *i.e.* what procedure has to be followed for obtaining blood or urine samples. This will vary according to whether the suspect is under a mandatory duty, or merely has an option under the Road Traffic Act s.8(2) or the Transport and Works Act, s.32(2), to supply blood or urine; and in the former case, whether or not he is a patient in a hospital and in the latter case, whether or not he exercises his option.

When the 1981 Transport Act amended the Road Traffic Act 1972 and allowed convictions to be based on breath analyses, the Home Office issued a circular (35/83) with an appendix containing a *proforma* recommended for use in drinking and driving cases. When the courts started to acquit because of defects in that form, each constabulary was left to make its own alterations. "The Report of the Working Group on Pre-Trial Issues" (Lord Chancellor's Department, 1992) recommended a standard *proforma* be used throughout England and Wales. The Director of Public Prosecutions instructed leading counsel, but each time his draft was ready, it had to be amended in view of another decision of the High Court.

The procedure to be followed in all cases is that laid down by the House **14–14** of Lords in *DPP v. Warren* [1993] A.C. 319. The background to this case is explained in great detail at (1994) 144 New L.J. 1669 and was summarised in his speech by Lord Bridge (at 322G–323J):

"The new code, while retaining the preliminary breathalyser test, provides that the normal method to be adopted at a police station in order to determine the amount of alcohol in the driver's body is by the provision by him of two specimens of breath for analysis by means of the approved device known as the Intoximeter. It is only in the specific circumstances defined by the statute (when it is either impossible or inappropriate to obtain or to rely on breath specimens) that it is either necessary or permissible to require the driver to provide a specimen of blood or urine. But when such circumstances do arise, questions with respect to the appropriate procedure to be followed in requiring drivers to provide specimens of blood or urine have given rise to some difficulties in the courts and it is to the resolution of those questions that this appeal is directed."

Although his Lordship uses the expression "driver" throughout his speech, what he said is just as applicable to somebody who had merely been in charge of a vehicle.

In *Hayes v. DPP* [1994] R.T.R. 163, it was held to be a satisfactory compliance with the requisite procedure if the correct information was given at any time prior to the actual provision of the specimen.

However, the procedure laid down in *Warren's case* has not been followed in, and does represent the law of, Scotland. In *Simpson v. McClory* [1993] S.L.T. 861, The Lord Justice Clerk (Ross) said that he did not understand the rationale of some of Lord Bridge's views (*ibid.*, 866A) and he found it "difficult to reconcile" part of that speech with other parts (*ibid.*, 866F). Clerk L.J. went on to state:

"The result may be that different constructions are placed upon the Act of 1988 in Scotland and in England but this is the result of different police procedures in the two countries." (*ibid.*, 867F.)

Lord Murray said: " . . . it may be that there is little option but to accept some divergence between the two jurisdictions on this matter, however undesirable that may be." (*ibid.*, 868L.)

(i) Compulsory body fluid specimen at a police station

14-15 Towards the end of his speech, Lord Bridge said ([1993] A.C. 319 at 332D/E): "Restating those views in summary form . . . what is required is no more and no less than the formula used in the instant case or words to the like effect." The formula told to Warren was as follows (at 324E/F):

"The approved evidential breath testing device cannot be used on this occasion because the calibration check has proved unsatisfactory. Accordingly, I require you to provide an alternative specimen, which will be submitted for laboratory analysis. The specimen may be of blood or urine, but it is for me to decide which. If you provide a specimen you will be offered part of it in a suitable container. If you fail to provide a specimen you may be liable to prosecution. Are there any reasons why a specimen of blood cannot or should not be taken by a doctor?"

Earlier on in his speech (at 328A/B), Lord Bridge had said:

"Again, on the face of the statute, I cannot see any reason why in this case the constable should do more than tell the driver the reason under section 7(3) why breath specimens cannot or should not be used; tell him that in these circumstances he is required to give a specimen of blood or urine but that it is for the constable to decide which; warn him that a failure to provide the specimen required may render him liable to prosecution; and then, if the constable decides to require blood, ask the driver if there are any reasons why a specimen of blood cannot or should not be taken by a doctor."

The impression one gains initially from Lord Bridge's speech is that less **14–16** information need be given to a driver than the Metropolitan Police imparted to Warren. However, at the end of his oration, he says that that "no less" than what was told to Warren must be said by the police. Except in one case (*Beaufont v. DPP*, unreported, May 15, 1996), where the issue was left open, no appeal has come before the High Court where a motorist who was told all that Lord Bridge said in that part of his speech which is reported on page 324 of the *Law Reports*, but was not also told all that Warren was told. (The differences are being informed that the specimen to be provided was required for a laboratory analysis and that part of it would be offered to its donor.) As these two parts of Lord Bridge's speech are (to quote The Lord Justice Clerk (Ross), see above) difficult to reconcile, the meaning most favourable to the defendant should be adopted, just as is done in interpreting criminal statutes. This view is supported by the decision in *Duffy v. DPP* [1994] R.T.R. 241, 258 G/H where Mitchell J. said:

> "For the avoidance of doubt, we repeat, in obligatory s.7(4) cases 'what is required is no more and no less than the formula used in the instant case' that is to say the *Warren* case. Lord Bridge's tag 'or words to like effect' is not to be regarded as an indication that the omission of any ingredient of his formula will or may be acceptable."

Thus, what was said to Warren must be told to all those whose are required to supply specimens of body fluid pursuant to the relevant provisions of the Road Traffic Act or the Transport and Works Act.

In *Ankrah v. DPP*, unreported, February 20, 1995, it was held that the **14–17** police must tell the defendant why he is being required to provide a specimen of body fluid rather than breath, even though that is obvious and is already known to him. If this was not done, the correct procedures would not have been followed. In that case, on being asked for a breath specimen, the appellant told the police that he suffered from asthma. He was then asked to provide blood. He was not told that this was because "for medical reasons he could not supply breath". The failure to tell him this meant the *Warren* formula had not been followed.

In *Edge v. DPP* [1993] R.T.R. 146 and *Beaufont v. DPP*, above, it was **14–18** held that merely asking the defendant to express a preference as to whether he would prefer to supply blood or urine was not sufficient, and he must be specifically asked if there was any reason why a sample of blood could not be taken by a doctor. In the words of Pill L.J. in that latter case, asking for a preference gives a "different and more limited opportunity" from that which Lord Bridge said had to be afforded to the motorist. Needless to say, it is not sufficient to ask "why won't you give a blood sample?": see *Williams v. DPP* [1994] R.T.R. 1107.

If the requirement is for urine, then there is no need to ask the motorist any questions about whether or not there are any reasons why a specimen of blood cannot or should not be taken by a doctor; see *DPP v. Garratt* [1995] R.T.R. 302. Apart from this exception, he must be told all the rest of the *Warren* formula.

(ii) Hospital patients

14–19 In *Warren's case*, Lord Bridge said that a motorist had to be told "the reason *under s.7(3)* why breath specimens cannot be taken or used" (328A— author's emphasis). In *Duffy v. DPP* [1994] R.T.R. 241 it was held that, although Lord Bridge was not considering hospital patients, nevertheless this requirement equally applied to such people, who should be told something like, for instance, that blood was required because breath specimens cannot be taken at a hospital. The opposite view (that such information need not be given to a patient) was taken by the court in *R. v. Burton-upon-Trent JJ., ex p Woolley* [1995] R.T.R. 139, where it was held that the applicant had been required to provide blood, not for a reason under section 7(3), but because under section 7(2) a requirement for a breath specimen could only be made at a police station and, therefore, since he was at a hospital, the police had no jurisdiction to ask him to exhale into the breathalyser. All that Lord Bridge had intended was that a driver should be given the factual reason under section 7(3) which allowed blood to be taken. There is force in that argument since Lord Bridge refers only to the person being told the reason under section 7(3) why he must give a body fluid, whereas a hospital patient must do this, not because of anything in subsections (3) but because of subsection (2).

14–20 In *ex p. Woolley*, above, Buxton J. also stated that it was sufficient merely to ask if there were any reasons why a specimen of blood could not be taken. There was no need to mention a doctor; the reason for this being that the doctor's permission had to be obtained before making the requirement. A few months earlier he had agreed with Leggatt L.J. in *White v. DPP* [1995] R.T.R. 287 that the doctor had to be mentioned. It is submitted that his earlier view was correct because, for all the motorist knows, the blood specimen could be taken by a police officer. The thought of this could make a patient decline to give blood. Also, because the Road Traffic Act, s.11(4) and the Transport and Works Act, s.38 only allow a medical practitioner to take a specimen, the motorist should be informed of that fact. The importance of section 11(4) is emphasised by the fact that it is repeated in section 15(4) of the Road Traffic Offender Act. The decision in *ex p. Woolley* loses a lot of its force since the applicant had in fact been told that a blood specimen would be taken by a doctor, before being asked about reasons for not supplying blood. Also, this was a point taken by the court of its own motion without argument from counsel.

Chapter 11 considers whether, if a patient was required to supply blood or urine, that specimen could be taken at a police station after he had been discharged from hospital or whether the procedure had to start all over again.

(iii) *The voluntary option—accepted*

In two places in his speech in *Warren*, Lord Bridge states what information **14-21** must be imparted to the motorist:

> "It is clear that under section 8(2) the driver, in order that he may decide whether or not to claim that the breath specimen be replaced, should be fully informed of the nature of the option open to him and what will be involved if he exercises it. He should be told that the specimen of breath which he has given containing the lower proportion of alcohol exceeds the statutory limit but does not exceed 50 micro-grammes of alcohol in 100 millilitres of breath; that in these circum-stances he is entitled to claim to have this specimen replaced by a specimen of blood or urine if he wishes; but that, if he does so, it will be for the constable to decide whether the replacement specimen is to be of blood or urine and that if the constable requires a specimen of blood it will be taken by a doctor unless the doctor considers that there are medical reasons for not taking blood, when urine may be given instead. I can see no ground whatever, on the face of the statute, why in a section 8(2) case the driver should be invited to state whether he prefers to give blood or urine or to state any reasons for his preference. Indeed, to invite him to do so, it seems to me, can only be misleading in suggesting that the driver is entitled to some say in the matter. The statute gives him no such say. The driver is faced with the prospect of conviction on the basis of the breath specimen which he has given containing the lower proportion of alcohol. His only chance of escape from that prospect is by opting to give and then in fact giving a replacement specimen of whichever kind the constable requires of him, subject only to his right to object to giving blood on medical grounds, and if they are accepted by the doctor, then to give urine instead. Again, so far as the language of the statute is concerned, I can see no reason in principle why the constable in the course of explaining to the driver his rights under section 8(2) should not tell him, if it be the case, that he, the constable, will require the replacement specimen to be of blood. (At 327B–H.)

> "In a case where the driver's option is to be explained to him under section 8(2), the driver should be told that if he exercises the right to have a replacement specimen taken under section 7(4), it will be for the constable to decide whether that specimen is to be of blood or urine and, if the constable intends to require a specimen of blood to be taken by a medical practitioner, the driver should be told that his only right to object to giving blood and to give urine instead will be for medical reasons to be determined by the medical practitioner." (At 332E/F.)

Strictly speaking, the above quotation is *obiter*, since that was a com-pulsory section 7(4) case. Nevertheless, in drivers' option cases, that extract from Lord Bridge's speech has been held by the High Court to be an accurate statement of the law, *e.g.* in *Charles v. DPP* [1996] R.T.R. 247, 265, where Lord Bridge's speech was analysed as containing five separate criteria:

> "1. The specimen of breath which he has given containing the lower proportion of alcohol exceeds the statutory limit but it does not exceed 50 microgrammes of alcohol in 100 millilitres of breath;
> 2. That in these circumstances he is entitled to claim to have the specimen replaced by a specimen of blood or urine if he wishes;
> 3. If he does so it will be for the constable to decide whether the replacement specimen is to be of blood or urine;
> 4. If the constable requires a specimen of blood it will be taken by a doctor unless the doctor considers that there are medical reasons for not taking blood, when urine may be given instead;
> 5. If the constable intends to require a specimen of blood to be taken by a medical practitioner he should be told that his only right to object to giving blood and to giving urine instead will be for medical reasons to be determined by the medical practitioner.
>
> Point 5 reflects Lord Bridge's re-formulation of Point 4 at the end of his speech."

These numbered criteria were approved in *Breenan v. DPP* and *Noscoe v. DPP*, unreported, October 13, 1994, where Gage J. said that they had to be "strictly followed".

In *Turner v. DPP* [1996] R.T.R. 274, 278G, the High Court echoed the words of Mitchell J. in *Ogburn v. DPP* supra: "The guidance given by Lord Bridge of Harwich in his speech [in *Warren*] is to be followed literally."

In *R v. Cheshire JJ., ex p. Cunningham* [1995] R.T.R. at 291F/G Leggatt L.J. said:

> "Since that decision of the House of Lords there have been other cases in this court, in particular *Edge v. Director of Public Prosecutions* [1993] R.T.R. 146, *Meade v. Director of Public Prosecutions* [1993] R.T.R. 151, and the more recent case of *Ogburn v. Director of Public Prosecutions* [1994] R.T.R. 241. Those subsequent cases have refuted attempts by the prosecution to blur the requirements enunciated by Lord Bridge, and to insist that the requirements which he stipulated were to be strictly complied with. There has been a suggestion made in one of the subsequent cases that the relevant parts of his speech were not to be read as though they were part of a statute. That is, of course, exactly what they were, or at all events they represented such rendition of the statute as the House of Lords thought appropriate. Accordingly, those requirements are to be strictly complied with."

14–22 On the other hand, Simon Brown L.J. stated in *Baldwin v. DPP* [1996] R.T.R. 238, 246:

> "It was not, [the Appellant] submits, made clear to him that he had a right to object. I disagree.
> It seems to me necessarily implicit in the course of the exchange that the officer, in stating that he proposed (note: not had decided) that the specimen should be one of blood, and in expressly inviting the defendant

to indicate any reasons why the specimen should not be blood, was properly notifying him of his rights in the matter. The fact that he was inviting objection to a blood specimen on grounds wider than for medical reasons is nothing to the point. Counsel sensibly refrains from arguing that the procedure was flawed on this ground.

I cannot accept that the decided authorities now so encrust and gloss the statute as to require not merely adherence to the procedure laid down in the main passage in Lord Bridge's speech in *Warren* at p. 327, but the slavish adoption of a form of words which, in terms, involves stating to the defendant at the earlier stage that he has 'a right to object'."

Those words must be taken in the factual context of the case. The defendant had been told items (1) to (4) of the *Warren* criteria. Instead of number (5) he was then told:

"I propose that the specimen be of blood. Are there any reasons why a specimen of blood cannot or should not be taken from you by a doctor?"

That was held to be sufficient. The defendant had the opportunity to object to giving blood as required by criterion (5). As he had been told criterion (4), he was aware that if there was such a reason, he could give urine. All that case is really saying is that a police officer can use his own words when explaining the *Warren formula* to a motorist.

In *Hayes v. DPP*, above, it was held that if the constable required a urine sample, then he need not mention criteria [4] and [5].

In *DPP v. Hill-Brookes* [1996] R.T.R. 279, the motorist was not told the full criteria (1). He was merely told instead:

"As the breath specimen with the lower proportion of alcohol shows an alcohol content of between 40 and 50 microgrammes inclusive of alcohol in 100 millilitres of breath you have an option to claim that it should be replaced by another specimen for a laboratory test."

In holding that the correct procedure had been followed, Balcombe L.J. said (p. 284):

"Lord Bridge's speech makes it clear that the reason why the formula should be followed is that in order that the driver ' . . . may decide whether or not to claim that the breath specimen be replaced, he should be fully informed of the nature of the option open to him and what would be involved if he exercises it'. Telling him that the pre-conditions of the existence of the option have been fulfilled can have no effect upon the driver being fully informed either of the nature of the option or what would be involved in its exercise; it is merely telling him that the conditions have been satisfied which you have given [sic] to the option. On that basis it cannot affect the driver if he is told of the pre-condition on the one hand by the words ' . . . the specimen of breath which he has given containing the lower proportion of alcohol exceeds the statutory limit' or that he is told that the alcohol content of his breath is in a bracket (figures given) which in fact establishes that the statutory limit has been exceeded. So as a matter of principle and applying the purpose with which Lord Bridge prefaces his procedure, there is no problem in this particular case."

14-23 Lord Bridge said in criterion (1) that a motorist should be told two things: (a) he is over the limit; but (b) his specimen does not exceed 50μg. His Lordship used the conjunctive not the disjunctive "or". If he had only intended part of the information in criteria (1) to be told to the motorist, he would surely have said so. Balcombe L.J. seems to have thought that telling a motorist that his breath specimen was "between 40 and 50μg" was sufficient, because those words meant that his breath alcohol concentration was above the prescribed limit. However, first any motorist will see the result of his breath analysis appear on the screen on the Intoximeter; yet Lord Bridge (in a part of his speech with which Balcombe L.J. does agree) said that a motorist must be told that the lower of his two readings does not exceed 50μg. Secondly, why should telling a motorist that his breath reading is between 40-50μg automatically convey to him that the alcohol in his breath was above the legal limit? As Alliot J. said *in argumento* in *DPP v. Charles*, above, many motorists think that "80" is the limit and do not know that there is any distinction between breath and blood, as was indeed the view of three members of the Court of Appeal in *R. v. Cook* [1996] R.T.R. 304, where they varied a sentence in the belief that the breath alcohol limit was 80μg, *i.e.* the blood limit (see the dicta of Lord Taylor C.J. in *R. v. Shoult* [1996] R.T.R. 298, 303D.) "80" is a figure that sticks in the mind of many motorists because of the great publicity campaign that followed the introduction of the Road Safety Act and which was not repeated when the Transport Act 1981 received the Royal Assent. If a person thinks that the legal limit is 80 and was told his breath specimen is between 40 and 50, he may well wonder why he should bother to give another specimen. In this situation, one cannot apply the principle that "everybody is deemed to know the law", otherwise there would have been no need for a motorist to have to be told anything other than the amount of alcohol in the lower of the two analyses. This is because if a person knew the law, he would then be aware of exactly what his rights were, but the decided cases do not make such an assumption; rather, they decree that all his rights must be explained to him. The rationale of this was given by Parker L.J. in *Walton v. Rimmer* [1986] R.T.R. 31, 35 A/B (see Chapter 15):

> "As the Lord Chief Justice observed in *Gaimster v. Marlow* ([1984] R.T.R. 49, 55), we are not here in a fanciful world, we are in a world of reality and the reality of this situation is this. On occasions when specimens are taken and measurements are taken by a Lion Intoximeter 3000, the defendant may well be in a state of intoxication such as makes it necessary that what is going on should be fully understood by him, or at least, fully understood by a reasonable person."

14-24 Also, the decision in *DPP v. Hill-Brookes* runs contrary to dicta in two other cases. In *Ankrah v. DPP* (for the facts, see above) it was held that a motorist must be told why a blood, rather than a breath, specimen is being required of him, even though he already knows the reason for that. In *Hayes v. DPP* [1994] R.T.R. 163, the custody sergeant read out to the defendant the Cheshire Constabulary drinking and driving *proforma*, which said that his breath specimen contained "not more than 50 microgrammes of alcohol" but did not inform him (in those days) that his alcohol level was above the prescribed limit. (He was, however, also shown the Intoximeter printout which displayed the exact amount of alcohol in his breath.) No point was taken on it in the trial. This was because at some stage, while trying to secure the attendance of a doctor, the defendant was told that his breath specimen showed him to be "over the limit". As not relevant to the appeal, this latter fact was not mentioned in the case stated and its omission led Kennedy L.J. in *DPP v. Charles*, above, to comment (p. 269):

> "In *Hayes* case it was submitted to this court that the option was not fully explained in accordance with the *Warren* formula in that [etc.] . . . In fact it could also have been said that the driver was not told that in relation to the breath specimens the lower proportion of alcohol exceeded the statutory limit (part of Point 1), and that if the Sergeant required a specimen of blood it would be taken by a doctor, so the criticism was incomplete, but the question of compliance with the *Warren* formula was directly in issue."

Miss Charles had been told the same about her breath specimen as had Mr Hill-Brookes, and about which Kennedy L.J. had said earlier in his judgment (p. 266):

> "She was not told that the lower proportion of alcohol exceeded the statutory limit (part of Point 1) and there was to reference to . . . Point 3 . . . "

It is submitted that the view of the law expressed by Kennedy L.J. (and **14–25** with which Alliot J. agreed) is in line with *Ogburn v. DPP*, above, *Breenan v. DPP*, above, and *ex p. Cunningham*, above, where three differently constituted divisional courts have all held that Lord Bridge's criteria must be strictly followed. In the latter case Leggatt L.J. specifically stated that any omission of any ingredient of Lord Bridge's criteria was not acceptable (at 258H). However, in *DPP v. Ormsby*, unreported, March 12, 1996, he held that *Hill-Brooke's case* had been correctly decided. He said that he had meant in his earlier judgment that only what Parliament had prescribed had to be told to the motorist. That is a *non sequitur* because the only express information which the legislature has stated must be given to a driver is that referred to in the Road Traffic Act, s.7(7), namely, a warning of possible prosecution if he fails to provide a specimen for analysis. All the other mandatory requirements are judged made. Indeed, Leggatt L.J. had specifically said in his earlier judgment that Lord Bridge's speech was "such a rendition of the statute as the House of Lords thought appropriate".

Another and possibly more likely interpretation of what Leggatt L.J. **14–25A** meant was that a motorist only had to be told what the statutory provisions actually enacted and therefore since section 8(2) only referred to a breath specimen not exceeding $50\mu g$, that was all that the motorist needed to be told about his breath alcohol concentration. There was no necessity also to tell him that his alcohol consumption exceeded the prescribed limit.

In *DPP v. Arnup* and *Gorman v. DPP*, New Law Digest November 11, 1996, Rose L.J. and Maurice Kay J. held that if blood was requested there was no need to tell a driver anything about urine unless and until the doctor had discovered that there were medical reasons preventing him from taking a blood sample. The motorist only had to be asked whether there was any reason (or any medical reason—both forms were acceptable) why he could not provide blood and he also had to be told that the blood would be taken by a doctor. This is the reverse of the concurring judgment of Rose L.J. in *DPP v. Hayes, supra*, where it was held that if urine was the fluid required, there was no need to mention anything about blood, save, presumably to say that the alternative specimen could be either of blood or urine. The word "presumably" is used by the author on account of the passage in Lord Bridge's speech at [1993] A.C. 332B/C. The appellant decisions in the *Arnup* and *Gorman* Cases follow the dicta of Pill L.J. in *Beaufont v. DPP, supra* (a hospital case) that in option cases the judiciary are taking a more liberal view of the oration delivered by Lord Bridge in the *Warren* case, *supra*.

14–26   In *Cartwright v. DPP*, unreported, May 18, 1994, it was held that there was nothing wrong with explaining part of the criteria for the statutory option prior to obtaining a breath specimen, *i.e.* before the option had arisen, and the remainder once a specimen not exceeding 50µg had been obtained.

(iv) Voluntary option declined

14–27   The courts have applied the same criteria for deciding if a motorist has declined his option under section 8(2) as they have to determining whether or not he has failed to provide a mandatory specimen for analysis (see Chapter 17).

In *Charles v. DPP*, above, the court followed the *obiter dicta* in *DPP v. Winstanley* [1993] R.T.R. 222 and *Ogburn v. DPP* and held that if the option was declined, the prosecution merely had to prove that the breath specimen was correctly taken and that the evidence of that specimen was not "tainted" by the failure to give the full *Warren* criteria, unless the absence of one of its ingredients had caused prejudice to the motorist. It should be noted that Lord Bridge does not draw such a distinction. He said (at 327) that a driver:

"... *should* be fully informed of the option open to him and what will be involved if he exercises it." (Author's emphasis.)

14–28   It is submitted that if somebody was not "fully informed" of exactly what would happen if he were to exercise his rights under section 8(2), then the correct procedure has not been followed, irrespective of whether or not he was prejudiced by that lack of information, and that *Charles v. DPP* has not correctly construed what Lord Bridge was saying. To be fair to Kennedy L.J., one can see the logic in *Charles v. DPP*, but the criminal law should be certain and the adequacy of the information supplied should not be judged retrospectively on whether or not the motorist decides to exercise his option, especially when somebody could claim his option but after an hour is no longer prepared to wait any longer for the arrival of doctor and, instead, leaves the station. However, until overruled by the House of Lords, *Charles v. DPP* accurately sets out how the law is currently being applied by the judiciary, *e.g. Robinson v. DPP*, unreported, April 23, 1996.

In *Rush v. DPP* [1994] R.T.R. 268, it was held that the onus of proving lack of prejudice lay on the prosecution.

DPP v. Poole [1992] R.T.R. 177 considered the case of a motorist who, as the police began to explain his rights to him under section 8(2), did not listen but just walked away from the area where the Intoximeter was located. It was held that in those circumstances the police had discharged their obligation to inform him of his statutory option.

In *Berry v. DPP, The Times*, November 7, 1995, the defendant was too drunk to understand the statutory option when it was explained to him. It was held that he was not able to assert that he had not been informed of what his legal rights were. The rationale was that self-induced intoxication could not be relied upon as a defence to a drinking and driving charge.

(f) The Consequences of the Correct Procedure not Having Been Followed

In *Fox v. Chief Constable of Gwent* [1986] A.C. 281 the House of Lords held **14–29** that the legal requirements prescribed for the taking of a specimen must be correctly followed. Lord Bridge (at 298) expressly approved the decision in *Howard v. Hallett* [1984] R.T.R. 353, and found "the reasoning of Goff L.J. in that case wholly convincing". In that latter case, Robert Goff L.J. had held that for the result of an analysis to be relied upon in court by the prosecution, the sample must have been provided strictly in accordance with the statutory procedure. His Lordship (at 360H–J) expressed his view of the matter in the most forthright way:

"It would be a most extraordinary consequence if, where the Act lays down a careful statutory procedure for requiring a suspected motorist to provide specimens of breath and for analysing them and prosecuting them before a Court, it is possible to disregard that procedure altogether. I cannot believe that was the intention of the legislature." (The facts of that case are set out later in this chapter.)

Thus it is now settled law that the correct procedure must be followed at the police station, otherwise evidence of the result of an analysis of any specimen supplied by an accused will not be admissible before the court. In the words of Buxton J. in *R. v. Burton-upon-Trent, ex p. Woolley* [1995] R.T.R. 139, 152 B/C:

"There is no doubt, however, that evidence obtained under the procedure now contained in the [Road Traffic] Act of 1988 is a special case, and it has long been accepted that where the requirements of the Act have not been followed the courts have no power to admit the resulting evidence of the accused's condition, however (as in the present case) reliable, cogent and unchallenged that evidence is."

Despite Lord Bridge thinking that the contrary would be "most extraordinary", Buxton J. said that for the law to be as he had expounded it (in the above quotation) led to "a striking conclusion" (at 152B). It is submitted that the law on this point is perfectly logical and rational, as was fully explained in *Murray v. DPP* [1993] R.T.R. 209, 220L–221B by none other than the Deputy Chief Justice himself:

> "As Ralph Gibson L.J. recognised in *Wakeley v. Hymans* [1987] R.T.R. 49, this result means that unmeritorious defendants may sometimes be acquitted. But it should be remembered that this legislation, contrary to the general traditions of the criminal law but for good and social reasons, compels a suspected person to provide evidence against himself. It is, therefore, in our judgement, not surprising that a strict and compulsory code is laid down as a set of pre-conditions which must be fulfilled before any specimen produced by the defendant, which may condemn him at the hearing of the charge against him, can be adduced in evidence: no matter that there may be some instances where breach of the code occasions no discernible prejudice."

III. THE PROCEDURE FOR OBTAINING SPECIMENS WHEN USED IN EVIDENCE FOR OFFENCES UNDER SECTIONS 1 TO 3 AND 4 OF THE ROAD TRAFFIC ACT

14–30 In *R. v. Thorpe* [1972] R.T.R. 118, it was held that a specimen lawfully obtained under the Road Traffic Act, s.7 could be used in evidence in any prosecution, no matter what the offence was. However, until 1986 there were conflicting authorities as to whether a sample of body fluid was admissible in evidence on a charge of driving while unfit if it was not admissible on a charge of driving with excess alcohol. The legal position was put beyond doubt when Lord Bridge in *Fox v. Chief Constable of Gwent* [1986] A.C. 281, 360 stated:

> "For my part, I see no reason to doubt the decision of the Divisional Court in *Howard v. Hallett* [1984] R.T.R. 353, that on the true construction of [section 15(2) of the Road Traffic Offenders Act 1988] the admissibility of a specimen of breath, blood or urine in proceedings for an offence under sections [4] or [5] depends on the correct procedure prescribed by [section 7] for obtaining such a specimen having been correctly followed."

Thus in *Archbold v. Jones* [1986] R.T.R. 186, a case of driving while unfit, it was held that, once a motorist had exercised his option under section 8(2), the prosecution could not rely on the breath analysis as evidence of the amount of alcohol consumed by the defendant, even though the Home Office Forensic Service were unable, for technical reasons, to analyse satisfactorily the blood provided by him.

Thus, the strict procedure proscribed by the Road Traffic Act, s.7 is applicable to the taking of specimens which that section compels a motorist to provide, namely those supplied during the course of an investigation into an offence under sections 3A, 4 and 5. Section 7 does not give a power to require specimens when the police are investigating any other offence, including those prescribed by the first three sections of the Road Traffic Act and the common law offence of motor manslaughter. There is no need to, because if drink is suspected in any of those cases, then an offence under section 3A, 4 or 5 may also have been perpetrated, which the police can then also investigate at the same time and which will allow them to use their powers under section 7 to obtain a specimen.

However, there are no decided cases on the following point: if, during an **14–31** investigation into an offence under sections 3A, 4 or 5 of the Road Traffic Act, the wrong procedure is used for obtaining a specimen, can that specimen be used as evidence in a prosecution for an offence other than one of those? There are a few cases under the Road Safety Act and the Road Traffic Act 1972 before it was amended by the Transport Act 1981. The provisions of those statutes for taking compulsory specimens only applied to driving or being in charge of a vehicle with excess alcohol. So in *R. v. Palfrey, R. v. Sadler* [1970] 1 W.L.R. 416, the Court of Appeal was of the opinion that the strict procedures for obtaining a body fluid specimen laid down by Parliament only applied to such offences; and that the result of an analysis was admissible at the trial of any other motoring offence, even though the police acted outside or contrary to the statutory procedure. However, one of the judges in that case was Lord Parker C.J. who recognised the flaws in that decision, as he acknowledged in *R. v. Bove* [1970] 2 All E.R. 20, 24:

"Counsel for the Crown, in directing our attention to the observation in *R. v. Palfrey, R. v. Sadler*, has very frankly pointed out the difficulties of reconciling that with the many cases up to and including *Pinner v. Everett* [1969] 3 All E.R. 257, and also to the somewhat absurd results which would follow from section 3(3)(a) of the 1967 [Road Safety] Act if the requirement of a specimen for the purposes of that subsection meant a requirement irrespective of whether the conditions precedent had been fulfilled."

Neither of those cases was cited, or mentioned by, the Court of Appeal in **14–32** *R. v. Richards* [1975] 1 W.L.R. 131, which held that the statutory procedure for obtaining a sample only applied in the case of (what is now) a section 5 offence and that Parliament had not intended to alter the law regarding driving while unfit, where, prior to 1967, there had been no restrictions on the taking of a specimen. (Then it was not an offence to refuse to provide one but such a refusal could be used by the prosecution as corroboration of its case.) This pronouncement was *obiter*. The facts of that case were that the defendant had been convicted of driving while unfit but had been acquitted of driving with excess alcohol, since he had imbibed after he had left his car at the scene of the accident. A forensic scientist testified that, even allowing for this post-driving consumption, the amount the motorist had consumed prior to driving would have made him unfit. Thus, the court decided that there was no reason why a conviction under section 4 could not be based on the quantity of alcohol detected by an analysis, after, of course, making due allowance for any consumed since the driving. (The House of Lords had held in *Rowlands v. Hamilton* [1971] 1 W.L.R. 647 that, on the true construction of the Road Safety Act, the offence created by that statute was driving with excess alcohol as ascertained from an analysis. Consequently, the police could only rely upon the actual amount of alcohol detected by the analyst. If this also included any consumed after the motorist had ceased to drive, then the specimen did not show what the alcohol level was at the time of driving, so the accused had to be acquitted.)

14–33   In *R. v. Trump* [1980] R.T.R. 274, the motorist had been unlawfully arrested and therefore had been wrongly told at the police station that he would be prosecuted if he did not give a blood specimen. Solely for that reason he provided such a sample, which was used as evidence to show that he was unfit to drive. The Court of Appeal held that on such a charge there was no requirement for the police to follow any statutory procedure. As the evidence only came into existence after the commission of the offence and was provided by the accused, the court accepted that under *R. v. Sang* [1980] A.C. 402, the judge had possessed a discretion to refuse to admit the result of the analysis in evidence but stated that, had he done so, he would have wrongly exercised that discretion. That decision must be contrasted with *R. v. Payne* [1963] 1 W.L.R. 637. There the accused was asked if he would consent to being looked at by a doctor to see if he was all right. He was also told that the police surgeon would not carry out an examination to see if his condition was due to drink. The doctor did just that, as he was unaware of what had been said to the defendant. The Court of Appeal ruled that the trial judge was wrong to allow him to give evidence as to whether or not the appellant had been under the influence of drink, since the latter might not have consented to being examined but for what he had been told by the police.

The only reason that can distinguish these two appeals is that nothing should be done to deter a person who might need medical treatment from seeing a doctor and that, accordingly, a prosecutor will be held to any representation made by the police about the purpose, etc., of the medical practitioner's examination.

14–34   If a person was charged with three offences, namely, [1] death by dangerous driving, [2] death by careless driving and [3] careless driving, it would be illogical if an analysis of a specimen obtained in breach of section 7 would be admissible evidence on charges [1] and [3], but not on [2]. (Nor should it make any difference if the Director of Public Prosecutions omitted to charge offence number [2] in order to overcome the problem.) Such an approach is in line with the above quoted view of Lord Parker C.J. in *R. v. Bove*, above, but, like all legal points, a definitive answer can only be obtained after a court has pronounced on it. It raises the whole issue (which is not particular to motorists) of how the courts should treat illegally obtained evidence. Should the Crown be allowed to adduce evidence which was obtained by a threat of prosecution when, unknown to the defendant, the threat was an idle one and when such evidence would never have been obtained if he had known the true legal position? This is an issue which could fill a book all on its own.

IV. RELIANCE ON THE WRONG ANALYSIS

(a) INTRODUCTION

The fact that a satisfactory sample has been provided does not auto- **14–35** matically mean that the prosecution can rely upon it if more than the requisite number had been obtained. A conviction will only be secured if the prosecution adduces evidence to the court of the result of the analysis of the correct specimen and not just of any specimen.

(b) OBTAINING A BLOOD ANALYSIS RATHER THAN RELYING ON ONE OF BREATH

Normally a constable can only require a specimen of breath and not one of **14–36** body fluid: see Road Traffic Act, s.7(3) and the Transport and Works Act, ss. 31(3) and (4). If the breathalyser is discovered not to have been working correctly, then a body fluid sample can be demanded, even though the motorist has already supplied two apparently satisfactory breath specimens which have been analysed: see Road Traffic Act, s.7(3) and the Transport and Works Act, s.31(5). What is the legal position if an officer mistakenly believes that the Intoximeter had malfunctioned? If that belief is a reasonable one and blood or urine is then provided, any conviction can only be for excess alcohol in that fluid: see *Badkin v. DPP* [1988] R.T.R. 401. An acquittal must still result even if, for any reason, the blood specimen turns out be inadmissible in evidence: see *McLellan v. DPP* [1996] R.T.R. 401. In *Badkin's case*, above, Glidewell L.J stated the above principle to be applicable if the blood sample had been analysed. He did not consider the possibility of the specimen not being analysed. In accordance with *McLellan v. DPP* and *Archbold v. Jones*, above, it is submitted that this principle also applies once the body fluid has been supplied to the police, even though the latter do not, or cannot, have it analysed. (It is submitted that the *obiter dicta* of Scott Baker J. in *Hague v. DPP* [1995] T.L.R. 586 to the contrary should not be followed.) If the belief about the malfunctioning of the breathalyser was an unreasonable one, the prosecution must be based on the breath analysis: see *Evans v. DPP*, *The Times*, May 30, 1996. This applies even if the motorist was not asked to exhale into an Intoximeter or Camic, as happened in *Stokes v. Sayers* [1988] R.T.R. 89, where the blood analysis revealed an alcohol level well in excess of the prescribed limit.

In *Hague v. DPP*, above, the defendant's two breath specimens were **14–37** analysed. At the time, the constable mistakenly thought that the machine had not properly calibrated itself and, accordingly, required a blood specimen, which was declined. The conviction for driving with excess alcohol in the breath was upheld by the High Court which stated that so long as no other specimen was provided the police could always rely on the breath analysis. The rationale of that decision was based on the Road Traffic Offenders Act, s.15(2) that the proportion of any alcohol found in a specimen shall in all cases be taken into account. To the same effect is

Burridge v. East [1986] R.T.R. 326. In such circumstances it is submitted that there could not be a conviction for failing to supply a specimen of body fluid, since (to quote defence counsel in *Cracknell v. Willis* [1988] A.C. 450, 459G/H):

> "The two offences [s.5 and s.6] were intended to be alternatives and that the Act should be construed so as to provide that they are mutually exclusive."

That submission was accepted by the House of Lords (*ibid.*, at 459G/H). In that case the defendant was charged with offences under both sections 5(1)(a) and 7(6) because he had supplied only a single breath specimen, but it is submitted that defence counsel's submissions are of universal application.

(c) Relying on Breath After Body Fluid Supplied Pursuant to Section 8(2) of the Road Traffic Act 1988 or Section 32(2) of the Transport and Works Act 1992

14–38 The reason that breath and body fluid samples are both provided is usually because the analysis of the former showed an alcohol content not exceeding 50µg, which gives the motorist an opportunity to have it substituted by an analysis of his body fluid (see Road Traffic Act, s.8[2] and Transport and Works Act, s.32[2]). If he does exercise that right and provides a specimen of blood or urine, then there can be no prosecution for excess alcohol in breath (see *Broadbent v. High* [1985] R.T.R. 359, 362, *per* Watkins L.J.). Nor can evidence be given as to the amount of alcohol in his breath, save for the sole purpose of showing why a specimen of some other substance was provided. The above statement of the law still applies even if the prosecution are unable to analyse the body fluid, as happened in *Archbold v. Jones*, above, where the sample became contaminated; or where the correct procedure for the taking of that specimen, as laid down in *DPP v. Warren*, above, was not followed, as occurred in *Wakeley v. Hyams* [1987] R.T.R. 49.

V. MULTIPLE BREATH SAMPLES

(a) Different Operating Cycles

14–39 The Road Traffic Act, s.7(1) (a) and the Transport and Works Act, s.31(1)(a) compel a person to provide two specimens of breath for analysis, whilst sections 8(1) and 32(1) respectively of those statutes enact that, of any two samples provided, the one with the lower proportion of alcohol must be used and the other disregarded. If both the breath analyses are the same, then either is admissible in evidence: see *Moscrop v. Wiseman*, unreported, July 4, 1988. However, sometimes more or less than two specimens of breath have been provided at the conclusion of the breathalyser procedure. This situation occurred in *Howard v. Hallet* [1984]

R.T.R. 353, where an inexperienced operator, having obtained the first reading, failed to ask for a second sample in the same operating cycle so that the machine closed down. After consultation with a senior officer he decided to start afresh and this time obtained two more specimens. When the matter came to court, the prosecutor relied upon the analysis of the second sample as being the lower of the last two to be provided. During cross-examination, the sergeant had said that the first reading was the lowest of all the three results. The High Court said that in order to comply with section 8(1), the prosecution had to rely upon the lower of the first two analyses. As no evidence was given of what the actual amount of alcohol in the first specimen was, the conviction had to be quashed. (For all the court knew, it could have been 35μg or even less.) The point was not taken by the prosecution that unless the Intoximeter (and the Camic) received and analysed two breath samples in one operating cycle, the device would not calibrate itself a second time; and, without such evidence, the result of the first breath analysis could not be considered reliable. Therefore it was not a valid specimen on which a conviction could be founded. The second and third were in fact the only two that could be relied upon to prove the amount of alcohol consumed.

In *Chief Constable of Avon and Somerset Constabulary v. Creech* [1986] **14–40** R.T.R. 87 the driver provided only one sample initially, but thereafter provided two more. The three readings were 95μg, 98μg and 100μg. At the trial no reliance was placed by the prosecutor on any printout and the operator gave oral evidence in relation to the first two samples. The justices acquitted on the basis that the two relied upon had been supplied in different operating cycles of the machine and that did not accord with the statutory procedure. Mustill L.J. (at 93G *et seq.*), with certain reservations about applying his conclusions to different facts, set out his understanding of the law to be as follows (the author's commentary is interposed in square brackets):

> "(a) The requirement in section 10(2) [now section 15(2) of the Road Traffic Offenders Act 1988] that the proportion of alcohol in a specimen of breath shall in all cases be taken into account must be read as referring only to specimens validly obtained, having regard to the express and implied requirements of the Act, at any rate so far as concerns reliance upon the specimen by the prosecution. [This was indeed the view of the House of Lords in *Fox v. Chief Constable of Gwent* [1986] A.C. 281.] (It may be that if a specimen came into existence in a manner not conforming to the statute, it could be relied upon by the defendant. We leave this question for consideration in a case where it is in point.)
>
> (b) The two specimens of breath referred to in section 8(6) [now s.8(1)] are specimens validly provided. [So in *Denny v. DPP* [1990] R.T.R. 417 where, after two readings had been obtained, the second calibration was incorrect, the police were entitled to take the appellant to another police station and there require two further breath specimens.]

(c) Since the constable has power to require no more than two specimens (section 8(1)(a) [now s.7(1)(a)]), once he has validly required and validly obtained two specimens of breath any third and subsequent specimens provided pursuant to a purported request are not valid, and are therefore not to be taken into account for the purposes of section 8(6) [now s.8(1)] or other provisions of the Act. [In *Revel v. Jordon* [1983] R.T.R. 497, and *R. v. Broomhead* [1975] R.T.R. 558, it was held that if a motorist did not at first provide sufficient breath to enable the device to measure the alcohol, the police were always entitled to give him another chance to try to do so. There the device was a roadside Alcotest breathalyser, but the same principle would apply in the case of a police station Intoximeter.]

(d) The ascertaining by means of an approved device of the proportion of alcohol in a specimen must be performed in conformity with the operating procedures of the device in question. Any deviation from these procedures sufficient to put in question the accuracy of any resulting measurement will invalidate the analysis, and make it unavailable for use in the procedures created by statute."

His Lordship accordingly concluded that there was no statutory requirement for the two specimens to be provided within one operating cycle of the instrument. That conclusion is legally correct but in practice erroneous, as the Intoximeter will not calibrate itself a second time unless both specimens are provided in the same cycle. Evidence of a second successful calibration, prior to the machine closing itself down at the termination of the relevant operating cycle, is a *sine qua non* of the admissibility of the result of any breath analysis (see, *e.g. Owen v. Chesters* [1985] R.T.R. 191, and *Mayon v. DPP* [1988] R.T.R. 281). The term "calibration" is used in the text as that is the expression used by the courts, although strictly speaking it is not a calibration but (to employ the manufacturer's terminology) "a standard check": see section 13–13.

14–41   Defences have been put forward based upon the argument that the police have simply failed to follow the statutory procedure because they had obtained more than the two specimens mentioned in the Act. In *Anderton v. O'Donnell*, unreported, October 4, 1985, the driver provided a sample at the beginning of the Intoximeter's cycle but then failed to provide the second before the device closed itself down. The officer restarted the instrument and requested O'Donnell to provide two samples in the same operating cycle, all of which exceeded the legal limit. The trial court accepted the submission of no case to answer on the simple basis that the officer had exceeded his powers in requiring three samples. That argument was dealt with by Lloyd L.J. who pointed out that once two samples had been successfully analysed as required by section 11(3) of the Road Traffic Act 1988, then any further specimens provided were irrelevant. Accordingly, it was held that the police could rely upon the first two samples obtained to secure a conviction. The point was not taken that the first result could not be considered to be reliable because there had been no second calibration by the Intoximeter in that first operating cycle, so that in fact the only two reliable analyses were those performed on the second and third specimens.

VI. A SINGLE BREATH SPECIMEN

In *Cracknell v. Willis* [1988] A.C. 450, the House of Lords overruled a **14–42** number of High Court cases and held that, where a person provided only one breath sample, the police could not rely upon its result to find a conviction under The Road Traffic Act, s.5, although the defendant could be convicted of an offence under section 7(6) (*i.e.* failure to provide a specimen). Their Lordships did hold that the result of the single analysis could be taken into account when deciding upon the sentence. In *Oldfield v. Anderton* [1986] R.T.R. 314, Tudor Evans J. was of the opinion that on a charge of failing to supply a specimen, the justices may be told that one sample had been successfully provided and this will enable them to form a view about the non-provision of a second one; but they should not be told the level of alcohol in that specimen because, if it was high, it could prejudice them against the defendant when deciding whether or not he had a reasonable excuse. It is also submitted that there is another reason why such evidence is inadmissible, namely that the result of an analysis is only admissible to prove the alcohol concentration in the specimen if the machine is proved to have calibrated itself after the motorist has finished blowing into it (see *Owen v. Chesters*, above). However, the Intoximeter and the Camic will not do this unless two satisfactory samples have been provided. In the case of large readings it is (in the author's experience) the invariable practice of Crown prosecutors to adduce in evidence the amount of the reading to support their contention that once the defendant realised just how high his alcohol level was, he thought it best not to supply a second specimen, but had been perfectly able to do so if he had wanted. As this is always done and since, apart from the actual non-provision of the second specimen, there is no evidential basis for such a contention, and bearing in mind the standard tactics of the Government Legal Service, as revealed by the Scott Inquiry into the Matrix-Churchill case, the author wonders if what is invariably the standard reason put forward for informing the court of the amount of the single Intoximeter reading, is not, in reality, an attempt to overcome the dicta of Tudor Evans J.

VII. NO READINGS AFTER BLOWING INTO THE BREATHALYSER

In *Morrison v. DPP*, October 12, 1995, the appellant had blown in twice but **14–43** no readings were obtained. He then blew two more times and obtained two readings. These were admissible in evidence as they were the only two results obtained. The failure to obtain readings on the first two exhalations was of no relevance. To the same effect is *Denny v. DPP* (see above).

C. Denying, depriving or not informing the defendant of his options under the Road Traffic Act, s.8(2) and the Transport and Works Act, s.32(2)

I. THE REQUISITE INFORMATION TO BE IMPARTED TO THE DRIVER

14–44 This has been set out in the preceding part of this chapter.

II. CANCELLING THE OPTION

14–45 In *Hope v. DPP* [1992] R.T.R. 305, it was held that a defendant can always change his mind and not exercise his option, in which case he can be prosecuted, but only for excess alcohol in breath. A constable can only treat the motorist as no longer wishing to exercise his option if he is told that in unequivocal terms. A short time after agreeing to provide blood, the appellant said that, to save the police the trouble of getting a doctor, he would supply urine. The court held that the appellant had not been saying that he had abandoned altogether the opportunity of providing a specimen under section 8(2).

III. INFORMING MOTORIST THAT OPTION UNDER SECTION 8(2) OR SECTION 32(2) IS MANDATORY

14–46 If a defendant provides a specimen of breath which is found to contain not more than 50µg of alcohol, it must be made plain to him that he merely has an option to provide a replacement specimen of body fluid and is under no legal obligation to do so. If that is not done, the prosecutor can not rely on either sample to obtain a conviction and there must be an acquittal. This happened in *Wakeley v. Hyams* [1987] R.T.R. 49. That was a case in which both litigants were police officers. The result of the analysis of the defendant's breath showed that its alcoholic content was 50µg. However, he was required to give a blood sample, instead of being offered the option of providing one, if he so chose. That proved fatal to the prosecution, although both analyses showed a level well over the statutory limit. The reasoning was that, although the reading did not exceed 50µg, the defendant had not been given the option of voluntarily substituting his breath sample with an alternative specimen and therefore any evidence from the Intoximeter was inadmissible. The result of his blood fluid analysis could also not be placed before the court, since none of the conditions precedent to the making of a mandatory requirement for such a fluid was present in this case.

In *Stevens v. DPP*, unreported, December 9, 1992, Rose L.J. held that the acquittal in *Wakeley v. Hyams* was based solely on the fact that there had been no mention of urine, only of blood. Where Rose L.J. obtained this idea is unknown, as this basis for allowing the appeal does not appear anywhere in the judgment.

However, *Wakeley v. Hyams* must be contrasted with *Jones v. DPP* [1991] **14–47** R.T.R. 41, where the constable at first gave the defendant the option of providing a blood or urine sample, as the lower Intoximeter reading was 45µg. The defendant opted to supply urine and it was only then that the officer told her that she had to give such a sample or face being prosecuted, as in the meantime he had concluded that the machine was unreliable. Schiemann J. held that the officer had been acting unreasonably in the conclusion he drew about the breathalyser (see section 12–11) and, therefore, the accused had the benefit of a section 8(2) option. Nevertheless, the High Court upheld the conviction because the motorist had been given the option of having her sample of breath replaced by one of blood or urine and she had chosen to provide the latter; what happened thereafter was irrelevant. In the words of Schiemann J. (at 48):

"In my judgment the justices were right in concluding that, since the defendant had claimed that the breath sample should be replaced by a urine sample and had provided such a sample, the requirements of section 8 are fulfilled."

The reasoning behind that decision was approved of and followed in *DPP v. Winstanley* [1993] R.T.R. 222. It would have been another matter if an accused were to testify that, but for the threat of prosecution, he might have decided before the doctor's arrival not to have bothered to exercise his option under section 8(2) or 32(2), as the case might be. The reason for this is, first, that he was no longer exercising his preference and, secondly, by virtue of section 15(4) of the Road Traffic Offenders Act 1988 (and the Transport and Works Act, s.38[5]), the result of a blood analysis is inadmissible unless the sample is taken with the consent of the accused. If the consent is obtained by duress and misrepresentation (*e.g.* an erroneous threat of prosecution), then such duress, etc., negates the consent. In *R. v. Palfrey, R. v. Sadler* [1970] 1 W.L.R. 416, the Court of Appeal recognised the invalidity of a motorist's consent in such circumstances, but made it clear (at 15) that in such a case it would be for "the accused person to raise the issue and show there was substance to it". It is submitted that the correct test is laid down in *R. v. Payne* [1963] 1 W.L.R. 637, namely that such evidence should be excluded if the defendant "might not have given his consent" had he known the true facts. It should be noted that there are no similar statutory provisions about urine specimens having to be given with consent but, if such were obtained by illegal threats, the court could always exercise its power of exclusion under section 78 of the Police and Criminal Evidence Act 1984; (see section 14–88).

(a) Doctor's Fees

14–48 The police must not, of course, do anything to discourage a motorist from exercising his option under section 8(2). In *Hammond v. Hunter*, unreported, March 6, 1985, the officer told the driver (who had registered 42µg on the Intoximeter) of his right under section 8(2) to opt to provide a blood sample, but added that the driver would have to pay for calling the doctor out to take such a sample. The defendant testified that he took this piece of information to mean that he would have to pay there and then, but he did not have any money with him and so declined his option. The justices acquitted him. The decision was upheld in the High Court. The rationale of the decision was that this piece of information had effectively destroyed the driver's freedom to choose to substitute a sample of blood for that of breath. However, in *Carberry v. Bettinson*, unreported, June 17, 1986, but mentioned at [1987] Crim. L.R. 420, the conviction was upheld when the defendant declined to exercise his option under section 8(2) to provide a blood specimen because he had been told that if the result of the analysis showed him to be over the limit, he would have to pay the doctor's fee of about £27. The difference between the two cases was that a demand for an immediate payment would prevent freedom of choice but such would not be lost through the incurring of a contingent liability which would only become an actual debt if it later transpired that there was a finding of guilt, which fact would not be known until a subsequent date when the specimen had been analysed. However, there may be cases where a person of limited means could well be deterred from exercising his rights through the mere possibility that he might have to pay money in the future which he could not afford.

(b) Misleading Information

14–49 In *Sharp v. Spencer* [1987] Crim. L.R. 420, the motorist asked if exercising her option under section 8(2) would make any difference, to which the reply was "probably not". Watkins L.J. held that the accused had been told what her rights were and that the constable's reply in no way removed that choice. However, as a result of that advice, the defendant did not opt to provide any body fluid for analysis. In his Lordship's view, the officer's reply was perfectly fair and involved no bullying. It is submitted that the answer was anything but fair. According to Home Office statistics for 1989, 22 per cent of those who exercised their option under section 8(2) were found to have a blood or urine alcohol concentration below the prescribed limit and 24 per cent in 1991. (After that year the Home Office stopped collecting and publishing such statistics). Consequently, the information given to the defendant was misleading, as she was deprived of a greater than one in five chance of an acquittal by being given erroneous information. However, it does not appear that their court was made aware of how advantageous the option under section 8(2) was to a driver. Should such evidence be forthcoming in a future case, then a court would be entitled to distinguish *Sharp v. Spencer*.

This reason why nearly a quarter of the people who exercise their option were acquitted is no doubt due to the time factor involved. A man's alcohol level begins to decline on average about an hour after finishing his last drink, although this can vary from 20 minutes to two hours or more depending on the duration needed for complete absorption into the bloodstream to occur. Prior to the elapse of that time, a person's alcohol level will still be increasing. (This topic is considered in greater detail in Chapter 9, above.) Until a breath specimen is taken (and this does not occur until after arrest, transportation to the police station and booking in), it will not be known whether or not the statutory option has arisen and whether it will be exercised. Only then is the doctor sent for and further time will elapse until his arrival. If the police opt for a urine specimen, then up to an hour is allowed for its provision (see the Road Traffic Act, s.7(5) and the Transport and Works Act, s.9). Table A9 of the Paton Report sets out the time interval between first breath analysis and the giving of the blood or urine specimen.

Table A9   **14–50**

Time interval (mins)	Frequency	Relative cumulative	
		Frequency (%)	Frequency (%)
0–4	71	0.6	0.6
5–9	138	1.1	1.7
10–14	273	2.2	3.9
15–19	532	4.3	8.2
20–24	1,131	9.1	17.3
25–29	1,700	13.6	30.9
30–34	1,760	14.1	45.0
35–39	1,631	13.1	58.1
40–44	1,324	10.6	68.7
45–49	962	7.7	76.4
50–54	715	5.7	82.1
55–59	519	4.2	86.3
60–64	413	3.3	89.6
65–69	279	2.2	91.8
70–74	245	2.0	93.8
75–79	163	1.3	95.1
80–84	142	1.1	96.2
85–89	101	0.8	97.0
90–94	97	0.8	97.8
95–99	59	0.5	98.3
100–104	39	0.3	98.6
105–109	37	0.3	98.9
110–114	28	0.2	99.1
115–119	27	0.2	99.3
120 and above or not known	104	0.7	100.0
Total 12,490			

14–51   In *Hobbs v. Clark* [1988] R.T.R. 36, the defendant, whose breath reading was 50μg, was told that he could give blood "to confirm" the Intoximeter reading. Roch J. (at 41) said that he would not have allowed the appeal solely because of this. However, in *DPP v. Warren* [1993] A.C. 319 the House of Lords took the opposite view. In the words of Lord Bridge (at 330E):

> "The next and perhaps most important case is *Hobbs v. Clark* [1988] R.T.R. 36. This was again a driver's option case. After taking breath specimens, neither of which contained more than 50 microgrammes of alcohol in 100 millilitres of breath, the only indication by the constable given to the driver of his right to provide a replacement specimen was in these words:
>
> 'You may have a doctor called if you so wish to take a sample of blood for the purpose of having it analysed to confirm the readings given by the machine. Do you wish to do this?'
>
> Not surprisingly, the defendant declined this offer. Now, in any view, this was both an inadequate and a misleading indication to the driver of the nature of his right under section 8(2) and what the exercise of that right would involve and I agree entirely with the decision of the Divisional Court allowing the defendant's appeal from his conviction of an offence under section 5 by justices based on the admission in evidence of the breath specimen."

In accordance with the views expressed by Lord Bridge, the information given to the defendant in *Sharp v. Spencer* was also misleading and the case should no longer be regarded as sound law.

In *Rush v. DPP* [1994] R.T.R. 268, it was held that the burden of proof was on the prosecution to show that no misleading information had been given.

IV. FAILING TO AVAIL ONESELF OF THE OPTION

14–52   A failure to provide an alternative specimen under section 8(2) of the Road Traffic Act automatically allows the prosecution to rely upon the breath analysis, no matter what the reason was for not providing a specimen of body fluid, at any rate according to the case of *DPP v. Winstanley* [1993] R.T.R. 222 and *Andrews v. DPP* [1992] R.T.R. 1, although that latter case recognised the discretion of the justices under PACE, s.78 to exclude any evidence of the breath analysis. In *Winstanley's* case the constable had asked for blood but, as he could not find an available doctor, he then required urine. Because the defendant had been to the toilet while the police were trying to obtain a doctor, he was unable to provide two specimens of urine. The High Court held that the Director of Public Prosecutions could rely upon the result of the breath analysis. It is submitted that this case was wrongly decided. The defendant was physically unable to supply urine and since at all times he was willing to supply blood, then if the police did not make available a doctor, surely the motorist had not properly been given his option?

D. Failure to produce sufficient evidence of the results of an analysis of a defendant's specimen

I. THE EVIDENCE

To prove the result of an analysis, the prosecution can either rely upon the **14–53** normal rules of evidence or upon documents served under the provisions of section 16 of the Road Traffic Offenders Act 1988 or the Transport and Works Act, s.35 (see Chapter 15). As well as proving the results of the analysis, it is also essential for the prosecution to establish that the sample which was analysed did indeed emanate from the defendant, as Watkins L.J. emphasised in *Bentley v. Chief Constable of Northumbria* [1984] R.T.R. 276, 281:

> "It was imperative, of course, to satisfy one of the essential require-
> ments of section 5, under which the information was laid, that the
> defendant was identified as the person who had acted in contravention of
> that section."

The result of the analysis will show that somebody's alcohol level exceeded the limit prescribed by Parliament. As was illustrated by *Dickson v. Atkins* [1972] R.T.R. 209, the material question for the court is whether the specimen supplied by the man in the dock can be identified with that to which the certificate (or other evidence) of analysis relates.

II. HEARSAY

(a) COMMON LAW

Body fluid analysis

In accordance with the normal rules of evidence, what is written on the **14–54** container in which the blood or urine is stored is, of course, hearsay evidence and will not be admissible to prove the truth of the writing. A good example of this is *Patel v. Comptroller of Customs and Excise* [1966] A.C. 356, where it was held that the markings on some packing crates, namely "Produce of Morocco", was no evidence that their contents came from Morocco. In the opinion of the Privy Council (at 365):

> "The decision of the House [in *Myres v. DPP* [1965] A.C. 1001],
> however, makes it clear beyond doubt that the list of exceptions to the
> hearsay rule cannot be extended judicially to include such things as
> markings or labels."

In *Paterson v. DPP* [1990] R.T.R. 329, the sample of blood received by the Home Office laboratory was in a phial with a label affixed to it containing various details, *e.g.* the time the sample was taken, etc. The truth of that information was proved by other testimony. However, the only evidence about the container on this point was that the custody sergeant had affixed a label to it but he did not say what, if anything, he had written on it. Accordingly, the defence argued that there was no link between the container sent by the police to the laboratory and the one examined there a few days later. The prosecutor replied that the justices could draw inferences from what was written on the label but that suggestion was not acceptable to Neil L.J. (at 343):

> "There is clearly force in that submission, but, as it seems to me, this being a criminal matter, the correct method of proof should be followed. It was not and [prosecuting counsel] very fairly concedes that there is a gap in the evidence. He suggests that it can be filled. But I think the matter is put beyond doubt by the fact that . . . on the label the police station concerned was Ashfordy Street, where [as] . . . the defendant was at Charles Street.
>
> In the circumstances I think the proof was not satisfactory in this case and the defendant is entitled to have the benefit of the lack of the correct procedure having been followed . . . I think that this appeal must succeed."

(b) CRIMINAL JUSTICE ACT 1988

14–55 Section 24 of the Criminal Justice Act 1988 (see section 16–11) will not assist as that section does not apply to documents prepared for the prosecution in question. It is obvious that labelling the specimen was part of the process of obtaining evidence for a possible criminal trial. To prevent a gap in the evidence, it is advisable to tender evidence of the markings applied to the phial containing the body fluid at the police station and then show that the same markings were on the one received by the analyst; see *R. v. Orrell* [1972] R.T.R. 14, where it was also held that it was not necessary for the prosecution to have to produce the capsule or its label in court. If the evidence does not show that exactly the same markings were on the phial received in the laboratory as were written on the label affixed to the one into which the police surgeon had put the defendant's blood or urine, then it is a question of fact whether or not the markings bear such similarity that the capsule from which the analysed body fluid came must indeed be the same one as that in which the defendant's specimen was placed, and that one of the witnesses, normally the police officer, must have made an error in his account of what was written on the container. In *Dickson v. Atkins* [1972] R.T.R. 209 the label showed the appellant's Christian name as "Joan", instead of "John" and the wrong surname of the arresting officer, namely "Faul" instead of "Gaul". The conviction was upheld on appeal.

In *R. v. Shaw* [1974] R.T.R. 458, there was no evidence that a label had ever been affixed to the container of blood, merely that it had been posted to the forensic science laboratory. There was a certificate of analysis which identified the sample by the details shown on its capsule. These corresponded exactly with the facts given in evidence by the police officer. The

Court of Appeal held that the jury were entitled to draw the inference that the sample analysed was indeed the defendant's blood. It is submitted that this decision undermines the force of *Myres v. DPP* [1965] A.C. 1001, regarding hearsay evidence. However, as the law stands, if all the details on the label correspond with the facts about the time, date, place and officer involved in the taking of the sample (as proved by other evidence) and there is evidence that the sample was posted to the laboratory, then those details on the label raise an inference that the specimen came from the appellant.

III. BREATH ANALYSES

The printout is real evidence, not hearsay; see section 15–02 *et seq*. There **14–56** must be evidence that the printout refers to the defendant. That can be proved either by oral evidence or by a certificate pursuant to either section 16(1) of the Road Traffic Offenders Act 1988 or the Transport and Works Act, s.35(1). The signature of the defendant on the printout is not sufficient evidence *ipso facto* to prove that the breath analysis was the defendant's; see *Garner v. DPP* [1990] R.T.R. 208, 216B. However, nowadays that would raise a prima facie case from which the justices could draw an adverse inference against the defendant if he did not give evidence (see the Criminal Justice and Public Order Act 1994, s.24; and *R. v. DPP*, *ex p. Mansfield* (1995) 160 J.P. 472 (a case concerning a certificate of conviction containing the same names as the accused)). The other way of proving the results of a breath analysis is by the testimony of a witness present during the test, that the readings on the device's video-display unit referred to the defendant's breath.

IV. HOME OFFICE CERTIFICATES OF ANALYSIS

It should be noted when considering the above authorities that the Home **14–57** Office certificate of analysis used by the police only identifies the sample by what is written on the label. It would, of course, be different if the certificate said "blood sample of Mr X contains 100mg of alcohol" as then the certificate would have identified the sample as actually being Mr X's and such evidence would be admissible under section 16 of the Road Traffic Offenders Act 1988 or the Transport and Works Act, s.35(1). However, the Home Office lawyers are well aware that their scientists' knowledge of whose blood is in the container is based solely on the label and it is for that reason that the certificate identifies the sample solely by what is written on its label. Nowhere does the certificate refer to the truth or otherwise of that writing.

V. FURTHER EVIDENCE AFTER THE CLOSE OF CASE

(a) AFTER SUBMISSION OF NO CASE TO ANSWER

If, after adducing all the evidence, a prosecutor has not established that the **14–58** sample analysed was the one provided by the accused, then it is possible for a submission of no case to answer to result in the acquittal of the defendant. The danger of such a submission is that the prosecution might seek to reopen its case to overcome the deficiency.

This happened in *MacDonald v. Skelt* [1985] R.T.R. 321, where it was in fact the magistrates who actually invited the prosecutor to call further evidence to defeat a submission of no case to answer made immediately after the close of his case. The High Court held that it was permissible, after a submission of no case to answer, for the justices to allow the prosecution there and then to call the requisite evidence to prove the necessary connection between the specimen analysed and that supplied by the defendant, so that the court could be satisfied that they were one and the same sample. It is submitted that a more appropriate course of action by a Bench in such circumstances was taken in *R. v. Uxbridge Justices, ex p. Conlon* [1979] Crim. L.R. 250. There the justices refused to allow the prosecutrix to call any evidence after she had closed her case. The High Court upheld that decision and said that magistrates should avoid giving the appearance of leaning towards the prosecution.

In *R. v. Central Criminal Court, ex p. Garnier* [1988] R.T.R. 42, after a submission of no case to answer, Judge Argyle had said that there was not sufficient evidence to convict, but he would not uphold the submission at that time. He then adjourned the hearing to a later date. The High Court granted prohibition preventing the Director of Public Prosecutions from calling any further evidence at the adjourned hearing. Its rationale was twofold. First, exactly the same point had been taken in petty sessions and secondly it involved an adjournment to another date. (There was no mention in the judgment that the affidavit evidence showed that the judge had told the main prosecution witness what facts were needed to raise a prima facie case and that it was for him to go to see if he could obtain such evidence!)

In *R. v. Francis* [1990] 1 W.L.R. 1264, the Court of Appeal declined to interfere with the trial judge's discretion to allow further evidence from the Crown after a submission of no case to answer and rejected defence counsel's argument that, even if the court had a discretion to allow the prosecution to reopen its case after such a submission, the exercise of that discretion in the prosecution's favour would only lead to such submissions not being made. Instead, the point would only be taken by the defence in their final speeches, after they had called their evidence. The reason for this, with which the court agreed, was that the later an application to reopen was made, the more likely it was to be refused. Lloyd L.J. (at 229) stated:

> "We would echo what was said in *R. v. Doran* [(1972) 56 Cr.App.R.429, 436–438] that the discretion [to admit further evidence] is one which should be exercised . . . on the rarest of occasions."

(b) AFTER THE COMMENCEMENT OF DEFENCE CASE

14–59 Once the defence case has opened, the prosecution can always call or recall a witness to deal with matters which have arisen *ex improviso, e.g.* to rebut an alibi. In *R. v. Pilcher* (1974) 60 Cr.App.R. 1, Lord Widgery C.J. said that the discretion to allow further prosecution evidence after the defence had started its case was a very limited one and that the judge in that case had exercised his discretion wrongly by allowing further evidence on the grounds that the interests of justice would be served by all the available evidence being called. In *R. v. Tate* [1977] R.T.R. 17, the Court of Appeal did not interfere with the discretion of the trial judge who allowed another analyst to be called by the Crown after the close of the defence case (the latter had called no evidence). Before the close of its case, the prosecution had called such a witness but his test results were based partly on an analysis carried out by another forensic scientist. The Court of Appeal said that the extra testimony only related to facts already placed before the jury when some of the evidence had been hearsay. It is submitted that this was correct. It was merely explaining how the first witness had calculated the amount of alcohol in the accused's blood. It is submitted that it would be another matter if the extra evidence dealt with a new point.

Until *R. v. Francis* [1990] 1 W.L.R. 1264, there were a number of cases which appeared to support the proposition that, once the defence case had opened, the prosecution could not call further witnesses except to deal with unforeseen matters or to prove a mere technicality. The latter does not include failure on the part of the police to follow the correct procedure; see *Wareing v. DPP* (section 23–14). Indeed, in view of that decision, it is hard to see when a technicality could play any part in an acquittal for drinking and driving. In *R. v. Godstone JJ., ex p. Dickson* [1971] Crim. L.R. 270, the prosecution called evidence of how a blood sample had been labelled, and produced a certificate of analysis under what is now section 16 of the Road Traffic Offenders Act 1988. After the defendant had started to give evidence, it was suggested by him that the certificate of analysis referred to somebody else. The trial was adjourned to enable the analyst to attend to give oral evidence. The High Court granted an order of prohibition to prevent the forensic scientist being called by the prosecution or the justices at the resumed hearing. The High Court held that the justices had no power to allow the prosecution to call further evidence after the close of the defence case, unless it was evidence in rebuttal.

In *R. v. Francis* [1990] 1 W.L.R. 1264, the Court of Appeal stated that the **14–60** discretion to allow further evidence was flexible and was not confined in any way, although it should only be rarely exercised. This is clearly an extension of the discretion but this pronouncement was *obiter*, as it was dealing with a discretion exercised after a submission of no case to answer. Whether it will be followed in later cases remains to be seen. In *James v. DPP* [1992] R.T.R. 312, 317H–J, the High Court stated that the prosecution should "normally" be precluded from calling further evidence once it had closed its case. Also, in no report of any case has rule 13 of the Magistrates' Courts Rules 1981 or its predecessors been mentioned. (However the note of the judgment in *ex p. Dickson* in the Criminal Law Review is only four lines, so maybe rule 13 was mentioned by the court.) That rule states:

> "(3) At the conclusion of the evidence, if any, for the defence, the prosecution may call evidence to rebut that evidence.

(4) At the conclusion of the evidence for the defence and the evidence, if any, in rebuttal, the accused may address the Court if he has not already done so."

Thus the Rules only allow testimony in rebuttal to be called by the prosecution after it has closed its case. "Evidence in rebuttal" means evidence to contradict matters which arise unexpectedly in the course of the defence: see *R. v. Whelan* (1881) 14 Cox C.C. 55 and *Price v. Humphries* [1985] 2 Q.B. 353. Applying the statutory rule of construction, "*inclusio unius, exclusio alterius*", then, because the Rules specifically allow evidence in rebuttal, no other type of prosecution evidence may be called once the defence has begun its case. Clearly, the Director of Public Prosecutions ought always to have foreseen that she must establish that the specimen supplied by the defendant did contain an amount of alcohol which exceeded the prescribed limit. Accordingly, if she does not adduce the facts necessary to prove that contention by the time she closes her case, rule 13 prevents her from plugging any gaps in the prosecution regarding this matter after the defence has opened its case.

(c) After Retirement to Consider Verdict

14–61 Once a jury has retired to consider its verdict, no further evidence is admissible in any circumstances (see *R. v. Owen* (1952) 36 Cr.App.R. 16). The same rule in effect applies once justices have retired to consider their final verdict (see *Phelan v. Back* [1972] 1 W.L.R. 273). In that case the High Court held it to be an exception to the rule where the recorder, hearing an appeal at quarter sessions, had recalled a witness after both sides' closing speeches in order to rehear the evidence which had already been given but of which the recorder had made no note. If any new evidence had been given, the High Court would have set aside the recorder's verdict.

E. Non-compliance with the statutory rules relating to the taking of body fluid, its division and provision to the defendant

I. INTRODUCTION

14–62 In *Dear v. DPP* [1988] R.T.R. 148, 155, Watkins L.J. stated that the procedure for the taking and supplying of a sample had to be complied with literally before the results of the analysis of that specimen became admissible in evidence for a prosecution under the relevant provisions of the Road Traffic Act. This section discusses what those procedures involve and considers them under following heads, *viz.*: (a) the taking of blood, (b) the supply of the urine, (c) the division of the specimen into two parts, (d) the provision of one of those parts to its donor, (e) what information must be given to him about this matter and (f) what is the position if a person supplies more specimens than the requisite number.

II. BLOOD

Section 11(4) of the Road Traffic Act 1988 and section 38(5) of the **14–63** Transport and Works Act 1992 lay down that a sample of blood is *only* provided if the person consents to it being taken by a medical practitioner and it is so taken.

In *Rowlands v. Harper* [1972] R.T.R. 469, the High Court refused to set aside an acquittal, where a police sergeant had assembled the syringe needle and the capsules into which the blood was poured from the syringe. The justices stated that this gave them doubts about the results of the analysis. In the case of *R.v. Burdekin* [1976] R.T.R. 27 the motorist had to guide the needle of the syringe into his vein since he was a heroin addict and the doctor could not find the vein. Once the needle was in the vein the doctor took over and withdrew the blood. The Court of Appeal upheld the majority verdict of the jury that the sample had been taken by a medical practitioner. The suggestion that this was not the case received very short shrift from Bridge J. (at 32):

"The proposition that in these circumstances the specimen was not taken by the medical practitioner within the meaning of section 11(4) is, with respect to [defence counsel] quite untenable."

In *Rathbone v. DPR*, January 20, 1995, it was held that it was not necessary for the doctor to testify that he took the blood with the accused's consent. That evidence could be given by a police officer.

III. URINE

(a) THE WORDS OF THE STATUTE

The provision of urine is governed by section 7(5) of the Road Traffic Act **14–64** 1988:

"(5) A specimen of urine shall be provided within one hour of the requirement for its provision being made and after the provision of a previous specimen of urine."

Identical provisions are also to be found in the Transport and Works Act 1992, s.31(7).

In *Roney v. Matthews* [1975] R.T.R. 273, it was held that if only a single specimen of urine was provided, it could not be used to prove the amount of alcohol in that fluid.

(b) MORE THAN ONE HOUR TAKEN TO PROVIDE THE TWO SAMPLES

In a number of pre-1981 Transport Act cases, it was held that evidence **14–65** could be given of the amount of alcohol in a urine sample, although it had been provided more than an hour after it was first requested. This happened, for example, in *Roney v. Matthews* [1975] R.T.R. 273, where the court said that the reason why the period of 60 minutes was specified was so that if the second specimen was not provided within that time, the police might treat the motorist as having failed to supply it. Likewise, in *R. v. Reynolds* [1976] R.T.R. 229, it was held that the analysis of the second sample was admissible in evidence even though the police had asked for it more than an hour after the initial requirement. Those cases were decided on the wording of section 9(5) of the unamended Road Traffic Act 1972, which stated:

> "9(5) A person shall not be treated . . . as failing to provide a specimen unless
>
> (b) he is then requested to provide two specimens of urine within one hour of the request but fails to provide then within the hour or refuses at any time within the hour to provide them."

This must be compared with the wording of the legislation now in force (see above). There is a clear difference. The 1972 Act did not say that the police could not allow more time. The 1988 Act specifically states that the specimen shall be provided within the hour. In the words of May L.J. in *Nugent v. Ridley* [1987] R.T.R. 412, 418G, section 7(5) has to be "read precisely as it reads". Thus, nowadays, both specimens of urine have to be provided within 60 minutes from when the constable first made his requirement for that fluid.

On the literal wording of the Act the 60 minutes would run from when the police told the defendant that he had to provide two samples. If that was not said to him until after the supply of the first specimen, then the hour would run from then; but see section 14–12.

(c) WHAT CONSTITUTES A SAMPLE

14–66 In *R. v. Radcliffe* [1977] R.T.R. 99, the motorist argued that, as he had not emptied his bladder when he had provided his first sample, the second specimen contained a higher level of alcohol than it otherwise would have done if he had emptied his bladder. The court dismissed the appeal as the Act merely said that two samples had to be provided. It did not lay down any further requirement that there was an obligation to empty all the urine in the bladder at the time of the first urination. In *Prosser v. Dickson* [1982] R.T.R. 96, the defendant was told to stop urinating which he did, but started again two minutes later. It was held that he had not provided a second sample, but that it was a mere continuation of the first. In *Over v. Musker* [1985] R.T.R. 84, the accused urinated and stopped of his own volition. A minute-and-a-half later he began urinating again and the High Court held that he had fulfilled the statutory requirement and had supplied two specimens.

(d) USE OF THE FIRST SAMPLE

14–67 In *R. v. Welsby* [1972] R.T.R. 301, the driver was told by the police to urinate into a lavatory. It was held that he had satisfactorily provided a first specimen of urine. The police were under no obligation to keep it. This decision was followed in *R. v. Beckett* [1976] Crim.L.R. 140, where Judge Barr held that a first specimen of urine had been provided when the defendant urinated into the lavatory, instead of the container supplied to him for the purposes of the provision of the first urine sample. The rationale of this judgment was that the statute required only the second specimen to be analysed so it was irrelevant what happened to the first sample.

IV. THE DIVISION OF THE SAMPLE

Section 15(5) of the Road Traffic Offenders Act 1988 provides:　　　**14–68**

"(5) Where, at the time a specimen of blood or urine was provided by the accused, he asked to be provided with such a specimen, evidence of the proportion of alcohol or any drug found in the specimen is not admissible on behalf of the prosecution unless—

(a) the specimen in which the alcohol or drug was found is one of two parts into which the specimen provided by the accused was divided at the time it was provided, and

(b) the other part was supplied to the accused."

Section 34(3) of the Transport and Works Act 1992 is framed in identical terms.

In *DPP v. Elstob* [1992] R.T.R. 45, it was held that "at the time" meant that the division had to be closely linked in time with, and performed as part of the same event as, the taking of the sample. In that case a conviction was ordered where, after taking the sample, the doctor had left the room and had returned about two minutes later with the sample divided into two. The court also held that there was no requirement that the division of the sample take place in the presence of the accused, although this was desirable whenever such was possible.

In *Kidd v. Kidd* [1969] 1 Q.B. 320, it was held that, although the statute referred to a division into two parts, it was in order for the sample to be split into a greater number (in that case three).

In *Dear v. DPP* [1988] R.T.R. 148, the doctor tried to draw blood from **14–68A** the right arm but only succeeded in getting a few droplets. He then drew blood from the other arm and put some of that specimen in an empty container and the other part in the phial containing the few droplets. The High Court held the results of the analysis not to be admissible in evidence on the ground that the specimen had to be divided into two parts and neither of them had to be mixed with any other blood.

V. THE PROVISION OF THE SAMPLE TO THE ACCUSED

(a) Mandatory Requirements of the Act

Subsection (15)(5) of the Road Traffic Offenders Act 1988 and section 34(3) **14–69** of the Transport and Works Act 1992 provide that if a person requests part of his sample, he must be supplied with it, otherwise the result of the analysis of the moiety retained by the police will be inadmissible in evidence. The same wording was used in section 2(4) of the Road Traffic Act 1962. In two cases on that section of the 1962 Act (*R. v. Price* [1964] 2 Q.B. 76 and *R. v. Mitten* [1966] 1 Q.B. 10) the High Court interpreted the phrase "a constable requiring any person . . . shall offer to supply", as requiring the offer to be made simultaneously with or in a manner so proximate to the requirement that the accused person must clearly have had the matter well in mind when the offer was made to him. In *R. v. Byers* [1971] R.T.R. 387, it was held that the accused must make his request for a sample at the time he provides it. In *Nicholson v. Watts* [1973] R.T.R. 208, it was held that the defendant must be allowed to choose which of the specimens he wanted to take with him. In the words of Lord Widgery C.J. (at 211G): "There is a procedure which must be meticulously followed."

What happens if that procedure is not followed? *R. v. Price*, above, regarded a breach of section 2 as automatically providing grounds for an acquittal while *R. v. Mitten*, above, said it gave a discretion to the trial judge to admit evidence of the analysis, provided he was satisfied that this would not cause prejudice to the accused. A breach of the relevant section manifestly means that the specimen would not have been taken in accordance with the statutory procedure. If such does occur, then the House of Lords has ruled in *Fox v. Chief Constable of Gwent*, above, that the result of any analysis of the specimen cannot be give in evidence. Thus the mandatory requirement laid down in *R. v. Price* has now been given its seal of approval by the House of Lords.

(b) Is a Request by the Accused Necessary?

14-70 Unlike previous legislation, the Road Traffic Offenders Act 1988 merely states that a sample must be supplied to the accused if he asks for one. It does not expressly state that he must be offered it. In *DPP v. Warren* [1993] A.C. 319 Lord Bridge said that a driver must be told exactly what had been told to Mr Warren (at 332E) and he had been informed that, if he supplied a specimen, he would be offered part of it in a suitable container (at 324E). His Lordship did not include that in the information which must be given to a motorist about the voluntary option. However, it is submitted that this did not mean that no mention of his rights under the Road Traffic Offenders Act, s.15(4) need be made to somebody who supplies blood pursuant to section 8(2). It would be neither rational nor logical to draw this distinction. There can be no reason why only those who are forced to give their specimens must be informed of their rights under the Road Traffic Offenders Act, s.15(5). What Lord Bridge must have had in mind was that this information was included in the mandatory requirement and had to be told as part thereof before any specimen was taken, but that in a driver's option case, this information only need be given to the motorist once he had actually exercised his option and had provided his sample. The importance of this provision is underlined by recent Court of Appeal decisions which have shaken public confidence in the reliability of Home Office forensic evidence.

In *R. v. Byers* [1971] R.T.R. 383 a provost lance-corporal told a more **14–71** senior non-commissioned officer of the Royal Corps of Signals who had been involved in a road accident when serving in Germany:

> "I request you to provide a specimen of blood or urine for a laboratory test. If you do provide such a specimen you will be offered a part. I must warn you that that failure to provide a specimen . . . may make you liable to imprisonment and a fine. Do you agree to provide a specimen of blood?"

The signaller replied in the affirmative. Nothing further was said about him being given some of his specimen, nor did he receive any part of it. The case turned on solely whether the answer "yes" was merely an agreement to give blood or also a request for part of the specimen. The court held the former, stating that, if he had wanted part of his sample, he would have asked for it. It does not appear to have been argued that by telling the soldier that he would be offered a part, this meant that he did not have to say anything else but would be given an opportunity of accepting it in due course. Whether that authority would be followed by the courts today is a moot point (see *Walton v. Rimmer*, 14–23 above). The author can do no better than to quote the view of this judgment expressed by B. Strachan in his book *The Drinking Driver and the Law* (1983) p. 219:

> "Here is an unfortunate decision that lacks a sense of reality of the language and circumstances of such occasions."

(c) Supply—How and When?

No time limit is prescribed in which the police must actually hand over a **14–72** part of his specimen to a person who asks for it. In *R. v. Sharp* [1968] 2 Q.B. 564, Widgery L.J. said that it must be given to him within a reasonable time and preferably before he leaves the police station. If that is not done, the court must consider all the circumstances of the case, and especially why he left the station without being given the phial containing his body fluid. By reasonable time, the court was clearly contemplating a matter of hours, not days. In *R. v. Jones (Colin)* [1974] R.T.R. 117, the Court of Appeal held that a sample had been supplied when it was placed with the property of the accused, who was detained on other charges.

In *Johnson v. DPP*, unreported, April 13, 1994, the High Court held that the appellant had been supplied with part of his blood specimen. He had selected the moiety which he wanted and that had been handed to him. The custody officer then took it back and stored it in the refrigerator to prevent its deterioration while the appellant remained in custody on other matters. When he was released 12 hours later, he did not request his specimen, not any time thereafter. The justices found as a fact that the blood remained in the police station refrigerator and could have been collected at any time after his release. McCowan L.J. held that the supply had occurred "when it was divided and he chose the one that he wanted". It is submitted that merely giving a sample and then immediately taking it back cannot amount to "a supply". The court held that the facts were "very similar" to *R. v. Jones*, above. However, in that latter case, the prisoner was kept in custody pending his trial and none of his property was returned to him. McCowan L.J. held that this difference was "in no way crucial". It is submitted that the opposite is the case. Here the appellant was released and all his other possessions were given back to him. The Road Traffic Offenders Act 1988, s.15(5)(b) states that part of the specimen shall be supplied to the motorist if, at the time of its provision, he requested it. Although not stated in the judgment, the decision is only explicable on the basis that there is a continuing duty on a driver to repeat his request on leaving the station.

(d) STORAGE AND THE CONTAINER

14-73 The purpose of making it mandatory to supply part of a specimen of body fluid to a motorist if he requests it is to enable him to be in a position to have his own analysis carried out, thus allowing him to obtain expert evidence to confirm or to contradict the accuracy of the tests carried out by the police. In *Ward v. Keene* [1970] R.T.R. 177, it was held that the sample supplied to the accused must remain capable of analysis for a reasonable length of time. It also held that if the prosecution sample could be analysed, there is a presumption that mishandling of the specimen by the accused was the cause of the latter's not being capable of analysis. In *Doctorine v. Watt* [1970] R.T.R. 305, it was held that there was no obligation on the police to supply instructions on how a sample should be kept and if, through ignorance, the motorist incorrectly stored his specimen so that it became incapable of accurate analysis, this did not prevent the result of the police's analysis being given in evidence. That decision was followed in *Clark v. Stenlake* [1972] R.T.R. 276, where the accused stored his sample on his window sill for 17 days. Samples should be kept in a refrigerator. In *Noscoe v. DPP*, above, evidence was given by a Home Office scientist of tests carried out to ascertain the loss of alcohol upon storage at room temperatures (see Table I, below). All the above cases (except *Noscoe*) were before the enactment of the Police and Criminal Evidence Act 1984. It is submitted that if the same situations were to occur today, the resulting inability of the defendant to dispute the results obtained by the prosecution analyst would have such a prejudicial effect on the proceedings that any court ought to exercise its power under section 78 of that Act (see below) to exclude such evidence. This is because the police should follow their normal procedure and give advice on storage. If the reason for it being incapable of analysis is due to the sample being supplied in a defective container, the accused must be acquitted because he will not have been supplied with a specimen within the meaning of the Act. This happened in *Hawkins v. Ebbutt* [1975] R.T.R. 363, where the court held that a phial on which the cap was not properly attached was an "unacceptable container". (There the blood had stuck to the lid with the result that it was not possible for the sample to be analysed by the type of equipment used by private analysts; see section 14-74 below.)

Table 1

Evidence given in DPP v. Noscoe, unreported, February 22, 1994, Widnes Magistrates' Court, by a Home Office analyst of experiments on loss of alcohol upon storage at room temperature from blood samples in the 5ml septum capped phial.

Case No.	Initial analysis date	Initial analytical figure	Analytical figure after 7–8 weeks' storage	Alcohol loss after 7–8 weeks' storage	Analytical figure after second storage period: 8–9 weeks	Alcohol loss after second storage period of 8–9 weeks	Total alcohol loss after storage
					ALCOHOL CONTENT (mg%)		
2401/92	April 30, 1992	77	60	−17	53	−7	−24
2418/92	May 1, 1992	85	68	−17	63	−5	−22
2440/92	May 5, 1992	83	64	−19	57	−7	−26
2453/92	May 5, 1992	85	65	−20	59	−6	−26
2461/92	May 5, 1992	79	57	−22	49	−8	−30

213

(e) CAPABLE OF ANALYSIS

14–74   In *Smith v. Cole* [1971] 1 All E.R. 200, it was held that the sample provided to the motorist must be "capable of analysis by ordinary methods by a reasonably competent analyst". Whether that be the case is entirely a matter of fact for the justices. There is a rebuttable presumption that if the police could analyse their sample, the same could be done to the defendant's (see *Kierman v. Willcock* [1972] R.T.R. 270). In earlier cases there were findings, on the facts, that clotted samples were only capable of analysis by gas chromatography and that the necessary equipment was not possessed by many analysts, so defendants were acquitted (*e.g. Earl v. Ray* [1969] 1 W.L.R. 1050, and *R. v. Nixon* [1968] 1 W.L.R. 577). A decision to the contrary was upheld in *Smith v. Cole*, above, as by then many analysts were using gas chromatographs. From that decision, it appears that the type of equipment possessed by the defendant's own analyst was irrelevant. What was material was whether the ordinary commercial laboratory could have analysed the actual sample supplied to the accused.

(f) INFORMATION IMPARTED TO THE MOTORIST

14–75   The police must not do anything, whether intentionally or unintentionally, to dissuade a motorist from carrying out his own analysis. In *Perry v. McGovern* [1986] R.T.R. 240, the defendant was acquitted because, having provided a sample of blood and having been given a portion of it, she was informed by a policeman that it was not capable of being analysed, so she took no further action. The High Court held that the justices should have excluded the result of the prosecution's analysis, which showed an alcohol level above the statutory limit. The basis of the decision was that the motorist had been misled, undoubtedly in good faith, into thinking that she did not have a specimen that could be submitted for independent analysis as contemplated by the statute. However, in *Butler v. DPP* [1990] R.T.R. 377, a scientist consulted by the defendant had refused to analyse the blood because its container had been accidentally labelled with the constable's name and not that of the defendant. The court said that it could see no reason why the sample could not have been analysed and upheld the conviction. However, it is implicit from the judgment that if the analyst had testified and given a reasonable explanation for his actions, then the High Court would most likely have ordered an acquittal.

14–76   Those two decisions must be compared with *Doyle v. Leroux* [1981] R.T.R. 438, where the defendant was informed that he was not going to be prosecuted for "an incident and accident" on a certain date. In writing that letter the police had in mind a possible charge of careless driving and had overlooked the excess alcohol offence. On receiving that communication and as a direct result of it the appellant had thrown away the specimen which had been given to him. The High Court upheld the conviction. They said that it could have amounted to a special reason for not disqualifying him but, as the analysis showed him to be twice the legal limit, he was obviously guilty and deserved to lose his driving licence. It is an open question whether, after the doubts cast on the reliability of prosecution scientific evidence in a number of recent appeals (see [1992] Crim. L.R. 466 *et seq.*), *Mokhra v. DPP*, *New Law Digest*, 10/12/96 reached the same conclusion on similar facts (240ml of alcohol). In *R. v. Anderson* [1972] R.T.R. 113, the circumstances were the same as in *Doyle v. Leroux*, save that the prosecution's analysis showed the alcoholic content of the sample to be only 1mg above the prescribed limit. The Court of Appeal said that this was no defence but held that special reasons applied and ordered the defendant not to be disqualified. This was because he had been misled by the police into not exercising his statutory right to have his own sample analysed, which may well have proved his innocence. The appeal was only against sentence, but Watkins L.J. and Nolan J. in *Perry v. McGovern* [1986] R.T.R. 240, were of the view that, had the appeal been against conviction, the latter should have been quashed. It is submitted that this view is preferable to that of the Court of Appeal but this is academic because nowadays the Court could always acquit by involving its powers under section 78 of P.A.C.E (see next paragraph) to exclude the evidence of the prosecution analysis.

However, as the authorities currently stand, it is clear that if the police **14–77** say anything which makes the accused believe that his sample can not be analysed, then he must be acquitted (*per* Glidewell L.J. in *Butler v. DPP* [1990] R.T.R. 377, 383J). If he does not have his sample analysed because he has been informed that he will not be prosecuted, he faces a conviction but will have special reasons for not being disqualified, provided the court does not consider that the result of the prosecution analysis showed the defendant to be so much over the limit that any analysis conducted on his behalf must confirm his guilt. However, it should be noted that *R. v. Anderson* and *Doyle v. Leroux* were decided before the Police and Criminal Evidence Act 1984 was in force. It is submitted that nowadays section 78 of that Act will cover the situation and allow the court to exclude the results of the analysis in such cases. This is because informing a motorist that he will not be prosecuted clearly has the necessary adverse effect on the fairness of the proceedings as contemplated by section 78, since the police, by their conduct, will have led the defendant into not taking the necessary steps to obtain evidence which might have contradicted the result of the analysis on which the charge was based and have, thus, secured his acquittal. This submission is in line with the view of the High Court in *DPP v. Snooks* [1993] Crim. L.R. 883. There the respondent had telephoned an analyst and was told that because the phial containing his blood specimen had not been supplied in a sealed envelope, any analysis would carry little weight in court proceedings. Accordingly, he took no further steps to have the specimen supplied to him independently tested. The High Court reversed the justices' decision to acquit the motorist because no specimen had been supplied to him, as required by section 15(5)(b) of the Road Traffic Offenders Act 1988. The High Court held that these had been such a supply and remitted the case to enable the justices to decide whether or not to exercise their discretion under section 78 to exclude evidence by the prosecution of the result of the analysis carried out on behalf of the police.

VI. MORE THAN THE REQUISITE NUMBER OF SPECIMENS AND SPILLED SPECIMENS

14-78 Once a person has supplied a sample (or two in the case of urine), he cannot be requested to supply any further ones and, if he does, the analyses of these cannot be relied upon in evidence by the prosecution. In *R. v. Hyams* [1973] 1 W.L.R. 13, the police officer wrongly but bona fide thought that the second urine specimen was insufficient to be analysed. As he was wrong about this, the Court of Appeal held that the subsequent requirement for blood was invalid. This decision was followed in *Pooke v. Lockwood* [1981] R.T.R. 285.

In *Beck v. Watson* [1980] R.T.R. 91, the doctor spilled the accused's blood sample as he was dividing it into two. The accused was asked for another sample which he provided. The High Court held that the police could only demand one sample and, once that was provided, they had no power to demand a second sample. Accordingly the latter had been improperly obtained and the result of its analysis was inadmissible in evidence. For a discussion of what amounts to "providing" a specimen the reader is referred to Chapter 17, below.

In *Gabrielson v. Richards* [1975] R.T.R. 223, the defendant provided three specimens in an hour, the third of which was analysed. It was held that this was not the correct specimen and the defendant could not be convicted on the result of that analysis. The same decision was reached in *R. v. Moore* [1978] R.T.R. 384, where the appellant supplied a third sample only after he had deliberately broken the police container and spilled his second sample after it had been received by the police (see section 17–37). In *Nugent v. Ridley* [1987] R.T.R. 412, the defendant was asked by the police surgeon to provide a specimen of urine in order to ascertain if he was capable of supplying such a sample. That specimen was discarded. A constable then required two samples which were provided. The prosecution relied upon the analysis of the second of these two samples. The conviction was upheld since the first specimen was not supplied pursuant to a requirement by an officer but at the request of the doctor made on his own initiative. Indeed, the court said that a third or subsequent sample could be analysed so long as it was provided within an hour of the original requirement. May L.J. said that the 1981 Transport Act merely laid down that a specimen had to be provided after a previous one. It did not say "after a single previous one", so there was no restriction on the number of urine specimens which could be supplied before the one that was analysed, provided they were all supplied with an hour of the requirement. It should be noted that this case was under what is now the 1988 Road Traffic Act, while the other cases mentioned in this section were under the unamended and differently worded 1972 Act (see section 14–65). That decision is in clear conflict with a number of cases which have held to be inadmissible a third breath specimen. There is nothing in the wording of the Act nor any jurisprudential or other reasons to justify such a distinction between a third specimen of liquid alcohol and one of gaseous ethanol. Thus, there must be great doubt about whether *Nugent's case* has correctly interpreted the relevant statutory provision.

F. No Printout

A number of appeals have featured cases where no printout from a breath **14–79** alcohol measuring instrument had been tendered in evidence. In *Garner v. DPP* [1990] R.T.R 208, the High Court made it clear that the statutory provisions of the Road Traffic Offenders Act 1988, s.16 (see Chapter 13) are only one way of presenting evidence concerning the amount of alcohol a person has consumed. That section was not intended to replace the common law mode of proof but to supplement it. Consequently, if the prosecution does not seek to rely upon the printout, this is not fatal to its case. Instead it must call oral evidence from somebody present at the relevant time to testify as to what happened when the defendant blew into the machine, including what appeared upon the visual display unit of the Intoximeter or Camic. In the words of Watkins L.J. in *Morgan v. Lee* [1985] R.T.R. 409, 413, 414:

> " . . . Evidence [of the result] could not be relied upon unless it was accompanied by evidence of the results in figures seen by the officer on the display panel of the self-calibrating exercise or evidence from him to the effect that the device would automatically abort if the results had not been satisfactory."

In two subsequent cases it was held that it was sufficient if there was **14–80** evidence of satisfactory calibration and there was no need for this to include the actual figures: namely, *Thomas v. DPP* [1994] R.T.R. 11, where two policemen merely testified that the breathalyser had calibrated itself correctly before the first, and after the second, breath analysis; and *Greenaway v. DPP, ibid.*, at 17, where the operator gave evidence that all the readings showed the Intoximeter to have been working correctly. The court held that by this he meant, *inter alia*, the calibration tests. It is submitted that the decision in *Morgan v. Lee*, above, is preferable to the subsequent cases. Whether or not a breathalyser has calibrated itself correctly is a question of fact for the justices. Therefore such evidence ought to be inadmissible and witnesses should be confined to saying what the calibration figures were. A good illustration of this principle is *R. v. Davies* 46 Cr.App.R. 12 where it was held that a witness can describe a motorist's condition but cannot testify if he was fit to drive, as that is a question for the tribunal of fact. By analogy it must be for the justices to say whether or not the figures proved the breathalyser to have calibrated itself correctly. Just as justices can take judicial notice that the Intoximeter has been approved by the Home Secretary, so they must also be able to take notice of the calibration figures which the Home Secretary has also approved, which will enable them to look at Home Office Circular 32/84 and discover from that if the figures given in court comply with those which were prescribed by (as he now is) Viscount Whitelaw.

Watkins L.J. in *Denneny v. Harding* [1986] R.T.R. 350 held that there **14–81** had to be testimony to confirm that the test had been carried out correctly and that such evidence must be given by a person "who has been trained upon the use of [the] device and its manner of performance". (For a discussion on that qualification, the reader is referred to section 16–22). He need not have been present when the test was carried out, but can base his opinion on the testimony given by an actual observer of the test. It was held in *DPP v. Parkin* [1989] Crim.L.R. 379 that it was not necessary for evidence to be given that the device had purged itself. It is submitted that this case is clearly contrary to the reasoning of the many authorities which say that there must be evidence of proper calibration (*e.g. Denneny v. Harding*, above). (They did not comment on purging as that was never raised.) It is surely just as important to know that there was no residual alcohol in the machine when it carried out its analysis as it is to know that it had successfully checked itself to confirm that it was functioning correctly. If purging is not important, why are its results shown on the printout? *Denneny v. Harding*, above, held that these must be evidence of the time at which the test was taken, but this time need not be from the Intoximeter, it can be from the operator's watch, at least according to *Van Flute v. DPP*, unreported, June 9, 1994.

I. THE RELEVANCE OF SECTION 69 OF THE POLICE AND CRIMINAL EVIDENCE ACT

14–82 A printout from the Intoximeter or Camic is a document produced by a computer and its admissibility as evidence is subject to the magistrates being satisfied that the conditions laid down in P.A.C.E. 1984, s.69 have been fulfilled (see section 15–08 *et seq.*). The prosecution cannot bypass section 69 merely by not placing the printout before the court, as that section will also apply to the result displayed on the screen. The reason for this is that, although section 69 refers to a "statement in a document produced by a computer", the expression "document" is defined in section 118 as having the same meaning as in the Civil Evidence Act 1968, s.10(1)(d). The definition of that word in this latter statute includes any device which stores visual images which are capable of being reproduced. Both the Intoximeter and the Camic store some of the information which is shown on their screens while a sample of breath is being blown in and analysed, and can display it at a later date if required.

Thus, according to *McKeown v. DPP* [1995] Crim.L.R. 69, the screen on the Intoximeter is a document for the purposes of P.A.C.E. 1984, s.69. If a constable merely reads out the result without putting the printout or a copy before the court, then section 69 does not apply; see *Sophocleous v. Ringer* [1988] R.T.R. 52 and *R. v. Shephard* [1993] A.C. 370. The author shares the view expressed in the commentaries at [1989] Crim.L.R. 361–363 and [1995] Crim.L.R. 233, and cannot see the logic of a document produced by a computer only being subject to section 69 if it is actually handed into the court and not governed by those provisions if its contents are merely read out to the Bench. Fortunately, the effect of those authorities have for practical purposes been nullified by *Burr v. DPP* [1996] Crim.L.R. 324, which held that secondary (in that case oral) evidence of computer documents were inadmissible and the original had to be produced. As the police always keep a copy of all Intoximeter printouts, if objection is taken to oral evidence of the results of analysis, the printout will have to be produced and that must comply with section 69. (The only exceptions will be those very rare cases where no printout was produced or it has been lost.) Also, if oral testimony of the breathalyser results was given, this will be by the witness reading out what he copied from the instrument's screen. The writing is therefore a copy of the original document and is, by virtue of the Criminal Justice Act 1988, s.27, admissible in evidence to the same extent as the original (*i.e.* what appeared on the screen). Accordingly, the constable should be asked to conform that he is reading to the court his note, or copy, of what appeared on the screen, and then be asked to make it an exhibit, so that it will then be governed by section 69. The same will apply if the officer tries to read, rather than produce to the court, the printout.

To invoke section 69, there must of course be evidence before the court that what appears on a breathalyser's video-display unit can be reproduced at a later date. So in *Prince v. DPP*, unreported, July 26, 1995, it was held to be sufficient merely to give evidence of the amount of the lower reading. In that case, the printout of the Intoximeter was not produced to the court and there was nothing to suggest that what appeared on its screen fell within the definition of "document" in section 118. The court also held that since the driver had exercised his option under section 8(2) of the Road Traffic Act 1988 to provide blood, there was no need for there to be any evidence of correct calibration.

If the evidence shows that no printout was produced by the machine because of a fault with the device, then in accordance with the ratio of *Jones v. DPP* [1995] Crim.L.R. 69, the device would not be an approved one and the result of its analysis would be inadmissible in court.

G. Inadmissible hearsay evidence

The normal rules of evidence apply to road traffic offences including the **14–83** usual exclusion of hearsay evidence. A good example of this is *Dye v. Manns* [1987] R.T.R. 90. The prosecution tried to prove that the police were entitled to demand a sample of body fluid for analysis, rather than a breath specimen by calling the arresting officer to testify what he had heard the Intoximeter operator tell the defendant. The High Court ordered an acquittal as this was inadmissible hearsay (see section 12–14).

The Road Traffic Offenders Act, s.16 and the Transport and Works Act, s.35 make provision for the admissibility of certain documentary evidence. This is a topic which is fully discussed in Chapter 15.

From the evidence given in *R. v. Tate* [1977] R.T.R. 17 it is apparent that, in order to be sure that they have obtained a correct result, the Home Office Forensic Science Service analyses a specimen of body fluid at least twice, using two separate chromatographs. Only if both analyses tally are they satisfied that its results are accurate. Normally each analysis is carried out by a different person who will state that his result was accurate because it was in agreement with the result of the analysis carried out by another scientist. It is submitted that logically both analysts must be called, as otherwise it would be hearsay evidence for one to give evidence of the readings obtained by the other. However, in two cases the Court of Appeal has held that an analyst can give evidence of the results of work carried out by his assistant (see *R. v. Kershbergh* [1976] R.T.R. 526 and *R. v. Rutter* [1977] R.T.R. 105, 112E). Nearly 20 years later in *R. v. Jackson, The Times,* May 21, 1996, the Court of Appeal reached the opposite view and held that such evidence was inadmissible. That case was about DNA evidence but its principle is of universal importance.

H. Special rules relating to specimens taken at hospitals

14-84   The meaning of "a patient at a hospital" has been considered in section 10–39 *et seq.* Under the Road Traffic Act 1988, s.9 and the Transport and Works Act 1992, s.33, a special procedure is laid down for the police whenever they require such a person to supply a specimen of body fluid. Failure to follow it will make the result of the subsequent analysis inadmissible in evidence. The prosecution must prove that the medical practitioner in immediate charge of the defendant had been notified of the proposal to make the requirement, and had not objected to the making of the requirement, the administration of the statutory warning or the provision of the specimen. The grounds on which he can object is that they would be prejudicial to the proper care and treatment of the patient. In *Baker v. Foulkes* [1975] 1 W.L.R. 1551 the House of Lords held that the doctor did not have to be informed of his right to object but merely had to be told of the proposal to make "the requirement" and those words in inverted commas did not include the warning of prosecution. However, in *DPP v. Warren* [1993] A.C. 319 at 332H/333A, Lord Bridge said that "questions with regard to the appropriate procedure to be followed in requiring drivers to give specimens" had arisen and it was "to the resolution of those questions" that the appeal was directed, so the House of Lords in that case was considering what the correct procedure was for making the requirement. The answer was the *Warren* formula. No distinction was made between any part of that formula, *i.e.* that which was part of the requirement and that which was extraneous to it. The requirement was the formula. As it included the warning of prosecution, it is doubtful whether *Baker v. Foulkes* is still good law.

    The reader is referred to Chapter 10 for a discussion of the following issues: (1) what evidence is needed to prove that the doctor to whom the police made the request was "the medical practitioner in immediate charge" of the patient; (2) that he did not object to what the police were proposing to do; (3) whether the doctor can be consulted within the patient's hearing; and (4) whether the doctor can withdraw a consent once given.

In *R. v. Green* (Note) [1970] 1 All E.R. 409, the Court of Appeal held that **14–85** the doctor must be told of the type of specimen which was going to be required and merely mentioning blood did not entitle a requirement for urine to be made.

In *Ratledge v. Oliver* [1974] R.T.R. 394, it was held that the medical practitioner could be given all the necessary information at one and the same time, and he did not need to be consulted for each stage individually.

I. Police and Criminal Evidence Act 1984

I. SECTION 36

Under section 36(6)(d) a custody officer may perform any of the powers **14–86** vested in a constable under sections 6 and 7 of the Road Traffic Act.

II. SECTION 69

Section 69 applies to breath alcohol measuring instruments, since they **14–87** incorporate a micro-computer. The application of that section is fully considered in Chapter 15.

III. SECTION 78

Section 78 gives a court the power to exclude evidence if its admission **14–88** would have such an adverse effect on the fairness of the proceedings that it ought not to be admitted. The courts have used this power to refuse to allow evidence to be given relating to the requirement for a specimen or its analysis. This latter has been considered earlier in this chapter (see section 14–05 *et seq.*).

IV. THE CODES OF PRACTICE

The procedure under the Road Traffic Act 1988, ss.7 *et seq.*, is not an **14–89** interview and therefore not subject to Code C of the Codes of Practice issued by the Home Secretary. Accordingly, there is no requirement for any conversation or question-and-answer session with an arrested motorist to be recorded or, if recorded, to be shown to him (see *DPP v. Rous* [1992] R.T.R. 246). Neither is he entitled to have his solicitor present during the breathalyser procedure nor, if an infant, to have his parents there (see *DPP v. Davies, ibid.*). Likewise, *Francis v. DPP, The Times*, May 2, 1996, held that the provisions of the Code did not apply to a mentally ill motorist who had been required to provide a specimen for analysis.

14–90   Since all those cases (save for *Francis v. DPP*), Notes to Guidance 6C were introduced into Code C on its revision in April 1991 and stated that procedures undertaken under section 7 of the Road Traffic Act did not constitute an interview for the purposes of the Code. In 1995 the Code was again revised and now the same paragraph 6C in the Notes to Guidance merely states "[Not Used]". The reason for this may be the fact that inferences can nowadays be drawn by a court from an accused's silence when questioned (see sections 36/7 of the Criminal Justice and Public Order Act 1994). So the police might find it advantageous to ask the defendant if he wishes to say anything about the offence, *e.g.* it will undermine the "hip flask" defence if it is only mentioned for the first time at the trial. Nevertheless, that will probably not be sufficient to persuade the judiciary to hold that carrying out a Road Traffic Act, s.7 investigation is an interview. However, Code C has been amended since *Rous's case* and in particular there is a new paragraph 11.13 which states:

"A written record shall also be made of any comments made by a suspected person, including unsolicited comments, which are outside the context of an interview but which might be relevant to the offence. Any such record must be timed and signed by the maker. Where practicable the person shall be given the opportunity to read that record and to sign it as correct or to indicate the respects in which he considers it inaccurate. Any refusal to sign shall be recorded."

Merely requiring a motorist to provide a specimen will not be covered by paragraph 11.13. However, if questions are asked about post-driving consumption of alcohol or things are said which are relevant to the reason why a specimen was refused, then it is submitted that all of this is subject to paragraph 11.13 (which was first introduced into Code C in 1991). If these are not recorded in accordance with that paragraph, then evidence should be excluded by the court of what was said or not said and, in certain cases, of the actual request by the police for a specimen. The court will exercise its discretion under section 78 to disallow such evidence if it considers that the failure to comply with the Code was unfair to the motorist. This will usually apply when there is a dispute about what occurred as then the motorist will have been deprived of the opportunity of making contemporaneous comments on the police record of this questioning (see *R. v. Canale* [1990] 2 All E.R. 187).

J. Cautioning

14–91   Paragraph 10 of the 1995 Code C states as follows:

"10 Cautions
(a) When a caution must be given
10.1 A person whom there are grounds to suspect of an offence must be cautioned before any questions about it (or further questions if it is

his answers to previous questions which provide the grounds for suspicion) are put to him regarding his involvement or suspected involvement in that offence if his answers or his silence (*i.e.* failure or refusal to answer a question or to answer satisfactorily) may (*sic*) be given in evidence to a court in a prosecution. He therefore need not be cautioned if questions are put for other purposes, for example, solely to establish his identity or his ownership of any vehicle or to obtain information in accordance with any relevant statutory requirement (see paragraph 10.5C) or in furtherance of the proper and effective conduct of a search, (for example to determine the need to search in the exercise of powers of stop and search or to seek co-operation while carrying out a search) or to seek verification of a written record in accordance with paragraph 11.13.

10.2 Whenever a person who is not under arrest is initially cautioned or is reminded that he is under caution (see paragraph 10.5) he must at the same time be told that he is not under arrest and is not obliged to remain with the officer (see paragraph 3.15).

10.3 A person must be cautioned upon arrest for an offence unless:

(a) it is impracticable to do so by reason of his condition or behaviour at the time; or

(b) he has already been cautioned immediately prior to arrest in accordance with paragraph 10.1 above."

In *Whelehan v. DPP* [1995] R.T.R. 177, a policeman saw the defendant sitting in a car and it was obvious that he had been drinking. The constable asked him if he had driven there. It was held that there was no need to administer a caution before answering that question. The High Court stated that a constable would not have grounds for suspecting an offence under section 5 had been committed until after he had obtained a positive breath test and therefore there was no need to caution a person before then. In *R. v. Beckford* [1995] R.T.R. 251, the driver had been involved in a fatal accident. A police officer arrived, smelt alcohol on his breath and asked him how much he had drunk. The officer did not caution him because (as he said) a smell of alcohol need only mean that he had consumed a small amount of liquor. The Court of Appeal upheld the judge's ruling that no caution was required at that stage. The accused had replied "a few pints" and, on being asked how many, stated "three pints". The Court of Appeal did not comment on the trial judge's ruling that it was only after the reply "three pints" that the need first arose for a caution to be administered. In *Whelehan v. DPP* the court also said that if Code C had been breached by the failure to administer a caution in that case, there was only one possible way that the justices could have exercised their discretion under section 78, namely in favour of the prosecution by allowing the evidence to be given.

K. Summary

The purpose of the Transport Act 1981, by amending the Road Traffic Act **14–92** 1972, was to prevent acquittals on grounds unrelated to the accuracy of the analysis. However, as the compulsory requirement of the motorist to give a sample amounts to compelling a person to incriminate himself, the judiciary has intervened to hold the balance, reserving to themselves the right to rule that a result of an analysis, even though accurate, was nevertheless inadmissible in evidence. In *Fox v. Chief Constable of Gwent* [1986] A.C. 281, 293, Lord Elwyn-Jones set out the position in a nutshell when he quoted with approval the words of the Lord Justice-General in *Lawrie v. Muir* (1950) J.C. 19, 26–27:

> "From the standpoint of principle it seems to me that the law must strive to reconcile two highly important interests which are liable to come into conflict: (a) the interest of the citizen to be protected from illegal or irregular invasions of his liberties by the authorities, and (b) the interest of the State to secure that evidence bearing on the commission of crime and necessary to enable justice to be done shall not be withheld from courts of law on any merely formal or technical ground. Neither of these objects can be insisted upon to the uttermost. The protection of the citizen is primarily protection for the innocent citizen against unwarranted, wrongful and perhaps high-handed interference, and the common sanction is an action of damages. The protection is not intended as a protection of the guilty citizen against the efforts of the public prosecutor to vindicate the law. On the other hand, the interest of the State cannot be magnified to the point of causing all the safeguards for the protection of the citizen to vanish, and of offering a positive inducement to the authorities to proceed by irregular methods. Irregularities require to be excused, and the infringements of the formalities of the law in relation to these matters are not likely to be condoned. Whether any given irregularity ought to be excused depends on the nature of the irregularity and the circumstances under which it was committed. In particular the case may bring into play the discretionary principle of fairness to the accused . . . "

14–93   In the case of the drinking and driving legislation, the judiciary has reconciled the "important principles" referred to by Lord Elwyn-Jones by ruling that any impropricty, no matter how unintentional, relating to the taking of the sample will render the evidence of the subsequent analysis inadmissible in court. However, in the absence of bad faith on the part of the police, the courts will consider all the circumstances of the case and will decide on its own individual merit any application by the defence to have prosecution evidence ruled inadmissible under P.A.C.E., s.78 on the grounds that there has been a contravention of one of the many statutory provisions governing the position prior to the time when a motorist reaches the police station. In *DPP v. Godwin* [1991] R.T.R. 303, Bingham L.J. specifically recognised that, in regard to exactly the same factual situation, two different benches of justices could exercise their discretionary powers under section 78 in totally opposite ways and neither decision would be appealable. In whose favour this discretion is exercised will often be dependent on the manner of the driving and the reason why the motorist was breathalysed.

Chapter 15

THE PRINTOUT, EVIDENCE BY CERTIFICATE AND OTHER FORMS OF DOCUMENTARY EVIDENCE

A. Introduction

At common law in a criminal trial facts must be proved by oral testimony **15–01** on oath (see *Paterson v. DPP* [1990] R.T.R. 329). Section 98 of the Magistrates Courts Act 1980 specifically enacts that, subject to any statutory exceptions, all evidence at petty sessions must be given on oath. Since 1967, provided the other side raises no objection, a litigant can adduce his evidence by written statements in accordance with section 9 of the Criminal Justice Act passed in that year. In addition, Parliament has made special provision for documentary evidence in drinking and driving cases by the Road Traffic Offenders Act 1988, s.16 and the Transport and Works Act, s.35. These allow evidence to be given by certificate from medical practitioners, constables and analysts about the taking and testing of specimens.

B. The Printout

I. WHEN IS IT IN EVIDENCE

In *Greenaway v. DPP* [1994] R.T.R. 17 the officer read from the printout to **15–01A** the magistrates. It was attached to his contemporaneous statement (which he used to refresh his memory) and was clearly visible to the justices. It had also been shown to defence counsel. The High Court held that all this did not make it an exhibit. It had to be formally produced to the court and made an exhibit. Unless that was done the magistrates were not entitled to see the document. In *Hasler v. DPP* [1989] R.T.R. 148 a police sergeant said in the witness box that the printout was in court and available to the justice if they wanted to see it. The High Court held that he had not made it an exhibit and the justices were not entitled to look at that document. This case was distinguished in *R. v. Pydar JJ., ex p. Foster*, unreported, May

5, 1996. There the witness was handed in the box the local constabulary's drinking and driving procedure form which he had contemporaneously filled in and he confirmed that he formally produced it. It was not physically handed into the court. The defendant made a submission of no case to answer and objected to the justice looking at the procedure form on the grounds that it had not been adduced in evidence. The High Court ruled that once a document had been formally produced, it became an exhibit even though the Bench had neither looked at, nor examined it, nor even had it in their possession during the prosecution case.

II. REAL EVIDENCE

15–02 When the Intoximeter and Camic devices were first introduced, there were a number of appeals to establish the precise nature of the evidence represented by the copies of the results of their tests, which those machines printed out automatically. Such documents are invariably referred to by the judiciary as "printouts". In *Castle v. Cross* [1985] R.T.R. 62, it was argued that such a document was only admissible to prove an offence under sections 5 and 6 of the amended Road Traffic Act 1972 by virtue of the specific provisions of section 10(3) [now section 16(1) of the Road Traffic Offenders Act] and, save for that statutory authority, it was inadmissible under the hearsay rule. Thus, the argument ran, magistrates could not look at it when, for example, trying an offence of failing without reasonable excuse to provide a sample of breath. This argument was firmly rejected by the High Court, which held that the printout needed no statutory authority to be produced as evidence of the truth of its contents since it was "real evidence" admissible under the common law. The court approved and followed the judgment of Simon P. in *The Statue of Liberty* [1968] 1 W.L.R. 739:

> " . . . real evidence . . . is conveniently defined in *Cockle's Cases and Statutes on Evidence*, 10th ed., (1963), p. 348: 'Real evidence is the evidence afforded by the production of physical objects for inspection or other examination by the Court.' If tape recordings are admissible, it seems that a photograph of radar reception is equally admissible—or indeed, any other type of photograph. It would be an absurd distinction that a photograph should be admissible if the camera were operated manually by a photographer, but not if it were operated by a trip or clock mechanism. Similarly, if evidence of weather conditions were relevant, the law would affront common sense if it were to say that those could be proved by a person who looked at the barometer from time to time but not by producing a barograph record. So, too, with other types of dial recording. Again cards from clocking-in-and-out machines are frequently admitted in accident cases. The law is now bound to take cognisance of the fact that mechanical means replace human effort."

15–03 What Simon P. was saying is that where mechanical and electrical instruments record factual information (*e.g.* a clock displaying the time), then that information is admissible as evidence of its own truth. As to proving what was recorded by the device, this can be done in one of two ways, either by calling people to say what they had seen appear on, or be displayed by, the instrument, or by producing to the court a document actually produced by the machine containing those facts.

III. STATUTE OR COMMON LAW

Castle v. Cross, above, was a case under section 7(6) (failure to provide). The **15–04** Road Traffic Offenders Act only refers to a printout proving the amount of alcohol in a breath specimen, so the question of whether its admissibility in those circumstances was solely governed by that statute was not actually before the court in *Castle's case* but, from the judgment of Steven Brown L.J., the answer was a clear "no". The same conclusion was reached in an appeal directly on the point, namely *Garner v. DPP* [1990] R.T.R. 208, where it was held that the admissibility was governed by the ordinary rules of the "common law as 'representing real evidence'", and not on any Act of Parliament.

Other members of the judiciary have taken the opposite view. In *Mayon* **15–05** *v. DPP* [1988] R.T.R. 281 at 285E/F and *Owen v. Chesters* [1985] R.T.R. 191 (which was approved in *Fawcett v. Gasparics* [1985] R.T.R. 375), it was held that a printout was only admissible to prove the result of a breath analysis if served in accordance with section 16 of the Road Traffic Offenders Act 1988. To the same effect is the decision in *Walton v. Rimmer* [1986] R.T.R. 31 (see below). The High Court of Justiciary (in *McDerment v. O'Brien* 1985 S.L.T 485) has taken a similar view to that of *Walton v. Rimmer*. The cases of *Chief Constable of Surrey v. Wickins* [1986] R.T.R. 162 and *Beck v. Scammell* [1988] R.T.R. 162, 166b–167a were concerned with whether or not the printout had been served in accordance with the provisions of section 16 of the Road Traffic Offenders Act. If service was not a prerequisite to admissibility, the court would have said so and not wasted its time on deciding whether or not service had been properly effected. The question of the printout being admissible at common law as "real evidence" was not referred to in the judgments, but it is impossible for the judges (especially as they included Watkins L.J.) to have overlooked any possibility of such a document being able to be produced to a court at common law.

IV. THE RATIONALE OF THE LAW

The reason why section 16 had to be complied with before a court could **15–06** look at the printout was explained by Watkins L.J. in *Owen v. Chesters* [1985] R.T.R. 191, 195c:

"The clear purpose of subsection [16(3)] . . . is to give the accused an adequate opportunity of studying the statement before the hearing, in order to see whether it discloses any possible ground for challenging the accuracy of the measurement."

Applying the principle of *inclusio unius est exclusio alterius* (Co. Lit. 210), since the legislature has made specific provision for it to be admissible if served on the accused in advance of the hearing, that excludes any other method of producing it in court (see *Blackburn v. Flavell* (1881) L.R. 6 App. Cas. 621).

V. SCOTTISH AND HOUSE OF LORDS CASES

15–06A   In *Smith v. McDonald* and *Smith v. Davie* [1984] S.L.T. 401 the High Court of Justiciary held that the prosecution could only rely on what is now RTOA, section 16(1)(a) if they put before the court both the printout and a certificate stating that the motorist had provided his specimen at the time and date shown on the printout. If the printout did not show the correct time and date, then a constable could not sign the certificate with the result that the prosecution could not take advantage of section 16. That argument does not appear to have been put forward in a case south of the Border but this line of reasoning appeared to find favour with the House of Lords *in argumento* in *DPP v. McKeown* (the decision in which was still awaited at the time that this treatise went to press). If the conditions in section 16 were not fulfilled, then the printout was only admissible at common law as "real evidence".

VI. TIME

15–07   In *Parker v. DPP* [1992] T.L.R. 163, it was held that a printout was still admissible in evidence even if during British Summer Time the time was shown in Greenwich Mean Time. (The accused had argued that the Summer Time Act 1972 combined with the Calendar (New Style) Act 1750 prevented a document referring to Greenwich Mean Time whilst British Summer Time was in force.)

B. Police and Criminal Evidence Act

I. THE RELEVANT PROVISIONS

15–08   At common law there was a presumption that a machine was working correctly; see *Castle v. Cross* [1985] R.T.R. 62 at 66H and *DPP v. Whittle* [1996] R.T.R. 154, 157J/K. With the increased use of computers, special rules governing their "evidence" in a court of law were introduced. These provisions are contained in P.A.C.E. 1984, which came into force on January 1, 1986 (S.I. 1985 No. 1934). The relevant section is number 69, which provides as follows:

> "(1) In any proceedings a statement in a document produced by a computer shall not be admissible as evidence of any fact stated therein unless it is shown:

(a) that there are no reasonable grounds for believing that the statement is inaccurate because of improper use of the computer;

(b) that at all material times the computer was operating properly, or if not, any respect in which it was not operating properly or was out of operation was not such as to affect the production of the document or the accuracy of its contents."

II. IS SECTION 69 APPLICABLE?

(a) A COMPUTER

One practical problem with invoking section 69 is that it must, of course, **15–09** be established that the actual breathalyser used by the constabulary does indeed incorporate a computer. Normally this can be achieved by cross-examination of the operator of such an instrument. Occasionally he will prove unhelpful. If this should occur, the defence may choose to adduce in evidence, under section 24 of the Criminal Justice Act 1988 (see Chapter 16–11), a copy of the Home Office publication "Field Trials of Three Substantive Breath Alcohol Measuring Instruments" which states:

"[The Intoximeter and the Camic] were selected for field trials. These were all microprocessor controlled, automating the subject sampling and calibration checking procedures."

The *proformas* used by the majority of police forces in drinking and driving cases have a printed page which, when filled in by the operator of the breathalyser in question, becomes a certificate under P.A.C.E., Sched. 3, para. 8. The fact that the police use such a certificate is clearly proof that section 69 applies to breath alcohol measuring instruments.

(b) THE INTOXIMETER AND THE CAMIC

A number of Court of Appeal decisions have held that section 69 only **15–10** applied to a computer where human intervention was required to activate it. Those cases were overruled by the House of Lords in *R. v. Shephard* [1993] A.C. 380, which held that section 69 applied to all computers and, at 386 B–G, that the requirements of that section were not fulfilled by the application of the maxim *omnia praesumuntur rite esse acta*. At first sight this case appears to be in conflict with their Lordships' earlier decision in *Cracknell v. Willis* [1988] A.C. 450, where they had referred to a presumption that the Intoximeter was working correctly and made no mention of section 69. However, in that case there was no finding by the justices that the Intoximeter incorporated a computer. From the report of *Cracknell v. Willis*, it is apparent that counsel in their argument did not cite or rely on section 69, which is not surprising as it is clear from the stated case that it was not a matter raised at first instance. Thus there was no factual basis on which the House of Lords could have considered the relevance of the provisions of P.A.C.E. 1984 when deciding whether or not there was a presumption of reliability to be invoked by a court when considering the accuracy of an analysis carried out by a breath alcohol measuring device. Accordingly, *Cracknell v. Willis* cannot be regarded as any binding authority governing a case where there is a finding of fact by the lower court that the Camic or Intoximeter incorporated a computer.

15-11 In *R. v. Medway JJ., ex p. Goddard* [1995] R.T.R. 207 the High Court held that section 69 applied to the Intoximeter and that its printout was not admissible unless there was affirmative evidence that the device was working correctly. Such proof could either be by oral evidence or by a certificate pursuant to paragraph 8 of Part II of Schedule 3. Such a certificate can only be signed by somebody whom the certificate "shows on its face . . . was a person who from their job description can confidently be expected to be in a position to give reliable evidence about the operation of the computer", *per* Lord Griffiths in *R. v. Shephard* [1993] A.C. 380 at 386F/G. *Ex p. Goddard*, above, also held that merely giving details of calibration did not comply with section 69. Indeed, from that case it would appear that the courts now take judicial notice that the Intoximeter is a computer.

15-12 In *Connolly v. Lancashire County Council* [1994] R.T.R. 79, there was evidence that the computer which produced the weighbridge tickets had been tested on July 11, 1990 and March 13, 1991, and had been found to have been working correctly on those dates. The offences were founded on the weights shown on the tickets and were alleged to have been committed on November 21, 1990 and January 15, 1991, but there was no evidence that the computer was operating properly on those two dates. The High Court held that the lapse of time between the dates of the tests and that of the alleged offences (in one case two months) did not enable the court to be satisfied that the weighbridge computer functioned correctly when it had weighed the defendant's lorries. In *McKeown v. DPP* [1995] Crim. L.R. 69, it was held that all the information on the printout had to be accurate for the document to be admissible in evidence. A court could not disregard an inaccurate time, even though that did not effect the accuracy of the result of the analysis. The High Court also upheld the motorist's submission that there can be no qualification to the word "accurate" in section 69 and rejected the prosecution argument that the words "to a material degree" should be read into the statute after the word "accurate". In that case the clock was 13 minutes slow. The courts have rejected attempts by the Director of Public Prosecutions to apply the principle of *de minimis*, thus leading to acquittals when the Intoximeter was five minutes fast (*Badkin v. DPP* [1988] R.T.R. 400); when it was three minutes slow (*Osborne v. DPP*, unreported, November 26, 1995, *per* Judge Petre); when it was two minutes slow (*Stibbard v. DPP*, unreported, February 15, 1995, *per* Judge Bathurst-Norman and *Hall v. DPP*, unreported, June 26, 1995, *per* Judge Holman). In *Waite v. Smith* [1986] Crim L.R. 405 (a case on calibration) it was held that the maxim *de minimis non curat lex* had no part to play where the accuracy of the Intoximeter was challenged, otherwise there would invariably be conflicting decisions between different courts and this would clearly be a wholly unacceptable state of affairs. In the words of Watkins L.J:

"There would therefore be uncertainty in this context through out magistrates' courts as to when justices could or could not regard a device as reliable. That would be a wholly unsatisfactory situation and one, which, in my judgment, should not be permitted to obtain."

It was held in *Slender v. Boothby* [1985] R.T.R. 385 that the accuracy of the information had to be judged objectively and the fact that the machine was operating within its manufacturer's specification was irrelevant. (There on February 29 the Intoximeter had shown March 1, as in those days it was not programmed to take account of leap years.)

In *Ashton v. DPP* (see below) Balcombe L.J., without deciding the **15–13** matter, tended to the view that if an Intoximeter performed within its specification, the document it produced was "accurate" within the meaning of section 69. This *obiter dictum* of Balcombe L.J. is contrary to the *ratio* of *Slender v. Boothby* and *McKeown v. DPP*, above, where Kennedy L.J. agreed with defence counsel's submission that the word "accurate" in section 69 had no qualification. It is submitted that the opinion of Kennedy L.J. is preferable to that of Balcombe L.J., since it accords with the wording of section 69. Also, the dicta of Balcombe L.J. is contrary to many decisions (the latest one being *Healy v. DPP* [1996] R.T.R. 247) which have held that evidence of the general unreliability of breathalysers was inadmissible. Thus evidence cannot be given to explain that, although the facts on the printout are inaccurate, they are the best the breathalyser can produce. This is because such evidence will be showing that all Intoximeters in this respect cannot perform accurately.

The actual grounds on which *Ashton v. DPP* [1995] T.L.R. 410 was decided are perfectly acceptable, namely that section 69 is complied with if the document contains shorthand which, when explained (by evidence, if need be), reveals perfectly accurate information. In that case, the High Court held that a printout showing "trace acetone" was admissible under section 69, even though medical evidence established that the defendant could not have had any of that substance on his breath. Expert evidence was adduced to show that "trace acetone" was shorthand to indicate that acetone or another chemical had been detected in the specimen and due allowance had been made for it when analysing the breath. The court was also of the opinion that "improper use" in section 69 meant that the operator had acted mala fides. This is yet another judicial attempt to "water down" section 69. It is submitted that this interpretation of the Act was contrary to the intention of Parliament, which, according to Lord Griffiths in *R. v. Shephard*, above, was to ensure that it was safe for a court to rely on computer evidence. There can be no rationale or justification for limiting the words "improper use" to where the operator acted with mala fides and to exclude the case when he has made a bona fide error.

In *Burdett v. Roberts* [1986] R.T.R. 391, and *Toovey v. Chief Constable of Northumberland* [1986] Crim. L.R. 475 (both pre-P.A.C.E. cases) it was held that the printout was admissible in evidence when a policeman had mistyped the names of the defendants into the breathalyser. The latter was because the device was merely attributing to those people the identification which it had been given for them.

15-14   Thus, if an Intoximeter only reproduces the actual information fed into it, that can be given in evidence, as the machine is accurately setting out what it has been told (*e.g.* a motorist's identity). On the other hand, if the device has to use its own knowledge (*e.g.* counting the number of vibrations of a quartz in order to obtain the time), then those facts must be accurate and, if not, section 69 has not been complied with, even though the information is as accurate as the Intoximeter can produce.

III. THE PRACTICAL EFFECT OF SECTION 69

15-15 The effect of section 69 is that even if there were correct calibration of the instrument, once there was some evidence of the possibility of the breathalyser having malfunctioned, the burden remained on the prosecution to show that this has not affected its accuracy. Thus section 69 has overruled the decision in *R. v. Ealing Justices, ex p. Wheeler (No.2)*, unreported, May 12, 1986. In that case the Metropolitan Police had supplied the defence with a copy of the Intoximeter's log. This revealed data corruption, so the prosecution was asked what data had been corrupted. While that consultation was taking place, the High Court held that defendants were not entitled to any Intoximeter documents (see section 16–10 *et seq.*). Accordingly, the Metropolitan Police solicitor declined to supply any further information. At the trial, the defence called an expert. All he could say was that the corruption might have affected the accuracy of the machine. It depended on which type of data had been corrupted and, without knowing this, he was not in a position to say whether or not the result of the analysis was correct. The High Court held that the justices were right to convict, as mere speculative evidence was not enough; the driver must establish (on a balance of probabilities) that the machine was not working properly. The effect of section 69 of P.A.C.E. 1984 is to reverse that decision, so that once there is some evidence of any possible malfunction, the prosecution must prove beyond all reasonable doubt that this had not prevented the breathalyser from producing an accurate result.

   Thus section 69 has overruled earlier cases such as *Gordon v. Thorpe* [1986] R.T.R. 358, where, although the Intoximeter was inaccurate, the motorist was convicted on the basis that his alcohol level must nevertheless have been over the legal limit. Nowadays, the inaccuracy would render the printout inadmissible under section 69. Nor is it any longer possible to convict if only one of the two analyses are correct. This is because a person can only be condemned on the results of both of the analyses of his breath (see *Cracknell v. Willis* [1988] A.C. 450).

15-16   *McKeown v. DPP* [1995] Crim. L.R. 69 held that section 69 applied to everything that was written on the document and that included the time. It held that pre-section 69 cases were of no relevance, such as *Fawcett v. Gasparics* [1986] R.T.R. 375, where a conviction was upheld when the wrong time was shown but expert evidence was called to show that this did not effect the result of the analyses. Similar evidence was adduced in

McKeown's case, above. The prosecution have to prove the accuracy of the Intoximeter clock. If its times are incompatible with those shown in the police drinking and driving *proforma* or the custody record, the prosecution will not be able to prove which time was correct so the printout will be inadmissible evidence. The times shown on the custody record and other constabulary documents are occasionally from the force computer but more often than not from either an officer's watch or the station chronometer. Indeed, as these are not computers, it could well be argued that those times are presumed to be correct (see section 15–08) and therefore the time displayed on the printout must have been wrong. Such a presumption has to be rebutted, in the case of the prosecution, by establishing, beyond all reasonable doubt, that it was wrong (*c.f. ex p. Wheeler (No. 2)* above). In comparing various times, it should be borne in mind that if the Intoximeter has not been used in the previous half-hour, then it would take a minimum of two-and-a-half to three minutes to obtain first STD after pressing the start button for the second time. It could take longer if the officer mistyped something and had to start again, or if there were problems with the acetone detector. If the machine has been used in the last half-hour, it will take the same time subject (1) to adding the time it takes for the operator to type in the relevant details (see Chapter 13) and (2) to subtracting the stand-by time of 90 seconds. It is useful to look at what time a defendant was given the printout and went back to the custody office, and at what stage of the proceedings these occurred. In considering these matters it should be noted that if the printer is switched on, typing will begin automatically and immediately after second STD and will continue until the requisite number of copies have been produced, which is usually three or four (each police force can programme their Intoximeters to produce up to 10 copies). Each printout takes 13 to 14 seconds to be produced and follows on immediately after the previous one.

In summary the law is thus: for a printout to be admissible in evidence, **15–17** it must display the times and dates when the samples were analysed (see *Parker v. DPP* [1992] T.L.R. 163). Since evidence of those facts (*i.e.* the times shown for analyses) is required to obtain a conviction, and if such facts are miscalculated by the computer, then even if only the analytical part of the printout were admissible in evidence, the prosecution would fail, as it would have been unable to adduce accurate evidence of what times the breathalyser showed for carrying out its analyses. In any case, the law applies the provisions of section 69 to all the information in a document and not merely that on which the prosecution choose to rely as part of their case.

IV. THE RESPONSE OF THE DIRECTOR OF PUBLIC PROSECUTIONS

The Director of Public Prosecutions has tried to counter the "clock **15–18** defence" in two ways, first by attempting to show the breathalyser time to be correct and secondly by establishing that it was no more than four minutes out and that an inaccuracy of such duration is irrelevant.

(a) WHICH IS THE ACCURATE TIMEPIECE?

15–19 The Director of Public Prosecutions has accepted that, where there was an inconsistency between two chronometers then, without any further evidence, a court cannot be satisfied beyond reasonable doubt as to which of the timepieces was accurate. What she now does, where appropriate, is to call a service engineer from Lion Laboratory to testify as to his last service before, and first one after, the date on which the defendant had blown into the machine. The engineer will swear that on the first occasion, he set the clock by the telephone talking clock and then state what time the clock was showing on the second occasion when he again checked with the talking clock. If the clock has not lost any time between these two visits, he will say that it must have been correct when the defendant blew into it because although the clock can go slow or go fast, it will not do both between his services. Whether that last statement is accurate is another matter. What he cannot say is that if the clock did go slow, the police did not alter the time back to that announced on the BBC (*i.e.* the right time). To change the time, the function code ET is typed on the keyboard and then the words "PASS CODE" appear on the screen. (The latter changes hourly but a police officer, who has been nominated as a supervisor and whose details have been supplied to Lion Laboratories, can telephone them up and will be given this code.) When that code has been entered, the instrument requests the input of the time. The Marketing Director of Lion Laboratories has testified that the time function code should not be given to police officers, although he cannot rule out that possibility. (To the author's knowledge it has become known to certain supervisors in the Metropolitan Police Force.) The hourly pass code will be supplied to supervisors because they need it for certain other purposes, *e.g.* to alter the number of printouts produced. Indeed, the hourly pass code is held at the Home Office Forensic Science Laboratory in Lambeth and will be supplied to specially designated police officers in the Metropolis.

(b) DISCREPANCY OF NO MORE THAN FOUR MINUTES

15–20 When the discrepancy between the clock in the Intoximeter and that used by the police does not exceed four minutes, the Director of Public Prosecutions relies on page 56 of the Intoximeter handbook, which states:

> "8.6 **Clock and Calendar Check**
> The clock should keep time to within better than plus or minus 4 minutes in 6 months."

The Director of Public Prosecutions argues that, because the handbook had been submitted to the Home Office Forensic Science Service when the Intoximeter was being evaluated, the approval of that instrument had also included the approval of the tolerance shown in the handbook. The answer to this are multifarious:

(1) In *Corps v. Dalton* [1983] R.T.R. 160, 165K; *DPP v. Carey* [1970] A.C. 1072 and *Walker v. Lovell* [1975] R.T.R. 377, it was held that the manufacturer's instructions were not included in the approval order. (These are to be found in the handbook.)

(2) *Inclusio unius est exclusio alterius.* The Home Secretary laid down a tolerance for the standard checks (*i.e.* between 32–37ug inclusive), but did not lay down any for the clock.

(3) Prior to the approval order and at the request of the Home Secretary, the British Calibration Service (part of the National Physical Laboratory and now NAMAS) set up a specification for breathalyser clocks in NPL Report BCS 2 (published by HMSO, ISSN 01422-7321). Paragraph 4 in Appendix A of that report reads as follows:

"4.1 The rate of the clock should be correct to better than 1.5 sec/day."

One-and-a-half seconds *per diem* does indeed equate to about four minutes in six months; but there is a vast difference between losing 1.5 seconds every day and slowing down by four minutes over a 24-hour period.

(c) ACADEMIA

In any case it is academic whether or not any accuracy for the clock was **15–21** approved by (as he now is) Viscount Whitelaw. The High Court has made it clear on numerous occasions (the last time being on May 28, 1994 in *Healy v. DPP*) that evidence of the general unreliability of the Intoximeter is inadmissible (see section 16–06 *et seq.*). So if all Intoximeters can lose up to four minutes, as the Director of Public Prosecutions claims, she cannot give such evidence in court because of the ruling in *Healy v. DPP*. In any case, whether or not the Home Secretary approved it is irrelevant. A clock's accuracy must be judged objectively. So in *Slender v. Boothby*, above, an Intoximeter which on February 29 showed March 1 was held to be an unreliable and non-approved machine, even though no Intoximeter in those days could deal with a leap year. Also, in *McKeown v. DPP* the High Court accepted defence counsel's submission that no qualification could be attached to the word "accuracy" in section 69 of P.A.C.E. Balcombe L.J. in *Ashton v. DPP* (reported at [1995] T.L.R. 410, but not on this point) was inclined to the contrary view but left the matter open; it is submitted that if the decisions in *Slender v. Boothby* and *McKeown v. DPP* had been cited to him, he would not have dissented from them. In any case a slow or fast clock causes that intoximeter to lose its approval by the Home Secretary. See *Jones v. DPP*.

It should be noted that the Director of Public Prosecutions has been granted leave and is pursuing an appeal to the House of Lords in the cases of *Jones v. DPP* and *McKeown v. DPP*.

(d) SCOTLAND

It is interesting to compare the approach of the judiciary in the south with **15–22** their brethren north of the Border, where the laws of evidence are totally different from those in England and Wales. In *Smith v. MacDonald* 1984

S.L.T. 398, it was held that if the Procurator Fiscal put the printout in evidence, the time shown for the test was conclusive of that fact. If it transpired that the actual time when the defendant supplied his specimen was different, then he must be acquitted, since it had not been proved that the defendant had blown into the Camic at the time when, according to the Camic, it had carried out its analysis. (The analysis is carried out immediately the breath specimen is provided.)

(e) Gas Chromatography

15–23 This is the technique used nowadays to analyse body fluids (see Chapter 9). A gas chromatograph is not a computer. It produces a graph and the Home Office Forensic Science Service have linked those machines to a computer which collates the results shown on the graph, converts them to digital numbers and then prints out in Arabic numerals the amount of alcohol found in the specimen which has been analysed. The admissibility of that printout is governed by section 69 of P.A.C.E.; see *East West Transport Ltd v. DPP*, [1996] R.T.R. 184, where it was held that a computer printout of a weighbridge was subject to section 69, and this applied even though the justices had found as a fact that the actual weighbridge was working correctly. (The weighbridge made all the necessary calculations and only used a computer to print out the weights of the lorries.)

C. Road Traffic Offenders Act 1988

I. SECTION 16

(a) Provisions

15–24 At common law, the only way to prove the results of a blood or urine test was to call the analyst. So far as the "breathalyser" is concerned, it would, *per* Watkins L.J. in *Owen v. Chesters*, above, be necessary to prove that the printout referred to the sample of breath provided by the accused. This could only be done by the testimony of somebody who saw the defendant blow into the machine and saw the results appear on its screen or the printing out of the results. In order to prevent the calling of such witnesses, whose evidence would often be unchallenged, special provision was made by section 16(1) of the Road Traffic Offenders Act 1988 for proof by written statements of certain facts. The following certificates are made admissible in evidence, namely, by subsection (a), one signed by a constable stating that the printout related to the accused and, by subsection (b), one purportedly signed by an authorised analyst (see below) as to the amount of alcohol or any drug found in a specimen of blood or urine. By section 16(2) the same applies to a certificate purportedly signed by a medical practitioner, stating that he took blood from the accused with his consent.

(b) AUTHORISED ANALYST

An authorised analyst is defined in subsection 16(7) of the RTOA (as **15–25** amended by the Road Traffic Act 1991) as a person who is qualified under regulations made under section 37 of the Food Safety Act 1990 for appointment as a public analyst or who has been authorised by the Secretary of State for making analyses for the purposes of section 16 of the Road Traffic Offenders Act 1988.

In *R. v. Kershbergh* [1977] R.T.R. 526, the Court of Appeal held that it was compulsory under the unamended Road Traffic Act 1972 for a certificate of analysis to be signed by an authorised analyst. In *Stevens v. DPP*, unreported, December 9, 1992, it was held that, under the differently-worded Road Traffic Offenders Act 1988, there was no similar mandatory requirement. This is not apparent from the wording of the Act but the decision was no doubt prompted by the fact that under the 1972 Act the certificate could also be evidence of the qualifications of the analyst, while the Road Traffic Offenders Act did not possess such a provision. This decision was therefore designed to prevent further evidence having to be adduced to establish that the signatory of the certificate did indeed possess the qualifications prescribed in section 16(7). However, the author is left wondering why, if anybody else could sign such a certificate, the Act refers to it being signed by "an authorised analyst" and also gives a definition of those two words.

D. Safeguards

I. GENERALLY

Certain safeguards have been laid down before the prosecution can invoke **15–26** section 16 of the Road Traffic Offenders Act 1988. First, there is subsection (3)(b), whereby no document may be produced to the court under subsection (1) unless a copy has been served upon the defendant at least seven days before the trial. The other protection for the motorist is that, under subsection (4), the provisions of section 16 do not apply if at least three days before the trial, or such further time as the court may allow, the defendant has served a notice requiring the attendance at court of the person who signed the certificate. Subsection (4) does not apply to the printout (see *Temple v. Botha* [1985] Crim.L.R. 517). At least, this appears to be what the court is saying but the report of the judgment is only four lines long. The reason for this is presumably because section 16(3) refers to a certificate and printout, while section 16(4) only refers to a certificate. By section 16(6A) (as inserted by Sched. 1, para. 37 of the Criminal Procedure and Investigations Act 1996) subsection 4 shall have no application to committal proceedings. If a notice under 16(4) is served on the DPP and if the latter then re-serves the certificate, another notice under 16(4) must be served by a defendant or he loses his right to insist on oral evidence by the signatory of the certificate, see *Ramsay v. DPP*, unreported, July 17, 1996.

II. COPY

15-27 The question of what is "a copy" has been considered in a number of cases. In *DPP v. Hutchinson*, unreported, June 16, 1990, the accused threw the original printouts into the pan of the police station lavatory. The operator printed out the Intoximeter results once more. The High Court held that this second batch of results were original printouts, admissible in evidence under the normal rules, and not just copies of the destroyed originals. In *Chief Constable of Surrey v. Wickens* [1985] R.T.R. 227, the officer handed an Intoximeter printout to the accused but forgot to sign the certificate at the bottom which gave the identity of the person who had blown into the device. This was held to be of no importance. The High Court stated that section 16(3) merely required that a copy be served and that an unsigned copy was nevertheless still a copy, notwithstanding that it bore no signature. In *Beck v. Scammel* [1986] R.T.R. 162, a policeman altered the time shown on the printout from Greenwich Mean Time to British Summer Time (which was then in force) by adding an hour to it. He did this with the best of intentions and in order to prevent the driver being misled. The High Court held that the printout was admissible in evidence, and said that it should be excluded from being produced to a court only if the served copy had been altered so materially as to affect the nature of it, and therefore to have disadvantaged the motorist in a manner which the legislation did not countenance.

III. SERVICE

(a) TIME LIMITS

15-28 For a document to be admissible under section 16, a copy must be served at least seven days before the actual date on which it is sought to put the original in evidence (see *Williams v. DPP* [1991] R.T.R. 214). In calculating the seven days, time begins to run from the day after that on which the certificate is received (see *Stewart v. Chapman* [1951] 2 K.B. 792.) The defence cannot waive this time limit (see *Tobi v. Nicholas* [1988] R.T.R. 343). The rationale of this is that the statute stated that such a document was admissible in evidence "only if a copy" had been served at least seven days before the trial. Consequently, the High Court held that Parliament's use of the words "only if" meant that the requirement of seven days was a *sine qua non* which could not be waived by the motorist. In *Tobi v. Nicholas*, above, the driver had only agreed to accept service of the analyst's certificate on the trial date because he had been told by the stipendiary magistrate that if he did not consent the case would be adjourned for a week. That appeal distinguished the decision in *R. v. Banks* [1972] 1 W.L.R. 346, on the grounds that it was decided on a differently-worded Act. There it had been held that if the defence wished to challenge the admissibility of a document on the grounds of non-service, the point must be taken at the time when the prosecution sought to adduce it as evidence.

In *R. v. Banks*, the first time the matter was raised was in a submission of "no case to answer". The Court of Appeal held that quarter sessions had been correct in refusing to uphold that submission. It is submitted that *R. v. Banks* was decided on the wrong grounds, since a person cannot waive a statutory requirement. Instead, the case should have been decided on the basis that, in the absence of any challenge to the admissibility of that evidence when the Crown proposed to adduce it, the court may assume that service to have been carried out correctly and, once the document was in evidence, it was too late to object. *R. v. Banks* was explained in *Anderton v. Kinnard* [1986] R.T.R. 11 as meaning the objection could conceivably be delayed until the end of the case but in almost all circumstances, the objection must be taken when the evidence is tendered or one waives one's right to do so. What *Tobi's case* decides is that, once the court is aware that section 16 has not been complied with, it cannot allow the certificate to put in evidence, even if no objection is raised to that by the accused.

(b) Upon Whom And By What Method

Service may be either personally or by recorded or registered letter (see **15–29** section 16(6)) or it can also be served in a similar manner on a defendant's solicitor (see *Anderton v. Kinnard*, above). That case also held that the use of the word "may" in the legislation means that the modes of services mentioned in the Act were not the only way in which service could be effected. Indeed, it can be served on anybody who has authority to accept it and in *Burt v. Kircaldy* [1965] 1 W.L.R. 474, it was held that in the absence of the addressee, his spouse has ostensible authority to accept the document. Likewise, in *Layton v. Shires* [1960] 2 Q.B. 294, it was held that a household servant has authority to receive letters on behalf of her master or mistress. A document can even be served on counsel but, in that case, only if the latter agrees to this (see *Penman v. Parker* [1986] 1 W.L.R. 882).

(c) Personal Service

In the case of the printout and the accompanying certificate, section **15–30** 16(3)(a) of the Road Traffic Offenders Act 1988 also allows them to be put in evidence if they were "handed to the accused when [they] were produced". In *Walton v. Rimmer* [1986] R.T.R. 31, it was held that the word "handed" meant "tendered". *i.e.* if the motorist declined an offer of the documents they could still be put in evidence under section 16. A Scottish court took a contrary view and held that only transferring actual physical possession of the documents to the accused would comply with the statutory requirement (see *McDerment v. O'Brian* 1985 S.L.T. 485). Its rationale was, why else would Parliament have used the word "handed" and not another word, such as "offered", if the latter was all that was required to comply with the Act? In *R. v. John* [1974] 1 W.L.R. 624, the Court of Appeal held that it was not possible to substitute any useful synonym for the word "supplied" when construing the predecessor section, *i.e.* section 10(5)(b) of the unamended Road Traffic Act 1972.

15-31 Accordingly, it is submitted that likewise it is not possible to substitute any useful synonym for the word "handed" in the 1988 Act and that the meaning given to that word by the Scottish courts is likely to be the correct interpretation, rather than the one given in *Walton v. Rimmer*, above. That case did, however, make it clear that for the subsection to apply, the intended recipient must have known that he was being offered a copy of the printout for him to take away. There the three printouts produced by the Intoximeter were placed on the station counter, where the defendant was requested to sign all of them, which he did. The police took away two of the copies and left the other one there, intending it to be taken by the motorist. The latter was not informed of this. The High Court rejected the argument by the prosecution that, as a matter of common sense, he must have known that the document left on the counter was for him to keep. In the words of Parker L.J. (at 35A–B):

> "As the Lord Chief Justice observed in *Gaimster v. Marlow* ([1984] R.T.R. 49, 55), we are not here in a fanciful world, we are in a world of reality and the reality of this situation is this. On occasions when specimens are taken and measurements are taken by a Lion Intoximeter 3000, the defendant may well be in a state of intoxication such as makes it necessary that what is going on should be fully understood by him, or at least, fully understood by a reasonable person."

(d) By Post

15-32 In *Hawkins v. DPP* [1988] R.T.R. 380, it was held that once the prosecution had proved posting, then there was a presumption under section 7 of the Interpretation Act 1978 that the document had been delivered in the normal course of the post. The court also held that posting could be proved at petty sessions by a certificate pursuant to rule 67(2) of the Magistrates' Court Rules 1981. The presumption in section 7 may always be rebutted. In *Wheeler v. Commissioner of Police*, unreported, May 21, 1984, the motorist objected to the analyst's certificate being tendered in evidence on the grounds that he had never seen it before. Prosecuting counsel tried to overcome this objection by relying upon an endorsement pursuant to rule 67(2) on the back of the analyst's certificate which stated that "a copy had been served by registered/recorded delivery". The justices ruled that it was inadmissible in evidence, since the court must be satisfied that a copy had been sent to the defendant by recorded delivery as against registered post or vice versa, and it was not sufficient merely to show that it had been served by one or other of those means. To overcome this difficulty, the prosecutrix produced to the court the envelope which had been sent. It exhibited a recorded delivery label and was marked "gone away–return to sender". On the basis that the means of postage had been established, the justices ruled the document admissible. The High Court took the opposite view and held that "service" meant "receipt" and, therefore, the return of the undelivered envelope to its sender rebutted the presumption that it had been received by the addressee. *Anderton v. Kinnard*, above, held that section 16(6), by using the words "may be served by recorded or registered delivery," was not stating the only way in which service could be effected. In that case ordinary post was held to be sufficient.

IV. SECTION 11

Section 11 of the Road Traffic Offenders Act 1988 allows the prosecution to **15–33** put in evidence a certificate purportedly signed by a constable which states that the accused had told him that he was driving a particular motor vehicle on a particular occasion. Such a certificate shall be evidence of the truth of those matters, provided it is served in the same manner as a certificate under section 16 and that no counter-notice requiring the signatory of the certificate to give oral evidence has been served not less than three days before the trial (or such further times as the court may allow)

E. Transport and Works Act 1992

The text of the Transport and Works Act, s.35 is slightly different from **15–34** that of the Road Traffic Offenders Act, s.16. However, save for the definition of "authorised analyst", its wording is more or less the same and appears to allow breathalyser printouts and certificates from doctors and analysts to be admissible evidence in exactly the same way as the Road Traffic Offenders Act allows such documents to be placed before a court. The only dissimilarity is that the Transport and Works Act defines an authorised analyst in the same terms as did the 1988 Road Traffic Act before it was amended by the 1991 Road Traffic Act, *i.e.* a person approved by the Secretary of State for carrying out analyses under section 35 or a person qualified for appointment as a public analyst under either of two statutes, both of which were repealed before the Transport and Works Act was even introduced into Parliament, namely the Food Act 1984 and the Food and Drugs (Scotland) Act 1956. With enactments like this, one can well understand why the Major administration is farming out the drafting of legislation that previously would have been undertaken by parliamentary counsel to the private sector.

F. Servicemen

By section 93 of the Road Traffic Offenders Act section 16 applies world- **15–35** wide to servicemen and a reference in it to an offence under the Road Traffic Act is also a reference to the corresponding service offence, and a "constable" includes a member of the provost staff.

G. Other Documentary Evidence

All police forces have issued a booklet to their members which sets out the **15–36** procedure for them to follow in drinking and driving cases. Included in it is the information to be given to the driver and spaces are left blank for the officer to write in the various matters, *e.g.* the replies given to his questions, details of what appears on the breathalyser's video-display unit, etc. That booklet is like any other document used by the police. Its evidential status was explained in *R. v. Epping JJ., ex p. Quy* [1993] Crim. L.R. 970 as being a contemporaneous record which can be used by the writer to refresh his memory when testifying to the court. It was equivalent to a police officer's note book. In *Murray v. DPP* [1993] R.T.R. 209, 221K the deputy Chief Justice said that prosecutors should ensure that the standard procedure book was produced in breathalyser cases. This remark must be read in the context of that case. The police officer had said that she had completed the standard procedure form but could not remember the exact words used. That prompted Watkins D.C.J. to say earlier in his judgment that the justices should have asked the officer to remind them of contents of the booklet and, *if necessary* (author's emphasis), to produce it. All the judgment means is that the advocate appearing for the Crown should ensure that he has it with him in court so that it can be put before the Bench in accordance with the normal rule of criminal evidence if the need arises, *e.g.*, where the constable is questioned about it by the defence when such cross-examination did not arise out of the replies given when testifying-in-chief.

Chapter 16

CHALLENGING THE ACCURACY OR RELIABILITY OF THE ANALYSIS

A. Introduction

Even if the correct procedures have been followed by the police and the **16–01** results of the analysis are admissible in evidence, this does not mean that those results are *ipso facto* accurate. The workings and reliability of breath testing machines in general have been discussed in Chapter 13. This chapter considers, in relation to any individual analysis, what indications will be given by the relevant apparatus regarding the accuracy and reliability of the tests it has performed.

I. WHAT HAS TO BE PROVED

On a charge under section 5 of the Road Traffic Act 1988, the prosecution **16–02** must establish that the accused's alcohol level was in excess of the prescribed limit. Although the Act does not place any limitation on how this can be done, as a matter of practicality the only way this can be achieved is by producing the result of an analysis of the defendant's breath, blood or urine. In *Lucking v. Forbes* [1986] R.T.R. 97, and *Gordon v. Thorpe*, *ibid.*, at 358, the High Court held that the prosecution did not have to prove a specific amount of alcohol in a motorist's body, but merely that it exceeded the legal level. However, in practical terms, if the result of the analysis is not shown to be accurate, it will be impossible to prove that a driver was over the prescribed limit. The condition of a person will never guarantee that he has imbibed sufficient drink to be guilty of an offence under section 5 of the Road Traffic Act 1988, and evidence of a motorist's demeanour, fitness to drive, etc., cannot found a conviction based on an excess of alcohol in the body (see *DPP v. Carey* [1970] A.C. 1072, 1092, *per* Lord Diplock). The roadside breath testing devices are not accurate enough to guarantee that a positive result automatically means that the motorist has excess alcohol in his body (see below).

In *Lucking v. Forbes* [1986] R.T.R. 97, it was held that if the justices were not satisfied with the accuracy of the analysis of the specimen relied on by the prosecution, they were not entitled to convict on the basis of another

243

specimen. There the justices had doubts about the accuracy of the breath reading because of the result of an analysis of a blood sample provided under the voluntary option scheme, even though the results of all the analyses showed the motorist to have had an alcohol level at the time of driving above the legal limit. There was, however, a substantial difference between the blood and breath analyses. The High Court upheld the acquittal. In *Gould v. Castle* [1988] R.T.R. 57 (a case of back-tracking), the High Court quashed a conviction when the magistrates found that the defendant's blood alcohol concentration was likely to have been above the statutory limit. A court had to be satisfied so that it was sure that the alcohol level was in excess of the prescribed limit (at 64K/L).

II. CHECKING THE RESULTS OF THE POLICE ANALYSIS

16–03 A successful challenge to the analysis undertaken on behalf of the police will result in an acquittal. If it was carried out on a body fluid, the person who supplied it will have been afforded his own opportunity of having the sample tested, as he will have been offered part of it. If the result differs from that alleged by the police, he can always call his own analyst as a witness. Due to the public disquiet caused by the introduction of breath alcohol measuring instruments (see *Lion Laboratories Ltd v. Evans* [1985] Q.B. 526), the Home Office advised chief constables to make arrangements for blood or urine samples to be obtained from persons providing breath samples at police stations (if the latter so opted). This was carried out so that motorists would be in a position to have their body fluid analysed and to make a direct comparison with the result of their breath analysis (see Home Office Circulars 28/84, 32/84 and 80/84). However, the failure of the police to comply with this Home Office advice would not result in a motorist being acquitted (see *McGrath v. Field* [1987] R.T.R. 349). This non-statutory option was terminated with effect from January 20, 1989 (see Home Office Circular 39/89).

16–04 This method of challenging the results of a breath analysis is not available to a person since he is not given a sample to enable him to obtain his own independent analysis. The best course of action for any motorist would be to telephone his doctor on his release from custody. He should arrange for the latter to take a sample of his blood as soon as practicable. He could then have it analysed to establish if it corroborated or undermined the breath analysis. Due allowance must, of course, be made for the time difference between the provision of the two samples (see section 9–24 *et seq.*). In theory a motorist could do likewise with a urine sample, but might encounter great difficulty in persuading a court of the time at which he had supplied it.

B. The Breathalyser

16–05 This section considers topics relevant to the question of whether or not the breathalyser has malfunctioned.

I. EVIDENCE OF GENERAL UNRELIABILITY OF THE BREATHALYSER

In *Lion Laboratories Ltd v. Evans* [1985] Q.B. 526, the Court of Appeal **16–06** indicated that documents, alleging that the Lion Intoximeter 3000 was unreliable and may lead to wrongful convictions, ought not to be made the subject of an injunction to prevent their publication. It held that in view of public disquiet, the information ought to be made known to the public. Despite the concern expressed by the Court of Appeal, a number of decisions of the High Court only served to increase the possibility of a wrongful conviction. In a number of cases (*e.g. R. v. Coventry Magistrates' Court, ex p. Perks* [1985] R.T.R. 74; *R. v. Teeside Justices*, unreported, December 24, 1984), defendants tried to obtain copies of documents relating to Intoximeters in general in order to support their contention that no reliance could be placed upon such machines. However, in all these cases it was held that evidence of the general unreliability of breath alcohol measuring instruments could not be given. This was because they were approved by the Secretary of State, and therefore their general performance was a matter for that Minister of the Crown, and not for the courts. In the words of Goff L.J. in *R. v. Skegness Magistrates' Court, ex p. Cardy* [1985] R.T.R. 49, 61:

" . . . the Lion Intoximeter 3000 device is and has been since 19 April 1983 an approved device for the purposes of the Act and, so long as that state of affairs continues, it is, in our judgement, wholly immaterial to mount a challenge to the general reliability of these approved devices in individual prosecutions brought under the Act."

However, his Lordship had confirmed earlier in his judgment that he **16–07** could see nothing untoward in a defendant trying to show that there was some individual fault with the relevant individual machine at the actual time when he had blown into it:

"In any event, it is one thing to challenge the reliability of the particular device upon which the defendant's breath was tested at the relevant time, which may be entirely proper in the circumstances of a particular case, and another thing to attempt to challenge the reliability of Lion Intoximeter 3000 devices generally."

To the same effect is *Hornigold v. DPP*, unreported, May 27, 1984. In the early 1990s a number of motorists whose Intoximeter readings were in the low forties were acquitted at petty sessions because of scientific evidence that the volatile hydrocarbons on their breath (see section 16–63) could have been the cause of them being shown to have an alcohol level above the legal limits. This was because the Intoximeter had failed to differentiate between alcohol and hydrocarbons. This defence did not find favour with the Director of Public Prosecutions who "resurrected" *R. v. Skegness JJ., ex p. Cardy* in *Healy v. DPP* [1996] R.T.R. 247, where the High Court held that since no Intoximeter could differentiate between alcohol and hydrocarbons, then such evidence pertained to general unreality and, accordingly, could not be adduced. The court held that this inadmissibility had not been altered by the House of Lords' decision in *Cracknell v. Willis* [1988] A.C. 450, which had overruled numerous High Court cases which had limited the evidence that could be used to challenge the unreliability of a particular Intoximeter. There Lord Goff stated:

" . . . It was open to Parliament to consider whether a specimen of breath so provided should constitute conclusive evidence of the quantity of alcohol in the defendant's breath . . . Parliament might have decided so to provide on the grounds that the public interest . . . was so great . . . But in my opinion, on the true construction of the present Act, no such provision has been enacted." (At 471A–C.)

Likewise, Lord Griffiths said:

" . . . Trial by machine is an entirely novel concept and should be introduced with a degree of caution . . . It would be *unthinkable that it could be intended that anyone should be convicted by an unreliable machine.*" (At 459A–Author's emphasis.)

16–08   That case involved an attack on the reliability of a particular Intoximeter but it is submitted that the above quotations from their Lordships' speeches show that there was no restriction of the evidence which can be used to impeach the accuracy of a breathalyser, even if that would undermine the reliability of all such devices and not just the one blown into by the defendant. This is especially so in view of Lord Griffiths' dictum (at 467F) that: "We all know that no machine is infallible."

Cases such as *Healy v. DPP* involved an attack on an Intoximeter which displayed no visible signs of inaccuracy. Where there is a visible defect, the prosecution cannot dismiss it by evidence that all breathalysers malfunction in the same way. So an Intoximeter which showed a wrong date was held to be inaccurate even though (in those days) no Intoximeter could deal with a leap year, and February 29 was always shown as March 1; see *Slender v. Boothby* [1986] R.T.R. 385.

Should the prosecution call evidence of reliability, then, in accordance with the principle in *Young v. Flint* [1987] R.T.R. 300, evidence in rebuttal can be called by the defence (*e.g.* an electrical engineer to testify about the analogue digital convertor; see Chapter 13).

II. THE EUROPEAN CONVENTION ON HUMAN RIGHTS

16–09   Article 6(3) states:

"3. Everyone charged with a criminal offence has the following minimum rights:
    a. to be informed promptly, in a language which he understands and in detail, of the nature and cause of the accusation against him;

b. to have adequate time and facilities for the preparation of his defence;

c. to defend himself in person or through legal assistance of his own choosing or, if he has not sufficient means to pay for legal assistance, to be given it free when the interests of justice so require;

d. to examine or have examined witnesses against him and to obtain the attendance and examination of witnesses on his behalf under the same conditions as witnesses against him;

e. to have the free assistance of an interpreter if he cannot understand or speak the language used in court."

The significant clause is (d). If the defence are not allowed to call any evidence to suggest that all Intoximeters are unreliable, then clearly the prosecution cannot adduce evidence of general reliability. However, it is submitted that clause 6(d) goes further and leads to the following result. If a court disallows any testimony relating to the performance of the actual Intoximeter used in the case being adduced by the defendant (because, *e.g.* that criticism would apply to all other Intoximeters), then the Director of Public Procecutions would likewise be stopped from calling any evidence to show that the machine was working accurately. Without such proof, she will not be able to satisfy section 69 of the Police and Criminal Evidence Act (see Chapter 15) and so will not be able to put before the court the result of the analysis. The Human Rights Convention is not incorporated into English law, so its provision will not assist in obtaining an acquittal; but, where evidence of unreliability is refused, the Convention will enable the motorist to obtain compensation from the Crown for all loss flowing from the driving disqualification imposed on conviction.

III. EVIDENCE OF PREVIOUS PERFORMANCE

(a) HEARSAY EVIDENCE

Although the accuracy of a particular breathalyser can always be called into **16–10** question, the defence will still be severely hampered if it is not entitled to see any of its logs, or the results of previous analyses, test records, services repair reports, etc., of the actual Intoximeter in question. When breath alcohol measuring instruments were first introduced, the High Court was faced with a flood of cases concerning attempts (some successful and others not so successful) in the lower courts to obtain discovery or production of such documents. All those attempts met with failure in the High Court. Part of the reasoning of these early decisions was that the only power to issue witness summonses in magistrates' courts was contained in section 97 of the Magistrates' Courts Act 1980, *i.e.* justices could only issue a witness summons to compel the attendance at court of what was "likely to be material evidence" and that these documents were not evidence, but inadmissible hearsay. In the words of Otton J. in *R. v. North Avon Justices, ex p. Davies*, unreported, July 3, 1985:

"The memory roll is simply a long printout showing all the breath tests carried out on the machine. Service repair reports speak for themselves. A document such as an Intoximeter log, or a service repair report on an Intoximeter at a police station is not evidence of the truth of its contents . . . "

Similar sentiments were expressed in *ex p. Cardy* [1985] R.T.R. 49 at 59B, *per* Robert Goff C.J.

(b) CRIMINAL JUSTICE ACT 1988

16–11 The hearsay rule has now been altered out of all recognition in criminal cases by the Criminal Justice Act 1988, so that the rationale of *ex p. Davies*, above, will no longer apply. Section 24 of that Act states:

"(1) . . . a statement in a document shall be admissible in criminal proceedings as evidence of any fact of which direct oral evidence would be admissible, if the following conditions are satisfied—
   (i) the document was created or received by a person in the course of a trade, business, profession or other occupation, or as the holder of a paid or unpaid office; and
   (ii) the information contained in the document was supplied by a person . . . who had, or may reasonably be supposed to have had, personal knowledge of the matters dealt with."

Clearly, that section makes "breathalyser documents" admissible in evidence as they will have been produced by people who (in the course of their employment) were present at the time the tests, repairs, etc., were carried out and would therefore have had personal knowledge of those facts. Although subsection (4) goes on to say that subsection (1) does not apply to documents brought into existence for a criminal investigation, the courts have interpreted this to mean that such a document cannot be used only in the actual proceedings for which it was prepared and it is perfectly admissible under that section in any other court case (see *R. v. Iqbal* [1990] 1 W.L.R. 756, 764). Thus breathalyser documents relating to other motorists will still be admissible in evidence under section 24, notwithstanding subsection (4).

(c) DISCOVERY

16–12 So far as appeals to, or trials in, the Crown Court are concerned, that court has power to issue witness summonses to compel a person to attend at a trial to give oral evidence or produce documents. The power to do this is contained in both the Criminal Procedure (Attendance of Witnesses) Act 1964 and in the Supreme Court Act 1981. Section 45(4) of that latter Act, so far as material, is as follows:

" . . . The Crown Court shall, in relation to the attendance and examination of witnesses, any contempt of court, the enforcement of its orders and *all other matters incidental to its jurisdiction*, have the like powers, rights, privileges and authority as the High Court."

Has that statute given the Crown Court much wider powers than a magistrates' court has in these matters? It could be argued that section 45 bestowed upon the Crown Court the same power as the High Court to order pre-trial discovery and inspection of all relevant documents, even if hearsay. This is most unlikely since that would present a radical departure from the established procedure for criminal trials. Accordingly, the best way to interpret the words in italics would be to construe them as being *ejusdem generis* with the preceding matters mentioned in the section and not as applying to discovery of documents.

(d) "Fishing Expeditions"

The other ground for refusing the motorist any access to such records has **16–13** not been reversed by legislation. As the defence does not know what information they may hold, any attempt to view them is regarded as a "fishing expedition" and is therefore not permissible. In *R. v. North Avon Justices, ex p. Davies*, above, Otton J. quoted with approval from the judgment in *R. v. Skegness Magistrates' Court, ex p. Cardy* [1985] R.T.R. 49, 60:

> "It must, we are sure, be a matter of the greatest concern to all those concerned with this device that a defective instrument should not result in the conviction of an innocent man of an offence under the Road Traffic Act of 1972. Solicitors acting for defendants must constantly be met with assertions by their clients that the amount of alcohol consumed by them was so small that it could not possibly have resulted in the reading revealed on the printout from the device which carried out the relevant sampling and testing. They may think it right, in the circumstances of a particular case, to challenge the reliability of the particular device at the hearing of the charge against their client. But they have no right to discovery of documents with a view to searching for material which might support a submission that the device in question was defective at the relevant time and, as the present case shows, they must not misuse the witness summons procedure for the purposes of obtaining discovery."

Thus, nowadays, the obstacle to obtaining Intoximeter documents is **16–14** relevance. If they are merely sought to try to support what the court thinks is a totally speculative defence, then they do not have to be disclosed. So even after *Cracknell v. Willis*, above, had been decided, the High Court in *R. v. Tower Bridge Stipendiary Magistrate, ex p. DPP* [1989] R.T.R. 118, held that the accused was on a "fishing expedition" when he sought to obtain the service record and the machine log of an Intoximeter on the grounds that its reading (61µg) was inconsistent with what he had consumed (a pint of shandy). Accordingly, the court quashed the witness summons. The lead judgment in that case was given by Paul Kennedy J. who, six years later, agreed with the judgment of Alliot J. in *McKeown v. DPP* [1995] Crim. L.R. 69. There the court was of the opinion that justices could order production of the circuit diagrams of the Intoximeter from its manufacturers where one of their directors had testified that any inaccuracy of its clock did not in any way effect its analytical functioning. The witness also said that such a diagram would show if his opinion on this point was correct. (In that case the clock was 13 minutes slow.) There the defence were not seeking the documents to prove malfunctioning. They were only relevant to rebut the specific testimony of an expert. Future cases will almost certainly not extend the limited decision in that case. Indeed, Kennedy L.J. was of the opinion that the justices at the trial (where the question of a witness summons was first raised) were entitled to refuse to order production if no request had been made to the Director of Public Prosecutions in advance that the witness should bring the documents to court. No witness summons could have been sought in advance of the hearing since the diagrams were only relevant if the director gave evidence. (A copy of his evidence had been served in advance but that was no guarantee that he would actually turn up in court and go into the box.)

16–15   At the time of going to press the decision in *DPP v. McKoewn* was awaited, the House of Lords having heard argument on the 10th and 11th November, 1996. While hearing counsels' submissions in that case, Lord Goff described *Ex p. Cardy, supra,* as the biggest fishing expedition he had ever come across. Lord Mustill expressed the tentative view that where there was clear evidence of some error (*e.g.* in that case the clock was thirteen minutes slow) then if the defence led convincing expert evidence that the fault could have effected the result of the analysis but without seeing certain documents the witness could not give a definite opinion, there was no reason why the justices should not, in those circumstances, order the relevant documents to be put in evidence by the breathalyser's manufacturers. Counsel for the Crown did not dissent from that suggestion. In the past, the major objection to such a course of action has been from Lion Laboratories Limited. The author suspects that in the very few cases where the justices will in future order disclosure, Lion Laboratories will prevail upon the DPP to offer no evidence and thus avoid having to obey a witness summons.

In *R. v. Bromley JJ., ex p. Smith* [1994] T.L.R. 62 the High Court held that in summary trials (as well as those on indictment) the prosecution must disclose all material documents in their possession to the defence. That decision still leaves open the question of what is "relevant". It is definitely not a "rod" with which an accused can fish out every breathalyser document in the possession of the Crown or the police. Exactly the same can be said about the obligation of disclosure imposed upon the DPP by Part I of the Criminal Procedure and Investigations Act 1996. (Not yet in force at the time of going to press.) Accordingly, that statute has not overruled the existing law on disclosure in drinking and driving cases. Section 1 of the Act imposes a duty on a prosecutor to reveal any material which might undermine the prosecution case. The prosecution will avoid disclosure by quoting McNeil J. in *R. v. Coventry JJ., ex p. Perks* [1985] R.T.R. 74, 76 that he could not see how the records of the Intoximeter over the previous month could have any relevance to its performance on a particular day. From the way it was said, one could read "previous day" for "previous month" and not alter the sense of his pronouncement. Also section 21 of Criminal Procedure and Investigation Act abolishes any obligation of disclosure at common law and section 1(2)(a) of the Act limits disclosure only to material which came into the prosecution's hands during the course of the investigation against the particular accused to whom the obligation of disclosure applies. Thus, under the 1996 Act, there is no obligation at law to disclose any fault concerning the Intoximeter which will have been discovered while another person was being breathalysed or while it was undergoing a routine check. Any obligation under common law to do so has been abolished. The Act should be renamed the Prevention of Useful Disclosure to the Motorist Act!

(e) CASES INVOLVING LARGE DIFFERENCES

In *R. v. Kingston-upon-Hull JJ., ex p. Walton*, unreported, May 17, 1983 and **16–16** *R. v. North Avon JJ., ex p. Davies*, unreported, July 3, 1983, the High Court held that witness summonses could not be issued for Intoximeter documents just because the defence were alleging unreliability because of the large difference (see sections 16–39 *et seq.*) between the two analyses. As can be seen from later in this chapter, that could be, but need not be, evidence of a malfunction. They do occur but are rare. If a machine was consistently producing readings with big discrepancies between them that would be highly cogent evidence of unreliability. It is submitted that in view of the changed judicial attitude to such matters, and in accordance with the decision in *R. v. Bromley JJ., ex p. Smith*, above (until overruled by the coming into force of section 21), nowadays the prosecution should in such cases be ordered to produce the log showing all previous readings recorded on the Intoximeter. (Such a document would be admissible under section 24 of the Criminal Justice Act). An application for any other document would still not be granted as that would be a fishing expedition.

The importance of these records relating to past performance can be seen by the case of *DPP v. McAll*, December 1990/February 1991, Dewsbury Magistrates' Court, a case of driving with excess alcohol. According to the written judgment of the justices, the reason for the acquittal was that they could not rely upon the Intoximeter in view of the large differences between the results of the analyses of the two samples provided by both the defendant (48 per cent difference) *and* (author's emphasis) the previous motorist to have been tested (a 52 per cent difference). Indeed, the latter was not prosecuted as he had opted to give blood pursuant to the Road Traffic Act, s.8(2) 1988 and this revealed an alcohol level below the prescribed limit.

(f) CRIMINAL JUSTICE ACT 1967, S.9

The reader may wonder how the Dewsbury Bench learned of the other **16–17** analysis. The answer is simple. Because of the large difference between Mr McAll's two breath readings, the prosecution consulted an expert. They then served his statement under section 9 of the Criminal Justice Act 1967. In that, the witness referred to having based his conclusions on, *inter alia*, the memory role. Once another document is mentioned in a "section 9" statement, then the defence is entitled to a copy of it. (Of course, if the expert is cross-examined on what material he took into account in reaching his conclusions, he is almost certainly bound to reply that it was based, *inter alia*, on the device's log, etc., so that the opposing litigant would then be entitled to look at those documents.) However, it will only be in a very rare case that the Director of Public Prosecutions will go to the trouble and expense of instructing an expert, namely where the defence discloses its hand in advance and this has forewarned the Director of Public Prosecutions, so that she has to consult her own expert.

(g) CROSS-EXAMINATION OF THE POLICE

16–18 If the defence does not accept evidence being given by certificate under the provisions of section 16 of the Road Traffic Offenders Act 1988 or the Transport and Works Act, s.35, then the prosecution will have to call an officer who can link the man in the dock with the breath analysis that is relied upon to prove the charge under section 5. That will almost certainly be the actual policeman who administered the breath test. The witness may be asked a question by the prosecutor relating to the past performance of the Intoximeter or to tests he has administered on other people at about the same time as the defendant's test; or the witness might volunteer such information in answering a question. In order to give his reply, he may need to refer to documents, in which case they will become available for inspection by the defence (see *Burnell v. British Transport Commission* [1956] 1 Q.B. 187).

However, he may answer from memory, in which case he should then be asked if he had made a note of such facts, to which he is bound to answer in the affirmative. (This is because all police forces require their constables to make a written record of everything that happens during the administration of the breathalyser procedure.) The witness can then be asked to check his answer with his notes. Once he has looked at them, the defence will be entitled to see them and to cross-examine upon them (see *Owen v. Edwards* (1984) 77 Cr.App.R. 191). That would not make them become exhibits (see *Senat v. Senat* [1965] P. 172), but they would almost certainly comply with the statutory requirements so that they would be admissible as evidence of the truth of their contents by virtue of section 24 of the Criminal Justice Act 1988. Having used this opportunity to see the documents, the defence would know if they contained any relevant information. For example, they might reveal some indication of a malfunction, *e.g.* the four people tested both before and after the accused might all have had a difference of at least 21 per cent between their two respective analyses (see sections 16–39 *et seq.*). Accordingly, the defence would now be entitled to demand that such documents be put in evidence. This could not be called a "fishing expedition" since their contents would already be know to the accused.

(h) OTHER EVIDENCE INDICATING AN INACCURATE ANALYSIS

Although discovery is not allowed to a motorist to enable him to learn **16–19** about the "track record" of a particular device, there may be indications from the material already available to him (*e.g.* the printout) which will enable him to form some conclusions about the accuracy of an analysis carried out by a particular device (see sections 16–26 *et seq.*).

IV. THE BURDEN OF PROOF

R. v. Medway JJ., ex p. Goddard [1995] R.T.R. 207 made it clear that under **16–20** P.A.C.E. 1984, s.69, it was for the prosecution to prove the accuracy of the results of any analysis displayed on a breathalyser's screen (see Chapter 14) and reproduced on its printout (see Chapter 15). If the equipment used for analysing body fluid is a gas chromatograph and this does not involve the use of a computer, then section 69 of P.A.C.E. will have no bearing on the matter. There will, therefore, be the presumption of *omnia praesumuntur rite et solemniter esse acta, i.e.* that the machine used to determine the alcohol level in the blood or urine was working correctly and has produced an accurate result. This presumption has been affirmed in a number of decisions, *e.g. Chief Constable of Kent v. Ellis*, unreported, April 15, 1985 and *Castle v. Cross* [1985] R.T.R. 62 at 66F–H. The reader should note that these are pre-P.A.C.E. cases, but their *ratio* is still applicable to instruments not incorporating a computer. However, nowadays, the Home Office Forensic Science Service link their gas chromatographs to a computer which converts the graph into figures and then prints the results. That printout is subject to section 69.

V. THE STANDARD OF PROOF

(a) EVIDENCE BY PRINTOUT

If its printout is tendered in evidence, then the only thing needed to **16–21** establish the reliability of a breath alcohol measuring instrument is a section 69 certificate (see Chapter 15).

(b) ORAL EVIDENCE

If the prosecution rely on oral evidence of the results of the analysis, they **16–22** must call an officer who can testify that the test was performed in a satisfactory manner and that the words and figures which appeared on the instrument's screen were all correct, *e.g.* as to calibration, etc. He will usually be the officer who conducted the test but need not be so. However, the witness must possess the qualifications laid down by Watkins L.J. in *Denneny v. Harding* [1986] R.T.R. 350, 356:

"The police officer is not in a position to give evidence unless he is one who has been trained upon the use of [the] device and its manner of performance. He has to be one who understands the calibration process and recognises that unless the result of that process lies within accepted limits the machine is not calibrating as it should and is therefore unreliable."

(c) How to Determine who is a Trained Officer

16–23 Whenever the prosecution calls somebody whom they claim to be "a trained officer", it is a matter for the court, after hearing the cross-examination of that policeman, to decide if the witness does indeed fulfil that requirement. Whether the court will regard him as "trained upon . . . the device" will depend on what questions were put to him by the defence and on what answers he gave.

Answers to the following questions would probably establish whether or not the witness could be regarded as sufficiently trained to give the requisite information regarding calibration and the administration of the breath analysis:

(i) What are the consequences of the machine failing to expel a printout?

(ii) How and why will the machine always print out the same figures as are shown on the video-display unit?

(iii) Has he ever come across a case where the figures shown on the screen and printout were different?

(iv) If the answer to (iii) is "no", how often has he checked that function on the machine?

(v) Can he explain the function keys and the meaning of the symbols which appear on the Intoximeter's display unit? (These have already been explained in Chapter 13.)

(vi) What would he do if various problems occur (*e.g.* no printout)?

Anybody can easily discover if the answers given to the above questions were correct by referring to the operator's handbook which is on sale to the public. The latter can always be put in evidence under section 24 of the Criminal Justice Act 1988 (see section 16–11) to contradict any of the answers given and thus disprove the prosecution's assertion that the witness is "a trained operator".

VI. THE NECESSITY FOR, AND THE SCOPE OF, EXPERT EVIDENCE

(a) The Justices' Own Knowledge

16–24 Subsequent sections discuss the means by which a breath alcohol measuring device may be challenged. In all these cases, it will be necessary to call an expert to explain to the court why the machine is unreliable. The magistrates can use their own knowledge solely with regard to what the correct calibration figures are (see section 16–27). Anything else must be established by evidence. In *Anderton v. Waring* [1986] R.T.R. 74, the motorist claimed that he had done his best to exhale into the machine. The police disputed this and said that he had blown round the mouthpiece but not into it. The High Court held that the justices could not dismiss the charge of failing to provide a specimen because they knew from their own experience of previous cases that the machine would have displayed "aborted", if the police officer was correct. (The reason was presumably that if a defendant was blowing around, instead of solely breathing into, the mouthpiece, some breath was bound to enter the Intoximeter so as to activate it, but it would not be of sufficient quantity to enable the machine to analyse it, with the result that the instrument would automatically abort and display this on its screen; see section 13–17.) However, May L.J. (at 80) made it clear that:

> "In my judgement, they were not entitled to make use of their experience of these machines nor to draw any inference from the absence of evidence that the visual display on the Lion Intoximeter 3000 showed the word 'Aborted', at least without raising the point in the course of the trial, hearing whatever evidence either side wished to call in consequence and then deciding the point on the evidence, rather than on what they have learned during, for instance, demonstrations of the machine or previous prosecutions of a similar nature."

To the same effect is *Jarvis v. DPP* [1996] R.T.R 192. There it was held that a metropolitan stipendiary magistrate was not allowed to use his own knowledge that no more than one Intoximeter was installed in any one police station in London.

In *Stokes v. Sayers* [1988] R.T.R. 89, the police officer testified that he had requested a body fluid as the Intoximeter had displayed "low abort". No evidence was given as to what this meant. The justices were of the opinion that, as they did not know what this meant, they could not be satisfied that this entitled the police to require a specimen of body fluid and accordingly acquitted the accused. That decision was upheld by the High Court. It is submitted that this is correct. The judiciary should only base a decision on the evidence in front of them and not on what they have learned in other trials. If they consider that something in the breathalyser procedure has occurred which could be favourable to the defendant, they could always adjourn the hearing and suggest to the accused that it would be in his interest to consult an expert. As a last resort justices could, of their own volition, call such a witness.

(b) ACCEPTANCE OF EXPERT EVIDENCE

It must always be borne in mind that, even in the absence of evidence to **16–25** the contrary, a court is under no obligation to accept the uncontroverted testimony of an expert. So in *Maharaj v. Soloman* [1987] R.T.R. 295, the High Court upheld the conviction where the Bench had rejected scientific evidence that the large difference between the two breath analyses threw doubt on the Intoximeter's reliability (see section 16–39). The magistrates were not convinced that the views of the witness were accepted by the scientific community; so it is always advisable for a party wishing to adduce scientific evidence to call at least two experts from different institutions. An expert must have the requisite knowledge to qualify as such: see *R. v. Inch*, *The Times*, November 28, 1989. It was held in *McKeown v. DPP* [1995] Crim L.R. 69 that a director of the manufacturers of the Intoximeter could give evidence of how it worked including its electronics even though he was a chemist and not an electrical engineer.

(c) Use of Experts not Called as Witnesses

16–26 In giving their evidence, experts can always refer to the opinion of other experts. In *R. v. Somers* [1963] 1 W.L.R. 1306 it was held that a police surgeon could base his evidence on the results obtained from experiments and tests undertaken by others, even though he himself had never conducted any research on the matter in question. In that case the Court of Criminal Appeal held that, as a doctor's training included a lecture on blood alcohol destruction rates, any medical practitioner could give evidence on that matter by reference to a table published by the British Medical Association, even though the witness was not "a man who had conducted any experiments himself, or indeed is in any real sense an expert in regard to [all the factors involved in] the conversion". Nowadays such tables and, indeed, the results of experiments carried out by a scientist (provided that they had been conducted in the course of his profession), would be admissible under the very wide-ranging provisions of section 24 of the Criminal Justice Act 1988 (see section 16–11).

VII. UNRELIABILITY APPARENT FROM THE DISPLAY ON THE SCREEN OR THE PRINTOUT

16–27 In considering the accuracy of breath alcohol measuring instruments, the first matter to be looked at is the information that appears on the printout or the visual display unit. The presence of the relevant trained operator should always be insisted upon, since his testimony will be necessary to establish everything that appeared on the screen of the breathalyser because not everything which is shown on the screen is reproduced on the printout. Such information is, of course, essential for the defence to be able to form a view on the reliability of the device used by the police.

(a) The STD Check

16–28 The Intoximeter's standard check (shown as STD on the printout) must be between 32 and 37μg. The Camic standard is 32–38μg (see Home Office Circular 32/84). The High Court held in *Waite v. Smith* [1986] Crim.L.R. 405 that the principle of *de minimis non curat lex* did not apply and if the check is only 1μg out from that approved by the Home Office, then the result of the analysis cannot be relied upon by the prosecution.

The reason why a tolerance of 5μg is allowed is because of slight variations in the strength of the alcohol solutions used in the breath simulators. The National Physical Laboratory BCS2, January 1983, Appendix A, para. 2 recommended that the two standard checks in each test cycle must be within 2μg. If the two STD readings are more than 2μg apart, a challenge to the accuracy can be made on the basis of BCS2.

(b) WHAT SHOULD APPEAR ON THE SCREEN

The "BLK" figure after the initial calibration and those immediately **16–29** following the two analyses must be shown as a zero. This is to ensure that the machine has purged itself, *i.e.* expelled all the alcohol from the sample previously tested. The printout should display the date and the time when the samples were provided. (It should be remembered that all times shown are Greenwich Mean Time.) The device cannot be considered to be functioning correctly if any of the above does not correctly appear on the printout or the screen. If any figures which appear on the screen or printout are wrong, then the analysis will not be admissible in evidence since the provisions of section 69 of P.A.C.E. 1984 will not have been complied with by the prosecution (see Chapter 15).

(c) A GREATER THAN 15 PER CENT DIFFERENCE

The difference between the two analyses should not normally exceed 15 per **16–30** cent of the lower reading. The specification for the next generation of breathalysers is that they must abort if the difference is greater than 15 per cent or 5μg, whichever is the greater. If this does occur, then it may well be possible to challenge the results of the analysis.

VIII. AN ANALOGUE/DIGITAL CONVERSION ERROR

An analogue/digital conversion error has previously been explained (see **16–31** Chapter 13) when considering the general reliability of breathalysers. Such an error can cause random figures to appear in the results of the analyses, without anybody being aware of this happening. Sometimes two random figures for the analyses will show a difference of more than 20 per cent, at other times two random numbers could be the same or very close to each other. The possibility of such an error can be used to support other allegations of malfunctioning, *e.g.* to explain the large difference between the two analyses or to account for the fact that the defendant has not drunk as much as the machine alleges he has. The possibility of an analogue/digital conversion error can also be used to rebut any prosecution suggestion of either general reliability or of impossibility for the machine to go wrong if the printout shows the calibration and purging to be correct. (In theory, such evidence of general reliability should be inadmissible for the same reason as any testimony about general unreliability is inadmissible.)

IX. THE AMOUNT OF ALCOHOL CONSUMED BY THE DEFENDANT IS NOT COMMENSURATE WITH THE RESULTS OF THE ANALYSIS

16–32 Until the decisions in *Jones v. DPP* [1995] Crim. L.R. 69 and *McKeown v. DPP, ibid.*, any challenge to the result of a breath analysis was invariably that the amount of alcohol consumed could not have put the defendant over the prescribed limit and therefore the analysis must be wrong. Despite the universal condemnation of, and the refusal to allow, such a defence by the High Court, the House of Lords, in the case of *Cracknell v. Willis* [1988] A.C. 450, finally gave recognition to the validity of such a defence. As Lord Griffiths asserted (at 467):

> "Suppose that a teetotaller after dining with people of the highest repute, two bishops if you will, forgets to turn on his lights and is stopped by the police. He is asked to take a roadside breath test and indignantly but inadvisedly refuses. He is arrested and taken to the police station. There he thinks better of his refusal. He agrees to supply two specimens of breath and the machine to his astonishment shows very high readings. He asks to be allowed to prove the machine wrong by supplying a blood or urine specimen. The police agree and he gives a blood sample. An analysis shows no alcohol in the specimen. It is virtually certain that the police would accept the analysis and he would not be prosecuted. But if he were prosecuted it is equally certain that the magistrates would prefer the analysis and he would be acquitted. But now suppose the police refuse his request to supply a blood or urine specimen because the reading on the machine was over 50 microgrammes. Is he to be convicted without the opportunity of calling the two bishops as witnesses to the fact that he had drunk nothing that evening and inviting the justices to draw the inference that the machine must have been unreliable. If he can invite the magistrates to draw such an inference from the work of the analyst, why should he not invite them to draw the inference from the word of the bishops.
>
> In my view it would require the clearest possible wording to show that Parliament intended such an unjust result. If Parliament wishes to provide that either there is to be an irrebuttable presumption that the breath testing machine is reliable or that the presumption can only be challenged by a particular type of evidence then Parliament must take the responsibility of so deciding and spell out its intention in clear language.
>
> *Until then I would hold that evidence which, if believed, provides material from which the inference can reasonably be drawn that the machine was unreliable is admissible.*" (Author's emphasis.)

The last sentence of the above quote has overruled all cases which attempted to limit the type of evidence which could be used to challenge the analysis.

However, justices were warned to examine such defences very carefully **16–33** by Lord Goff who advised them (at 472):

> "I have little doubt that the point will be taken time and time again. I place greater faith in the good sense of magistrates who, with their attention drawn to the safeguards for defendants built into the Act to which I have referred earlier in this opinion, will no doubt give proper scrutiny to such defences and will be fully aware of the strength of evidence provided by a printout, taken from an approved device, of a specimen of breath provided in accordance with the statutory procedure."

X. THE BASIS AND NATURE OF SUCH A CHALLENGE

Motorists all over the country have invited magistrates to listen to a variety **16–34** of pieces of evidence intended to persuade them that reasonable doubt existed about the accuracy of the figures on the printout. Justices listen patiently to drivers' accounts of their pre-test drinking, to testimony from highly-paid experts as to the likely breath alcohol levels which such imbibing would produce, from bystanders (some interested and some not) and police officers as to the driver's behaviour when arrested, and so on. In each and every case the object was to persuade the court that the breath alcohol level on the printout could not be reconciled with all the surrounding facts and that there was therefore a real doubt as to the accuracy of the readings. In many cases such submissions were doomed to failure for want of credible evidence, while others were wholly successful, supported by highly believable accounts of what (if anything) had actually been imbibed. The evidence which magistrates are prepared to accept can clearly be seen from the facts of the cases that they were asked by aggrieved informants to state for the opinion of the High Court. This is an extract from a case stated by the Colehill justices in *Chief Constable of Warwickshire v. Singh*, unreported, March 6, 1985:

> "We believe that the respondent had drunk no more than four pints of shandy. We are of the opinion that this intake of alcohol could not have resulted in a reading of 49μg of alcohol in a 100ml of breath and that the only possible explanation for this state of affairs was that the Intoximeter must have been faulty."

In the case of *Price v. Nicholls* [1986] R.T.R. 155, the defendant was a reformed alcoholic. The Intoximeter printout showed a lower reading of 170μg. Its operator's handbook contains a table relating breath alcohol levels to clinical symptoms. According to that table, if the Intoximeter was correct and the respondent had consumed just under five times the legal limit, then he should have been displaying signs of coma and anaesthesia, depressed or abolished reflexes, hypothermia and impaired circulation and respiration. Indeed, he was quite likely to have died. Yet the police in this case gave evidence that at the time of being arrested the motorist was quiet, polite, calm and co-operative. The magistrates acquitted as they accepted the accused's evidence that all he had drunk was three glasses of barley wine and a very small quantity of table wine. They heard expert testimony that in order to achieve a level of 170μg, the defendant would have had to have drunk three-quarters of a bottle of spirits, in addition to his admitted consumption of liquor.

16–35   In *Hughes v. McConnell* [1986] R.T.R. 244, the High Court had before it a case stated by the Shifnal justices in which they had dismissed a charge under the Road Traffic Act, s.5(1), where the reading had been 120μg. The magistrates accepted the defendant's evidence that he had only consumed three pints of shandy together with some non-alcoholic drinks and for that reason acquitted him. This was in spite of the fact that the Bench also believed prosecution evidence that as the accused drove home, he was stopped by a constable because he kept swerving across the white line in the middle of the road and, on swerving back, kept clipping the pavement. When speaking to the police his speech was slurred and he smelt of intoxicating liquor. That adjudication prompted Lord Griffiths to remark ([1988] A.C. 450, 463) that he was not at all surprised at the Divisional Court being disturbed by that decision!

16–36   The High Court is indeed sceptical of justices who accept the word of a motorist as to what he had drunk, rather than the results of an analysis by the Intoximeter. In *Young v. Flint* [1987] R.T.R. 300, the magistrates had found as a fact that Mr Young had drunk only three glasses of wine, although a breath analysis had showed him to have been over twice the legal limit. This prompted Watkins L.J. to remark that the wine must have been of "a very potent type"!

In the appeal of *DPP v. Hill* [1991] R.T.R. 351, the High Court reversed the justices' decision that the amount of alcohol imbibed by the respondent was below the legal limit. He had worked as a doorman in a licensed club for four-and-a-half hours, until 2.30 a.m. The only drink he had consumed was at the conclusion of his duty, when he had half a pint of lager. A fellow employee and his boss both gave evidence that they had not seen him drinking during that evening and the latter testified that he would have been dismissed if he were to be found drinking at work. However, neither of them had had him under observation at all times. His reading was 46μg of alcohol per 100ml of breath. He attributed his smell of intoxicants to the fact that he had been working in licensed premises that night, but there was no evidence of any liquor having been spilled on him. The High Court's reasons for ordering a conviction were given by Neil L.J. (at 356):

16–37   "[Believing that the defendant had drunk less than alleged by the Intoximeter] would involve three very surprising consequences: one that the Intoximeter itself was faulty, two not only was that faulty but the Draeger Alert device also was faulty and, finally, that there was some explanation other than drink to account for the evidence of glazed vision which was not only given by the police, but was accepted by the justices.

It seems to us, with the utmost respect to the justices, that they may perhaps have misinterpreted the effect of the decision in *Cracknell v. Willis* [1988] A.C. 450, and have thought that, because it was possible as a matter of law to rebut the presumption by evidence, that meant that might be a comparatively easy thing to do.

On the facts of this particular case it really was quite impossible to come to the conclusion that the justices reached in this case."

It is submitted that this decision has usurped the function of the Bench, **16–38** who have seen the witnesses. It can just about be explained on the grounds that the lower court drew the wrong inference from the evidence of the police that the defendant had glazed vision and that this testimony, which had been accepted by the court, had undermined the account of the respondent as to what he had to drink. In addition, the defence witnesses had not kept him constantly in sight, so he may well have had a few drinks without being seen. Indeed, any finding of fact that he did not have any alcoholic beverages without being seen would have been directly contrary to both the police accounts of his mode of driving and his state when arrested. No suggestion was made of there being any fault with the Intoximeter. It is submitted that all this case decided was that once the magistrates had accepted the police account of the facts, then in law there was only one inference that could be drawn from them, namely that the defendant had obviously been drinking far more than he had told the court and therefore there was nothing to show the Intoximeter to have been other than a reliable device. Thus was an appeal decided on its own facts and has no further bearing on subsequent cases. If the justices had rejected the evidence of the police, then the High Court would no doubt have upheld their verdict. It does demonstrate that a court will attach great importance to the defendant's physical and mental state when he is arrested and whether his condition is consistent with the amount of alcohol revealed by the analysis.

In *DPP v. Hill*, above, petty sessions accepted that the defendant was in **16–39** the condition alleged by the police, which was totally inconsistent with his account of his alcoholic intake. However, on other occasions such evidence could work in an accused's favour if he took advantage of it. He should arrange for a doctor to observe him consume alcohol until he reaches the same level at which the police allege that he drove. The doctor will confirm this by taking a blood specimen which is then analysed. The latter also observes his reaction and response to that amount of intoxicants. The medical practitioner can then be called to inform the court of the motorist's responses, compared with those alleged by the police, in relation to the same amount of alcohol. This could be of great advantage, especially in cases of very high readings, if the defendant was found by the doctor to be totally incapable of behaving (and driving) in the manner alleged by the prosecution. Often he will be incapable of driving a car or even standing upright. It will also be necessary for there to be expert evidence to establish that the amount which the defendant actually drank did not produce an alcohol level consistent with the breathalyser result. The fact that his admitted consumption must have put him over the limit is not fatal to the case, provided that it cannot be at all compatible with the Intoximeter: see *Lucking v. Forbes*, above. Also, there should be as many witnesses as possible to confirm the defence account of what the motorist had drunk. However, in view of the narrow construction placed by the High Court in *Hill's case* on the speech of Lord Griffiths in *Cracknell v. Willis*, it is doubtful if the testimony of a mere suffragan, as opposed to a diocesan, bishop would be sufficient. Also, it will often be necessary to undermine prosecution suggestions that the device could not possibly have gone wrong, if the results of its calibration and purging exercises were in order. The only way this can be achieved is by an electronic engineer testifying to the unreliability which can be caused by the occasional malfunctioning of the analogue digital converter (see Chapter 13). Indeed, it is probably best always to call such an expert, if such testimony is not ruled to be inadmissible on the grounds that it refers solely to the general unreliability of the device. Also, under section 24 of the Criminal Justice Act 1988, the Paton Report can be produced in court and the passage quoted which showed that in no less than one out of every 1,000 of the tests examined in that Report, no explanation could account for the difference between the result of the analyses of the specimens of, on the one hand, breath and, on the other hand, of blood or urine provided by the same motorist on the same occasion. The manufacturers and others would no doubt argue that an error rate of 0.19 per cent proved the machine's reliability. However, to a driver facing the potential loss of his licence, such a failure rate could have dire consequences.

XI. A LARGE DIFFERENCE BETWEEN THE TWO ANALYSES

(a) GENERALLY

(i) *The Paton Report*

16–40 Unlike blood and urine specimens which can be tested several times, a breath sample can only be analysed once. Additionally, each breath sample supplied by a motorist could well contain a different amount of alcohol, due to the manner of exhalation. For example, after a person realises on his first attempt how easy it is to blow into the machine, he may well breath more shallowly the next time, so that less deep lung air (which contains the true alcohol equivalent to that in the blood stream) enters the device. In the survey leading to the Paton Report, breath tests on 32,007 motorists were examined. In half of those tests, the difference between the two analyses was not more than 5 per cent. Only in 1.6 per cent of the tests was the disparity greater than 20 per cent. After considering all relevant matters, Sir William Paton recommended that where a breath alcohol measuring instrument showed a discrepancy between the two analyses "which exceeded some value such as 20 per cent" of the amount of the lower reading, then the person who had provided the specimens of breath should have the option of replacing them with one of blood or urine. The response of the Home Secretary is set out in his letter to Sir William dated May 23, 1985 (reproduced at pp. 5–6 of the Report):

"I also have it in mind to have the machines modified so that if the difference between two successive breath samples exceeds 20% the machine will abort with the consequences that any evidential testing will need to be by way of blood test."

In those days the major cause of a large difference was a faulty acetone detector. That cause has been virtually eliminated by the new software.

The working group on evidential breath analysers of L'Organisation **16–41** Internationale de Metrologie Legale have produced a draft report which recommends:

"Measuring Cycle
In normal operation, the measuring cycle involves two measurements that each correspond to an exhalation. The result of each measurement is delivered at the end of the measuring cycle. However, if is not possible to perform the second measurement, it shall be possible to obtain the first measurement result upon special order or after a specific period of time. In this case, it shall be indicated by the instrument that the measurement cycle has not been completed.

Note: Users should be aware that it is advisable to perform further investigations (for example, a second measurement cycle) when the difference between the two measurements of a cycle exceeds the greater of the following two values:
— 10% in relative value of the smallest value.
— 0.040mg/l [4µg/100 ml]."

Mainly on the basis of that draft and partly as a compromise between the two schools of thought (*i.e.* the academics who regard a difference of more than 10 per cent to be unacceptable and the view of Home Office Forensic Science Service that up to 20 per cent is in order), the Home Office specification (HMSO 1994, ISBN 0113411367) for the next generation of breathalysers is that they must abort if the difference exceeds 15 per cent of the lower reading or 5µg, whichever is the greater. As they are far more reliable than the present generation, if a difference of over 15 per cent makes their results suspect, then the same must also apply to the Intoximeter and the Camic.

K. L. Dubouski wrote the following letter to the *American Journal of* **16–42** *Forensic Medical Pathology* which published it in (1988) Volume 9, No. 3 at 272.

"The following position statement on duplicate breath-alcohol testing was adopted by the National Safety Council Committee on Alcohol and Other Drugs:
'National Safety Council Committee on Alcohol and Other Drugs, October 1986
Duplicate Breath-alcohol Testing
At least two separate breath samples should be collected and analysed individually in performing any quantitative evidential breath-alcohol analysis. The breath samples should be collected at intervals of not less than 2 nor more than 10 min after an initial deprivation period of at least

15 min. Reported breath-alcohol analysis results shall be truncated to two decimal places and all results obtained shall be reported. Consecutive breath-alcohol analysis results within 0.02g/210L [10µg/100 ml] without regard to sign (*sic.*), shall be deemed to be in acceptable agreement.' "

(ii) The Consequences of a Large Difference

16–43 The Home Secretary did not put into practice what he had in mind at the time when he wrote the above letter. Consequently any two successive readings with a difference greater than 10 per cent (and definitely 20 per cent) will throw doubt on the reliability of the device. However, such a discrepancy in the two readings produced by a breathalyser does not *ipso facto* entitle a court to dismiss the charge. This may only be done on the basis of expert testimony that the difference was so large that it would be unsafe to rely upon the analysis (see *Lloyd v. Morris* [1986] R.T.R. 299). Even if such evidence is given, it will be solely a question of fact, in any particular case, whether or not the difference between the two results is found to be an indication of the unreliability of the device. In *Maharaj v. Solomon* [1987] R.T.R. 295 and *Lodge v. Chief Constable of Greater Manchester* (reported on another point [1988] Crim. L.R. 533) the High Court made it plain that, if experts gave evidence about the matter, it was entirely for the magistrates to decide whether or not to accept it. The High Court would not interfere if the lower court did not accept the explanation given in the testimony of the defence expert, even if no witnesses to the contrary had been called by the prosecution. In *Lodge v. Chief Constable of Greater Manchester* it was specifically recognised that two Benches could come to opposite results on exactly the same evidence and neither verdict would be appealable. It is submitted that whenever the difference in the two analyses exceeds 15 per cent (see above), an accused should challenge the accuracy of the breathalyser. He should call at least two scientists who are familiar with breath alcohol measuring instruments and who are prepared to say that the difference between the two results was so large that the test cannot be relied upon as being correct.

(iii) Cause of a Large Difference

16–44 There are a number of reasons why a large difference may occur, not all of which are due to any error on the part of the machine. In his evidence in *DPR v. McAll*, unreported, December 16, 1990, P.M. Williams (the international marketing director of Lion Laboratories Limited) classified the cause of large disparities into two type, one being "subject factors" and the other "machine factors". The former are due to the characteristics of the person who blows into the device. P.M. Williams also subdivided each category into four subdivisions. Each of these will be considered separately. (Unless otherwise stated, the commentary on each subdivision is that of the author.) If one of these factors were to occur, it could well cause an erroneous reading, which might be either much smaller or larger than the true one; and if it effected only one, and not both, of the two analyses, it would cause a large variation between the two.

(b) SUBJECT FACTORS

P.M. Williams described these as (i) mouth alcohol; (ii) hyperventilation; **16–45**
(iii) blowing technique; and (iv) other substances.

(i) Mouth Alcohol

Its causes (apart from the obvious one) and its effects are dealt with later in **16–46**
this chapter (see section 16–59). All that need be said about it here is that it
evaporates very rapidly and, provided none is drunk in the interval
between them, it will be the cause of a large difference between the two
readings.

(ii) Hyperventilation

This is the technique of taking rapid breaths before blowing into the **16–47**
mouthpiece. The breathalysers approved by the Home Secretary for
analysing breath samples work on the principle of Henry's Law, namely
that the same volume of alcohol in the blood is transferred to the air in the
lungs when those two substances are at the same temperature. Hyperventilation has the effect of cooling down the mouth and the throat and
condensing some of the alcohol out of the respiratory tract before it enters
the mouth. This will produce a much lower reading than normal and, if
done before only one of the analyses, it will lead to a large disparity
between the two results. In a paper for the Karolinski Institute in
Stockholm in 1982, A.W. Jones reported that 20 seconds' hyperventilation
had reduced the temperature of the air in the lungs by 1°C, which had the
effect of reducing the alcoholic content of the breath therein by 10 per cent.

(iii) Blowing Technique

It is possible to inhale fresh air and exhale it without it passing through the **16–48**
lungs, thereby avoiding it being contaminated with ethanol. This is a
technique used by players of certain wind instruments but requires a lot of
practice to perfect it.

(iv) Other Substances

If, very shortly before blowing into the machine, or between blows, a **16–49**
motorist drinks certain non-alcoholic liquids, or consumes certain substances, *e.g.* a patent medicine, this could have the same effect on the
reading as mouth alcohol.
    The instructions in the operator's handbook specify that the operator
should ensure that the motorist has not drunk for 20 minutes, nor smoked
for five minutes, before the test. (It normally takes at least this amount of
time for an arrested person to arrive at the police station, be documented
and then be requested to provide breath specimens.) Provided the police
have waited the requisite time, unless there is evidence that the defendant

had been seen doing one of the things mentioned above it will not be open to the prosecution to suggest that any of those respective matters caused the big difference between the two readings. This is because all of these would clearly have been visible either to the arresting officer or to the operator of the breathalyser. The only exception is regurgitation of alcohol from the stomach to the mouth which is then exhaled.

(c) MACHINE FACTORS

16–50 According to P.M. Williams there are four possible machines errors, namely (i) acetone deduction; (ii) incorrect breath volume requirement; (iii) analogue/digital conversion error; and (iv) an unspecified fault.

(i) Acetone Deduction

16–51 The frequency used by the Intoximeter for its infra-red beam in the analytical chamber is one which will be absorbed by both the alcohol and by any acetone present in the breath (see Chapter 13). Accordingly, the Intoximeter uses a semi-conductor to detect the acetone, and the necessary adjustment is made from the amount of "alcohol" which has already been detected in the breath. A large difference in the two readings will naturally occur should the Intoximeter under- or over-compensate for acetone in one of the samples but correctly allow for it in the other. According to the Paton Report, over-compensating for acetone, where there was in fact none, was the major cause of the blood analysis not correlating with that of the breath. This will most likely be the prosecution's answer to a large disparity when there is no evidence of "subject error". Since the Paton Report, Lion Laboratories have introduced new software to test the acetone detector during calibration and the execution of this test is indicated to the operator by the sound of a click. If there is a malfunction in the Taguchi cell, the words "*A.D. FAULT*" will appear on the screen. However, Lion Laboratories admit that the new software has not completely solved the problem and that over- or under-compensation for acetone can still occur for one of the two analyses, but only very rarely. It is submitted that if such an error did occur, then by virtue of P.A.C.E., s.69 (see Chapter 15), at least one of the readings would be inadmissible in evidence. By applying the logic of *Cracknell v. Willis* [1988] A.C. 450, the defendant would have to be acquitted, since the prosecution could not obtain a conviction by relying solely upon the single analysis if, that is, the whole printout has not been ruled inadmissible by section 69.

(ii) Incorrect Breath Volume Requirement

16–52 Breath alcohol measuring instruments are all designed to analyse deep lung air. To ensure that sufficient air is expelled from the lungs to enable it to receive deep breath, a minimum of 1.5 litres of air has to be blown into the Intoximeter in order to achieve an analysis. If the machine malfunctions and carries out its analysis before the requisite volume has been exhaled into it, it is likely to give an artificially low reading.

(iii) *An Analogue/Digital Conversion Error*

The causes and effects of an analogue/digital conversion error have already **16–53** been considered in Chapter 13, above. Lion Laboratories readily admit that such a malfunction could be the cause of large difference between the two analyses. It is submitted that an electronic engineer should always be called whenever the defence cannot offer any other explanation for it. He can explain a large discrepancy between the two readings as probably being due to a conversion fault and that no reliance can accordingly be placed on either reading.

(iv) *An Unspecified Fault*

This error speaks for itself. Anything can go wrong with a box of **16–54** electronics!

In *Varma v. DPP*, unreported, January 31, 1995 (Knightsbridge Crown **16–55** Court), Professor V. Marks gave his views to the court on this topic:

"There are a number of possible reasons why breath alcohol measurements might differ by more than 10μg/100ml.

The first, but amongst the less likely (though possible), is that the measuring instrument is giving erroneous analytical results.

Another is that alcohol is still being very rapidly absorbed from the intestine. In this case the concentration of alcohol in the blood is itself rising with the passage of time and this would be reflected in a (genuine) rise in the breath alcohol concentration with the passage of time. Although I have no knowledge of experiments undertaken to investigate the minimum, average and maximum rate at which such changes in blood alcohol can occur I would be surprised if it was ever fast enough to account for a 10μg per minute increment in breath alcohol concentration (corresponding to a 4.5mg/100ml blood) over a one minute period. This explanation cannot account for decrements in breath alcohol concentrations, only differences in which the first value is the lower of the two measurements.

Another, and commoner reason for such large (or even much larger) discrepancies between two successive breath alcohol measurements is the presence of high concentrations of alcohol in the mouth and upper respiratory passages, *i.e.* the pharynx or throat, that are not reflected in the concentration of alcohol in the body as a whole. This fact was appreciated quite early on in the history of breath alcohol testing and is the reason why an interval of 20 minutes must elapse between a person ceasing to drink and a breath alcohol test being performed.

Exactly the same effect can, however, be produced by the regurgitation of alcohol-rich stomach contents as would be present in the stomach of someone who had recently consumed an alcoholic beverage—especially if the stomach had previously been empty. This phenomenon, referred to in the medical literature as gastro-oesophageal reflex, can cause entry into the mouth of gastric contents which can be detected by the 'sufferer' but not by anyone else. As pointed out in *Cecil's Essentials of Medicine*, 3rd ed., p. 285: 'Many otherwise healthy individuals have occasional heartburn or regurgitation.' It only 'becomes a disease when the symptoms are severe and frequent . . . 'Regurgitation differs from eructation or 'belching' which is the expulsion of swallowed gas from the stomach.

There are very few data of which I am aware showing how high a breath alcohol measurement can be, or is, achieved by the occurrence of regurgitation."

In that case the difference was 13 per cent. Judge Munro-Davies, sitting with lay justices, quashed the conviction on the basis of the above evidence.

XII. INTERFERING SUBSTANCES IN THE BREATH

(a) GENERALLY

16–56 As these affect all Intoximeters, such testimony is evidence of general unreliability and is not admissible: see *Healy v. DPP*, above. The fact that such substances do exist was recognised in the Paton Report (at p. 13):

"Acetone is just one example of the class of interfering substances, *i.e.* substances other than alcohol that might appear in the breath, be detected as alcohol and (if not measured separately) cause the Intoximeter or the Camic to give a false reading."

By comparing the results of the analyses of both breath and blood provided by the same person, the Paton Report found no real evidence of other interfering substances save acetone, except in a very few special cases, usually involving glue sniffers. The Report was also of the opinion that taste and smell would be a poor guide to what these special substances could be, but they would have to be of relatively low molecular weight. A good example would be an ex-hospital patient with a residue of volatile anaesthetics. In an article in (1990) Vol. 30, No. 3, *Medical Science Law* 203, entitled "The Effect of Respiratory Aerosol Inhalers and Nasal Sprays on Breath Alcohol Testing Used in Great Britain", the authors (P.J. Gomm, S.I. Weston and M.D. Osselton) are of the view that:

"In practice, very few substances occur naturally in breath which exhibit absorption in the appropriate region of the infra-red spectrum and which are likely to be present in sufficiently high concentrations to affect the quantitative measurements of alcohol. The exception to this is acetone; however both of the instruments used for evidential purposes are capable of discriminating against this compound."

Most of the substances that could cause an artificially high reading will cease to have that effect a short time after their consumption. Thus their effect on a breathalyser's reading will be nil if the police follow the manufacturer's instructions and wait 20 minutes after the motorist has last eaten or drunk anything before administering the test. Indeed, it is highly unlikely that less than 20 minutes will have elapsed between a person's arrest on the highway, his transportation back to the police station, his documentation and finally his provision of a breath sample.

The most likely substances to cause a fairly high reading on the **16–57** Intoximeter are:

(1) acetone
(2) mouth alcohol
(3) volatile hydrocarbons

(i) Acetone

When the Intoximeter was produced it was believed that acetone was **16–58** commonly found on the breath. Since then it has been learnt that it was inversely proportional to the amount of alcohol in the body and that if a non-pregnant lady or a non-diabetic had drunk sufficient alcohol to have taken his or her alcohol level beyond the prescribed limit, his or her body should contain none of this substance; see "Breath Acetone Concentrations in Fasting Male Volunteers: Further Studies and Effect of Alcohol Administration" by A.W. Jones (1988) 12 *Journal of Alcohol Toxicology*. The reason for this is that the main cause of acetone is fasting. When a person has not been eating and accordingly has not replaced his carbohydrates, he makes up for this deficiency by breaking down and "eating up" his own keytone bodies. A by-product of this break-down is acetone. If somebody had drunk sufficient alcohol to have exceeded the legal limit allowed for driving, then that imbibing will have provided him with sufficient carbohydrates to prevent him from breaking down his body fat, so that there will be no acetone on his breath. There are also some medical conditions which cause acetone, but, save for diabetes and pregnancy, are very rare. In those circumstances, where acetone is not due to the break-down of body fat, it can coexist with alcohol.

It is one of the substances which will be wrongly treated as alcohol by the infra-red absorption method of analysis used by the Intoximeter. Accordingly, the latter incorporates a semi-conductor to detect acetone and to make the necessary deduction from its analysis. The Paton Report found that over-compensation for acetone resulting in a falsely low reading was far more likely than under-compensation. Nevertheless, the latter remains a possibility. Acetone is produced by certain diabetics and if the printout does not indicate that an allowance for acetone has been made in the case of a person suffering from diabetes, then there is a possibility that the result of the analysis was too high. This is discussed further in section 16–28.

(ii) Mouth Alcohol

Its Effects

The devices approved by the Secretary of State are designed to measure **16–59** gaseous alcohol (*i.e.* that found on the breath), not liquid alcohol. If the latter is blown into the analytical chamber, the breathalyser will produce a reading far in excess of the true breath alcohol concentration. However, liquid alcohol evaporates very quickly, as is illustrated by a test mentioned in the Intoximeter handbook. A breath test was administered to a person who had consumed a quantity of whisky immediately beforehand and this produced a reading of 240μg. Twelve minutes later the reading was down to a single figure. Experiments carried out by R. Denny show that the effect of mouth alcohol is roughly halved every minute, so on two readings of, say, 80 and 60μg one minute apart, half of the mouth alcohol (*i.e.* 20μg) will have dissipated in that minute. Deduct the other half from 60 and one will obtain the true level of 40μg. Thus, if the manufacturers' instructions are followed and the police allow 20 minutes to elapse between the provision of the specimen and the last drink, by then any alcohol in the mouth will have evaporated.

Its Causes

16–60 Besides the residue of the alcohol drunk remaining in the mouth, the most usual causes of mouth alcohol are regurgitation (*i.e.* a gastro-oesophageal reflex, from which, on occasion, everybody suffers), vomiting or belching. Belching causes droplets of alcohol to be deposited in the mouth. If those droplets are then blown into a breathalyser, it will give an inaccurate reading. As to vomiting the reader is referred to the evidence of Sellwood (the consultant in charge of the casualty unit) at Truro General Hospital:

> "Following a head injury patients are more prone to vomiting . . . Vomiting is so common after a head injury that it is one of the symptoms which we directly question the patient for in trying to determine whether they have a head injury . . .
>
> Vomiting is an active process combining the action of involuntary gastric muscles and voluntary muscles in the abdominal wall and produces a forceful ejection of stomach contents through the mouth. This is as opposed to regurgitation which is a passive process whereby in a patient whose conscious level is diminished for whatever reason, their stomach contents may passively well-up into the *pharynx*, and if the patient is in a suitable position, out of the mouth.
>
> Whatever is in the stomach will be vomited back. This includes any food or ingested drinks."

(Reproduced by permission of Messrs Frank and Caffin from the proof of evidence of Sellwood in the case of *DPP v. McCarthy*, May 1991, Truro Magistrates' Court.)

16–61 There are, as well, certain medical and dental conditions which will result in liquid alcohol being retained in a motorist's mouth or throat for far longer than 20 minutes, with the result that if a person with such a condition were to exhale into the breathalyser, he would breath out liquid alcohol and thereby obtain an artificially high reading. The most common cause of this is large cavities in the teeth which will retain the alcohol in the mouth. The latter would be expelled by blowing into the breathalyser. A more rare condition was that of the defendant in *LaFaiffe v. DPP*, unreported, September 11, 1991, Southwark Crown Court. He had under-gone an operation for oesophageal cancer, which had caused irregularities to the lining of his oesophagus, *i.e.* pouches in which fluids could linger. His medical condition also caused regurgitation. Therefore when he was breathalysed, he blew liquid alcohol from his oesophagus as well as gaseous alcohol from his breath into the Intoximeter, which caused a spuriously high reading. He was duly acquitted of driving with a breath alcohol concentration above the prescribed limit. The same occurred when a defendant had extensive dental work to three bridges in his mouth: see (1994) 18 Jo. Ana. Tox. 255. The bridge trapped the alcohol which was blown back into the Intoximeter when he provided his two specimens.

There are also various medications which contain ethanol (*e.g.* a patent **16–62** mouthwash) and which, if consumed by a motorist, could cause a falsely high reading. There are also tinctures on sale which contain a fairly high percentage of alcohol. If such a substance was applied to a motorist's gums, the alcohol in it would remain for longer than 20 minutes; and should he blow into a breathalyser, some of the alcohol in the tincture would also be expelled into the machine and accordingly produce a falsely high reading.

(b) VOLATILE HYDROCARBONS

Apart from alcohol the most common substances found in the breath are **16–63** ketones, aldehydes and volatile hydro carbons, especially (in the latter case, according to Professor Peters) ethane, methane and ethylene. The presence of these three hydrocarbons in the breath is quite common. Evidence by a service engineer of Lion Laboratories and P.M. Williams in *DPP v. McAll*, above, and also by the latter in *DPP v. Cameron*, unreported, July 30, 1992, Lichfield Magistrates' Court, was that volatile hydrocarbons could give a false reading of up to 5µg when the person breathalysed had not been drinking alcohol. (The infra-red analysis could not differentiate them from ethanol.) Dr Williams was also of the opinion that this error would not occur with a person who had been drinking more than the prescribed limit. This was because the Taguchi cell (see Chapter 13) could not detect small amounts of volatile hydrocarbons, but would detect them when mixed with about 35µg of alcohol, thus enabling the Intoximeter to give an accurate analysis. Unfortunately, the strength of the evidence about the Taguchi cell operating correctly when hydrocarbons are mixed with alcohol leaves a lot to be desired.

So far as the author can ascertain, the only witness called by the prosecution about the Taguchi cell has been the marketing director of Lion Laboratories. He is an eminent chemist, readily admits to not being an electrical engineer, and is not familiar with its design. The Taguchi cell is imported into this country by Envin Scientific Products Limited. As to its level of performance, the reader is referred to a copy of a proof of the evidence of P. Thrift which is reproduced in Appendix 10.

(c) Acetaldehyde

(i) Structure

16–64 The reason why acetaldehyde and alcohol will both absorb the infra-red in the Intoximeter's analytical chamber is because their molecular structures are much alike with similar carbon-hydrogen bondings (see Figure A).

Figure A

Molecular structure of ethanol

Molecular structure of acetaldehyde

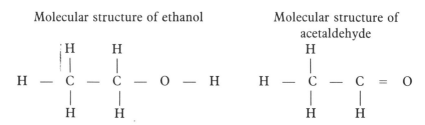

(ii) The Amount in the Breath

16–65 Research carried out by A.V. Jones in Sweden and verified by Lion Laboratories shows that the infra-red analysis will not detect any acetaldehyde below $25\mu g$. The generally accepted view (*e.g.* T. Peters, the Director of Pathology at King's, London, and A. V. Jones) is that such a level of acetaldehyde is virtually impossible but if such a level was reached, it would be obvious to any observer as the cheeks would be flushed. However, a recent article by Wong, Keys Scott and Peterson found that people who had been drinking could have well over $25\mu g$ of acetaldehyde in 100ml of their breath. The summary of this article in (1992) 9 *Alcohol* 189 reads:

"Five pairs of volunteers were studied to determine the effect of drinking ethanol on breath acetaldehyde levels. On a given study day, samples of breath were obtained for measurement of acetaldehyde and ethanol from both participants at t = -1h, t = -0.5 h, and at t = 0 to obtain baseline values. The drinkers were then given ethanol (0.3g/kg bodyweight), and the controls given an equal volume of tap water. Breath samples were then taken at 0.5, 1, 1.5, 2h and hourly until t = 6h. The last sample taken was at t = 23.5h. Acetaldehyde levels in breath were quantified with a fluorigenic high-performance liquid chromatographic assay. Blood ethanol was approximated using a breath analyser. Acetaldehyde in breath rose 50-fold at the 0.5-h time point and returned to levels not significantly different from baseline values by 3–4h. The mean peak blood ethanol values reached 0.055%. The t1/2 elimination for ethanol was 1.6h, and that for acetaldehyde was 2.25h. Elimination of both acetaldehyde and ethanol in breath were initially 0 order. A significant correlation (r = 0.74) was found between baseline breath acetaldehyde levels and peak acetaldehyde levels. We conclude that acetaldehyde resulting from ethanol intake rapidly partitions into breath. The correlation of baseline breath acetaldehyde values with peak values found after an ethanol challenge indicate that measurement of breath acetaldehyde may be useful in the identification of individual differences in ethanol metabolism."

In a letter to the *New Law Journal*, April 3, 1992, P.M. Williams wrote that any acetaldehyde in the breath would all be blown out when the first reading was obtained on the Intoximeter and none would be left in the breath when the motorist provided his second sample. Professor Peters agrees that this could happen in some cases but that it was more likely that equalisation would have occurred by the time the motorist came to provide his second specimen for the Intoximeter. (Equalisation means that all the substances on a motorist's breath when he first blew into the machine will also be present in the same proportions when he provides his second breath sample.) In addition, the male lungs hold 4.5l of breath, but only 1.5l is needed to obtain an analysis from an Intoximeter. Therefore, acetaldehyde would remain on the breath in the mouth and when more air was breathed in, equalisation would occur more or less instantaneously. Indeed, if all the acetaldehyde was expelled from the breath on the first blow and none had returned by the time of the second blow into the breathalyser, the same would have happened to the alcohol on the breath, with the result that the breathalyser's second reading would be zero.

(d) THE BURDEN OF PROOF

In *Sophocleous v. Ringer* [1988] R.T.R. 52, a metropolitan police scientist **16–66** testified that there was always a possibility of a blood specimen producing micro-organisms which manufactured alcohol but she had never personally come across this. The High Court held that such evidence did not raise a reasonable doubt as to possible contamination of the blood sample. That decision must be contrasted with that in *Collins v. Lucking* [1983] R.T.R. 312, where the prosecution analyst said that micro-organisms were found in the accused's urine sample but that these would not have affected the analysis unless he was a diabetic. In the absence of any evidence as to whether or not the accused was such a person, the High Court directed an acquittal. This was because, without knowing whether he was a diabetic, the justices could not be sure of his guilt.

XIII. THE PRESENCE OR ABSENCE OF AN ACETONE MESSAGE ON THE INTOXIMETER PRINTOUT

The Intoximeter is designed to prevent acetone being wrongly treated as **16–67** alcohol by the infra-red analysis and thus producing a falsely high reading. If acetone is detected, the device should make the necessary deduction from the result of the analysis before it is shown on its video-display unit and printed out (see section 13–09). If there is no reference to acetone on the printout, then the Intoximeter will have made no allowance for this chemical when producing the results of its analysis.

The view of Lion Laboratories is set out in the Intoximeter's handbook at p.21:

"The concentration of acetone likely to be found in breath is generally so low that, by itself, it would not cause the 3000 to read an apparent breath alcohol level. However, if the diabetic subject had been drinking alcohol, the acetone in his breath could cause the alcohol reading to be falsely high."

16–68   As well as showing the presence of acetone, the printout also gives an indication of the amount. If less than $5\mu g$, has been detected no indication will be given. If more has been found in the breath specimen, the following messages will be given, "trace acetone" for 5–$9.9\mu g$, "moderate acetone" for 10–$14.99\mu g$, and "large acetone" for 15 or more micrograms. Thus, it is only in exceptional cases that there will be a genuine acetone message. This will normally occur only in the case of diabetic ketosis (caused by not taking insulin) or a person who has been fasting for at least three days (see section 16–58). Pregnant women can suffer from what is known as accelerating fasting and that condition can also cause acetone. If an Intoximeter indicates that anybody other than the aforementioned people had acetone on his breath, then that machine has almost certainly malfunctioned and the information about this displayed on its printout will be inaccurate, so that the latter document will not comply with PACE, s.69 and will accordingly be inadmissible in evidence in a criminal court.

In *Ashton v. DPP* [1995] T.L.R. 410, the printout showed "trace acetone" and it was accepted by the court that the person to whom it related did not have such a substance on his breath. The Director of Public Prosecutions called P.M. Williams to testify that sometimes saliva would be blown into the Intoximeter and this would be detected by the Taguchi cell and cause it to give an acetone message, as happened in that case. He also explained that such a message was shorthand and meant that the breath contained the amount of alcohol shown in the printout plus another substance. It is submitted that this evidence is not altogether convincing. The Intoximeter mouthpiece contains a spit trap. If the spit trap does not prevent saliva entering the machine, then one would expect an acetone message to be fairly common. However, since the Intoximeter's software was modified as a result of the publication of the Paton Report, that is a rare occurrence. The author would also draw the reader's attention to the fact that there was no mention in the Intoximeter handbook of saliva activating an acetone message nor in any of the manufacturer's handouts about the acetone detection system. Nor was there any mention of this by the same P.W. Williams when he gave evidence in the case of *DPP v. McCall* (see above) when it would have been highly relevant as a possible explanation of the large difference between the two readings, i.e. that the second analysis was lowered by saliva having been blown in and activating the Taguchi cell. If that cell was so activated, one would expect to see a large number of printouts carrying an acetone message but this is not the case. In fact, for the reasons set out in Appendix 10, it is impossible for any saliva to reach the Taguchi Cell.

XIV. A READING NOT EXCEEDING 43μg ON THE INTOXIMETER

As a matter of justice, a reading on an Intoximeter of no more than 43μg **16–69** should not found a conviction. The Intoximeter cannot distinguish between ethanol and certain volatile hydrocarbons and its reading could, on occasion, be the combined total of the two substances. That is the view of certain Home Office Forensic Scientists (*e.g.* Dr. J. W. Mundy). It is submitted that it may well be possible for hydrocarbons to represent up to 5μg of the result, *i.e.* the maximum amount that is found in the breath. The Intoximeter is allowed an accuracy of plus or minus three by the Home Secretary: see *R. v. Cambridge Crown Court, ex p. Wong* [1992] R.T.R. 382, 384A. Thus if the true amount of alcohol in the breath was 35μg, this could produce a reading of 43μg. This is because 5μg of that total could be accounted for by volatile hydrocarbons, thus reducing the alcohol content of the reading to 38μg. Further, because of the 3μg tolerance allowed to the device, an alcohol reading of 38μg can only be relied upon as actually proving 35μg of alcohol in the breath, *i.e.* within the legal limit. Nor would it be possible for the police to allege that a reading of 35μg must have meant that the defendant had more alcohol in his breath at the time of driving. This is because it can take up to two hours (or even longer) after a male person ceases to drink for the alcohol in his breath to reach its peak concentration. The above was argued by the defence in *DPP v. Moyne*, unreported, December 19, 1991, Basildon Magistrates' Court, where the Intoximeter reading was 43μg. The justices dismissed a charge under the Road Traffic Act s.5, because evidence confirming the above facts raised a doubt in their minds as to whether or not the driver's alcohol level had in fact been above the legal limit. The above argument depends on the Taguchi cell not being able to detect hydrocarbons mixed with alcohol as well as being unable to detect them in the absence of ethanol. However, the subsequent judgment of the High Court in *Healy v. DPP* (see above) now prevents petty sessions from acquitting on those grounds.

The Paton Report compared samples of body fluid and breath which were not taken simultaneously. It assumed the most favourable rate of metabolism, so as to get corresponding breath and blood analyses. Where that assumption was erroneous, the reason why the breath and blood samples still appeared to correspond was because the presence of hydrocarbons in the breath counterbalanced a rate of alcohol dissipation which was greater than that which had been assumed.

XV. EXTERNAL FACTORS TENDING TO SHOW ACCURACY AND THE RELEVANCE OR OTHERWISE OF THE ROADSIDE BREATH TEST

(a) STATE OF THE MOTORIST

16–70 The most important indicators of the reliability of an analysis will often be the state, condition and demeanour of the motorist. This is so where a large amount of alcohol is alleged and the evidence shows the defendant to be "rolling drunk". The opposite will be the case of somebody with an analysis of three times the legal limit who was driving perfectly normally and was stopped in a routine document check; then his condition would raises doubts as to the accuracy of the analysis. In these situations it will be most helpful for the motorist to drink, in the presence of a doctor, the amount of alcohol which the police allege he had consumed. The doctor could then verify the amount by taking a blood sample which is then analysed. If appropriate, the doctor would also be able to give evidence as to the effects that this amount of alcohol had on the defendant and show that it was inconsistent with that purportedly shown by the analysis.

(b) THE SCREENING BREATHALYSER

16–71 Most of the arrested motorists will have provided a positive roadside breath test, indicating that they were driving in contravention of section 5. They may also have been detained in a police station for several hours until such a test showed them to be below the limit. In *Lomas v. Bowles* [1984] Crim. L.R. 178, the High Court held that in considering a challenge to the accuracy of a urine analysis, the justices were entitled to taken into account the fact that the appellant had provided a positive test on the Alcotest 80. However, three years later, in *Maharajah v. Solomon* [1987] R.T.R. 295, 299L–300B, Watkins L.J. said:

> "[Defence counsel] argues that [the justices] could not possibly be permitted to take into consideration the fact that the defendant had been brought to the police station as a result of failing the screening test at the roadside. He says that it is a wholly irrelevant factor, seeing that the device used at the road side is not as accurate a device as the Intoximeter 3000. I agree with that. There have been instances when a motorist has failed the screening device at the roadside, and yet has been found, upon taking the Intoximeter 3000, to be below the permissible limit. Justices cannot be guided to a conclusion by the mere fact that a motorist has failed the screening test at the roadside. I agree that it was wrong of these justices to take into consideration that factor." (At 299L—300B.)

16–72 Those words were quoted with approval by Glidewell L.J. in *Lodge v. Chief Constable of Greater Manchester* (reported on another point at [1988] Crim. L.R. 533). That quotation repeats what Watkins L.J. had said in *Snelson v. Thompson* [1985] R.T.R. 220. In that case counsel had argued that the Intoximeter must be inaccurate because it had given a reading of 56µg, while on his client's release just over an hour later, an Alcometer breath screening device had showed him to be below the legal limit, and that such an elimination rate of alcohol was four times the normal rate. Watkins L.J. said (at 224):

"However it has to be borne in mind that the Lion Alcometer SL-2 is but a screening device. The designers and the manufacturers of it do not pretend that it contains a mechanism which enables it to calculate, with any kind of precision, the level of alcohol in the breath; whereas the Intoximeter 3000, as I have already indicated, is an instrument for which the designers claim a level of precision which permits of almost no, or very little, error."

The Lord Justice appears later to have contradicted himself by saying that "the justices were perfectly entitled to take account of this", *i.e.* that the defendant had failed a roadside breath test. However, it is submitted that what Watkins L.J. was saying was that the failed roadside breath test had cancelled out the passed test at the police station. In other words, the justices could take cognisance of the roadside test as a counterbalance to the police station test.

Lafferty v. DPP, unreported, March 11, 1994, disapproved of the above quoted dicta of Watkins L.J. and held that a court could take into account the roadside breath test when deciding if an Intoximeter was, or was not, accurate, provided it was kept in mind that the roadside breath test was a screening device and not 100per cent accurate. (Lion Laboratories claim the Alcometer to be accurate to within 10per cent.)

In *DPP v. Hill* [1991] R.T.R. 351, 356, Neill L.J. said 16–73

"There was not only the accident which might be equivocal because animals do run across the road, but also the positive evidence of two devices . . . there was the roadside test provided by an approved Draeger Alert device, which is an electronic machine, and a machine which in the ordinary way is a carefully examined machine."

The Alert is one of the later roadside devices used to ascertain if a motorist's alcohol level is likely to be above that allowed by the law. In their case stated, the only reference to that machine's performance is at paragraph (f) where the justices say (at 353):

"They were not assisted by the expert as to whether the Lion Intoximeter or the Draeger in question were working properly at the material time."

In the case, there was no finding about the reliability of the Draeger 16–74 Alert and it would therefore appear that the views of Neill L.J. on that topic were not supported by the decision in the lower court. It would be another matter if credible evidence was given of how an Alert worked, and of its reliability. A court might then be entitled to take into account the result of a test by that device as conclusive evidence of the accuracy of the analysis. The mere fact that it is an approved instrument will not prevent an attack on its reliability, since Watkins L.J. has quite rightly referred to the unreliability of other approved devices. The type of device used by the police in *Maharaj v. Solomon*, above, or in *Lodge v. Chief Constable of Greater Manchester*, above, is not stated in either report. As the constabularies in these two cases were the Metropolitan and Greater Manchester Police Forces, it would appear that the machine in question was the Alcometer, which uses a fuel cell. (The Alert uses a semi-conductor to determine the amount of alcohol on the motorist's breath; see Chapter 13.) However, in the judgment in *DPP v Hill* [1991] R.T.R. 351, above, there is no mention of these two earlier cases or that they apparently involved a different type of breathalyser and so no attempt was made to distinguish them on that basis.

In view of these apparently conflicting authorities, it would appear that the law, as it now stands, is that the results of a screening device can be used to corroborate the accuracy of a Camic or Intoximeter.

XVI. SUMMARY

16–75 Where the details on the printout do not cast any suspicion on the results of the breath analysis, there will only be an acquittal if sufficient doubt is raised about the particular breathalyser used by the accused, so that the court thinks that the case before it could be one of the 0.19 per cent of analyses where an error has been made by what is normally a very reliable machine. For this to occur, the magistrates will need very cogent evidence, such as very convincing testimony of what the accused had drunk. Indeed, what is interesting in this field of law is the way the judiciary have put their faith in boxes of wires and silicone chips. The prime example of this is the fact that for many years it had not been possible, as a matter of substantive law, to challenge the accuracy of breath alcohol measuring instruments by showing that the amount of drink consumed by the accused could not possibly have produced the same breath alcohol concentration as that indicated by the result of the analysis.

C. Body fluids

I. CERTIFICATE OF ANALYSIS

16–76 In *Thomas v. Henderson* [1983] R.T.R. 293, Woolf J. was of the opinion that whenever a motorist wished to challenge the results shown on a certificate of analysis served by the prosecution, he must request the presence of the analyst at court.

II. GAS CHROMATOGRAPHY

Nowadays, the prosecution always analyses samples of body fluid by gas **16–77** chromatography. This is a very accurate method (see Chapter 9). It is fully automated and is not beset by the problems facing the breathalyser. The cause of an erroneous analytical result will almost invariably be due to the method of taking of the sample in the case of blood, or the storage of the sample in the case of urine.

III. DISAGREEMENT BETWEEN EXPERTS

In a number of cases it has been held that an appeal court cannot interfere **16–78** with the decision of the tribunal of fact as to which of two disputed analyses is, in fact, the accurate one (*e.g. R. v. Sodo* [1975] R.T.R. 357; *Froggat v. Allcock* [1975] R.T.R. 372; *R. v. Elliot* [1976] R.T.R. 308). This applies no matter how large the difference (see *R. v. Dawson* [1976] R.T.R. 533, where it was 119mg).

IV. BLOOD

(a) ALCOHOL STERILISATION

Before veinapuncture the surrounding skin is sterilised. The swabs nor- **16–79** mally used for this purpose are impregnated with alcohol. The Home Office supply alcohol-free swabs to police surgeons for use in drinking and driving cases. In the past, some constabularies have purchased their own supply from other sources. These were of the normal variety, with the result that their alcohol consequently contaminated the blood sample via the syringe needle. This occurred in Greater Manchester in the 1980s, the discovery of which led to the High Court subsequently quashing numerous convictions for driving with excess alcohol (see *R. v. Bolton JJ., ex p. Scally* [1991] 1 Q.B. 537).

(b) NON-DISPOSABLE SYRINGES

Most police surgeons use disposable syringes. However, if this is not the **16–80** case and alcohol is used to sterilise them and they are subsequently used to obtain blood, the same result is likely to occur as happened in *ex p. Scally, above.* Cases in which this has occurred are known to H. J. Walls, a former director of the Metropolitan Police Forensic Science Laboratory; see H.J. Walls and A.R. Brownlie, *Drink, Drugs and Driving* (2nd ed., 1985, p. 76).

(c) PRODUCTION OF ALCOHOL

To prevent organisms producing alcohol a preservative is added to the **16–81** sample. The phials supplied by the Home Office should already contain such a substance. It is normally sodium fluoride and should be at a

279

concentration of about ½—1 per cent in the blood sample. It should be put in the container by its manufacturer together with an anti-coagulant, normally an oxide. If a sample coagulates this probably mean there is also no preservative.

V. URINE

16–82 In the case of urine, there is always the possibility of the sample containing some sugar and yeast which have fermented and produced alcohol. Alternatively, if the specimen has not been properly preserved, there is the likelihood of micro-organisms appearing in it which produce ethanol. To ensure that there has not been any such occurrence, the analyst must always check that a urine specimen contains the necessary preservative and no sugar. It is therefore essential that the relevant forensic scientist is always questioned about these matters in the witness box, in order to ensure that the alcohol found in the urine was in it when it left the accused's body and has not been produced afterwards by yeast, or micro-organisms. Even if no sugar or yeast is found in a specimen when analysed, that is no proof that some was not present when the specimen was provided by the motorist and has not fermented and produced alcohol.

Chapter 17

NO SAMPLE

A. Introduction

Section 6(4) of the Road Traffic Act 1988 and section 29(5) of the **17–01** Transport and Works Act 1992 make it an offence for a person, without reasonable excuse, to fail to provide a sample of breath for a breath test. Likewise, section 7(6) of the Road Traffic Act and section 31(1) of the Transport and Works Act make it an offence for a person, without reasonable excuse, to fail to provide a specimen for analysis when required to do so. The grounds which entitle the police to make such a requirement have been discussed in Chapters 10 (breath tests) and 11 (specimens for analysis), while the procedure to be followed is set out in Chapters 14. If those grounds do not exist or the prescribed procedure at the police station or hospital is not followed, then any requirement for a sample is unlawful and the motorist commits no offence if he refuses to supply one (see *Anderton v. Lythgoe* [1985] 1 W.L.R. 222 and *Ankrah v. DPP*, unreported, February 20, 1995). In *Sykos v. DPP* [1988] R.T.R. 129, the High Court upheld a conviction for failing to supply a breath specimen. The accused had been asked for one on four occasions and had always refused. He was then asked to give blood but he also declined this request. As the police had no lawful authority to request that fluid, the requirement for breath remained valid, and his failure to supply blood gave rise to no offence.

In *Vines v. Cameron*, unreported, November 25, 1985, the High Court held that to secure a conviction the prosecution must prove two things; first, that the defendant did fail to supply a specimen and, secondly, that he had no reasonable excuse for so doing. The subsequent parts of this chapter will consider these two matters separately.

B. A failure

I. THE NECESSITY FOR A REQUEST

The Road Traffic Act, ss. 6(4) and 7(6) and the Transport and Works Act, **17–02** ss. 29(5) and 31(1) all make it an offence to fail to provide a specimen when "required to do so in pursuance of this section". In *Kuldip Singh Gill v.*

DPP, January 16, 1995, it was held that a driver could not be convicted of failing to supply a specimen of blood or urine if he was not requested to do so. Thus there must be a requirement by the constable, *i.e.* the officer must have actually asked for one. If a person deliberately and successfully takes a course of action for the express purpose of preventing a constable from being in a position to speak to him (*e.g.* by running off when approached), he cannot be convicted of failing to provide a specimen (see *Cunliffe v. Bleasdale* [1973] R.T.R. 90). He could, of course, always be prosecuted for obstructing the police but that would not entail the loss of his driving licence.

II. WHAT IS A FAILURE?

17–03 It is, of course, up to the prosecution to prove that there has been "a failure on the part of the defendant to supply a specimen". The Road Traffic Act 1988, s.11(2) and the Transport and Works Act 1992, s.38(1) define the word "fail" as including the word "refuse". The Road Traffic Act, s.11(3) and the Transport and Works Act 1992, s.38(4) give a definition of failure, but only for breath. If the accused is willing to supply such a specimen then, of course, the police must make the necessary arrangements for its provision (see *Hoyle v. Walsh* [1969] 2 Q.B. 13 and section 17–26). A refusal by a motorist can be conveyed by his conduct. In *R. v. Mackey* [1977] R.T.R. 146, the accused took some peppermints from his pocket. A policeman told him that he was not to eat any sweets and, should he attempt to do so, the officer would treat it as a refusal to take the test. The motorist made no reply but went as if to put a mint into his mouth. He was restrained from so doing and the High Court held that his actions amounted to a refusal. In a number of cases, the question has arisen of whether the police are entitled to come to the conclusion that the motorist is unwilling to provide a sample. Lane J. in *R. v. Clark* [1969] 1 W.L.R. 1109, 1113 stated that the test to be applied was as follows:

"Any words, or indeed any actions, on the part of a defendant, which in the eyes of a jury make it clear that in all the circumstances of the particular case he is declining the policeman's proper invitation, amount to a refusal within the section."

In *R. v. Kelly* [1972] R.T.R. 447, 449, Lawton L.J. said:

"In the view of this court the word 'fails' has its ordinary meaning, namely, he does not do that which he is required to do—it may be that there are good reasons or bad reasons for failing. If he fails to do what he is required to do because he is obstinate, that is a bad reason. On the other hand if he fails to do that which he is required to do because he is suffering from either a temporary or permanent disability that is a good reason but he has still failed. If he has a good reason he cannot be convicted under section 2(3) of the Act of having failed to provide a sample because he will have had a reasonable excuse."

17–04 In *DPP v. Shuker*, unreported, March 7, 1995, the respondent was unable to blow into the breathalyser and claimed to be suffering from bronchitis. Although he did not believe him, the Intoximeter operator called a doctor, who held that the respondent was able to provide such a specimen, so the latter was duly charged with failing to provide a breath specimen. The justices brought in a not guilty verdict and held that once a doctor had been called, the breath procedure was suspended and, if the police still wanted that substance, they had to make another request. That was rejected by the High Court who ordered a conviction. In the words of Balcombe L.J.:

> "I should add that it seems to me that Mr Geey, for the Appellant prosecutor, was quite right in his contention that if the decision of the Magistrates in this case was correct, it gives virtually a charter to recalcitrant motorists to succeed in getting some sort of delay. In this case the delay was, in fact, minimal; it was only about half an hour. One can envisage cases where it might take longer for the police surgeon to arrive.
>
> The section is quite clear; it is quite simple. Once you are required to provide specimens of breath for analysis, as this Respondent was, you are guilty of an offence if, without the reasonable excuse, you fail to provide a specimen. As I have already made it clear, this Respondent did fail to provide the specimen. He did not seek to raise by way of his defence before the Magistrates any reasonable excuse, and that seems to me to be the end of the matter."

At no time was the motorist asked to supply a body fluid. Four-and-a-half months later, a differently constituted divisional court took the opposite view in *DPP v. Whythe* [1996] R.T.R. 137, where the defendant declined to supply blood, giving a potential medical reason for not doing so. A doctor was called but no evidence was adduced of what occurred thereafter, save that no specimen of any sort was provided. The prosecution sought to rely upon the initial failure to supply breath as founding the offence under section 7(6). Butterfield J. rejected this (at 141/2):

> "For my part, I think it likely that the constable was told by the doctor that there was no medical reason why the defendant could not provide a specimen of blood and in those circumstances the constable relied on the answer given before the medical examination as amounting to a failure on the part of the defendant. If that is what happened, and I emphasise that there was no finding to that effect, it was an understandable approach carried out, no doubt, in perfectly good faith, but was wrong in law."

The approach of Butterfield J. (with whom Stuart-Smith L.J. agreed) is much preferable to that of Balcombe L.J. and French J. An initial demurrer on medical grounds should not be regarded as a failure if the police surgeon does not concur in those reasons. The motorist might have genuinely believe that a medical condition prevented him providing the type of sample first requested. If a doctor then pronounced him fit to do so, it would be unfair not to allow him the opportunity of there and then complying with what had originally been requested of him.

In *Singh Dhillon v. DPP* (1992) 157 J.P. 420, the defendant was asked (in **17–05** an option case) whether he would give blood or urine, to which he replied: "No, I don't like needles."

Laws J. said that those words, however they were spoken, were equivocable and could not (without further inquiry) have been construed as refusing to provide a specimen for analysis. At that stage the appellant was merely telling the police that he was not prepared to give a blood sample and not that he was also unwilling to supply one of urine.

It is submitted that the above decision is preferable to that of *DPP v. Fountain* [1988] R.T.R. 385, where the defendant replied when asked to provide blood: "In view of the danger of AIDS, I would prefer not to give blood." The High Court held that the justices were wrong not to treat that as a refusal. It is submitted that the justices were right, and that the defendant was merely expressing a preference not to give blood and should (as the justices found) have had more explanation given to him. Also, the court never considered the question of the absence of any mention at all of urine, even though it was heard five months after *Hobbs v. Clark, ibid.*, at 35. On this latter ground alone, the case was clearly wrongly decided.

III. WHICH SPECIMEN HAS NOT BEEN PROVIDED?

17–06 In *Sykes v. Chief Constable* [1988] R.T.R. 129, the motorist was requested to provide a specimen of breath but refused, so the constable then asked for one of blood, which was also not provided. The High Court upheld the conviction for failing to supply a breath specimen because the police had no grounds for requesting blood and the fact that such a request had been made was irrelevant. In the words of Parker C.J. (at 133):

> "As I have already indicated, the requirement to provide a specimen of blood was improper. Does the making of that requirement in any way render inadmissible the evidence in relation to the specimen of breath? I cannot for myself see why it should do so."

In *Boden v. DPP* [1988] R.T.R. 188, the accused was charged with failing to provide a specimen of breath. He had refused to give one on medical grounds, so the constable required a sample of blood but the latter substance was also not provided. It was held to be irrelevant as to whether the request for blood was, or was not, lawful. The defendant had failed to provide a breath specimen after a legal requirement and was guilty of the offence as charged, unless he had a reasonable excuse.

In *Durbin v. DPP*, unreported, June 28, 1994, the defendant, on being asked to provide breath for analysis, replied that he had stomach pains and suffered from ulcers. Accordingly, the constable decided that for medical reasons a breath specimen could not be provided, so he requested blood and sent for a doctor, who confirmed that the accused was suffering from stomach pains but said that these were not continuous and that a specimen of breath could be provided between spasms. He was again asked to blow but said that he could not do so. The High Court upheld his conviction for failing to provide a specimen of breath. The court rejected the submission that, once blood had been asked for, the defendant could only be convicted of failing to supply that substance. The court held that if a motorist failed to provide a specimen immediately, an officer was always entitled to require another one; and if an officer requested blood because he thought there were medical grounds which prevented breath being supplied, there was nothing to stop him asking for breath once he learnt that he had been mistaken about the medical reason.

Hague v. DPP [1995] T.L.R. 589 held that where an accurate breath analysis had been obtained and no body fluid was provided, even though a lawful requirement for the latter had been made, then the defendant was guilty of driving with excess alcohol, and not of failing to provide a specimen. (The operator mistakenly thought that the machine had not correctly calibrated itself.)

In *Worsley v. DPP*, unreported, November 11, 1995, the High Court upheld a conviction for failing to supply "a specimen of breath/blood/urine" on the grounds that section 7(6) only created one offence. By analogy with *Garfield v. Maddocks* [1974] Q.B. 7, it is submitted that if the information specifies the actual substance which the driver had failed to supply, the prosecution must prove the non-provision of that very thing which includes showing that the request for it had been lawfully made. (In *Garfield v. Maddocks*, above, the appellant had been charged with using threatening behaviour contrary to section 5 of the Public Order Act 1936. That section created one offence of using threatening, abusive or insulting behaviour. The High Court held the appellant could have been charged with having committed all three types of conduct and convicted if he had perpetrated only one type; but as only one method of committing the crime was alleged, a conviction could only be obtained if the appellant had actually behaved in the way specified in the information.)

IV. OBJECTIVE TEST

In *Rawlins v. Brown* [1987] R.T.R. 238, it was held that whether or not the **17–07** defendant had refused to give a sample must be judged objectively and he would be guilty of failing to provide a specimen if he objectively appeared to be refusing, even though in fact he was perfectly agreeable to doing so.

V. SILENCE

In *Campbell v. DPP* [1989] R.T.R. 256, it was held that mere silence on the **17–08** part of an accused when asked to provide a sample could amount to "a refusal".

VI. CONDITION OR INDULGENCE

In *DPP v. Billington* [1988] R.T.R. 231, the High Court emphasised the **17–09** difference between a motorist, on the one hand, refusing to give a sample at all or only under certain conditions and, on the other hand, not refusing to provide one but merely requesting that, if possible, he would like to do something else first. In the words of Lloyd L.J. (at 243K *et seq.*):

"1. A defendant is not in general entitled to impose a condition on his willingness to provide a specimen under section 8 of the Act of 1972. If, for example, he says that he will only provide a specimen after he has seen his solicitor or if his solicitor is present, that is treated by the courts as tantamount to a refusal.

2. If, on the other hand, a defendant says that he is willing to provide a specimen but asks if he can see his solicitor first, that is not tantamount to a refusal since he is not in those circumstances imposing a condition. He is seeking a favour. It is then up to the police to decide, in the exercise of their discretion, whether to grant the favour or not.

3 . . . the distinction between imposing a condition and asking a favour is one which may be narrow and may depend on the precise language used by the defendant when asked to provide a specimen . . . "

To the same effect were the words of Lord Widgery C.J. in *Pettigrew v. Northumbria Police Authority* [1976] R.T.R. 177, 182:

" . . . a distinction must be made between the motorist who says 'I will not unless . . . " and the motorist who says 'I will but may I do so and so before hand?'. In the second instance there is no refusal of the request because it is quite clear that the matter is being treated as one of discretion of the police. In the first instance, however, there is a refusal because the purported acceptance is in fact destroyed by the condition which is being attached to it."

Likewise in *Smith v. Hand* [1986] R.T.R. 265, the High Court upheld the acquittal of a motorist, who when asked to supply a specimen replied: "May I speak to my solicitor before deciding whether to give a specimen?"

VII. A CHANGE OF MIND

17–10 A less stringent approach was taken by the Court of Appeal than that of the jury in *R. v. Reid* [1973] 1 W.L.R. 1283. There the defendant refused to provide any body fluid on the grounds that the constable was not entitled to make such a requirement. The sergeant then explained the correct legal position to the accused who thereupon agreed to provide a sample, but the arresting officer was not prepared to allow him to change his mind. The court upheld the conviction for failing to supply a sample but stated that the jury had taken a somewhat stern view of the matter (at 1298H). It is implicit from their comments that the members of the court would not have considered an acquittal to be perverse. Thus a quick change of mind does not automatically mean there has been a refusal. The court did hold that those facts amounted to a special reason for not imposing a disqualification.

17–11 Of course, a defendant cannot escape punishment by changing his mind much later. In *Smith v. DPP* [1989] R.T.R. 159, the High Court was of the view that a failure occurred unless the motorist immediately agreed to provide a specimen when requested to do so. The court was unhappy at the suggestion that if a police officer allowed a driver later on to change his mind and to supply a specimen, then no offence of refusing a sample would have occurred. Schiemann J. stated that (at 164):

"I am not attracted by the idea that the police officer has a discretion in these circumstances . . . If the court decides that the time has passed and the statutory procedure has come to an end by reason of somebody having firmly rejected the option of providing an alternative specimen, then the court in my judgement is entitled to do so, not withstanding that a co-operative police officer has given the motorist an opportunity of giving an alternative sample."

Although that case was about a motorist who, at first, declined his statutory option of providing blood or urine under section 8(2) of the Road Traffic Act 1988 but later changed his mind, the same principle applies in the case of a motorist who was under a legal obligation to provide a specimen. From the decision in *R. v. Reid*, above, it would appear that the law is that anything done or said by a defendant indicating an unwillingness to give a sample is prima facie evidence of a refusal, but that assumption may be rebutted by a very quick change of mind. If there is a sudden change of mind, it is entirely a matter of fact whether there has been in law "a failure" to supply a specimen.

Thus the High Court held in *Smyth v DPP* [1995] R.T.R. 391 that there had been no failure to provide a specimen when the accused changed his mind five seconds after initially declining to comply with a requirement for a specimen. The court stated that there was no absolute bar to a person changing his mind: it all depended on the facts. The court drew the analogy with a person being arraigned who said "guilty" and almost immediately thereafter said "not guilty", where in such circumstances any judge would allow a change of plea. Contrasted to that case is the decision in *Procaj v. Johnson* [1970] R.T.R. 49, where a change of mind after 26 minutes was held to be too late. It might well be advantageous to call expert evidence of the small amount of alcohol metabolism that occurred in the interval between the refusal and the offer to supply a specimen.

VIII. THIRD PARTY INTERVENTION

In *R. v. Miles* [1979] R.T.R. 509, it was held that there was a failure to give **17–12** a breath sample when the accused's wife prevented him from taking the test. Thus interference by a third party is not an *actus novus interveniens* which has any bearing on the question of whether or not there had been a failure to supply a specimen. Of course, it is another matter as to whether or not such third party action would amount to a "reasonable excuse" (see below).

IX. MANUFACTURER'S INSTRUCTIONS

The Home Office specification for the Intoximeter and Camic is that they **17–13** allow a motorist three minutes in which to supply his specimen. In *DPP v. Thomas*, [1996] R.T.R. 293, the High Court held that there was no obligation to inform the motorist of that time limit. In that case the sole reason for the failure to give a specimen was that the accused had chosen to argue that a second one was unnecessary as his first one had revealed an alcohol level in excess of the statutory limit. The court was of the view that he had been told to blow a second time into the machine. He was therefore under an obligation to do that forthwith, and should have attempted to do so straight away and not have argued with the police. In those circumstances, it was irrelevant that the machine would in fact allow him three minutes in which he could blow into it. To the same effect is *Coyle v. DPP* [1995] T.L.R. 427, where Buxton J. also said, *obiter*, that it could be a defence if the accused had been prejudiced by not having been informed of the manufacturer's instructions. That, of course, would not include the fact that he chose to waste time before he started to exhale into the machine, as his obligation is to do that as soon as he is so required.

In *Cosgrove v. DPP*, *The Times*, March 29, 1996, the High Court held that if a motorist was not attempting to blow into the device properly, then a constable could treat such conduct as a "refusal" and need not afford him the full three minutes allowed by the machine for providing a breath specimen. However, if an officer did that, he ran the risk that a court might form a different view of the accused's endeavours and acquit him because he had not been deliberately trying to avoid providing a specimen. In other words, if no specimen is provided by the time the machine has closed itself down, a conviction will ensue, unless there was a reasonable excuse for its non-provision. If, however, a motorist was not afforded his full three minutes to provide his specimen, he must be acquitted (*i.e.* there will not have been a "failure"), unless the Bench are satisfied that he was not making a proper attempt to blow into the machine.

X. ILLEGALITY

17-14 Any illegality involved in demanding a roadside breath test or any unlawfulness which occurs at the police station in connection with the requirement for a specimen for analysis will automatically result in an acquittal on a charge under the Road Traffic Act, ss. 6(4) and s.7(6) respectively. What is not so certain is if the same principle applies in the latter case to the events occurring prior to the arrival at the police station. In *Morris v. Beardmore* [1981] A.C. 446, the House of Lords held that under the (unamended) Road Traffic Act 1972 any illegality on the part of the police automatically rendered unlawful a request for a sample for a laboratory test; and, if such a sample was refused the defendant had to be acquitted. In *Fox v. Chief Constable of Gwent* [1986] A.C. 281, the House of Lords specifically refused to overrule their earlier decision in *Morris v. Beardmore*. In *Fox* it was specifically recognised that this point "may one day call for judicial determination" (*per* Lord Edmund-Davies at 295G). In *Hartland v. Alden* [1987] R.T.R. 253, and *Gull v. Scarsborough, ibid.*, at 261, the High Court held that the Transport Act 1981 (now replaced by the Road Traffic Act 1988) had overruled *Morris v. Beardmore*, and that the principle of *Fox's case* applied to refusals to give a specimen as well as to driving with excess alcohol. However, it must be remembered that there is a great difference between the two crimes. In the latter case, the *actus reus* has already been perpetrated by the time the police arrive on the scene and all they have to do is collect the evidence. In the former case, no offence will have been committed until after the defendant has arrived at the police station and has then refused a request to provide a specimen. If, but for the illegal acts of the constable, the defendant would never have been at the station, then there is a powerful argument for saying that since without this illegality the offence would never have been committed, then no evidence should be allowed of what happened during his sojourn at the station. Whether such rhetoric would appeal to the House of Lords when such a case comes before them is another matter, especially as P.A.C.E. s.78 (see Chapter 14) has given the judiciary a far greater power to exclude evidence than they possessed in 1985, when the appeal in *Fox's case* was heard.

XI. FAILURE TO UNDERSTAND THE REQUIREMENT

In *R. v. Nichols* [1972] R.T.R. 308, it was held that not understanding a **17–15** valid requirement did not prevent a person from having failed to provide a specimen. A contrary view was taken in *Chief Constable of Avon and Somerset v. Singh* [1988] R.T.R 107 where it was held that, if the motorist did not comprehend the mandatory warning of prosecution, then there had not been a valid request which complied with the statutory requirements, in that case section 7(6). Which case was correctly decided is of academic interest only since that lack of comprehension would, if there was a valid requirement, manifestly be a reasonable excuse for the non-provision of a sample.

C. Breath specimens

I. THE STATUTORY REQUIREMENTS

Section 11(3) of the Road Traffic 1988 gives an extensive meaning of what **17–16** is meant by a failure in relation to a breath test or a breath analysis:

> "A person does not provide a specimen of breath for a breath test or for an analysis unless the specimen —
> (a) is sufficient to enable the test or the analysis to be carried out, and
> (b) is provided in such a way as to enable the objective of the test or analysis to be satisfactorily achieved."

The above definition of what was meant by "not providing" was first enacted in the Transport Act 1982. The Road Traffic Act, s.7(1)(a), empowers the police to require two specimens of breath for analysis, each of which must comply with what is now section 11(3) and, if that is not done, then there has been a failure to provide a breath specimen: see *DPP v. Byrne*, unreported, October 1, 1991.

It is submitted that the statutory definition means that, provided the breathalyser was working correctly, then, unless the police were able satisfactorily to analyse or to test a defendant's specimen (as the case might be), there would have been a "failure" within the meaning of the Act.

Section 38(4) of the Transport and Works Act 1992 is framed in identical terms to section 11(3) of the R.T.A. 1988.

17–17 Subsection (a) had always been part of the breathalyser law but subsection (b) was introduced by section 59 of the Transport Act 1982 to overrule the decision in *Corps v. Dalton* [1983] R.T.R. 160; see H.L. Deb., col. 983/4 (October 14, 1982). In that latter case the High Court upheld the acquittal of a motorist who had inflated the bag for 40 seconds in two attempts (with a negative result), when the manufacturer's instructions had stated that it must be fully inflated in one continuous exhalation lasting between 10 and 20 seconds. The justices found, as a fact, that the method by which the specimen was provided would have produced a positive reading if the alcohol level had been in excess of the prescribed limit. That finding of fact was not disturbed by the High Court, although there appears to have been no evidence to support it, and the accused's blood alcohol concentration was found to be 149mg. The court did say that it would have been another matter if the defendant had deliberately ignored the manufacturer's instructions in the hope of falsely producing a negative result. He would then have been guilty of an offence under what is now section 6(4).

H.M. Government did not agree with the justices and were of the opinion that Dalton had been able to obtain a "false negative" result, to quote the words of the Lord Advocate in the debate on what became section 59 of the Transport Act. (In breathalyser language, a positive result means that the driver has been shown by the device to have consumed alcohol in excess of the prescribed limit, while a negative results means the opposite.)

II. THE INTERVAL BETWEEN THE REQUEST AND THE ARRIVAL OF THE BREATHALYSER

17–18 In *R. v. Wagner* [1970] R.T.R. 422, it was held that a motorist had failed to supply a specimen when, having been asked to take a test, he declined to wait for the arrival of the breath testing equipment, although the court did say that he was only required to wait a reasonable length of time. In *Ely v. Marle* [1977] R.T.R. 412, it was held that 10 minutes was a reasonable length of time to await the arrival of the breathalyser. These cases concerned screening tests which usually have to be administered at or near the place where the motorist was stopped, so that if the officer making the request did not have a breathalyser with him, everybody had to wait at the roadside until the breath testing apparatus arrived (see Chapter 10). Likewise, in *R. v. Auker-Howlett* [1974] R.T.R. 109, it was held that there was a failure when the motorist, having been told that he must wait 20 minutes after his last drink before blowing into the breathalyser, refused to wait that length of time.

III. A POSITIVE RESULT

In *R. v. Holah* [1975] R.T.R. 74, it was held that so long as a positive result **17–19** is obtained, the motorist will have satisfactorily taken the test, no matter how much he may have disregarded the manufacturer's instructions.

IV. VERIFYING THE RESULT

The prosecution must prove that there has been "a failure". This means **17–20** that they must prove that insufficient breath had been blown into the breathalyser to obtain a positive result. If the officer sees any exhalation into the device, he must check to see if a positive result has been obtained. Neglect to do this will lead to an acquittal, since the prosecution would be unable to show that no result had been achieved on the breathalyser. So in *Walker v. Lovell* [1975] 1 W.L.R. 1141, the officer saw that the bag of the Alcotest had only been inflated to one-third of the required amount but did not check to see if the crystals had turned green because the manufacturer's instructions said that the bag must be fully inflated by the motorist. Accordingly, the House of Lords (by a three to two majority) upheld the acquittal for failing to provide a specimen. In the words of Lord Edmund-Davies (at 1169):

> "Upholding *R. v. Holah* [1973] 1 W.L.R. 127, as I do . . . appears to me to place upon a police officer who has subjected a motorist to a breath test, however imperfectly it appears to have been performed, a duty to inspect the bag to see the effect (if any) produced upon the crystals inside and, if he sees the result is positive, then to proceed to arrest under section 8(4). In the light of *Holah*, I hold that it is not open to a constable who fails to make that inspection to say that he nevertheless had reasonable cause to suspect that the motorist had failed to provide the requested specimen of breath. No duty could be lighter or more easily discharged than that of inspecting the bag before proceeding further."

Likewise in *Fawcett v. Tebb* [1984] Crim. L.R. 175, it was held that if a **17–21** motorist blew into an Alcometer SL-2, and the officer did not press the "read" button, then there was no proof that he had failed to supply sufficient breath for the test to be carried out correctly. The instructions from Lion Laboratory (who make the machine) are that the suspect must blow hard enough for the "A" light to come on and for sufficient duration for the "B" light to become illuminated. In *Fawcett's case* only the "A" light lit up and therefore the constable thought that the defendant had committed an offence under section 6(4), so he did not bother to press the read button to check if a positive or negative result had been obtained. However, it was perfectly possible for somebody who was very drunk to produce a positive reading on the Alcometer by blowing into it without light "B" showing. It would be another matter if the prosecution could show that the amount of breath blown into the device could not under any circumstances have produced a positive reading. So in *Wilson v. Cummings* [1983] R.T.R. 347, the High Court upheld the conviction when the justices found as a fact that the amount of breath blown into the Alcotest 80 was so infinitesimal that none of it would have reached the crystals. Thus there was no possibility of a positive reading being obtained. If the police examine the breathalyser for a result and discover that no positive reading has been obtained, then it is a question of fact and degree whether non-compliance with the manufacturer's instructions has prevented the machine from correctly performing its function.

17–22 In *Hall v. DPP*, unreported, June 26, 1995, Judge Holman ruled that section 11 (3)(b) had overruled *Fawcett v. Tebb* above. In *Hall's case* the defendant had exhaled some breath into an Alcometer. The constable was clearly of the view that insufficient breath had been blown into the device for the test to be carried out but could not be certain that the "A" light had not been illuminated. The judge held that, unless the "B" light came on, a false negative result might be obtained, so the appellant had not complied with section 11(3)(b) and was guilty of failing to take a breath test. However, it is submitted that in view of the interpretation given to section 11(3)(a), Judge Holman's ruling was wrong. If a constable cannot tell if sufficient breath has been provided without looking at the result, how can he also tell, without doing the same thing, whether the breath has been exhaled in such a way as to achieve the object of the test? On the facts of *Hall's case*, so long as it was possible to obtain a positive result if the "A" light had come on then, until the read button has been pressed, the officer could not have known for certain whether the object of the test had been achieved, *i.e.* a true reading. If the test was negative, a true reading may not have been obtained; but if a positive result has been achieved, then the reading was accurate. In *Walker v. Lovell* [1975] R.T.R. 377 at 384D–F, Lord Diplock said that the purpose of the test was to ascertain if the defendant's alcohol level exceeded the prescribed limit. If the test gave that result (*i.e.* above the limit), then the test has been satisfactorily taken even though it has not been carried out in accordance with the manufacturer's instructions. There the motorist should have exhaled in one single breath, lasting between 10 to 20 seconds; instead he obtained a positive reading after blowing in with two breaths each of four seconds duration. He was held to have satisfactorily taken the test. If (as was held to be the case in *Fawcett v. Tebb*) the fact that a possible false negative might have been obtained does not *ipso facto* mean that subsection (a) has not been satisfied if a positive result could also have been obtained, then the same must apply for subsection (b). Until the read button is pressed, nobody can say if a positive result has, or has not, been obtained. Indeed, the debates in Parliament (October 14, 1982 H.L. Debates Col. 983 *et seq.*) make it manifest (as does Home Office Circular 35/83) that what is now enacted in section 11(3)(b) was intended to overrule *Corps v. Dalton*, above, and not *Fawcett v. Tebb*, above.

V. PROOF OF FAILURE

The prosecution must always prove that no test result or breath analysis **17–23** has been obtained. Clearly, if no breath is blown into the Camic or Intoximeter, then there cannot have been an analysis. If some breath is exhaled into those latter two machines, there must be evidence of the lack of an analysis. The only way of knowing this is by the display on their screen and (in the case of the Intoximeter) by the printout showing "no sample". Both what appears on the screen and on the printout are documents produced by a computer (see section 10 of the Civil Evidence Act 1968) and, therefore, to be admissible must comply with section 69 of the Police and Criminal Evidence Act 1984 (see Chapter 15). If they do not accord with the requirements of that section, they cannot be adduced in evidence and there will, accordingly, be nothing before the court to show that no satisfactory analysis of the defendant's breath had taken place; in which case the prosecution must fail.

It is accepted that the preceding paragraph about verifying the result of the Intoximeter does not accord with *Oldfield v. Anderton* [1986] R.T.R. 314, where Lloyd L.J. said (at 319):

"Suppose, after providing the first specimen, the defendant had simply walked away from the machine and refused to take any further part in the exercise. It would be idle to suggest in such a case that he could not be convicted on the oral evidence of the police officer. There could be no conceivable purpose in such a case of the police officer producing the printout or giving oral evidence as to what he saw on the visual display unit. There is nothing in the Act of 1972 to require such further evidence to be given in such a case; nor can I see how any such requirement can be implied, whether as a safeguard to the defendant or for any other purpose.

That is essentially, as I see it, what this case is about. The police officer gave evidence that the defendant made several short blows into the machine instead of one long, continuous blow. The defendant gave evidence to the contrary. The justices were entitled to accept the police officer's evidence and to convict on the strength of that evidence without supporting evidence of the printout or as to what the officer saw on the visual display unit. Accordingly, I would reject both [of the appellant's] arguments on this appeal."

If the justices had found as a fact that the defendant's several short blows could never under any circumstances have produced an analysis, then the dicta of Lloyd L.J. is in line with other authorities. However, in that case there was no such evidence. Accordingly, Lloyd L.J. erred in saying that no evidence was required to show that the breathalyser's screen or printout had indicated that no sample had been provided. That statement is expressly contrary to the decision of the House of Lords in *Walker v. Lovell*, above. Accordingly, that part of his judgment must be regarded as having been uttered *per incuriam* and should not, it is submitted, be followed in later cases. To be fair to Lloyd L.J., none of the cases mentioned in the preceding paragraphs of this book were cited by him.

VI. A SINGLE BREATH SAMPLE FOR ANALYSIS

17–24 In *Stepniewski v. Commissioner of Police of the Metropolis* [1985] R.T.R. 330, it was held that a failure occurred when a motorist had only provided one breath sample, even though that was shown to be below the legal limit. There the defendant blew into the Intoximeter and the result was 34µg, which meant that, whatever the second result, he could not be charged with an offence under section 5 of the Road Traffic Act. However, he failed to provide a second sample and duly found himself convicted of failing to provide a specimen of breath contrary to section 7(6). Upholding the conviction, May L.J. (at 335) pointed out that if a defendant failed to provide a sample without a reasonable excuse, then he fell foul of section 7(6) and the actual level of alcohol in his body was irrelevant. Nolan J. concurred in this. However, it would appear that the argument that the police could only require a sample of breath if they were bona fide investigating a possible offence under section 4 or 5 was not advanced. Such an argument was subsequently put forward in *Anderton v. Lythgoe* [1985] 1 W.L.R. 222, although the factual matrix was slightly different (see section 11–03). Nolan J., in the latter case, held that if there were no grounds for suspecting an offence under either section 4 or 5, then the police could not be said to be investigating such a crime. Accordingly, they had no power to require a breath sample and the result of any analysis would be inadmissible as it would be based on an unlawful request. (That decision was not cited in the contrary decision of *R v. Norfolk JJ., ex p. Keymer*, unreported, October 12, 1994 [*q.v.* Chapter 11], which should accordingly be considered as having been decided *per incuriam*.) It is, therefore, submitted that, once a reading appears on the screen showing the defendant's breath alcohol concentration to be below the legal limit, there can be "no further investigation into whether a person has committed an offence under s.4 or 5 [of the R.T.A.] which an officer could carry out under s.7(1)" (*per* Ralph Gibson L.J. in *Haghigat-Khou v. Chambers* [1988] R.T.R. 95, 100B, who was actually referring to the police having obtained two analyses but which, it is submitted, equally applies to one analysis not exceeding 35µg). Consequently, the police would not be entitled to require another specimen. The only exception might be if the police were investigating an offence under section 4 of the Road Traffic Act, when the manner of the driving or of his demeanour led the police to believe that a motorist was unfit to drive. Then, it could be argued, a second specimen would be necessary to obtain an accurate measurement of his blood alcohol concentration since a reading of 34µg might corroborate other evidence of unfitness to drive, while no second reading would prevent the result of the single analysis being adduced in evidence. (This is because, *inter alia*, there would be no second calibration; *q.v.* section 16–27.)

VII. AN UNAPPROVED DEVICE

Section 7(6) only makes it an offence to refuse to supply a specimen which **17–25** has been required in accordance with that section, and subsection (1)(a) only empowers the police to require two specimens of breath "by means of a device of a type approved by the Secretary of State". To the same effect is section 31 of the Transport and Works Act. Thus, no offence is committed if a motorist fails to blow sufficient breath to obtain an analysis by a breathalyser which does not carry the Home Secretary's approval: see *Jones v. DPP* [1995] Crim. L.R. 69, where the clock was fifteen minutes slow. A list of approved breath testing devices are set out in Chapter 8 and of approved breath analysing machines in Chapter 11. Those chapters also consider when malfunctioning can cause an instrument to lose its seal of approval.

D. Machine error

It should not be forgotten that there is always the possibility of a breath **17–26** alcohol measuring device developing an intermittent fault which could prevent it, on occasion, from correctly receiving breath samples. This was discovered to have happened in Cumbria between May 1983 and February 1984. Accordingly, the Home Secretary announced a free pardon for those wrongly convicted in Carlisle of failing to supply a specimen, since it had subsequently been discovered that the cause of their failure could have been due to the refusal of the Intoximeter to recognise that the motorist had, in fact, supplied sufficient breath to enable an analysis to be undertaken (see *The Guardian*, November 15, 1984).

I. BADLY ASSEMBLED OR WRONGLY OPERATED DEVICE

In *Hoyle v. Walsh* [1969] 2 Q.B. 13, the police officer failed to secure the **17–27** bag to the tube so that it came off while the defendant was blowing into it and before he was able satisfactorily to complete the test. The High Court held that had not been a "failure" of the part of the motorist. In the words of Lord Parker C.J. (at 21):

"[Prosecuting counsel] claims, however, if equipment is provided, even if it is not in working order, there has been a failure to give a specimen of breath. I am quite unable to accept that. The very word failure denotes that the defendant has not done something which is possible, and if no equipment is provided, or defective equipment is provided, I cannot read the inability to provide a specimen of breath for that reason as a failure to do so within the meaning of [the statute]."

With an Intoximeter, the constable has to fix the mouthpiece to a tube, which is housed inside the device and is spring loaded to return to its housing when not in use. The Handbook states:

"When the subject is to blow, a new mouthpiece should be unwrapped and pushed firmly into the sampling tube. Then pull out the tube at least half-way and offer it to the subject. Although the tube is flexible so that it may adapt to different subject heights, care should be taken to ensure that the tube is not bent so hard as to restrict the flow of breath through it. This is most likely to occur at the point where the tube emerges from the instrument casing, as shown in diagram 1. If excessive condensation does accumulate in the breath tube then it should be pulled fully out and shaken."

Thus the officer must always be cross-examined about the angle at which the tube was held by the motorist. If the constable cannot remember, or if it was at the wrong angle, then the principle of *Hoyle v. Walsh* will apply and there will have been no failure to provide a sample by the accused.

II. BURDEN OF PROOF AND THE PRESUMPTION OF *OMNIA PRAESUMUNTUR RITE ET SOLEMNITER ESSE ACTA*

17–28 In *Vine v. Cameron*, unreported, November 25, 1985, the High Court said that if the alleged failure to provide a specimen was due to faulty analytical or test equipment, then the question of where there had been a failure was embedded in the issue of the instrument working correctly. It is submitted that this is the correct approach, although the accused would have to raise this issue himself. This is because of the application of the principle *omnia praesumuntur rite et solemniter esse acta*: see section 15–08. This is borne out by the decision in *Oldfield v. Anderton* [1986] R.T.R. 314, where it was held that evidence as to calibration checks (*q.v.* section 16–27 was not required in prosecutions for failing to supply breath. Section 69 of the Police and Criminal Evidence Act 1984 will only be of relevance if the prosecution are forced to rely upon a document from a computer to prove that no specimen was provided. That will occur when some breath is breathed into a breath alcohol measuring device (*i.e.* not the hand-held equipment used at the roadside). However, once section 69 becomes applicable, then the burden passes to the prosecution to prove that the device into which the accused was required to blow was both reliable and approved.

E. Body fluids

I. BLOOD

(a) WHICH DOCTOR?

It was held in *Bayliss v. Thames Valley Police Chief Constable* [1978] R.T.R. **17–29** 328 that the police were merely entitled to demand that the motorist allow a specimen of blood to be taken by any medical practitioner and could not insist that it be taken by a particular doctor. In that case, the accused had asked for his own doctor to be present and an officer accordingly telephoned the latter. He arrived at the same time as the police surgeon. The defendant said that he was quite willing to give blood but it had to be taken by his own doctor. The High Court ordered his acquittal. They held that there had been no refusal to supply a sample. The court explained that the Act did not state that the fluid must be taken by a particular type of doctor but allowed it to be obtained by any medical practitioner present at the relevant time and place. Their Lordships emphasised that it would be a totally different matter if the defendant's own doctor had not been present at the police station. What the court was saying was that a motorist could not delay giving a sample by insisting on a particular doctor, but if there were more than one present at the relevant time, he could chose which one he wanted. So in *R. v. Godden* [1971] R.T.R. 462, it was held that the defendant was guilty of refusing to give a blood sample when he insisted that his own doctor, who was not at the station, must take the sample.

(b) WHICH PART OF THE BODY?

It is solely the choice of the police surgeon as to which part of the body he **17–30** shall take the blood from and the motorist must comply with whatever the doctor decides. In *Solesbury v. Pugh* [1969] 1 W.L.R. 1114, the defendant was convicted of failing to supply a specimen as he would only allow a sample to be taken from his big toe, which the doctor was not prepared to do. Likewise, a motorist was found guilty by offering a capillary specimen when the medical practitioner required that it be taken intravenously (see *Rushton v. Higgins* [1972] R.T.R. 456). That decision must be compared with *R. v. Taylor* [1974] R.T.R. 554, where the doctor made various attempts to take blood but was unsuccessful. The police therefore asked for a urine sample but the defendant refused, although he made it plain that he was willing to give blood, despite the fact that the doctor had said that he could not extract that fluid without causing considerable discomfort to the defendant. It was held that there had been no refusal to supply a sample, since at all times he had been willing to do just that. That case was decided in the days when the accused could choose which type of body fluid he would give. As that decision is now vested in the police, there is nothing today to stop the police deciding in a similar situation that, as the doctor preferred not to take blood, then the defendant must supply urine, as happened in *Garrett v. DPP* [1995] T.L.R. 55.

(c) AT WHOSE RISK?

17–31 In *Rawlins v. Brown* [1987] R.T.R. 238, the defendant told the surgeon that he had an allergy to needles but he could take blood at his (the doctor's) risk. The accused was told that he must freely consent to giving blood without any conditions attached. He replied that he wished to give blood but the doctor would be responsible for the consequences. The High Court held that there had not been an unconditional consent to supply a specimen, so that the doctor was right to decline to take a sample. It is submitted that the decision is right in saying that a motorist must give his permission unreservedly and "without any strings attached", but was wrongly decided on its facts. All the accused was telling the doctor was that the latter must take the responsibility for the consequences. In law that must have been the position already because, if the police surgeon was negligent, he could always end up being sued by the motorist. It is submitted that there was no failure to give a sample as the motorist was willing at all times to supply one. Merely reminding the doctor of the law of negligence could not amount to a failure to supply a blood specimen. That case in fact concerned the statutory option under section 8(2). It is submitted that what occurred there should definitely not be considered "a failure" for the purposes of section 7(6).

(d) THE CONSENT FORM

17–32 In *Hier v. Read* [1978] R.T.R. 114, it was held that agreeing to give a sample but then refusing to sign the consent form did not automatically amount to a refusal to give blood. *R. v. McAllister* [1974] R.T.R. 408 held that declining to sign that form was merely one of the matters to be taken into account in deciding whether an offence under section 7(6) had been committed. In *Hier*, it was also held that merely insisting on reading such a form before agreeing to sign it does not amount to a refusal, even if the police officer thought that this was merely delaying tactics.

II. URINE

(a) WAITING THE HOUR

17–33 In *Jones v. Roberts* [1973] R.T.R. 26, it was held that once a defendant had said that he would not provide a urine sample, the police could treat that as a failure, even though one hour had not expired (*i.e.* the length of time which the Act states shall be allowed for supplying the two samples). In *R. v. Coward* [1976] R.T.R. 425, 429E, Lawton L.J. held that a motorist ought not to be held to have failed to provide a urine sample until the 60 minutes allowed by the legislation for its provision had elapsed. In that case, the accused never said that he would not supply a specimen.

(b) First Sample

In *R. v. Beckett* [1976] Crim. L.R. 140, Judge Barr at first instance held that **17–34** the prisoner had not failed to supply urine but had satisfactorily given his first sample by urinating into a lavatory, even though that was contrary to the police's requirement that he should provide it in the container supplied to him. Judge Barr held that as the first specimen was not for the purposes of analysis, the police should have asked the accused for his second sample, and were wrong to have treated the urination into the toilet as a refusal to provide a specimen of that fluid.

(c) The Requirement for the Second Sample

In *R. v. Reynolds* [1976] R.T.R. 229, it was held that once he had been **17–35** asked for two urine specimens, it is up to the defendant to supply the same without any further requests by the police, *e.g.* to remind him when his hour is up. It is also up to the accused to ask for a suitable container if the police have not supplied one. The Court of Appeal said that, as he was a patient at a hospital, he could always have asked a nurse for one.

III. GENERALLY

(a) Size of Specimen

In *R. v. Coward* [1976] R.T.R. 425, it was held that a sample was not to be **17–36** regarded as having been provided unless there was enough fluid for it to be divided into two parts, each of which was of sufficient size to be analysed.

(b) When Requirement Satisfied

Once a specimen of blood is in the syringe, or the jug with the urine has **17–37** been handed over to the police, the motorist will have supplied his specimen. What happens thereafter to it is irrelevant.

In *Ross v. Hodges* [1975] R.T.R. 55, 59A/B Lord Widgery C.J. said:

> "I am not prepared to hold that the mere passing of urine was a provision of urine for present purposes unless and until the police officer was given the opportunity of taking charge of it and did take charge of it."

In that case it was held that there had been no provision of his urine when the defendant dropped the jar containing the fluid as he handed it over to the police. It was held to be irrelevant whether or not the spillage was deliberate. In *Beck v. Watson* [1980] R.T.R. 95, the High Court was of the opinion that the removal of the syringe from the vein by the doctor was the provision of the specimen. The fact that the doctor spilled it as he was transferring it into another container did not alter the fact that the specimen had been obtained. *R. v. Rothery* [1976] R.T.R. 550 held that stealing the specimen back from the police did not mean that one had not been provided pursuant to the Road Traffic Act, s.7(4).

In *R. v. Moore* [1978] R.T.R. 384, it was held that a second specimen of urine had been provided. There the defendant was only convicted of criminal damage when he knocked the bottle off the police station desk. It broke and its contents were lost.

F. Reasonable excuse

I. INTRODUCTION

17–38 Unless the Intoximeter clock is inaccurate, in 999 cases out of a thousand in which a motorist has been charged with failing to provide a specimen, his only hope of avoiding a conviction is to proffer a "reasonable excuse" for not having done so. Unless this matter is raised by the defence, the courts south of the border will assume that none existed but, once it is made an issue in the case, the prosecution must prove beyond all reasonable doubt that the defendant had no such excuse (see *Rowlands v. Thorpe* [1970] 3 All E.R. 195). In Scotland the police must inquire of the motorist why he is not willing to supply a specimen. Without such inquiry the prosecution cannot prove the absence of a reasonable excuse: see *Duncan v. Norman* [1995] S.L.T. at 1995L. Parliament has not given any guidance as to what it meant by those words. When this question was raised in the House of Commons Committee considering the Road Safety Bill, the Under-Secretary of State for the Home Department (D. Taverne, Q.C., M.P.) stated:

> "It would be rather dangerous if we tried to give a definition of what that reasonable excuse would be when, in fact, it would be entirely a matter for the courts. It may be that the example which was given [an M.P. wanting to vote in a division] is the kind of example that the Courts would accept." (Standing Committee E, December 6, 1966.)

> Thus the Wilson administration left it entirely in the hands of the judiciary to decide what ambiguous words in an Act of Parliament meant. Until there was case law on it, how could a motorist know if the reason which he believed allowed him not to provide a specimen was indeed a legitimate one? It is a sad state of affairs that peers and Members of Parliament are prepared to pass legislation without knowing what it means and how it is intended to work in practice. This is especially so where the liberty of the subject is involved.

II. INABILITY OR A WIDER DEFINITION

(a) THE COURT OF APPEAL

17–39 A difference of judicial opinion exists over what can amount to "reasonable excuse". The most cited authority for what is meant by those words is *R. v. Lennard* [1973] 1 W.L.R. 483, where Lawton L.J. said:

". . . No excuse can be adjudged a reasonable one unless a person from whom the specimen is required is physically or mentally unable to provide it or the provision of the specimen would entail a substantial risk to his health."

That decision was considered by the Court of Appeal in *R. v. John* [1974] 1 W.L.R. 624. The judgment was given by Roskill L.J. who said (at 629):

" . . . one returns to consider the language used in *R. v. Lennard* [1973] 1 W.L.R. 483. It may be—and we say this with the utmost respect to Lawton and Scarman L.JJ.—that the language used, if construed too strictly, might involve an over-rigid approach to the language of the section. Certainly, in view of this court and in the light of what was said by Scarman L.J. in *R. v. Reid (Philip)* [1973] 1 W.L.R. 1283, 1289, the court did not intend to lay down something rigid and exhaustive. In truth what the court was there saying was that for an excuse to be capable of being a reasonable excuse, it must be an excuse which is related to the capacity of the person concerned to supply a sample, be it of urine or be it of blood. It is not related to his [religious] belief . . . "

In that case religious grounds were not a reasonable excuse for failing to supply a sample. It also held that "a reasonable excuse" must merely relate to the "capacity of the person concerned to provide a sample".

(b) Conflicting Decisions of the High Court

R. v. Lennard had been cited in a number of appeals in differently **17–40** constituted courts of the Queen's Bench Division, in which conflicting views have been expressed on how rigidly the judgment of Lawton L.J. should be followed.

In *DPP v. Billington* [1988] R.T.R. 231, Lloyd L.J. held that the above quoted dicta of Lawton L.J. in *R. v. Lennard* were for guidance only as the statute did not give any indication as to what could or could not constitute a special reason. In *Spalding v. Paine* [1985] Crim. L.R. 673, and *DPP v. Pearman* [1992] R.T.R. 407, the High Court upheld the acquittal of motorists where stress and shock were the respective causes of their inability to provide breath samples (for the facts, see below).

Cotgrove v. Cooney [1987] R.T.R. 124 also took a less stringent view of what constituted a reasonable excuse. The facts were that the defendant had done his best to provide a sample but had been unable to do so. No medical evidence was called. The acquittal was upheld on appeal but that decision did not find favour with either Glidewell L.J. in *Grady v. Pollard* [1988] R.T.R. 316, or with Watkins D.C.J. in *DPP v. Whalley* [1991] R.T.R. 161, 168, where his Lordship reaffirmed the above quoted dicta of Lawton L.J. in *R. v. Lennard* [1973] 1 W.L.R. 483:

" . . . the motorist understood perfectly well what was being asked of him. In such a situation there can be no reasonable excuse for not complying unless what the motorist contends for, and the justices accept as genuine, is a refusal to comply with the request, as was said in *R. v.*

Lennard [1973] R.T.R. 252, because there is a physical or mental reason which would entail a substantial risk to health in complying with the proper request of a police officer that a specimen of breath be provided . . . The circumstances, if any there can be, in which the principle there stated can be departed from will I imagine be extremely rare."

17–41 In *DPP v. Eddowes* [1991] R.T.R. 35, Watkins D.C.J. stated specifically that *Cotgrove v. Cooney* [1987] R.T.R. 124 should no longer be followed. The facts of the former case were that the defendant had supplied one satisfactory breath sample. The justices had found that he had tried his best to supply a second sample and, therefore, brought in an acquittal. That was reversed on appeal because the defendant had proffered no reason for his inability to have given a second sample, other than that he had tried his best. The justices had assumed that he was under stress, but the High Court held this assumption to be wrong, as many motorists had successfully provided a breath sample after an accident, even though they had been in the same condition as the man who had appeared before them.

In *Webb v. DPP* (decided in 1988 but not reported until [1992] R.T.R. 299) the court declined to speculate as to whether or not *Cotgrove v. Cooney* was correctly decided. *DPP v. Fountain* [1988] R.T.R. 385, 389K, describes the dicta of Lawton L.J. as a "helpful guide upon what is capable of being a reasonable excuse".

(c) The Decisions of the 1990s

17–42 Appeals on what amounts to a "reasonable excuse" still continued to occupy the Divisional Court. A three-judge court was convened to hear the case of *DPP v. Ambrose* [1992] R.T.R. 283—no doubt because of the conflicting authorities. It approved the above quoted dictum of Lawton L.J. in *R. v. Lennard* and held that it was no defence to have done one's best to blow in, unless there was medical evidence showing that there was a mental or physical incapability preventing the provision of sufficient breath to enable a breath alcohol measuring device to carry out an analysis. That proposition was also approved of by the court (Woolf L.J. and Pill J.) in *Daniels v. DPP* [1992] R.T.R. 140. On the other hand, earlier in the year in *DPP v. Beech* [1992] R.T.R. 239, one of those judges, Woolf L.J., had said:

"[Prosecuting counsel] submitted that it is wrong to regard the words of Lawton L.J. in *Lennard* as if they were a statutory provision . . . For my part I agree with that proposition."

In *DPP v. Curtis* [1993] R.T.R 72, Watkins D.C.J. and Tucker J. again reiterated that the correct definition of "reasonable excuse" was that given by Lawton L.J. in *R. v. Lennard*.

In *DPP v. Radford* [1994] T.L.R. 195, the High Court stated that where a "defence of reasonable excuse" was raised to a charge under the Road Traffic Act, s.7(6), the prosecution should draw to the attention of the justices the decision in *Curtis' case* and paragraph 8–1378 of *Stones' Justices' Manual* (1993 ed.). However, that manual makes no mention of the decisions of the House of Lords in *Morris v. Beardmore* [1981 A.C. 446 and *DPP v. Warren* [1993] A.C. 319 (see section 17–45). More significantly, in no High Court case on this issue has the former (or indeed the latter) decision of their Lordships' House been cited or referred to by counsel. Accordingly, in so far as they regarded *R. v. Lennard* as a correct statement of the law, they were decided *per incuriam*. For the same reason, the comments in *Radfords' case* about *Stones' Manual* should not be treated too seriously.

(d) Salus Populi Est Suprema Lex

The High Court has recognised that injustice may well flow from their **17–43** insistence that merely doing one's best to exhale into the breathalyser was not a sufficient reason for failing to provide a specimen. This can only be explained on the basis of *salus populi est suprema lex*. The judges are aware of this, as can be seen from the judicial pronouncement in the case of *Dawes v. Taylor* [1986] R.T.R. 81, 86 (*per* Kennedy J.):

> "Although it may seem unjust that somebody who may be said in common parlance to have done his best to provide a sample should nevertheless be convicted of failing to provide a sample, with all the penal consequences to which such a conviction may give rise, this conclusion has to be viewed in the context of the legislation which, of necessity, makes some inroads into individual freedom in order to try to prevent those who have taken too much alcohol from driving on the roads. That point was made by Roskill L.J. in *R. v. John* [1974] R.T.R. 332, 337H and it seems appropriate to reiterate it here."

A totally different (and, it is submitted, correct) approach was taken by Pain J. (with whom Croom-Johnson L.J. agreed) in *Cotgrove v. Cooney* [1987] R.T.R. 124, 127F, where the justices had found that the accused had done his best to blow into the breathalyser:

> "For myself I am happy to find that the authorities permit that conclusion on that finding of fact because otherwise one would find that if a person had really tried as hard as he could and was none the less to be convicted, then a man would be convicted in a case where there was no *mens rea* which is a matter, for myself, that I would be sorry to see happening in a case of an offence which is not a technical offence, as so many road traffic offences are, but is an offence which ordinary people would regard as morally blameworthy conduct."

Watkins D.C.J. has made clear his views on the above dicta. In *DPP v. Eddowes* [1991] R.T.R. 35, 39, he said that the judgment was "contrary to a broad spectrum of authority". In *DPP v. Daley* [1992] R.T.R. 155, 160, he said that he was "very firmly still of that view". It is submitted that the Deputy Chief Justice is right about it being contrary to authority but those appeals seem to have been decided *per incuriam*, as they do not cite the House of Lords' case of *Morris v. Beardmore*, above, which lays a good foundation for the later decision in *Cotgrove v. Cooney* [1987] R.T.R. 124.

17-44   In *Dawes v. Taylor* [1986] R.T.R. 81, the defendant had been given a breath test inside a police car and had been told to blow long enough and hard enough for the lights to come on. Owing to his position in the vehicle, he was unable to see the lights, so he stopped blowing before they became illuminated. The High Court upheld his conviction for failing to give a sample as he was physically and mentally capable of providing sufficient breath for the test. As the defendant did not know when he had to stop exhaling the decision shows the harshness of invariably applying the above quoted dictum of Lawton L.J. in *R. v. Lennard*. It is submitted that the accused in *Dawes v. Taylor* was in the same position as somebody whose lack of English prevented him from understanding how hard or for how long he had to blow. In that latter case, there would have been an acquittal (*q.v.* section 17–58).

Just as the House of Lords in *Cracknell v. Willis* [1988] A.C. 450 was quite satisfied to leave it to justices to determine whether a defendant was, or was not, telling the truth when he swore that he had not drunk as much alcohol as the result of the analysis indicated, so inferior judges should also have relied upon the good sense of the magistracy to decide where the truth lay when they are told by a person appearing before them that he did his best to blow into the breathalyser.

In *DPP v. Curtis* [1993] R.T.R. 72 Watkins D.C.J. made it clear that in his opinion the usual stress and nervousness felt by most people when in a police station could never amount to a reasonable excuse, otherwise every driver could claim that excuse to avoid the consequences of not providing a specimen for analysis.

DPP v. Coyle [1995] T.L.R. 427 and *DPP v. Pearman* [1992] R.T.R. 407 both held that "doing one's best" was not a reasonable excuse for failing to supply a specimen for analysis but in neither appeal was any House of Lords' case cited. In *Pearman*, Lloyd L.J. noted that the attitude of the judiciary was hardening.

(e) THE VIEW OF THE HOUSE OF LORDS AND THE CORRECT INTERPRETATION OF SECTION 7(6)

17-45   In *Morris v. Beardmore* [1981] A.C. 446, the House of Lords thought (*per* Lord Roskill, at 468): "The suggested limitation [by Lawton L.J.] on 'reasonable excuse' may be somewhat too narrow . . . [although] that defence must be kept within strict confines."

In the view of Lord Edmund-Davis (at 461):

> "But, not withstanding such decisions as *R. v. Lennard* [1973] 1 W.L.R. 483, and *R. v. John* [1974] 1 W.L.R. 624, I am not at present wholly persuaded that only physical or mental inability to comply with a constable's request can constitute a 'reasonable excuse' for non-compliance. It is a phrase commonly found in the law, and it is difficult to see why it should necessarily have any special and restricted connotation in the Road Traffic Acts. It gives rise to what is largely, if not entirely, a question of fact: see *Leck v. Epsom Rural District Council* [1922] 1 K.B. 383 . . . I am meanwhile not prepared to commit myself in the matter, which in any event is unrelated to the facts of the case."

In *DPP v. Warren* [1993] A.C. 319, 326G, Lord Bridge said:

"There is no need to consider what is capable of amounting to a reasonable excuse but it suffices to say that the defence is clearly of very limited scope."

His Lordship went on to say later in his speech:

" . . . and then, if the constable decides to require blood, ask the driver if there are any reasons why a specimen cannot or should not be taken from him by a doctor. This will certainly give the driver the opportunity to raise any objection he may have to giving blood, either on medical grounds or indeed *for any other reason* which might afford a 'reasonable excuse' under section 7(6)" (at 328B/C—author's emphasis).

It is clear that the House of Lords has given a wider meaning to "reasonable excuse" then Lawton L.J. did in *R. v. Lennard,* above. If Lawton L.J. was right, Lord Bridge would have referred only to "a medical", and not to "any other", reason.

In *McLaren v. McLeod* [1994] S.L.T. 1281, 1284, the High Court of **17–46** Justiciary held that "reasonable excuse" in section 7(6) was wider than medical reasons and there was "no warranty" for so restricting it. In *Andrews v. DPP* [1992] R.T.R. 1, 12H/J, Bingham L.J said:

"Where there was no specimen of breath and the driver was prosecuted under section 7(6) for failing to provide a specimen when required to do so in pursuance of the section, the prosecutor would have to establish that the driver had no reasonable excuse. I do not suggest that these provisions would avail a driver very often, but they could be relied on by the court if obvious injustice would otherwise result."

It is submitted that, as a matter of common sense, what Parliament intended is accurately set out by Bingham L.J. in the above quotation. If a driver did his best to blow in, surely no Member of Parliament voted for such a person to be convicted and lose his driving licence? One can only hope that before too long the House of Lords will give a definitive ruling on what excuses can be considered reasonable for failing to provide a specimen.

(f) GENUINE BELIEF OF, RATHER THAN ACTUAL, INCAPACITY

Mann J., who was one of the three judges in *DPP v. Ambrose* [1992] R.T.R. **17–47** 283, had previously taken a somewhat less rigid view of the law in *McGrath v. Vipas* [1984] R.T.R. 58, 66:

"It may be that a defendant's bona fide belief on reasonable grounds that he was mentally or physically unable to supply a specimen although he was mentally or physically able to do so would, in the light of the authorities, constitute a 'reasonable excuse'. However, such a belief was not asserted in this case."

However, he seemed to have revised his views when he came to deliver his judgment in *DPP v. Fountain* [1988] R.T.R. 385. In *DPP v. Shuker,* unreported, March 7, 1995, Balcombe L.J. said:

"For my part, I would say, without it being necessary to decide this (we have not been referred to any authorities on the point) that it might have been a reasonable excuse if he genuinely believed he had bronchitis, but that was not the way the case went before the Magistrates."

(g) FAILURE TO BLOW

17–48 In *Teape v. Godfrey* [1986] R.T.R. 213 and *DPP v. Judge*, unreported, November 27, 1988, it was held that a defence of "reasonable excuse" could not be raised unless the defendant had done his best to blow into the breathalyser. It is submitted that this should not apply where the motorist reasonably believed in advance that for medical reasons he was incapable of providing sufficient breath to obtain an analysis.

(h) MAGISTRATES USING THEIR OWN KNOWLEDGE AND THE NECESSITY FOR EXPERT EVIDENCE

17–49 In *DPP v. Ambrose* [1992] R.T.R. 283, 288, Mann L.J. stated that justices should not of their own volition conclude from the evidence (and introduce into their decision a finding) that the accused had had a reasonable excuse for failing to supply a sample, unless he had specifically raised the matter as a defence to the charge.

17–50 In *Wetherall v. Harrison* [1976] R.T.R. 126, the defendant testified that he had been seized by a fit at the police station because of his fear of needles. A police surgeon and a sergeant both gave evidence that in their opinion it was not a genuine fit. The High Court held that a justice who was a doctor was able to use his professional knowledge to hold that the symptoms displayed by the accused showed that he was having a genuine fit and another justice was able to use his experience of wartime inoculations and the fear which they could create in certain individuals. A justice was entitled to tell his fellow justices how he viewed the evidence but was not allowed to give evidence to them contrary to that given in court. In *DPP v. Curtis* [1992] T.L.R. 432, Watkins D.C.J. said that magistrates were not entitled to go beyond the testimony given in the case they were trying and should be wary of using whatever knowledge they had of physical or mental conditions to form an opinion about what was affecting a motorist when she was asked to provide a breath specimen. They had to adhere to the facts and could not rely on experiences of their own which the testimony given before them could not support. In that case the defendant said that, when she was in the police station, she had a cold. Her doctor said that she had been treated for asthma. She said she was nervous but did not say that she was suffering any breathing difficulties. The justices acquitted her since, from their experience, they knew that nervousness could cause an asthmatic attack. One of them had been a member of the St John's Ambulance Brigade. Watkins D.C.J. held that justices were not entitled to go beyond the evidence, which in that case they had done; there had been no suggestion by the defendant that she had been suffering from asthma and that this was the cause of her non-provision of a breath specimen. It is submitted that it would have been another matter if there had been a thoracic surgeon or other medical practitioner who had the specialist knowledge to know whether or not the evidence indicated an asthma attack.

In *Parker v. Smith* [1974] R.T.R. 500 a motorist had refused to provide a specimen. He had cut his head. The justices accepted counsel's submission that his client was dazed, as evidenced by the cut, and he did not therefore understand what was being required of him. The defendant did not give evidence and called no witnesses. The High Court held that justices could only find a "reasonable excuse" on the evidence before them. Here there was no none to suggest that the defendant was dazed. It was a mere surmise by counsel in his closing speech. In *DPP v. Hammond*, unreported, March 4, 1994, the doctor who had been at the hospital disagreed with the defendant over whether the latter had been fit enough to understand the requirement. The High Court held that the justices could not in the absence of evidence assume that the respondent's ability to understand fluctuated, so they were ordered to convict. They were also warned to be wary of rejecting medical evidence not contradicted by other medical practitioners.

Thus the law is that there must be some evidence of a special reason but, once raised, the prosecution must negative it beyond all reasonable doubt. If the Bench think from their own knowledge that the facts justify a finding of reasonable excuse, they could always, of their own motion, call an expert witness and thus not exceed their role as judges.

The necessary testimony could indeed come from the motorist himself. **17–51** In *DPP v. Pearman*, above, Lloyd L.J. held that even in the absence of medical evidence it was still open to magistrates to make a finding that the accused was incapable of providing a specimen and he cited with approval the words of Glidewell L.J. in *Grady v. Pollard* [1988] R.T.R. 316, 323:

> "Such evidence will normally be the evidence of the medical practitioner, but it need not be, and one can envisage situations in which there is other evidence; indeed in some circumstances, the evidence of the defendant himself would suffice . . . "

This was followed in *DPP v. Crofton* [1994] R.T.R. 279, where the High Court upheld the acquittal of a defendant whose reasonable excuse was his *ipse dixit*, namely, breathlessness caused by a pre-existing depression.

Despite the views expressed by Glidewell and Lloyd L.JJ. (and quoted above), it is nevertheless submitted that whenever an accused has done his best to provide a breath specimen, he should regard it as most prudent to call a doctor to explain post-accident stress to the justices. A clinical examination by a psychiatrist might well reveal that an accused suffered above-average stress. Likewise, anybody who has been unable to provide sufficient breath to obtain a reading on a breath alcohol measuring device should visit a physician to see if he has a lung capacity which is capable of providing the requisite amount of breath in the time allowed (*q.v.* section 17–54). In a letter to the *Law Society Gazette* (August 31, 1988), a solicitor referred to four unsuccessful attempts by a magistrate to provide a breath sample for a Lion Intoximeter, when the latter "tried out" such a device during the hearing of a case brought under section 7(6).

(i) Relying on Reasons not Given to the Police

17-52 In *Teape v. Godfrey* [1986] R.T.R. 213, it was held that if a person knew that he had a medical condition, which might prevent him from giving a sample, he must inform the police, at the time, of this fact. Failure to do so would cause him to lose the right, at his subsequent trial, to rely upon that condition as his reason for failing to supply a specimen. In *DPP v. Kinnersley, The Times*, December 29, 1992, Rose L.J. held that there was no obligation on the motorist to tell the local constabulary anything at all. He said that dicta to the contrary in *Teape v. Godfrey* were *obiter* and in that case the court had overloaded the effect of the police caution, *i.e.* telling the arrested motorist that he was under no obligation to say anything. The Scottish courts have taken a similar view to that of Rose L.J. and have held that a motorist is under no obligation to inform the police of any known medical condition which prevents him blowing into the breathalyser (see *McClory v. Owen Thomas* 1989 S.C.C.R. 402).

Those cases were decided before the enactment of sections 36 and 37 of the Criminal Justice and Public Order Act 1994 which nowadays allows a court to draw such inferences as it sees fit from a defendant's silence at a police station (or elsewhere), provided he has been duly warned that those consequences will follow from his silence. So today a failure to tell the police of medical reasons preventing a specimen being given will not stop such a defence being put forward but, in considering the veracity of such a claim, a court will be able to draw an adverse inference from this silence, if the defendant had been made aware of this consequence by the police.

(j) The Relevance of One Successful Breath Sample Being Provided

17-53 In *Oldfield v. Anderton* [1986] R.T.R. 314, Tudor Evans J. was of the opinion that it was only right, on a charge of failing to give a breath specimen, that evidence could be given that the accused was able to supply one satisfactory breath sample. (The reading given by it, however, should not be revealed to the court, since if it was a high one, this could prejudice the magistrates against the defendant: *q.v.* section 14–42.)

(k) The Medical View

17-54 The following are the requirements of some approved breathalysers:

The Camic
Minimum pressure: 15cm of water
Minimum volume: 1.5 litres
Maximum breath period: 6 seconds

The Alcometer
Minimum breath pressure: 7.5cm of water
Minimum breath discard volume: 1.25 litres
Minimum breath period: 2.3 seconds
Minimum breath flow rate: 28 litres per minute

The Intoximeter
Minimum pressure: 10.2 cm of water.
Minimum flow rate: 10 litres per minute
Maximum breath period: 9 seconds

A very informative article was published by M. J. Morris ([1990] 45 *Thorax* 717) about breath tests. Her main conclusions were:

> "When Briggs *et al.* asked 26 patients with an FEV1 [forced expiretory volume in one second]/FVC [forced vital capacity] below 60% to use an Alcometer simulator only 10 were able to produce a flow rate of 28 litres/ min for 2.7 seconds. Subjects with an FEV1 below 1.5 litres or an FEV below 50% were very unlikely to be able to activate the results of the analysis.
>
> Thus there are difficulties in requiring breath samples from patients with respiratory disease and from people with small lungs. There may also, I believe, be problems with the Lion Intoximeter for people with a vital capacity above 3 litres who do not carry out breathing manoeuvres well in response to commands, because of nervousness, age, or some degree of respiratory dyspraxia."

A healthy person should be able to provide sufficient breath for an analysis or for a breath test, but this is not universal. The most common cause of failing to provide a breath specimen by those who genuinely try will be asthma or bronchitis. When a subject blows into the Intoximeter all the breath passes along a series of convoluted tubes inside the machine. The resistance to flow offered by the Intoximeter is consequently quite high. The harder a person blows, the more breath is required to obtain an analysis (*q.v.* section 13–11).

A study by Gomm, Ossecton, Johnson and Upton published in (1991) 31 **17–55** *Medical Science and the Law* 221 concluded that most people whose FEV1 was less than 2 litres or whose peak flow rate was below 290 litres per minute lacked the lung capacity to blow sufficient breath into the Lion Intoximeter, while all those whose FVC exceeded 3 litres were able to provide a satisfactory specimen. A later study by Gomm, Broster, Johnson and Hammond, published in (1993) 33 *Medical Science and the Law* 311, concluded that people of small stature (*i.e.* 5ft, 5in. or less) whose FEV1 did not exceed 2.3 litres or whose FVC did not exceed 2.6 litres respectively were incapable of providing a satisfactory specimen for the Intoximeter. (The above figures were accepted as being accurate by P.M. Williams, the Marketing Director of Lion Laboratories, when giving evidence in a case before the Basildon Magistrates.) The studies also concluded that people under 35 years old were more likely to be able to provide sufficient breath then those over that age. The older the person, the more difficulty they experienced in using the Intoximeter.

An editorial in [1993] 35 *Thorax* 218 asked the following question and then supplied the answer:

"Can patients with respiratory disease give an adequate breath sample for analysis? The Lion Alcometer SL-2, one of the roadside screening devices commonly used in Britain, is activated by a flow rate of 28 litres a minute or more, which turns on a light and a timer. A second light is triggered if the flow rate is maintained for 2.7 seconds—giving a minimum expired volume of 1.25 litres. The reading is indicated as being above, roughly the same as, or below the legal limit of 35μg/100ml. As a screening device it performs well. When Briggs *et al.* asked 26 patients with an FEV1/FVC below 60% to use an Alcometer simulator only 10 were able to produce a flow rate of 28 litres/min for 2.7 seconds. Subjects with an FEV1 below 1.5 litres or an FEV1 below 50% predicted were very unlikely to be able to activate the Alcometer."

17–56 M.J. Morris and A.G. Taylor wrote in *The Lancet*, January 3, 1987, about four acquittals of failing to provide a specimen for the Intoximeter:

"During the past year five people (see Table B) have been investigated in our lung function laboratory because they had not been able to provide a breath sample and had therefore been arrested or summonsed for 'failure to provide a specimen of breath for analysis without reasonable excuse'. Subject D pleaded guilty but the other four have been acquitted on the evidence of lung function tests and other data reported here."

Table B

Lung function tests in five people unable to provide a breath sample

Patient	Vital capacity (1) (and % predicted)	Diagnosis
A (62a M)	2.37 (61)	Obesity, angina, cardiomegaly
B (59 M)	2.63 (70)	Ankylosing spondylitis
C (40 M)	4.73 (118)	Asthma*
D (321 F)	3.20 (90)	Normal lungs
E (321 M)	2.80 (58)	Glottic closure, respiratory dyspraxia

* Peak flow rate 470l/min. on day of lung function testing (280l/min at police station).

The authors of that letter then refer to the fact that Lion Laboratories merely state that only 1.5 litres of breath is required in nine seconds for the Intoximeter and go on to comment:

"The requirement for 1.5 litres at a flow rate greater than 10l[itres]/min[ute] under-represents what is really required. This, however, is the information given to general practitioners and chest physicians who are asked to assess whether someone has a medical excuse for failing to provide a breath sample. In general such physicians are unaware that only two or three attempts have been allowed. Perhaps all five of our patients could have satisfied the requirements, given adequate instruction as to the type of breath required and the opportunity of repeated attempts. However, we do not think that their failure to do so within the statutory 3 minutes justifies the conclusion that they were unwilling to provide a sample. In the lung function laboratory patients often have difficulty in following instructions and doing breathing manoeuvres to command. As an additional safeguard, we think that the law should be changed to allow anyone who has not succeeded in providing a breath sample acceptable to the Intoximier to provide a blood or urine sample instead."

(1) BLOOD

A phobia or fear of needles is a reasonable excuse, see *ex. p. Quy* [1993] Crim.L.R. 970.

III. FAILURE TO UNDERSTAND THE REQUIREMENT

(a) MENTAL INCAPACITY

In *Spalding v. Paine* [1985] Crim L.R. 673, the accused had been found by **17–57** the police sitting in the front seat of her illegally parked car with a partially empty whisky bottle. She was in an emotional state because her boyfriend had broken off their relationship and repeatedly said that she wanted to die. The High Court upheld her acquittal:

" . . . the justices were saying in this case that they had come to the conclusion that, because of the emotional condition of this lady, she was not in a condition to go through the mental processes which the statute contemplated. Accordingly there was a reasonable excuse shown by this lady . . . "

Neill L.J., in giving the above judgment, made it clear that this was not a case of self-induced intoxication and stated that he was deliberately saying nothing about such a situation.

(b) LACK OF UNDERSTANDING OF THE ENGLISH LANGUAGE

In *Beck v. Sager* [1979] R.T.R. 475, the defendant was an Arab who did not **17–58** speak much English. As he did not understand what was being asked of him, nor the statutory warning, the magistrates acquitted him, which verdict was upheld on appeal. That decision was approved by *Simpson v. Spalding* [1987] R.T.R. 221, which emphasised that the Arab's inability to understand what the police were telling him made him mentally incapable of providing a specimen within the meaning given to those words in *R. v. Lennard, q.v.* section 17–39, above. Even Watkins D.C.J. in *DPP v. Whalley* [1991] R.T.R. 161, 168, accepted that lack of English would be a reasonable excuse for failing to give a sample:

> "It follows therefore that the observation [in *Singh*] that a failure to understand the obligation to provide a specimen of breath was capable of amounting to a reasonable excuse was an obiter dictum. Nevertheless I agree with it in principle."

In *Chief Constable of Avon and Somerset Constabulary v. Singh* [1988] R.T.R. 107, and in *DPP v. Beech* [1992] R.T.R. 239, the High Court stated that an acquittal would result when an accused had not understood the statutory warning of prosecution because of lack of English or perhaps because of mental stress and anxiety. This would apply where the warning "did not impinge upon the mind of the person to whom it was given and was not understood by [him] as a warning". *DPP v. Beech* was of the opinion that this lack of comprehension would amount to "a reasonable excuse"; while *Singh* regarded the same factual matrix as a failure by the police to comply with section 7(7), in that no warning (within the meaning of the Act) had been given.

It is submitted that the above cases were correctly decided as, if a person does not understand what the local constabulary require of him and the penal consequences of failure, then he could not be blamed for any non-compliance with their requirements.

IV. SELF-INDUCED INTOXICATION

17–59 In *DPP v. Pearman* [1992] R.T.R. 407, it was held that shock combined with inebriation which had rendered a person physically incapable of providing a sample of breath for analysis could amount to a reasonable excuse for not supplying such a specimen. To the contrary is *Berry v. DPP* [1995] T.L.R. 571, where it was held that a person did not have a reasonable excuse where alcohol was a contributory factor. In *DPP v. Beech*, above, the justices found that the procedure was explained to the accused, but he was too drunk to understand it. Woolf L.J. held:

> "It would, in my view, defeat the object of the legislation, which is intended for the protection of the public, to hold that the fact that the defendant was too drunk to understand what was said to him could provide him with a reasonable excuse. It would also be an abuse of language so to describe it."

However, the court agreed with the Crown's concession that a drunken motorist who had lapsed into total unconsciousness would have a reasonable excuse for not giving a specimen.

17–60 Thus a person can rely upon self-induced intoxication where it is obvious to the police that he was either incapable of supplying a sample or of understanding what was being told to, or required of, him. Where this is not apparent, he cannot submit that he had drunk too much alcohol. The rationale of this is, presumably, that where the police knew (or possibly ought to have known) that his drunken state rendered him incapable of doing or understanding what he was being told, then they could always have preferred a charge of driving while unfit; but it would make a mockery of the law if somebody who appeared to be capable of providing a breath sample was able to avoid punishment for not having done so by merely establishing at his trial that his failure to blow into the machine was solely due to having been too inebriated to have done so. (By that time the limitation period for laying an information for driving while unfit would probably have expired.)

V. EX TURPI CAUSA

In *DPP v. Szarzynski* [1993] R.T.R. 364 the respondent, having been **17–61** arrested after a roadside breath test, ran off and was recaptured half an hour later. He was taken to a police station but failed to provide a specimen of breath for analysis. On medical evidence, the Crown Court ordered an acquittal because the respondent had been suffering from hyperventilation, even though he might not have been aware of it at the time. The Director of Public Prosecutions appealed by way of case stated, submitting that since the hyperventilation had been caused by the exhaustion, etc., of fleeing from justice, it therefore could not be relied upon on the principle of *ex turpi causa*. The High Court said that the Crown Court did not make that finding of fact about the cause of the respondent's medical condition; and therefore did not adjudicate on the merits of the argument put forward by the Director of Public Prosecutions. It is submitted that it could well be argued that the judiciary should treat a medical condition brought about solely by an illegal act as being analogous to self-induced intoxication and not capable of affording a reasonable excuse for not supplying a satisfactory specimen.

VI. THE CODES OF PRACTICE AND SECTION 78 OF THE POLICE AND CRIMINAL EVIDENCE ACT 1984

(a) CONSULTING THE CODE

There have been a number of cases about people who would not supply a **17–62** sample until they had read the Code of Practice issued by the Home Secretary under the provisions of section 66(b) of the Police and Criminal Evidence Act 1984. In *DPP v. Whalley* [1991] R.T.R. 161, the accused was given a notice stating that the Code of Practice was available on request. He was also orally informed that he had a right to consult it forthwith. He was then asked to provide a sample of breath. He replied: "No, I want to read the Code of Practice first."

He was thereupon charged with failing to supply a specimen. The justices acquitted him on the grounds that he had been misled into believing that he had the right to read the Code before exhaling into the Intoximeter. Watkins D.C.J. (at 168) held that to be no excuse:

"It does not, in my view, avail the defendant in this case that he claims to have been confused or misled by anything the officer may have said as to his right to see Codes of Practice, to consult his solicitor or other matters of that kind. The justices failed, it seems to me, to comprehend the real impact of the judgments in *R. v. Lennard* [1973] R.T.R. 252, and *Grennan v. Westcott (Note)* [1988] R.T.R. 253. I would like to make it perfectly clear—I say this by way of repetition, I appreciate—that in my judgment *R. v. Lennard* must be strictly followed by justices."

Watkins D.C.J. (at 166B) said that the justices were right not to have invoked their powers under section 78 of the Police and Criminal Evidence Act 1984 (see Chapter 14). That statute bestows upon the judiciary a discretion to refuse to admit evidence on the grounds that it would be unfair to the accused to allow such testimony to be given. It is submitted that, as the defendant had been misled by the police, it would have been unfair not to have excluded any evidence which showed that he had been required to supply a specimen of breath. The fact that such a discretion exists was recognised in *Hudson v. DPP* [1992] R.T.R. 27, where the conviction was set aside and the case remitted for the Crown Court to decide how they would exercise that discretion. (There the facts were more or less identical with *Whalley's case*.) Indeed, Hodgson J. stated that the notice given to arrested motorists should make it clear that they had no right to delay the Road Traffic Act procedure by reading the Code or consulting their solicitors. If that was not done, justices could (and it is submitted should) exercise their discretion under section 78 to exclude any evidence of a requirement being made for a specimen for analysis.

17–63   In *DPP v. Skinner* [1990] R.T.R. 254, the police gave the defendant a copy of the Code of Practice to read. He was then asked to give a specimen, but insisted that he should be allowed to finish reading the Code and then speak to a solicitor, before providing a specimen. The stipendiary magistrate acquitted him. That decision was reversed on appeal. Lloyd L.J. pointed out that the relevant code (Code C) was printed with "Notes for Guidance", and those for section 6 said that the procedure under section 5 of the Road Traffic Act was not an interview for the purposes of the Code. Lloyd L.J. went on to say that the Notes were not part of the Code and it was for the court to decide what had occurred. He was clearly of the opinion that merely asking a person to supply a specimen was manifestly not "an interview". Thus the High Court held that it was not a reasonable excuse for a defendant to refuse to give a blood sample until he had spoken to a solicitor. It is submitted that (provided the police make it clear that the Road Traffic Act procedure is not "an interview" for the purposes of the Code) this was a correct decision because, if a person was allowed to delay giving a sample until his lawyer arrived, some of his alcohol would have metabolised by the time the specimen was provided.

(b) Revision of the Code

Note for Guidance 3E of the 1995 Code C states: **17–64**

> "3E. The right to consult the codes of practice under paragraph 3.1 above does not entitle the person concerned to delay unreasonably any necessary investigative or administrative action while he does so. Procedures requiring the provision of breath, blood or urine specimens under the terms of the Road Traffic Act 1988 need not be delayed."

VII. NO WARNING OF PROSECUTION

Although there is a mandatory statutory requirement for a warning of **17–65** prosecution when requiring a specimen for analysis, the absence of which will result in an automatic acquittal (see sections 14–09 *et seq.*), there is no similar requirement when requesting a breath sample for the roadside screening device. In *R. v. Dolan* [1969] 1 W.L.R. 1479, it was held that failure to give such a warning could amount to a reasonable excuse for not taking the breath test. The rationale of this according to the Court of Appeal was (at 1428A):

> "Unless he is given the warning . . . he may not know the law and may have no idea that he has a statutory obligation to comply with the request and is committing a criminal offence if he refuses to do so . . . If any jury came to the conclusion that the accused had not been given the mandatory warning and was ignorant of his legal obligations, it is hard to see how they could properly convict."

That was a decision on the Road Safety Act 1967 which enacted that a warning had to be given. It also stated that, in the absence of such a warning, the court had a discretion to direct an acquittal. As the lack of a warning does not automatically lead to the dismissal of the charge under section 6(4), it is submitted that *R. v. Dolan* is still good law; and that if a court is not satisfied that the defendant was aware of the fact that a failure to take a test was an offence, he would be able to invoke the defence of reasonable excuse.

This submission is still made despite the contrary decision in *Worsley v.* **17–66** *DPP*, unreported, November 11, 1994, which stated that because Parliament had only enacted a mandatory warning for those required to provide specimens under section 7(1), there was no duty to give any such warning when demanding a breath test and therefore the absence of a warning of prosecution could never amount to a reasonable excuse for not complying with a request under section 6 of the Road Traffic Act.

VIII. OTHER REASONABLE EXCUSES FOR REFUSING TO PROVIDE A SAMPLE

In *Rowland v. Thorpe* [1970] 3 All E.R. 195, the High Court did not dismiss **17–67** out of hand the proposition that, because of the embarrassment that it could involve, the refusal by a woman to supply urine could amount to a reasonable excuse, if there was no female officer present. In *Anderton v. Goodfellow* [1980] R.T.R. 302, it was held that embarrassment at having to urinate in front of a constable of the same sex was not a reasonable excuse for not having supplied a specimen. In *R. v. Harling* [1970] R.T.R. 441, the Court of Appeal thought that an accused could have a reasonable excuse for refusing to give blood if a police surgeon had already made three unsuccessful attempts to take blood and that had caused the defendant to lose confidence in the doctor.

17–68 The following reasons have been held not to be legitimate excuses for failing to supply a specimen:

1. Genuinely believing that the police had not been acting bona fide (*McGrath v. Vipas* [1984] R.T.R. 58).

2. Not having committed any moving traffic offence (*R. v. Downey* [1970] R.T.R. 257), or indeed any offence (*Hawes v. DPP* [1993] R.T.R. 116).

3. Having been told by one's solicitor that there was no need to supply a specimen (*Dickinson v. DPP* [1989] Crim. L.R. 741).

4. Having a genuine fear of catching AIDS (*DPP v. Fountain* [1988] R.T.R. 385). It would be another matter if the defendant could produce medical evidence to show that his fear of AIDS had caused a phobia which prevented him putting his lips to the mouthpiece of the Intoximeter and blowing into it, as happened in the case of *DeFreitas v. DPP* [1992] T.L.R 337.

5. Being a patient at a hospital who had, prior to the arrival of the police surgeon, already provided a blood sample for the hospital (*Kemp v. Chief Constable of Kent* [1987] R.T.R. 66).

6. Having been assaulted by a policeman who had punched him and cut his eyebrow causing bleeding (*R. v. Wallace* [1972] R.T.R. 9, where the assault had been committed by a constable, while the requirement for a sample had been made by a sergeant. The Court of Appeal did say that if the assault had been more serious and had been by the same officer who had requested the specimen, then mistrust of the officer might have constituted a reasonable excuse).

7. Being wrongly arrested as a burglar, being handcuffed and man-handled into a cell. However, the state of mind caused by this could be special reasons for not disqualifying (*Chief Constable of Avon and Somerset Constabulary v. O'Brien* [1987] R.T.R. 182).

8. Wanting a solicitor to be present when giving a sample (*Law v. Stephens* [1971] R.T.R. 358).

9. Willing to give a specimen for analysis of a different substance from that required by the police (*Francis v. Chief Constable of Avon and Somerset Constabulary* [1988] R.T.R. 250 and *Grix v. Chief Constable of Kent* [1987] R.T.R. 193).

10. Not being told that one was only allowed three minutes in which to provide a breath specimen before the Intoximeter automatically closed itself down (*DPP v. Thomas* (1993) 157 J.P. 480, where the defendant, instead of blowing in as required, argued with the police until the breathalyser closed itself down; and *DPP v. Coyle* [1995] T.L.R. 427,

where Buxton J. held that this could amount to a reasonable excuse but only if the defendant could show there was a good reason why he would have been able to provide a specimen if he had been told of the three-minute time limit).

11. Only having consumed alcohol after ceasing to drive (*R. v. Lennard*, above, overruling *Glendinning v. Bell* [1973] R.T.R. 52).

12. Religious reasons (*R. v. Najran* [1993] R.T.R. 451, and *R. v. John* [1974] 1 W.L.R. 624).

13. Wanting diplomatic representation (*R. v. Seaman* [1971] R.T.R. 456).

IX. SUMMARY

To summarise, a reasonable excuse for failing to supply a sample will **17–69** normally be either a medical condition which made the motorist physically or mentally incapable of providing the specimen requested, or that the provision of a specimen would cause him a serious risk of injury. However, the court will, on occasion, consider other excuses as being reasonable, if the special circumstances were such that one could not really have expected a defendant to have supplied a sample; but the judiciary will not allow that defence to become (in the words of Lord Roskill in *Morris v. Beardmore* [1981] A.C. 446, 468) "an easy escape route from conviction for the obviously guilty motorist". Also, the courts can use their powers under P.A.C.E., s.78 to exclude evidence of the requirement for the specimen and accordingly dismiss the charge. This will happen when the reason for the "failure" was due to the motorist having been misled by the police.

Chapter 18

UNFIT THROUGH DRINK OR DRUGS

A. Introduction

Section 4 of the Road Traffic Act 1988 makes it an offence to drive or to be **18–01** in charge of a mechanically-propelled vehicle on a road or other public place when unfit to drive through drink or drugs. In *Thomson v. Knights* [1974] K.B. 336, it was held that any information alleging unfitness to drive through "drink or drugs" was not bad for duplicity, as there was only one offence of unfitness to drive, although it could be committed in more than one way, *i.e.* either through drink, or through drugs, or through a combination of those two substances. In *R. v. Carr* (1934) 24 Cr.App.R. 199 it was stated that a charge should avoid the word "drunk" when giving particulars of the offence.

B. Drink or Drugs

"Drug" is defined in the Road Traffic Act 1988, s.11(2) and the Transport **18–02** and Works Act 1992, s.38(1) as including "any intoxicant other than alcohol". This definition was introduced into the law by the Transport Act 1981. Prior to that its meaning was solely a question for the jury. No definition of the word "drink" is given in the statute. In *Armstrong v. Clark* [1957] 2 Q.B. 391, 394, Lord Goddard C.J. held that this word meant "alcoholic drink" and that "drug" meant "a medicament or medicine, given to cure, alleviate or assist an ailing body". In that case the accused was a diabetic and his insulin was held to be a "drug". In *Bradford v. Wilson* (1984) 78 Cr.App.R. 77 it was held that *Armstrong v. Clark* was not an authority for the proposition that only a medicine could be "a drug" and the latter was any substance taken by a person which affected the control of the human mind and which was neither a beverage nor taken as food. Accordingly, the High Court upheld the conviction under what is now section 4 of the Road Traffic Act 1988 of a glue sniffer who had inhaled toluene.

In *Watmore v. Jenkins* [1962] 2 Q.B. 572 the accused had a high body level of hydrocortisone because of a liver infection and this meant that he had to take a larger than normal dose of insulin for his diabetes. Without warning, his hydrocortisone level fell and ceased to counteract the extra insulin, so that the latter made him go into a hypoglycaemic state while driving his car. The High Court upheld the acquittal on the ground (at 585) that the insulin was no more than a predisposition or a historical cause taken to obtain an equilibrium and that it was the reduction of the hydrocortisone that was responsible for the motorist's hypoglycaemic episode.

In *R. v. Ealing JJ., ex p. Woodman* [1994] R.T.R 189 the defendant, a diabetic, became unfit to drive when he suffered a hypoglycaemic attack caused by a low blood sugar level. The attack could have been due, *inter alia* to an excessive injection of insulin or lack of food after taking the correct dosage of that drug. However, it happened 12 hours after his last injection, and there was no evidence to show that there was any insulin left in his body to produce the blood sugar imbalance which caused the attack. As it could not be established that his unfitness was caused by a drug, the High Court quashed his conviction.

The vast majority of convictions under section 4 are for being unfit through drink. The number involving drugs is increasing, especially in Scotland. Over half the motorists arrested for reckless driving in Tennessee during the summer of 1993 were found to be under the influence of drugs (see Brookhoff and Cook, "Testing Reckless Drivers for Cocaine and Marijuana [1994] *The New England Journal for Medicine*).

C. Unfit

(a) DEFINITION

18–03 Unfitness is clearly defined in section 4(5):

" . . . a person shall be taken to be unfit to drive if his ability to drive properly is for the time being impaired."

(b) EVIDENCE OF DRINKING AND MEDICAL EVIDENCE

18–04 There must be proof of impairment and not merely that the accused had been drinking and driving (see *R. v. Hawkes* (1931) 22 Cr.App.R. 172).

In *R. v. McBride* [1962] 2 Q.B. 167 and *R. v. Woodward* [1995] 1 W.L.R. 1375, it was held that evidence merely that the accused had been drinking was inadmissible (as it was prejudicial), unless there was also evidence that the amount of drink consumed could have made him unfit to drive. The latter could no doubt be achieved by testimony about the motorist's condition, *e.g.* unable to stand after alighting from his vehicle, etc. (They were both cases of death by dangerous driving but it is submitted the same principle would apply to driving while unfit.) Nowadays, evidence of impairment due to drink or drugs is usually provided by a police surgeon. In *R. v. Lanfear* [1968] 2 Q.B. 77, it was held that such a person should be regarded as an independent witness and not just as somebody who has come to court solely to help the prosecution.

(c) OTHER EVIDENCE

A motorist's unfitness to drive can also be proved by non-medical **18–05** witnesses. Anybody who saw the defendant at the relevant time can testify how much the latter had imbibed but cannot state that he was unfit to drive, because that is the very question which the court must answer on the evidence before it (see *R. v. Davies* [1962] 1 W.L.R. 1111). To help the court to reach a decision, evidence may be adduced of the manner of driving. An example of such testimony being relied upon by the prosecution can be seen in the opening speech of counsel for the Crown in *R. v. Owen (Philip)*, *The Times*, April 26, 1978:

> "[The police] saw that [the defendant's] car was veering from the nearside to the offside lane, being driven at 45–50m.p.h.
> The police flashed their head lamps to try to stop Mr Owen's car but there was no response. Later, Mr Owen's car slowed down and continued at about 5 m.p.h. for about a quarter of a mile. Police Constable Edwards ran up to Mr. Owen's car.
> He ran alongside the car and the driver still seemed oblivious of his presence. He opened the driver's door and put the footbrake on himself."

(d) EXPERT AND OTHER EVIDENCE AS TO THE EFFECTS OF ALCOHOL

In *R. v. Hunt* [1980] R.T.R. 29, the defendant had collided with a parked **18–06** van. His blood was analysed and showed his alcohol intake to be two-and-a-half times the legal limit. The Court of Appeal held that, without expert evidence as to the effects of intoxicants, a jury could assume that a motorist whose alcohol level was so much above the prescribed limit was unfit to drive.

In *R. v. Thorpe* [1972] 1 W.L.R. 342, it was held that a jury could draw a similar inference about a person whose alcohol level exceeded the prescribed limit. This is probably unfair to the motorist as the view of the British Medical Association is that where the alcohol is twice the legal limit, this is the level at which a person would definitely be unfit to drive. In *R. v. McBride*, above, it was held to be permissible for a doctor to say that the prisoner's alcohol level would have adversely affected the average driver.

(e) REFUSAL TO UNDERGO A MEDICAL EXAMINATION OR TO SUPPLY A SAMPLE

Under the Road Traffic Act 1962 a jury could regard a refusal to give a **18–07** specimen for analysis both as corroborating other prosecution evidence that the accused was unfit to drive and as rebutting defence assertions to the contrary. (In those days no offence was committed by a refusal.) It is submitted that, although that provision has now been repealed, justices can still today use such evidence in a similar way. *R. v. Hillman* [1978] R.T.R. 124 held that if the accused gave a reasonable explanation as to why he had declined to give a sample and this was accepted, then no question of corroboration or rebuttal would arise.

(f) REBUTTING EVIDENCE

18–08   In *R. v. Hegarty* [1977] R.T.R. 337, a doctor examined the accused and formed the opinion that he was unfit through drink. His urine analysis showed only 4mg of alcohol. The Court of Appeal said that the analysis raised sufficient doubt about the doctor's evidence and accordingly quashed the conviction.

D. Alcohol absorption and consequences for the driver

18–09   Absorption of alcohol from the gastrointestinal tract (including the stomach) occurs by simple passive diffusion along concentration gradients and does not involve an active transport system. As alcohol is completely water soluble it readily permeates cell membranes. Its distribution is largely governed by the water content of the various organs and tissues. Alcohol is usually rapidly absorbed from the stomach. This absorption may be slowed down if the stomach contains food or especially fat such as milk. Although alcohol can be absorbed while in the stomach, the upper portion of the small intestine represents the principal site of its absorption. Absorption in this portion is rapid and virtually complete so that the rest of the intestinal tract is exposed to very little alcohol.

The critical determinant of the rate of absorption appears to be the emptying time of the stomach, which is subject to various influences. The presence of food slows gastric emptying, as do high concentrations of alcohol which can produce gastric irritation and pylorospasm, hence the popular advice that drinking on any empty stomach will result in faster intoxication whereas having a meal first will delay intoxication. The delayed intoxication is in fact due to the food causing delayed gastric emptying rather than the food "lining the stomach" as is popularly supposed.

The important role of the stomach as a temporary impediment to absorption is graphically illustrated by findings made in patients who have undergone massive gastrectomies, *i.e.* removal of part of the stomach. These patients become intoxicated rapidly with relatively small quantities of alcohol because it is delivered almost immediately to the site of its rapid absorption in the small intestine.

18–10   The rate of entrance of alcohol into various tissues varies directly with the blood supply of the tissue. The concentration in the highly vascularised central nervous system therefore rapidly comes into equilibrium with that in the systemic arterial blood. Concentrations in the poorly perfused tissues increase more slowly. This explains the popular observation that a person who takes a few drinks without food quickly becomes inebriated and then in the next half-an-hour becomes more sober. This is because blood is carried to the brain by the extra rich blood supply of brain tissue. The concentration of alcohol in the brain then falls as the alcohol is redistributed slowly to other body tissues.

Elimination of the alcohol from the body is slower than its absorption. More than 90 per cent of the alcohol absorbed is metabolised chiefly in the liver to carbon dioxide and water. The average rate of metabolism is 10ml per hour, equal to a fall of 15mg per 100ml per hour in the blood level of alcohol. However, the rate of alcohol absorption after oral intake is greatly influenced by the nature and concentration of the alcoholic beverage, food intake and a multitude of other physical and biological factors that combine with the individual's sex, body weight and body water to determine the peak alcohol concentration and other characteristics of the time course of the blood alcohol concentration.

The metabolism of alcohol takes place chiefly in the liver. The remainder of the alcohol is excreted largely unchanged in urine and in expired air. Small quantities may also be found in saliva, sweat and tears. It has been found that in severe chronic alcoholism the rates of metabolism can in time become double the accepted average. This is popularly known as the increased capacity of chronic drinkers to tolerate fairly large doses of alcohol which in the occasional drinker would cause profound intoxication.

The phenomena and characteristics which have been described above are **18–11** illustrated in the diagram which describes the theoretical time course of blood (or breath) alcohol concentration. This is subdivided schematically into four phases:

1. Absorption
2. Plateau
3. Diffusion/equilibration
4. Elimination.

These are illustrated in Figure 1. The time lag from initial absorption of alcohol to the beginning of the post-absorptive phase is a key variable in relation to highway safety. The peak blood alcohol concentration and the time for its achievement are important in that the peak often marks the changeover between rising and falling alcohol concentration which is related to acute adaptation to the effects of alcohol. These variables also illustrate the substantial biological variability in alcohol pharmacokinetics. Dubowski, in 1976, found elapsed time from end of alcohol intake to peak alcohol concentration varying from 14–138 minutes; a nearly tenfold variation. (See Dubowski, "Human Pharmacokinetics of Ethanol" (1976) 22 Clin.Chem. 1199.)

It must be stressed that the rate of decrease of blood alcohol concentration does not directly and exclusively reflect the metabolic disposition of alcohol, because the changes in concentration are also in part a product of alcohol elimination through urine, breath and perspiration. Excretion through these routes would be expected to be positively correlated with the plasma alcohol concentration because it involves passive diffusion of alcohol in accordance with its concentration gradients for the route involved. Breath alcohol analysis is by far the most commonly employed form of chemical testing in traffic law enforcement. The principle of the Intoximeter is that alcohol is partitioned between blood and alveolar air, and that this alcohol is measured by comparison with a standard alcohol concentration.

18–12 There has been a surge of interest in self-testing equipment; the personal breathalyser. The rationale is simply that the driver can ideally check his own alcohol level and thus ensure that it is safe to have another drink before driving home. Although this would seem to offer a fail-safe in that the driver would know his exact level, this logic is in fact delusory. Reference to Figure 1 illustrates the fallacy of these methods since some knowledge of the four phases of alcohol absorption are required to interpret the result. A single reading will not indicate which of the four phases has been reached, namely absorption, plateau, equilibration/diffusion or elimination. One might be at a level of 60mg per cent, yet be in the absorptive phase and thus be at a level of 95mg per cent half-an-hour later.

Figure 1

Diagram illustrating alcohol absorption phases

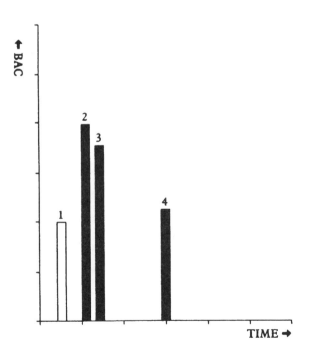

The second fallacy which can be deduced from Figure 1 is the presumption that the consumption of known amounts of alcoholic beverages of known strengths will give rise to known and reproduceable levels of blood alcohol concentration. Clearly this cannot be the case. It will depend upon which phase has been reached and thus reliance upon a set calculation may give misleading results. However, the concept of alcohol units is very useful and will be part of any consideration of the alcohol problem and so will be mentioned. Standard alcohol units are a way of calculating the quantity of alcohol which has been drunk. Each drink has a known alcoholic strength, *e.g.* whisky has a higher percentage alcohol concentration than beer. However, beer is consumed in larger quantities. The unit of whisky contains an identical amount of alcohol to a unit of beer. This therefore is a convenient means of alcohol standardisation. Table 1 gives the average alcohol concentrations of different drinks and the measures which contain one unit.

It is appropriate to mention the measurement of urine alcohol in **18–13** connection with Figure 1. In the absorptive phase the concentration of alcohol in the blood is greater than that in the urine. However, in the elimination phase the concentration in the urine becomes greater than that in the blood. It has been determined that in this phase the ratio of alcohol in the urine to that in the blood is 4:3. This is because the urine obtained at a particular time is derived from blood passing through the kidneys earlier, when the blood alcohol concentration was greater. This is likely to be so when the doctor examines the patient. The known ratio makes it possible to calculate the concentration of alcohol in the blood from an examination of the urine only. However, due to the number of assumptions made, the blood and breath alcohol concentrations are much more accurate and the offence of driving under the influence of alcohol is statutorily defined in terms of the concentration of alcohol in the blood and breath. The relationship between alcohol in the blood and alcohol in the urine is shown in Figure 2 (overleaf).

Table 1

The alcohol concentration of different drinks

Drink	Average strength	Measure containing one unit
Wine	10%	One glass
Spirits	40%	One single
Sherry	18%	Onc single
Beer	3.5%	One half-pint
Beer Strong-brew	6%	One third
Low alcohol beer (1%)	1%	Two pints
Low alcohol beer (0.5%)	0.5%	Four pints

The characteristic pharmacokinetics of alcohol are responsible for many aspects of road safety. The partition of alcohol between body tissues and the consequent alcohol concentration ratios for blood and breath are necessary subjects for study, without which it would be difficult to comprehend the major phenomena of alcohol absorption and metabolism. The key characteristic of alcohol pharmacokinetics is the unpredictability of peak alcohol concentration, time to peak after end of drinking and the rate of alcohol elimination from blood. This variability is apparent even on ingestion of identical weight-adjusted doses. This great biological variability when combined with sex, age and time-related differences makes the blood alcohol information in widely disseminated alcohol consumption tables based on average data inappropriate as a guide for the drinking behaviour of individual drivers.

18–14 It is often difficult to decide whether the post-absorptive phase has been reached in any given time—thus it is almost impossible to convert the alcohol level of breath or urine to blood alcohol with acceptable degrees of accuracy. Whilst this has been held out as the model indicating the ideal state of alcohol absorption, short-term fluctuations do occur. Whilst the general trend and the four stages are reliable, the typical pattern may not be followed. The elimination phase may not be strictly as in the diagram. More importantly, alcohol absorption is not always complete within 30–90 minutes as often claimed. Peak alcohol concentration consequently cannot be reliably predicted in an individual. It is not possible to reliably establish whether an individual is in the absorption or elimination phase or even establish the mean overall rate of alcohol elimination from the blood or breath. It has been determined also that large short-term fluctuations occur in some patients and result in marked departures from the mean. It is also documented that there are marked oscillations in blood or breath concentrations which can give rise to large and significant variations above or below a given concentration for hours.

Figure 2

Diagram illustrating the relationship between alcohol in the blood and alcohol in the urine

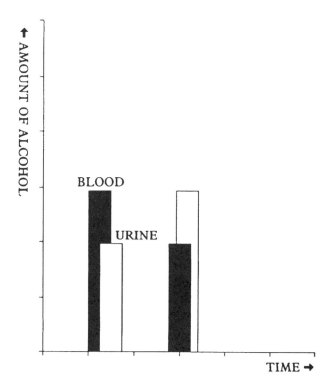

With regard to the pharmacokinetic properties of alcohol, research 18–15 studies have indicated very marked differences with regard to age and sex. The definitive studies of Dubowski confirmed that the average time to peak alcohol concentration after end of drinking was 1.35 times as long in males as in females, and the average blood alcohol concentration for identical amounts consumed was 12.8 per cent higher in women than in men. He also confirmed that the average alcohol decrement in blood concentration was 23.6 per cent greater in women than in men. The reason for these large differences is asserted to be due to differences in body water and adipose tissue proportions. Zeiner, in 1983, contended the use of oral contraceptives and the stage of menstrual cycle was important. Women taking oral contraceptives achieved lower peak alcohol concentrations and had lower rates of alcohol elimination than women not taking oral contraceptives (see Zeiner, *Effects of Female Sex Steroids on Ethanol Pharmacokinetics* (1983, U.S. Government Printing Office), p. 63). The premenstrual phase of the ovulation cycle was marked by higher peak alcohol concentrations and greater absorption rates. Schweitzer in 1968 showed increases in blood alcohol elimination rates with increasing age. (See Schweitzer, *Statistische Untersuchungen zur Alkohol Elimination* (1968), p. 63.)

The key characteristic of the pharmacokinetics of alcohol is the unpredictability of the blood alcohol concentration at any time, making nonsense of easy nomograms and glib predictions. The short-term fluctuations of the blood and breath alcohol and the variability of the peak concentration and timing of the post-absorptive state, combined with sex and age-related variability must spell caution to those drivers who drink and plan to stay under the limit.

E. Impairment and the risk of accident

18–16   There is a popular misconception that a drunk driver is "too drunk to be injured", so relaxed that, like a rubber man, on collision he will bounce and thus avoid injury. This is an appealing story but completely false. The drunken driver is more likely to be seriously injured.

Warren *et al.* concluded that alcohol-related crashes were likely to be more severe both in terms of personal injury and damage to property (see R.A. Warren, *et al.*, Twenty-fifth Proceedings of the American Association of Automotive Medicine). Honkanen and Visuri confirmed that head injuries were more commonly associated with alcohol (47 per cent) than arm injuries (25 per cent). Thirty-nine per cent of tibial and ankle fractures were associated with alcohol (see R. Honanken and T. Visuri, (1976) 65 *Annales Chirurgica Gynaecologica* 287). The drunken driver is far less likely to be cautious. He is less likely to use a seat-belt and thus prevent or lessen any potential injury. The intoxicated driver brakes too late and the whole event is uncontrolled. Alcohol increases the risk of an accident by increasing risk-taking behaviour. It prolongs reaction times, diminishes perception and impairs judgmental decision-making involved in driving. It also gives false confidence and inco-ordination of movement, both of which exert deleterious effects on the skills utilised in driving. The physician's task of treating trauma is also complicated by alcohol. Neurological injury may be masked by intoxication and the acute state of intoxication can be linked to a considerable range of metabolic disturbances, as well as altered responses to anaesthesia.

There is a significant and direct relationship between increasing blood alcohol concentration in a motor vehicle driver and increasing risk of his involvement in a road crash. Studies by Norman confirm this direct relationship (see L.G. Norman, *Road Traffic Accidents: Epidemology, Control and Prevention*, (1962), World Health Organisation, Geneva). These studies show that alcohol impaired drivers are believed to be responsible for 25–35 per cent of all crashes causing serious injury and 6 per cent of all crashes. In single vehicle crashes 55–65 per cent of fatally injured drivers have blood alcohol concentrations of 100mg per 100ml of blood or greater. In 1982, one in three persons killed in Australian road crashes had a blood alcohol concentration of 50mg per cent or more.

18–17   Global studies leave no doubt that alcohol and accidents are causally related. In 1982 Fell described that there were 48,000 motor vehicle fatalities in the United States and Canada. Such fatalities, he showed, accounted for 37 per cent of all deaths in 15–24-year-olds and 10 per cent in 25–54-year-olds. He demonstrated that alcohol was involved in 50–55 per cent of fatal accidents, 18–25 per cent of injury accidents and 5–8 per cent of property damage accidents (see J.C. Fell, *Alcohol Involvement in Traffic Accidents*, 1982, U.S. Department of Transport Publication, p. 806). In Canada, despite the continuing decline between 1973 and 1978 in the number of Canadian motor vehicle fatalities, the percentage of blood alcohol levels in driver fatalities remained constant with 38–39 per cent at the legally impaired level of 80mg per cent or above (see H.M. Simpson, D.R. Mayhew and R.A. Warren, "Epidemiology of Road Accidents Involving Young Adults" (1982) 10 Drug. Alc. Depend. 35). Other studies found that drivers with alcohol levels of 50mg per cent or more have a greatly increased risk of being involved in a road crash causing injury or death.

The Grand Rapids study (R.F. Borkenstein, R.E. Crowther *et al.*, *The Grand Rapids Study*, 1964, Indiana University) which was the first and most influential case-control study, compared 5,978 drivers involved in accidents during 1962–1963 with a control group of 7,590 drivers during the same period. This quantified the relation between accident involvement and blood alcohol concentration. The risk of accident increases sharply beyond 80mg per cent from twofold at that level to tenfold at 150mg per cent and twentyfold at 200 mg per cent compared with the base line risk at 0–10 mg per cent. The sharp increase occurs at much lower levels for younger and more inexperienced drivers. These results are depicted in Table 2.

Table 2

The Grand Rapids study

Blood alcohol level	Risk of accident
0–10mg%	Baseline
80mg%	Twofold
150mg%	Tenfold
200mg%	Twentyfold

Focusing on the incidence of accidents in Great Britain, the figures for **18–18** the period 1977–1988 are displayed in Table 3. The figures regarding car drivers involved in accidents show a remarkably constant incidence with 275,098 car drivers involved in 1978 and 303,693 involved in 1988. The per centage of such drivers breath tested is also shown in Table 3. It can be seen how with increasing awareness of the association between alcohol and accidents the number of drivers breath-tested has almost doubled from 31,531 in 1978 to 60,798 in 1988. The number of drivers who have failed breath tests has also declined, but very slightly, from 10,543 in 1978 to 8,549 in 1988. The figures for two-wheel motor vehicles are also shown in Table 3. Again, the number of drivers breath-tested in this category has increased. The number of those who failed breath tests has decreased from 1,313 in 1978 to 987 in 1988.

Table 3

Breath tests and breath test failures: by car drivers and two-wheeled motor vehicle riders involved in accidents: 1977 to 1988

Number/Percentage

	1978	1979	1980	1981	1982	1983	1984	1985	1986	1987	1988
Car drivers involved:	275,098	265,327	262,979	265,531	275,507	261,714	279,954	278,517	290,560	287,636	303,693
Breath tested:											
Number	31,531	32,447	32,735	32,640	34,472	33,769	35,192	36,655	49,559	52,760	60,798
Percentage of drivers involved	11%	12%	12%	12%	13%	13%	13%	13%	17%	18%	20%
Failed breath test[1]:											
Number	10,543	11,329	10,777	10,121	11,145	10,200	10,422	10,432	10,014	9,222	8,549
Percentage of drivers tested	33%	35%	33%	31%	32%	30%	30%	28%	20%	17%	14%
TWMV riders involved:	71,382	69,173	73,054	70,949	73,033	65,962	65,340	57,822	53,562	47,024	44,279
Breath tested:											
Number	4,486	4,990	5,673	5,180	5,592	5,230	4,958	4,354	5,178	5,136	5,390
Percentage of riders involved	6%	7%	8%	7%	8%	8%	8%	8%	10%	11%	12%
Failed breath test[1]:											
Number	1,313	1,573	1,716	1,432	1,546	1,510	1,390	1,286	1,176	1,075	987
Percentage of riders tested	29%	32%	30%	28%	28%	29%	28%	30%	23%	21%	18%
Other drivers involved:	68,099	63,095	55,837	54,256	52,920	49,613	51,441	53,134	53,549	52,861	56,599
Breath tested:											
Number	3,444	3,546	3,224	3,207	3,277	3,266	3,311	3,693	6,481	7,130	8,793
Percentage of drivers involved	5%	6%	6%	6%	6%	7%	6%	7%	12%	13%	16%
Failed breath test[1]:											
Number	1,109	1,183	928	750	803	722	745	839	756	745	689
Percentage of drivers tested	32%	33%	29%	23%	25%	22%	23%	23%	12%	10%	8%
Total involved:	414,579	397,595	391,870	390,736	401,460	377,289	396,735	389,473	397,671	387,521	404,571
Breath tested:											
Number	39,461	40,983	41,632	41,027	43,341	42,265	43,461	44,702	61,218	65,026	74,985
Percentage of driver/ riders involved	10%	10%	11%	10%	11%	11%	11%	11%	15%	17%	19%
Failed breath test[1]:											
Number	12,965	14,085	13,421	12,303	13,494	12,432	12,557	12,557	11,946	11,042	10,225
Percentage of driver/ riders tested	33%	34%	32%	30%	31%	29%	29%	28%	20%	17%	14%

[1] Failed or refused to provide a specimen of breath.

Table 4

Deaths: by age, sex, deaths from all causes, all accidental deaths and all road deaths: 1988

	0–4	5–9	10–14	15–19	20–24	25–34	35–44	45–54	55–59	60–64	65 and over	Retirement age	All[1] ages
Male													
Deaths from all causes	2,657	413	444	1,460	2,048	3,847	6,663	15,616	16,539	28,249	231,228	231,228	309,159
All accidental deaths	186	166	185	707	891	1,058	876	726	340	379	2,305	2,305	7,817
Road deaths (registered)	47	106	125	540	643	570	378	283	138	143	628	628	3,601
% of accidental deaths	25%	64%	68%	76%	72%	54%	43%	39%	41%	38%	27%	27%	46%
% of all deaths	2%	26%	28%	37%	31%	15%	6%	2%	1%	1%	0%	0%	1%
1988 Stats 19 fatalities	56	104	112	550	642	560	380	288	139	138	620	620	3,589
Female													
Deaths from all causes	1,917	254	239	596	713	1,867	4,495	9,563	10,049	17,305	273,787	291,092	320,785
All accidental deaths	139	57	57	161	159	247	240	227	158	212	3,856	4,068	5,508
Road deaths (registered)	46	42	44	134	113	150	113	95	72	77	604	681	1,491
% of accidental deaths	33%	74%	77%	83%	71%	62%	47%	42%	46%	36%	16%	17%	27%
% of all deaths	2%	17%	18%	22%	16%	8%	3%	1%	1%	0%	0%	0%	0%
1988 Stats 19 fatalities	49	38	50	135	126	144	100	105	60	72	584	656	1,463
All persons													
Deaths from all causes	4,574	667	683	2,056	2,761	5,709	11,158	25,179	26,588	45,554	505,015	522,320	629,944
All accidental deaths	325	223	242	868	1,050	1,298	1,116	953	498	591	6,161	6,373	13,325
Road deaths (registered)	93	148	169	674	756	720	491	378	210	220	1,232	1,309	5,092
% of accidental deaths	29%	66%	70%	78%	72%	55%	44%	40%	42%	37%	20%	21%	38%
% of all deaths	2%	22%	25%	33%	27%	13%	4%	2%	1%	0%	0%	0%	1%
1988 Stats 19 fatalities	105	142	162	685	768	704	480	393	199	210	1,204	1,276	5,052

[1] Includes age not reported

Crown copyright, Reproduced with the permission of the Controller of Her Majesty's Stationery Office.

331

In order to appreciate the magnitude of the problem Table 4 shows the deaths by age from all causes including accidental deaths and all road deaths for the year 1988. It shows that a high percentage of accidental deaths is caused by road traffic accidents. Indeed, for the 15–19 age group, it is 78 per cent of all accidental deaths and for the 20–24 age group it is 72 per cent of all accidental deaths. These figures will be considered in greater detail later.

It is worthwhile noting that pedestrians must bear some proportion of the blame. In 1985 there were 1,400 road deaths which were attributed to alcohol of which about 400 were due to drinking pedestrians. The risk of pedestrian fatality increases with increasing levels of alcohol (see A.B. Clayton *et al.*, *A Controlled Study of the Role of Alcohol in Fatal Adult Pedestrian Accidents* (1977), p. 332).

18–19   Whilst the association between alcohol and accident is beyond argument, the incidence of drink driving remains stubbornly high. This is due to the different perceptions, priorities and values of the driver who drinks. He is not a pharmacologist or a physician or an epidemiologist. He does not perceive alcohol as a drug which depresses the nervous system. He sees alcohol as his well-known pint, full of camaraderie and the values he loves and trusts. He feels alcohol must be a stimulant because he sees the inebriation, talkativeness and stimulation only. The driver who has drunk is relaxed, released from inhibitions and confident. He feels a euphoria which is of particular significance since it increases risk-taking. There is reduced motor and intellectual performance but the driver himself feels an increased ability. He feels he is a better driver who can cope with greater risks. The higher the blood alcohol the more the judgment is lost but this tends to lead the driver to feel that his performance is improving. The skill most allied to driving is that of divided attention. Diligent research has proved that this is the skill impaired at the lowest blood alcohol concentration. Information acquisition and processing are rendered slower and less efficient and thus cause many of the other defects which contribute to driver impairment.

18–20   The studies of Loomis and West in 1958 demonstrated a direct relationship between blood alcohol concentration and impairment of driving concentration. (See T.A. Loomis and T.C. West (1958) 19 Q.J. Stud.Alcohol. 30). In assessing the effects of alcohol on driving, two methods have been developed, that of closed-course driving and the use of driving simulators. Closed course driving has the disadvantage of low speeds and the absence of unknown dangers (Mack C. Mitchell (1985) 10 *Journal Studies on Alcohol* 109). However, allowing for these drawbacks Attwood found in 1980 that drivers with a blood alcohol concentration of 60–80mg per cent demonstrated greater unpredictability of braking, steering and maintenance of lane position.

In programmed simulator studies Rafaelson *et al.* (1972) 179 *Science* 920 found that a blood alcohol concentration of 95mg per cent prolonged braking time up to one-half.

Erwin *et al.* described an unequivocal decremental effect of alcohol on vigilance performance. He also frequently encountered drowsiness. He concluded that these soporific and vigilance effects of alcohol confirmed the well-recognised phenomenon that 30 per cent of all single vehicle accidents are caused by the driver becoming too drowsy to control his vehicle, or actually falling asleep (see C.W. Erwin *et al.*, "Alcohol-Induced Drowsiness and Vigilance Performance" (1978) 39 J.Stud.Alcohol 505).

The simulated automobile apparatus used by Loomis and West (see above) demonstrated that all subjects showed some impairment of function at blood alcohol concentrations of 50mg per cent. They detailed impairment of perception of time, loss of attentiveness and inability of the driver to react in an emergency situation with his normal efficiency.

Rates of information processing are impaired by alcohol (see Moscowitz and Roth (1971) 32 Q.J.Stud.Alcohol 969). Steering errors were increased in the range of 70–100mg %, (see Mortimer and Sturgis (1975) *Alcohol, Drugs and Traffic Safety* 329). Research by Newman and Fletcher in 1940 revealed a significant diminution in glare recovery in 40 per cent of subjects in the range of 100–125mg % (see Newman and Fletcher (1940) 115 J.A.M.A. 1600).

According to Wallgren and Barry, with blood alcohol levels of 80–100mg% there was a 10 per cent diminution of simple reaction times (see Wallgren and Barry, *Actions of Alcohol*, (1970), Elsevier, New York). In well-designed experiments intended to reproduce the reactions responsible for avoiding mechanisms Linnoila found an increment in the number of mistakes with higher doses of alcohol (0.15–1.2g/kg) (see M. Linnoila (1973) 51 Annls. Med.Exp.Biol. Fenn. 118).

Alcohol impairs short-term memory. Burns and Moskowitz found that with divided attention tasks there was marked deterioration with blood alcohol levels above 50mg % (see Burns and Moskowitz (1980) 17 Eur.J.Clin.Pharmacol 259) Divided attention studies are complex tests which therefore more closely resemble driving.

Driving is a complex skill. There are hundreds of separate behavioural **18–21** components which comprise the ordinary driving experience. Epidemiological studies have aided analysis of the error which contributes to accident. Alcohol is causally linked to accident. There is a direct relationship between increasing blood alcohol concentration in drivers and increasing risk of a motor vehicle crash. It is incumbent upon doctors to educate their patients about the dangers of alcohol abuse in general and operating a motor vehicle under the influence of alcohol in particular.

F. The complications of chronic alcohol ingestion

A great deal has been written about the acute effects of alcohol. The **18–22** problem is always portrayed as being acute. The driver drinks alcohol which impairs his muscular co-ordination, perception and judgment. The alcohol is absorbed and metabolised. Then he returns completely to the normal baseline state without any defect at all. Should he drink again the cycle will begin again. This however, may not be the whole truth.

During the Christmas period a driver may drink socially as an isolated occurrence and then be breathalysed. He may not normally drink any alcohol at all. However, most cases will not fall within this category. During their drinking life, alcoholics show a marked fluctuation in their alcohol intake with periods of light drinking alternating with binges. It is after these periods that the patient may portray some symptoms of alcohol-related illness. The first major medical problem can be expected after about 10 years of drinking. The early presentations will usually be trauma or gastritis in the late twenties or early thirties or neurological or psychiatric in the mid-forties. Liver disease is a presenting feature in one-third. Popper found peripheral neuropathy in some 10 per cent of alcoholics with a history of 10 years daily ingestion of 120g of ethanol (see H. Popper *et al.* (1974) 66 *Gastroenteology* 1227). Mellor noted a strong correlation between alcoholism and male mortality (see Mellor, *Alcohol and the Risk of Accident Involvement: Proceedings of the Eighth International Conference on Alcohol, Drugs & Traffic Safety*, Stockholm, 1980). Schukit, 1978, found that the leading cause of death in young alcoholics was accident (see M.A. Schukit *et al.* 1977 4(4) Am.J. Drug Alcohol Abuse 581). In young alcoholics (15–39 age group) mortality is 11 times the average for males, and 17 times the natural average for females (see A.M. Adelskin and C. White (1976) 6 *Population Trends* 7).

18–23   Turner *et al.*, 1977, found that the majority of patients with organ or psychiatric disease have a history of daily intakes in excess of 150g T.B. Turner *et al.* (1977) 141(6) John Hopkins Med.J. 273. Brain atrophy visible by computed tomography (CT) scanning and accompanied by intellectual impairment has been noted in some 50 per cent of young males with intakes greater than 100g daily for three years (average 200g for 10 years). In a review, the Royal College of Psychiatrists concluded that to show physical or mental disease primarily from long-continued use of alcohol, the critical level of daily intake which must be exceeded by the majority of persons seems to be in the order of 80–100g of ethanol adjusted up or down from the 70kg weight (Turner *et al.*, 1977). The upper limit of safe drinking is now widely advocated as 80g ethanol per day for males and 40g for females, with 60g and 30g daily respectively as the preferred limit.

Alcohol is responsible for a wide variety of clinical conditions. The major conditions associated with alcohol abuse are shown in Table 5 (overleaf).

Table 5

Accidents

Trauma

Liver (*e.g.* cirrhosis, alcoholic hepatitis)

Gastrointestinal (*e.g.* cancer of tongue, oseophagus and pharynx, gastritis, malabsorption, pancreatitis)

Cardiovascular (*e.g.* hypertension, cardiomyopathy)

Skeletal (*e.g.* osteoporosis)

Neurological (*e.g.* Wernicke-Korsakoff syndrome cerebral atrophy, peripheral neuropathy)

Haematological (*e.g.* macrocytosis, megaloblastic anaemia)

Metabolic (*e.g.* hypoglycaemia, iron overload, gout)

Endocrine (*e.g.* gonadal atrophy)

Fetal (*e.g.* alcohol syndrome)

Drug interactions

The most renowned complication of alcohol abuse is cirrhosis. Not all **18–24** excessive drinkers develop liver disease (see S. Sherlock, *Diseases of the Liver and Biliary System*, (1989, Blackwell Scientific Publications)). It has been estimated retrospectively that the probability of an individual developing cirrhosis after consuming 210g of ethanol daily is 50 per cent after 22 years. In a group of 526 unselected male alcoholics receiving treatment, liver function tests showed severe liver damage in a quarter, with less damage in a half (see W.K. Lelbach (1975) 252 *Annals of the New York Academy of Science* 85).

Acute alcoholic hepatitis usually appears as severe hepatic decompensation after particularly heavy drinking. Nutritional changes include peripheral neuritis. With established cirrhosis loss of memory and concentration, hallucinations, convulsions, fits and tremors may be the stigmata of alcoholism. Alcohol cannot be stored and thus the alcohol must be oxidised. Alcohol induces enzymes used in its catabolism. One gram of alcohol gives seven calories and these calories make no contribution to nutrition other than to give energy.

Above a daily intake of 80g of alcohol the possibility of an individual developing cirrhosis varies linearly with time. All alcoholics are at risk of developing cirrhosis, though the time of heavy consumption required to develop it varies. Patients with established cirrhosis may present with one or more of its complications such as bleeding from oesophageal varices, secondary to portal hypertension or with ascites. Loss of memory and concentration, hallucinations and tremor may also be stigmata of alcoholism but it is important to distinguish the picture from that of early hepatic precoma.

18–25   Porta-systemic encephalopathy is a metabolic abnormality of the brain associated with disturbances of the mental state and neuromuscular system. It may be acute, particularly if following fulminant hepatic failure, or chronic and often intermittent in patients with cirrhosis of the liver. Chronic hepatic encephalopathy is almost invariably associated with cirrhosis resulting from shunting of blood from the portal circulation past the liver. Clinical features are disturbances of mental state, depression, irritability, disturbances of concentration, impairment of judgment, flapping tremor and muscular inco-ordination. Further clinical features are ataxia, intellectual impairment and constructional apraxia.

Cirrhosis is a diffuse process characterised by fibrosis and conversion of normal nodules into structurally abnormal nodules. Clinical signs are related to development of two major complications, hepatocellular failure and portal hypertension. Cirrhosis results from hepatocellular damage followed by regeneration and fibrosis. Clinically unapparent impairment in mental function, sufficient to cause disruption in the routine of everyday living is frequent in patients with cirrhosis. The picture is of the type associated with lesions of the fronto-parietal regions of the brain. Using psychomotor testing abnormalities can be shown in 80 per cent of patients following a selective porta-caval shunt operation. Only 15 per cent of patients with chronic liver disease and portal hypertension clinically not encephalopathic were judged fit to drive. It is important to realise that although a driver may be severely incapacitated because of the complications of chronic alcohol abuse he may at the time of driving have drunk no alcohol and thus be negative to both breath and blood testing.

18–26   Hypoglycaemia with fits or altered behavioural states or chronic deterioration is a possible consequence of alcohol abuse. The metabolism of alcohol by alcohol dehydrogenase utilises NAD and the resulting NADH/NAD elevation prevents gluconeogenesis, which is the breakdown of liver glycogen stores into glucose. If food is not eaten and liver stores of glycogen reduced, then hypoglycaemia may result. Long-term consequences are not uncommon, particularly dementia.

Alcohol abuse leads to potentiation of the effects of the sedative and tranquilliser group of drugs. This is due to them being metabolised at a reduce rate, because alcohol competes for the liver enzymes which metabolise them. This means that a given dose of drug will have a larger clinical effect which will last longer because there will be reduction in the metabolism of the drug due to alcohol or the chronic effects of alcohol on the liver. This has serious implications for driving and is the reason that drink and drugs should not be mixed.

18–27   The neurological manifestations of alcohol abuse are also well known. The Wernicke and Korsakoff syndromes are both the consequence of thiamine deficiency. In the Wernicke syndrome, the mental symptoms comprise a confusional state, inattentiveness, indifference, impaired memory, disorientation and disordered perception. Neurological signs occurring in the majority of cases include nystagmus, truncal ataxia and peripheral neuropathy. Frequently, patients have the skin changes and redness of tongue characteristic of nutritional deficiency. The Korsakoff syndrome almost always occurs in association with the Wernicke syndrome. This is an amnestic syndrome with inability to recall past events and the impairment of ability to retain new information.

Whilst abuse of alcohol causes severe complications, the withdrawal of alcohol itself can be the cause of severe disturbance. Very few can be unfamiliar with the headache, nausea, tremulousness and sweating that comprise the hangover. As legend has it, the severity of the hangover is proportional to the duration of the "binge". The term "ethanol withdrawal" refers to the symptoms which occur after cessation of drink in the patient addicted to alcohol.

The most common symptom is tremor. It will be relieved by alcohol but **18–28** on prolonged withdrawal it becomes more marked with agitation, sweating, nausea and insomnia. About one-quarter of such cases develop perceptual disturbances. These are usually visual but may be auditory or tactile. Fits occurring during withdrawal in non-epileptic patients occur within 48 hours after cessation of alcohol. These are popularly known as "rum-fits". These symptoms of tremor, fits or perceptual disturbances usually occur within one or two days of withdrawal.

Delirium tremens is a late but dramatic and potentially serious complication of alcohol withdrawal (see Lewis P. Rowland, *Merritt's Textbook of Neurology* (7th ed., 1984, Lea and Febiger, Philadelphia). It usually begins two to three days after the commencement of withdrawal. There will be confusion, agitation, tremor, fever, sweating and a fast heart rate. There will also be hallucinations. Mortality can be up to 15 per cent. It is for this reason that the incarcerated alcoholic may be in danger unless the diagnosis of delirium tremens is made and appropriate treatment instituted immediately. Table 6 depicts the alcohol withdrawal syndromes.

Table 6

Early withdrawal syndrome	*Late withdrawal syndrome*
Within one or two days of commencement of withdrawal.	Two or three days after commencement of withdrawal.
Tremor, agitation, sweating.	Delirium tremens.
Perceptual disturbance.	Confusion, agitation, sweating, tachycardia.
Fits.	Hallucinations.

This chapter attempts to outline the complications of chronic alcohol abuse. Table 5 lists the main categories and some of those which will cause impairment of driving skills have been considered further. For greater detail the reader should be referred to medical textbooks. The conclusion must be drawn that the chronic effects of alcohol abuse may cause profound impairment in the skills used for driving even though the driver may not have drunk any alcohol in the recent past. He will thus be negative to both breath and blood alcohol testing.

G. Malnutrition and chronic alcohol abuse

18–29 The nutritional status of the chronic alcohol abuser is at the heart of the physiological impairment that results in the accident. There is impairment of the normal physiological and biochemical function at the cellular level so that cells are less able to carry on their normal functional role. The factors contributing to malnutrition in chronic alcohol abusers are found in Table 7. Ethanol has a calorific value of 7.1kcal/g. However, ethanol uncouples oxidative phosphorylation, which means that it interferes with energy production and a proportion of the energy is dissipated as heat. The metabolism of alcohol itself requires a number of vitamins. Thus, paradoxically, the chronic alcohol abuser has an increased requirement for vitamins yet has a reduced quantity of them.

Table 7

Mechanisms responsible for malnutrition in chronic alcohol abusers.

1. Decreased absorption.
2. Poor intake.
3. Financial impoverishment resulting in a poor diet.
4. Decreased "active forms" of vitamins.
5. Poor storage.
6. Enhanced breakdown.
7. Enhanced excretion.
8. Enhanced requirement.
9. Poor conversion of vitamins into chemically working forms.
10. The supply of "empty calories" from alcohol.

Approximately 10 per cent of alcohol is excreted unchanged in the urine and breath. The remainder is metabolised exclusively in the liver. There are three enzyme systems which can contribute to the metabolism of alcohol:

1. ADH
2. Microsomal ethanol oxidising system (MEOS)
3. Catalase

Alcohol is metabolised to acetaldehyde by each of these systems initially but there are marked differences in co-factors. These systems are shown schematically in Figure 3.

18–30 The acetaldehyde formed in each of these reactions is further metabolised to acetate by aldehyde dehydrogenase (ADH) as shown in Figure 3 (overleaf).

The relative importance of the enzyme systems responsible for the initial oxidation of alcohol to acetaldehyde is controversial. Most important pharmacologically is that involving aldehyde dehydrogenase, with a K_m for ethanol of about 1000×10^{-6}M. This system is probably active at relatively low concentrations of alcohol. The contribution of MEOS is not clear. The activity of this system can be increased by inducers of drug metabolising enzymes such as barbiturates, but alcohol itself does not appear to possess this property. Nevertheless, the K_m of MEOS for alcohol of about 8000×10^{-6}M is considerably higher than that of ADH and it may therefore play a significant role at higher blood ethanol concentrations above $10,000 \times 10^{-6}$M. Even at this level however, ADH still accounts for over 60 per cent of the alcohol metabolised. Catalase is almost certainly not important physiologically (see L.J. Kricka and P.M.S. Clark, *Biochemistry and Alcoholism*, Ellis Horwood).

Figure 3

1. $CH_3CH_2OH + NAD^+ — CH_3CHO + NADH + H^+$
ADH
2. $CH_3CH_2 OH + NADPH + H^+ + O_2 — CH_3CHO + NADP^+ + 2H_2O$
MEOS
3. $CH_3CH_2OH + H_2O_2 — CH_3CHO + 2H_2O$
CATALASE

The acetaldehyde formed in each of these three reactions is further metabolised to acetate by aldehyde dehydrogenase, ADH.

4. $CH_3CHO + NAD^+ + H_2O — CH_3COOH + NADH + H^+$
ADH

In the last section the Wernicke-Korsakoff syndrome was described and its occurrence was linked to thiamine depletion. If recognised early, it may be reversed by thiamine replacement, if not, irreversible damage will occur. Reference to Table 7 shows that all these mechanisms are responsible for thiamine deficiency. There is insufficient dietary intake and increased metabolic requirement. Alcohol is known to inhibit the carrier mechanism in the gut responsible for absorption of thiamine. Liver damage can cause loss of thiamine reserves. In addition there is decreased conversion of thiamine to its active form: thiamine pyrophosphate (TPP) (see *Harper's Review of Biochemistry*, (20th ed., Lange Medical Publications). The liver is the principal storage organ for thiamine. TPP acts as a co-factor for a number of key enzymes in metabolic processes. There is marked evidence of thiamine deficiency in chronic alcohol abusers.

Nicotinamide is another of the vitamin B group which is often deficient **18–31** in chronic alcohol abusers. The co-factors nicotinamide adenine dinucleotide (NAD) and nicotinamide adenine dinucleotide phosphate (NADP) are obligatory for almost every metabolic reaction in the cell. Reference to Figure 3 shows that the metabolism of alcohol requires many reactions which depend on the presence of NAD. Its deficiency mirrors the protein deficiency in chronic alcohol abusers. Thus there is the classic combination of poor and deficient intake, enhanced requirement, poor storage, reduced absorption and lessened conversion to the active form.

Vitamin B_6, pyridoxine, is absorbed in the small intestine and then converted into its active form, pyridoxal-5-phosphate, mainly in the liver. Clinical signs of pyridoxine deficiency include neuromuscular irritability and peripheral neuropathy. Depression frequently attends chronic alcoholism and pyridoxine deficiency may be the cause, by virtue of reduced synthesis of brain neuro-transmitters. Chronic alcohol abuse can lead to a deficiency of pyridoxine by the usual mechanisms of reduced storage absorption, diet and utilisation. Interestingly, however, pyridoxine is specifically inhibited by alcohol as regards the activation and breakdown reactions. Acetaldehyde, the metabolic oxidation product of ethanol, specifically inhibits the enzyme responsible for conversion to the active form. It also stimulates the enzyme responsible for breakdown of the active form. Protein malnutrition, a common consequence of liver dysfunction, may lead to urinary loss of the active form since there will be decreased serum albumin binding. Alcohol also causes reduced uptake of the vitamin by the mechanism of lessened ability to liberate the vitamin from bound substrates contained in food in the gastrointestinal tract.

18–32   Vitamin B_2, riboflavin, is absorbed in the small intestine. The vitamin is phosphorylated in the liver to one of its active forms, flavin mononucleotide. It serves as a co-factor for a number of metabolically important enzymes. FAD is another riboflavin derivative that acts as a co-factor in many enzymes in intermediary metabolism. Alcohol interferes with absorption and utilisation of riboflavin in similar ways to those set out for the other B group vitamins. Thus diminished uptake, enhanced requirements and lessened storage are involved. A good daily intake of good quality protein promotes a positive balance of riboflavin. However, in alcoholic malnutrition, there is increased loss of riboflavin in the urine (see G.A. Goldsmith, *Riboflavin Deficiency* (R.S. Rivlin ed., 1975, Plenum, London)).

Folic acid and vitamin B_{12} are requirements for red blood cell formation, as is bone marrow synthesis of DNA. Both these depend upon the oxidation reduction of repeating one-carbon fragments which are attached to tetrahydrofolate, the active form of folic acid. Reference to Figure 3 shows that metabolism of alcohol generates NADH and hydrogen ions which indicates a state of reduction (see S.B. Rosalki, *Clinical Biochemistry of Alcohol* (1984)). This state of reduction is not capable of reversal with large amounts of alcohol metabolism and the oxidation necessary to divert these one-carbon fragments into DNA synthesis is not present. This alcohol inhibitory effect on folate one-carbon fragments is responsible for the two major blood parameters which characterise chronic alcohol abuse. These are macrocytosis and megaloblastic anaemia.

18–33   Macrocytosis is considered a very sensitive and reliable parameter of alcohol intake. It is very frequent amongst ethanol abusers and is unaccompanied by any evidence of anaemia. As its name implies it refers to the fact that the volume of the red blood cell is raised. It is a sensitive, early sign of chronic alcohol abuse and it takes several weeks to become normal after abstaining from alcohol. The mean corpuscular volume which is the degree of macrocytosis present is considered a very useful early sign of ethanolic tissue damage. It has merits as a screening test for alcohol abuse and likewise is indicative of relapse. It is likely that megaloblastic anaemia is due to the inhibitory effects of alcohol on folate metabolism. Megaloblastic anaemia accompanies changes in the blood with changes in the bone marrow unlike macrocytosis.

Vitamin B_{12} has a dual supply. It is is eaten in bound form and is also liberated by the action of bowel enzymes. The vitamin is bound to intrinsic factor, a protein produced by the stomach. B_{12} levels are usually normal in alcoholics. B_{12} is liberated from damaged liver cells in alcohol-related liver disease. This causes a high circulating blood level. High serum B_{12} levels can thus be used as a parameter of liver disease. In this way alcoholic liver disease releases liver stores of B_{12}. Increased quantities are lost in the urine.

Folate deficiency is found in over half of chronic alcohol abusers. Folate **18–34** and B_{12} deficiency cause similar neurological symptoms of which peripheral neuropathy is the most relevant. However, B_{12} deficiency causes subacute degeneration of the spinal cord. Since beer contains more folate than spirits, beer drinkers are less likely to suffer from folate deficiency.

The nutritional status of the chronic alcohol abuser is central to the physiological impairment that causes the accident. Alcohol supplies a large proportion of the daily calorie intake of many chronic alcohol abusers. Yet many alcoholic drinks contain almost no vitamins or minerals. Since, as this chapter shows, the vitamins and co-factors and derivatives play such a crucial role in metabolism, the alcohol abuser needs more, yet actually receives less by the many mechanisms enumerated. There is consequently impairment of the normal physiological and biochemical function at the cellular level so that cells are less able to perform their normal functional role.

H. The profile of the accident

The accident caused by the fusion of alcohol and driving has certain **18–35** characteristics. It is mandatory to analyse critically the characteristics in order to advance solutions and remedies which have a reasonable prospect of success. The first characteristic is the magnitude and constancy of the problem. The number of road accidents in Great Britain from 1971 to 1989 is shown in Table 8. Road accidents are the greatest cause of accidental death. Table 8 shows the difference in statistics between the incidence of road accidents and railway accidents. This table does show, however, that during 1971–1989, the total number of road accidents did fall considerably while still remaining substantial.

Table 8

Cause of death	1971	1981	1986	1989
Railway accident	212	95	99	84
Road accident	7,970	4,880	5,565	5,501

Figure 4 shows the relationship between drinking and road accidents.

The graph is restricted to accidents which caused death within 12 hours of the accident. The number of drivers and riders who were killed in road traffic accidents and whose blood alcohol levels exceeded the legal maximum fell from 28 per cent in 1981 to 21 per cent in 1989. This is an important characteristic since it illustrates that the energetic campaign to reduce road deaths caused by driving whilst over the legal limit is capable of achieving results.

Figure 4

Figures for 1987 onwards are for the United Kingdom

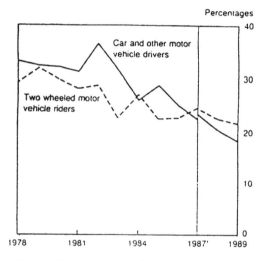

Figures for 1987 onwards are for the United Kingdom

Source: Social Trends, Central Statistical Office (1991).

Analyses of the times at which accidents occur yield important and interesting characteristics. Statistics are almost three times as high on Friday or Saturday night than on any other night during the week. Of those pedestrian casualties who are killed between 10 p.m. and 4 a.m. and who are aged over 16, 70 per cent have elevated levels of blood alcohol. During the night period, one-half of all fatal casualties amongst motorcycle and car drivers and passengers of motorcycle riders have elevated blood alcohol levels in excess of the legal limit. These statistics all refer to casualties in Great Britain.

18–36   In the United States, studies for the Fatal Accident Reporting System (FARS) indicate that during the period 1977–1981 there was an increasing incidence of elevated blood alcohol levels, and their magnitude in fatal crashes in the 16–25 driver age group. In the 16–19 age group there was the highest incidence of alcohol involved in fatal crashes. (Council on Scientific Affairs, (1986) 255 J.A.M.A. 522.) Analysis of the statistical data from

FARS indicate that younger drivers killed in crashes have lesser values of blood alcohol concentration than older drivers. This trend has been seen when the data from several years has been analysed. Table 9 shows a model developed by Simpson. It shows the risk by age of suffering a fatal crash with driver impairment due to blood alcohol concentration of 80mg per cent or over. The risk of a sober driver having a fatal crash is set at one. The largest risk is that of the 16–17 year-old who is suffering from impairment and this is set at 165. (See H.M. Simpson, "The Impaired Driver Problem vs. The Impaired Problem Driver" (1978) 61 Trans.Assoc.Life.Ins.Med.Dir. 178.)

Table 9

Age (blood alcohol over 80 mg%)	Risk of fatal crash
16–17	165
18–19	70
20–24	31
25–29	27
30–34	17
35–44	22
45–49	24
50 +	39
Sober driver	1

Source: H.M. Simpson, "The Impaired Driver Problem vs. The Impaired Problem Driver" (1978).

Young drivers are disproportionately represented in crashes and especially in alcohol-related crashes with low blood alcohol concentrations. Increased incidence with even low blood alcohol concentrations may be due to decreased tolerance of younger drinkers compared with their older and more experienced counterparts. In addition, the enhanced judgment and skill of older drivers will clearly be a factor which tends to reduce the incidence of accidents.

In the United States analysis of the data for alcohol associated crashes yields interesting data on the profile of the accident. In 1981 there were 43,979 fatal motor vehicle accidents (see A. Richman "Human Risk Factors in Alcohol-Related Crashes" (1985) 10 *Journal of Studies on Alcohol* 21). Cerrelli, 1983, found that single vehicle crashes occurred more frequently during nights and weekends. He also found a 71 per cent alcohol involvement during weekend nights. (See E.C. Cerrelli *Alcohol in Fatal Accidents* (1983), prepared for the U.S. Department of Transportation.) The study by Terhune and Fell, 1982, reported a 94 per cent incidence of alcohol involvement after midnight and before 6 a.m. in a business area. Most studies show a striking preponderance of crashes at nights and at weekends. (See Terhune and Fell, "The Role of Alcohol, Marijuana, and

Other Drugs in the Accidents of Injured Drivers", *Proceedings of the 25th Annual Conference of the American Association for Automotive Medicine* (1981), p.117.)

18–37 Statistics almost uniformly show an increased proportion of males in those groups of drivers who drink. Males are also more likely to have higher blood alcohol concentrations. Jones and Joscelyn, 1978, thought that this might be a consequence of the social pressures which compel them to do most night driving, which is the type most often associated with drinking. (See R. K. Jones and K. B. Joscelyn, *Alcohol and Highway Safety* (1978, U.S. Department of Transportation Publication.))

There is evidence that young men who experience difficulties at school, work and in family and social relationships are overrepresented in statistics for alcohol associated crashes (R. L., Douglas, *Youth, Alcohol and Traffic Accidents* (1982, National Institute on Alcohol Abuse and Alcoholism), p. 197.) Cameron, 1982, noted the strong association with hostility, anger and rebellion. Drivers who are alcoholic have a higher incidence of crashes than non-alcoholic drivers. (See T. Cameron, "Drinking and Driving Among American Youth" (1982) 10 Drug Alc.Depend. 1.) They also drive after drinking more frequently than non-alcoholic drivers (Jones and Joscelyn, 1978). Vingilis in 1983, after a review of the literature, concluded that alcoholics and drivers who drink and drive are not the same group. Many of the drivers who drink and drive are not alcoholics. However, he concluded that drinking and driving and crashes may be one of the first manifestations of alcoholism (See E. Vingilis, "Drinking Drivers and Alcoholics" (1983) 7 *Research Advances in Alcohol and Drug Problems 299*.) Richman (1985, see above), concluded after an exhaustive study of accident statistics that young men under 25 were more likely to be legally impaired. These statistics are shown in Table 10. Characteristics such as lifestyle and risk-taking which are associated with alcohol use increase the hazards of drinking and driving. An important example of this is the wearing of seatbelts. These are used less frequently in alcohol associated accidents than in non-alcohol associated crashes. Table 11 shows the proportion of drivers involved in single vehicle accidents by age; illustrating that these tend to occur more often among younger drivers.

Table 10

Drivers with legal impairment (BAL > 10%)

	Men under 25		Other groups	
	N	%	N	%
All accidents	20,189	38	43,917	30
Night-time accidents	11,046	50	16,748	50
Single vehicle accidents	7,704	55	11,792	55
Night-time single vehicle accidents, weekend	2,999	64	2,946	77

Source: U.S. Fatal Accident Reporting System, 1980.

The alcohol consumption statistics for Great Britain analysed into socio- **18–38** economic groups are interesting. It is a popular misconception that, as in smoking, where those in manual occupations are less likely to be non-smokers, so with alcohol, those in manual occupations would be less likely to be non-drinkers. However, alcohol statistics show the exact opposite. Those in manual occupations are the most likely to be non-drinkers or to consume very little alcohol. Amongst women, non-manual groups consumed consistently higher levels of alcohol than those in manual groups. Amongst men, there was very little variation by socio-economic group amongst those who consumed more than a medium amount of alcohol.

Table 11

Age	Number	% in single vehicle accidents
Under 16	481	42.4
16–19	8790	47.8
20–24	13012	46.8
25–34	16764	41.6
35–49	11432	36.7
50–64	7156	34.3
Over 65	3999	29.4

Source: U.S. Fatal Accident Reporting System, 1981.

Chapter 19

CAUSING DEATH BY CARELESS DRIVING WHEN UNDER THE INFLUENCE OF DRINK OR DRUGS

A. Introduction

Ten new offences were created by section 3 of the Road Traffic Act 1991 **19–01** (*q.v.* Chapter 3) which was inserted by section 3A into the 1988 Road Traffic Act. This was based on a recommendation of the North Committee to deal with a case where a person had killed somebody while under the influence of drink but whose driving could only be classified as careless rather than dangerous. Thus it is now punishable with up to 10 years' imprisonment to kill somebody at the same time as committing two offences against the Road Traffic Act, namely contravening both sections 4(1), 5(1)(a) or 7(6) and section 3. The reason why so many offences are created by section 3A is because there have been a number of cases which have held that alleging all the elements in section 3 in the same information, and likewise with section 5(1)(a), made the charge duplicitous.

How sections 4, 5 and 7 can be contravened has already been considered **19–02** earlier in this treatise. Section 3 makes it an offence to drive on a road or other public place without due care and attention or without reasonable consideration for other road users, or those in a public place. The type of conveyance to be driven depends on what the motorist was doing. If he was unfit to drive, he contravenes section 3A if he was merely in a mechanically propelled vehicle. In any other case, he must have been travelling in a motor vehicle (*q.v.* Chapter 7). The best description of what amounts to an infringement of section 3 was given by Lord Hewett C.J. in *McCrone v. Riding* [1938] 1 All E.R. 158/9:

> "The words of the section are that it is an offence when a person drives a motor vehicle 'without due care and attention or without reasonable consideration for other persons using the road'.
> That standard is an objective standard, impersonal and universal, fixed in relation to the safety of other users of the highway. It is in no way related to the degree of proficiency or degree of experience attained by the individual driver.
> I think that it is not without significance that the statute uses both the word 'care' and the word 'attention'. In other words, the driver, whoever

he may be, experienced or inexperienced, must see what he is about. He must pay attention to the thing he is doing, and, perceiving that which he is doing or entering upon, he must do his best, and he must show proper care in the doing of that thing upon which he is intent."

Thus the *actus reus* of driving without "due care and attention" is simply falling below the standard of the competent driver. In *Simpson v. Peat* [1952] 2 Q.B. 24, 27, Lord Goddard C.J. said:

"The question for the justices: was the defendant exercising that degree of care and attention which the reasonable and prudent driver would exercise in the circumstances?"

B. Preservation of Evidence and Prejudice

19–03 In *R v. Beckford* (1994) 159 J.P. 305 a driver was convicted of an offence under section 3A. He had driven into a concrete block at the end of a barrier on a flyover. The police collected his car and delivered it to a garage where it was scrapped, the proprietor having been given no instructions to preserve it. An examination by a Ministry of Transport vehicle examiner showed that its steering had locked. The motorist alleged that this was the cause of the accident and that the failure to preserve his car had prevented him having it looked at by an expert of his choice, so he asked the judge to stay his trial or to exercise his discretion under P.A.C.E., s.78. Those applications were refused. The Court of Appeal upheld the conviction, stating that on the facts, no prejudice had been caused to the defence. There was no evidence of any problems with the steering beforehand, there had been no marks on the road to indicate that the brakes had been applied and the experts called by the Crown had opined that the position of the car was inconsistent with the defence hypothesis.

C. The Victim

19–04 In *Attorney-General's Reference (No. 3 of 1994)* [1996] 2 W.L.R. at 426 the Court of Appeal approved the decision of the High Court of Justiciary in *McCluskey v. Lord Advocate* [1989] R.T.R. 182 that a person could be convicted of an offence under the Road Traffic Act s.1 for killing a child who was *en ventre sa mère* at the time of the accident, was born prematurely and died because of the injuries sustained by the defendant's dangerous driving. The same would obviously apply to a fatality under section 3A.

D. Limitation

19–05 At common law a person could only be tried for an offence involving death if the victim dies within a year and a day of the infliction of his injuries (see *R. v. Dyson* [1908] 2 K.B. 454). That rule was abolished in the case of injuries received on or after June 17, 1996 by the Law Reform (Year and a Day Rule) Act 1996. Charges can be brought if the death occurs more than three years later, only with the consent of the Attorney-General. His fiat is also needed if the person to be indicted has already been convicted of an offence arising out of the circumstances leading to the fatality.

(a) ARREST AND REMISSION

The Road Traffic Act 1991, Sched. 4, para. 39 makes an offence of death by **19–06** careless driving a "serious arrestable offence" for the purposes of P.A.C.E., Sched. 5, P. II. Paragraph 17 of the same Schedule of the R.T.A. excludes the power of the Home Secretary to grant an early release from prison under the Criminal Justice Act to any one serving a sentence imposed for contravening section 3A.

Chapter 20

PENALTIES

A. Introduction

As has been shown in Chapter 3, there are a number of different sanctions **20–01** which can be imposed for drinking and driving offences. Almost invariably a fine will be imposed. As an additional financial punishment, a defendant can always be ordered to pay the costs of the prosecution and have his vehicle confiscated. Normally magistrates have to record upon an offender's driving licence the details of any conviction and can, and in some cases must, disqualify him from holding or obtaining such a licence. A court can also impose a community service order or as a last resort a custodial sentence, either to take effect immediately or only to come into effect if the person upon whom it was imposed subsequently commits another offence punishable by imprisonment. Each of the above penalties is considered separately in subsequent sections of this chapter. The final section sets out the "tariff" for drinking and driving offences recommended by the Magistrates' Association.

B. Fines

Upon conviction on indictment, there is no statutory financial restraint on **20–02** the amount of the fine which can be imposed by the Crown Court. On summary conviction, justices fix the exact amount of the fine payable, subject to statutory maxima which depend on the level of the offence.

Level	Maximum fine
1	£200
2	£500
3	£1,000
4	£2,500
5	£5,000

(Amounts fixed by the Criminal Justice Act 1991, s.17 and Sched. 4.)

C. Penalty Points

When a person is convicted of an offence for which the justices have the **20–03** power to impose disqualification, the court must order a certain number of penalty points to be indorsed upon the offender's licence. If a person is convicted of more than one offence committed on the same occasion, he normally only receives the penalty points for the offence which attracts the maximum number. Only if special reasons exist does a court have a discretion not to order a licence to be so indorsed; see below.

D. Disqualification

20-04 On conviction for certain offences the court may, and indeed in some cases must, order a motorist to be disqualified from driving. In *Owen v. Imes* [1972] R.T.R. 489 it was held that a discharge was a conviction and did not enable a driver to avoid mandatory disqualification. In *R. v. Meese* [1973] 1 W.L.R. 675, it was held that every disqualification started on the date of its imposition and always ran concurrently with any other similar orders.

Where legislation has provided that a crime shall carry a mandatory period of disqualification, then the minimum length (in the absence of special reasons) which a court must impose is one year, or two years in the case of an offence under section 3A of the Road Traffic Act 1988. That minimum duration is increased to three years if the offence has been committed within 10 years of a previous conviction for an offence involving compulsory disqualification (see section 34 of the Road Traffic Offenders Act 1988). This three-year rule applies even if the motorist had not been disqualified after his first conviction because of special reasons (see *Bolliston v. Gibbons* [1985] R.T.R. 176). An application can be made for the removal of a disqualification at any time after two years, provided that the offender had served half of its length, or after five years, whichever was the shorter. This enables a motorist to make such an application after two years, even where he had originally received a mandatory three-year ban; see *Dawes v. Davidson* [1976] R.T.R. 44, where the court thought that a good reason for granting such an application was where the offender had kept his licence on the previous occasion because his plea of special reasons (see below) had been upheld. Under the Road Traffic Offenders Act 1988, s.34(A), as inserted by the Road Traffic Act 1991, s.31, when a court imposes a mandatory disqualification (other than under the totting-up provisions), it will also have the power to order that if the offender undergoes a course approved by the Secretary of State, his disqualification shall be reduced by a specified period (being not less than three months nor more than a quarter of the length of the original sentence). At the time of going to press, only certain magistrates' courts had been given such a power, namely those authorised by Schedule I of the Courses for Drink-Driving (Designation of Areas) Order, S.I. 1992 No. 3014, Schedule 1, which is set out below:

PETTY SESSIONS AREAS

Petty sessional divisions of non-metropolitan counties and metropolitan districts:
  Birmingham

Carmarthen South
Carmarthen North
Corby
Exeter
Exmouth
Felixstowe
Hartlepool
Lincoln District
Maidenhead
Maidstone
Medway
Newcastle and Ogmore
Shrewsbury
Southampton
Stoke-on-Trent
Swindon
Taunton Deane
West Allerdale
Woodbridge

Metropolitan districts not divided into petty sessional divisions:
Sheffield
South Tyneside
Wolverhampton

Outer London Borough not divided into petty sessional divisions:
Bromley

Petty sessional divisions of the inner London area:
South Central
South Westminster

MEANING OF "CONVICTED"

It should be noted that when ascertaining whether the conviction for the **20–05** first offence was within 10 years of the commission of the second offence, the word "convicted" in this context means the date upon which a person was found guilty, which is not necessarily the date on which he was sentenced. The latter could be after an adjournment for the police to obtain a copy of the convicted person's driving record from the Driving and Vehicle Licensing Centre at Swansea (see *Jones v. Ridley* [1981] R.T.R. 341). The Magistrates' Association has made recommendations about the length of disqualification to be imposed (see below).

DURATION

Since 1978 there have been only two reported cases of the Court of **20–06** Appeal considering the length of disqualification for offences under sections 4 to 7 of the Road Traffic Act. In *R. v. Cook* (see below) the motorist was a man of good character who had been involved in a minor road accident. His breath alcohol concentration was 140μg. The Court of Appeal reduced his disqualification from four to two years. However, it transpired that the judges got confused and thought that the legal level was 80 (*i.e.* the blood alcohol limit); see *R. v. Shoult*, [1996] R.T.R. 298. In *R. v. Moore* [1994] R.T.R. 360, the appellant had been sent to prison for 15 months for burglary and also disqualified for three years for failing to provide a specimen. The trial judge thought that he was dealing with a conviction under section 7(6) and, as the defendant had a previous similar conviction within the last 10 years, he imposed the statutory minimum period of disqualification, namely three years. In fact, the offence was under section 6. The Court of Appeal said that even if the judge had known of this he might still have passed such a sentence, since it was a second conviction for a drinking and driving offence (at 365D). The Court of Appeal held that because of the special circumstances of the case and the fact that the defendant had served 14-and-a-half months of his disqualification before it was suspended pending appeal, they would reduce it to 15 months. The case is best explained on the basis that the Court was merely reducing the sentence to the length which had already been served. It should not be regarded as an indication of what should have been passed at first instance. The Court no doubt also took into consideration the fact that for most of his disqualification he was in prison.

20–07   In *R. v. Ealing J.J., ex p. Scrafield* [1994] R.T.R. 195, the High Court held that certiorari would only be granted to quash a sentence when it was "irrational, harsh and truly astonishing"[1] and that was not the description which could be applied to a 10-year disqualification for having been convicted on the third occasion within three years of driving with excess alcohol and when on the latest occasion the breath alcohol concentration was more than twice the permitted level. A similar conclusion was reached in *Tucker v. DPP, ibid.*, at 203 where the High Court did not disturb an 18-month discretionary disqualification for a section 7(6) offence, although Pill J. described it as "severe". That was a pre-*Butterworth* case when the penalty for failing to provide a specimen for analysis was thought to depend on what the police suspected the motorist of and not on what he had actually been doing. There the charge was brought on the basis that the police were investigating an in charge offence, although the evidence showed that the accused had in fact driven. Accordingly, that judgment in that case should be regarded as restricted to its own facts.

E. Special Reasons

I. GENERALLY

20–08   Only if there are "special reasons" will a driver manage to avoid losing his licence if convicted of an offence involving obligatory disqualification.

[1] *i.e.* the test to be applied in granting judicial review of a sentence imposed at petty sessions.

"Special reasons" mean a special circumstance which led to the commission of the offence but which does not amount to a defence to the charge; see *Whittal v. Kirby* [1947] K.B. 194, 201, *per* Lord Goddard C.J.:

> "What then can be said to be a special reason beyond saying that it must be one that is not of general character? This was expressly considered by the King's Bench Division of Northern Ireland in the case in *R. v. Crossan* [1939] N.I. 106. In that case the court adopted a test that I had ventured to use in an address that I gave to the magistrates assembled at the Summer Assizes for Essex in 1937. I suggested that the reasons must be special to the offence, and not to the offender and the court in adopting what I had said used these words:
>
> > 'A special reason within the exception is one which is special to the facts of the particular case, that is, special to the facts which constitute the offence. It is, in other words, a mitigating or extenuating circumstance, not amounting in law to a defence to the charge, yet directly connected with the commission of the offence, and one which the court ought properly to take into consideration when imposing punishment. A circumstance peculiar to the offender as distinguished from the offence is not a "special reason" within the exception.'
>
> I respectfully and entirely agree with and adopt this passage."

On very rare occasions the courts have applied a wider interpretation. Where a driver puts forward a special reason, it is for him to prove those facts on a balance of probabilities (see *DPP v. O'Connor, Same v. Allatt, Same v. Connor, Same v. Chapman, R. v. Chichester Crown Court, ex p. Moss, DPP v. Allen* [1992] R.T.R. 66). The normal rules of evidence apply (see *Flewitt v. Horvath* [1972] R.T.R. 121). Even though special reasons exist, the magistrates can still impose a disqualification, although it need not be for a full 12 months.

Lane v. DPP, unreported, March 10, 1995, held that in deciding whether **20–09** or not to disqualify, justices had to ask themselves three questions: (1) Was the evidence capable of amounting to a special reason? (2) If it was, did the evidence, on a balance of probabilities, establish a special reason? (3) If so, should they exercise their discretion? In answering the third question, the justices can only consider the reasons for committing the offence and nothing else. It is submitted that this last proposition is contrary to a number of other decisions, *e.g. Taylor v. Rajan* (see below) where Lord Widgery C.J. was clearly of the view that the manner of driving was most important and should be taken into account by the justices when they came to consider whether or not to exercise their discretion not to order disqualification. Accordingly, *Lane's case* should be restricted to its own facts, *i.e.* that the hardship which a disqualification might cause the defendant is not a relevant consideration. If only the reason why the offence was perpetrated can be considered, and the justices are not allowed to take into account anything else (*e.g.* the manner of the driving), then they would in effect have no discretion but not to disqualify, seeing that they had found the reasons for perpetrating the offence were special ones and anything else was irrelevant. As Parliament has given them a discretion, then justices must be able to take into account more than the actual reason which caused the offender to transgress the law. Nevertheless, it is submitted that where special reasons do exist, it would often be unjust to impose the full rigour of the law.

20-10   In *DPP v. O'Connor*, above, Woolf L.J. quite sensibly said that the prosecution should be warned in advance of an intention to plead special reasons so that they might be in a position to meet that averment and thus avoid an adjournment. His Lordship also thought that if such information was not given in advance, that would throw doubt on the bona fides of such a plea. Should the failure to do so be due to his solicitor (not an unknown occurrence) it will always be open to a defendant to rebut the inference of "recent fabrication" implicit in the pronouncement of Woolf L.J. In the words of Lord Radcliffe in *Fox v. General Medical Council* [1960] 1 W.L.R. 1017, 1025:

> "If in cross-examination, a witness's account of some incident or set of facts is challenged as being a recent invention, thus presenting a clear issue as to whether at some previous time he said or thought what he has been saying at the trial, he may support himself by evidence of earlier statements by him to the same effect. Plainly the rule that sets up the exception cannot be formulated with any great precision, since its application will depend on the nature of the challenge offered by the course of cross-examination and the relative cogency of the evidence tendered to repel it."

Thus the easiest way of denying the prosecutor's allegation of recent fabrication will often be for a driver to produce to the court the proof of evidence taken by his solicitor which contained the factual information relied upon in support of the plea of "special reasons". This would show that he had told his solicitor of the matter when he first instructed him and it was not something which he thought up later.

Under the Road Traffic Offenders Act, s.47, if a court finds "special reasons" it must state what they are in open court and in the case of petty session it must also record them in its Register. This provision is not, however, mandatory, according to *Barnes v. Gevaux* [1981] R.T.R. 236.

II. DE MINIMIS NON CURAT LEX

20-11   An alcohol level just above the prescribed limit will not amount to a special reason for not disqualifying; see *Delaroy-Hall v. Tadman* [1969] 2 Q.B. 208 and *R. v. Anderson* [1972] R.T.R. 113 at 117G.

III. "LACED" DRINKS OR OTHERWISE UN-KNOWINGLY CONSUMING EXTRA ALCOHOL

(a) GENERALLY

20-12   The most frequently tendered special reason is that the accused, without any negligence on his part, reasonably believed that he had consumed either no alcohol or less alcohol than he had in fact done. This is normally caused by "laced drinks", *i.e.* where somebody has added extra alcohol to whatever beverage had been requested (see *Pugsley v. Hunter* [1973] 1 W.L.R. 578). In addition, the defendant must establish that it was only this extra amount of alcohol which had put him over the limit. This must be proved by admissible evidence and not hearsay, but justices can draw an inference of laced drinks if the amount of alcohol consumed by the motorist is incompatible with the analysis: see *James v. Morgan* [1988] R.T.R. 85 at 88 and *Flewitt v. Horvath* [1972] R.T.R. 121. In *Pridige v. Grant* [1985] R.T.R. 196, the High Court held that a Bench should approach the matter with the following three considerations in mind, when adjudicating on such a plea:

1. The motorist must not have known at the time that his drinks had been laced or that he had "consumed" more alcohol than he intended.

2. He must neither have known, nor ought he have known, when he came to drive, that he was (to use the vernacular) over the limit or was unfit to drive. The High Court was of the opinion that, in the case of unfitness, it would be rare indeed for a person not to have realised that his ability to drive was impaired.

3. It was solely the amount of the laced drinks which had taken the accused over the *de facto* prosecution alcohol limit or had made him unfit to drive. (The former must normally be proved by expert evidence.) The court also said that if laced drinks were proved, it would be difficult to say that the discretion not to disqualify should not be exercised (at 201E.) Each of the above matters will be considered separately.

(i) Knowledge of the Extra Alcohol

In *Adams v. Bradley* [1975] R.T.R. 233, it was held that there were no **20–13** special reasons for not disqualifying the defendant when he had consumed a stronger lager than he had anticipated without realising it. In that case the defendant did not stipulate what type of lager he wanted. If, however, he had not been given the brand which he had specifically requested, that can amount to a special reason. In *Alexander v. Latter* [1972] R.T.R. 441, the accused asked for lager. He was offered diabetic lager without being told that it was double strength. As he was told the type of lager it was reasonable for him to have expected the publican to have warned him if it was more potent than the average beverage. Likewise, there were special reasons in *R. v. Krebbs* [1977] R.T.R. 406, where the driver requested Harp lager but later, without his knowledge, he was given Lowenbrau which was double the strength of his desired beer. In *Brewer v. Metropolitan Police Commissioner* [1969] 1 W.L.R. 267, it was held in the High Court that there were special reasons when, while at work, the defendant had unknowingly inhaled trichoroethylene fumes containing ethanol even though the magistrates had found that he ought to have been aware of this fact. Likewise, in *R. v. Holt* [1962] Crim. L. R. 565, it was held that there were special reasons when the defendant took amytal without being warned of the effect it could have if taken with even a little alcohol.

(ii) Knowledge of Unfitness or Excess Alcohol

20-14 The accused must show that he had no knowledge, nor ought to have known, that if he drove he would be committing an offence under sections 4 or 5 of the Road Traffic Act 1988. In *DPP v. Barker* [1990] R.T.R. 1, the motorist's drinks had been laced so that her breath alcohol concentration was more than three times the legal limit. She testified that she could remember nothing about it. After hearing expert evidence about the effect that such alcohol would have had on her, the Bench did not disqualify her. That decision was upheld on appeal in the High Court, despite a prosecution plea that the justices had not asked themselves if the respondent had appreciated that she was unfit to drive. In *DPP v. O'Connor* [1991] R.T.R. 335, Woolf L.J. emphasised that in cases where there was erratic driving or where the accused had consumed a substantial amount of alcohol above the prescribed limit, the justices would want to consider carefully whether or not he should have appreciated that he was in a condition where he ought not to have driven.

In *Donahue v. DPP* [1993] R.T.R. 156, the High Court upheld the justices' refusal to exercise their discretion not to disqualify in a laced drinks case. The defendant entertained his employer's guests in a hospitality tent at the Cheshire Show and asked to be served with non-alcoholic drinks. The justices found that he must have realised that he was unfit to drive, and also that he was foolish just to accept the liquids brought to him as being alcohol-free.

(iii) Evidence that the Unknown Consumption was Responsible for the Alcohol Level being over the *de facto* Prosecution Limit

20-15 It used to be thought that to establish "special reasons" the motorist had to prove that the unknown alcohol consumption was solely responsible for him being over the prescribed limit. In *R. v. Cambridge Crown Court, ex p. Wong* (1991) 155 J.P. 554, it was held that it would be sufficient if it was established that the unknown consumption had taken him over the *de facto* prosecution limit of 39μg. Wong's breath alcohol concentration was 40μg. He had been taking a cough linctus (Benylin) which, unknown to him, contained ethanol. Expert evidence showed that the dosage taken by him was responsible for 1.7μg of the alcohol analysed by the Intoximeter. Subtracting that amount from the breathalyser reading of 40μg, then left a figure of 38.3μg which was below the level at which the Director of Public Prosecutions would prosecute. The High Court held that "special reasons" existed since the accused would never have been tried but for the alcohol he had unknowingly consumed when taking his cough medicine.

That decision was followed in *Woodward v. DPP*, unreported, February 25, 1995. It is also submitted that since it takes, on average, about an hour after the last drink for the alcohol in the male body to reach its maximum level, the prosecution would not normally be in a position to allege that a person's alcohol level had decreased in the interval between the driving and the provision of the specimen, and thus negate the plea of "special reasons" by a back-calculation (see Chapter 9 and 20–18).

Unless it is obvious that the extra ethanol which he unintentionally **20–16** consumed must have put him over the *de facto* level for being prosecuted, a motorist must produce expert testimony of that fact. So in *DPP v Younas* [1990] R.T.R. 22, it was held that an expert need not be called when it was obvious that the laced drink must have put the respondent over the limit. The High Court did not consider it perverse for the magistrates to have held that the one-and-three-quarter pints of beer which he had intentionally consumed would not have made his blood alcohol concentration exceed the prescribed limit. That appeal must be contrasted with *Smith v. DPP* [1990] R.T.R. 17 where a differently constituted divisional court of the Queen's Bench would not interfere with the findings of the Crown Court that they were not satisfied that the admitted consumption of one-and-a-half pints of beer would not have caused a person to contravene section 5. As a matter of science that decision was undoubtedly wrong, and illustrates the importance that whenever there is an allegation that somebody's drinks have been laced, an expert should always be called to show that without the "lacing," the alcohol level would not have been above the legal limit.

The facts of those cases show that the judiciary have adopted the wrong **20–17** approach to the issue. The correct way should be to deduct the amount of the alcohol in the laced drink from the result of the analysis and to see if that would produce an alcohol level below the prosecution limit. If that reasoning had been applied in those two cases, both would have been decided in the opposite way to that in which they were actually decided. The alcohol in Younas's breath was 72µg and, deducting from that the two double brandies with which his drinks had been laced (*i.e.* 26µg), would leave 46µg as the amount which he had knowingly consumed. On the other hand, in *Smith's case* [1990] R.T.R. 17, his drink had been laced by a single vodka which would account for 15mg of alcohol. The amount of the latter fluid in his blood was 86mg. Therefore without the lacing the analysis would have been 69mg. Indeed, in both cases, the evidence of the total quantity of intoxicants consumed, including the laced drinks, would not have produced as much alcohol as was in fact discovered by the analyses. It is submitted that the fact that a driver might have drunk more than he remembered would be irrelevant so long as the court approached the matter by subtracting the amount of the alcohol which had been unintentionally consumed from the level revealed by the analysis. This approach overcomes the problem that often people forget what they had to drink, and the more they imbibe, the less they remember about it!

In *Smith v. Geraghty* [1986] R.T.R. 222, it was held that the accused had **20–18** to establish that it was at the actual time of driving that his alcohol level would have been within the *de facto* legal tolerance but for the laced drinks and not at some other time. In deciding whether that was the case, magistrates were entitled to add on to the amount of alcohol revealed by the analysis the additional ethanol which would have been metabolised in the interval between the driving and the provision of the specimen (see Chapter 9). However, the court made it clear that such back-calculations should only be done in the clearest of cases. There the defendant's blood sample was taken well over an hour after he had ceased driving. On analysis, it was shown to contain an alcohol concentration of 92mg. It was found as a fact by the Bench that, but for the laced drinks, the result of the analysis would only have been 77mg. The prosecution submitted to the lower court that an extra 15mg per hour should be added on to the figure of 77mg, to allow for the difference in time between the driving and the taking of the specimen. (The average blood alcohol loss of a person is about 15mg per hour.) The defence argued that the blood alcohol concentration did not reach its peak until a considerable time after the last drink and that instead of the accused's alcohol level falling (as the prosecution alleged), it was in fact rising. The Bench said that they were not prepared to become involved with complicated back-calculations of this nature with so many variables (*e.g.* whether the alcohol was in its absorption of elimination phase and at what rate this might occur, etc.). The High Court upheld that finding of special reasons. In the words of Glidewell L.J. (at 232G/H):

> "But as a generality, it is my view most undesirable that justices should be drawn into or allow themselves to be drawn into detailed calculations with all the variations which necessarily have to be built into such calculations, with the margins of error which there are."

IV. A SUDDEN EMERGENCY

20–19 In *DPP v. Whittle* [1996] R.T.R. 154 Simon Brown L.J. was of the view that nowadays such cases should be treated as cases of duress of circumstances, which is a complete defence, see sections 4–17 *et seq.* In *Brown v. Dyerson* [1969] 1 Q.B. 45, it was held that there would be a "special reason" if a person who did not intend to drive was faced with a sudden emergency which necessitated him having to drive (*e.g.* to take somebody who had collapsed to hospital). However, he would have to prove that he had considered the matter and that there was no other way to meet the emergency save by driving, *e.g.* if was not possible for him to get a taxi (see *Evans v. Bray* [1977] R.T.R. 24 and *R. v. Baines* [1970] R.T.R. 455). However, the greater the urgency of the situation, the less time for thought. In *DPP v. Cox* [1996] R.T.R. 123, a steward of a club was the key holder. Late at night he received a telephone call from the police saying that intruders were reported inside the club. He immediately drove the 300 yards there, half of which was on a public road. He never thought about alternative transport, walking or waiting for a lift from the police. The High Court upheld the finding of special reasons. The intruders could have been vandals smashing the place up, with the situation getting worse by the minute. Time was of the essence. Also, he would be safer going by car. If he were to be attacked he had a means of retreat. Thus, judged objectively, the steward had special reasons and that being so, then failure to consider any alternative did not prevent special reasons if the circumstances were such that the resultant loss of time did not justify attempting to make other transport arrangements, even though he never even bothered to think about this aspect of the matter. In *Achreeth v. Cottee* [1954] 1 W.L.R. 1124 the High Court overruled quarter sessions and held that special reasons existed for driving while disqualified when the defendant had driven at 5.00 a.m. to his place of work. The dough-making machine had broken down and he was the only person who had the keys to the storage area where the special tools needed to repair it were kept. If the machine had not been repaired at least 5,000 customers of the bakery would not have received their bread. The case was remitted for the justices to decide if there had been other transport available to take the accused from West Norwood to Hampstead at that time in the morning.

Normally, the driving must cease as soon as the emergency is over. In **20–20** *DPP v. Feeney* (1989) 89 Cr.App.R. 173, the defendant was at a party where a young lady found her colostomy bag had become detached, leaving her in a very embarrassing state such that a taxi driver would not be willing to take her home. Although he had not intended to drive, the accused saw no alternative but to drive her home, which he did. He then set off to drive the 1,000 yards to his residence but was stopped and breathalysed on the way. The High Court upheld the magistrates' finding that driving the girl home was an emergency but held that there was no reason why he could not have walked the 1,000 yards to his home and, accordingly, ordered him to be disqualified. The approach to be adopted in these cases was laid down by Lord Widgery C.J. in *Taylor v. Rajan* [1974] R.T.R. 304, 310:

> "the manner in which the defendant drove, because if he committed traffic offences, such as excessive speed or driving without due care and attention, this again is a consideration which tells against his having the discretion exercised in his favour, and they should generally have regard to whether the defendant acted reasonably or otherwise."

In *Park v. Hicks* [1979] R.T.R. 259, the defendant was at Heathrow Airport **20–21** waiting to fly abroad when he received a message that his daughter had not arrived at her school. This was held not to be a special reason for driving as there was nothing that he could have done about his child's disappearance so there was no necessity for him to have driven. In *Thompson v. Diamond* [1985] R.T.R. 316, it was doubted whether it could ever be a special reason that a person was driving to hospital to see a patient. A defendant worrying about the patient's well-being could never amount to a special reason. It might be different if the patient's condition had depended on seeing the accused. There the defendant had merely been told that his mother had been taken to hospital so he drove to see her, with the result that no special reason existed for him having driven with excess alcohol.

The motorist must have made all reasonable attempts to use alternative transport before he gets into the driving seat. In *Evans v. Bray* [1977] R.T.R. 24, the accused drove 40 miles to his wife at about 2 a.m. in response to a telephone call that she urgently needed her pills. The High Court ordered the driver to be disqualified as he had set off on his journey without checking to see if there was any alternative means of transporting the medicine, *e.g.* ringing the police or contacting the local hospital.

In *Taylor v. Rajan* [1974] R.T.R. 304 at 309L the Lord Chief Justice said: **20–22** "The justices should only exercise their discretion in favour of the driver in clear and compelling circumstances."

In *Powell v. Gilha* [1979] R.T.R. 127, it was held that there were no "special reasons" if the emergency could have been reasonably foreseen in advance. The defendant had made no provision for the possibility of her husband, whom she had taken to a party, requiring a special toilet because he was a paraplegic.

In *DPP v. Knight* [1994] R.T.R. 375, the High Court upheld the findings of "special reasons". A mother on telephoning her baby-sitter was told that there had been a number of telephone calls which contained a threat of attacking her daughter with a knife. After unsuccessfully trying to get a taxi, she drove home, fearing an imminent assault upon her daughter. (She would not otherwise have driven back to her house.) Her breath alcohol concentration was 44ug. In *DPP v. Upchurch, ibid.*, at 366, the High Court made a wasted costs order against the Director of Public Prosecutions when she appealed against the finding of "special reasons". There the defendant had walked to a restaurant where he got innocently caught up in a disturbance involving 200 people. A friend was injured in the head and was believed by him to be seriously unwell, so he went back to where he was staying, collected his car and then drove his friend miles to hospital. He only got into his car after being told by a policeman that no ambulances were available and after telephoning a taxi company who said that because of the situation no cab would come. His breath alcohol level was 45μg. Blofeld J. said that any other decision by justices would have been perverse (at 373J). Russell L.J. expressed the view:

"I feel bound to say that I am disturbed and surprised that the Director of Public Prosecutions should have chosen in this case to have a case stated by the justices and to bring the matter before this court, no doubt at great public expense. The case, in my view and in agreement with Blofeld J. was a clear one for the exercise of the justices' discretion in the way that they exercised it."

As a mark of their disapproval, instead of awarding the successful respondent his costs out of central funds as is usual, their Lordships made an order for costs against the Director of Public Prosecutions. Unfortunately that has no deterrent effect as the First Division of Civil Servants has negotiated that any order for costs made against a named civil servant shall be paid by the Crown.

In *Williams v. Tierney* [1988] R.T.R. 118, 123 C–E, it was held that driving a short distance after the emergency had ceased did not preclude special reasons if in all the circumstances it was reasonable to do so (see sections 14–17 *et seq.*). That would depend on the availability of other transport, the weather, time of day, etc. In *Taylor v. Rayan* Widgery L.J. said:

"Another factor which arises in this case, and may arise again, is that there will often be a distinct difference in the situation presented to the driver on his outward journey when he goes to deal with the emergency, and on his homeward journey when the emergency has been dealt with. It will generally be very much more difficult for the driver to justify using his car to go home, the emergency having been dealt with, than it may be for him to justify using the car to go to the place where the trouble has arisen which requires attention." [1974] R.T.R. at 309.

Also, the higher the alcohol level the less likelihood of the discretion not **20–22A** to disqualify being exercised. In *Taylor v. Rajan*, above, the court was manifestly of the opinion that a person with a blood alcohol concentration of 230mg should definitely be disqualified. The Lord Chief Justice stated:

> "Lastly, but by no means least, if the alcohol content in the defendant's blood is very high, this is a very powerful reason for saying that the discretion should not be exercised in his favour. Indeed, if the alcohol content exceeds 100mg per 100ml. of blood the justices should rarely, if ever, exercise this discretion in favour of the defendant driver."

Exactly when the amount of alcohol consumed is such that the driver must be disqualified has still to be laid down by the court. Some guidance can be gained from *Evans v. Bray* [1977] R.T.R. 24, where the High Court was of the opinion that a blood alcohol concentration of 179ml "militated against" not imposing a disqualification. In *DPP v. Cox*, above, special reasons were upheld where the breath reading was 66μg (152ml in blood). These pronouncements about levels were concerned solely with cases of "emergency" driving. Special reasons were found in *DPP v. O'Connor* [1992] R.T.R. 66, where the breath alcohol level was 95μg (172ml in blood) but that was a laced drinks case.

In *DPP v. Doyle*, *The Times*, December 19, 1992, it was held that there could be no special reasons if the defendant, having learnt of the emergency, continued to drink before setting off in her car.

It is submitted that the real questions for the magistrates are: **20–23**

1. What would the consequences have been if the defendant had not driven?

2. Was there alternative transport which could have prevented those consequences?

3. If the answer to 2 is "no", was the avoidance of those consequences of such magnitude that it justified the defendant driving—in the way that he actually did—when it was clearly against the law for him to do so?

In *DPP v. Bristow*, *The Times*, October 26, 1996, the High Court held **20–23A** that the "key question" which justices should ask themselves in emergency cases was: "What would a sober and sensible friend of the defendant who was present but who was a non-driver have advised in the circumstances, to drive or not to drive?"

Only if there was a real possibility of the former answer would there be special reasons. In deciding that matter, the crucial circumstances to be considered were:

(i) how much the defendant had had to drink;

(ii) what threat he would pose to others when driving in an inebriated condition, given the distance he was proposing to drive, the likely state of roads and the condition of his car;

(iii) how acute the problem was;

(iv) what alternatives had been open to the defendant to solve the problem.

In that case the respondent's daughter came home and said that her sister and cousin had been sexually assaulted and were being detained against their will in a house. The respondent drove to the house which was 500 hundred yards away with a breath alcohol limit twice the permitted maximum. (The police at the scene had smelt alcohol on his breath and had breathalysed him.) The High Court held that the justices were wrong not to disqualify him in view of the fact that he had drunk far too much and that there had been other solutions readily available. (The brief report available to the author does not say what they were.)

V. BLACKMAIL

20-24 In *DPP v. Enston* [1996] R.T.R. 324, the defendant had given a lift to a young lady under the threat of a false accusation of rape if he did not do so. When stopped by police the defendant was too frightened to tell them why he was driving. The threat of blackmail was held to amount to special reason for not ordering disqualification.

VI. THE DISTANCE DRIVEN

20-25 In *James v. Hall* [1972] R.T.R. 228, it was held that special reasons could also exist when moving a vehicle off a busy road in order to park it a very short distance away out of the traffic in circumstances where no danger was caused or was likely to be caused to other road users. *Coombs v. Kehoe* [1972] R.T.R. 224 held that where the short distance driven was down a main road this would not amount to special reasons. In that case Lord Widgery C.J. held that a *James v. Hall* situation must be confined to "a man who drives literally a few yards by which [he] meant 10 or 15 yards, something of that kind". Other judges have taken a less restrictive view.

In *Chatters v. Burke* [1986] 1 W.L.R. 1321, Taylor J. said that shortness of distance driven (which was not defined and on which no limitation was placed) was not by itself a special reason. There were in fact seven matters which must be taken into account (at 1327):

> "First . . . how far the vehicle was in fact driven [no maximum distance was mentioned by the judge]; secondly, in what manner it was driven; thirdly, what was the state of the vehicle; fourthly, whether it was the intention of the driver to drive any further; fifthly, the prevailing conditions with regard to the road and traffic on it; sixthly, whether there was any possibility of danger by contact with other road-users; and finally, what was the reason for the vehicle being driven at all."

In that case the owner of a car was being driven home by somebody else who suddenly lost control, with the result that the vehicle rolled over and ended up in a field. The car passenger then drove the car out of the field and parked it on the road, not intending to drive any further. The High Court upheld the finding of the justices that there were special reasons for not disqualifying the owner.

In *Redmond v. Parry* [1986] R.T.R. 146, it was held that there were **20–26** special reasons where a man, who did not intend to drive, moved his car a few feet to the rear in a public house car park, as his wife, who was going to drive home, did not like reversing. Unfortunately, while manoeuvring out of the parking bay, he collided with another vehicle, but the High Court emphasised that he had not intended to drive any further and that there had been no pedestrians in the vicinity. In *DPP v. Corcoran* [1991] R.T.R. 329, the High Court upheld the justices' finding of special reasons where the defendant had driven his car, in order to park it, a distance of 40 yards without causing any danger. (His breath reading was 56μg.)

No judge has laid down the maximum permitted distance beyond which **20–27** it cannot amount to special reasons. The dicta of Lord Widgery C.J. about distance in *Coombs' case*, above, are really *obiter*, as the *ratio* was that there were no special reasons for not disqualifying a man who had driven 200 yards through a busy street and was a potential source of danger. (He had collided with two cars.) Lord Widgery's view on the 10–15 yards has not been followed. In *DPP v. Corcoran*, above, Lloyd L.J. stated that what distinguished that case from *Coombs's case*, above, was not so much the distance travelled but the fact that there were no other vehicles on the road and no danger to other road users. In other words, he thought that there could be special reasons when a person had driven for 200 yards. In *Haime v. Walklett* [1983] R.T.R. 512, 516, the court said that 200 yards was a significant distance but also that it was a journey which, at the time it was undertaken, was unlikely to encounter other traffic. It is submitted that the latter part of that sentence was the significant part of the judgment. *Reay v. Young* [1949] 1 All E.R. 1102 held that driving 150 yards on a moorland road where the only other person was a police motorcyclist was a special reason. (That was a case of no insurance but the principle is the same.) On the other hand, in *R v. Mullarkey* [1949] Crim.L.R. 406, it was held that driving 440 yards with few other road users around was not a special reason. Reconciling that case with *Corcoran's case*, above, the law would appear to be that travelling less than a quarter of a mile would not prevent special reasons being pleaded.

Different considerations apply to a section 7(6) offence. In *DPP v. Rose* **20–28** (1988) 156 J.P. 733, the High Court allowed the appeal and held that there were no special reasons when the motorist had driven two feet and had only intended to go a few feet further. The court does not really deal with the shortness of "the journey", but concentrated on the reason for the failure to have provided a specimen, namely, that he would not do unless a third party was present as a witness. That, of course, could not amount to a special reason, and the case should only be regarded as an authority for this last proposition. In *DPP v. Williams*, unreported, June 22, 1994, the High Court held that shortness of distance driven could never be a special reason for not supplying a specimen as that matter had no connection whatsoever with not blowing into a breathalyser.

VII. THE OFFENDER'S PERSONAL CIRCUMSTANCES

The personal circumstances of an offender can never amount to special **20–29** reasons. Thus the following lost their licences:

(i) A driver who retained alcohol longer than the average person because of a liver condition (see *R. v. Scott* [1970] 1 Q.B. 661);

(ii) A driver whose ability to drive was not impaired (see *Taylor v. Austin* [1969] 1 W.L.R. 264);

(iii) A driver who would lose his job if he were to be disqualified from driving (see *Glendinning v. Batty* [1973] R.T.R. 405);

(iv) A driver who was a cripple (see *R. v. Hart* [1969] Crim.L.R. 321);

(v) A doctor in an area which was remote and designated by the Ministry of Health (*i.e.* there was a shortage of doctors) and who needed his licence to be able to see his patients, and without which he would be forced to give up his practice and it was unlikely that a replacement for him would be found (see *Holroyd v. Berry* [1973] R.T.R. 145);

(vi) An army driver who was about to be posted to Northern Ireland (See *Gordon v. Smith (Robert Stanley)* [1970] R.T.R. 52);

(vii) A driver who had telephoned the police after an accident and requested their attendance at the scene (see *Kerr v. Armstrong* [1974] R.T.R. 139);

(viii) A driver of unblemished character (see *R. v. Steel* (1968) 52 Cr.App.R. 510); and

(ix) Being deprived of the opportunity to put forward a post-driving consumption of alcohol defence because of wrong advice by his solicitor (see *Dickinson v. DPP, The Independent*, June 19, 1989). (The driver had been advised not to provide a specimen for analysis.)

(x) Unhappiness causing one to drink to excess, see *DPP v. Phillips*, unreported, June 22, 1994.

(xi) Being granted bail subject to a condition of not driving (*R. v. Kwame* [1975] R.T.R. 106).

VIII. OTHER SPECIAL AND NON-SPECIAL REASONS

(a) FAILING TO PROVIDE A SPECIMEN

20–30 In *Anderton v. Anderton* [1977] R.T.R. 424, it was held that the special reasons must relate exclusively to why no specimen had been provided and not to the driving nor to why the journey had been undertaken in the first place. The defendant would have had a special reason (*i.e.* a sudden emergency) if the charge had been one of driving with excess alcohol. However, he did not have a special reason for not providing a specimen and the justices were ordered to disqualify him from driving for at least the statutory minimum period of 12 months. To the same effect is *Williams v. DPP*, unreported, June 22, 1994. That principle was not followed in *Bunyard v. Haynes* [1985] R.T.R. 348, where it had been held to be a special reason for not indorsing a licence that, although the defendant had refused to provide a specimen, he had neither been driving, attempting to drive nor in charge of a motor vehicle (see Chapter 10). Likewise, in *McCormick v. Hitchins* [1988] R.T.R. 182, the defendant refused to exhale into a breathalyser because he had not been driving and because he was not going to drive for as long as his consumption of alcohol made it illegal for him to do so. The High Court held that this amounted to special reasons for not indorsing his licence. If in both of the last two mentioned cases, the defendants had provided a specimen and that had contained alcohol above the legal limit, they would have been acquitted of a charge under section 5 because they had not, and would not have, driven while they had alcohol (in excess of the prescribed limit) in their body.

In *R. v. Reid* [1973] 1 W.L.R. 1283, a very strong Court of Appeal **20-31** (Lawton, Scarman L.JJ. and Ackner J.) held that there were special reasons for not disqualifying when the defendant had initially refused to provide a specimen for analysis but very shortly afterwards had retracted his refusal, and there was nothing in the evidence to suggest that he had committed an offence under section 5. The facts were that he had declined to give a sample on the grounds that the police were not entitled to require one. A sergeant, whom he knew, then correctly explained the law to him, at which he immediately agreed to provide a sample, but the arresting officer who had made the initial request was not prepared to allow him to change his mind. This is a most interesting decision as really it is saying that, although the defendant was guilty under the strict rigours of the law, nevertheless, since he had acted in a reasonable way and there was nothing to suggest that he had contravened sections 4 or 5, then those facts amounted to "special reasons".

In *Chief Constable of Avon and Somerset Constabulary v. O'Brien* [1987] **20-32** R.T.R 182, a motorist had been wrongly arrested and roughly treated by the police. The High Court held that his frame of mind flowing from that incident had caused him to refuse to give a breath sample and that this amounted to a special reasons for not ordering disqualification. A similar interpretation has been given to the phrase "special reasons" in *Daniels v. DPP* [1992] R.T.R. 140. There the defendant helped another man to bump start a motorcycle. It suddenly fired, and in order to keep it going, he jumped on the cycle and drove it for no more than 35 yards before stopping. The police questioned him about the ownership of the cycle and arrested him on suspicion of having stolen it. He was then taken to a police station and detained on the theft charge. Over an hour later, he was asked to provide a specimen for analysis. He refused as his mind was directed to the theft allegation and he regarded the accusation of unfitness to drive as relatively trivial. If he had not been distracted by the allegation of theft, he may have taken a different view of the request to supply a specimen. The High Court held that those facts amounted to special reasons.

In *DPP v. Kinnersley*, The Times, December 29, 1992, the High Court held that a fear of AIDS not amounting to a phobia could constitute special reasons for not providing a breath sample.

In *White v. Metropolitan Police Commissioner* [1984] Crim. L.R. 687, Judge Birkett-Baker held that providing a single breath specimen below the legal limit was a special reason and imposed only a 12-month disqualification, instead of a mandatory three years. It is submitted that no disqualification should have been imposed, as section 7 is designed to punish those who refuse to provide a specimen in order to avoid being found to have driven with excess alcohol—which was not the fact in *White's case*. In *DPP v. Rose* (1988) 156 J.P. 733, the High Court expressed no opinion on whether special reasons had existed in *White's case*.

DPP v. Daley [1994] R.T.R. 107 held that doing one's best to provide a specimen was not a special reason.

(b) DRIVING WHILST UNFIT OR OVER THE PRESCRIBED LIMIT

20–33   In *Harding v. Oliver* [1973] R.T.R. 497, the defendant sent his sample to a hospital to have it analysed, whereupon it was lost. The prosecution analysis revealed a blood alcohol concentration of 82mg. The justices held this to be a special reason and did not impose any disqualification. Their decision was reversed on appeal. (If a similar situation were to occur nowadays, the magistrates may well be able to use their discretion under section 78 of the Police and Criminal Evidence Act 1984 (see chapter 14) to exclude evidence of the results of the prosecution analysis.) This case should be compared with *R. v. Anderson* [1972] R.T.R. 113, where the driver was told by the police that he was not going to be prosecuted, as a result of which he threw away the specimen which had been given to him. The High Court held that this amounted to a special reason for not disqualifying him. The prosecution's analysis showed the alcoholic content of the sample to be only 1mg above the prescribed limit and he had been misled by the police into not exercising his statutory right to have his own sample analysed, which may well have proved his innocence. (The appeal was only against sentence and the Court of Appeal made it clear that in their view that there could be no appeal against conviction. However, in *Perry v. McGovern* [1986] R.T.R. 240, 245 Watkins L.J. (with whom Nolan J. concurred) said that he agreed with the commentary on that case in [1972] Crim.L.R. 245, which was of the view that the Court of Appeal should have quashed the conviction.)

20–34   A somewhat similar thing occurred in *Doyle v. Leroux* [1981] R.T.R. 438, where the defendant was told by the police that they were going to take no further action in relation to the accident and the incident. In writing that letter, the Chief Superintendent intended to refer only to a possible charge of driving without due care and attention and had overlooked the breathalyser offence. That communication caused the defendant to throw away the specimen which had been given to him. The High Court held that this could have amounted to a special reason for not imposing a disqualification on the defendant, but not where (as in that case) the prosecution analysis showed him to be twice the legal limit. Ormrod L.J. said the accused was obviously guilty and deserved to be disqualified.

In *Lodwick v. Brow* [1985] T.L.R. 394, the defendant was suffering from post-traumatic amnesia, which caused him to forget about his blood specimen so that it got lost. The High Court held there were no special reasons and went on to state that the comments in *Doyle v. Leroux*, above, about the existence of special reasons if the blood analysis had revealed a much lower level of alcohol nearer to the prescribed limit were *per incuriam*. *Harding v. Oliver*, above, was not cited. The relevant dicta in *Doyle v. Leroux* were wholly in accordance with the decision of the Court of Appeal in *R. v. Anderson*, above.

In *Vaughn v. Dunn* [1984] R.T.R. 376, 380D, the High Court was doubtful if the following could ever amount to special reasons, namely a detective who had to go out drinking in order to obtain information and who received expenses of £2 *per diem* to pay for his beverages. In any event, the court had no doubts that the justices were wrong to have exercised their discretion in his favour since he was so drunk that he drove straight into a lamp post. He had gone out with the deliberate intention of drinking and should have got a taxi or a lift home.

In *DPP v. O'Meara* [1989] R.T.R. 24, a bus driver was found to be still **20–35** over the limit 12 hours after his last drink. It was held that it was not a special reason that he did know that the effect of alcohol could last so long. That case was followed in *DPP v. Williams*, unreported, June 22, 1994.

In *R. v. McIntyre* [1976] R.T.R. 330, the accused had been to a club. Due to the amount he had drunk, he decided not to drive. A policeman spoke to him, but he misunderstood what was being said and thought that the constable was instructing him to remove his parked car which was blocking part of the road. The Court of Appeal stated that obeying a constable's request to drive was a special reason, and the same applied if there was a genuine misunderstanding of what the officer was saying. On the other hand, in *DPP v. White* [1988] R.T.R. 267, it was held that there were no special reasons when a defendant had been stopped by the police, gave a negative breath test and was allowed to continue driving. During the same journey he was again stopped but this time provided a positive breath test and a subsequent breath analysis showed him to have contravened section 5.

In *Bullen v. Keay* [1974] R.T.R. 559, it was held not to be a special reason that drugs had been taken to commit suicide.

F. Totting up

Under section 35 of the Road Traffic Offenders Act 1988, unless there are **20–36** mitigating circumstances, a motorist must be disqualified if the penalty points awarded by the court bring the total number on his licence to 12 or more. Under section 29 no account is to be taken of points awarded for any offence committed more than three years before the commission of the present offence or since he was last disqualified. By virtue of the Road Traffic Act 1991, s.48 and Schedule 24, para. 95, a disqualification no longer cancels out the existing penalty points on a licence unless the disqualification was imposed under the totting up provisions, in which case all existing penalty points will still continue "to be wiped off" the driving licence. The length of such a driving ban is six months, or one year, if the offender has been disqualified for 56 days or longer on one occasion (or two years if he has been disqualified more than once) for any offence perpetrated within three years of the commission of the offence for which he is then being disqualified. However, totting up merely means a disqualification has to be imposed: it does not mean that such a disqualification is consecutive to any other disqualification. See *Learmont v. DPP* [1994] R.T.R. 108.

20–37   Under subsection 35(4) mitigating circumstances, in order to prevent an otherwise mandatory disqualification, cannot merely be the hardship which the offender would suffer through loss of his licence, unless it is "exceptional hardship". This will normally mean the loss of one's job or a forced resignation through no longer being able to travel to work. The same subsection also does not allow the trivial nature of the offence from amounting to mitigating circumstances and prohibits the same facts being put forward as mitigating circumstances, if a court has already taken them into consideration within three years of the commission of the present offence, when ordering the offender not to be disqualified under the "totting up" provisions.

20–38   Mandamus will not lie to force the magistrates to impose a totting up disqualification if the previous penalty points were not disclosed to them. In *R. v. Northamptonshire Justices, ex p. Nicolson* [1974] R.T.R. 97, the defendant's licence was eaten by his dog and his new licence accidentally omitted his past convictions. When the police discovered this, they applied for an order of mandamus to compel the justices to disqualify the defendant. That application was refused as the magistrates were *functus officio* and a prerogative order would not be issued to make them hear fresh evidence (*i.e.* the driver's previous convictions). Nowadays, under section 142 of the Magistrates' Courts Act 1980, petty sessions have been given a statutory power which allows them to alter any sentence imposed by them where it is in the interests of justice to do so. The Crown Court has a similar power under section 42 of the Supreme Court Act 1981 to alter any sentence but can only do so within 28 days of its imposition.

G. Recently qualified drivers

20–39 Under the Road Traffic (New Drivers) Act 1995, there is an automatic revocation by the Secretary of State of the driving licence of a motorist who has only passed his driving test within the previous two years if his licence is indorsed so that it contains six or more penalty points. The revocation comes into effect on the day it is notified to the motorist by the Secretary of State and that date must be after any appeal which is pending against the order indorsing the licence. The motorist can only obtain his full licence back by passing a driving test. In other words, the person becomes a learner driver again.

H. Restoration of licence by the Secretary of State

20–40 A disqualification for up to 56 days merely suspends a driving licence; any ban for longer revokes the licence (see Road Traffic Offenders Act s.37(1)). Once a disqualification lasting more than 56 days has expired, the motorist is entitled to reapply for his licence. At one time such an application automatically led to the restoration of the licence. Nowadays, before a motorist's licence is restored, the Secretary of State requires that those whom he regards as "high risk drivers" must satisfy him that their drinking habits no longer pose any danger to other road users. This normally involves a medical check-up by a doctor nominated by the Department of Transport. The high risk categories are those who have been convicted of either (a) two drinking and driving offences within 10 years, or (b) once refusing to supply a sample for analysis, or (c) having a blood (breath or urine) alcohol concentration which was two-and-a-half times the prescribed limit (see DVLC Publication INS 157, rev. 1/94). Shortly before the end of a driving ban, it is the Secretary of State's policy to send a reminder to those disqualified, informing them that they will soon be able to drive again and to remind them to apply for a new licence. If there is a prompt application, the Secretary of State will arrange for a high risk applicant to be seen by a doctor prior to the conclusion of his driving ban.

Sometimes, however, no reminder is sent to a disqualified driver who **20–41** may then naturally not apply for his licence back until a few days before the end of his disqualification. If that person is a high risk driver, he will be denied his licence until sometime after the end of his disqualification. If the Secretary of State forgets to give any advance notice of his intention not to grant automatically a licence until after a satisfactory medical report, so that a motorist does not apply in advance for his licence, the latter will discover that, although he has served his sentence, he still cannot drive until he has been given a clean bill of health by a Ministry of Transport doctor. Such a situation occurred in the case of *Richardson-Probert v. Ministry of Transport,* unreported, 1988, where the plaintiff accordingly sued for negligence. Rose J. struck out the proceedings on the grounds that they disclosed no cause of action. That case started life as an application for judicial review but, after she had obtained her licence, a Divisional Court (presided over by Russell L.J.) ordered her claim for damages to continue as if commenced by writ. This indicates that at least two judges had taken a contrary view from that of Rose J. about whether such an action would lie against the Secretary of State, and their opinion is supported by *R. v. Knowsley Metropolitan Borough Council, ex p. Maguire, The Independent,* June 19, 1992, where Schiemann J. accepted that a local authority could be held liable for negligently refusing a hackney carriage licence.

I. Confiscation

The Road Traffic Act 1991, s.36 extended the power of forfeiture to any **20–42** offence punishable with imprisonment under the Road Traffic Act 1988. This is more a theoretical, rather than a real, power, because in *R. v. Highbury Corner Magistrate, ex p. Di Matteo* [1991] 1 W.L.R. 1374 it was held that in deciding whether or not to make a confiscation order, a court had to take into account the value of the vehicle and the effect that such an order would have on the convicted motorist. The value of most cars is well beyond the amount of the normal tariff for such offences, so that the criteria laid down by the judiciary will rarely be met and it will, therefore, not be possible to make a confiscation order in the average drinking and driving case.

J. Imprisonment

20–43 In *R. v. Craig*, *The Times*, July 25, 1993, Turner J. said:

> "Courts could be expected to respond to justified public concern and to pass tougher sentences on drivers who drank and then caused death by reckless driving."

Nowadays, a conviction under section 3A and, when drink is a factor, under section 1 will invariably lead to a long sentence of imprisonment. In *Attorney-General's References No. 14 and 24 of 1993* [1994] R.T.R. 49, the Court of Appeal said since guidelines were laid down in *R. v. Boswell* the maximum sentence had doubled and that five years' imprisonment was the starting point for drivers who drove with reckless disregard for the safety of others after consuming alcohol. The Court also approved *R. v. Pettipher* [1991] R.T.R. 183, where it was held that an aggravating feature was the number of deaths. The reports are full of such cases where sentences (even after allowing for the principle of double jeopardy) have been increased by the Court of Appeal to four years (*R. v. Brown* [1995] Crim.L.R. 437), or even longer, as happened in *R. v. Vickers* (1995) 12 W.R.T.L.B. 33 (an increase to six years where the accused, who pleaded guilty, had driven on the pavement killing a pedestrian when his breath alcohol level was 115µg). The only exception was the very unusual circumstances of *R. v. Asquith* [1995] R.T.R. 51, where a man of good character was convicted of a causing death by careless driving with an alcohol level of nearly twice the permitted amount. He killed the father of a four-year-old son. He then acted *in loco parentis* to that infant. The Court of Appeal did not interfere with a sentence of community service because the child had found a "new father" and it would be unfair to deprive him of this second father figure.

20–44 The Court of Appeal held in *R. v. Jordan* [1994] T.L.R. 572 that the decisions on sentencing in cases of fatalities where the consumption of alcohol was a factor were not applicable where the defendant's driving was affected by drugs rather than drink. There the driver had pleaded "guilty" to causing death by dangerous driving and the court reduced a term of imprisonment from three years to two, because as a result of the consumption of amphetamines the driver had made a bad misjudgment but he had not followed a persistent course of bad driving.

20–45 Even where nobody has been killed, the Court of Appeal has upheld custodial sentences for drinking and driving offences in two circumstances: where the defendant had a bad record or where the imbibing was accompanied by bad driving. In *R. v. Nokes* [1978] R.T.R. 101, 103K, a custodial sentence was upheld where the motorist's antecedents were described as "show[ing] a disregard for the law relating to road traffic". In other cases such sentences were not disturbed on appeal where there was also a conviction for dangerous driving, *e.g. R. v. Jenkins, ibid.*, at 104. In *R. v. Newman, ibid.*, at 107, a man of good character had his sentence reduced to 28 days' imprisonment. He had collided with the back of a stationary car. With the abolition of the right to trial by jury, unless somebody was killed, the Court of Appeal only has the opportunity of pronouncing on the sentences passed on drunken motorists if, at the same time as they were committed to the Crown Court on matters triable on indictment, they were also sent to that court to be sentenced for road traffic offences. In view of the sentences they received for the indictable crimes, any appeal on the traffic matters would almost certainly have been of academic interest only, and therefore not brought. The Criminal Law Act 1977 also reduced the maximum sentence from two years to six months' imprisonment for contravening (what are now) sections 4, 5 and 7 of the Road Traffic Act. The maximum sentence naturally has to be kept for the worst cases, so that conduct which merited a short prison sentence when the maximum term was two years no longer attracts a custodial sentence when the maximum is only six months. The only reported decision since 1978 appears to be the appeal of *R. v. Cook* [1995] Crim.L.R. 966. There the defendant had been committed to the Crown Court under section 41 of the Criminal Justice Act 1988 for driving with excess alcohol. The Crown accepted a plea to careless driving and the section 5 offence. The facts were that while driving, he failed to correct his steering after turning right. His car continued to turn and collided with the offside door of a stationary car. The appellant and the driver of the other car were exchanging names when a police officer appeared. He was arrested and subsequently gave two specimens of breath, the lower of which gave a breath alcohol level of 140 microgrammes per 100 millilitres of breath. He had no previous convictions. He was sentenced to two months' imprisonment, disqualified from driving for four years and ordered to take a driving test.

His appeal against sentence was allowed. The court said:

> "The sentences were utterly inappropriate. It could never be appropriate to send a man to prison for this criminality, at the lower end of the scale. The appellant's car only just collided with the other vehicle and was going very slowly; minimal damage was caused. The sentence of imprisonment was quashed, and a fine of £500 substituted. The disqualification was reduced to two years. The order requiring him to take a driving test and a notice to the Secretary of State that he was suffering from alcoholism were set aside."

In *R. v. Shoult* [1996] R.T.R. 298, Lord Taylor C.J. said the decision in **20–46** *R. v. Cook* [1996] R.T.R. 304, was based on a misunderstanding of the amount of the alcohol involved. (The court evidently thought that the legal limit was 80, *i.e.* the blood level.) The Lord Chief Justice expressed his agreement with the Magistrates' Association that justices should consider imprisonment for those whose breath alcohol exceeded 100µg.

20–47   If a fine is not paid, the debtor may be committed to prison, the length of the period of incarceration depending on the outstanding balance. The maximum length is laid down in Schedule 4 to the Magistrates' Courts Act 1980, amended by the Criminal Justice Act of 1992, ss. 88 and 91.

Balance outstanding	*Maximum length of imprisonment*
Not exceeding £200	7 days
Over £200 but not exceeding £500	14 days
Over £500 but not exceeding £1,000	28 days
Over £1,000 but not exceeding £2,500	45 days
Over £2,500 but not exceeding £5,000	3 months
Over £5,000 but not exceeding £10,000	6 months
Over £10,000	12 months

K. Recommended penalties

20–48 Although the maximum duration of any particular driving ban or the quantum of any fine is at the discretion of the tribunal hearing the case, as a matter of practice it will tend to follow the recommendations made by the Magistrates' Association with such modifications as the local petty sessions has decided is appropriate for their area. These recommendations are as follows:

The legal limits are:
Breath: 35 micrograms per 100 millilitres.
Blood: 80 milligrams per 100 millilitres.
Urine: 107 milligrams per 100 millilitres.

Between 40 and 52 micrograms per 100 millilitres of breath the suggested fine is £480 and disqualification for 12 months. For amounts in excess of 52 micrograms (breath) or 120 milligrams (blood) or 160 milligrams (urine) then refer to the chart below and read off a datum or entry point for your deliberations.

For breath: Take the reading on the left-hand side of the chart and go to the diagonal line. Where the reading meets the diagonal, drop vertically to the base line and read off the associated fine and disqualification.

For blood: Above 120, go to the right of the diagonal, drop vertically and read off fine and disqualification. Below 210, go left and proceed as above.

For urine: Take the reading on the right-hand side of the chart and go left to the diagonal line. Where the reading meets the diagonal, drop vertically to the base line and read off fine and disqualification.

Important: This only provides a starting point. Always apply circumstances to increase or decrease fine or disqualification.

RECOMMENDED PENALTIES

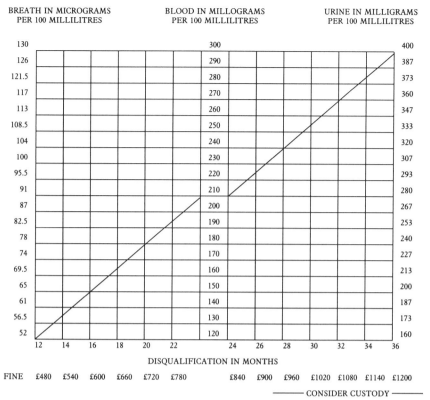

BREATH IN MICROGRAMS PER 100 MILLILITRES	BLOOD IN MILLOGRAMS PER 100 MILLILITRES	URINE IN MILLIGRAMS PER 100 MILLILITRES
130	300	400
126	290	387
121.5	280	373
117	270	360
113	260	347
108.5	250	333
104	240	320
100	230	307
95.5	220	293
91	210	280
87	200	267
82.5	190	253
78	180	240
74	170	227
69.5	160	213
65	150	200
61	140	187
56.5	130	173
52	120	160

DISQUALIFICATION IN MONTHS

12 14 16 18 20 22 24 26 28 30 32 34 36

FINE £480 £540 £600 £660 £720 £780 £840 £900 £960 £1020 £1080 £1140 £1200

———— CONSIDER CUSTODY ————

REFUSING BREATH, BLOOD OR URINE SPECIMENS (DRIVING ETC.)—£720 AND DISQUALIFY 18 MONTHS

Offence	Length of disqualification	Amount of Fine
In charge while unfit (s.4)	Note 1	£360
In charge with excess alcohol (s.5)	Note 1	£360
Refusing to give a sample for the screening device (s.9)	Note 1	£180
Refusing to give a sample for analysis having driven (s.7)	18 months	£720
Refusing to give a sample for analysis having been in charge (s.7)	Note 1	£360
Driving with excess alcohol (s.5)	[See Fig. 1, above]	

Note 1. Discretionary qualification. Therefore no recommendation is made.

The above guidelines were published in 1993. They are being reviewed and new ones will be issued in 1997.

In *Cracknell v. Willis* [1988] A.C. 450, 461, Lord Griffiths stated in effect that where a single breath specimen had been provided and analysed, the penalty under section 7(6) should be the same as if the accused had been

375

convicted of driving with the amount of alcohol in his single sample. If it is a high reading the defendant can always successfully object to the amount being given in evidence because there will have been no second calibration so that the printout will be inadmissible because of PACE, s.69 (see Chapter 15). Also without a second reading, one cannot tell if it is artificially high because of mouth alcohol. A large difference between the two readings would indicate the presence of that fluid.

L. Mitigation for guilty pleas

20–49   The "standard credit" given by the Crown Court for a guilty plea is usually (in the case of prison sentences) a reduction of one-third off the "normal tariff". In drinking and driving cases involving fatalities, about a year seems to be the credit given for not contesting the case. In *R. v. Hastings* [1995] T.L.R. 256, the Court of Appeal said that no discount needed be given to those who pleaded guilty and whose driving had been very dangerous and where there had been no realistic option open to them except to confess their guilt. The author's experience of summary road traffic trials is that no discount is given by justices for a guilty plea, and this was confirmed by a survey conducted among magistrates, the results of which were published in (1995) 12 W.R.T.L.B. 38. This showed that 75 per cent of justices did not give any discount for guilty pleas in drinking and driving cases.

M. Conclusions

20–50   Unlike most other crimes, a minimum sentence for certain drinking and driving offences has been laid down, namely mandatory disqualification for a year, although in certain special circumstances a court may mitigate that penalty. As to the maximum length of any particular driving ban, or the amount of any fine, that is at the discretion of the tribunal hearing the case, although, as a matter of practice, it will tend to follow the recommendations made by the Magistrates' Association with such modifications as the local justices have decided as appropriate for their area. A monetary penalty is invariably imposed and, where a serious accident occurs, then a custodial sentence is likely to be passed. In the case of a fatality the length of imprisonment will rarely be less than five years, even for a man of previous good character.

One promising hope for the future is that the new drinking and driving course for motorists seems to be achieving a good result. To quote from a very brief summary from the first report on rehabilitation courses run in 1993/94:

"The course aims to promote positive attitudes towards drink driving by increasing participants' knowledge about alcohol, its abuse and its effects. There were startling improvements in the participants' knowledge scores. On the alcohol knowledge scores, at the start of the courses only 32% scored 7 or more. 785 (79%) improved their scores in the end test and 11% scored the same, of these 75% had scores of 7 or more.

On the tests designed to explore attitudes towards alcohol, 85% improved their scores by the end of the course. By way of example, the number of offenders strongly disagreeing with the statement 'It's quite safe to drive after one or two drinks' rose from 12 to 43%. There was an even greater improvement in the number who strongly disagreed with the statement 'Driving when over the legal limit doesn't really increase your chances of having an accident, as long as you drive carefully', rising from 32% to 68%. The course, however, had very little effect on the average amounts of alcohol consumed amongst the participants. One quarter reported reducing their weekly consumption by up to 10 units, with a further 14% reporting a reduction of more than 10 units per week. It should be said, however, that 42% of the participants were still drinking in excess of the levels recommended by the Health Education Council." (Sweet and Maxwell's *Road Traffic Indicator*, June 1995.)

The Minister for Road Safety said that the figures showed only 0.2 per cent of those who attended the course to have re-offended, compared with 1.2 per cent of those who had not attended such a course.

Chapter 21

POLICE POWERS OF ARREST AND DAMAGES FOR THE AGGRIEVED MOTORIST

A. Introduction

Forcing a motorist to give a blood sample, or detaining him in a police **21–01** station until he provides a specimen would, without the intervention of statute, amount to the tort of trespass. Accordingly, the Road Traffic Act 1988 bestowed extra powers on the police. They are entitled to require a specimen for analysis at a hospital or at a police station (see Road Traffic Act, ss. 7(2) and (3)). Normally, the only way to get a motorist to go to the police station is to arrest him. However, should the police apprehend somebody in excess of their powers, then the court has a discretion under P.A.C.E., s.78, to refuse to admit in evidence anything that occurs thereafter (see Chapters 14 and 17). In addition, every unlawful incarceration gives rise to a potential claim for damages. This chapter considers what are the powers of the police to arrest a motorist whom they suspect of drinking and driving, and the redress that exists for those who have been wrongly apprehended.

B. Power of arrest

The power of arrest for drinking and driving offences has only been vested **21–02** in the police. There is no right of "a citizen's arrest," except in one case, namely for a contravention of the Road Traffic Act, s.3A. This is because the latter is a "serious arrestable offence" (see P.A.C.E. 1984, s.24(1)(b) and Sched. 5, pt. II). Accordingly, anybody may arrest any person whom he reasonably suspects to be guilty of such a crime, provided (except in the case of a constable) that such an offence has actually been perpetrated (*ibid.*, s.24[5]). A policeman need only have reasonable suspicion that one has been committed (*ibid.*, s.24[6]). In view of the *actus reus* such a distinction is academic.

Under the Road Traffic Act 1988, unless the person concerned is a **21–03** patient at a hospital, a constable has the authority to arrest anybody whom he reasonably suspects is or has been driving or attempting to drive, or is or has been in charge of, a motor (or, in the case of section 4, a mechanically propelled) vehicle on a road or other public place, if any one of the following three conditions is satisfied:

(1) that the arrested person was suspected of having been unfit to drive (see s.4(6)); or

(2) that the arrested person had given a positive breath test (see s.6(5)(a)); or

(3) that the arrested person, having been required to provide a breath specimen, had failed to blow sufficient breath into the breathalyser for a test to be carried out and there was reasonable cause to suspect him of still having alcohol in his body (see s.6(5)(b)).

Under the Transport and Works Act 1992, s.30, a constable may arrest a person whom he has reasonable cause to suspect is committing, or has committed, an offence under section 27(1) of the Act (unfit to carry out work), or whom he has reasonable cause to suspect has either (i) given a positive reading on a breath test carried out pursuant to section 29, or (ii) failed to take such a breath test and still has alcohol in his body.

Under P.A.C.E., ss. 25(1)(d)(i) and (iii) the police can arrest for any offence if they reasonably believe this to be necessary in order to prevent injury to the person or damage to property. As drivers who have been drinking are a danger to the public, it is submitted that, provided the arrested person would, but for his apprehension, have driven on a road or public place, a constable may arrest him for a summary offence under section 5 of the Road Traffic Act 1988, if it appeared that his driving ability was impaired.

The fact that the motorist has a reasonable excuse for failing to take a breath test is irrelevant, according to *R. v. Kelly* [1972] R.T.R. 447, where the defendant had undergone a tracheotomy. The Court of Appeal held that he had, accordingly, been lawfully arrested for failing to take a test, even though his failure was not an offence, as he had a reasonable excuse for what had occurred.

C. Suspicion

21-04 It should be noted that the suspicion need not be based upon the officer's personal knowledge but can be based on information received (see *R. v. Moore* [1970] R.T.R. 486), including an anonymous tip off (see *Topping v. Scott* [1981] Crim.L.R. 780).

In *R. v. Way* [1970] R.T.R. 348, it was held that the smell of alcohol on a motorist's breath did not amount to reasonable suspicion that he had committed an offence under section 4. In *Joiner v. DPP*, unreported, December 14, 1995, it was held to be reasonable to suspect a motorist of being unfit to drive, who, while being followed by a police car, accelerated and overtook another vehicle, turned into a side street and extinguished his car's lights, and who subsequently mounted the kerb and parked on the verge. He then alighted from the car and ran off, pursued by the police. The latter, on catching up with him, smelt alcohol on his breath and asked him what he was doing, to which he replied "Well, you've got to try, haven't you?"

D. Impossibility of a conviction

In *R. v. Moore* [1975] R.T.R. 285, two constables saw the appellant run off **21–05** from his car, so they approached the vehicle and removed its rotor arm, thus making it immobile. Subsequently he came back and entered his car, where he fell asleep. While in that state, the officers returned and arrested him for being in charge while unfit. The Court of Appeal held his apprehension to be lawful and rejected the suggestion that the police had no power to arrest him since they knew that he had the statutory defence of there being no possibility of him driving while unfit. (This was because of the missing rotor arm.) The court said that the police did not have to consider what possible defences a suspect might have before detaining him. It is submitted that this decision should no longer be regarded as correct in view of the later case of *Flange v. Chief Constable of South Humberside* [1992] T.L.R. 137, where a differently constituted Court of Appeal held it to be unreasonable, and therefore illegal, for somebody to be arrested if it was known at the time of his apprehension that there was no possibility of a charge being brought against the person who was being detained. By analogy, it is submitted that it would be unreasonable for a constable to arrest somebody whom he knew must be acquitted of the offence for which he was being apprehended. This submission is in accordance with the House of Lords' decision in *Mohammed-Holgate v. Duke* [1984] A.C. 437, 443B, where it was held that a police officer must exercise his powers of arrest in accordance with the *Wednesbury* principles of reasonableness (see [1948] 1 K.B. 223). It is surely unreasonable to arrest a man known to have committed no offence.

E. Powers of entry

I. EXPRESS STATUTORY POWERS

Even if the local constabulary are entitled to apprehend a motorist, their **21–06** powers of entry on to private property to make such an arrest are limited. They may always go on to private property without permission to make an arrest for an offence under either section 3A (because it is an arrestable offence; see PACE, s.17[1][b]) or section 4 of the Road Traffic Act 1988, which expressly incorporates a power of entry in subsection (7). Also, if the motorist is a trespasser, then the police can follow him on to the land (see *R. v. Burdekin* [1976] R.T.R. 27). The only other time the police can enter uninvited on to private property where the motorist is lawfully present, in order to apprehend him, is if he has either (a) failed to take a breath test and is suspected of having alcohol in his body or (b), having taken such a test, he has given a positive result and (i) there has been an accident arising out of the use of a motor vehicle on a road or other public place and (ii) the arresting officer reasonably believes that the person whom he wishes to detain had been involved in the accident and (iii) the arresting officer also reasonably suspects that the accident had involved personal injury being caused to somebody, other than the person to be arrested (see Road Traffic Act, s.6[6]). Also, under the Transport and Works Act, s.30(4)(b) a constable has similar powers to go on to land without the authority of the occupier in order to effect an arrest of a person who works on a transport system as a driver, guard, conductor, signalman or in any other capacity in which he can effect the movement of a vehicle or who works in a maintenance capacity or as a supervisor of, or look-out for, persons working in a maintenance capacity and who, pursuant to section 29, has provided a positive test on the breathalyser or has failed to take the test and the constable suspects him of still having alcohol in his body, where there has been an accident which the arresting officer reasonably suspects has caused death or injury to a person other than the one arrested.

II. IMPLIED LICENCE TO ENTER

21–07 The police, like anybody else, are deemed to have permission to enter the land or gardens of somebody else. This licence is implied even in the case of policemen whose sole purpose is to effect an arrest of the lawful occupier (see *Pamplin v. Fraser* [1981] R.T.R. 494). It does not, however, extend to entering the actual dwelling-house without an express invitation (see *Fox v. Chief Constable of Gwent* [1986] A.C. 281). (For a further discourse on the implied powers of entry by the local constabulary and their revocation, the reader is referred to Chapter 10.)

F. Recapturing an arrested person who is unlawfully at large

21–08 Once a person has been legally arrested, if he then escapes, he will be unlawfully at large and therefore can be pursued on to private property, including into his own house, and recaptured therein. This power to enter private property, uninvited, is contained in section 17(1)(d) of the Police and Criminal Evidence Act 1984 but is limited to cases of hot pursuit (see *D'Souza v. DPP* [1992] 1 W.L.R. 1073).

G. Common law

21–09 P.A.C.E., s.17(5) abolished all common law powers of entry without warrant, save to prevent a breach of the peace.

H. What constitutes an arrest and its formalities

I. PHYSICAL APPREHENSION OR SUBMISSION

In *Spicer v. Holt* [1977] A.C. 987, 999G, Viscount Dilhorne quoted with **21–10** approval the definition in *Halsbury's Laws of England* (4th ed., Vol. 11, para. 99):

> "Arrest consists in the seizure or touching of a person's body with a view to his restraint; words may, however, amount to an arrest if, in the circumstances of the case, they are calculated to bring, and do bring, to a person's notice that he is under compulsion and he thereafter submits to the compulsion.
>
> Whether or not a person has been arrested depends not on the legality of the arrest but on whether he has been deprived of his liberty to go where he pleases."

Thus for an arrest there must be either an act of submission by the arrested person or a touching of the man or woman to be detained by the police officer making the arrest. This is well illustrated by *Nichols v. Bulman* [1985] R.T.R. 236. The defendant opened his front door but remained inside the house. He was asked to take a breath test but refused. A constable then told him that he was under arrest, so the latter tried to close the door but was prevented by the officer. A scuffle took place with the accused being overpowered inside the premises. It was held that there was no lawful arrest as the police could not effect an arrest merely by words which were not accepted and they, therefore, had no power to step inside the house (see Chapter 10). The decision was followed in *R. v. McMillan*, unreported, July 9, 1986, where Judge A.A. Edmondson directed an acquittal on an assault charge. The prisoner at the Bar had been pursued into the car park of the public house where he lived with his wife, who was the innkeeper. (It was then closing time.) He provided a positive breath test. The constable told him that he was under arrest, so he ran into his residence and was followed inside by the constable. He then attempted to eject the officer with physical force. The judge held that mere words, without any submission thereto, could not amount to an arrest. Therefore the police had no right to enter private property and the lawful occupier was entitled, as he did, to use no more force than was necessary to expel a trespasser.

II. INFORMATION TO BE GIVEN ON ARREST BY THE POLICE

In addition, for an arrest to be lawful, it must comply with P.A.C.E., s.28, **21–11** *i.e.* the police must both inform a detained person that he has been arrested and give him details of the offence for which he had been apprehended even if those facts are obvious. The details must include the date, time and venue of the offence (see *Murphy v. Oxford*, unreported, February 15, 1985). This information must be supplied at the time of the arrest or as soon thereafter as is practical. In *Nicholas v. Parsonage* [1987] R.T.R. 199, it was held that the words "at the time of the arrest" did not just mean simultaneously with the actual apprehension (*i.e.* the touching or the submission to the words of arrest) but also encompassed a reasonable period both before and after that. In *Wheatley v. Lodge* [1971] 1 W.L.R. 29, it was held to be sufficient if the arresting officer did all that he reasonably could to impart the relevant information, even though the detained person did not hear or understand it, *e.g.* he was deaf or did not speak English.

One particular problem which arises for the police is whether a person should be arrested for failing to take a breath test or for having given a positive one. In *R. v. Holah* [1973] 1 W.L.R. 127, it was held that the driver of a Rolls Royce had been unlawfully arrested when he was told that the grounds for his apprehension were that he had failed to give a breath sample. He had blown into the breathalyser for less than the requisite 10 seconds but had drunk so much that he had in fact given a positive reading. The Court of Appeal held that, as he had given a positive reading, he had not failed to give a satisfactory breath specimen and should have been arrested for providing a positive one. That decision was approved by a three to two majority in the House of Lords' case of *Walker v. Lovell* [1975] W.L.R. 1141. In *Woon v. Maskell* [1985] R.T.R. 289, it was held that the officer was entitled to make an arrest for giving a positive sample as soon as the red (over the limit) light appeared on the Alcometer, instead of having to keep the "read" switch depressed and waiting the full 40 seconds specified by the manufacturers. If a motorist on the first attempt fails to provide sufficient breath for a test to be carried out, he can always be requested to blow again into the instrument (see *Price v. Davies* [1979] R.T.R. 204); and if he gives a positive reading on a subsequent test, he must be arrested under subsection 6(5)(a) and not under subsection 6(5)(b) for having failed to take a test.

III. CHALLENGING THE LAWFULNESS OF AN ARREST

21-12 If the validity of an arrest is challenged in court, the police can only justify their actions upon the grounds which they had communicated to the detained person at the time of this apprehension (see *Christie v. Leachinsky* [1947] A.C. 572). They cannot rely upon their suspicions in relation to any other matters, save those communicated to him at the time he was detained. A good example of this principle is *R. v. Holah* (see section 21–11, above), where the arrest was held to be unlawful. The appellant had been told that the grounds for his apprehension were that he had failed to provide a breath sample, whereas he should have been arrested for giving a positive test.

I. Duration of the detention

I. GENERALLY

Once arrested, a person can, of course, be taken to a police station and **21–13** requested to supply a specimen for analysis. This requirement must, it is submitted, be made as soon as is practicable after the arrival at the station. The driver can be kept there until he has provided, or has failed to give, a sample after being requested so to do (whichever is the sooner.) Thereafter the police can only detain him for so long as there is any likelihood of him actually driving a mechanically propelled vehicle while he is either unfit to do so or while his alcohol level is in excess of the statutory limit (see Road Traffic Act 1988, s.10(1) as amended by Road Traffic Act 1991, Sched. and *Bourlet v. Porter* [1973] R.T.R. 293, 308 F–I, *per* Viscount Dilhorne). However, under section 10(2), a person must be released even though he is still either unfit to drive or over the prescribed limit, if it appears that there is no likelihood of him driving or attempting to drive while in that condition.

If the police consider that a motorist's ability to drive is or may be impaired through drugs, then a doctor must be consulted before a decision is taken as to whether or not that person should be detained or released in accordance with section 10(3). This is subject to PACE, s.38(1) (see section 21–14 below).

II. BAIL OR CUSTODY

It is submitted that as statute has expressly defined the power of detention **21–14** of persons who have been requested to supply specimens, the police are limited to those powers and have no other right to keep such people in custody (*expressio unius est exclusio alterius*). Thus, when section 10(1) no longer applies, the police must release the motorist by virtue of PACE, s.34(5)(b). If the police are contemplating bringing charges against him or further inquiries are necessary relating to drinking and driving, then his release can be made subject to conditions of bail, *i.e.* that he attends at a police station, at a time appointed by the custody officer (*ibid.*, subsection 47(3)). If the police had sufficient evidence to charge him (*e.g.* when he had failed to give a specimen) and they do so, then they can bail him to appear at a fixed date in court and are entitled to withhold bail if one of the conditions set out in section 38(1) of the 1984 Act applies, *i.e.* reasonable belief that he will not turn up in court, detention is necessary to prevent interference with the administration of justice, necessary to prevent injury to anybody or damage to property or the arrested person's name and/or address has not been sufficiently ascertained.

III. THE ARRESTED PERSON'S VEHICLE

In *Liepins v. Sperman* [1986] R.T.R. 24, it was held that if a driver was **21–15** arrested, the police were under a duty to insure that his vehicle and other road users were safeguarded and this included the power to remove the vehicle to a police station. In *Stunt v. Bolton* [1972] R.T.R. 435 it was held that in such circumstances the driver was under a duty to hand over his car keys.

J. Damages

I. GENERALLY

21–16 If the police exceed their statutory powers and a motorist is wrongly detained, he can sue the chief constable of the relevant force for the tort of false imprisonment. An example of this happened in about 1990 to one of the author's clients. A motorist satisfactorily provided two samples of breath which, on being analysed by the Lion Intoximeter, showed him to be well above the legal limit. A taxi then arrived to take his wife to their house. The husband told the police to keep his car and its keys and that he would go home in the cab with his spouse. The custody officer refused to allow him to leave the station and continued to detain him for about three hours until his alcohol level was below the prescribed limit. In an out-of-court settlement of the subsequent false imprisonment action, the Hampshire Constabulary paid him £3,000 and his reasonable costs. (As for the offence of driving over the prescribed limit, the motorist received a two-year driving disqualification, which was reduced on appeal to 15 months.)

II. BURDEN OF PROOF

21–17 If a plaintiff alleges trespass, he must prove the *actus reus* but if he succeeds, the onus on justifying it is on the defendant. In a malicious prosecution action the burden of establishing that tort remains solely on the plaintiff.

K. Quantum

21–18 In a false imprisonment action, a jury must award a person sufficient damages to compensate him for his loss of liberty and the fact that he may have contributed to such loss of liberty is irrelevant in assessing his compensatory damages (see *Holden v. Chief Constable of Lancashire* [1987] Q.B. 380). If as a result of an illegal arrest, a motorist was breathalysed and lost his licence because of the result of the analysis, he would be entitled to recover damages for the loss of his licence, including any loss of earnings directly flowing from his inability to drive. In addition, a jury can always award extra damages to act as a deterrent to try to prevent the police from committing such a tort in the future and or to mark their disapproval of the conduct of the local constabulary (see *Holden's case*, above).

L. Trial by jury

If the police are sued, and if the writ includes a claim for false imprison- **21–19** ment or malicious prosecution, such an averment will automatically entitle a plaintiff to a trial by jury (see sections 69(1)(b) of the Supreme Court Act 1981 and 66(3)(b) of the County Courts Act 1984). The latter will always be far more generous than the judiciary. An example of this is the case of *Reynolds v. Commissioner of Police for the Metropolis* [1982] Crim.L.R. 600, where the female plaintiff had been falsely imprisoned for nearly a day. The jury awarded £12,000. A wrongful requirement by the police for a blood sample while a person was illegally detained will probably be considered by a jury to be an aggravating feature which might lead to them awarding a few thousand pounds more as damages. Similar sums of money are likely to be recovered in malicious prosecution actions, *i.e.* where it is not a case of a genuine mistake of law but where the police have come to court and told lies. With juries there is no certainty. There is always the distinct possibility that they might award a very modest sum if they disapproved of the plaintiff's driving, *e.g.* his alcohol level had been well over the prescribed limit or he had injured somebody. Nowadays, the Court of Appeal has wide powers to interfere with a jury's verdict and can substitute its own award instead of ordering a retrial by another jury. In libel actions it has laid down guidelines that juries should follow. So far there has been only one reported case of the Court of Appeal making an award itself rather than ordering a retrial of a false imprisonment action, namely *Cumber v. Chief Constable of Humberside* [1995] L.S.Gaz. 39. The Court awarded a 16-year-old girl of good character £350 for just under four-and-a-half hours' unlawful incarceration. On her release she had appeared frightened, tearful and distressed. This case illustrates the grounds put forward by the appellant's counsel in *Holden's Case*, above, for not agreeing to the Court of Appeal assessing the damages: "A jury would be far more generous than your Lordships." A good example of this is an unreported case in which the author appeared at St. George's Hall, Liverpool in 1982. A jury awarded the plaintiff £6,500 for about half-an-hour's false imprisonment and an illegal search of his house while so incarcerated. The Family Division judge who tried it would have awarded £1,000 while the local circuit judges decided over lunch that the correct amount was £3,500. Nowadays, police forces are more cost-conscious, so most police forces are likely to make reasonable offers to settle out of court, especially if the matter is in the hands of their insurers. Others will almost certainly defend every case as a matter of principle.

Chapter 22

APPEALS AND JUDICIAL REVIEW

A. Appeals to the Crown Court

I. RIGHT OF APPEAL

Nowadays, motorists charged with any drinking and driving offence (other **22–01** than one under section 3A of the Road Traffic Act 1988), can no longer be tried by jury, but must be tried summarily. Under section 108 of the Magistrates' Courts Act 1980, an appeal lies of right by a defendant from petty sessions to the Crown Court against both conviction and sentence and is by way of rehearing. A motorist wishing to appeal must, within 21 days of the date of his sentence, give notice to the clerk to the justices at the court where he was convicted and to the Director of Public Prosecutions; (see rule 7(2) of the Crown Court Rules 1982). The Crown Court can always, if it wishes, extend the time for serving the notice of appeal (see rule 7(5)).

II. POWERS EXERCISABLE ON HEARING AN APPEAL

By virtue of section 48(2) of the Supreme Court Act 1981, the Crown Court **22–02** can make any order which a magistrates' court could have made or can remit the case to the latter with their opinion. However, it cannot allow an amendment to the information (see *Garfield v. Maddocks* [1974] Q.B. 7). It can always apply the provisions of section 123 of the Magistrates' Courts Act 1980, which allows it to convict notwithstanding any difference between the evidence and the facts alleged in the information. However, despite its wide words, section 123 is not a cure-all for every defect, *e.g.* duplicity (see *Griffiths v. Freeman* [1970] 1 W.L.R. 659) nor does it allow a conviction for a different legal offence from that specified in the information, see *Garfield v. Maddocks*. The question of costs is considered in Chapter 23.

B. Appeals to the High Court

I. RIGHT OF APPEAL

There is a right of appeal by both the prosecution and the defence by way **22–03** of "case stated" from either a magistrates' court or the Crown Court to the High Court, but only on a point of law. The time limit in both cases is 21 days but in the case of an appeal from the magistrates, no extension of time can be granted (see Magistrates' Courts Act 1980, s.111(2) and rule 26 of the Crown Court Rules). If either a magistrates' court or the Crown Court refuse to state a case, they can be ordered to do so by the High Court (see section 111(6) of the Magistrates' Courts Act 1980 and section 29 of the Supreme Court Act 1981). Provided no further evidence could have been called on the point, the High Court will allow a point of law to be taken which was not raised in the lower court; see *Hoyle v. Walsh* [1969] 2 Q.B. 13, 20D.

II. POWERS EXERCISABLE ON HEARING AN APPEAL

22-04 The High Court can uphold or reverse the decision of the lower court or remit the case to the court appealed from with its opinion (see sections 6 and 10 of the Summary Jurisdiction Act 1857, as amended by the Magistrates' Courts Act 1980). In *Griffith v. Jenkins* [1992] 2 A.C. 76 the House of Lords held that, if on a case stated, the High Court finds that there was an error of law by the lower court, it can order a retrial by a differently constituted Bench. Whether such an order is made is entirely up to the appeal court and the House of Lords has declined to lay down any hard and fast rules on how that discretion should be exercised. It is submitted that the power to order a retrial should only be used, if at all, where there was sufficient evidence at the first trial to have obtained a conviction (including testimony which had erroneously been ruled inadmissible). According to Pill L.J. in *R. v. Faversham and Sittingbourne JJ, ex p. Stickings et al., The Times*, May 9, 1996, it should not be assumed that a Divisional Court would always order a retrial on the basis of an error by the lower court on the admissibility of evidence. By analogy it is submitted that such should never be ordered where the prosecution could only succeed by having to call witnesses additional to those who attended the first hearing. This submission is based on the analogy with the rule that once the defence have called their evidence, no further witnesses for the prosecution are normally allowed to testify (see Chapter 14). It is also submitted that where a motorist had been disqualified for some time before the finding of guilt was set aside, it would be wrong to order a retrial if on a fresh conviction there had to be a compulsory driving ban, as any time spent disqualified before the successful appeal would not count towards any new sentence. Nor could the mandatory penalty be mitigated by the justices: see *R. v. Kwame* [1975] R.T.R 106. This is because such can only be done where there are special reasons and the latter can only refer to why the offence was committed in the first place.

C. Appeals to the Court of Appeal

I. RIGHT OF APPEAL

22-05 Under the Criminal Appeal Act 1968, a person convicted on indictment can appeal to the Court of Appeal (Criminal Division) against both conviction and sentence, by the amended section 1(2), leave is needed either from the trial judge or the appeal court. Under section 36 of the Criminal Justice Act 1988, the Attorney-General may, with leave of the appeal court, appeal against sentence on the grounds that it was unduly lenient. (Many such cases have concerned drunken motorists who have been involved in fatal accidents.) In addition, he may, under section 36 of the Criminal Justice Act 1972, refer to the Court of Appeal, for their opinion, a point of law which arose in a case where the accused has been acquitted.

II. POWERS EXERCISABLE BY THE COURT

(a) APPEAL BY THE ACCUSED

As well as upholding or quashing a verdict, the court can substitute a **22–06** conviction on a lesser charge, if it was open to the jury to have found the defendant guilty of that offence. If the court sets aside a conviction, it has an unfettered power to order a retrial (see section 43 of the Criminal Justice Act 1988). On the dismissal of an application for leave or of an appeal by a convicted person, the court may always order that any time spent in custody pending the hearing of the application or the appeal shall not count towards the sentence. This will be done where the application or appeal is regarded as devoid of merit (see Practice Note [1980] 1 All E.R. 555).

(b) APPEALS AND REFERENCES BY THE ATTORNEY-GENERAL

On an appeal by the Attorney-General under section 36 of the Criminal **22–07** Justice Act 1988, the Court of Appeal may impose such sentence as the lower court had jurisdiction to pass. However, irrespective of the outcome of a reference under section 36 of the 1972 Act, the court has no power to order a conviction but will merely set a precedent for future similar cases.

D. Appeals to the House of Lords

I. RIGHT OF APPEAL

An appeal lies to the House of Lords by either party from both the High **22–08** Court and Court of Appeal but only if the court appealed from certifies that the case raises "a point of law of general public importance" and they or the House of Lords grant leave to appeal (see section 1 of the Administration of Justice Act 1960 and section 33 of the Criminal Appeal Act 1968). The application for leave and a certificate must be made to the High Court or the Court of Appeal, as appropriate, within 14 days of its judgment beginning with the date of the decision. If a certificate is granted but leave is refused, an application for leave can be made to the House of Lords within 14 days beginning with the date of the refusal. These time limits can only be extended on an application made by the defence (*ibid.*, section 2 and section 34, respectively). Unless the House orders otherwise, once leave has been granted, a petition of appeal should be lodged within a month.

II. THE POWERS OF THE HOUSE OF LORDS

22-09 The House of Lords has the same powers as the court from which the appeal is brought and can also remit the case thereto (*ibid.*, section 1(4) and section 35(3), respectively).

E. Appeals against conviction by those who pleaded guilty

22-10 A convicted motorist cannot normally appeal against his conviction, if he had pleaded guilty to the charge. There are a few exceptions (see below). Since the amendments made by the Criminal Appeal Act 1995 to section 142 of the Magistrates' Courts Act 1980 which came into force in January 1996, petty session now has power to set aside any finding of guilt whenever it is in the interest of justice to do so. This is now an ideal way to have removed from a licence an indorsement for a drinking and driving offence to which a driver had admitted his guilt in ignorance of the fact that his specimen had not been required in accordance with the correct procedure and that that he could therefore never have been convicted, as a matter of law, in the first place.

I. THE CROWN COURT

22-11 The Crown Court can quash a conviction and order a retrial before the justices if the plea had been equivocal, *i.e.* the appellant or indeed the prosecutor had said something before sentence which cast doubt on his original plea: see *Ankrah v. DPP*, unreported, February 20, 1995, and *R. v. Crown Court at Huntingdon, ex p. Jordan* [1981] Q.B. 857. A person who pleaded guilty can also appeal against conviction if he wishes to raise a plea in bar (see *Cooper v. New Forest District Council* [1992] Crim.L.R. 877).

II. THE HIGH COURT

22-12 The High Court can only hear an appeal on the facts set out in the case stated. Therefore the only remedy for a person who wrongly pleaded guilty is judicial review (see below).

III. THE COURT OF APPEAL

The Court of Appeal will quash a conviction whenever the verdict was **22–13** unsafe, see the Criminal Appeal Act 1995, s.2. By analogy with the previous practice, this will normally arise in five circumstances: first, where the plea was equivocal; secondly, where on the prosecution evidence the accused could never have been convicted; thirdly, where new evidence comes to light which (usually) was not available at the trial and which casts doubt on the conviction; fourthly, where a guilty plea was entered only after an erroneous ruling on the law by the trial judge; and fifthly, error on the face of the record (*e.g.* duplicity, no offence known to law, etc.).

F. The advantages and disadvantages of appealing directly to the High Court rather than the Crown Court

Once a request for a case stated has been made, it is no longer possible to **22–14** appeal against conviction to the Crown Court, even if the proceedings in the High Court are not pursued and no case is ever lodged in the Crown Office (see *R. v. Winchester Crown Court, ex p. Lewington* [1982] 1 W.L.R. 1277). Indeed, in *R. v. Surrey Justices, ex p. Curl*, unreported, March 8, 1992, the High Court was inclined to the view that the mere request for a case stated extinguished all right of appeal against conviction to the Crown Court, even if the magistrates refused to state a case and their decision was upheld by the High Court. Therefore, unless a motorist can be certain that the magistrates have made no adverse finding of fact, he must seriously consider whether it would be more advantageous for him to try to obtain a more favourable finding of fact from the Crown Court, before going on to the High Court. If, on the other hand, the prosecution could, on a rehearing, easily "plug the gaps" in their case that became apparent in the lower court, then it would be best for an appellant to go straight from petty sessions to the Queen's Bench Division.

One problem with requesting a case stated is that the accused may get a **22–15** shock when he receives it and sees what it has set out as findings of fact or what it states had happened in court. It is submitted that as soon as something occurs in the trial which the accused thinks may afford an appeal to the High Court, he should ask the clerk to make a contemporaneous note of the Bench's legal ruling and of anything which might be significant, *e.g.* a specific answer given by a witness. If this is not done, the contents of the case stated could come as a complete surprise when first read. An example of this occurred in the case of *R. v. Surrey Justices, ex p. Curl* above. This was an application to compel the justice to state a case in which affidavits were filed by the Bench, their clerk, the prosecution and defence, and, where the justices' recollection of what was said in court bore little relation to the accounts given by their clerk, the prosecutrix or by the clerk of the defendant's solicitor. If the court is reluctant to put anything in writing, it will be necessary for the defence advocate to make his own note and to ask the Bench or the clerk to confirm that an accurate record has been made. It should also be requested that a copy of the note be appended to the court file. On another occasion, the case stated might be completely silent on a basic point. If this occurs, the High Court can always order the case to be sent back to the magistrates for them to set out further facts which they have found. Such an application should be made promptly, otherwise it is likely to be refused on the grounds that it would by then be too late to expect the Bench to remember the matter. That was the reason why the prosecution's request for the justices to find further facts was refused in the case of *Young v. Flint* [1987] R.T.R. 300.

Another and, in some cases, by no means insignificant advantage of appealing direct to the High Court is that the latter cannot increase the penalty, while the Crown Court has such a power which it can exercise even when the appeal was only against conviction (see section 48(4) of the Supreme Court Act 1981.) If a sentence appears on the lenient side, then any appeal should go straight to the High Court.

G. Judical review

I. GENERALLY

22–16 Judicial review will lie against inferior courts and the Crown Court, except in relation to the latter's jurisdiction over trials on indictment. (An extended meaning has been given to those last six words by the judiciary; see *R. v. Manchester Crown Court, ex p. DPP, The Independent*, July 2, 1992). In *R. v. Morpeth Ward Justices, ex p. Ward* [1992] Crim.L.R. 497, it was held that the appropriate route to the Divisional Court from the magistrates' court was by way of case stated. That was the route prescribed by Parliament and judicial review of justices' decisions should be sought only when it was for some reason inapposite or clearly inappropriate to proceed by way of the case stated. In the words of Lord Templeman in *R. v. Inland Revenue Commissioners ex p. Preston* [1985] A.C. 835, 862C:

> "Judicial review is available where a decision-making authority exceeds its powers, commits an error of law, commits a breach of natural justice, reaches a decision which no reasonable tribunal could have reached, or abuses its powers. Judicial review should not be granted where an alternative remedy is available."

In *R. v. Bristol JJ., ex p. Rowles* [1994] R.T.R. 40, it was held that a breach of natural justice entitled a litigant to obtain judicial review of the decision, even though he had an alternative remedy, in that case an appeal; the reasons being that he was entitled to a fair hearing, both in the lower of the Court as well as an appeal. The opposite view was taken in *R. v. Peterborough JJ., ex p. Dowler*, [1996] T.L.R. 331. It is submitted that *ex p.*

Rowles is preferable and a litigant should be entitled to a fair trial at first instance and not just on an appeal.

II. NO CONVICTION IN LAW WAS POSSIBLE ON THE FACTS

In the past the High Court was prepared to quash a conviction where, on 22–17 the prosecution's own evidence, the person could never in law have been convicted, at any rate if there was some fault on the prosecution, *e.g.* withholding evidence or other relevant information from the defence, through mere inadvertence or otherwise. In *R. v. Bolton JJ., ex p. Scally* [1991] Q.B. 537, the defendant had pleaded guilty to driving with excess alcohol in her blood. It was later discovered that the police surgeon had used an alcohol-impregnated swab to disinfect her skin prior to veinapuncture. This may have caused extra alcohol to contaminate the blood sample. In quashing the conviction, Watkins D.C.J. stated (at 256):

> "What happened here was that, there being no dishonesty, the prosecutor (a combination of the police and the Crown Prosecution Service) corrupted the process leading to a conviction in a manner which was unfair, for it gave the defendants no proper opportunity to decide whether to plead guilty or not guilty; indeed it wrongly denied them a complete defence to the charge. In my view, that conduct was analogous to fraud, collusion or perjury if ever there was."

This applies irrespective of why the plea of guilty was entered, whether through negligent advice from a solicitor or otherwise. In *R. v. Kingston-upon-Thames JJ., ex p. Kganna* [1986] R.T.R. 364, both the defence and prosecuting solicitors failed to realise that the Intoximeter had malfunctioned. The conviction was quashed because the police had misled the motorist because they had told his solicitor that the Intoximeter had been working correctly. (It had in fact incorrectly calibrated itself at 38μg.) However, a divergence of judicial opinion arose in two cases heard within a fortnight of each other over whether the High Court could grant certiorari where no complaint is made against the justices and no impropriety is alleged against the prosecution; see *R. v. Cheshire JJ., ex p. Sinnott* [1995] R.T.R. 281 and *R. v. Burton-upon-Trent JJ., ex p. Woolley, ibid.*, at 139. The latter decision was approved and followed in *R. v. Penrith JJ., ex p.* Marks [1996] R.T.R. 207. In view of the amendments to section 142 of the Magistrates' Act (see section 22–10) it is now of academic interest when such a writ (as it used to be) will lie. Indeed, now there is an alternative remedy, a prerogative order would be refused on those grounds alone: see *ex p. Preston*, above.

III. QUASHING AN ACQUITTAL

In *R. v. Hendon Justices, ex p. DPP* [1992] T.L.R. 349, Mann L.J. held that 22–18 the old rule was no longer appropriate and nowadays certiorari would lie to quash an acquittal. That decision is in line with *Griffith v. Jenkins* [1992]

A.C. 76, where the House of Lords overruled previous authority and held that, if a conviction was quashed on the hearing of a case stated, there was nothing to prevent a retrial being ordered.

IV. DISCRETION

22-19 Judicial review is a discretionary remedy and a prerogative order can always be refused even though an applicant may have "proved his case". Previously it was thought that any discretion would not be exercised against the defendant in a criminal matter: see *R. v. Jeffrey Noel, ex p. Perry* [1992] T.L.R. 70, *per* Mann L.J. That is clearly no longer so. In *Shaw v. DPP* [1993] R.T.R. 45, a three-judge court held that, even if the applicants had been convicted on duplicitous informations, the applications would have been refused on the grounds that they were all outside the three months' time limit prescribed by R.S.C. Order 53, r.4(1). (In appropriate cases time will not be a bar to obtaining relief, *e.g. Re Sampson* [1987] 1 W.L.R. 194, where the House of Lords granted leave to appeal nearly four years out of time because a subsequent decision had cast grave doubts on the original decision in the Crown Court.) In *ex p. Woolley*, above (where the application was made timorously) Beldam L.J. and Buxton J. both said that even if they had jurisdiction and if the wrong procedure had been used to take the driver's blood specimen, they would, at their discretion, still not have quashed the conviction.

H. Power to suspend a disqualification pending appeal or judicial review

22-20 A notice of appeal does not *ipso facto* suspend a driving disqualification: see *Taylor v. Metropolitan Police Commissioner, The Times,* November 3, 1986. An appellant must apply for such an order. Under section 39(1) of the Road Traffic Offenders Act 1988 any court which imposes a sentence of disqualification from driving can suspend it pending appeal. Also, where a person has appealed to the Crown Court, that court can grant a stay and, likewise, the Court of Appeal, where there is an appeal to it or an application for leave to do so (section 40[2]). The High Court has a similar power where a motorist has applied to a magistrates' or a Crown Court for a case stated (section 40[4]). The High Court will exercise this power before the case is stated or when the justices have refused to state a case and the motorist is applying for an order of mandamus to compel them to do so. (The author has never known the High Court to refuse a suspension where the court below has agreed to state a case: see *ex p. Smith*, below.) Both the High Court and the Court of Appeal (depending on which court is appealed against) have similar powers when a motorist has appealed to the House of Lords or has applied for leave to do so (section 40[3]). Also, the High Court can suspend a disqualification pending the hearing of the motion where an application is made for leave to move for certiorari to quash the proceedings in which the order for disqualification was made (section 40[5]). A similar power is contained in R.S.C. Order 53, r.3(10)(a). Thus in *R. v. St Albans Crown Court, ex p. Smith*, unreported, December 20, 1995, the applicant had been convicted of driving with excess alcohol and had appealed to the Crown Court (the grounds being the "slow clock defence": see section 15–10, above). That court, as well as petty sessions, had refused to suspend the sentence of disqualification, so the applicant sought judicial review of that refusal by the Crown Court. Popplewell J. granted leave to move, suspended the disqualification and ordered the substantive motion not to be listed until after the hearing of the Crown Court appeal.

A court which does make an order of suspension must inform the **22–21** Secretary of State thereof (sections 39[1] and 40[7]). There have been out of court settlements of threatened negligence actions where such information has not been passed on to the Secretary of State and a motorist has been arrested for driving while disqualified because the police national computer (which obtains its information automatically from DVLC, Swansea) still showed him as not being entitled to drive.

By section 43 of the Road Traffic Offenders Act, any time during which either an offender was not disqualified pending appeal, or his disqualification was suspended, does not count towards the length of his sentence.

Chapter 23

COSTS

A. Legal aid

I. INTRODUCTION

Unfortunately, like any other labour-intensive industry, employing a **23–01** lawyer can involve a litigant in considerable expense. Since 1949 Britain has had a legal aid system whereby the state will pay for the costs of impecunious litigants and, in view of decisions by the European Court of Human Rights, it is in practice no longer feasible for Parliament to contemplate abolishing it at least in criminal cases.

II. THE AUTHORITIES WITH POWER TO GRANT LEGAL AID

Initially the decision as to whether or not financial assistance should be **23–02** given in any particular prosecution lies with the magistrates' court. If the defendant is committed to the Crown Court or appeals thereto, that later court can also grant a criminal legal aid order. The Court of Appeal has a similar power for appeals and must exercise it as if it were a first instance trial court. For appeals to the High Court and for proceedings therefrom to the House of Lords, the Legal Aid Board can grant a civil legal aid certificate. In the case of appeals or applications to the House of Lords from decisions of the Court of Appeal, the power to grant legal aid is vested in the latter court.

III. FINANCIAL ELIGIBILITY AND THE COST TO THE LITIGANT

The government has regulated the financial eligibility which will entitle a **23–03** person to receive a contribution from the general body of taxpayers towards his legal costs. This has been done by Schedule 4 to the Legal Aid in Criminal and Care Proceedings (General) Regulations 1989 (S.I. 1989 No. 343), which is amended periodically, normally each April. Legal aid can be refused where it appears that the contribution under the Regulations would exceed the amount of legal fees likely to be incurred. If it subsequently transpires that the contribution exceeded the amount of the legal costs, then the surplus must be returned to the defendant (*ibid.*, regulation 39). At the conclusion of a trial or appeal which results in an acquittal the court may (and usually will) order the repayment of any contributions paid or payable under a criminal legal aid order.

(a) CRIMINAL LEGAL AID

23–04 At the time of writing the following were the current legal aid figures (see S.I. 1996 No. 646):

Disposable income and capital limits (as defined in Schedule 3 to S.I. 1989 No. 343)	*£ per week*
Free legal aid income limit	£49 disposal income
Weekly contributions	£1 for every £3 of disposable income over £48

(*N.B.* Automatically qualify free of contribution if in receipt of income support, family credit or disability working allowance)
No upper income limit

Free legal aid capital limit	£3,000

Contribution from capital is of all the excess over £3,000

IV. THE CRITERIA FOR GRANTING LEGAL AID

23–05 The factors which have to be taken into account in making a decision on whether to grant or to refuse a legal aid order are laid down in section 22(2) of the Legal Aid Act 1988. Two of the criteria militating in favour of granting legal aid will often apply to breathalyser cases. First, subsection (a) makes the loss of livelihood a relevant factor. The mandatory driving disqualification in drinking and driving cases can often render an accused unable to perform his job, which in turn usually leads him to lose his employment. In *R. v. Brigg Justices, ex p. Lynch* (1984) 148 J.P. 214, the High Court stated that, subject to his financial eligibility, a person should always be given legal aid where his livelihood would be threatened by a conviction.

23–06 Secondly, such cases will often be within subsection (b), a substantial question of law, because they can easily involve highly technical legal issues where there are conflicting authorities. One only need to look at the size of this treatise to realise just how difficult this topic has become. A layman could never hope to grasp the legal niceties, *e.g.* whether or not the police have complied with the statutory requirements entitling them to request a sample of breath or body fluid.

23–07 Thirdly, the criteria referred to in subsection (d) (expert cross-examination of witnesses) (see *R. v. Liverpool JJ., ex p. McGhee* [1993] Crim.L.R. 609) will arise more often than people would imagine, namely when the reliability of a breath alcohol measuring instrument or the accuracy of the results of an analysis of body fluid are being disputed by a motorist, a defence which has become quite a common occurrence since the decision of the House of Lords in *Cracknell v. Willis* [1988] A.C. 450 (see section 16–31). In such cases it will be necessary to cross-examine expert scientists most skilfully.

The Justices Clerk's Society has issued guidelines to magistrates' courts **23–08** (see (1992) 21 L.S.Gaz. 31). These state that, irrespective of the plea, legal aid should always be awarded for a charge of causing death by careless driving when under the influence of drink or drugs (Road Traffic Act, s.3A) and should be refused for an offence of failing to provide a screening breath test (*ibid.*, section 6). The Society also recommends that legal aid should normally be refused for a guilty plea to excess alcohol or failing to supply a specimen for analysis (*ibid.*, sections 5 and 7) but it might be appropriate in a serious case or when sentencing consequences are likely to be serious. When such matters are contested, the guidelines say that there may be defences involving technical issues of complex law, which make the grant of legal aid appropriate.

Nowadays the law relating to drinking and driving has become so **23–09** complicated that, without the benefit of legal representation, there is a substantial risk of a driver suffering real injustice, especially with the draconian penalties that ensue from a conviction. In this context the words of Roch J. in *R. v. Cambridge Crown Court ex p. Lindsey* [1991] R.T.R. 127, 133 are most apposite:

> "He conducted his own case. That is to be regretted because, had he been represented, much of the difficulty which has arisen in this case might have been avoided."

V. REMEDIES FOR REFUSALS TO GRANT LEGAL AID

A defendant can ask the area committee of the Legal Aid Board to review a **23–10** refusal by a magistrates' court to grant legal aid, but this right does not extend to crimes which can only be tried summarily. Accordingly, it applies only to one of the drinking and driving offences, namely that created by the newly inserted section 3A of the Road Traffic Act 1988 (causing death by careless driving when under the influence of drink or drugs). To be eligible to seek a review, the application for legal aid must have been lodged with the court not later than 21 days before the date fixed for the holding of the committal proceedings (see regulation 15 of the Legal Aid in Criminal and Care Proceedings (General) Regulations 1989).

Unlike in the case of an indictable offence, judicial review is the only **23–11** recourse open to a person accused of a summary offence who is refused legal aid. For such an action, the granting of legal aid is in the hands of the Legal Aid Board and applications are made through the appropriate area office for a (civil) legal aid certificate. More often than not, once a successful application for leave to move has been granted in the High Court and the consequent notice of motion has been served on the chief clerk of the relevant court, then the latter will send the appropriate legal aid order to the motorist rather than an affidavit from the magistrate, attempting to justify his action in refusing legal aid in the first place. This is despite the Review of Justices' Decisions Act 1872 which was passed to enable the magistracy, in judicial review proceedings, to file affidavits in support of their decisions without also having to appear by counsel, and thereby avoid having to pay any costs should the judgment of the High Court go against them (see *R. v. Llandiloes Licensing Justices, ex p. Davies* [1975] 1 W.L.R. 809, *per* Lord Goddard C.J.).

B. Central funds

I. AWARD MADE FROM CENTRAL FUNDS

23–12 For many years courts had had the power to award to prosecutors and successful defendants in indictable cases their costs out of the local rate fund but this power was used most sparingly in the case of those who were acquitted. As a result of the Beeching Report, central government took over the administration of justice and replaced local court of quarter sessions with the Crown Court, which is administered by the Lord Chancellor's Department. Consequent upon this change, the liability to pay the costs of successful defendants was transferred from the local rate fund to central funds, *i.e.* money provided by Parliament. During the passage of the Prosecution of Offences Bill 1985 through the House of Lords, their Lordships passed amendments which led to magistrates' courts being given, in section 16 of that Act, the same power to award costs out of central funds to the accused in summary matters as they already possessed in the case of indictable offences. An award of costs out of central funds to an accused is called "a defendant's costs order". The Court of Appeal and the Crown Court (when sitting both in its appellant capacity and as a court of first instance) can award a successful defendant his costs out of central funds. The High Court and House of Lords can award them to a defendant irrespective of the outcome of the appeal.

II. SPECIAL RULES FOR LEGALLY-AIDED LITIGANTS AND PROSECUTORS

23–13 The other major change under the Prosecution of Offences Act 1985 was that the power to award prosecution costs out of central funds was limited to cases which were brought by private prosecutors. Additionally, a defendant's costs order cannot include any costs that are covered by a legal aid certificate (*ibid.*, section 16[B]), but can include any contribution payable under a civil legal aid certificate.

III. WHEN SUCH COSTS SHOULD BE AWARDED

23–14 How the discretion to make a defendant's costs order is to be exercised has been laid down by the Lord Chief Justice in Practice Directions. At the time of writing, the current one is Practice Direction (Crime: Costs) [1991]

1 W.L.R. 498. Such orders should be made in favour of successful litigants save in three types of cases, *i.e.* where the accused has misled the police as to the strength of his case or has been acquitted on a technicality. (Failure of the police to follow the correct statutory procedure is not a technicality *per se*, and in such cases the justices have no discretion but to make a defendant's costs' order, in accordance with the decision in *Wareing v. DPP* [1990] R.T.R. 188.) The Practice Direction also states that, where the conduct of the prosecutor warrants that he should be made to pay the costs, then an order for costs should be made against him rather than a defendant's costs' order. (It should be noted that (save in the High Court or House of Lords) such an order can only be made against the prosecution in accordance with the provisions of section 19 of the Prosecution of Offences Act, *i.e.* a wasted costs order (see below)).

In the High Court, guilty drivers will normally only be awarded their costs if the judges consider the point of law to be a genuinely novel one. This happened in *Rawlins v. Brown* [1987] R.T.R. 238 (see section 17–07). In the words of Woolf L.J. in that case:

> "In the circumstances of this case, bearing in mind that this is a new point which has not previously been decided, we do feel it appropriate that costs [of the motorist who lost his appeal] should come out of central funds."

IV. WITNESSES

Further, whether or not an accused is legally aided, the fees of expert and **23–15** other witnesses for attending court on his behalf are paid out of central funds irrespective of the result of the case, unless the court orders otherwise (see paragraphs 16 *et seq.* of the Costs in Criminal Cases (General) Regulations (S.I. 1986 No. 1355)). A "witness" is defined in section 21(1) of the Prosecution of Offences Act 1985 as:

> "Any person properly attending to give evidence whether or not he gives evidence or is called at the instance of one of the parties or the court, but does not include a person attending as a witness to character only unless the court has certified that the interests of justice require his attendance."

C. Inter partes costs

I. POWERS AND DISCRETION TO MAKE AWARDS

A convicted motorist, or one who unsuccessfully appeals to the Crown **23–16** Court, or Court of Appeal, or makes an unsuccessful application for leave to appeal to the House of Lords, may be ordered to pay all or part of the prosecution costs by virtue of section 18 of the Prosecution of Offences Act

1985. A similar power to award costs against an unsuccessful litigant is also possessed by the High Court (see R.S.C. Order 62) and the House of Lords. The sum awarded cannot be more than the costs reasonable incurred by the prosecution (see *R. v. Highgate Justices, ex p. Petrou* [1954] 1 W.L.R. 485). Under paragraph 6.4. of Practice Direction (Crime: Costs) [1991] 1 W.L.R. 498, issued by Lord Lane C.J., an order for costs should normally be made against a convicted defendant, provided he has the means to pay. Likewise, in the High Court, the normal practice is to order a motorist who loses to pay costs, unless he is in receipt of legal aid and accordingly has the protection of section 17(1) of the Legal Aid Act 1988. A typical example of this is *Broadbent v. High* (reported on other grounds [1985] R.T.R. 359):

PROSECUTING COUNSEL:	"My Lord, there is the question of the respondent's costs . . . "
WATKINS L.J.:	"Are you legally aided, Mr Goldbergh?"
DEFENCE COUNSEL:	"No. This man has brought the matter privately before your Lordships."
WATKINS L.J.:	"Then I am afraid that you have no alternative but to pay the costs."

II. THE HOUSE OF LORDS AND THE HIGH COURT

23–17 The costs of appealing to the House of Lords can be very high. Even if a litigant was successful in the High Court, this will not protect him if the Director of Public Prosecutions successfully appeals to the House of Lords (see *DPP v. Shah* [1984] 1 W.L.R. 886). The only way a motorist might be able to escape this is to ask the High Court to make it a condition of granting a certificate under section 1(2) of the Administration of Justice Act 1960, or of granting leave to appeal, that the prosecutor undertakes to pay the defendant's costs in any event, as happened in *Spicer v. Holt* [1977] A.C. 987 and *DPP v. Warren* [1993] A.C. 319.

Because of the provisions of section 17(1) of the Legal Aid Act 1988, the High Court and the House of Lords on appeal therefrom will only make, against a legally aided litigant, what is know as a "football pools" order, *i.e.* the order for costs against him is not to be enforced without leave of the court. This means effectively that they are never paid, unless the defendant suddenly comes into a large sum of money. Also, the High Court might decline to make an *inter partes* order for costs if the appeal raised a novel point of law which needed to be resolved by a superior court. Indeed, in the latter circumstances, the losing defendant will probably be awarded his costs out of central funds, if he is not in receipt of legal aid.

III. ABSENT DEFENDANTS

23–18 In *DPP v. Shah* [1984] 1 W.L.R. 886, the House of Lords affirmed the principle that if an informant brings a case in the magistrates' court and then appeals, he will not be awarded his costs if the defendant does not turn up to oppose the appeal. The same principle applies in the High Court on an appeal by way of case stated (see *Lee v. Barton* (1909) 101 L.T. 603n, *per* Alverstone C.J.). The only doubt thrown on this principle appears to be some hesitation by Woolf L.J. in *DPP v. Beech* (reported only on other points [1991] Crim.L.R. 64). Nevertheless, he followed the principle but said that this was not to be quoted as a precedent.

In *DPP v. Daley* [1992] R.T.R. 155, the High Court refused to make a costs order against a losing defendant who neither attended nor was represented at the appeal.

In *Canterbury City Council v. Cook, The Times*, February 23, 1995, the Crown Court took a point of its own motion and allowed the appeal. The respondent indicated that she would not be appearing at the hearing of the case stated. The High Court refused an application for costs against her and said to make such an order would be most unjust when she had not been asked to consent to the appeal being allowed.

IV. WASTED OR WRONGLY INCURRED COSTS

Under section 19 of the Prosecution of Offences Act 1985, a party may be **23–19** ordered to pay the costs where he has caused the other party to incur those costs through "an unnecessary or improper act or omission". In *DPP v. Denning* [1992] Q.B. 532, the High Court held that this merely meant that there had been an act or omission which would not have occurred if the litigant had conducted his case properly. Such an order can be made in favour of a legally-aided litigant. By section 19A (as inserted by section 111 of the Courts and Legal Services Act 1990) a similar order can be made against a legal representative if he is the cause of the wasted costs.

V. APPLICATIONS FOR RESTORATION OF DRIVING LICENCE

On an application for the restoration of a driving licence under section 42 **23–20** of the Road Traffic Offenders Act 1988 (see Chapter 20) the court may, irrespective of whether or not it allows the application, order the applicant to pay all or any part of the costs of the application (see subsection 5(b) of section 42).

VI. ABANDONED APPEALS

A litigant who appeals and then withdraws it before the hearing may be **23–21** ordered to pay the costs of the respondent, just as if the appeal had been dismissed. It should be noted that the notice of hearing date (form 5011) sent by the Crown Court to the parties is misleading. It does correctly state that if the appeal is abandoned more than three working days before the date set for its hearing, the Crown Court cannot make an order for costs. It omits to mention that a respondent can always apply to the magistrates' court under section 109 of the Magistrates' Court Act 1980 for an order that the appellant pay the costs incurred by him in the appeal prior to its withdrawal.

D. Assessment and taxation of costs

I. BY WHOM CARRIED OUT

(a) INTER PARTES AWARDS

23–22 Parliament has laid down who shall quantify the amount payable when an *inter partes* award of costs has been made. By section 18 of the Prosecution of Offences Act 1985, the actual amount that may be awarded is determined by the tribunal convicting the accused or, in the case of the Crown Court or Court of Appeal, the tribunal which dismissed the appeal. It cannot delegate this power to a taxing officer or its clerk, although it can seek his assistance in assessing the amount (see *Bunston v. Rawlings* [1982] 1 W.L.R. 473, a case concerning justices). The principle would apply equally to the Crown Court and Court of Appeal, as the relevant wording of the statute is identical for all three forums. Under Order 62 of the Rules of the Supreme Court, in the High Court the costs can either be assessed by the court or, as usually happens, be taxed by a Taxing Master or (if not exceeding £25,000) by a Principle or Senior Executive Officer in the Supreme Court Taxing Office. In the House of Lords any award of costs must be taxed by the Principal Clerk to the Judicial Office.

(b) CENTRAL FUNDS

23–23 As regards central funds, a defendant has the choice of accepting the sum the Bench awards (see section 16(9)(a) of the Prosecution of Offences Act 1985) or, if he does not wish to accept that amount, he is entitled to have his bill of costs taxed by the appropriate court officer (*ibid.*, subsection 16(9)(b)).

(c) LEGAL AID

23–24 Except for proceedings in the magistrates' court, where legal aid costs are assessed by the Legal Aid Board, all legal aid bills are taxed by the appropriate court officer.

II. TIME LIMITS

Certain time limits are laid down for taxing costs. Any bill to be paid out of **23–25** central funds must be lodged in court within three months (regulation 6(1) of the Costs in Criminal Cases (General) Regulations 1986), but the time limit may be extended for good reason (regulation 12(1)) or (if no good reason) in exceptional circumstances which need not relate to the failure to apply for costs within the time limits: see *R. v. North Kent JJ., ex p. Goldrich* [1995] T.L.R. 56. The same time limit also applies in the High Court to an *inter partes* taxation, save that time runs from when the final order is perfected (see R.S.C. Order 62, r.29(1)). (An order is perfected in the case of appeals by way of case stated when the associate enters the result in his book, which is normally the same day as the hearing.) There is a general power to extend time in the High Court (*ibid.*, Order 62, r.21); but delay in taxing a bill can cause the costs to be disallowed in part or in total (*ibid.*, rule 28(1)). The taxing officer will make such a disallowance where prejudice might have been occasioned to the paying party by the delay. In the case of *Pamplin v. Fraser (No. 2)* [1984] 1 W.L.R. 1385 Parker J. held that prejudice could be inferred when a defendant has had hanging over him an unquantified bill of costs with the knowledge that if it came to more than he could afford, he could end up in prison if he did not pay it. (By section 76 of the Magistrates' Courts Act 1980, any order for costs made against a defendant can be enforced in a criminal cause by committal to prison.) So in *Pamplin*, above, a bill of £550 was taxed down to £5 because the prosecution were 10 months out of time in lodging their bill for taxation.

A bill of costs for the House of Lords should be lodged for taxation within three months of the date of the judgment. Any request for an extension of time should be made before the three months has expired. Only in exceptional circumstances will an extension be granted if the application is made outside the three-month time limit.

III. QUANTUM

(a) CENTRAL FUNDS

(i) *Non Legally-aided Litigants*

The quantum of costs payable out of central funds is stated in sections **23–26** 16(6) and 17(1) of the Prosecution of Offences Act 1985 to be "such amount as the court considers reasonable to compensate the [litigant] for any expenses properly incurred by him in the proceedings". Similar words were used in section 1(2) of the Costs in Criminal Cases Act 1952 and were explained in Practice Direction (Crime: Costs) [1968] 1 W.L.R. 389 as meaning:

> "The proper approach is to assume the [litigant] to be of adequate but not abundant means and to ask oneself whether the expenses were such

as a sensible solicitor in the light of his then knowledge would consider reasonable to incur in the interests of his client . . . "

(ii) *Legally-aided Litigants*

23–27   On a taxation of costs to be paid out of central funds, no sum can be allowed in respect of costs which are covered by a legal aid certificate (see section 21(4A)(a) of the Prosecution of Offenders Act 1985 as inserted by paragraph 15 of section 5 of the Legal Aid Act 1988). Thus a legally-aided litigant can normally only recover from central funds the amount of his contributions payable to the Legal Aid Fund (where the court has no power to order a refund) and his costs of travelling to court. It is submitted that any judicial pronouncements to the contrary were made *per incuriam*, overlooking what was then section 16(8), now section 21(4A)(a). An example of this occurred in *DPP v. Barry* (1989) 133 S.J. 784:

> Stoker J.: "It is simply a question of which public fund pays is it not?"
> [Defence counsel agreed]
> Stoker J.: "You can have your costs out of central funds. I doubt if it will make any practical difference as they are all public funds in any case, but it protects the legal aid fund."

The sentiments are entirely right, as the inability of the Criminal Legal Aid Fund to recover costs from other sources distorts expenditure, which could have important repercussions as the Treasury seeks ways to limit legal aid spending.

(iii) *Witnesses*

23–28   In the case of a witness, by virtue of section 21(4) of the Prosecution of Offences Act 1985, he or she is entitled to receive "compensation for the expenses, trouble or loss of time properly incurred in or incidental to his attendance", but the amount of such compensation must be calculated in accordance with regulations made by the Lord Chancellor (see section 21(3)). The amounts allowed under these regulations are increased at regular intervals.

(b) INTER PARTES COSTS

23–29   *Inter partes* costs are nowadays assessed on the same basis as those payable out of central funds (see sections 18(1) and (2) of the Prosecution of Offences Act 1985 and R.S.C. 1965, Order 62, r. 12(1)), except that the fact that a party is legally-aided is not to be taken into account. Where pleas of guilty are tendered in the magistrates' court and refused, but at the Crown Court the defendant is convicted only of those offences which she was prepared to admit to at petty sessions, the costs awarded against her should be limited to what she would have been ordered to pay on a guilty plea in the lower court. In a straightforward case these costs would have been about £25: see *R. v. Hughes*, March 24, 1994.

(c) Litigants Under Seventeen Years

A person under 17 cannot be ordered to pay more costs to the prosecutor **23–30** than the amount of any fine imposed upon him; see section 18(5) of the Prosecution of Offences Act 1985.

(d) Interest

Interest cannot be awarded on costs in a criminal case (see *Westminster City* **23–31** *Council v. Wingrove* [1991] Q.B. 652).

Appendix 1

LEGISLATION

I. ROAD TRAFFIC ACT 1988

The statutory provisions reproduced in this Appendix are printed as inserted, amended or substituted by the Road Traffic Act 1991 and the Transport and Works Act 1992 and the Criminal Procedure and Investigations Act 1996.

Motor vehicles: drink and drugs

Causing death by careless driving when under influence of drink or drugs

3A.—(1) If a person causes the death of another person by driving a mechanically propelled vehicle on a road or other public place without due care and attention, or without reasonable consideration for other persons using the road or place, and—

(a) he is, at the time when he is driving, unfit to drive through drink or drugs, or

(b) he has consumed so much alcohol that the proportion of it in his breath, blood or urine at that time exceeds the prescribed limit, or

(c) he is, within 18 hours after that time, required to provide a specimen in pursuance of section 7 of this Act, but without reasonable excuse fails to provide it,

he is guilty of an offence.

(2) For the purposes of this section a person shall be taken to be unfit to drive at any time when his ability to drive properly is impaired.

(3) Subsection (1)(b) and (c) above shall not apply in relation to a person driving a mechanically propelled vehicle other than a motor vehicle.

Driving, or being in charge, when under influence of drink or drugs

4.—(1) A person who, when driving or attempting to drive a mechanically propelled vehicle on a road or other public place, is unfit to drive through drink or drugs is guilty of an offence.

411

(2) Without prejudice to subsection (1) above, a person who, when in charge of a mechanically propelled vehicle which is on a road or other public place, is unfit to drive through drink or drugs is guilty of an offence.

(3) For the purposes of subsection (2) above, a person shall be deemed not to have been in charge of a mechanically propelled vehicle if he proves that at the material time the circumstances were such that there was no likelihood of his driving it so long as he remained unfit to drive through drink or drugs.

(4) The court may, in determining whether there was such a likelihood as is mentioned in subsection (3) above, disregard any injury to him and any damage to the vehicle.

(5) For the purposes of this section, a person shall be taken to be unfit to drive if his ability to drive properly is for the time being impaired.

(6) A constable may arrest a person without warrant if he has reasonable cause to suspect that that person is or has been committing an offence under this section.

(7) For the purpose of arresting a person under the power conferred by subsection (6) above, a constable may enter (if need be by force) any place where that person is or where the constable, with reasonable cause, suspects him to be.

(8) Subsection (7) above does not extend to Scotland, and nothing in that subsection affects any rule of law in Scotland concerning the right of a constable to enter any premises for any purpose.

Driving or being in charge of a motor vehicle with alcohol concentration above prescribed limit

5.—(1) If a person—

(a) drives or attempts to drive a motor vehicle on a road or other public place, or

(b) is in charge of a motor vehicle on a road or other public place,

after consuming so much alcohol that the proportion of it in his breath, blood or urine exceeds the prescribed limit he is guilty of an offence.

(2) It is a defence for a person charged with an offence under subsection (1)(b) above to prove that at the time he is alleged to have committed the offence the circumstances were such that there was no likelihood of his driving the vehicle whilst the proportion of alcohol in his breath, blood or urine remained likely to exceed the prescribed limit.

(3) The court may, in determining whether there was such a likelihood as is mentioned in subsection (2) above, disregard any injury to him and any damage to the vehicle.

Breath tests

6.—(1) Where a constable in uniform has reasonable cause to suspect—

(a) that a person driving or attempting to drive or in charge of a motor vehicle on a road or other public place has alcohol in his body or has committed a traffic offence whilst the vehicle was in motion, or

(b) that a person has been driving or attempting to drive or been in charge of a motor vehicle on a road or other public place with alcohol in his body and that that person still has alcohol in his body, or

(c) that a person has been driving or attempting to drive or been in charge of a motor vehicle on a road or other public place and has committed a traffic offence whilst the vehicle was in motion,

he may, subject to section 9 of this Act, require him to provide a specimen of breath for a breath test.

(2) If an accident occurs owing to the presence of a motor vehicle on a road or other public place, a constable may, subject to section 9 of this Act, require any person who he has reasonable cause to believe was driving or attempting to drive or in charge of the vehicle at the time of the accident to provide a specimen of breath for a breath test.

(3) A person may be required under subsection (1) or subsection (2) above to provide a specimen either at or near the place where the requirement is made or, if the requirement is made under subsection (2) above and the constable making the requirement thinks fit, at a police station specified by the constable.

(4) A person who, without reasonable excuse, fails to provide a specimen of breath when required to do so in pursuance of this section is guilty of an offence.

(5) A constable may arrest a person without warrant if—

(a) as a result of a breath test he has reasonable cause to suspect that the proportion of alcohol in that person's breath or blood exceeds the prescribed limit, or

(b) that person has failed to provide a specimen of breath for a breath test when required to do so in pursuance of this section and the constable has reasonable cause to suspect that he has alcohol in his body,

but a person shall not be arrested by virtue of this subsection when he is at a hospital as a patient.

(6) A constable may, for the purpose of requiring a person to provide a specimen of breath under subsection (2) above in a case where he has reasonable cause to suspect that the accident involved injury to another person or of arresting him in such a case under subsection (5) above, enter (if need be by force) any place where that person is or where the constable, with reasonable cause, suspects him to be.

(7) Subsection (6) above does not extend to Scotland, and nothing in that subsection shall affect any rule of law in Scotland concerning the right of a constable to enter any premises for any purpose.

(8) In this section "traffic offence" means an offence under—

(a) any provision of Part II of the Public Passenger Vehicles Act 1981,

(b) any provision of the Road Traffic Regulation Act 1984,

(c) any provision of the Road Traffic Offenders Act 1988 except Part III, or

(d) any provision of this Act except Part V.

Provision of specimens for analysis

7.—(1) In the course of an investigation into whether a person has committed an offence under section 3A, 4 or 5 of this Act a constable may, subject to the following provisions of this section and section 9 of this Act, require him—

(a) to provide two specimens of breath for analysis by means of a device of a type approved by the Secretary of State, or

(b) to provide a specimen of blood or urine for a laboratory test.

(2) A requirement under this section to provide specimens of breath can only be made at a police station.

(3) A requirement under this section to provide a specimen of blood or urine can only be made at a police station or at a hospital; and it cannot be made at a police station unless—

(a) the constable making the requirement has reasonable cause to believe that for medical reasons a specimen of breath cannot be provided or should not be required, or

(b) at the time the requirement is made a device or a reliable device of the type mentioned in subsection (1)(a) above is not available at the police station or it is then for any other reason not practicable to use such a device there, or

(bb) [*Not yet in force*] a device of the type mentioned in subsection (1)(a) above has been used at the police station but the constable who required the specimens of breath has reasonable cause to believe that the device has not produced a reliable indication of the proportion of alcohol in the breath of the person concerned, or

(c) the suspected offence is one under section 3A or 4 of this Act and the constable making the requirement has been advised by a medical practitioner that the condition of the person required to provide the specimen might be due to some drug;

but may then be made notwithstanding that the person required to provide the specimen has already provided or been required to provide two specimens of breath.

(4) If the provision of a specimen other than a specimen of breath may be required in pursuance of this section the question whether it is to be a specimen of blood or a specimen of urine shall be decided by the constable making the requirement, but if a medical practitioner is of the opinion that for medical reasons a specimen of blood cannot or should not be taken the specimen shall be a specimen of urine.

(5) A specimen of urine shall be provided within one hour of the requirement for its provision being made and after the provision of a previous specimen of urine.

(6) A person who, without reasonable excuse, fails to provide a specimen when required to do so in pursuance of this section is guilty of an offence.

(7) A constable must, on requiring any person to provide a specimen in pursuance of this section, warn him that a failure to provide it may render him liable to prosecution.

Choice of specimens of breath

8.—(1) Subject to subsection (2) below, of any two specimens of breath provided by any person in pursuance of section 7 of this Act that with the lower proportion of alcohol in the breath shall be used and the other shall be disregarded.

(2) If the specimen with the lower proportion of alcohol contains no more than 50 microgrammes of alcohol in 100 millilitres of breath, the person who provided it may claim that it should be replaced by such specimen as may be required under section 7(4) of this Act and, if he then provides such a specimen, neither specimen of breath shall be used.

(3) The Secretary of State may by regulations substitute another proportion of alcohol in the breath for that specified in subsection (2) above.

Protection for hospital patients

9.—(1) While a person is at a hospital as a patient he shall not be required to provide a specimen of breath for a breath test or to provide a specimen for a laboratory test unless the medical practitioner in immediate charge of his case has been notified of the proposal to make the requirement; and—

(a) if the requirement is then made, it shall be for the provision of a specimen at the hospital, but

(b) if the medical practitioner objects on the ground specified in subsection (2) below, the requirement shall not be made.

(2) The ground on which the medical practitioner may object is that the requirement or the provision of a specimen or, in the case of a specimen of blood or urine, the warning required under section 7(7) of this Act, would be prejudicial to the proper care and treatment of the patient.

Detention of persons affected by alcohol or a drug

10.—(1) Subject to subsections (2) and (3) below, a person required to provide a specimen of breath, blood or urine may afterwards be detained at a police station until it appears to the constable that, were that person then driving or attempting to drive a mechanically propelled vehicle on a road, he would not be committing an offence under section 4 or 5 of this Act.

(2) A person shall not be detained in pursuance of this section if it appears to a constable that there is no likelihood of his driving or attempting to drive a mechanically propelled vehicle whilst his ability to drive properly is impaired or whilst the proportion of alcohol in his breath, blood or urine exceeds the prescribed limit.

(3) A constable must consult a medical practitioner on any question arising under this section whether a person's ability to drive properly is or might be impaired through drugs and must act on the medical practitioner's advice.

Interpretation of sections 4 to 10

11.—(1) The following provisions apply for the interpretation of sections 3A to 10 of this Act.

(2) In those sections—

"breath test" means a preliminary test for the purpose of obtaining, by means of a device of a type approved by the Secretary of State, an indication whether the proportion of alcohol in a person's breath or blood is likely to exceed the prescribed limit,

"drug" includes any intoxicant other than alcohol,

"fail" includes refuse,

"hospital" means an institution which provides medical or surgical treatment for in-patients or out-patients,

"the prescribed limit" means, as the case may require—

    (a) 35 microgrammes of alcohol in 100 millilitres of breath,

    (b) 80 milligrammes of alcohol in 100 millilitres of blood, or

    (c) 107 milligrammes of alcohol in 100 millilitres of urine,

or such other proportion as may be prescribed by regulations made by the Secretary of State.

(3) A person does not provide a specimen of breath for a breath test or for analysis unless the specimen—

    (a) is sufficient to enable the test or the analysis to be carried out, and

    (b) is provided in such a way as to enable the objective of the test or analysis to be satisfactorily achieved.

(4) A person provides a specimen of blood if and only if he consents to its being taken by a medical practitioner and it is so taken.

Cycling when under influence of drink or drugs

30.—(1) A person who, when riding a cycle on a road or other public place, is unfit to ride through drink or drugs (that is to say, is under the influence of drink or a drug to such an extent as to be incapable of having proper control of the cycle) is guilty of an offence.

(2) In Scotland a constable may arrest without warrant a person committing an offence under this section.

(3) [. . .]

Application to the Crown

Application to the Crown

183.—(1) Subject to the provisions of this section—

    (a) Part I of this Act,

    (b) Part II of this Act, except sections 68 to 74 and 77,

    (c) Part III of this Act, except section 103(3),

    (d) Part IV of this Act, and

(e) in this Part, sections 163, 164, 168, 169, 170(1) to (4), 177, 178, 181 and 182.

apply to vehicles and persons in the public service of the Crown.

Application of sections 5 to 10 to persons subject to service discipline

184.—(1) Sections 5 to 10 of this Act, in their application to persons subject to service discipline, apply outside as well as within Great Britain and have effect as if—

(a) references to proceedings for an offence under any enactment included references to proceedings for the corresponding service offence,

(b) references to the court included a reference to any naval, military or air force authority before whom the proceedings take place,

(c) references to a constable included references to a member of the provost staff,

(d) references to a police station included references to a naval, military or air force unit or establishment,

(e) references to a hospital included references to a naval, military or air force unit or establishment at which medical or surgical treatment is provided for persons subject to service discipline, and

(f) in section 6(1) the reference to a traffic offence included a reference to the corresponding service offence.

(2) In relation to persons for the time being subject to service discipline, the power to arrest conferred on a constable by section 4(6) of this Act is also exercisable by a member of the provost staff and is so exercisable outside as well as within Great Britain.

(3) In this section—

"corresponding service offence," in relation to an offence under any enactment, means an offence under section 42 of the Naval Discipline Act 1957 or an offence against section 70 of the Army Act 1955 or section 70 of the Air Force Act 1955 committed by an act or omission which is punishable under that enactment or would be so punishable if committed in Great Britain,

"member of the provost staff" means a provost officer or any person legally exercising authority under or on behalf of a provost officer,

"persons subject to service discipline" means persons subject to that Act of 1957, to military law or to air force law and other persons to whom section 42 of that Act of 1957 or section 70 of either of those Acts of 1955 for the time being applies,

"provost officer" means a person who is a provost officer within the meaning of that Act of 1957 or either of those Acts of 1955.

Hover vehicles

188.—(1) For the purposes of the Road Traffic Acts, a hovercraft within the meaning of the Hovercraft Act 1968 (in this section referred to as a hover vehicle)—

(a) is a motor vehicle, whether or not it is intended or adapted for use on roads, but

(b) apart from that is to be treated, subject to subsection (2) below, as not being a vehicle of any of the classes defined in section 185 of this Act.

(2) The Secretary of State may by regulations provide—

(a) that any provisions of this Act which would otherwise apply to hover vehicles shall not apply to them or shall apply to them subject to such modifications as may be specified in the regulations, or

(b) that any such provision which would not otherwise apply to hover vehicles shall apply to them subject to such modifications (if any) as may be specified in the regulations.

Certain vehicles not to be treated as motor vehicles

189.—(1) For the purposes of the Road Traffic Acts—

(a) a mechanically propelled vehicle being an implement for cutting grass which is controlled by a pedestrian and is not capable of being used or adapted for any other purpose,

(b) any other mechanically propelled vehicle controlled by a pedestrian which may be specified by regulations made by the Secretary of State for the purposes of this section and section 140 of the Road Traffic Regulation Act 1984, and

(c) an electrically assisted pedal cycle of such a class as may be prescribed by regulations so made,

is to be treated as not being a motor vehicle.

(2) In subsection (1) above "controlled by a pedestrian" means that the vehicle either—

(a) is constructed or adapted for use only under such control, or

(b) is constructed or adapted for use either under such control or under the control of a person carried on it, but is not for the time being in use under, or proceeding under, the control of a person carried on it.

General interpretation of Act

192.—(1) In this Act—

"bridleway" means a way over which the public have the following, but no other, rights of way: a right of way on foot and a right of way on horseback or leading a horse, with or without a right to drive animals of any description along the way,

"carriage of goods" includes the haulage of goods,

"cycle" means a bicycle, a tricycle, or a cycle having four or more wheels, not being in any case a motor vehicle,

"driver", where a separate person acts as a steersman of a motor vehicle, includes (except for the purposes of section 1 of this Act) that person as well as any other person engaged in the driving of the vehicle, and "drive" is to be interpreted accordingly,

"footpath", in relation to England and Wales, means a way over which the public have a right of way on foot only,

"goods" includes goods or burden of any description,

"goods vehicle" means a motor vehicle constructed or adapted for use for the carriage of goods, or a trailer so constructed or adapted,

"highway authority", in England and Wales, means—

(a) in relation to a road for which he is the highway authority within the meaning of the Highways Act 1980, the Secretary of State, and

(b) in relation to any other road, the council of the county, metropolitan district or London borough, or the Common Council of the City of London, as the case may be;

"international road haulage permit" means a licence, permit, authorisation or other document issued in pursuance of a Community instrument relating to the carriage of goods by road between member States or an international agreement to which the United Kingdom is a party and which relates to the international carriage of goods by road,

"owner", in relation to a vehicle which is the subject of a hiring agreement or hire-purchase agreement, means the person in possession of the vehicle under that agreement,

"petty sessions area" has the same meaning as in the Magistrates' Courts Act 1980,

"prescribed" means prescribed by regulations made by the Secretary of State,

"road",

(a) in relation to England and Wales, means any highway and any other road to which the public has access, and includes bridges over which a road passes, and

(b) in relation to Scotland, means any road within the meaning of the Roads (Scotland) Act 1984 and any other way to which the public has access, and includes bridges over which a road passes,

"the Road Traffic Acts" means the Road Traffic Offenders Act 1988, the Road Traffic (Consequential Provisions) Act 1988 (so far as it reproduces the effect of provisions repealed by that Act) and this Act,

"statutory", in relation to any prohibition, restriction, requirement or provision, means contained in, or having effect under, any enactment (including any enactment contained in this Act),

"the Traffic Acts" means the Road Traffic Acts and the Road Traffic Regulation Act 1984,

"traffic sign" has the meaning given by section 64(1) of the Road Traffic Regulation Act 1984,

"tramcar" includes any carriage used on any road by virtue of an order under the Light Railways Act 1896, and

> "trolley vehicle" means a mechanically propelled vehicle adapted for use on roads without rails under power transmitted to it from some external source (whether or not there is in addition a source of power on board the vehicle).

(2) In this Act—

> "carriageway"
> "footway"
> "local roads authority"
> "public road"
> [. . .]
> "roads authority"
> "special road" and
> "trunk road",

in relation to Scotland, have the same meanings as in the Roads (Scotland) Act 1984, and "footpath", in relation to Scotland, means a way over which the public have a right of way on foot only (whether or not associated with a carriageway).

(3) References in this Act to a class of vehicles are to be interpreted as references to a class defined or described by reference to any characteristics of the vehicles or to any other circumstances whatsoever and accordingly as authorising the use of "category" to indicate a class of vehicles, however defined or described.

192A.—(1) Sections 4 to 11 of this Act shall not apply (to the extent that apart from this subsection they would) to vehicles on any transport system to which Chapter I of Part II of the Transport and Works Act 1992 (offences involving drink or drugs on railways, tramways and certain other guided transport systems) applies.

(2) Subject to subsection (1) above, the Secretary of State may by regulations provide that sections 4 to 11 of this Act shall apply to vehicles on a system of guided transport specified in the regulations with such modifications as he considers necessary or expedient.

(3) Regulations under subsection (2) above may make different provision for different cases.

(4) In this section—

> "guided transport" means transport by vehicles guided by means external to the vehicles (whether or not the vehicles are also capable of being operated in some other way), and
> "vehicle" includes mobile traction unit."

General index

194. The expressions listed in the left-hand column below are respectively defined or (as the case may be) fall to be construed in accordance with the provisions of this Act in the right-hand column in relation to those expressions.

Expression	Relevant provisions
Bridleway	Section 192
Carriage of goods	Section 192
Carriageway	Section 192
Cycle	Section 192
Drive	Section 192
Driver	Section 192
Footpath	Section 192
Footway	Section 192
Goods	Section 192
Goods vehicle	Section 192
Goods vehicle test certificate	Section 49(2)(b)
Heavy locomotive	Section 185
Heavy motor car	Section 185
Highway authority	Section 192
International road haulage permit	Section 192
Invalid carriage	Section 185
Light locomotive	Section 185
Local roads authority	Section 192
Motor car	Section 185
Motor cycle	Section 185
Motor tractor	Section 185
Motor vehicle	Section 185, 186(1), 187, 188, 189
Owner	Section 192
Plating certificate	Section 49(2)(a)
Prescribed	Section 192
Public road	Section 192
Road	Section 192
Roads authority	Section 192
Road Traffic Acts	Section 192
Special road	Section 192
Statutory	Section 192
Test certificate	Section 45(2)
Traffic Acts	Section 192
Traffic sign	Section 192
Trailer	Section 185
Tramcar	Section 192
Trolley vehicle	Section 192
Trunk	Section 192
Unladen weight	Section 190

II. ROAD TRAFFIC OFFENDERS ACT 1988

(as amended by the ROAD TRAFFIC ACT 1991 and the CRIMINAL PROCEDURE AND INVESTIGATIONS ACT 1996)

Evidence by certificate as to driver user or owner

11.—(1) In any proceedings in England and Wales for an offence to which this section applies, a certificate in the prescribed form, purporting to be signed by a constable and certifying that a person specified in the certificate stated to the constable—

(a) that a particular mechanically propelled vehicle was being driven or used by, or belonged to, that person on a particular occasion, or

(b) that a particular mechanically propelled vehicle on a particular occasion was used by, or belonged to, a firm and that he was, at the time of the statement, a partner in that firm, or

(c) that a particular mechanically propelled vehicle on a particular occasion was used by, or belonged to, a corporation and that he was, at the time of the statement, a director, officer or employee of that corporation,

shall be admissible as evidence for the purpose of determining by whom the vehicle was being driven or used, or to whom it belonged, as the case may be, on that occasion.

(2) Nothing in subsection (1) above makes a certificate admissible as evidence in proceedings for an offence except in a case where and to the like extent to which oral evidence to the like effect would have been admissible in those proceedings.

(3) Nothing in subsection (1) above makes a certificate admissible as evidence in proceedings for an offence—

(a) unless a copy of it has, not less than seven days before the hearing or trial, been served in the prescribed manner on the person charged with the offence, or

(b) if that person, not later than three days before the hearing or trial or within such further time as the court may in special circumstances allow, serves a notice in the prescribed form and manner on the prosecutor requiring attendance at the trial of the person who signed the certificate.

(3A) Where the proceedings mentioned in subsection (1) above are proceedings before a magistrates' court inquiring into an offence as examining justices this section shall have effect with the omission of—

(a) subsection (2), and

(b) in subsection (3), paragraph (b) and the word "or" immediately preceding it.

(4) In this section "prescribed" means prescribed by rules made by the Secretary of State by statutory instrument.

(5) Schedule 1 to this Act shows the offences to which this section applies.

Proof, in summary proceedings, of identity of driver of vehicle

12.—(1) Where on the summary trial in England and Wales of an information for an offence to which this subsection applies—

(a) it is proved to the satisfaction of the court, on oath or in manner prescribed by rules made under section 144 of the Magistrates' Courts Act 1980, that a requirement under section 172(2) of the Road Traffic Act 1988 to give information as to the identity of the driver of a particular vehicle on the particular occasion to which the information relates has been served on the accused by post, and

(b) a statement in writing is produced to the court purporting to be signed by the accused that the accused was the driver of that vehicle on that occasion,

the court may accept that statement as evidence that the accused was the driver of that vehicle on that occasion.

(2) Schedule 1 to this Act shows the offences to which subsection (1) above applies.

(3) Where on the summary trial in England and Wales of an information for an offence to which section 112 of the Road Traffic Regulation Act 1984 applies—

(a) it is proved to the satisfaction of the court, on oath or in manner prescribed by rules made under section 144 of the Magistrates' Courts Act 1980, that a requirement under section 112(2) of the Road Traffic Regulation Act 1984 to give information as to the identity of the driver of a particular vehicle on the particular occasion to which the information relates has been served on the accused by post, and

(b) a statement in writing is produced to the court purporting to be signed by the accused that the accused was the driver of that vehicle on that occasion,

the court may accept that statement as evidence that the accused was the driver of that vehicle on that occasion.

Admissibility of records as evidence

13.—(1) This section applies to a statement contained in a document purporting to be—

(a) a part of the records maintained by the Secretary of State in connection with any functions exercisable by him by virtue of Part III of the Road Traffic Act 1988 or a part of any other records maintained by the Secretary of State with respect to vehicles, or

(b) a copy of a document forming part of those records, or

(c) a note of any information contained in those records,

and to be authenticated by a person authorised in that behalf by the Secretary of State.

(2) A statement to which this section applies shall be admissible in any proceedings as evidence (in Scotland, sufficient evidence) of any fact stated in it to the same extent as oral evidence of that fact is admissible in those proceedings.

(3) In the preceding subsections—

(a) "document" and "statement" have the same meaning as in section 10(1) of the Civil Evidence Act 1968 or, in Scotland, section 17(3) of the Law Reform (Miscellaneous Provisions) (Scotland) Act 1968, and

(b) the reference to a copy of a document shall be construed in accordance with section 10(2) of the Civil Evidence Act 1968 or, in

Scotland, section 17(4) of the Law Reform (Miscellaneous Provisions) (Scotland) Act 1968.

Nothing in this subsection shall be construed as limiting to civil proceedings the references to proceedings in the preceding provisions of this section.

(4) In any case where—

(a) a statement to which this section applies is produced to a magistrates' court in any proceedings for an offence involving obligatory or discretionary disqualification,

(b) the statement specifies an alleged previous conviction of an accused person of any such offence or any order made on the conviction,

(c) it is proved to the satisfaction of the court, on oath or in such manner as may be prescribed by rules under section 144 of the Magistrates' Courts Act 1980, that not less than seven days before the statement is so produced a notice was served on the accused, in such form and manner as may be so prescribed, specifying the previous conviction or order and stating that it is proposed to bring it to the notice of the court in the event of or, as the case may be, in view of his conviction, and

(d) the accused is not present in person before the court when the statement is so produced,

the court may take account of the previous conviction or order as if the accused had appeared and admitted it.

(5) Nothing in the preceding provisions of this section enables evidence to be given in respect of any matter other than a matter of a description prescribed by regulations made by the Secretary of State.

(6) The power to make regulations under this section shall be exercisable by statutory instrument, which shall be subject to annulment in pursuance of a resolution of either House of Parliament.

(7) Where the proceedings mentioned in subsection (2) above are proceedings before a magistrates' court inquiring into an offence as examining justices this section shall have effect if—

(a) in subsection (2) the words "to the same extent as oral evidence of that fact is admissible in those proceedings" were omitted;

(b) in subsection (4) the word "and" were inserted at the end of paragraph (a);

(c) in subsection (4), paragraphs (c) and (d) and the words "as if the accused had appeared and admitted it" were omitted.

Use of specimens in proceedings for an offence under section 4 or 5 of the Road Traffic Act

15.—(1) This section and section 16 of this Act apply in respect of proceedings for an offence under section 3A, 4 or 5 of the Road Traffic Act 1988 (driving offences connected with drink or drugs); and expressions used in this section and section 16 of this Act have the same meaning as in sections 3A to 10 of that Act.

(2) Evidence of the proportion of alcohol or any drug in a specimen of breath, blood or urine provided by the accused shall, in all cases (including cases where the specimen was not provided in connection with the alleged offence), be taken into account and, subject to subsection (3) below, it shall be assumed that the proportion of alcohol in the accused's breath, blood or urine at the time of the alleged offence was not less than in the specimen.

(3) That assumption shall not be made if the accused proves—

(a) that he consumed alcohol before he provided the specimen and—

(i) in relation to an offence under section 3A, after the time of the alleged offence, and

(ii) otherwise, after he had ceased to drive, attempt to drive or be in charge of a vehicle on a road or other public place, and

(b) that he had not done so the proportion of alcohol in his breath, blood or urine would not have exceeded the prescribed limit and, if it is alleged that he was unfit to drive through drink, would not have been such as to impair his ability to drive properly.

(4) A specimen of blood shall be disregarded unless it was taken from the accused with his consent by a medical practitioner.

(5) Where, at the time a specimen of blood or urine was provided by the accused, he asked to be provided with such a specimen, evidence of the proportion of alcohol or any drug found in the specimen is not admissible on behalf of the prosecution unless—

(a) the specimen in which the alcohol or drug was found is one of two parts into which the specimen provided by the accused was divided at the time it was provided, and

(b) the other part was supplied to the accused.

Documentary evidence as to specimens in such proceedings

16.—(1) Evidence of the proportion of alcohol or a drug in a specimen of breath, blood or urine may, subject to subsections (3) and (4) below and to section 15(5) of this Act, be given by the production of a document or documents purporting to be whichever of the following is appropriate, that is to say—

(a) a statement automatically produced by the device by which the proportion of alcohol in a specimen of breath was measured and a certificate signed by a constable (which may but need not be contained in the same document as the statement) that the statement relates to a specimen provided by the accused at the date and time shown in the statement, and

(b) a certificate signed by an authorised analyst as to the proportion of alcohol or any drug found in a specimen of blood or urine identified in the certificate.

(2) Subject to subsections (3) and (4) below, evidence that a specimen of blood was taken from the accused with his consent by a medical practitioner may be given by the production of a document purporting to certify that fact and to be signed by a medical practitioner.

(3) Subject to subsection (4) below—

(a) a document purporting to be such a statement or such a certificate (or both such a statement and such a certificate) as is mentioned in subsection (1)(a) above is admissible in evidence on behalf of the prosecution in pursuance of this section only if a copy of it either has been handed to the accused when the document was produced or has been served on him not later than seven days before the hearing, and

(b) any other document is so admissible only if a copy of it has been served on the accused not later than seven days before the hearing.

(4) A document purporting to be a certificate (or so much of a document as purports to be a certificate) is not so admissible if the accused, not later than three days before the hearing or within such further time as the court may in special circumstances allow, has served notice on the prosecutor requiring the attendance at the hearing of the person by whom the document purports to be signed.

(5) In Scotland—

(a) a document produced in evidence on behalf of the prosecution in pursuance of subsection (1) or (2) above and, where the person by whom the document was signed is called as a witness, the evidence of that person, shall be sufficient evidence of the facts stated in the document, and

(b) a written execution purporting to be signed by the person who handed to or served on the accused or the prosecutor a copy of the document or of the notice in terms of subsection (3) or (4) above, together with, where appropriate, a post office receipt for the registered or recorded delivery letter shall be sufficient evidence of the handing or service of such a copy or notice.

(6) A copy of a certificate required by this section to be served on the accused or a notice required by this section to be served on the prosecutor may be served personally or sent by registered post or recorded delivery service.

(6A) [*Not yet in force*] Where the proceedings mentioned in section 15(1) of this Act are proceedings before a magistrates' court inquiring into an offence as examining justices this section shall have effect with the omission of subsection (4).

(7) In this section "authorised analyst" means—

(a) any person possessing the qualifications prescribed by regulations made under section 27 of the Food Safety Act 1990 as qualifying persons for appointment as public analysts under those Acts, and

(b) any other person authorised by the Secretary of State to make analyses for the purposes of this section.

III. TRANSPORT AND WORKS ACT 1992

Preliminary

26.—(1) This Chapter applies to transport systems of any of the following kinds—

(a) a railway;

(b) a tramway;

(c) A system which uses another mode of guided transport and is specified for the purposes of this Chapter by an order made by the Secretary of State.

(2) This Chapter shall not apply to a transport system unless it is used, or is intended to be used, wholly or partly for the carriage of members of the public.

(3) The power to make orders under this section shall be exercisable by statutory instrument, which shall be subject to annulment in pursuance of a resolution of either House of Parliament.

Principal offences

Offences involving drink or drugs on transport systems

27.—(1) If a person works on a transport system to which this Chapter applies—

(a) as a driver, guard, conductor or signalman or in any other capacity in which he can control or affect the movement of a vehicle; or

(b) in a maintenance capacity or as a supervisor of, or look-out for, persons working in a maintenance capacity,

when he is unfit to carry out that work through drink or drugs, he shall be guilty of an offence.

(2) If a person works on a transport system to which this Chapter applies—

(a) as a driver, guard, conductor or signalman or in any other capacity in which he can control or affect the movement of a vehicle, or

(b) in a maintenance capacity or as a supervisor of, or look-out for, persons working in a maintenance capacity,

after consuming so much alcohol that the proportion of it in his breath, blood or urine exceeds the prescribed limit, he shall be guilty of an offence.

(3) For the purposes of this section, a person works on a transport system in a maintenance capacity if his work on the system involves maintenance, repair or alteration of—

(a) the permanent way or other means of guiding or supporting vehicles,

(b) signals or any other means of controlling the movement of vehicles, or

(c) any means of supplying electricity to vehicles or to the means of guiding or supporting vehicles,

or involves coupling or uncoupling vehicles or checking that they are working properly before they are used on any occasion.

(4) For the purpose of subsection (1) above, a person shall be taken to be unfit to carry out any work if his ability to carry out that work properly is for the time being impaired.

Offences by operators of transport systems

28.—(1) If a person commits an offence under section 27 above, the responsible operator shall also be guilty of an offence.

(2) In this section "the responsible operator" means—

(a) in a case where the transport system on which the offence under section 27 above is committed has only one operator, that operator;

(b) in a case where the transport system on which the offence under section 27 above is committed has more than one operator, whichever of them is responsible for the work giving rise to the offence.

(3) No offence is committed under subsection (1) above if the responsible operator has exercised all due diligence to prevent the commission on the transport system of any offence under section 27 above.

(4) If a person commits an offence under section 27 above in the course of his employment with a person other than the responsible operator, his employer shall (without prejudice to any liability of that operator under subsection (1) above) also be guilty of an offence.

(5) No offence is committed under subsection (4) above if the employer has exercised all due diligence to prevent the commission on the transport system by any of his employees of any offence under section 27 above.

Police powers, etc.

Breath tests

29.—(1) where a constable in uniform has reasonable cause to suspect—

(a) that a person working on a transport system to which this Chapter applies in any capacity mentioned in section 27(1) and (2) above has alcohol in his body, or

(b) that a person has been working on a transport system to which this Chapter applies in any capacity mentioned in section 27(1) and (2) above with alcohol in his body and still has alcohol in his body,

he may require that person to provide a specimen of breath for a breath test.

(2) Where an accident or dangerous incident occurs on a transport system to which this Chapter applies, a constable in uniform may require a person to provide a specimen of breath for a breath test if he has reasonable cause to suspect that—

(a) at the time of the accident or incident that person was working on the transport system in a capacity mentioned in section 27(1) and)2) above, and

(b) an act or omission of that person while he was so working may have been a cause of the accident or incident.

(3) In subsection (2) above "dangerous incident" means an incident which in the constable's opinion involved a danger of death or personal injury.

(4) A person may be required under subsection (1) or subsection (2) above to provide a specimen either at or near the place where the

requirement is made or, if the requirement is made under subsection (2) above and the constable making the requirement thinks fit, at a police station specified by the constable.

(5) A person who, without reasonable excuse, fails to provide a specimen of breath when required to do so in pursuance of this section shall be guilty of an offence.

Powers of arrest and entry

30.—(1) A constable may arrest a person without warrant if he has reasonable cause to suspect that that person is or has been committing an offence under section 27(1) above.

(2) A constable may arrest a person without warrant if —

(a) as a result of a breath test under section 29 above he has reasonable cause to suspect that the proportion of alcohol in that person's breath or blood exceeds the prescribed limit, or

(b) that person has failed to provide a specimen of breath for a breath test when required to do so in pursuance of section 29 above and the constable has reasonable cause to suspect that he has alcohol in his body.

(3) For the purpose of arresting a person under subsection (1) above, a constable may enter (if need be by force) any place where that person is or where the constable, with reasonable cause, suspects him to be.

(4) A constable may, for the purpose of—

(a) requiring a person to provide a specimen of breath under section 29(2) above in the case of an accident which the constable has reasonable cause to suspect involved the death of, or injury to, another person, or

(b) arresting a person in such a case under subsection (2) above,

enter (if need be by force) any place where that person is or where the constable, with reasonable cause, suspects him to be.

Provision of specimens for analysis

31.—(1) In the course of an investigation into whether a person has committed an offence under section 27 above, a constable may require him—

(a) to provide two specimens of breath for analysis by means of a device of a type approved by the Secretary of State, or

(b) to provide a specimen of blood or urine for a laboratory test.

(2) A requirement under this section to provide specimens of breath shall only be made at a police station.

(3) A requirement under this section to provide a specimen of blood or urine shall only be made at a police station or at a hospital; and it shall not be made at a police station unless subsection (4) below applies.

(4) This subsection applies if—

(a) the constable making the requirements has reasonable cause to believe that for medical reasons a specimen of breath cannot be provided or shall not be required,

(b) at the time the requirement is made, either a device (or reliable device) of the type mentioned in subsection (1)(a) above is not available at the police station or it is for any other reason not practicable to use such a device there, or

(bb) [*Not yet in force*] a device of the type mentioned in subsection (1)(a) above has been used at the police station but the constable who required the specimens of breath has reasonable cause to believe that the device has not produced a reliable indication of the proportion of alcohol in the breath of the person concerned, or,

(c) the suspected offence is one under section 27(1) above and the constable making the requirement has been advised by a medical practitioner that the condition of the person required to provide the specimen might be due to a drug.

(5) A person may be required to provide a specimen of blood or urine in pursuance of this section notwithstanding that he has already provided or been required to provide two specimens of breath.

(6) If the provision of a specimen other than a specimen of breath may be required in pursuance of this section, the question whether it is to be a specimen of blood or a specimen of urine shall be decided by the constable making the requirement; but if a medical practitioner is of the opinion that for medical reasons a specimen of blood cannot or should not be taken, the specimen shall be a specimen of urine.

(7) A specimen of urine shall be provided within one hour of the requirement for its provision being made and after the provision of a previous specimen of urine.

(8) A person who, without reasonable excuse, fails to provide a specimen when required to do so in pursuance of this section shall be guilty of an offence.

(9) A constable shall, on requiring a person to provide a specimen in pursuance of this section, warn him that a failure to provide it may render him liable to prosecution.

Choice of specimens of breath

32.—(1) Of any two specimens of breath provided by a person in pursuance of section 31 above, the one with the lower proportion of alcohol in the breath shall be used and the other shall be disregarded.

(2) But if the specimen with the lower proportion of alcohol contains no more than 50 microgrammes of alcohol in 100 millilitres of breath, the person who provided it may claim that it should be replaced by such specimen as may be required under section 31(6) above and, if he then provides such a specimen, neither specimen of breath shall be used.

(3) The Secretary of State may by regulations substitute another proportion of alcohol in the breath for that specified in subsection (2) above.

(4) The power to make regulations under this section shall be exercisable by statutory instrument; and no such regulations shall be made unless a draft of the instrument containing them has been laid before, and approved by a resolution of, each House of Parliament.

Protection for hospital patients

33.—(1) While a person is at a hospital as a patient, he shall not be required to provide a specimen of breath for a breath test or to provide a specimen for a laboratory test unless the medical practitioner in immediate charge of his case has been notified of the proposal to make the requirement; and—

(a) if the requirement is then made, it shall be for the provision of a specimen at the hospital, but

(b) if the medical practitioner objects on the ground specified in subsection (2) below, the requirement shall not be made.

(2) The ground on which the medical practitioner may object is that the requirement or the provision of a specimen or (in the case of a specimen of blood or urine) the warning required under section 31(9) above would be prejudicial to the proper care and treatment of the patient.

(3) A person shall not be arrested under section 30(2) above while he is at a hospital as a patient.

Evidence in proceedings for offences under section 27

Use of specimens in proceedings

34.—(1) In proceedings for any offence under section 27 above—

(a) evidence of the proportion of alcohol or any drug in a specimen of breath, blood or urine provided by the accused shall be taken into account, and

(b) it shall be assumed that the proportion of alcohol in the accused's breath, blood or urine at the time of the alleged offence was not less than in the specimen.

(2) That assumption shall not be made if the accused proves—

(a) that he consumed alcohol before he provided the specimen and after he had stopped work on the occasion of the alleged offence, and

(b) that, had he not done so, the proportion of alcohol in his breath, blood or urine would not have exceeded the prescribed limit and, where the offence alleged is an offence of being unfit to carry out the work in question through drink, would not have been such as to impair his ability to carry out that work properly.

(3) Where, at the time a specimen of blood or urine was provided by the accused, he asked to be provided with such a specimen, evidence of the proportion of alcohol or any drug found in the specimen shall not be admissible in the proceedings on behalf of the prosecution unless—

(a) the specimen in which the alcohol or drug was found is one of two parts into which the specimen provided by the accused was divided at the time it was provided, and

(b) the other part was supplied to the accused.

Documentary evidence as to specimens

35.—(1) In proceedings for any offence under section 27 above, evidence of the proportion of alcohol in a specimen of breath may be given by the production of a document (or documents) purporting to be—

(a) a statement automatically produced by the device by which the proportion of alcohol in the specimen was measured, and

(b) a certificate signed by a constable (which may but need not be contained in the same document as the statement) that the specimen was provided by the accused at the date and time shown in the statement.

(2) In such proceedings, evidence of the proportion of alcohol or a drug in a specimen of blood or urine may be given by the production of a document purporting to be a certificate signed by an authorised analyst identifying the specimen and stating the proportion of alcohol or drug found in it.

(3) In such proceedings, evidence that a specimen of blood was taken from the accused with his consent by a medical practitioner may be given by the production of a document purporting to be a certificate to that effect signed by the practitioner.

(4) A document such as is mentioned in subsection (1) above shall be admissible in evidence on behalf of the prosecution in pursuance of this section only if a copy of it either was handed to the accused when the document was produced or was served on him not later than seven days before the hearing.

(5) A document such as is mentioned in subsection (2) or (3) above shall be admissible in evidence on behalf of the prosecution in pursuance of this section only if a copy of it was served on the accused not later than seven days before the hearing.

(6) A document purporting to be a certificate (or so much of a document as purports to be a certificate) shall not be admissible in evidence on behalf of the prosecution in pursurance of this section if the accused, not later than three days before the hearing or within such further time as the court may in special circumstances allow, has served notice on the prosecutor requiring the attendance at the hearing of the person by whom the document purports to be signed.

(7) In this section "served" means served personally or sent by registered post or recorded delivery service.

(8) In subsection (2) above "authorised analyst" means—

(a) any person possessing the qualifications prescribed by regulations made under section 76 of the Food Act 1984 or section 27 of the Food and Drugs (Scotland) Act 1956 as qualifying persons for appointment as public analysts under those Acts, or

(b) any other person authorised by the Secretary of State to make analyses for the purposes of this section.

Penalties

Penalties

36.—(1) A person guilty of an offence under this Chapter other than an offence under section 29(5) above shall be liable on summary conviction to imprisonment for a term not exceeding six months, to a fine not exceeding level 5 on the standard scale or to both.

(2) A person guilty of an offence under section 29(5) above shall be liable on summary conviction to a fine not exceeding level 3 on the standard scale.

Miscellaneous and supplementary

Special provision for Scotland

37.—(1) Section 30(3) and (4) above shall not extend to Scotland, and nothing in those subsections shall affect any rule of law in Scotland concerning the right of a constable to enter any premises for any purpose.

(2) In proceedings for any offence under section 27 above in Scotland—

(a) a document produced in evidence on behalf of the prosecution in pursuance of section 35 above and, where the person by whom the document was signed is called as a witness, the evidence of that person, shall be sufficient evidence of the facts stated in the document, and

(b) a written execution purporting to be signed by the person who handed to or served on the accused or the prosecutor a copy document or notice under section 35 above, together with, where appropriate, a post office receipt for the relevant registered or recorded delivery letter, shall be sufficient evidence of the handing or service of the copy document or notice.

Interpretation of Chapter 1

38.—(1) In this Chapter—

"breath test" means a preliminary test for the purpose of obtaining, by means of a device of a type approved by the Secretary of State, an indication whether the proportion of alcohol in a person's breath or blood is likely to exceed the prescribed limit;

"drug" includes any intoxicant other than alcohol;

"fail" includes refuse;

"hospital" means an institution which provides medical or surgical treatment for in-patients or out-patients.

(2) In this Chapter "the prescribed limit" means, as the case may require—

(a) 35 microgrammes of alcohol in 100 millilitres of breath,

(b) 80 milligrammes of alcohol in 100 millilitres of blood, or

(c) 107 milligrammes of alcohol in 100 millilitres of urine,

or such other proportion as may be prescribed by regulations made by the Secretary of State.

(3) For the purposes of this Chapter, it is immaterial whether a person who works on a transport system does so in the course of his employment, under a contract for services, voluntarily or otherwise.

(4) For the purposes of this Chapter, a person does not provide a specimen of breath for a breath test or for analysis unless the specimen—

(a) is sufficient to enable the test for the analysis to be carried out, and

(b) is provided in such a way as to enable the objective of the test or analysis to be satisfactorily achieved.

(5) For the purposes of this Chapter, a person provides a specimen of blood if and only if he consents to its being taken by a medical practitioner and it is so taken.

(6) The power to make regulations under subsection (2) above shall be exercisable by statutory instrument; and no such regulations shall be made unless a draft of the instrument containing them has been laid before, and approved by a resolution of, each House of Parliament.

Amendment of scope of offences involving drink or drugs under Road Traffic Act 1988

39. The following section shall be inserted in the Road Traffic Act 1988 after section 192—

"Tramcars and other guided vehicles: drink and drugs
192A.—(1) Sections 4 to 11 of this Act shall not apply (to the extent that apart from this subsection they would) to vehicles on any transport system to which Chapter 1 of Part II of the Transport and Works Act 1992 (offences involving drink or drugs on railways, tramways and certain other guided transport systems) applies.

(2) Subject to subsection (1) above, the Secretary of State may by regulations provide that sections 4 to 11 of this Act shall apply to vehicles on a system of guided transport specified in the regulations with such modifications as he considers necessary or expedient.

(3) Regulations under subsection (2) above may make different provision for different cases.

(4) In this section—
'guided transport' means transport by vehicles guided by means external to the vehicles (whether or not the vehicles are also capable of being operated in some other way), and
'vehicle' includes mobile traction unit."

Consequential amendment

40. In section 17 of the Railway Regulation Act 1842 (punishment of persons employed on railways guilty of misconduct) the words "who shall be found drunk while so employed upon the said railway" shall be omitted.

Appendix 2

ENDORSEMENT CODE

Drink or drugs

DR10   Driving or attempting to drive with an alcohol level above the prescribed limit.

DR20   Driving or attempting to drive while unfit through drink.

DR30   Driving or attempting to drive, then failing to supply a specimen for analysis.

DR40   In charge of a vehicle while alcohol level above the prescribed limit.

DR50   In charge of a vehicle while unfit through drink.

DR60   Failing to supply a specimen for analysis, not having driven or attempted to drive.

DR70   Failing to provide specimen for breath test (roadside).

DR80   Driving or attempting to drive while unfit through drugs.

DR90   In charge of a vehicle while unfit through drugs.

NOTE: Aiding and abetting, counselling or procuring: the 0 in the code for the substantive offence becomes 2.

Inciting: the 0 in the code for the substantive offence becomes 6.

Appendix 3

THE BREATH ANALYSIS DEVICES
(APPROVAL) ORDER 1983

In pursuance of the power conferred upon me by section 8(1) of the Road Traffic Act 1972(a), I, the Right Honourable William Whitelaw, one of Her Majesty's Principal Secretaries of State, do by this Order approve, as a means by which specimens of breath may be provided for analysis under the said section 8(1), each of the types of device described in the Schedule hereto for the use of police forces in England and Wales.

W.S.I. Whitelaw
One of Her Majesty's Principal
Secretaries of State

Home Office
18th April 1983

SCHEDULE

The device comprised of two components which are respectively known as the "Camic Simulator" and the "Camic Breath Analyser", each being manufactured by Camic Car and Medical Instrument Company Limited.

The device comprised of two components which are respectively known as the "Lion Breath Simulator" and the "Lion Intoximeter 3000" the first-mentioned component being manufactured by Camic Car and Medical Instrument Company Limited and the other component being manufactured by Lion Laboratories Limited.

(a) 1972 c. 20, as amended by 1981 c. 56, Schedule 8.

EXPLANATORY NOTE

(This Note is not part of the Order)

Section 8 of the Road Traffic Act 1972, as amended by Schedule 8 to the Transport Act 1981, empowers a constable, in specified circumstances, to require a person to provide two specimens of breath for analysis by means of a device of a type approved by the Secretary of State. This Order approves two devices for that purpose, Schedule 8 comes into force on 6th May 1983 (S.I. 1983/576) and, accordingly, this Order will have effect from that date.

Appendix 4

LION INTOXIMETER 3000 SAMPLE PRINTOUT

TEST RECORD

LION INTOX. 3000/3030   *Machine number*
WIDNES POLICE STN   *Station*
CHESHIRE CONSTAB   *Constabulary*

THU JAN 24, 1991   *Date of test*

SUBJECT NAME =

DOB. = 28/03/55

SIGNATURE   *Signature of subject*

TEST UG% TIME

STD 36	01:17GMT	*First calibration*
BLK 0	01.18GMT	*Purging*
ONE 39	01:18GMT	*First analysis*
BLK 0	01:18GMT	*Purging*
TWO 39	01:20GMT	*Second analysis*
BLK 0	01:20GMT	*Purging*
STD 36	01:20GMT	*Second calibration*

OPERATOR NAME =

I CERTIFY THAT IN THIS STATEMENT, READING ONE RELATES TO THE FIRST SPECIMEN OF BREATH PROVIDED BY THE SUBJECT NAMED ABOVE, AND READING TWO TO THE SECOND, AT THE DATE AND TIME SHOWN HEREIN.

Certificate pursuant to Road Traffic Offenders Act 1988, s.16(1)

SIGNATURE   *Signature of operator*

439

LION INTOXIMETER
OPERATOR INSTRUCTION CARD

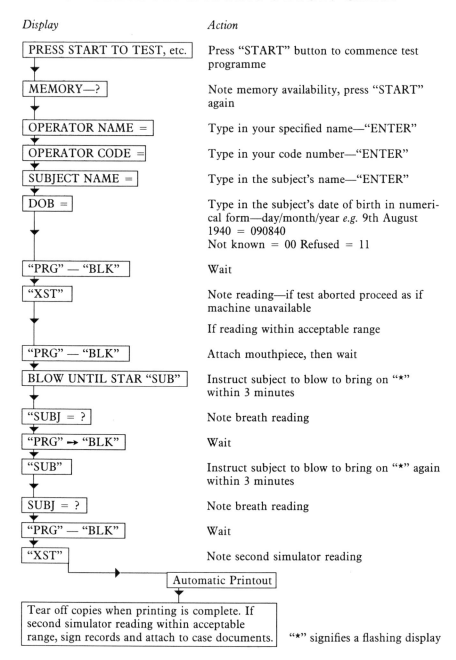

Display	*Action*
PRESS START TO TEST, etc.	Press "START" button to commence test programme
MEMORY—?	Note memory availability, press "START" again
OPERATOR NAME =	Type in your specified name—"ENTER"
OPERATOR CODE =	Type in your code number—"ENTER"
SUBJECT NAME =	Type in the subject's name—"ENTER"
DOB =	Type in the subject's date of birth in numerical form—day/month/year *e.g.* 9th August 1940 = 090840 Not known = 00 Refused = 11
"PRG" — "BLK"	Wait
"XST"	Note reading—if test aborted proceed as if machine unavailable If reading within acceptable range
"PRG" — "BLK"	Attach mouthpiece, then wait
BLOW UNTIL STAR "SUB"	Instruct subject to blow to bring on "★" within 3 minutes
"SUBJ = ?	Note breath reading
"PRG" → "BLK"	Wait
"SUB"	Instruct subject to blow to bring on "★" again within 3 minutes
SUBJ = ?	Note breath reading
"PRG" — "BLK"	Wait
"XST"	Note second simulator reading
Automatic Printout	
Tear off copies when printing is complete. If second simulator reading within acceptable range, sign records and attach to case documents.	"★" signifies a flashing display

Appendix 5

DRINKING AND DRIVING: SUMMARY OF BREATH TESTING REQUIREMENTS AND OUTCOMES

England and Wales 1991★: Numbers and percentages

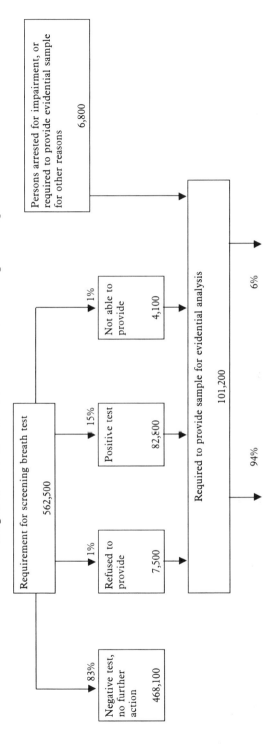

★ This is the last year in which the figures have been available for compiling such a chart. Since 1992 the Home Office has not kept all the relevant statistics as they were not considered to be of sufficient interest.

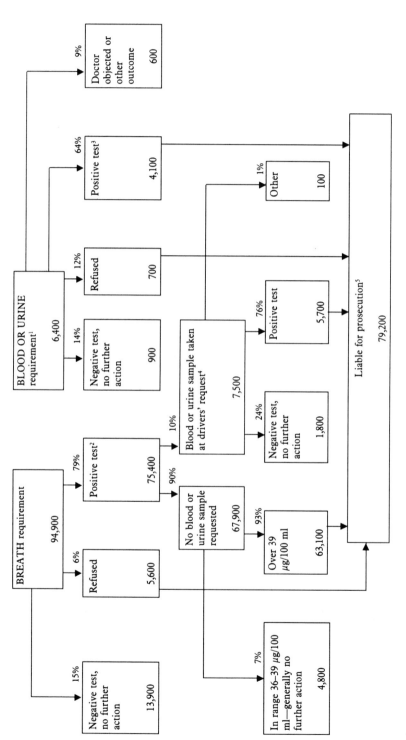

1 Only is there is a legitimate reason why an evidential breath test cannot be taken.
2 Over 35 µg alcohol per 100 ml of breath. Persons in range 36–39 µg per 100 ml are not normally prosecuted.
3 Over 80µg alcohol per 100 ml blood or 107 mg per ml urine.
4 Between April 16, 1984 and January 20, 1989, drivers with an evidential breath reading of over 50 µg alcohol per 100 ml breath were able to request a blood or urine test. This right was for a trial period and on a non-statutory basis. It was withdrawn after a review.
5 This figure is expected to be lower than the number actually prosecuted, partly because of under-recording of breath tests. Breath test statistics are derived from a return to the Home Office by police forces in respect of each alcohol test required. Most forces return confirmation on negative tests on an aggregated basis. Reporting of breath tests is not comprehensive; negative tests are less well reported than positive tests. The introduction of simplified returns in 1987 raised the level of recording; and so the figures for 1987 and later are not comparable with earlier figures.

Table 1

SCREENING BREATH TESTS TOTALS AND OUTCOME, BY MONTH
England and Wales 1995

Numbers and percentages

Month	Total tests	Positive/refused	% Positive/refused
January	54,100	7,000	13
February	48,100	7,000	15
March	49,700	7,700	16
April	47,200	8,200	17
May	46,100	7,700	17
June	49,400	7,200	15
July	53,300	7,700	14
August	52,000	8,200	16
September	47,500	7,900	17
October	54,000	8,600	16
November	59,800	8,300	14
December	141,400	8,900	6
Total	702,700	94,400	13

Reporting of breath tests is not comprehensive: negative tests are less well reported than positive tests. Up until 1992, breath test statistics were derived from a return to the Home Office by police forces in respect of each alcohol test required. Most forces returned information on negative tests on an aggregated basis. During 1992 a new return was introduced, which required police forces only to give the total number of screening tests, and the sum of positive and refused tests. The introduction of this new return may have altered the level of recording compared with earlier years. This was discussed in the 1992 *Breath Test Statistics Bulletin* (Issue 12/93).

Table 2

Proceedings at magistrates' courts by offence type and outcome
England and Wales 1994

Number of offences

Offence group	Offence type	Total proceedings	Proceedings discontinued[1]	Committals for trial	Charges withdrawn/dismissed	Total Findings of guilt
	Driving etc. after consuming alcohol or taking drugs:					
	Unfit to drive through drink or drugs (impairment)	3,932	213	117	1,810	1,792
	Driving with alcohol in the blood above the prescribed limit	80,628	2,146	713	4,603	73,166
	Driving and failing to provide specimen for analysis (breath, blood or urine)	10,080	389	298	1,403	7,990
	In charge of motor vehicle, while unfit through drink or drugs (impairment)	977	59	13	542	363
	In charge of motor vehicle with alcohol in the blood above the prescribed limit	2,752	193	6	888	1,665
	In charge of motor vehicle and failing to provide specimen for analysis (breath, blood or urine)	862	38	18	150	656
	Failing to provide specimen for initial breath test	5,458	196	83	2,068	3,111
	Total	104,690	3,234	1,248	11,464	88,743

(1) Also includes discharges under section 6 of the Magistrates' Courts Act 1980, and hospital and guardianship orders without conviction.

Table 3

Findings of guilt at magistrates' courts by offence type and sentence or order imposed England and Wales 1994

Number of offences

Offence group / Offence type Dealt with	Total findings of guilt	Sentence or order										
		Absolute or conditional discharge or recognisance	Probation or supervision order	Fine	Community service order	Attendance centre order	Combination order	Young offender institution	Young offender institution	Imprisonment — Fully suspended	Imprisonment — Unsuspended	Committed for sentence
Otherwise dealt with												
Driving etc, after consuming alcohol or taking drugs:												
Unfit to drive through drink or drugs (impairment)	1,792	57	188	1,005	138	4	73	19	11	192	11	93
Driving with alcohol in the blood above the prescribed limit	73,166	554	4,203	57,998	3,838	39	1,637	242	224	3,894	101	434
Driving and failing to provide specimen for analysis (breath, blood or urine)	7,990	172	665	5,162	539	10	267	50	32	740	41	311
In charge of motor vehicle, while unfit through drink or drugs (impairment)	363	12	27	244	19	—	6	1	4	19	2	28
In charge of motor vehicle with alcohol in the blood above the prescribed limit	1,665	42	96	1,322	69	3	22	5	4	60	5	37
In charge of motor vehicle and failing to provide specimen for analysis (breath, blood or urine)	656	16	46	448	44	1	13	2	—	51	2	33
Failing to provide a specimen for initial breath test	3,111	140	202	1,627	46	2	15	—	—	—	11	1,067
Sub-total	88,743	994	5,427	67,807	4,694	60	2,034	320	275	4,957	173	2,003

Table 4

Sentences of immediate imprisonment imposed at magistrates' courts by length of sentence

England and Wales 1994 — Number of offences

Offence Offence type group	Total	Length of sentence				
		14 Days and under	Over 14 days up to 1 month	Over 1 Month up to 2 months	Over 2 months up to 3 months	Over 3 months up to 6 months
Driving etc, after consuming alcohol or taking drugs:						
Unfit to drive through drink or drugs (impairment)	192	8	29	39	51	65
Driving with alcohol in the blood above the prescribed limit	3,894	75	534	737	1,124	1,423
Driving and failing to provide specimen for analysis (breath, blood or urine)	740	17	123	138	225	238
In charge of motor vehicle, while unfit through drink or drugs (impairment)	19	–	3	4	12	–
In charge of motor vehicle with alcohol in the blood above the prescribed limit	60	2	19	16	17	6
In charge of motor vehicle and failing to provide specimen for analysis (breath, blood or urine)	51	1	12	11	19	8
Total	4,957	103	720	945	1,448	1,740

Table 5

Sentences of young offender institution imposed at magistrates' courts by length of sentence

England and Wales 1994 — Number of offences

Offence group / Offence type	Total	Length of sentence				
		14 days and under	Over 14 days up to 1 month	Over 1 month up to 2 months	Over 2 months up to 3 months	Over 3 months up to 6 months
Driving etc, after consuming alcohol or taking drugs:						
Unfit to drive through drink or drugs (impairment)	19	–	4	4	8	3
Driving with alcohol in the blood above the prescribed limit	242	2	53	53	62	71
Driving and failing to provide specimen for analysis (breath, blood or urine)	50	–	8	13	18	11
In charge of motor vehicle, while unfit through drink or drugs (impairment)	1	–	–	1	–	–
In charge of motor vehicle with alcohol in the blood above the prescribed limit	5	–	3	2	–	–
In charge of motor vehicle and failing to provide specimen for analysis (breath, blood or urine)	2	–	2	–	–	–
Total	320	2	70	73	88	85

447

Table 6

Fines imposed at magistrates' courts by offence group and amount

England and Wales 1994

Offence group	Offence type	Total Number of fines	Amounts of fines									Number of offences Average amount of fines £
			Up to and Incl £5	Over £5 up to £10	Over £10 up to £20	Over £20 up to £50	Over £50 up to £100	Over £100 up to £200	Over £200 up to £400	Over £400 up to £800	Over £800 up to £5000	
	Driving etc. after consuming alcohol or taking drugs (*i.e.* all offences under R.T.A. sections 4–7)	67,807	8	26	47	1,049	5,727	17,551	29,674	12,924	800	306

Table 7

Proceedings for trial (1) at the Crown Court by offence type and outcome

England and Wales 1994

Number of offences

Offence group	Offence type	Total proceedings for trial	Not tried	Acquitted	Total findings of guilt	Sentence or order						Imprisonment		Otherwise dealt with
						Absolute or conditional discharge or recognisance	Probation or supervision order	Fine	Community service order	Combination order	Young offender institution	Fully suspended	Unsuspended	
Driving etc, after consuming alcohol or taking drugs:														
	Unfit to drive through drink or drugs (impairment)	131	9	15	107	1	7	7	5	2	10	–	36	39
	Driving with alcohol in the blood above the prescribed limit	602	16	19	567	10	28	53	40	12	32	8	230	154
	Driving and failing to provide specimen for analysis (breath, blood or urine)	224	5	17	202	1	6	21	9	2	4	3	80	76
	In charge of motor vehicle, while unfit through drink or drugs (impairment)	10	1	4	5	–	3	–	–	–	–	–	1	1
	In charge of motor vehicle with alcohol in the blood above the prescribed limit	7	–	2	5	–	1	–	–	–	–	–	1	3
	In charge of motor vehicle and failing to provide specimen for analysis (breath, blood or urine)	11	–	1	10	–	1	2	–	–	–	–	3	4
	Failing to provide specimen for initial breath test	78	2	15	61	2	2	10	1	–	–	–	6	40
Total		1,063	33	73	957	14	48	93	55	16	46	11	357	317

(1) Some trials take place at the Crown Court in a different year from that in which the committal took place in the magistrates' court, and so the totals do not agree with those shown under "Committals for trial" in Table 2.

Table 8

Proceedings at the Crown Court for sentencing after summary conviction (1) by offence type and sentence or order

England and Wales 1994   Number of offences

Offence Offence type group	Total	Sentence or order						Imprisonment		Otherwise dealt with
		Absolute or conditional discharge or recognisance	Probation or supervision order	Fine	Community service order	Combination order	Young offender institution	Fully suspended	Unsuspended	
Driving etc. after consuming alcohol or taking drugs:										
Unfit to drive through drink or drugs (impairment)	16	–	–	2	–	–	1	–	9	4
Driving with alcohol in the blood above the prescribed limit	124	1	10	11	4	3	10	1	65	19
Driving and failing to provide specimen for analysis (breath, blood or urine)	45	1	4	4	–	1	2	–	23	10
In charge of motor vehicle, while unfit through drink or drugs (impairment)	1	–	–	–	1	–	–	–	–	–
In charge of motor vehicle with alcohol in the blood above the prescribed limit	3	–	1	1	–	–	–	–	1	–
In charge of motor vehicle and failing to provide specimen for analysis (breath, blood or urine)	5	–	–	–	1	–	–	–	1	3
Failing to provide a specimen for initial breath test	5	2	–	1	–	–	–	–	–	2
Total	199	4	15	19	6	4	13	1	99	38

(1) Some sentences are given in the Crown Court in a different year from that in which the conviction took place in the magistrates' court, and so the totals do not agree with those shown under "Committed for sentence" in Table 3.

Table 9

Sentences of immediate imprisonment imposed at the Crown Court by length of sentence
England and Wales 1994

Number of offences

Offence group	Offence type	Total	Length of sentence						
			6 Months and under	Over 6 months up to 12 months	Over 12 months up to 18 months	Over 18 months up to 2 years	Over 2 years up to 3 years	Over 3 years up to 5 years	Over 5 years
	Driving etc. after consuming alcohol or taking drugs (*i.e.* all offences under R.T.A. sections 4–7)	456	456	—	—	—	—	—	—

Table 10

Sentences of young offender institution imposed at the Crown Court by length of sentence
England and Wales 1994

Number of offences

Offence group	Offence type	Total	Length of sentence						
			6 Months and under	Over 6 months up to 12 months	Over 12 months up to 18 months	Over 18 months up to 2 years	Over 2 years up to 3 years	Over 3 years up to 5 years	Over 5 years
	Driving etc. after consuming alcohol or taking drugs (*i.e.* all offences under R.T.A. sections 4–7)	59	58	1	—	—	—	—	—

Table 11

Fines imposed at trials at the Crown Court by offence group and amount

England and Wales 1994 — Number of fines

Offence group	Offence type	Total Number of fines	Amounts of fines									Average amount of fines £
			Up to and incl £5	Over £5 up to £10	Over £10 up to £20	Over £20 up to £50	Over £50 up to £100	Over £100 up to £200	Over £200 up to £400	Over £400 up to £800	Over £800	
	Driving etc. after consuming alcohol or taking drugs (*i.e.* all offences under R.T.A. sections 4-7)	93	5	5	–	3	13	24	30	13	–	232

Table 12

Fines imposed at the Crown Court on sentencing after summary conviction by offence group and amount

England and Wales 1994

Offence group	Offence type	Total Number of fines	Amounts of fines									Number of fines — Average amount of fines
			Up to and Incl £5	Over £5 up to £10	Over £10 up to £20	Over £20 up to £50	Over £50 up to £100	Over £100 up to £200	Over £200 up to £400	Over £400 up to £800	Over £800	
	Driving etc. after consuming alcohol or taking drugs (*i.e.* all offences under R.T.A. sections 4–7)	19	3	—	—	4	4	2	4	2	—	154

Table 13

Driving licence endorsements and disqualifications imposed at magistrates' courts by offence group and period of disqualification(1)

England and Wales 1994 — Number of offences

Offence group	Offence Type	Endorsements without disqualification	Total Disqualifications imposed	Period of disqualification													Disqualifications in which driving test requirement imposed
				Until driving test passed	Under 6 months	6 months and under 1 year	Over 6 months and under 1 year	1 Year	Over 1 year and under 2 years	2 Years and under 3 years	3 Years	Over 3 years and under 4 years	4 Years and under 5 years	5 Years and under 10 years	10 Years & over, less than life	Life	
Driving etc after consuming alcohol or taking drugs.(2)		6,577	80,625	57	266	421	458	31,110	18,970	7,652	18,179	226	1,145	1,986	148	6	691

(1) Excludes those persons disqualified by magistrates' courts under section 35 of the Road Traffic Offenders Act 1988 (penalty points system).
(2) *i.e.* all offences under R.T.A. sections 4–7.

Table 14

Driving licence endorsements and disqualifications imposed at the Crown Court by offence group and period of disqualification (1)

England and Wales 1994   Number of offences

Offence group	Offence Type	Endorsements without disqualification	Total Disqualifications imposed	Period of disqualification													Disqualifications in which driving test requirement imposed
				Until driving test passed	Under 6 months	6 months	Over 6 months and under 1 year	1 Year	Over 1 year and under 2 years	2 Years and under 3 years	3 Years	Over 3 years and under 4 years	4 Years and under 5 years	5 Years and under 10 years	10 Years & over, less than life	Life	
Driving etc. after consuming alcohol or taking drugs.(3)		320	610	5	2	5	1	190	53	73	232	3	19	22	5	—	69

(1) Excludes persons disqualified by the Crown Court under section 35 of the Road Traffic Offenders Act 1988 (penalty points system).
(2) Included in "Total disqualifications imposed".
(3) *i.e.* all offences under R.T.A. sections 3A–7.

Table 15

Findings of guilt for offences of driving etc. after consuming alcohol or taking drugs by offence type and age group of offender

England and Wales 1994

Number of offences

Offence Type	All Ages	Under 17	17 and under 21	21 and under 25	25 and under 30	30 and under 40	40 and under 50	50 and under 60	60 and over
					Age Group				
Unfit to drive through drink or drugs (impairment)	1,899	13	200	359	357	508	309	105	48
Driving with alcohol in the blood above the prescribed limit	73,733	214	6,265	11,430	14,402	21,029	13,190	5,303	1,900
Driving and failing to provide specimen for analysis (breath, blood or urine)	8,192	26	430	1,002	1,721	2,710	1,525	620	158
In charge of motor vehicle while unfit through drink or drugs (impairment)	368	1	30	49	65	103	75	34	11
In charge of motor vehicle with alcohol in the blood above the prescribed limit	1,670	7	144	249	304	510	285	127	44
In charge of motor vehicle and failing to provide specimen for analysis (breath, blood or urine)	666	–	42	82	125	232	124	50	11
Failing to provide specimen for initial breath test	3,172	4	178	374	638	1,042	635	238	63
Total all offences	89,700	265	7,289	13,545	17,612	26,134	16,143	6,477	2,235

457

Table 16

Findings of guilt at all courts by offence group and police force area
England and Wales 1994

Number of offences

Offence Offence type group	England and Wales	Police Force area								
		Avon and Somerset	Bedfordshire	Cambridgeshire	Cheshire	Cleveland	Cumbria	Derbyshire	Devon and Cornwall	Dorset
Driving etc. after consuming alcohol or taking drugs(1)	89,700	1,981	1,114	890	1,746	893	971	1,442	2,011	1,032

	Police Force Area									
	Durham	Essex	Gloucestershire	Greater Manchester	Hampshire	Hertfordshire	Humberside	Kent	Lancashire	Leicestershire
Driving etc. after consuming alcohol or taking drugs(1)	938	2,420	840	5,439	2,846	1,505	1,129	2,509	2,645	1,271

	Police Force area									
	Lincolnshire	London City of	Merseyside	Metropolitan Police	Norfolk	Northamptonshire	Northumbria	North Yorkshire	Nottinghamshire	South Yorkshire
Driving etc. after consuming alcohol or taking drugs(1)	550	437	2,677	15,259	806	880	2,134	1,210	1,580	2,119

	Police Force area									Total England
	Staffordshire	Suffolk	Surrey	Sussex	Thames Valley	Warwickshire	West Mercia	West Midlands	West Yorkshire	Wiltshire
Driving etc. after consuming alcohol or taking drugs(1)	1,685	977	1,421	2,140	3,304	756	1,975	5,851	4,038	966	84,387

	Police Force area				Total Wales
	Dyfed-Powys	Gwent	North Wales	South Wales	
Driving etc. after consuming alcohol or taking drugs(1)	812	689	1,353	2,459	5,313

(1) *i.e.* all offences under R.T.A. sections 4-7.

458

Table 17

Findings of guilt at all courts by offence group, sex and age of offender

England and Wales 1994

Number of offences

Offence Offence type group	Male			Female			Total 21 and over	Total offences		% Male 21 and over	% 21 and over
	Under 21	21 and over	Total	Under 21	21 and over	Total		by persons	by (1) others		
Driving etc. after consuming alcohol or taking drugs(2)	7,127	76,200	83,327	427	5,946	6,373	82,146	89,700	–	93	92

(1) Companies, local authorities etc.
(2) *i.e.* all offences under R.T.A. sections 4–7.

459

Table 18

Written warnings for motoring offences by offence group and police force area

England and Wales 1994

Number of warnings

Offence group / Offence type	England and Wales	Police Force area								
		Avon and Somerset	Bedfordshire	Cambridgeshire	Cheshire	Cleveland	Cumbria	Derbyshire	Devon and Cornwall	Dorset
Driving etc. after consuming alcohol or taking drugs(1)	325	6	3	–	–	2	7	3	5	–

Offence type	Police Force area									
	Durham	Essex	Gloucestershire	Greater Manchester	Hampshire	Hertfordshire	Humberside	Kent	Lancashire	Leicestershire
Driving etc. after consuming alcohol or taking drugs(1)	1	–	–	2	20	–	3	7	6	–

Offence type	Police Force area									
	Lincolnshire	London, City of	Merseyside	Metropolitan police	Norfolk	Northamptonshire	Northumbria	North Yorkshire	Nottinghamshire	South Yorkshire
Driving etc. after consuming alcohol or taking drugs(1)	2	–	6	24	21	5	5	6	1	87

Offence type	Police Force area										Total England
	Staffordshire	Suffolk	Surrey	Sussex	Thames Valley	Warwickshire	West Mercia	West Midlands	West Yorkshire	Wiltshire	
Driving etc. after consuming alcohol or taking drugs(1)	2	1	2	5	7	4	–	41	4	9	293

Offence group / Offence type	Police Force area				Total Wales
	Dyfed-Powys	Gwent	North Wales	South Wales (1)	
Driving etc. after consuming alcohol or taking drugs(1)	2	28	–	2	32

(1) i.e. all offences under R.T.A. sections 4–7.

Appendix 6

ACCIDENT STATISTICS AND CONSEQUENCES FOR THE DEVELOPMENT OF MODELS FOR THEIR PREVENTION

Legal policies for the prevention of accidents caused by drunken driving focus on the human factor. The goal is to change the association between drinking and driving. Legal policies in many jurisdictions move from data to policy with alacrity, but without justification. It is important to note that the reason why deterrence is so difficult to achieve and, when achieved, is so transient, may be because the statistics from which such prevention studies emanate may not themselves reveal the whole story. They may not indicate who is the drinking driver, his destination or companions. These factors may be just as important, and should be considered when studying prevention data statistics.

For this reason, it is necessary to focus on the data concerned before constructing alcohol control policies on safety. Further evaluation of accident statistics will therefore take place, but by focusing on building a structure for accident prevention. Research does not exist in isolation. It has a context and this entire picture will point in some directions with the exclusion of others. Whilst public concern will immediately focus on the presence of alcohol in the crash equation as the sole factor requiring prevention, this merely underlines the preoccupation with the personal characteristics of drivers. However, it may be social contexts which are of equal or greater importance. Crashes are complex events. Whilst driving may statistically raise the risk of injury, it does not guarantee a crash will occur. Alcohol is related to other elements that increase the chance of an accident happening, such as alcohol, youth and night driving, which, when occurring together, may raise the chance of an accident.

The conundrum is whether the presence of alcohol is related to other factors in the behaviour of a motorist that might be more directly related to the accident. An example of this reasoning was advanced by Fell in 1982, who concluded that drivers with raised blood alcohol levels were less likely to wear safety belts (see J. C. Fell *et al.* (1982) 4 Q.J.Am.Ass.Auto.Med. 31). A further question is whether drivers who have elevated blood alcohol concentrations are more likely to drive lighter or older cars, as a study by Bako *et al.*, 1979, has indicated. His study indicates that income, car use and alcohol interact and that this interaction is possibly the causative factor (see G. Bako *et al.*, *Proceedings of the 7th International Conference on Alcohol, Drugs and Traffic Safety* (1979), p. 137).

It is important to realise that alcohol is not the only element in the process which may be modified. Those who drink and drive must be identified in order to direct attempts at prevention towards them. Drinking drivers are significantly male. Fell's statistics indicate that over 85 per cent of those driving whilst intoxicated and indeed over 85 per cent of crash fatalities are male. Drinking, driving and masculinity are more strongly associated than driving and masculinity. The group aged 16–25 is at the greatest risk of death and injury from alcohol-impaired driving (see J. Headlund *et al.*, National Highway Traffic Safety Administration (1983)). Young drivers are more likely to have fatal accidents with low blood alcohol levels than older drivers (see H. M. Simpson *et al.*, (1982) 10 Drug Alc. Depend. 35). There is also the combination of alcohol abuse and risk-taking night driving which has a high risk of death and injury (see D. Pelz and P. Williams, University of Michigan Highway Safety Research Institute (1975)). The pattern of driving, in this context, will be more highly predictive of a bad outcome than alcohol alone. The young certainly seem to be more impaired by lesser amounts of alcohol (see T. Cameron (1982) 10 Drug Alc. Depend. 1) and the pattern of drinking is different in the young (see H. T. Blane, *Middle-Aged Alcoholics and Young Drinkers* (1979, Plenum Press, New York) p. 5). Alcoholism is more prevalent in middle age. However, heavy drinking episodes or "binges" are more common in the 18–24 age group. Drinking and driving is more common in this age group (Cameron, 1982).

Socio-economic analysis of this age group indicates selfish, exhibitionist and careless driving (see D. Pelz and S. Schuman, *Proceedings of the 3rd Annual Alcoholism Conference of the National Institute on Alcohol Abuse and Alcoholism* (1974), p. 50). This study also found a correlation between bad school records and lower social groups. Lower income and job status, lower educational status and minority membership are frequently present. Divorced and separated individuals and single men testify to the social instability which provides the background to drink driving (see R. K. Jones and K. B. Joscelyn, Department of Transportation Publication (1978)). The relation between youth, leisure activities and alcohol is borne out by studies in which maturity slowly develops. In this process alcohol, anti-social traits and truancy decrease as youth attains its mature phase of steady employment, marital stability and adult values (see J. E. Donovan *et al.* (1983) 44 J.Stud.Alcohol 109). However, the question is not so much the analysis of the drinking driver, but his destination and companions. It is thus not so much the person but the environment that can be equally as important. This may be the reason why deterrence has been found to be so difficult to achieve and, even when achieved, has been found to be so transient.

Fundamental to all studies of the problem is the low risk of detection for the drinker in any single event of drinking and driving. Estimates of between 200 and 2,000 occurrences of driving whilst intoxicated for every arrest indicate the minute chance of detection in American society (see R. B. Voas, *Alcohol, Drugs and Traffic Safety* (1975, Addiction Research Foundation, Toronto), p. 21). Accidents and death are rare, even with alcohol as an aggravating factor. This probably increases the risk threefold. The risk of either arrest or accident is less than one in 1,000 (see H. L. Ross, *Deterring the Drinking Driver* (1982, D. C. Heath and Co., Lexington, Mass.)). This clearly is very small and is perceived as such.

It is inappropriate to consider drinking drivers as being capable of making sensible decisions concerning risks. Indeed, this process may not be possible at all. Joseph R. Gusfield, 1985, in his studies of bar culture over three months, indicated that drinking and driving was the

" . . . assumed, customary way in which men transported themselves. Failure to do so was something to be excused, to be explained. Competent drivers were presumed able to carry out the expected activities of life which included drinking and driving. Those exempt from such expectations were those who could obtain the protection and aid of others, that is, women, the elderly, alcoholics (incompetent drivers), or those whose prior D.W.I. [driving while intoxicated] arrests increased the cost of risk."

Gusfield summarises exactly why many of those who drink and drive are immune to the normal principles of deterrence.

There is a social structure which governs drinking and driving, based on recreation and mobility. The bar studies analysed four bars in San Diego with intensive observations for three months. Intervention in drinking and driving was influenced by two facets of the bars and their drinkers. In a neighbourhood bar with regular members there was an interdependent relationship between the drinkers and the bar, which was both economic and personal.

The second major factor affecting intervention by others in the drinking driving act was the relationship between customers. Relationships through marriage or friendship may lessen drinking and driving. The institutional settings did control behaviour. "Trouble" means things that occur within the bar. Authority prevented trouble such as fights within the bar. The intervention of police inside the bar was something to be feared. Serving those under legal age was something to be prevented since it would inevitably result in intervention. Drinking and driving is thus not an important concern of the bar staff since not enough consequences to heighten concern (see J. R. Gusfield, (1985) 10 J. Stud. Alcohol 70).

Practical intervention took place at Notre-Dame University some years ago. The University was disturbed by serious drinking accidents involving students crossing the state line on drinking sprees. The University solved the problem by providing transport for the students to and from their haunts. Advice to use taxis is often given yet there is no reliable study of the cost and feasibility. Drinking and driving may in many, or even almost all, instances be a problem concerning travel.

Hamilton and Collins, 1981, quoted the "malevolence assumption". This indicates that whenever alcohol has been imbibed it has always caused the accident (see C. Hamilton and J. J. Collins, *Perspectives on the Relationships Between Alcohol Consumption and Criminal Behaviour* (1981, Guildford Press, New York) p. 253). This in itself may be an oversimplification. An automobile accident in which alcohol is present is one in which the non-drinker is automatically innocent. There is a strong feeling of outrage. An old, defective or unserviced car, or a driver who drives too fast, without seat-belts, does not attract the same blame even though the responsibility for accident may be greater or the same. A driver who is too young or too old, who drives when tired, or inappropriately for the conditions of the road or visibility is not guilty to the same extent.

Study, policy and intervention must consider each of these aspects. It must also take into account other misconceptions, particularly concerning the availability of alcohol.

The availability of alcohol, the effect of alcohol advertising and its impact on consumption are matters of controversy. However, several well-designed studies have attempted to clarify matters that are often obscured by emotional arguments. Very many would have us believe that advertising must of necessity increase consumption, but this is not so. Ogborne and Smart (1980) analysed data from Canada designed to test this hypothesis. In 1974 the government in Manitoba introduced new legislation restricting alcohol advertising of beer. Subsequent to this restriction, beer consumption in that province rose at a similar rate as in a control province in Alberta where no such restriction was in force. They concluded that it was unlikely that restrictions on advertising would reduce consumption (see A. C. Ogborne and R. G. Smart (1980) 75 *British Journal of Addiction* 293).

Similarly, in the United States, using data from 51 states, Ogborne and Smart (1980), similarly found that advertising restrictions were unrelated to per capita beer, wine or spirit consumption, to total per capita consumption or to alcoholism. They found, importantly, that the best predictor of consumption was personal income, whilst total consumption was the best predictor of alcoholism rate. It is noteworthy that the rapid growth of alcohol sales in Russia occurred even though there was no alcohol advertising (see V.G. Treml (1975) 36 J. Stud. Alcohol 285). Advertising tends to alter brand preference rather than quantity consumed.

Attempts at curbing the association between drinking and driving must take into account these provisions. Channelling effort and resources into wasteful directions cannot achieve success. This may be the reason why deterrence has been found to be so difficult to achieve and, when achieved, has been found to be so transient. The failure to deter permanently the population of institutionalised drinkers who drive constitutes the challenge to prevention.

Appendix 7

BREATH/BLOOD/URINE CHART

Prescribed limit

If a blood specimen was provided by the defendant the prescribed limit is 80 mg, of alcohol in 100ml of blood; if a urine specimen, 107mg of alcohol in 100ml of urine; if breath, 35µg of alcohol in 100ml of breath.

	— Alcohol —	
Breath (µg/ml)	Blood (mg/ml)	Urine (mg/ml)
35	80	107
36	83	110
37	85	113
38	87	116
39	90	119
40	92	122
41	94	125
42	97	129
43	99	132
44	101	135
45	103	138
46	106	141
47	108	144
48	110	147
49	113	150
50	115	153
51	117	156
52	120	159
53	122	162
54	124	165
55	126	168
56	129	171
57	131	174
58	133	177
59	136	181
60	138	184
61	140	187
62	143	190
63	145	193
64	147	196
65	149	199
66	152	202
67	154	205
68	156	208
69	159	211

Appendix 8

SUBSTANCES OTHER THAN ETHYL ALCOHOL WHICH CAN GIVE A READING ON THE INTOXIMETER

There are other alcohols apart from those drunk as a beverage which will give a reading on the Intoximeter. They can, for example, be inhaled. It is necessary to realise that there are other alcohols besides ethyl alcohol. Whilst they may not be as pleasant to drink they are for the most part cheaper and more readily available than ethyl alcohol and for that reason they can be and are abused. The family of alcohols which begins with methyl and ethyl alcohols and continues to propyl, butyl and amyl is used in industry. The toxicity of this series increases paradoxically with decreasing molecular weight. Thus methyl alcohol is extremely toxic and can cause blindness or death, whereas ethyl alcohol is merely an intoxicant. Isopropyl alcohol, the next member of the chain, will not even cause euphoria. The chemical structures of these compounds are shown in Figure 1.

Figure 1

Chemical formulae of the first four members of the saturated monohydric alcohols

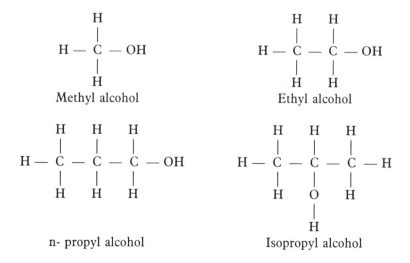

Industrial use depends on the fact that the volatility of these alcohols is in proportion to their molecular weight. Methyl alcohol, the compound with the lowest molecular weight, has the greatest volatility and is, therefore, extremely hazardous because of its use as a solvent for paints. This hazard is heightened by the use of spray guns.

A. Methyl alcohol

This is used in antifreeze, as a fuel for running cars, as a denaturant of ethyl alcohol, as a solvent for paints, varnishes, shellacs, paint removers and in dry cleaning. It is a colourless liquid. It is the most volatile of the alcohols with a smell somewhat like ethyl alcohol. It is both common and prevalent as an industrial solvent. It is possible to become intoxicated by inhaling the vapour of methyl alcohol. The boiling point of methyl alcohol is 64.1°C. Most will be familiar with it as methylated spirits. The beloved drink of meths drinkers is a mixture of 5–10 per cent methyl in ethyl alcohol to which has been added extra flavour and colour. The obvious attraction of such a cocktail is its cheapness and constant availability. Other standard beverages may also be added to increase palatability. The intoxication and impairment caused by inebriation with methyl alcohol is similar to that caused by ethyl alcohol, so that the ability to drive would be seriously impaired. Violence, however, is a more frequent accompaniment.

The metabolics of methyl alcohol are formaldehyde and formic acid. They are extremely toxic and account for the pathology of methyl alcohol poisoning. The retina is especially sensitive to these metabolites and blindness can therefore be a consequence of methyl alcohol ingestion and poisoning.

When methyl alcohol is ingested, there follows a latent period, usually about 24 hours, during which the person may have become sober. The illness then progresses rapidly with a return of nausea and vomiting. There is photophobia and dilated or fixed pupils may be associated with loss of vision. There will also be excitement, dyspnoea and prostration and collapse. Cardiac irregularity can be associated with poisoning. There will be a metabolic acidosis and renal failure may occur. The signs and complications of methyl alcohol poisoning include:

Photophobia;
excitement;
visual loss;
dyspnoea;
vomiting;
stupor;
collapse;
metabolic acidosis;
cardiac irregularity;
renal failure;
dilated and sluggish or fixed pupils.

The problem of specificity is amply illustrated by a study from Sweden by Jones (1989). In the first case described, the Swedish police suspected a 44-year-old man of driving whilst drunk. When he was stopped by traffic control, his breath smelled of alcohol and his walk was unsteady. A breath test reading with the Alcotest 7310 was 0.27g/210l. A duplicate test six minutes later showed 0.26g/210l. A blood test was taken, and the mean from four independent determinations was 0.0g/dL. This was confirmed by gas chromatography. The forensic method for the determination of ethanol was enzymatic oxidation with yeast alcohol dehydrogenase. This is described in section 9–11. It is highly selective, for ethyl alcohol as a substrate and methyl alcohol is not oxidised under the conditions used. Due to the difference between the breath alcohol analysis and the blood laboratory analysis, a further investigation was conducted. The blood alcohol enzyme method again yielded zero results. Yet a more detailed analysis of the gas chromatography result yielded a peak at the time of methanol.

This result was reported to the police. However, the man was discovered dead at home 24 hours after the incident. This is typical of methyl alcohol poisoning, which allows sobering up until 12–24 hours. The patient later dies of the toxic metabolites of methyl alcohol, namely formic acid and formaldehyde.

The results of this case illustrate the different specificities of different tests. The Alcotest 7310 breath alcohol machine incorporates a semiconductor sensor (Taguchi cell) which responds to both methanol and ethanol, as well as ketones and hydrocarbons. Thus both methanol and ethanol, as indeed other aliphatic alcohols, will give a positive result with the Alcotest. Certainly a positive result is not specific for ethanol. The yeast ADH enzyme method is highly specific for ethanol and methanol is not oxidised under the conditions used. Gas chromatography is highly specific. However, in the first instance, the only purpose of the gas chromatography analysis was to confirm the concentration by an independent technique. The electronic integrator was set at the retention time of ethanol. Thus, it would not have measured methanol. On the second occasion, a more detailed examination of the gas chromatography trace showed a large mass at the retention time of methanol. Initially, gas chromatography was not meant as a general screening test for other low molecular weight volatiles. (See A.W. Jones, "Observations on the Specificity of Breath Alcohol Analyses Used for Clinical and Medical Purposes" (1989) 10 *Journal of Forensic Sciences* 842). A summary of these results in tabulated form is shown in Table 1.

Table 1

	Ethanol	Methanol
Enzymatic oxidation with yeast alcohol dehydrogenase	+ve	−ve
Gas chromatography	Peak at retention time of ethanol	Peak at retention time of methanol
Alcotest reading	+ve	+ve
Clinical signs of alcoholic intoxication	+ve	+ve

A second case illustrating the lack of specificity of the Alcolmeter (SM-I) in failing to distinguish between methanol and ethanol was described by Salum in 1984. The Alcolmeter incorporates a fuel-cell sensor. These machines are widely used as roadside testing machines and also as hospital monitors to measure blood alcohol levels in patients. The case concerned a patient who visited a psychiatric ward because he had been drinking heavily. He smelled of alcohol and the result of the Alcolmeter SM-I test was 0.23g/210*l*. He spent the night elsewhere and returned the next day and denied that he had drunk any further alcohol. The Alcolmeter reading was 0.20g/210*l*. He complained that he felt unwell and had vomited. He was admitted and a sample of blood was sent for a toxicological screening analysis. The results indicated a serum methanol of 0.304g/dL, but no ethanol. He was treated for methanol poisoning but nevertheless died two days laters. (See I. Salum and O. Wahlund (1984) 81 *Swenska Lukartioningen* 32).

B. Isopropyl alcohol

This is a clear and colourless liquid with an odour characteristic of spirits. It has a strong and burning taste. Isopropyl alcohol has no initial euphoric action and vomiting and gastric irritation are extremely prominent. The symptoms of intoxication of isopropyl alcohol are similar to that of ethanol, although isopropyl alcohol is about twice as toxic as ethyl alcohol. Gadsden (1958) described several cases of isopropyl alcohol intoxication. This was caused by a cheap, alcoholic beverage called "scrap iron". The main constituent was isopropyl alcohol and the mixing process took place in galvanised iron drums which was responsible for the metallic taste. The outstanding symptom was toxic psychosis which reversed on withdrawal. (See R.H. Gadsden (1958) 168 J.A.M.A. 1220.) Transient renal failure, haemolysis and myopathy have been described as has the presence of acetone in the absence of hypoglycaemia or glycosuria. McFadden and Haddow (1969) described a case of coma developing after topical application of isopropyl alcohol for the relief of fever in an infant (see S.W. McFadden and J.E. Haddow (1969) 6 Int.Pharm.Abstr. 551).

Isopropyl alcohol is slowly absorbed through the intact skin. Some is converted in the body to acetone which is excreted in the breath. Isopropyl alcohol persists in the circulation longer than ethyl alcohol. It is used as a skin cleansing agent such as in medi-swabs and in sterile pack fluid. It can also be used for preserving pathological specimens and for dehydrating tissues.

This is hardly the place for an exhaustive list of each member of the alcohol series together with exact descriptions of the signs and symptoms of intoxication. The purpose of this Appendix has been merely to introduce the concept that there are other members of the alcohol series besides ethyl alcohol which can be abused. Those most common have been described as regards the symptoms. The purpose behind the descriptions has been the problems raised by specificity in testing.

The third case described by Jones (1989) (see above) excellently illustrates the role of analytical toxicology. A driver was above the legal limit according to a preliminary roadside test. He was taken to the police station and was tested with the IR Intoximeter 3000. This machine uses spectrometry at 3.4μm for its determination. This single wavelength is able to measure volatile hydrocarbons, ketones and methanol. The result of the intoximeter analysis was 0.345g/210l. A blood analysis using the ADH method indicated 0.212g/dL. This is a very unsatisfactory correlation and so a specimen was examined by gas chromatography using the headspace method. The gas chromatograph for this indicated the presence of several additional low molecular weight compounds. These peaks are identified from their mass spectra by comparison with standard known reference substances. Table 2 lists and identifies these chemical compounds. It exemplifies what a problem cross-reacting substances can be.

Table 2

Peak	Chemical compound
1	Methanol
2	Acetaldehyde
3	Ethanol
4	Acetone
5	2-Propanol
6	2-Butanone
7	2-Butanol

In Sweden, a technical alcohol called T-Red contains 92 per cent ethanol, traces of methanol, 2 per cent acetone and 5 per cent 2-butanone. Interestingly, both primary and secondary alcohols can be metabolised by liver ADH. These reactions are reversible. Ketones can therefore be converted into the corresponding secondary alcohols by suitable reduction with liver ADH. In this way, acetone is the precursor of 2-propanol, and 2-butanone is converted into 2-butanol. It must be that this denatured alcohol is constantly available and can be bought without restriction at all hours. One litre costs $2 compared with $25 for a comparable bottle of spirits bought at a liquor store. Not only is this drink prevalent amongst down-and-out alcoholics in Sweden, but it is also a problem amongst drinking drivers.

C. Solvents

At the beginning of this Appendix, it was stated that there were other alcohols besides ethyl alcohol which may be abused and these could cause problems with specificity. There is another group of compounds which are capable of causing problems of specificity. These are not other alcohols but solvents. Much has been made recently of the intentional inhalation of volatile chemicals. Whilst currently very topical, nitrous oxide was misused as early as the nineteenth century.

There is a wide diversity of origins for inhaled solvents, ranging from glue and cleaning substances to petrol and nail varnish remover. A list of solvents and their easily obtainable commercial preparations is shown in Table 3. These products are universal, cheap, easily available and act quickly. Although most solvent inhalation and abuse is intentional, it is not beyond the bounds of possibility that inhalation could be innocent. Any of the solvents in Table 3 may be abused. Glue, the most notorious abused solvent, can be sniffed from a potato crisp bag but any solvent may be placed on a cloth and sniffed. Most abusers of solvents are male and abuse is often a group activity.

Table 3

Product	Solvent contained
Glue	Toluene
Adhesive	Toluene, hexane
Dry cleaning fluid	Trichlorothane
Stain remover	Carbon tetrachloride
Petrol	Complex mixture of hydrocarbons
Paint thinners	Toluene, ethyl acetate
Disposable lighter refills	Butane
Dyes	Acetone
Adhesives	Toluene
Nail polish remover	Acetone
Typing eraser	Methylene chloride, trichloroethane
Aerosol	Fluorinated hydrocarbons

It is important to realise that the clinical signs and symptoms of solvent abuse are similar to the effects of alcohol inebriation. There is an initial phase of stimulation which is then followed by central nervous system depression. Those who abuse solvents are often those who abuse alcohol, and these abuses are often concurrent. The main clinical manifestations of solvent abuse are listed below:

Initial stimulation;
Depression;
Slurring of speech;
Ataxia;
Feelings of omnipotence;
Headache;
Impaired judgment;
Excitement;
Blurring of vision;

Vomiting;
Nausea;
Abdominal pain;
Irritability;
Delirious state;
Clouding of consciousness;
Illusions;
Hallucinations;
Toxic psychosis;
Anti-social and self-destructive acts.

One variant of solvent abuse is petrol sniffing. The constituents of petrol are lipid soluble and therefore the vapour is rapidly absorbed from the lungs. It is this rapid absorption which accounts for the fast onset of symptoms, such as excitement. It is reported that less than 20 inhalations of the petrol vapour can produce an intoxication lasting from three to six hours.

In this Appendix the concept of specificity has been introduced. There are substances besides ethyl alcohol which may react positively in tests for ethyl alcohol. These substances may be the cause of confusion or controversy and are listed below:

Solvents;   Petrol;
Butane;   Acetone;
Glue;   Toluene.

IN "A GUIDE TO TYPE APPROVAL PROCEDURES FOR EVIDENTIAL BREATH ALCOHOL TESTING INSTRUMENTS USED FOR ROAD TRAFFIC LAW ENFORCEMENT IN GREAT BRITAIN"

Published by HMSO in October 1994.

Possible interfering substances

There is the following list of substances which may occur on the breath of a person required to supply a sample of breath for alcohol analysis, in addition to ethanol. It gives the test vapour concentration and maximum permitted response for each compound. The indicated concentration of each substance is in addition to a nominal concentration of ethanol of 35 μg/100ml.

Substance	Vapour concentration μg/100ml $\pm$ 5%	Maximum response μg/100ml
Water	3,000	3
Carbon dioxide	20,000	3
Acetone	75	15
Acetaldehyde	20	15
Methanol	20	20
Isopropanol	20	20
Carbon monoxide	25	12.5
Toluene	25	12.5
Xylene (1:1 meta:para)	25	12.5
Benzene	25	12.5
Perchlorethylene	25	12.5
Methyl ethyl ketone	30	15
Ethyl acetate	30	15
Methane	50	15
n-Pentane	50	15
n-Hexane	50	15
n-Heptane	50	15
n-Octane	50	15
Diethyl ether	50	15

Appendix 9

ACETONE—THE CAUSES OF PRODUCTION IN THE HUMAN BODY

Acetone is the commonest interfering substance which may appear in the breath. The Lion Intoximeter will confuse acetone with ethanol. In the case of a driver having breath acetone, this would result in an anomalously elevated breath ethanol reading when a part of the reading would be due to acetone. The reading would thus be too high. For this reason, the Intoximeter incorporates a mechanism to measure the concentration of breath acetone. A correct deduction is therefore made from the alcohol reading before printout. This correction will prevent a miscarriage of justice, since otherwise a driver could be convicted of driving with excess alcohol in his breath specimen, when all or part of the reading could be due to the cross-reacting substance, acetone.

Acetone will cause infra-red absorption in the same wavelength as ethanol. The atomic structure of acetone is very similar to that of ethanol and is shown in Figure 12. Once the breath specimen has passed through the analytical chamber, together with its photo-electric cell, it passes in series through a Taguchi cell. This is a semi-conductor and works on the principle that there is a change in conductivity when any acetone is absorbed on the surface. This results in a change in current which produces a signal corresponding to the concentration of acetone in the breath. The Taguchi cell is especially sensitive to acetone.

Acetone is one of the compounds produced in the body called ketone bodies. In normal metabolism they are not produced. It is popularly expressed that fats burn in the flame of carbohydrates. When fats and fatty acids are oxidised, then acetyl CoA is formed. This acetyl CoA will enter the citric acid cycle, or energy cycle, only if carbohydrate and fat breakdown are balanced. However, if fat degradation predominates, then acetyl CoA cannot enter the citric acid cycle, since oxaloacetate is not present for the formation of citrate. The concentration of oxaloacetate is diminished if carbohydrate is unavailable or improperly used. In fasting or in diabetes, oxaloacetate is used to form glucose and thus there is none left to condense with acetyl CoA. In this situation, acetyl CoA is shunted to the formation of acetoacetate and D-3-hydroxybutyrate. Acetone, acetoacetate, and D-3-hydroxybutyrate are known as ketone bodies. Because it is a beta-keto acid, acetoacetate undergoes a slow, spontaneous decarboxylation to acetone. The smell of acetone may be detected on the breath of a person who has a high level of acetoacetate in the blood. The structure of the ketone bodies is shown in Figure 12, together with the reactions by which they are formed.

Higher than normal quantities of ketone bodies in the blood and urine constitute ketosis. The simplest form of ketosis occurs in starvation and this involves depletion of available carbohydrate. This is accompanied by mobilisation of free fatty acids. This constitutes the general pattern of ketosis. The energy requirements of the body are provided by fatty acid oxidation. Release of free fatty acids and aminoacids is enhanced by decreased levels of insulin. This provides glucose at the expense of proteolysis.

Figure 12

$$2\ CH_3CO\text{-}S\text{-}CoA \leftrightarrow CH_3COCH_2CO\text{-}S\text{-}CoA \leftrightarrow COO^-CH_2OHCCH_3CH_2CO\text{-}S\text{-}CoA$$

Acetyl CoA   Acetoacetyl CoA   3-Hydroxy-3-methylglutaryl CoA

3-Hydroxy-3-methylglutaryl CoA → Acetoacetate

$$CH_3CHOHCH_2COO^- \leftrightarrow CH_3COCH_2COO^- \rightarrow CH_3COCH_3$$

D-3-Hydroxybutyrate   Acetoacetate   Acetone

Non-pathologic forms of ketosis are found under conditions of high-fat feeding and after severe exercise in the post-absorptive state. No condition in which ketosis occurs differs qualitatively from this general pattern of metabolism but quantitatively it may be exaggerated to produce the pathologic states found in diabetes mellitus.

Diabetes mellitus is the most notable condition in which ketosis occurs. The basic defect is due to reduced insulin activity. This may be due to a missed or mistaken dose of insulin. It also may be due to an infection, other intercurrent illness or accident. The general pattern of metabolism leading to ketosis and the production of ketone bodies has been outlined above. There is decreased carbohydrate utilisation and enhanced fatty acid oxidation. There is accumulation of acetyl CoA and this is diverted into the pathways shown in Figure 12 to produce ketone bodies.

Because of the rise in ketone body levels in the blood, there is acidosis. Because of the increased blood glucose (hyperglycaemia) and loss of glucose in the urine (glycosuria) there is an osmotic diuresis. Dehydration will result. This will be exacerbated by vomiting. Clinically, the features reflect the biochemical changes. There will be dehydration. The skin will be dry with an absence of sweating. Breathing will be fast and deep. The pulse will be of small volume and the lips, tongue, and mouth will be dry because of the dehydration. Acetone will be present on the breath. It has a characteristic odour. However, not everyone is able to smell the characteristic odour. Because the onset of this state may take hours or days, the patient or driver may appear mildly drowsy or sleepy, whilst at the most extreme end of the spectrum he may be unconscious. A list of the signs in diabetic ketosis is given in Table 32. If the patient is a known diabetic, then the diagnosis of diabetic ketoacidosis will depend upon the history, physical signs and the fruity odour of acetone on the breath. The urine will be tested for glucose and ketones. Plasma examination will be performed for glucose and ketones using either ketone reagent strips or tablets. Treatment will require insulin, fluids and electrolytes to correct the dehydration.

In addition to diabetes, a ketoacidotic state can be induced by alcohol. Alcoholic ketoacidosis occurs in chronic alcoholics. Often it occurs after a binge, but the alcoholic may not have imbibed any alcohol for 24 hours or more. It occurs in association with starvation and is accompanied by abdominal pain and vomiting. Pancreatitis is invariably present. There are extremely high plasma-free fatty acid levels. In contrast to diabetic ketoacidosis, this syndrome is rapidly reversible with intravenous glucose. Thiamine should also be given. There are also much rarer causes of metabolic ketoacidosis. For instance, there are inherited disorders of aminoacid catabolism of the aminoacids valine, leucine and isoleucine, which result in metabolic ketoacidosis. The description of such rare conditions would not be merited in a work of this scope. Table 33 lists the causes of ketosis which may result in acetone being present in the breath.

Thus, there are many metabolic disorders, both pathological and non-pathological, which may result in the production of acetone in the breath. To this must be added the acetone-containing solvents which may be abused.

Table 32

Signs in diabetic ketosis

Dehydration
Rapid and deep breathing
Fruity smell of acetone on breath
Absence of sweating
Pulse thin and of poor volume
Dry mouth and tongue
Drowsiness
Coma
Hyperglycaemia
Glycosuria
Ketonuria
Ketonemia

Table 33

Causes of ketosis which may result in acetone being present in breath

Diabetic ketosis
Alcoholic ketoacidosis
Starvation
High-fat feeding
After severe exercise, in the post-absorptive state
Acetone containing solvents, whilst not a cause of ketosis, may result in acetone being present in the breath, after solvent inhalation

Appendix 10

VOLATILE HYDROCARBONS AND THE LION INTOXIMETER

The proof of evidence of Dr. Peter Thrift in the case of *Griffiths v. DPP* (Birmingham Crown Court). Reproduced by permission of Jennings, Perks and Breakwell, Solicitors.

Contents

1.0 Principles of operation: the Lion Intoximeter

The Lion Intoximeter 3000 works on the principle of analysing the alcohol level in the exhaled breath. Two chambers are employed within the Intoximeter, one of which is used to contain the sample of the exhaled breath. The sample of the subject's breath to be analysed is fed into a chamber through which a beam of infra-red light, which has a wavelength centred on 3.41 microns, passes. The presence of alcohol in the sample reduces the transmissibility of the infra-red light beam. As the level of attenuation of this beam is dependent upon the alcohol level in the sample, it is possible for the Intoximeter to calculate the alcohol level by carefully measuring the attenuation of the beam as it travels through the sample.

Such systems can suffer from drift of the measured results, with respect to time, which leads to inaccurate results. The Lion Intoximeter attempts to minimise such inaccuracies by bifurcating the infra-red beam through two chambers. One of these chambers is used to contain the sample, whilst the second is used as a reference standard. An infra-red sensor, which is used to detect the intensity of the infra-red beam, is switched alternately between these two chambers. It is therefore possible to generate a reading which is the difference in transmissibility of the beam in the sample and the reference standard chambers. By measuring the relative transmissibility of the beam, as opposed to its absolute value, the major factors causing drift are eliminated from the calculations subsequently generated.

Unfortunately, infra-red light absorption occurs with a number of other gaseous substances, particularly, volatile hydrocarbons. Therefore, the infra-red method cannot be used on its own to generate accurate measurements of alcohol density.

Acetone: a common substance found naturally in the breath, absorbs infra-red light, and therefore will generate a reading in a system that uses such methodology to measure ethanol. Figure 2.0.2 gives the molecular structure of acetone. Note the similarity of the structure to that of ethanol.

Figure 2.0.1   *Figure 2.0.2.*

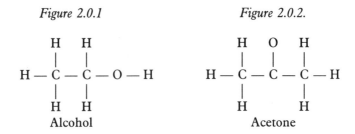

Alcohol   Acetone

3.0 Taguchi cell

An important, if not the most important, design objective for an Intoximeter should be to detect alcohol (ethanol) in the breath. Clearly, the detection of any other substance, no matter how closely chemically related, is undesirable. However, if it is an inherent characteristic of the design that a substance other than ethanol can generate readings, then readings attributable to this other substance should be clearly identifiable. Should the detection of a substance other than ethanol not be identified as another substance, then this can only degrade the accuracy of any readings obtained.

Unfortunately, the virtues of the infra-red detection system do not extend to the individual identification of other closely related substances which could be found in the breath. Therefore a secondary detection system is necessary to establish the presence of other substances which the infra-red measurement system could assume were alcohol.

A semi-conductor sensor, known as a Taguchi cell, has a spectrum such that it is particularly sensitive to certain substances. This sensitivity is selective and may be modified by the addition of small amounts of certain chemicals during the course of its manufacture. In the semi-conductor world this is usually referred to as doping. A range of sensors can therefore be produced, each of which will be particularly sensitive to a particular substance. The Taguchi cell, model TGS 822, is particularly sensitive to acetone, a substance commonly found in the breath. The Lion Intoximeter 3000 uses such a cell to monitor the breath sample after it has passed through the analytical chamber and its infra-red measuring system.

3.1 PRINCIPLE OF OPERATION OF THE TAGUCHI CELL

When a deposition, composed mainly of tin dioxide, is exposed to certain gases, there results a decrease in the electrical resistivity of the material. To be effective, the deposition needs to operate at a temperature of some 400°C.

In practice the deposition of the tin dioxide is made on a ceramic tube containing a small electrical heater which, when powered, enables the deposition to reach the required operating temperature. In uncontaminated air, oxygen, which traps free electrons by its electron affinity, is absorbed on to the tin dioxide particle surface, forming a potential barrier to the grain boundaries. This potential barrier, eVs in air, restricts the flow of electrons, resulting in an increase in the electrical resistance of the material. Upon exposure to reducing gases, *e.g.* acetone, ethanol, carbon monoxide, etc., the mainly tin dioxide alloy absorbs gas molecules, which results in oxidation.

The relative absorption rates of the gases is dependent upon the particular alloy used in the deposition. By small changes in the materials used it is possible to tailor a sensor to respond to particular gases.

The oxidation lowers the potential barrier, thereby reducing the electrical resistance. The sensor is quite sensitive, so a small quantity of the gas in a sample of air is sufficient to result in a measurable change in resistance. This reduction in resistance of the sensor is a function of the relative gas density in the sample: thus, the measurement of resistance may be used to quantify the density of the gas in the air found in that sample.

In general, the sensors are designed to operate at 400°C: however, the sensitivity of a particular design of sensor to various gases may be modified by varying the heater temperature. Additionally, it may be modified by changing the composition of the deposition. If the sensor is run at a low temperature, to permit the detection of gases, which would normally be outside its range of detection, it will be necessary to run the heater periodically at full temperature to purge the surface of the sensor.

3.2 CONSTRUCTION

The Taguchi TGS 822 cell is a small cylinder some 17mm in diameter and 10mm in height, with an outer case moulded in Nylon 66. Its electrical connections are made through six nickel pins extending some 6.5mm from the base. For convenience these pins are configured to the well-established B7G thermionic valve base standard, thereby permitting the use of a standard base that has been produced and proven by the million over the last half-century.

A small circular hole at the top and a second circular hole at the bottom allow gases to pass through the cell. During this passage, the gases pass over the sensor itself, and are measured for contaminants, such as acetone. Ingress of small particles is prevented by a double layer of 100 mesh stainless steel gauze, conforming to SUS 316, over the holes. In addition to this function, the fine mesh has the beneficial effect of making the cell flameproof. Tests have demonstrated that this fine mesh will prevent a spark produced inside the cell from igniting an external explosive mixture of oxygen and hydrogen.

The sensor itself is made from a small ceramic tube though which 60 micron wire is threaded, with a nominal resistance of 30 Ω, which is used as a heater, when an electric current is passed through it. Sintered bulk semiconductor material, composed mainly of tin dioxide, SnO_2, is deposited on the outside of the ceramic tube. Electrical connections to this material are made through electrodes deposited on the surface. Gold alloy wires of 60 micron diameter are used to make electrical connections between electrodes and the pins at the header end of the B7G base.

A sectioned drawing of the cell is given in Figure 3.2.1.

Figure 3.2.1

Stainless steel mesh cover

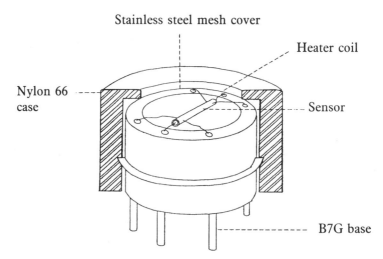

Heater coil

Nylon 66
case

Sensor

B7G base

Construction of TGS 822

3.3 SENSITIVITY TO VOLATILE HYDROCARBONS

Section 3.1 described how selective doping of the material used in the deposition on the sensor modifies its sensitivity to particular gases. In the case of the Taguchi 813, the deposition material has been modified to make it sensitive to acetone. Figure 3.3.1 is a graph of its sensitivity to acetone. The graph shows the variation in the ratio of electrical resistance, with air taken as a reference, in a mixture of air and acetone, for varying densities.

However, as stated in section 2.0, the molecular structure of acetone is similar to that of ethanol, and hence the Taguchi cell produces a response curve, Figure 3.3.2, which is some what similar to Figure 3.3.1.

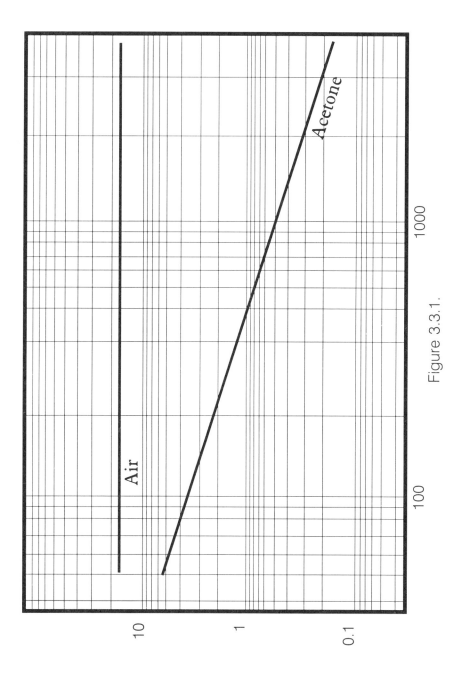

Figure 3.3.1.

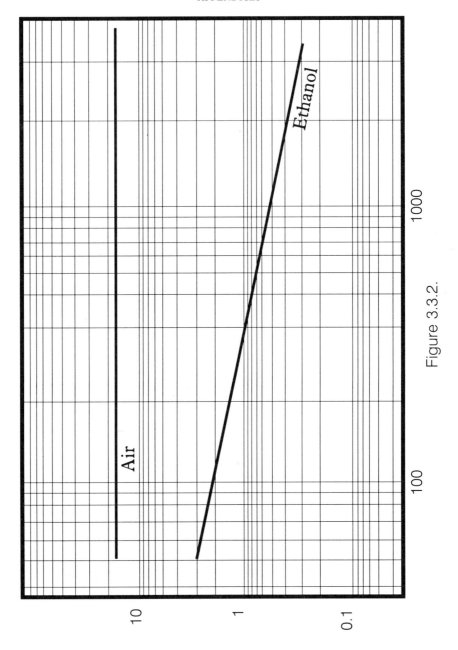

Figure 3.3.2.

3.4 APPLICATION OF THE CELL

To illustrate how the Taguchi cell is used in the system, consider the following cases:

(i) Assume that a pure ethanol/air mixture is drawn into the analytical chamber. Then the readings produced by the infra-red beam would tally with those of the Taguchi 813 cell. Therefore, the system would correctly conclude that the sample in the analytical chamber had been a mixture of ethanol and air.

(ii) Assume that a very low density of acetone/air is drawn into the analytical chamber. Then the reading from the Taguchi 813 cell would considerably exceed that which would have been generated had an identical density of ethanol/air been used. The infra-red system will produce a reading based on the latter; comparison of the two readings would show a wide disparity, and the system would therefore be able to correctly identify the presence of acetone.

(iii) Assume that a sample drawn into the analytical chamber is a low density mixture of acetone and ethanol in air, such that they are in similar proportions. Both the infra-red system and the Taguchi 813 system will have their readings inflated by the presence of the acetone but, resulting from their differing sensitivities to acetone, the readings would not tally. By comparing their difference with the reading of the infra-red system, it is possible to calculate the amount of acetone and hence the amount of ethanol in the sample.

The principle used in (iii) to ascertain the quantities of two variables from the readings from two independent sensors, each having a differing sensitivity to the two gases, is a valid scientific principle. The accuracy to which the quantities of the gases can be established is good for similar quantities, but decreases rapidly as the quantities become unbalanced (see Appendix 1).

It follows that other volatile hydrocarbons may be readily detected and identified when little or no ethanol is present in the air sample.

However, as the level of ethanol is progressively increased, it becomes progressively more difficult to identify these other volatile hydrocarbons, although they still make a full additive contribution to the reading.

At this level the other volatile hydrocarbons will not be discernable as an individual entity but will be added to the reading resulting from the ethanol, and hence give a falsely high reading.

3.5 TIME STABILITY

Tests to ascertain the stability of the TGS 822 cell versus time were conducted in air with a heater voltage set to its nominal five volts. The TGS 822 under test was connected in series with a resistive load which was connected to a DC supply. The heater was switched on and the voltage drop across the sensor was measured on a laboratory standard digital voltmeter at fixed time intervals. It was found that the characteristic of the sensor, when measured over a period of time, is for its voltage to rise rapidly, then to fall slowly in an exponential fashion before stabilising.

The general shape of the curve can be seen from the characteristic shown in Figure 3.5.1.

Figure 3.5.1

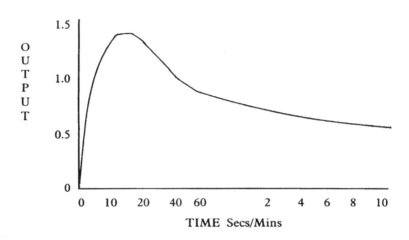

It was also found that the amplitude of this signal was a function of how long the cell had been switched off. Figure 3.5.1 is typical of a cell being powered after a rest period of half an hour. If the cell was left for some days, then the amplitude of this graph has been observed to be up to five times the figure given, but the shape of the characteristic does not appear to alter.

4.0 Calculating the level needed to show exceedence of the statutory level

A number of factors must be considered:

(a) It is well established that the breath of a subject may contain volatile hydrocarbons, ketones, aldehydes and alcohols in various forms, including ethane, methane, ethylene, etc. Evidence by Dr P.M. Williams in *DPP v. Cameron*, July 30, 1992, established that this level could be up to 5μg.

(b) The Home Office allows an accuracy of plus or minus 3μg for the Lion Intoximeter 3000.

Taking an example of a reading on the Lion Intoximeter 3000 of 43μg, this must be reduced to 38μg to allow for the contribution made by the natural volatile hydrocarbons in the subject's breath and further reduced to $35\mu g$ to allow for the tolerance permitted by the Home Office.

Therefore any reading up to, and including, $43\mu g$ obtained on a Lion Intoximeter 3000 should be regarded as within the legal limit.

5.0 Saliva

When an individual is requested to blow from the mouth into an instrument there is always a possibility that in blowing an individual may release some saliva. The possibility of this most certainly will not be reduced if that individual, who is blowing into the instrument, is in an intoxicated state; as would be the norm. Therefore, it is sensible design requirement for any instrument designed to analyse the contents of an individual's breath that it does not take cognisance of the presence, or otherwise of saliva.

The primary path to prevent saliva entering the Lion Intoximeter 3000 is a disposable "Spit-Trap Mouthpiece". Any saliva not trapped by this device would need to negotiate the convoluted path to where the Taguchi cell is situated. This path does not present a problem for gases, but liquids such as saliva will drop out of the gas due to their relatively higher density, and tend to adhere to the walls thereby failing to reach the Taguchi cell.

A further obstacle to the path of the saliva is the stainless steel mesh which covers the active sensor within the cell (see section 3.2). Tests in my laboratory have established that saliva is trapped by the very small holes in the mesh. The heater in the sensor has the secondary effect of driving off the liquid. Furthermore, the effect of this saliva upon the Taguchi cell to measure acetone is insignificant in respect to accuracy.

To ascertain how effective design objectives have been met in service, it is common practice with any equipment to review the performance of the instrument over many trials, and observe its performance. The Lion Intoximeter 3000 is used widely throughout the United Kingdom, resulting in thousands of tests each year. In fact some 600 were introduced approximately 13 years ago. The distinct lack of evidence that the equipment is affected by saliva is evidence to the effectiveness of the design in eliminating the effects of saliva.

Appendix 10A

ACCURACY AS A FUNCTION OF RELATIVE DENSITY

In section 3.4 it was stated that, "The accuracy to which the quantities of the gases can be established is good for similar quantities, but decreases rapidly as the quantities become unbalanced."

Perhaps an explanation of the foregoing statement should be given. Viewed from a purely mathematical stance there is no lower limit to separating the readings for two gases mixed in the manner suggested.

However, in practice each of the two readings will have their own finite tolerance. With each tolerance being made up of both fixed and variable errors. The latter are largely as a result of the small instability found in the sensors. These errors are relatively small compared to the readings. However, when the difference between two readings is required, the absolute magnitude of the errors will not change, and therefore the error associated with the difference reading is of a higher percentage magnitude than either of the two individual readings.

It follows that when the readings are very different, then the difference is large and the error is acceptable. As the difference narrows between the readings, the errors, taken as a percentage of the difference, grow.

A point is reached where the errors mask out the difference, and hence no useful data may be obtained.

Appendix 11

DRIVING OFFENCES CHARGING STANDARD AGREED BY THE POLICE AND CROWN PROSECUTION SERVICE

DRIVING OFFENCES CHARGING STANDARD

Index

1 CHARGING STANDARD—PURPOSE

1.1 The purpose of joint charging standards is to make sure that the most appropriate charge is selected, in the light of the evidence which can be proved, at the earliest possible opportunity. This will help the police and Crown Prosecutors in preparing the case. Adoption of this joint standard should lead to a reduction in the number of times charges have to be amended which in turn should lead to an increase in efficiency and a reduction in avoidable extra work for the police and the Crown Prosecution Service.

1.2 This joint charging standard offers guidance to police officers who have responsibility for charging and to Crown Prosecutors on the most appropriate charge to the preferred in cases relating to driving offences. The guidance:

- *should not be used* in the determination of any *pre-charge* decision, such as the decision to arrest;
- *does not* override any guidance issued on the use of appropriate alternative forms of disposal *short of charge*, such as cautioning;
- *does not* override the principles set out in the Code for Crown Prosecutors;
- *does not* override the need for consideration to be given in every case as to whether a charge/prosecution is in the public interest;
- *does not* remove the need for each case to be considered on its individual merits or fetter the discretion of the police to charge and the CPS to prosecute the most appropriate offence depending on the particular facts of the case in question.

2 INTRODUCTION

2.1 The purpose of road traffic legislation is to promote road safety and to protect the public. The principal driving offences are contained in the Road Traffic Act 1988 ("RTA 1988"). This joint standard gives guidance about the charge which should be preferred if the criteria set out in the Code for Crown Prosecutors are met.

2.2 This standard covers the following offences:

- careless driving or inconsiderate driving—section 3 RTA 1988;
- dangerous driving—section 2 RTA 1988;
- causing death by careless driving when under the influence of drink or drugs—section 3A RTA 1988;
- causing death by dangerous driving—section 1 RTA 1988;
- manslaughter—contrary to common law;
- causing bodily harm by wanton or furious driving, etc.—section 35 of the Offences Against the Person Act 1861.

3 GENERAL PRINCIPLES: CHARGING PRACTICE

3.1 You should always have in mind the following general principles when selecting the appropriate charge(s):

(i) the charge(s) should accurately reflect the extent of the defendant's alleged involvement and responsibility thereby allowing the courts the discretion to sentence appropriately:

(ii) the choice of charges should ensure the clear and simple presentation of the case particularly where there is more than one defendant;

(iii) it is wrong to encourage a defendant to plead guilty to a few charges by selecting more charges than are necessary;

(iv) it is wrong to select a more serious charge which is not supported by the evidence in order to encourage a plea of guilty to a lesser allegation.

4 GENERAL COMMENTS ABOUT DRIVING OFFENCES

4.1 The manner of the driving must be considered objectively. In practice, the differences between the two types of bad driving will depend on the degree to which the driving falls below the minimum acceptable standard. If the manner of the driving is *below* that which is expected, the appropriate charge will be careless driving; if the manner of the driving is *far below* that which is expected, the appropriate charge wil be dangerous driving. There is no statutory guidance about what behaviour constitutes a manner of driving which is "below" and "far below" the required standard.

4.2 The purpose of this charging standard is to make sure that once a decision to prosecute has been taken, police officers and prosecutors select the most appropriate charge where there is a choice of two or more charges. The following factors are not relevant when deciding whether an act of driving is careless or dangerous:

- the injury or death of one or more persons involved in a road traffic accident, except where Parliament has made specific provision for the death to be reflected in the charge. Importantly, injury or death does not, by itself, turn an accident into careless driving or turn careless driving into dangerous driving;
- the age or experience of the driver;
- the commission of other driving offences at the same time (such as driving whilst disqualified or driving without a certificate of insurance or a driving licence);
- the fact that the defendant has previous convictions for road traffic offences;
- the disability of a driver caused by mental illness or by physical injury or illness, except where the disability adversely affected the manner of the driving.

4.3 There is no clear cut dividing line between acts of careless driving and acts of dangerous driving. True, momentary inattention will not usually have very serious adverse effects and therefore does not usually warrant criminal proceedings. Something more than momentary inattention (which may minimal or serious results) is generally careless driving. Substantial/gross/total inattention (which may have miminal or serious results) is generally dangerous driving, even though it may take place over a period of a few seconds. The factual examples set out in this standard are merely indicative of the sort of behaviour which may merit prosecution under either section 2 or section 3 RTA 1988.

4.4 It is important to put the facts of the case in context. Athough the test is objective, the manner of the driving must be seen in the context of the circumstances in which the driving took place.

Behaviour which may not be criminal in certain conditions may merit proceedings in other conditions, for example, a safe lane change in slow-moving traffic may become unsafe on a motorway where speeds are faster, there is less time to react and the consequences of any accident are likely to be more serious. Similarly, behaviour which might merit proceedings under section 3 in certain conditions may merit a prosecution under section 2, for example, if there is poor visibility; increased volume of traffic; adverse weather conditions; or difficult geography, such as blind corners.

(a) DRIVING IN EMERGENCY SITUATIONS

4.5 When a member of the emergency services commits an offence while responding to an emergency call discretion should be used in deciding whether or not a prosecution is needed. Generally, a prosecution is unlikely to be appropriate in cases of genuine emergency unless the driving is dangerous or indicates a high degree of blameworthiness. For example, a prosecution of a driver who caused a minor accident while responding to an urgent, life-threatening emergency may not be appropriate; but a prosecution may be appropriate when a serious accident is caused by an over-enthusiastic driver responding to a less urgent emergency call in which life is not threatened. In each case it is necessary to weigh all the circumstances of the case, particularly the nature of the emergency known to, or reasonably perceived by, the driver and the nature of the driving.

4.6 There will be cases when persons who are not members of the emergency services drive in an emergency situation. Examples include doctors who receive an urgent call for assistance and a driver taking a sick child to hospital. As with members of the emergency services, all the circumstances of the case must be weighed, particularly the nature of the emergency known to, or reasonably perceived by, the driver and the nature of the driving.

DRIVING AND ALCOHOL/DRUGS

4.7 The road traffic legislation treats the consumption of alcohol and drugs alike. The following principles apply to driving affected by the consumption of alcohol or drugs, though the case law, and the following paragraphs, focus or alcohol.

4.8 Assessing the relevance of the consumption of alcohol is a difficult area. The leading authority is *R. v. Woodward (Terence)* [1995] 1 W.L.R. 375 (Court of Appeal). The following general principles come from that case:

- the merge fact that the driver has had drink is not of itself relevant to or admissible on the question of whether his driving is careless or dangerous;
- for such evidence to be admissible, it must tend to show that the amount of drink taken in such as would adversely affect a reasonable driver, or alternatively, that the accused was in fact adversely affected.

4.9 In practice, however, there will need to be some further evidence to show that the manner of the driving fell below or far below that which is to be expected in order to justify proceedings under section 3 or section 2 respectively.

5 CARELESS DRIVING—SECTION 3 RTA 1988

5.1 The offence of driving without due care and attention is committed when the driving falls below the standard expected of a reasonable, prudent and competent driver in all the cirumstances of the case. It is a summary only offence carrying a level 4 fine (£2,500), discretionary disqualification for any period and/or until a driving test has been passed. The court must endorse the driver's licence with 3–9 penalty points unless there are special reasons not to do so.

5.2 The test of whether the standard of driving has fallen below the required standard is an objective one. It apples both when the manner of driving in question is deliberate and when the manner of driving occurs as a result of an error of judgment or simply as a result of incompetence or inexperience.

5.3 Section 38(7) RTA 1988 states that failure on the part of a person to observe a provision of the Highway Code shall not of itself render that person liable to criminal proceedings, but a failure, particularly a serious one, may constitute evidence of careless or dangerous driving.

5.4 In general, prosecution for careless driving will be appropriate when the manner of the driving demonstrates a serious miscalculation or a disregard for road safety, taking into account all the circumstances including road, traffic and/or weather conditions.

5.5 There will be rare occasions where an accident occurs and yet there is no evidence of any mechanical defect, illness of the driver or other explanation to account for why the accident happened. In these cases, a charge of careless driving may be appropriate. The prosecution can provide evidence to the court about the accident on the basis that in the absence of any explanation—such as the ones indentified above—it is inevitable that the defendant must have been driving below the standard expected of a reasonable, prudent and competent driver, since otherwise the accident would not have happened.

5.6 The following are examples of driving which may support an allegation of careless driving:

(1) Acts of driving caused by more than momentary inattention and where the safety of road users is affected, such as:
  (a) overtaking on the inside;
  (b) driving inappropriately close to another vehicle;
  (c) driving through a red light;
  (d) emerging from a side road into the path of another vehicle;
  (e) turning into a minor road and colliding with a pedestrian.

(2) Conduct which clearly caused the driver not to be in a position to respond in the event of an emergency on the road, for example:
  (a) using a hand-held mobile telephone while the vehicle is moving, especially when at speed;
  (b) tuning a car radio;
  (c) reading a newspaper/map;
  (d) selecting and lighting a cigarette/cigar/pipe;
  (e) talking to and looking at a passenger which causes the driver more than monetary inattention;
  (f) leg and/or arm in plaster;
  (g) fatigue/nodding off.

The above examples explain the driver's conduct rather than demonstrate a course of driving which necessarily falls below the objective standard of the driving itself. For example, they may explain why the driver veered across carriageways, passed through a red light or otherwise caused a danger to other road users. In these cases, it is necessary to go beyond the explanation for the driving and consider whether the particular facts of the case warrant a charge or careless driving. The reason for the driver's behaviour is not relevant to the choice of charge: it is the acts of driving which determine whether the driver has fallen below (careless driving) or far below (dangerous driving) the standard required.

These examples are placed here because *usually* when this conduct occurs the appropriate charge will be section 3. But police officers and prosecutors must always consider the manner of the driving in the context of the other facts in the case to decide the *most* appropriate way forward.

5.7 In deciding whether a charge of careless driving is appropriate, you will want to consider whether the act of driving concerned was the result of either momentary inattention or an isolated misjudgment, or something more serious. A moment's inattention which causes the manner of the driving to fall below the objective standard required of the reasonable, prudent and competent driver need not, of itself, lead to a prosecution. It is acts caused by more than momentary inattention—especially where the manner of the driving adversely affects the safety of other road users—which will normally result in a charge of careless driving.

5.8 In cases where there has been an accident and the evidence suggests that more than one driver may have been at fault, it will be necessary to establish that there is independent evidence against each driver before charging any individual driver, or that the facts speak so strongly for themselves in relation to any individual driver that the only conclusion possible to draw is that he departed from what a reasonable, prudent and competent driver would have done in the circumstances.

5.9 The public interest in favour of a prosecution is proportionate to the degree of blameworthiness: the greater the blameworthiness, the greater the public interest in favour of prosecuting. In addition, the public interest will favour prosecuting in cases when the court may wish to make an order under section 36 of the Road Traffic Offenders Act 1988, disqualifying the driver until he passes a driving test; or where it appears that the court ought to notify the Secretary of State that the driver may be suffering from any relevant disability within the meaning of section 22 of the Road Traffic Offenders Act 1988.

5.10 However, the public interest does not call for a prosecution in every case where there is a realistic prospect of conviction for careless driving; prosecution for an act of slight carelessness is unlikely to have a deterrent effect; and it is not the function of the prosecution to conduct proceedings merely to settle questions of liability for the benefit of insurance companies.

5.11 The public interest will tend to be against a prosecution for careless driving where:

(1) the incident is of a type such as frequently occurs at parking places, roundabouts, junctions or in traffic queues, involving minimal carelessness such as momentary inattention or a minor error of judgment;

(2) only the person at fault suffered injury and damage, if any, was mainly restricted to the vehicle or property owned by that person.

5.12 In addition, there is often an overlap between careless driving and some other offences such as driving with excess alcohol, regulatory offences, offences of strict liability, or offences under the Road Vehicles (Construction and Use) Regulations 1986. The merits of many individual cases can be adequately met by charging the specific statutory or regulatory offence which Parliament made available, subject to paragraphs 5.13 and 5.14 below.

5.13 Sometimes, there will be evidence of a course of conduct which involves the commission of a number of different statutory or regulatory offences, or the commission of the same statutory or regulatory offence on a number of occasions which are very close in time with one another. For example, a driver may drive through a red traffic light, ignore a pelican crossing and fail to give way at a junction within what might reasonably be described as the same course of driving. Alternatively, a driver may drive through two or more sets of red traffic lights, one after the other, within what may reasonably be described as the same course of driving.

5.14 In these situations, it is not appropriate simply to charge a number of individual statutory or regulatory offences: the court needs to be made aware of the link between what might otherwise appear as isolated incidents, when in reality they form part of a more serious course of bad driving. This course of bad driving should be reflected in a more serious charge. Where this type of situation arises, the manner of the driving has, in reality, fallen far below that expected of a competent and careful driver because of the driver's systematic failure to pay heed to the relevant traffic directions. Accordingly, consideration should be given to prosecuting the driver under section 2 of the Act: see paragraph 7.6.

6 DRIVING WITHOUT REASONABLE CONSIDERATION—SECTION 3 RTA 1988

6.1 The offence of driving without reasonable consideration is committed when a vehicle is driven on a road or other public place as a result of which other persons using the road or place are inconvenienced. It is a summary only offence carrying a level 4 fine (£2,500), discretionary disqualification for any period and/or until a driving test has been passed. The court must endorse the driver's licence with 3–9 penalty points unless there are special reasons not to do so.

6.2 The accused must be shown:

(1) to have fallen below the standard of a reasonable, prudent and competent driver in the circumstances of the case; and
(2) to have done so without reasonable consideration for others.

6.3 The difference between the two offences under section 3 is that in cases of careless driving the prosection need not show that any other person was inconvenienced. In cases of inconsiderate driving, there must be evidence that some other user of the road or public place was inconvenienced.

6.4 An allegation of inconsiderate driving is appropriate when the driving amounts to a clear act of selfishness, impatience or aggression. There must, however, also be some inconvenience to other road users, for example, forcing other drivers to move over and/or brake as a consequence. Examples of conduct appropriate for a charge of driving without reasonable consideration are:

(1) flashing of lights to *force* other drivers in front to give way;
(2) misuse of any lane to avoid queuing or gain some other advantage over other drivers;
(3) unnecessarily remaining in an overtaking lane;
(4) unnecessarily slow driving or braking without good cause;
(5) driving with undipped headlights which dazzle oncoming drivers;
(6) driving through a puddle causing pedestrians to be splashed.

6.5 A person who drives without reasonable consideration for other road users can be convicted of driving without due care and attention although the reverse does not apply.

7 DANGEROUS DRIVING—SECTION 2 OF THE ACT

7.1 A person drives dangerously when:

(1) The way he drives falls *far below* what would be expected of a competent and careful driver; *and*

(2) It would be obvious to a competent and careful driver that driving in that way would be dangerous.

7.2 Both parts of the definition must be satisfied for the driving to be "dangerous" within the Act. Dangerous driving is an either way offence. In the magistrates' courts the maximum penalty is a level 5 fine (£5,000), and/or six months' imprisonment; in the Crown Court, the maximum penalty is two years' imprisonment and/or an unlimited fine. In both instances, the court must disqualify the driver from driving for at least one year and must endorse the driver's licence with 3–11 penalty points unless in either case there are special reasons not to do so.

7.3 The test of whether a driver has fallen far below the required standard is an objective one. It applies both when the manner of driving in question is deliberate and when the manner of driving occurs as a result of an error of judgment or simply as a result of incompetence or inexperience.

7.4 There is no statutory definition of what is meant by "far below", but "dangerous" must refer to danger either of injury to any person or of serious damage to property: section 2A(3) of the Act. Additionally, section 2A(2) of the Act provides that a person is to be regarded as driving dangerously if it would be obvious to a competent and careful driver that driving the vehicle in its current state would be dangerous. When considering the "state" of the vehicle, regard may be had to anything attached to or carried by the vehicle: section 2A(4) of the Act. Therefore, you must consider whether the vehicle should have been driven at all, as well as how it was driven.

7.5 The standard of driving must be objectively assessed. It is not necessary to consider what the driver thought about the possible consequences of his actions. What must be considered is whether or not a competent and careful driver would have observed, appreciated and guarded against obvious and material dangers.

7.6 In deciding whether a charge of dangerous driving is appropriate, you will want to consider whether the act of driving concerned was undertaken deliberately and/or repeatedly. Although the test of danger is an objective one, deliberate or repeated disregard, for example, of traffic directions (be they "stop" or "give way" signs or traffic lights) may be evidence that the manner of the accused's driving has fallen far below the standard required, thereby making a charge of dangerous driving appropriate.

7.7 In addition, the following are examples of driving which may support an allegation of dangerous driving:

(1) racing or competitive driving;

(2) prolonged, persistent or deliberate bad driving;

(3) speed which is highly inappropriate for the prevailing road or traffic conditions;

(4) aggressive or intimidatory driving, such as sudden lane changes, cutting into a line of vehicles or driving much too close to the vehicle in front, especially when the purpose is to cause the other vehicle to pull to one side to allow the accused to overtake;

(5) disregard of traffic lights and other road signs, which, on an objective analysis, would appear to be deliberate;

(6) failure to pay proper attention, amounting to something significantly more than a momentary lapse;

(7) overtaking which could not have been carried out with safety;

(8) driving a vehicle with a load which presents a danger to other road users.

8 CAUSING DEATH BY CARELESS DRIVING WHEN UNDER THE INFLUENCE OF DRINK OR DRUGS— SECTION 3A RTA 1988

8.1 This offence is commited when:

(1) the driving was without due care and attention or without reasonable consideration for other road users; *and*

(2) the driving has caused the death of another person; *and*

(3) the driver is either unfit through drink or drugs, or the alcohol concentration is over the prescribed limit, or there has been a failure to provide a specimen in pursuance of the RTA 1988.

8.2 It is an offence triable only on indictment and carries a maximum penalty of 10 years' imprisonment and/or an unlimited fine and an obligatory disqualification for at least two years (three years if there is a previous relevant conviction). The driver's licence must be endorsed with 3–11 penalty points.

8.3 The examples given in paragraph 5 of careless driving apply to this offence; in the context of section 3A, less serious examples of careless driving (which may not of themselves require a prosecution under section 3 alone) may also merit proceedings under section 3A.

8.4 The accused's driving must have been a cause of the death but need not be the sole one.

8.5 Proper procedures have to have been adopted in the requesting and/ or obtaining of any sample of breath, blood or urine. In cases where the procedures are flawed, there is a risk that the evidence may be excluded. Where this is possible, careful consideration must be given to whether the remaining evidence will support an alternative allegation of causing death by careless driving while unfit to drive through drink/drugs, in which case, evidence other than that from an intoximeter machine can be relied upon to demonstrate the defendant's unfitness to drive.

8.6 It is not necessary to add a further charge relating to drink-driving when the defendant is charged with a section 3A offence, because a guilty verdict to the relevant drink/drive offence can be returned by the jury under the statutory provisions: see paragraph 14.

9 CAUSING DEATH BY DANGEROUS DRIVING—SECTION 1 RTA 1988

9.1 This offence is committed when:

(1) the driving of the accused was a cause of the death of another person and

(2) the driving was dangerous within the meaning of section 2A of the Act (see paragraph 7.3 of this standard).

9.2 The offence is triable only on indictment and carries a maximum penalty of 10 years' imprisonment and/or an unlimited fine with an obligatory disqualification for a minimum of two years. The driver's licence must be endorsed with 3–11 penalty points.

9.3 The accused's driving must have been a cause of the death but need not be the sole one.

9.4 The examples given in paragraph 7 of dangerous driving apply to this offence.

9.5 Where a section 1 offence can be proved and there is sufficient evidence of a section 4, 5 or 7 offence, the appropriate summary offence should be charged and adjourned *sine die* pending the outcome of the section 1 offence—these offences cannot be committed to the Crown Court under section 41(1) Criminal Justice Act 1988. If the defendant is convicted of the section 1 offence, the court will often make it clear that the sentence imposed reflects the element of drink/driving, in which case the summary offence should not subsequently be pursued. Where the defendant is acquitted of the section 1 offence (or is convicted but it is clear the court has not taken the element of drink/driving into account) prosecutors should consider reactivating the drink/drive offence.

10 RELATIONSHIP BETWEEN SECTION 1 AND SECTION 3A RTA 1988

10.1 Offences under section 1 and section 3A carry the same maximum penalty, so the choice of charge will not inhibit the court's sentencing powers. The courts have made it clear that for sentencing purposes the two offences are to be regarded on an equal basis. (*Attorney-General's Reference (No. 49 of 1994) R. v. Brown* [1995] Crim.L.R. 437; *R. v. Locke* [1995] Crim.L.R. 438.)

10.2 The court will sentence an offender in proportion to his criminality. The consumption of alcohol is an aggravating feature increasing the criminality of the offender and therefore the sentence passed. The consumption of alcohol is an aggravating feature within the definition of section 3A. The consumption of alcohol is not part of the definition of section 1 but may be treated as an aggravating feature in appropriate cases.

10.3 Where a section 1 offence can be proved, it should be charged. However, you may on occasions have to decide which is the more appropriate charge: section 1 or section 3A. This will almost always occur when the manner of the driving is on the borderline between careless and dangerous. The prosecution is likely to be put to election if the two offences are charged in the alternative. In borderline cases, section 3A should be chosen provided all the other elements of that offence can be proved. The prospects of a conviction will be greater and the court's sentencing power remains unaffected.

11 MANSLAUGHTER—CONTRARY TO COMMON LAW

11.1 Manslaughter is committed when the driver, in breach of a duty of care, is criminally negligent and causes the death of the victim.

11.2 The offence is triable only on indictment and carries a maximum sentence of life imprisonment and/or an unlimited fine. The driver must be disqualified for at least two years and there is a compulsory re-test. The driver's licence must be endorsed with 3–11 penalty points.

11.3 The driver must be shown to have been in breach of a duty of care towards the person who died. The ordinary principles of the law of negligence apply to ascertain whether there is such a duty. There is a general duty of care on all persons not to do acts imperilling the lives of others. To show a breach of a duty of care will require proof that the driving:

(1) fell far below the minimum acceptable standard of driving; *and*

(2) involved a risk of death; *and*

(3) was so bad in all the circumstances as, in the opinion of the jury, to amount to a crime: *R. v. Adomako* [1994] 3 All E.R. 79.

11.4 The examples of driving which fall far below the minimum acceptable standard of driving set out in paragraph 7.7 apply here as well.

11.5 This charge will very rarely be appropriate in road traffic fatality cases because of the existence of the statutory offences.

11.6 Manslaughter should be considered when a vehicle has been used as an instrument of attack (but where the necessary intent for murder is absent) or to cause fright and death results.

11.7 Manslaughter should also be considered where the driving has occurred other than on a road or other public place, or when the vehicle driven was no mechanically propelled, and death has been caused. In these cases the statutory offences do not apply.

12 CAUSING BODILY HARM BY WANTON AND FURIOUS DRIVING—SECTION 35 OFFENCES AGAINST THE PERSON ACT 1861

12.1 It is an offence for any person in charge of a vehicle:

(1) to cause *or cause to be done* bodily harm to any person; by

(2) wanton or furious driving, or other wilful misconduct, or by wilfult neglect.

12.2 It is a offence triable only on indictment and carries a maximum penalty of a two years' imprisonment and/or an unlimited fine.

12.3 This offence should be used rarely as it does not carry endorsement or disqualification. It should normally only be used on those occasions when it is not possible to prosecute for an offence under the road traffic legislation, for example:

(1) when the driving was not on a road or other public place;

(2) when the vehicle used is not a mechanically propelled vehicle within the RTA 1988;

(3) when the statutory notice of intended prosecution is a prerequisite to a prosecution and has not been given.

12.4 This offence is useful in cases when a victim suffers serious injury though there has been no direct contact between the victim and the vehicle. For example, when the driving caused the victim to take avoiding action and as a result of which sustained serious injury by, say, falling down a ditch.

12.5 When a vehicle has been deliberately used as a weapon and has caused injury, alternative charges of dangerous driving under section 2 of the Act or section 18 Offences Against the Person Act 1861 should be considered if all the elements of those offences can be proved.

13 ROAD TRAFFIC FATALITY CASES: "NEAREST AND DEAREST"

13.1 In addition to the public interest considerations set out in the Code for Crown Prosecutors, special considerations apply to cases when there is a family or other close personal relationship between the deceased and the accused driver. These are often referred to as "nearest and dearest" cases. The considerations are unlikely to be relevant in any case where the evidence would support proceedings for manslaughter.

13.2 In each case, the particular circumstances and the nature of the relationship will have to be considered. The closer the relationship between the deceased and the accused driver, the more likely it will be that the guidance which follows will apply.

13.3 In cases of causing death by dangerous driving involving the death of a "nearest and dearest", where there is evidence to suggest an aggravating feature which imperils other road users or that the accused is a continuing danger to other road users, the proper course will be to prosecute for dangerous driving (section 2). The focus of the case will then be imperilling of other road users.

13.4 Additionally, if the accused drove in such a way as to show serious disregard for the lives of the "nearest and dearest" or other road users, notwithstanding that a "nearest and dearest" has been killed, proceedings for causing death by dangerous driving should be considered.

13.5 However, in cases of causing death by dangerous driving involving the death of a "nearest and dearest", where there is *no* evidence either of an aggravating feature imperilling other road users nor that the accused is a continuing danger to other road users, the proper course is not to prosecute.

13.6 In cases of causing death by careless driving while under the influence of drink, etc. involving the death of a "nearest and dearest", the proper course will be to prosecute for careless driving and the appropriate drink/driving offence.

13.7 In cases of careless driving which caused the death of a "nearest and dearest" where there is evidence to suggest that the accused is a continuing danger to other road users, the proper course is to prosecute for careless driving (section 3).

13.8 However, in cases of careless driving which caused the death of a "nearest and dearest" where there is *no* evidence that the accused is a continuing danger to other road users, the proper course is not to prosecute.

13.9 Evidence that an accused presents a continuing danger to other road users may be found in his/her previous convictions or medical condition. In such cases, the court may wish to make an order under section 36 of the Road Traffic Offenders Act 1988, disqualifying the driver until he passes a driving test; or when it appears that the court ought to notify the Secretary of State that the driver may be suffering from any relevant disability within the meaning of section 22 of the Road Traffic Offenders Act 1988.

13.10 If a person other than a "nearest and dearest" is killed as a result of the dangerous driving, notwithstanding the fact that a near relative has also been killed, a charge for causing death by dangerous driving should normally follow. In order to present the case fully to the court a separate charge for the death of the close relative cannot, in these circumstances, be avoided.

14 ALTERNATIVE VERDICTS

14.1 In certain circumstances, it is possible for a jury to find the accused not guilty of the offence charged but guilty of some other alternative offence. The general provisions are contained in section 6(3) Criminal Law Act 1967 and are supplemented by other provisions which relate to specific offences.

14.2 Section 24 of the Road Traffic Offenders Act allows for the return of alternative verdicts where the allegations in the indictment amount to, or include, an allegation of an offence specified in the table set out in that section. The relevant statutory provisions are:

Offence charged	Alternative verdicts
Section 1: death by dangerous driving	Section 2: dangerous driving Section 3: careless, and inconsiderate driving
Section 2: dangerous driving	Section 3: careless, and inconsiderate driving

Section 3A: causing death by careless driving while under the influence of drink or drugs	Section 3: careless, and inconsiderate driving
	and/or the relevant offence from:
	Section 4(1): driving whilst unfit
	Section 5(1)(a): driving with excess alcohol
	Section 7(6): failing to provide a specimen.

14.3 Where the accused is charged with an offence under section 3A of the RTA 1988 he may not be convicted as an alternative with any offence of attempting to drive: section 24(2) of the Road Traffic Offenders Act 1988.

14.4 In the very rare cases when manslaughter is charged, it will normally be prudent to prefer an alternative charge for causing death by dangerous driving if the driving took place on a road or other public place. Further, when manslaughter is charged there should be no difficulty in also charging as an alternative a section 3A offence if it is made out, although such a situation is most unlikely to arise.

14.5 It is essential however, that the charge which most suits the circumstances is always preferred. It will never be appropriate to charge a more serious offence in order to obtain a conviction (whether by plea or verdict) to a lesser offence.

INDEX

Abetting. *See* ACCESSORIES

ABSORPTION OF ALCOHOL,
age factors, 18–15
biological process, 9–03
breakdown in body, 9–03
delayed intoxication, 18–09
determinant, 18–09
drugs preventing breakdown, 9–04
elimination from body, 9–03, 18–10
emptying time of stomach, 18–09
entrance rate, 18–10
enzyme breaking down alcohol, 9–03
factors affecting, 18–09
fermentation in stomach, 9–04
full stomach, 18–09
inhalation, 9–04
menstrual cycle, 18–15
molecular structure of alcohol, 9–03
phases, 18–11, 18–12
post-absorptive phase, 18–14
process, 18–09
self-testing equipment, 18–12
sex differences, 18–15
site of, 18–09
stomach, role of, 18–09
theoretical time course, 18–11
urine alcohol, 18–13

ABSORPTION OF ALCOHOL. *See* ALCOHOL

ACCESSORIES,
actus reus, 4–12
agreement between principal and
    accessory, 4–12
circumstances, duress of, 4–19
defences,
    duress, 4–17—4–19
    emergencies, 4–19
    necessity, 4–17—4–19
driving instructors, 4–16
duress, 4–17—4–19
emergencies, 4–19
generous host, 4–15
inability to prove driver, 4–16
joint enterprise, 4–16
knowledge requirement, 4–14
lacing drinks, 4–14, 4–15
mens rea, 4–13

ACCESSORIES,—*cont.*
nature of offence, 4–13
necessity, 4–17—4–19
recklessness, 4–14
requirements, 4–13

ACCIDENT,
construction of word, 10–20
dangerous incident, 10–23
definition, 10–18
deliberate acts, 10–18, 10–19
entry powers after, 10–51
impairment and risk of, 18–16—18–21
involvement of vehicle, 10–21
location, 10–22
meaning, 10–18
ordinary man, in opinion of, 10–18
profile, 18–35
statistics, App. 6
vehicle involvement, 10–21

ACETALDEHYDE, 16–64, 16–65

ACETONE, 13.09, 13.20, 16.51, 16.58,
App. 10

ACQUITTAL, QUASHING, 22–18

ACTUS REUS,
accessories, 4–13
"being in charge" offence,
    blood, excess alcohol in, 3–18
    breath, excess alcohol in, 3–17
    faiure to provide specimen, 3–20
    unfitness to drive, 3–13
    urine, excess alchohol in, 3–19
blood, excess alcohol in,
    "being in charge" offence, 3–18
    careless driving, causing death by,
        3–04
    carrying out work, 3–26
    driving with, 3–15
    without reasonable consideration,
        causing death, 3–09
breath, excess alcohol in,
    "being in charge" offence, 3–20
    careless driving, causing death by,
        3–03
    carrying out work, 3–25

507

MAINTENANCE WORK, 3–24

MALE METABOLISM OF ALCOHOL, 9–24

MALNUTRITION,
chronic alcohol abuse, 18–29—18–34

MECHANICAL DEFECTS,
impossibility, 4–05

MECHANICALLY PROPELLED VEHICLE,
ceasing to be, 7–08
conditions, 7–08
definition, 7–08
electrically assisted pedal cycle, 7–08
invalid carriages, 7–08
lawnmowers, 7–08
motor vehicles, 7–02

MELLANLY FACTOR, 9–39

MENS REA,
accessories, 4–14
"being in charge" offence, 3–31
driving a vehicle, 3–31
transport offences, 3–31

MENSTRUAL CYCLE, 18–15

MENTAL INCAPACITY, 17–57

METABOLISM OF ALCOHOL,
alcoholics, 9–25
appeals on, 2–04
data on, 9–24
females, 9–24
males, 9–24
meaning, 9–24
Paton report, 9–25
rate, 9–24
variability, 9–24

MITIGATION FOR GUILTY PLEAS, 20–49

MODE OF TRIAL, 3–33

MONORAILS, 7–09

MOPEDS, 7–04

MORTALITY STATISTICS,
pre-legislation, 1–12
reductions in deaths, 1–23

MOTOR VEHICLES,
appearance of being, 7–07
autocross cars, 7–03
ceasing to be, 7–05

MOTOR VEHICLES,—cont.
definition, 7–02
electrically assisted pedal cycle, 7–06
engine removed, 7–04, 7–05
evidence, 7–07
exceptions, 7–06
generally, 7–02
go-karts, 7–03
hover vehicles, 7–03
intended or adapted for use on road,
7–03
invalid carriages, 7–06
lack of repair, 7–04, 7–05
lawnmowers, 7–06
looking like, 7–07
mechanically propelled, 7–02
mopeds, 7–04
no practical likelihood of being driven,
7–05
presumption of, 7–07
removal of engine, 7–04, 7–05
repair lacking, 7–04, 7–05
scrambling bikes, 7–03
statutory exceptions, 7–06
tramcars, 7–06

MOUTH ALCOHOL, 16–59—16–62

NECESSITY,
accessories, 4–17—4–19

NO CASE TO ANSWER SUBMISSION, 14–58

NO SAMPLE. See FAILURE TO GIVE SPECIMEN

OATH, EVIDENCE GIVEN ON, 15–01

OFFENCES,
See also individual offences
alternative verdicts, 3–34
autrefois acquit or convict, 3–35, 3–36
discretion to prosecute, 3–42
duplicity, 3–38—3–41
mode of trial, 3–33
relationship between, 3–33—3–37
time limits, 3–33

OMNIA PRAESUMUNTUR RITE ET SOLEMNITER
ESSE ACTA, 17–28

OPERATORS OF TRANSPORT SYSTEMS, 3–28

OPTION, STATUTORY,
cancelling option, 14–45
doctor's fees, 14–48
failing to avail oneself, 14–52
failure to be given, 2–13
information to be given, 2–05—2–07

WITHOUT REASONABLE CONSIDERATION, CAUSING DEATH,—*cont.*
failure to provide sample, 3–11
unfitness to drive, 3–07
urine, excess alchohol in, 3–10

WITNESSES,
costs, 23–15

WORK, CARRYING OUT. *See* CARRYING OUT WORK